Public Opinion, Democracy, and Market Reform in Africa

This book is a ground-breaking exploration of public opinion in sub-Saharan Africa. Based on the Afrobarometer, a comprehensive cross-national survey research project, it reveals what ordinary Africans think of democracy and market reform, subjects about which almost nothing is otherwise known. The authors find that support for democracy in Africa is wide but shallow and that Africans feel trapped between state and market. Beyond multiparty elections, people want clean and accountable government. They will accept economic structural adjustment only if it is accompanied by an effective state, the availability of jobs, and an equitable society. What are the origins of these attitudes? Far from being constrained by social structure and cultural values, Africans learn about reform on the basis of knowledge, reasoning, and experience. Weighing supply and demand for reform, the authors reach sober conclusions about the varying prospects of African countries for attaining full-fledged democracy and markets.

Professor Michael Bratton is professor of Political Science and African Studies at Michigan State University. He is cofounder and codirector of the Afrobarometer, a comparative series of national political attitude surveys covering more than a dozen African countries. He is the recipient of numerous grants and awards for his ongoing research on Africa. He is also a member of the editorial board for the *Journal of Modern African Studies* and is the coauthor (with Nicolas van de Walle) of *Democratic Experiments in Africa: Regime Transitions in Comparative Perspective*.

Professor Robert Mattes is associate professor of Political Science at the University of Cape Town. Through his work with the Institute for Democracy in South Africa (Idasa) he is cofounder and codirector of the Afrobarometer. He is the author of numerous articles on African politics and has received many grants for his work on the subject. He is also currently the director of the Democracy in Africa Research Unit at the University of Cape Town.

Professor E. Gyimah-Boadi is associate professor of Political Science at the University of Ghana at Legon. He is cofounder and codirector of the Afrobarometer along with Professors Bratton and Mattes. He is also executive director of the Ghana Center for Democratic Development (CDD-Ghana) in Accra. He frequently contributes to scholarly journals and books on Africa.

Cambridge Studies in Comparative Politics

General Editor
Margaret Levi   *University of Washington, Seattle*

Assistant General Editor
Stephen Hanson   *University of Washington, Seattle*

Associate Editors
Robert H. Bates   *Harvard University*
Peter Hall   *Harvard University*
Peter Lange   *Duke University*
Helen Milner   *Columbia University*
Frances Rosenbluth   *Yale University*
Susan Stokes   *University of Chicago*
Sidney Tarrow   *Cornell University*

Other Books in the Series

Lisa Baldez, *Why Women Protest: Women's Movements in Chile*
Stefano Bartolini, *The Political Mobilization of the European Left, 1860–1980:
    The Class Cleavage*
Mark Beissinger, *Nationalist Mobilization and the Collapse of the Soviet State*
Nancy Bermeo, *Unemployment in the New Europe*
Carles Boix, *Democracy and Redistribution*
Carles Boix, *Political Parties, Growth, and Equality: Conservative and Social
    Democratic Economic Strategies in the World Economy*
Catherine Boone, *Merchant Capital and the Roots of State Power in Senegal,
    1930–1985*
Catherine Boone, *Political Topographies of the African State: Territorial Authority
    and Institutional Choice*
Michael Bratton and Nicolas van de Walle, *Democratic Experiments in Africa:
    Regime Transitions in Comparative Perspective*
Valerie Bunce, *Leaving Socialism and Leaving the State: The End of Yugoslavia,
    the Soviet Union, and Czechoslovakia*
Daniele Caramani, *The Nationalization of Politics: The Formation of National
    Electorates and Party Systems in Western Europe*
Kanchan Chandra, *Why Ethnic Parties Succeed: Patronage and Ethnic Head Counts in
    India*

Continues after the Index

Public Opinion, Democracy, and Market Reform in Africa

MICHAEL BRATTON
Michigan State University

ROBERT MATTES
University of Cape Town

E. GYIMAH-BOADI
University of Ghana

CAMBRIDGE
UNIVERSITY PRESS

PUBLISHED BY THE PRESS SYNDICATE OF THE UNIVERSITY OF CAMBRIDGE
The Pitt Building, Trumpington Street, Cambridge, United Kingdom

CAMBRIDGE UNIVERSITY PRESS
The Edinburgh Building, Cambridge CB2 2RU, UK
40 West 20th Street, New York, NY 10011-4211, USA
477 Williamstown Road, Port Melbourne, VIC 3207, Australia
Ruiz de Alarcón 13, 28014 Madrid, Spain
Dock House, The Waterfront, Cape Town 8001, South Africa

http://www.cambridge.org

First published 2005

Printed in the United States of America

Typeface Sabon 10/12 pt.   *System* LATEX 2ε [TB]

A catalog record for this book is available from the British Library.

Library of Congress Cataloging in Publication Data

Bratton, Michael.
Public opinion, democracy, and market reform in Africa / Michael Bratton, Robert
Mattes, E. Gyimah-Boadi.
    p. cm. – (Cambridge studies in comparative politics)
Includes bibliographical references and index.
ISBN 0-521-84191-7 – ISBN 0-521-60291-2 (pb.)
    1. Africa, Sub-Saharan – Politics and government – 1960– – Public opinion. 2. Democracy –
Africa, Sub-Saharan – Public opinion. 3. Legitimacy of governments – Africa,
Sub-Saharan – Public opinion. 4. Africa, Sub-Saharan – Economic conditions – 1960– –
Public opinion. 5. Africa, Sub-Saharan – Economic policy – Public opinion.
6. Capitalism – Africa, Sub-Saharan – Public opinion. 7. Free enterprise – Africa,
Sub-Saharan – Public opinion. 8. Public opinion – Africa, Sub-Saharan.
I. Mattes, Robert B. II. Gyimah-Boadi, Emmanuel. III. Title. IV. Series.
JQ1879.A15B74   2004
320.967–dc22   2004043555

ISBN 0 521 84191 7 hardback
ISBN 0 521 60291 2 paperback

To
the 21,531 Africans
who graciously took time
to answer our interminable questions.
May they achieve the democracy and development that
they say they want.

Contents

List of Tables and Figures

FIGURES

Acknowledgments

As will soon become apparent, we owe heavy intellectual and other debts, especially to Richard Rose and Larry Diamond, who are godfathers to many of the ideas expressed in these pages. Great benefit was also gleaned from exchanges with Barry Ames, Joel Barkan, Robert Bates, Stephen Burgess, Yun-Han Chu, Stephen Ellis, George Ellison, Steve Finkel, Richard Gunther, Ron Inglehart, Tim Kelsall, Marta Lagos, Peter Lewis, Don Mead, Kwabenah Amoah Awuah Mensah, Pippa Norris, H. Kwesi Prempeh, Mampela Ramphele, Mitch Seligson, Doh Chull Shin, Nic van de Walle, and Jennifer Widner. We were stimulated too by the implicit debate between Claude Ake and Amartya Sen over the ways that poor people view democracy and development. Above all, we were inspired by the courageous lifelong commitment to democratic reform of our dear colleague Masipula Sithole, who, sadly, passed away as this book was nearing completion.

Our presentation is based on the Afrobarometer, an international survey research project to which many people contribute. The authors represent the Afrobarometer's three core partners: The Institute for Democracy in South Africa (Idasa), the Center for Democratic Development (CDD-Ghana), and Michigan State University (MSU). Our national partners in twelve African countries broke new ground by conducting thousands of face-to-face interviews, often under challenging field conditions. Hearty thanks are due to the following people and their survey teams (in country alphabetical order): in Botswana – Mogopodi Lekorwe, Mpho Molomo, and Wilford Molefe; in Lesotho – John Gay and Thuso Green; in Malawi – Stanley Khaila and Maxton Tsoka; in Mali – Massa Coulibaly; in Namibia – Christiaan and Erna Keulder; in Nigeria – Shola Fatodu, Bola Adedoyin, Samson Arekete, and Tunde Durosimi-Etti; in Tanzania – Joseph Semboja, Deogratius Mushi, and Amon Chaligha; in Uganda – Robert Sentamu and Francis Kibirige; in Zambia – Neo Simutanyi and Mbiko Msoni; and in Zimbabwe – Annie Chikwana, Nyasha Madzingira, and Eldred Masunungure. They helped design questionnaires, organize fieldwork, enter data, and write reports describing the results of country surveys. The Afrobarometer rests on their efforts, which made this study possible.

In addition, we have leaned on other capable researchers. At MSU, Carolyn Logan compiled the first cross-national compendium of Round 1 survey results and coordinated Round 2 surveys. Fabiana Machado worked long and hard to clean and merge data sets and to establish the Afrobarometer website. Other research assistants, including Paloma Bauer, Wonbin Cho, Cheryl Coslow, Gina Lambright, Kimberly Ludwig, Virginia Parish, Rakesh Sharma, and Kimberly Smiddy, made numerous contributions in the field and on campus. Karen Battin, Rhonda Burns, Laurie Cooper, and Jill Tirnauer lent their superior skills at project and grants management. The invaluable time series of democracy surveys in South Africa, dating back to 1994, owes its existence to Idasa's Paul Graham and Wilmot James. At Idasa's Cape Town office, Derek Davids took charge of interviewer training for the Afrobarometer in Southern Africa and Cherrel Africa was responsible for data management. At CDD in Accra, Charles Wiafe, Kojo Sakyi, Edem Selormey, and Jon Temin did the same for West Africa. Zeric Smith and Rod Alence helped guide surveys in Mali and Tanzania respectively. We are grateful to all of them for their diligence and dedication.

As for methodological advice, Rajen Govender taught us structural equations modeling, Bill Reed guided us in how to address problems of missing data, and Gary King, James Honeker, and Matthew Welch helped us unravel the mysteries of *Amelia*.

Several sources of funding supported Round 1 of the Afrobarometer. The National Science Foundation provided the first seed grant for fieldwork in Ghana and for preliminary comparative analysis. Other costs were covered by various field missions of the United States Agency for International Development (USAID), for example in Southern Africa, Nigeria, and Uganda. The Swedish International Development Cooperation Agency provided a major grant to cover not only survey research in Tanzania, but core activities like international networking, capacity-building, and outreach. The Danish Governance Trust Fund, administered by the World Bank, funded the Mali survey. We thank Kathy Peterson, U.S. Ambassador to Lesotho and the responsible program officers in each funding agency – notably Sean Hall, Liz Hart, Per Nordlund, Steve Snook, and Ozias Tungwarara – for having the vision to recommend support for public opinion research in Africa. The Mellon Foundation and Michigan State University provided support for writing. Revisions to the manuscript were made at the Center on Democracy, Development, and the Rule of Law at Stanford University, where we greatly enjoyed Larry Diamond's warm hospitality.

For insightful commentaries on a draft manuscript we wish to single out three valued colleagues: Joel Barkan, Carolyn Logan, and Nic van de Walle, whose close and critical readings saved us from numerous egregious errors. We also benefited from the hard-hitting comments of two anonymous reviewers appointed by Cambridge University Press. Our early findings were also floated before audiences at Harvard, Princeton, Stanford, and Uppsala Universities; at the Universities of Notre Dame, Michigan, and Cape Town; and at the national universities in Taiwan and Chile. We thank the participants in these seminars for their incisive critiques, as well as our copanelists at meetings of the African Studies, Midwest Political Science, International Political Science, and American Political Science Associations.

For permission to use selected findings and ideas from early explorations of the themes of this book, we thank the publishers of the *British Journal of Political Science, Comparative Political Studies, World Development*, the *Journal of Modern African Studies, African Affairs*, and the *Journal of Democracy*. In the same vein we gratefully acknowledge Praeger Publishers and Lynne Rienner Publishers.

Although we are indebted to all these colleagues, publishers, and sponsors, we absolve them from any errors of fact or judgment that follow. While each of us did a little of everything, Mattes took the lead on technical analysis, Gyimah-Boadi provided contextual interpretation, and Bratton wrote most of the text. The three of us assume joint responsibility for the end product. If readers want to arrive at their own conclusions, or simply wish to know more, we invite them to use the resources at www.afrobarometer.org.

Michael Bratton,
East Lansing

Robert Mattes,
Cape Town

E. Gyimah-Boadi,
Accra

November 2003

Introduction

This book explores public opinion in the parts of Africa that have recently experienced political and economic reforms. What views do Africans hold about democracy and a market economy? How do they behave in response to liberalization? Why do citizens think, feel, and react as they do? And what are the implications of mass opinion for the consolidation of fragile new regimes? In short, we explore the nature of public opinion – its content, origins, and outcomes – in all its glorious diversity in the leading reformist countries of the sub-Saharan subcontinent.

Needless to say, very little is presently known about these subjects. Thus, our first task is descriptive: to fill a gaping empirical hole and to help give voice to otherwise silent majorities of ordinary men and women. But we also harbor theoretical ambitions and an abiding interest in public policy. Why does public opinion vary cross-nationally and among different social and opinion groups within countries? What sort of theory – of interests, identities, or institutions – best explains African patterns of mass attitudes and action?[1] By accounting for popular demands and satisfactions – or, more likely, dissatisfactions – this book enters evidence into long-standing, often heated, debates on the suitability of political democracy and market-friendly policies to African needs and conditions.

To introduce our topic, we present two vignettes – one apiece about democratic and market reforms – that illustrate the above preoccupations. These short stories point to a variety of regime paths being taken by African countries and to distinctive patterns of popular response. In the process, we begin to situate public opinion as both a cause and a consequence of change.

A TALE OF TWO PRESIDENTS

In Africa today, civilian leaders who ignore the constitution pose a more insidious threat to democracy than coup plotters in the military. As elected rulers have come to enjoy the benefits of public office, they often have been tempted to cling to power by bending the law. It is not uncommon for leaders to try to amend the national constitution, either to sideline opponents for the presidency, or to extend the number of terms that a president can serve. Among others, Sam Nujoma of Namibia and Frederick Chiluba of Zambia have used these tactics. Both tried to persuade their compatriots that they deserved a third term in office, even in the face of explicit constitutional prohibitions. In wanting to overturn presidential term limits, they sought to circumvent democratic reforms made a decade earlier.

Nujoma, Namibia's founding father, was first elected in 1989 with 57 percent of the vote, a solid mandate that was increased in presidential elections in 1994. As his second term unfolded, Nujoma gave conflicting signals about his intentions: at first he declared he would step down to make way for a younger candidate; but he later allowed that his future would be left up to the ruling South West Africa Peoples' Organization (SWAPO). Feigning response to a popular groundswell and arguing that the country could ill afford a damaging succession struggle, Nujoma accepted the unanimous acclamation of an extraordinary party congress in 1998 that he should stay on. An amendment to the constitution was rammed through the National Assembly, where SWAPO enjoyed a comfortable super-majority, which allowed Nujoma to run again in the 1999 presidential elections. He won a third term, now with 77 percent of the vote.

Chiluba had similar ambitions, but was less effective in realizing them. He took office after resoundingly defeating Zambia's founding father, Kenneth Kaunda, in a landmark transition in 1991. Chiluba was reelected five years later with an almost undiminished majority. In this election, however, he eliminated competition from Kaunda (whose parents were born in Malawi) by trumping up a charge that the latter was not a Zambian citizen. Belatedly, in May 2001, just six months before he was due to step down, Chiluba publicly floated the possibility of a third term. He managed to persuade the ruling Movement for Multiparty Democracy (MMD), to renominate him as its presidential candidate, but in the process precipitated a split in the party. Lacking enough votes in parliament to change the constitution, Chiluba expelled all his leading opponents from the MMD, including the national vice-president and several cabinet ministers. A few days later – in the face of popular protests by student, labor, and church groups and moves by parliamentarians to begin impeachment – the president dramatically reversed himself: he went on national television to announce that he would *not* seek a third term.

Many factors explain why Nujoma's power play succeeded and Chiluba's failed. The former president could capitalize on his reputation as the liberator of his country from colonial rule, whereas the latter came to power as a second-generation, compromise candidate. Nujoma was apparently more skillful than Chiluba in managing splits within his own party and turning them to his own advantage. And perhaps Zambians, unlike Namibians, had already learned from bitter experience that a single leader should not be permitted to stay in office too long.

To fully appreciate whether leaders can get away with manipulating the core rules of the democratic game, we contend that attention should be paid to public opinion. As third-term debates came to a head in both countries, we conducted national probability sample surveys in Namibia and Zambia that, among other questions, asked people about their attitudes to government by a strong leader. Specifically, did they approve or disapprove of a form of government in which "we abolish parliament and political parties so that the president can decide everything?" The results were strikingly different across the two countries: in Namibia, only a bare majority (of 57 percent) rejected one-man rule; yet in Zambia, an overwhelming majority (91 percent) did so.

Thus the profile of public opinion in Namibia, where almost half of the population indicated they would not resist a strong leader, was acquiescent to Nujoma's bid to change the constitution to suit his own ambitions. In Zambia, however, Chiluba confronted a much more politicized populace that clearly rejected any seizure of power by another would-be strongman. While these popular preferences may or may not have been communicated directly by the people to the president, they certainly found expression via civic organizations, political parties, and the parliament. As a reflection of popular disaffection with a leader's machinations, public opinion apparently played a role in determining whether a nondemocratic gambit would succeed.

TAKING ACCOUNT OF ADJUSTMENT

As well as influencing the course of events, public opinion is shaped by policy performance. In recent years, African countries have undertaken economic reform programs that aim to encourage economic growth by adjusting the structure of the national economy. The scope of such reforms, including actual implementation, has varied greatly from country to country, as illustrated by the divergent paths recently taken by Mali and Nigeria.

Originally an agricultural economy, Nigeria was self-sufficient in food at the time of independence and an exporter of cocoa, palm oil, groundnuts, and cotton. The development of oil resources in the 1970s, however, led to an economic boom that financed the rapid expansion of the state sector. Numerous public enterprises were established in industry and manufacturing that, together with the civil service, came to account for more than 60 percent of formal employment. Imports of capital goods and raw materials to support these enterprises, along with the consumer luxuries that Nigerians increasingly demanded, produced a ballooning trade deficit. By the 1980s, the government could no longer finance its own expenditures and was forced into debt.

When General Ibrahim Babangida grabbed power in 1985, he moved quickly to restructure the Nigerian economy. Following a referendum on international borrowing that revealed a strong streak of popular economic nationalism, Nigerian policy experts undertook to design their own structural adjustment program (SAP) in 1986. It aimed to restore fiscal discipline, diversify the economy away from dependence on oil, and address the growing debt burden. This homegrown product won the approval of the World Bank and the International Monetary Fund (IMF), which made the country eligible for the disbursement of loans and the rescheduling of arrears.

Yet the economic reform program became severely distorted by corruption. From the outset, the oil boom allowed the personal enrichment of top public officials who entered into lucrative deals with foreign oil companies. An economic downturn in the 1980s due to falling world oil prices created even greater incentives for graft, which infamously led successive military administrations in Nigeria into spectacular avarice. By the mid-1990s, General Sani Abacha allowed Nigeria's oil refineries to collapse and maneuvered himself, his cronies, and members of his family into controlling positions in the oil import business. By the time Abacha died in mid-1998, the government had dropped all pretense of systematic economic management. Public enterprises were looted and capital took flight. Life worsened for ordinary people as education and health services collapsed, average life expectancy stalled at about fifty years, and Nigeria slipped from being a middle-income country to being a low-income one.

Under these circumstances, public confidence in the government's economic strategy was bound to be extremely low. In the first place, only 40 percent of the respondents in a national probability sample survey in January 2000 had even heard of the SAP, in part because many respondents were too young to remember the public debates about a program introduced in 1986. Among those who had heard of the SAP, a mere 14 percent were prepared to express satisfaction with the way it had been implemented. This judgment accords with a World Bank assessment that, by 1997, Nigeria had demonstrated poor compliance with an orthodox package of recommended reforms.

The case of Mali presents a different picture. Much less well endowed with natural resources than Nigeria – it has no oil and two thirds of its land area is desert – Mali embarked on a promising path of policy reform that attracted a measure of support from both international donors and the general public.

Malian governments were initially opposed to a market-based economy. From 1960 to 1968, the independence government of Modibo Keita attempted to install a regime of rural socialism whose political bankruptcy was signaled when party militants resorted to confiscating food grains from farmers. The succeeding military government of Moussa Traoré opened the door to World Bank and IMF support by, among other reforms, allowing staple foodstuffs to be traded privately. Unwilling to surrender control, however, Traoré permitted only token privatization of the rural economy and violently repressed demands for political freedoms raised in the streets by urban demonstrators. He was finally ousted in a coup in 1991, which was followed by a democratic election in 1992 that installed Alpha Omar Konaré, a reformer with a more wholehearted commitment to restructuring the economy.

Like other West African governments, the Konaré administration had no choice but to accept a 50 percent devaluation of the national currency (the CFA franc) in January 1994. But, of its own accord, it also adopted measures to resume the liberalization of agricultural marketing, introduce a value added tax, and initiate the sale of publicly owned utility companies. Gradually, Mali began to harvest the fruits of these reforms. Growth in real domestic product averaged 5 percent between 1994 and 1998, though it later slowed again. The export of rice increased substantially and the country approached self-sufficiency in this staple food. Although cotton prices dropped, livestock exports boomed. And, for the first time in years, improvements in the management of the government's finances allowed public employees to be paid on time.

Accordingly, survey research shows that Malians are much more satisfied than Nigerians with their country's economic reform program. Interestingly, exactly the same proportion of adults in both countries (40 percent) is aware of the existence of an official SAP, though in Mali, where reforms are more recent, lack of policy knowledge is due less to age than to lack of education. The big difference between the two countries, however, is that many more Malians (39 percent) say they are satisfied with the reform package as implemented, a figure nearly three times higher than in Nigeria. To be sure, SAPs attract only minority satisfaction in both countries, but Nigerians express an almost total lack of confidence in the economic policies implemented by corrupt military dictators. These findings suggest that significant proportions of Africans attend to national policy developments and form their opinions accordingly. In the contrasting cases of Nigeria and Mali, the policy performance of governments apparently affected the size of any popular constituency for economic reform.

SETTING AN AGENDA

On the basis of these case comparisons, we find it worthwhile to explore more systematically the role of public opinion in the evolution of democratic and market regimes in Africa. Several avenues for elaboration immediately come to mind.

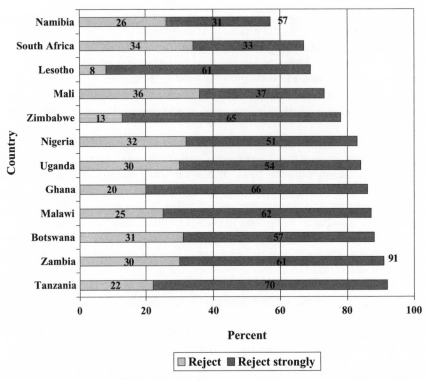

FIGURE 1.1. Rejection of One-Man Rule

Do these findings apply elsewhere? The countries mentioned so far –
Namibia, Zambia, Mali, and Nigeria – were chosen because their national
populations display extreme values on relevant public attitudes. Figure 1.1
shows that, across twelve African countries for which we have data,
Namibians express the very lowest rates of rejection of one-man rule,
whereas Zambians are second highest. Figure 1.2 shows that, across nine
African countries that had implemented a SAP, Nigerians were among the
most dissatisfied and that Malians were among the most satisfied.

Thus, the cross-national results point in the same directions as the case
comparisons. In countries where, in the past, strong leaders entrenched themselves in power for multiple terms in office (as did Nyerere in Tanzania, Banda
in Malawi, and Rawlings in Ghana), public opinion runs strongly against
one-man rule. In Malawi, widespread popular opposition (87 percent, almost Zambian levels) contributed to President Muluzi's reluctant decision
in March 2003 to forego a third term bid. In countries where the authorities have abandoned SAPs and incited economic nationalism against global
financial institutions, satisfaction with SAPs is low. In Zimbabwe, for example, satisfaction is even lower than in Nigeria (just 3 percent). And vice

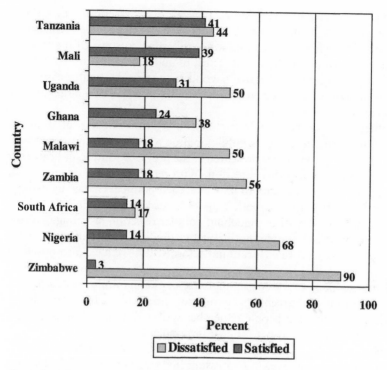

Percent who say they are "satisfied/very satisfied" or "dissatisfied/very dissatisfied"

FIGURE 1.2. Satisfaction with Economic Reform Programs

versa: in countries that have demonstrated a measure of compliance with the market-based policy recommendations of the World Bank and IMF and people have seen modest improvements in the economy (for example, in Tanzania and Uganda), public opinion shows relative satisfaction with SAPs. Strikingly, in Tanzania, almost as many people say they are satisfied with the country's economic reform program as express dissatisfaction (41 percent versus 44 percent).[2]

But cross-national comparisons also raise new questions. One-man rule is roundly rejected in Botswana in a context where leaders have refrained from ruling in brutal fashion or attempting to outstay their welcome. This case raises other possibilities, including that the rejection of one-man rule is a product of a popular syndrome of democratic preferences based on extended experience with open, multiparty politics. Moreover, satisfaction with structural adjustment is very low in South Africa, plumbing Nigerian depths. In this case, public unease cannot be attributed to a failure of orthodox stabilization measures because, under the guidance of African National Congress's (ANC) economic team, the government has balanced the public budget and controlled inflation. Nor has creeping corruption in South Africa reached anything resembling Nigerian levels. Instead, dissatisfaction with SAPs in South Africa must be due to other factors such as the poor performance of the economic regime at generating jobs and reducing some of the starkest economic inequalities in the world. Thus, to understand the diverse sources of public opinion, we must move beyond monocausal, country-case comparisons in favor of more rigorous multivariate analyses of a large number of observations.

Another item on the agenda for this book is the theoretical status of mass attitudes and behavior. Is public opinion a cause or a consequence of regime change? The vignettes presented in the previous sections indicate that the arrow can point in either direction. With reference to presidential term limits, public opinion appears to have preceded political change by making a formative contribution to both Nujoma's success and Chiluba's failure. In the language of statistical modeling, popular rejection of strongman rule was an independent variable that helped to predict the fate of presidential efforts to reverse recent constitutional reforms. But we have also observed that populations that have experienced government at the hands of "life" presidents are likely to overwhelmingly reject one-man rule. In this regard, public opposition to the reemergence of strongmen is also a reaction to harsh political experience that people remember well and do not wish to repeat. Thus, public opinion is also a product of popular learning.

In the case of structural adjustment programs, we have portrayed public opinion mainly as reactive. In expressing low satisfaction with SAPs, citizens were seen as responding to relatively effective policy implementation in Mali and to the serious corruption of the economic reform effort in Nigeria. Thus public opinion was treated as a dependent variable, a phenomenon to be explained, in this case principally in terms of the government's record at policy performance. At some stage in the process of reform, however, public attitudes take on an independent existence. For example, as satisfied customers of a SAP begin to emerge, as in Tanzania when small-scale vendors welcomed the lifting of trading regulations, constituencies congeal in favor of sustaining and extending market-based reforms. Thus, attitudes and behaviors that start out as reactions to an external policy stimulus can, in turn, become catalysts of reform in their own right.

In this book, we start and end with whole regimes. At this macro level, we are interested in big questions about the status of, and prospects for, democratic and market reforms in Africa. We would like to know whether public opinion helps or inhibits the probability of consolidating new forms of political and economic organization in various countries. At the core of the book, however, is a microlevel investigation. For most of the presentation, we treat public opinion as a set of mass initiatives for reform or public reactions to reforms introduced by national and international elites. The bulk of the chapters that follow are devoted to describing the profile of public opinion and analyzing its origins and outcomes.

OVERVIEW OF CONTENTS

Part I of this book proposes a framework for analyzing popular orientations. Chapter 1 sets the scene by summarizing recent trends in political and economic liberalization, noting variations across African countries. It also dissects the literature's prevailing theory of the consolidation of democracy, finds it wanting, and substitutes a model of supply and demand for a range of regimes. We also derive a series of propositions about the profiles of public opinion that might be expected to prevail in Africa's new, hybrid systems.

Chapter 2 introduces the Afrobarometer and discusses the survey research methodology of this study. It situates Round 1 Afrobarometer surveys in relation to previous similar work in Africa and abroad, and emphasizes the comparative ambition of the present enterprise. A key element of this chapter is a literature-based review of competing explanatory frameworks. In examining what others have written about popular attitudes to emergent democracies and markets, we derive hypotheses for tests with African data. We note in other world regions, for example, that democratization attracts more widespread public support than reforms to introduce a market economy. As it happens, the Africans we interviewed feel the same way.

The book then proceeds by successive steps to document Afrobarometer results, to propose explanations, and then to test these. In the process, we gradually increase the sophistication of statistical techniques, beginning with univariate description, exploring tentative bivariate connections, introducing controls via single-stage multivariate regression models, and concluding with comprehensive path analyses. Readers may wish to pick and choose extracts from the text depending on their interests: those intrigued by empirical African realities will find Parts II and III most engaging; those concerned with the testing of theory may wish to spend more time on Parts I and IV.

Part II describes how people think, as well as what they do, in relation to reform. Chapter 3 records attitudes to democracy in African countries, characterizing popular support for this type of political regime as wide but shallow. Chapter 4 narrates economic attitudes, stressing popular ambivalence to market-based capitalism. Chapter 5 adds new information on the extent of popular engagement among Africans in informal economic activities and formal political processes. While it would be wrong to assume that public opinion is uniform across social groups within a country, we start by emphasizing cross-national variations. For example, we find that about two thirds of Africans interviewed say that they prefer democracy to any other form of government, but that Batswana (the citizens of Botswana) exceed, and Basotho (the citizens of Lesotho) fall short of, this average.

In Part III we ask why liberalization reforms attract differential levels of popular support and mass satisfaction. Applying candidate theories to the Afrobarometer data, we test the impacts of social demography, cultural values, and institutional influences, as well as considerations of cognitive awareness and performance evaluation (see Chapters 6 through 10). Contrary to the historical and anthropological emphases of African studies, we find that explanations of public opinion on the sub-Saharan subcontinent are not well served by frameworks based on social structure or cultural values. Instead, we substitute a popular learning approach that posits that people arrive at opinions about democracy and markets on the basis of knowledge, reasoning, and experience. In our view, the evolution of public opinion depends on two key considerations: first, emerging popular understandings of what a democracy or a market actually *is*; and second, mass perceptions of what, in practice, these regimes actually *do*.

Part IV (Chapters 11 and 12) expands and refines this emerging explanation. The object is to comprehensively model both popular attitudes (demand for, and perceived supply of, democracy and a market economy) and mass behavior (specifically, various forms of participation in the political process). We confirm that demand for reforms hinges critically on the quantity and quality of scarce information available to citizens. And the perceived supply of democratic and market regimes is a function of popular evaluations of the performance of leaders, institutions, and regimes. Weaving these strands of explanation together, we find that demand for democracy is largely intrinsic (as a goal valued in and of itself), but that evaluations of the supply of economic reform are highly instrumental (depending on improvements in the material conditions of life). Moreover, political participation is mostly a product of institutional mobilization. In all cases, Africans develop their orientations to reform less from formal education and more from direct experiences in adulthood.

The book concludes (in Chapter 13) with interpretation of "country" differences. What does it mean that being a Nigerian is a significant predictor of popular satisfaction with democracy or that being a Tanzanian powerfully explains support for market reforms? Precisely which economic or institutional attributes are signified by these geographic attributes? Analysis returns to country characteristics as represented by aggregate data derived from Afrobarometer surveys and other independent sources. By this last step we find that political legacies matter. Among other paths, a history of settler colonialism is not conducive to the consolidation of democracy; but past episodes of multiparty rule – however brief – are extremely helpful. Based on such findings, the book ends with some broad-gauged speculations about the sustainability of recent democratic and market reforms in the parts of Africa we have studied.

PART I

FRAMEWORK

Africa's Hybrid Regimes

The late twentieth century was an era of reform. Most often, change ran in a liberalizing direction. Closed polities and economies became more open. The disintegration of the Soviet Union and the emergent hegemony of the United States heralded much more than the end of the Cold War. This period was characterized by the global diffusion of democracy and markets as organizing principles for society. The 1980s and 1990s were periods of fundamental regime change around the world, in which prevailing strategies for the development of poor countries were stood on their heads. In the realm of ideas and policies – and more gradually within institutions – an ascendant democratic capitalism displaced the doctrine of state socialism.

The spread of democratic and market values has been global in scale but uneven in impact. In much of Eastern Europe and Latin America, reformers effected a dual regime transition by transforming elements of both political and economic life. They pried open ossified bureaucratic systems by reducing the role of the state and increasing the amount of freedom available to individuals and groups. Wholly or partly, contested elections and competitive markets began to replace authoritarian rulers and centrally planned economies. The relaxation of official controls held out the promise that, henceforth, citizens and consumers would exercise a greater measure of choice in the governance of the state and the direction of the economy. In the Middle East, Central Asia, and China, however, political elites were cautious and selective in their embrace of the new orthodoxy, attempting to reap the benefits of market-based growth while maintaining the privileges and presumed stability of nondemocratic rule.

Yet the triumph of democratic capitalism has provoked resistance. On one hand, conservative and religious elements have reacted – most dramatically in the fanatic attack on the World Trade Center – against the excessive liberalism and materialism of a secular society. On the other hand, progressive political groups have rallied around a banner of antiglobalization to protest – at the doorsteps of the World Bank and the International Monetary

Fund – the dangers of consuming the planet's natural resources and deepening the plight of the world's poor.

The countries of sub-Saharan Africa, which inhabit the outer periphery of the global economy and international state system, have not escaped these crosscurrents. Indeed, the continent's very marginality and weakness in the world system exposes African peoples and governments to external pressures for liberalization that often run well ahead of domestic demands for reform. As latecomers, Africans scramble to catch-up with trends – of emancipation or backlash – that emanate from other parts of the world. In seeking a balance appropriate to the continent's cultures and socioeconomic status, African leaders and peoples have started to experiment with their own versions of political competition and economic privatization. So far, reforms have been tentative, partial, and incomplete, leaving Africa with hybrid regimes that awkwardly mix old and new principles of organization.

However pressing the need for reform – and the coexistence of political and economic crises in Africa makes reform imperative – the context is hardly conducive to development. Because per capita incomes and basic literacy remain low, an independent middle class has yet to emerge that can serve as the sponsor of democratization and marketization. Moreover, the top stratum of political leaders in Africa remains wedded to a political economy in which wealth and power derive from personal control of the resources of the state. As such, incumbent elites are predisposed to resist reforms to a system that has served them well in the past. And, importantly, ordinary African people have been slow to make known their views on the desirability (or otherwise) of political and economic reforms. At face value, one would expect that shortfalls in education, literacy, and media exposure would inhibit popular awareness of the issues at stake. Yet, because men in the street and women in the villages have borne the brunt of Africa's crises, one might expect that they would support changes that promise to end their deprivation. Alternatively, they may regard democracy and markets as imported constructs that are poorly suited to African conditions and useful only to the extent that they can be turned to local purposes. All these speculations, however, remain to be inspected and explored.

This chapter sets the scene at the macro level for investigating, in subsequent chapters, microlevel attitudes to reform in sub-Saharan Africa. It begins by sketching out some of the tectonic movements that occurred in the continent's political and economic firmament during the era of liberalization. We report that African leaders have undertaken reforms to different degrees and in different combinations in various countries and that the incompleteness of the reform process gives rise to a range of hybrid regimes. As a result, the theoretical apparatus in the current political science literature – which hinges on the ideal concept of the consolidation of democracy – is not well suited to explaining diverse African realities. Instead, we propose that African political and economic regimes may remain unstable for extended periods or harden prematurely in embryonic or low-quality forms. Only in exceptional cases have African regimes consolidated as recognizable democratic or market models. Beginning in this chapter and as this book progresses, we will identify the key contours of public opinion that help to distinguish these outcomes.

A DECADE OF POLITICAL REFORMS, 1990–2001

In the struggle for political independence in the 1950s and 1960s, African nationalists struck a social contract with colonized populations. Follow us, they said, and we will lead you to political freedom and material prosperity. As is now well known, these promises were seldom fulfilled. In retrospect, the pledge to alleviate poverty was destined to face daunting objective obstacles – poor soils, intermittent rains, huge distances, undereducated populations, single-product economies, low-producer prices – that were largely beyond the control of leaders, though their own mistaken development strategies and inexperience at management surely also hindered economic takeoff. The construction of political regimes, however, was almost entirely within leaders' discretion, and they must bear the blame for making choices that sacrificed popular freedoms at the altar of elite desires for wealth, security, and power. African one-party states and military governments were not the most repressive regimes in the world at the time, but they did systematically fail to deliver the civil liberties and political rights that previously had been promised. As the social contract unraveled, ordinary Africans discovered that autocrats had constructed political systems that made no provision for changing leaders.

By the 1990s, however, citizens demanded change. Students, workers, and civil servants took to the streets to insist on an end to mismanagement, corruption, and repression. Responding principally to these internal mass protests, but also pushed by international donors and lenders, incumbent rulers had little choice but to ease restrictions on political life. Reluctantly, African presidents released political prisoners, unfettered the independent press, and recognized opposition political parties in preparation for competitive elections. Together, these liberalization reforms put an end to the political monopoly enjoyed by African one-party states and made it difficult for military officers to again stake a legitimate claim to rule. As analysts now agree, the liberalization of authoritarian rule amounted to the most significant political shift on the continent since independence was won a generation earlier.[1]

But political openings in Africa led in multiple directions, and not always toward democracy, which we understand as an institutionalized, competitive, electoral regime embedded in a matrix of civil liberties. Contemporary political transitions have tended to stall in "a political gray zone ... between full-fledged democracy and outright dictatorship."[2] As

Diamond notes, the problem of classifying political regimes has intensified in recent years as "more regimes than ever before are adopting the *form* of electoral democracy...but fail to meet (a) substantive test, or do so only ambiguously."[3] Around the world, intransigent incumbents go through the motions of holding competitive elections but impose political restrictions that make it extremely difficult, if not impossible, for opposition candidates to win. Analysts have yet to reach consensus on what to call these regimes – whether "electoral authoritarian," "competitive authoritarian," or "semiauthoritarian"[4] – but would probably endorse McFaul's view that a variegated "fourth wave of regime change" is producing both "democracy *and* dictatorship."[5]

Based on Freedom House data, Table 1.1 displays the distribution of political regime types in sub-Saharan Africa in 2001.[6] According to this classification, Diamond rates only five African regimes, containing just 7 percent of the continent's population, as *liberal democracies*. The governments of these countries came to power peacefully in free multiparty elections and subsequently held regular polls at intervals prescribed by national constitutions. Alternations of leadership have occurred in the island states of Mauritius and Cape Verde, events rarely seen before in African politics.[7] As the label implies, liberal democracies embody respect for civil and political liberties, for example, by tolerating press criticism, even as leaders have not actively encouraged or embraced dissent.[8] Liberties are upheld by relatively effective legislative and judicial institutions, which act fairly independently within a largely rule-governed political process. South Africa has led the way by establishing a constitutional court that undertakes rigorous judicial review of test cases based on an expansive bill of rights. And, to date, Africa's liberal democracies have benefited from moderate to low levels of corruption.

A larger group of transitions, numbering nine in sub-Saharan Africa by 2001, brought forth second-best, hybrid *electoral democracies*. These civilian, constitutional systems clearly meet minimal democratic standards, namely that legislative and chief executive offices are filled via popular choice under universal suffrage. The regime is founded and renewed by elections that observers, monitors, and losing candidates judge as fundamentally free and fair.[9] In electoral democracies, however, civil and political liberties, especially between elections, are not universally secure. Political minorities are sidelined from the protections of the constitution and justifiably complain, as in Malawi and Namibia, of neglect or even repression. Moreover, freedom of speech is compromised by government domination of the electronic media, which endows the ruling party or coalition with the loudest voice in the land. Most importantly, political power remains concentrated in the hands of executive presidents to the point that significant arenas of decision making lie beyond the control of other elected officials. While legislatures try to assert independence, for instance on budget matters (as in Benin), parliamentarians usually perform as docile handmaidens of the executive

TABLE 1.1. *Political Regimes in Sub-Saharan Africa, 2001*

Liberal Democracy		Electoral Democracy		Ambiguous		Liberalized Autocracy		Unreformed Autocracy	
Cape Verde	(1,2)	Ghana	(2,3)	Mozambique	(3,4)	**Competitive**		Swaziland	(6,5)
Mauritius	(1,2)	Mali	(2,3)	Tanzania	(4,4)	Lesotho	(4,4)	Burundi	(6,6)
São Tomé and Principe	(1,2)	Namibia	(2,3)	Djibouti	(4,5)	Central African Republic	(4,5)	Congo, Kinshasa	(6,6)
South Africa	(1,2)	Benin	(3,2)	Nigeria	(4,5)	Guinea-Bissau	(4,5)	Eritrea	(7,6)
Botswana	(2,2)	Madagascar	(2,4)	Sierra Leone	(4,5)	Côte d'Ivoire	(5,4)	Rwanda	(7,6)
		Seychelles	(3,3)	Zambia	(5,4)	Gabon	(5,4)	Somalia	(6,7)
		Senegal	(3,4)			Gambia	(5,5)	Sudan	(7,7)
		Malawi	(4,3)			Togo	(5,5)		
		Niger	(4,4)			Ethiopia	(5,6)		
						Kenya	(6,5)		
						Cameroon	(6,6)		
						Zimbabwe	(6,6)		
						Hegemonic			
						Burkina Faso	(4,4)		
						Congo, Brazzaville	(5,4)		
						Comoros	(6,4)		
						Mauritania	(5,5)		
						Chad	(6,5)		
						Guinea	(6,5)		
						Uganda	(6,5)		
						Angola	(6,6)		
						Liberia	(6,6)		
						Equatorial Guinea	(6,7)		

Note: Figures in parentheses are Freedom House political rights and civil liberties scores for 2001 on a scale of 1 (high) to 7 (low). Diamond subdivides liberalized autocracies into "competitive authoritarian" and "hegemonic authoritarian" regimes according to the degree that the executive branch of government restricts political competition.

Source: Adapted from Larry Diamond, "Thinking About Hybrid Regimes," *Journal of Democracy* 13, 2 (2002): Table 2.

branch.[10] And as ruling parties increase their parliamentary majorities in second and subsequent elections, executive and legislative powers become further fused.[11]

The most common way of organizing national politics in Africa however, is what we call *liberalized autocracy* (and what others call semi-, electoral, or competitive authoritarianism). Covering more than half the continent's countries and over two thirds of its population, liberalized autocracies are also hybrid systems; their genesis lies in previous military and one-party arrangements, now adapted for survival in a more open environment. Leaders have learned how to manipulate the rules of the democratic game and to stage manage low-quality elections to their own advantage. As evidenced by recent multiparty contests in Nigeria, Cameroon, Côte d'Ivoire, and Kenya before 2002, elections are nominally competitive but are seriously flawed by ethnic conflict, political intimidation, vote buying, and questionable ballot counts. With fairer elections, countries like Mozambique, Tanzania, and Zambia potentially could graduate to the status of electoral democracy (Diamond calls them "ambiguous," see Table 1.1). At the other extreme, however, as in Chad and Liberia, elections are the only available antidote to violence: voters calculate that the best prospects for peace lie in voting armed strongmen into power rather than allowing them to continue to prosecute a civil war (Diamond labels these de facto power monopolies as "hegemonic").

In liberalized autocracies, leaders may pay lip service to basic political freedoms, for example, by allowing token opposition. But they govern in heavy-handed fashion, typically placing strict limits on independent press, civic organizations, and political parties to the point of imprisoning their strongest opponents or barring them from contesting elections. The executive branch of government, personified in the presidency, is so dominant that, *in extremis*, the regime amounts to one-man rule. Even once-democratic regimes like Gambia and Zimbabwe, may slide back into autocracy due to power grabs by military or civilian elites.

Finally, we count seven *unreformed autocracies* where governments make no pretense at legitimizing themselves through competitive elections. In some cases, leaders came to power through heredity (as in Swaziland), military coup (as in Burundi), or armed insurgency (as in Eritrea or Rwanda). In other cases (for example, Sudan), sham elections are held in the parts of the country that the government controls, but major segments of the electorate are excluded, as are the opposition forces that represent such areas. These countries are often embroiled in extended internal conflicts that preoccupy their governments and can lead to the collapse of central state authority (as in Somalia and Congo, Kinshasa). As official control breaks down and weapons flood society, people are increasingly exposed to violence and extortion at the hands of local gangs or warlords. In these countries, political liberalization either is never attempted or is captured and distorted by faction leaders who stand to gain from the demise of central authority.

Thus, sub-Saharan Africa has undergone political change while also experiencing considerable continuity. In practice, inherited monopolies of power remain embedded in the heart of African political systems. Especially in countries where soldiers once ruled, the various armed forces resist domestication and continue to arrogate a wide range of reserve powers.[12] In Nigeria, for example, the army has unilaterally launched pogroms against protesters in minority ethnic enclaves that the elected civilian administration of Olusegun Obasanjo appears powerless to halt. Until civilians exert reliable control over the military, officials with guns remain capable of intervening, either to combat perceived opponents in society, or to seize control of the state. Moreover, within the realm of civilian authority, the task of dividing and distributing presidential power has barely begun. Election to office has not prevented ambitious leaders from resorting to arbitrary and personalistic tactics of rule, whereby power and patronage emanate principally from one "big man."[13] Even in post-Mandela South Africa, Thabo Mbeki has added extensive powers to the office of the president, overturned party preferences to install loyalist leaders in the provinces, and shown himself willing to set policy priorities, including treatment for AIDS victims, on the basis of personal whim.

The missing links in the further development of democracy in Africa are procedures for public accountability and a rule of law. To effectively reallocate power, institutions are required to counterbalance the centralizing impulses of military and civilian strongmen. Accountability can be asserted either horizontally within the state by legislative, judicial, and specialized oversight bodies, or vertically by institutions in society like political parties, civic associations, and the mass media. But these institutions must possess both autonomy, that is, their own budgets and bases of recruitment, and capacity, being able to check abuses by the executive branch. Ideally, a universal, secular body of law would be a key resource for enforcing accountability. Unfortunately, democratization in Africa has often occurred "backwards," at least in comparison to the sequence in which political development unfolded in the West. In the African context, universal suffrage has preceded rather than followed the establishment of a functioning state, as represented by the supremacy of constitutional rules and the institutional separation of powers.[14] In the absence of political institutionalization under a rule of law, Africa's democracies remain few and fragile.

TWO DECADES OF ECONOMIC REFORM, 1982–2001

In a parallel trend, independence leaders first sought to close African economies, but were later compelled to open them. International financiers required movement toward a market economy, defined as a regime in which private actors engage in production, distribution, and exchange without intervention by state institutions. In practice, as with political reforms, economic liberalization in African countries has been both partial and in-complete. It has been partial in the sense that reforms have been uneven across sectors and institutions, and incomplete to the extent that, in many places, the reform process has stalled or been rescinded.[15]

In a bid to consolidate political power after independence, African leaders first adopted a development strategy that favored the distribution of re-sources to political supporters rather than investments in economic growth. Policies during this period typically included an overvalued exchange rate, which guaranteed that urban elites could afford to import luxury goods, and subsidies on staple foods, which helped to ensure the political qui-escence of urban masses. This distorted policy regime, which discouraged producers and abetted state consumption, ultimately proved unsustainable because it led inexorably to fiscal and trade deficits. It also undermined the creation of wealth: for the continent as a whole, GDP per capita declined fully 15 percent between 1977 and 1985 alone, meaning that the average African had become poorer than she was at independence twenty-five years earlier.[16]

Faced with this economic crisis, African governments had little choice but to liberalize their approach to development by means of comprehen-sive programs of policy reform. With the admonition of Washington-based international financial institutions, but with varying degrees of political com-mitment, governments agreed to restore macroeconomic balance (short-term stabilization) and to try to recover economic growth (through longer-term adjustments to the structure of the economy).[17] Between 1982 and 1997, some thirty-seven African countries accepted stabilization and adjustment loans from the World Bank or International Monetary Fund, in return for which they promised to reduce the state's economic interventions and to en-courage the freer play of market forces.[18] While critics questioned whether an orthodox structural adjustment package would work in Africa, especially in places where a formal private sector had barely begun to function,[19] a consensus emerged that growth could never be restored unless government overspending and external payments were reined in.[20]

In early stages, the typical reform package included measures to bring the macro economy into equilibrium and to create new opportunities for agricul-tural production and international trade. Governments attempted to restore budget balance by reducing public spending, cutting deficits, and containing inflation. Outside the West African franc zone (where, until 1994, foreign exchange rates were fixed), the real value of national currencies was allowed to depreciate, thus closing the gap between official exchange rates and those on parallel, or "black," markets. Interest rates were deregulated, including by withdrawing subsidies on loans to small farmers. At the same time, farm-ers received tax relief as real producer prices were increased, sometimes to world market levels. Finally, governments unlocked international trade by curbing tariffs on imports and creating incentives to promote exports.

In later stages of the economic reform process, as conditional lending for structural adjustment supplanted emergency stabilization measures, African governments were encouraged to undertake far-reaching changes to economic institutions. For example, lenders and donors insisted that governments pull back from buying and selling farm products by allowing private traders to enter previously controlled agricultural markets. As a means of ending the drain on the national treasury of loss-making public corporations, governments had to come up with privatization plans to offload their holdings in airlines, railways, and public utilities, as well as in marketing and manufacturing. And the banking sector was deregulated, allowing the entry of private finance houses. Finally, governments were urged to downsize the public bureaucracy by eliminating patronage jobs from the civil service. In short, structural adjustment involved shrinking the size of the state.

Many of these economic reforms were controversial. Easterly argues that "the most important failing of adjustment lending (was) the failure to put in place policies that would promote growth."[21] Because the IMF and World Bank were concerned about debt service, they perversely rewarded poor economic performers with a string of loans and paid insufficient attention to incentives for economic expansion. The net effect of lending in the 1980s and 1990s was often economic contraction, even recession – economic growth remained "maddeningly hard to detect."[22] Stiglitz stresses the social costs of adjustment. Rapid and premature trade liberalization exposed the vulnerabilities of African farmers and manufacturers, who could not compete against the mass-produced or subsidized goods from Europe and America that soon flooded local markets. Jobs were lost as farms cut production and factories closed, and tight monetary policies discouraged entrepreneurs from taking on new workers. Additionally, "because trade liberalization occurred before safety nets were put in place, those who lost their jobs were forced into poverty."[23] Finally, van de Walle questions the appropriateness of state retrenchment. He compares public expenditures across various regions of the developing world in order to show that "the African state is not unusually large," "does not provide many services," and "is largely absent outside the capital."[24] Under these circumstances, economic development requires a longer and stronger bureaucratic reach – as well as an improved quality of public services – rather than further contraction of already limited state capacity.

In any event, economic reforms were rarely implemented in full. Attempts to restore fiscal health were uneven, with many governments failing to co-ordinate budgetary and monetary policies and thus never achieving even the primary goal of economic stability. Because many African politicians and civil servants were skeptical of the professed benefits of reform, adjustment agreements were abandoned or implemented only half-heartedly. Often, the most difficult structural transformations in the adjustment package were never systematically pursued. For example, although governments curbed the expansion of loss-making public enterprises, they often refused to sell off ("privatize") such enterprises.[25] And, even where privatization was undertaken, it usually did more harm than good in places that were rife with corruption. African governments also routinely dug in their heels when confronted with the need to reduce the number of public employees in the civil service. In acute cases, certain countries even reversed in the 1990s the hard-won trade and agricultural policy reforms that they had adopted with fanfare in the 1980s. For example, the liberalization of maize prices in Kenya was an on-again, off-again affair for two decades and, in Senegal and Zambia, the state began to intervene again to control international trade and agricultural marketing during the late 1990s.

Just as African countries attained differing degrees of liberalization in the political sphere, so they can be classified by the extent to which policymakers adopted an orthodox package of macroeconomic reforms. Reporting on its adjustment-lending operations in sub-Saharan Africa, the World Bank has provided a typology based on compliance with recommended reforms over time.[26] An underlying indicator – of multiple reforms in three policy arenas: macroeconomic stabilization, public-sector management, and private-sector development – captures both initial loan agreements and eventual policy shortfalls and reversals. After aggregating numerical scores for every reform in each policy arena, World Bank researchers grouped countries into three broad categories: good, poor, and weak compliance. We add a category for countries without World Bank adjustment loans that, for their parts, may or may not have undertaken homegrown economic reform programs (see Table 1.2).

By these standard, just ten African countries (what the World Bank calls "good compliers"), containing some 17 percent of sub-Saharan Africa's population, made a genuine policy effort to put their economies on a market-led course. Even if we add countries that, of their own accord, adopted a liberal package of economic policies (like Botswana, Namibia, Seychelles, and South Africa), then fewer than one quarter of all Africans now live under a predominantly market regime. As with democratization, market reform is an attribute of small states, with five high performers having populations of less than 2 million, two of which are islands (Mauritius and Seychelles). But a couple of decades of market reforms have yielded fewer positive results than one decade of political reforms, in good part because populous Nigeria managed to transit to electoral democracy while exhibiting "poor compliance" with macroeconomic adjustment.

Across Africa, reluctant reformers (that is those that the World Bank saw as achieving poor compliance) soon discovered that partial policy measures did not restore growth, and even avid reformers (that is, those with good compliance) found adjustment did not bring about sustained economic recovery. Conditions improved somewhat between 1995 and 1998 as sub-Saharan Africa's GDP expanded at a real average rate of 4 percent per annum,

TABLE 1.2. *Extent of Compliance with Economic Reform Programs, Sub-Saharan Africa, 1997*

Good Compliance	Weak Compliance	Poor Compliance	No World Bank Program
Benin	Burkina Faso	Burundi	Angola
Gambia	Côte d'Ivoire	Cameroon	Botswana
Ghana	Guinea	Central African Republic	Lesotho
Malawi	Guinea-Bissau	Chad	Namibia
Mali	Madagascar	Congo, Brazzaville	Seychelles
Mauritania	Niger	Equatorial Guinea	South Africa
Mauritius	Senegal	Gabon	
Mozambique	Togo	Kenya	
Sierra Leone	Uganda	Nigeria	
Tanzania	Zambia	Rwanda	
	Zimbabwe	Sào Tomé and Principe	
		Somalia	
		Sudan	
		Congo, Kinshasa	

Note: Data unavailable for Cape Verde, Comoros, Djibouti, Eritrea, Ethiopia, Liberia, and Swaziland.
Source: World Bank, *Adjustment Lending in Sub-Saharan Africa: An Update* (Washington, DC, World Bank, Operations Evaluation Department, Report No. 16594, 1997).

while inflation and trade imbalances fell.[27] But these gains were cut short by the Asian economic crisis of 1997–99 and the global economic slow-down that started in 2001 as demand for Africa's key commodities slumped, along with their prices. Moreover, growth rarely exceeded the anemic economic expansion experienced in the years immediately after independence; and because growth rarely outpaced the population boom, living standards continued to stagnate.

International policy advisers therefore began to insist that initial adjustment measures be supplemented with an array of second-generation institutional reforms. These included: a rule of law to guarantee rights in property and enforce contracts; more aggressive policies to build up the stock of human capital in terms of health and education; and a program of good governance to ensure the transparency, accountability, and effectiveness of the public bureaucracy. Thus, reformers drew an explicit connection between the two types of liberalization: in order to grow economically it was also necessary to embark on democratization.

DUAL TRANSITIONS: COMPATIBILITIES AND CONTRADICTIONS

Have democratic and market regimes emerged simultaneously in the countries of sub-Saharan Africa?[28] A simple analysis of the ranked categories in Tables 1.1 and 1.2 indicates a strong prima facie case for the coincidence of these two forms of regime.[29] The empirical evidence suggests that democracy – whether electoral or liberal – is likely to go together with good compliance with internationally mandated structural adjustment programs. A subset of leading African countries – including Botswana, Ghana, Malawi, Mali, Namibia, and South Africa, whose profiles of public opinion we examine closely in this book – is currently embarked on a dual transition on both political and economic fronts. By contrast, a dismal record on both types of liberalization marks unreformed autocracies such as Burundi, Rwanda, Congo (Kinshasa), Somalia, and Sudan, a laggard category that we do not systematically study here.

With reference to countries outside Africa, Dahl notes that, "by the end of the twentieth century, although not all countries with market economies were democratic, all countries with democratic political systems also had market economies."[30] Thus, a good deal of mutuality informs the makeup of liberalized regimes, not least because power and wealth are often distributed in societies according to shared patterns. The direction of the linkage runs both ways. On one hand, democratically elected governments tend to follow policies that are market friendly. Democratization requires a foundation in law, the presence of which gives investors confidence that politicians will be restrained from arbitrary intervention in economic life and that the proceeds of entrepreneurship will be protected. Also, political leaders who must account to a mass electorate are inclined to deliver welfare services, which in turn increase the stock of human capital required for economic advancement. On the other hand, market reforms undercut the advantages enjoyed by political elites in capturing rents from official monopolies and applying these to the consolidation of their own power. Instead, in market economies, resources are generated at various locations beyond the boundaries of the state, thus providing a material foundation for building countervailing political institutions.

Democracy and capitalism are also theoretically compatible. As Bunce has argued, these regimes "institutionalize uncertainty"; they combine firm rules with uncertain outcomes.[31] Thus, the institutionalization of liberal reforms does not put an end to change. Precisely because democracy and markets are constructed to allow open-ended solutions to emerging problems, they are more adaptable to changing environmental circumstances, and, in principle therefore should be better equipped for survival over the long run. By contrast, authoritarian rule and central planning are each a variation on a theme of top-down administration, and each has built-in rigidities. In Africa, postindependence regimes (which featured ambitious economic plans in a one-party state with a weak bureaucracy) were unable to deliver the range of public goods that national populations demanded. And existing institutions collapsed when ordinary people withdrew support and sought their own ways to get things done. By contrast, systems based on institutionalized uncertainty offer Africans opportunities to experiment with various solutions to the continent's deep-seated problems without having to repeatedly tear down whole regimes and then reconstruct them from the ground up.

As mentioned at the outset, however, democracy and markets may not flourish in Africa's inhospitable terrain. Old regimes will certainly prove resistant. We have already noted that the institutional skeletons of one-party and militarized states endure after transition, especially in liberalized autocracies. And we have shown that a state-centered approach to economic management lives on in African countries that display "poor" or "weak" compliance with market reforms, even as the state loses capacity to formulate policy and administer programs. Informal practices of patronage and clientelism surely persist (or even increase) after liberalization, negating the intent of formal-legal reforms. In certain countries, criminal elements within the political elite may even take advantage of new opportunities to evade laws and to create clandestine networks of personal power. As Bayart says, "the sequences of political and economic liberalization in Africa no doubt hold in store some very odd forms of deregulation indeed,"[32] including the continued privatization of the state through corruption and cronyism.

Moreover, the relationship between democratization and market reform embodies contradictions, some of which are quickly felt in the short term. On one hand, structural adjustment programs are almost invariably adopted by nondemocratic means. International bankers, technical advisers, or finance ministry officials make the critical decisions about economic policy behind closed doors, usually without popular consultation. Mkandawire condemns the absence of domestic policy debate about alternative strategies to orthodox adjustment as a manifestation of "choiceless democracy."[33]

On the other hand, the demands of governing democratically may tempt African governments to ignore the conditions attached to adjustment loans. As Block has demonstrated for Africa's electoral democracies, a political business cycle is already evident in the fiscal year before elections in which politicians "indulge in spending sprees and monetary expansions in an effort to retain office."[34] One would also expect that constituency pressures for social spending would tempt representatives to break austerity budgets even after elections. By enfranchising the population at large and unleashing popular demands, democratization inhibits economic discipline. In an ironic twist, the very political constituencies that were in the forefront of the prodemocracy movements – urban workers in formal wage employment – are asked to shoulder the burdens of austerity that accompany economic stabilization and adjustment. This has led some authors to argue that efforts at economic reform will derail when urban interest groups organize to resist austerity, either through unionized lobbying or spontaneous street protests.[35] According to this argument, democratic governments find it much more difficult to implement economic reform programs than more autocratic governments that can insulate policymakers, allowing them room to make unpopular policy choices.[36]

Above all, by widening income gaps, market reforms undermine the political equality on which democracy is based. While the democratic principle of one person–one vote endows all citizens with equally loud voices, the concentrations of wealth that arise in market economies permit some citizens to accumulate undue political influence. Whether through legal campaign contributions to political candidates or illegal bribes to sitting officeholders, rich people are able to purchase privileged access to the government's decisions. Moreover, capitalist firms are themselves internally autocratic; governed by powerful chief executives or small managerial teams, these organizations fit uncomfortably within the political culture of a democratic society. Thus, even though market reforms may provide a favorable environment for launching democracy, the tendency of capitalism to evolve into monopoly later acts as a brake on democracy's full institutionalization. As Dahl concludes, "In a country with a market-capitalist economy, it appears, full political equality is impossible to achieve . . . consequently, there is a permanent tension between democracy and a market-capitalist economy."[37]

DEMAND, SUPPLY, AND REGIME CONSOLIDATION

To the extent that democratization and market reform are compatible, a common framework of theory should encompass both types of regime change. At the same time, recognizing inherent tensions, space must be left for politics and economics to interact. In this book, we employ concepts from political economy – including popular demand for reform, the institutional supply of reform, and regime consolidation – that are inclusive enough, yet sufficiently discriminating, to suit these theoretical objectives. Given our disciplinary backgrounds as political scientists, we focus attention mainly on political regimes and leave the elaboration of a theory of the consolidation of market economies to colleagues more qualified than ourselves. We nonetheless wonder which comes first: political or economic reform?

For better or worse, the current discourse among political scientists about regime prospects revolves around the concept of "the consolidation of democracy." According to Linz and Stepan, democracy is consolidated when the procedures for electing leaders and holding them accountable become "the only game in town."[38] The critical elements are twofold: the rules, which codify a set of democratic political institutions; and a normative consensus among individual political actors, who agree to observe these rules.

As such, two distinct intellectual traditions – institutional and cultural – infuse the recent literature on democracy's consolidation. An institutional approach starts with rules. It seeks to discover whether familiar macropolitical structures – like elections, the separation of powers, and civilian control of the military – are being built on a foundation of law. For example, Huntington emphasizes elections and civil-military relations, linking the consolidation of democracy to the turnover of leaders and the professional training of the officer corps.[39] Grindle looks for the conversion of patron-client relations into political parties and at the decentralization of the functions of government.[40] And O'Donnell demands arrangements of "horizontal accountability" embedded in legislative and judicial bodies to check and balance the overweening powers of executive presidents.[41] Whichever agencies are emphasized, all these authors see the development of democracy as an interlocking set of macropolitical institutions.

An alternative, cultural approach begins at a micro level with personal attitudes and values. The logic is that democracy cannot take root without democrats, that is, individuals who will sponsor a democratic project and, if failure threatens, stand up to defend it. Higley and Gunther focus on the attitudes of political elites, a neglected topic; they show that "settlements and convergences" among top leaders are required to sustain programs of democratic reform.[42] Most culturalists, however, emphasize mass orientations, seeing these as essential to democracy's durability and safety. To cite just two examples: Shin tracks the evolution of public opinion in Korea during the 1990s, revealing a mixed record of democratic acculturation;[43] and Colton looks at electoral behavior in Russia during the same period, concluding, against expectations, that many ordinary Russians are transforming from subjects into citizens.[44]

In our opinion, political institutions and political cultures coevolve, each shaping the other. The consolidation of political regimes is best understood, therefore, as mutually reinforcing processes of *institutionalization* (at a macro level) and *legitimation* (at a micro level). Such convergence is implied in Linz and Stepan's recommendation to conceive consolidation constitutionally, as well as attitudinally and behaviorally.[45] Along these lines, Diamond proposes a mixed, multilevel matrix of indicators to tap both institutionalization and legitimacy.[46] And Hadenius reminds us that "political learning" about democratic citizenship occurs only under the institutional conditions of an "interactive state."[47]

However, because institutional and cultural developments inhabit disparate spheres of analysis, researchers usually make sweeping inferences about regime consolidation from limited bodies of evidence. On one hand, institutionalists are inclined to focus on the façade of legal procedures and formal organizations, without inquiring too closely whether such institutions are effective or accepted. On the other hand, culturalists place too much store on expressed levels of public support for democracy as if mass acclaim for an abstract regime alone were enough to ensure the deepening of actual democratic practice. To be sure, formal institutions and popular support for democracy are both necessary conditions for regime consolidation. But neither alone is sufficient.

Instead, for democracy to take root, popular *demands* for democracy must be accompanied by a *supply* of democratic institutions provided mainly, though not exclusively, by political elites. In the words of Rose, Mishler, and Haerpfer:

What happens to a new democracy is the outcome of a continuing process of interaction between what elites supply and what the populace demands. . . . Uninterrupted progress towards the *completion* of a new democracy will occur if popular demands for reforms to improve the regime are met by political elites. This positive equilibrium is often described as a stable or established democracy.[48]

An equilibrium model has several valuable features. It allows that regimes stabilize when equilibrium is attained. In this study, we measure the consolidation of democracy as a *high-level equilibrium* between popular democratic demands and the perceived supply of democratic institutions that is maintained over some period of time. Moreover, when equilibrium occurs at lower levels, it can indicate the consolidation of various nondemocratic, autocratic, and hybrid regimes. And, in principle, the same logic of supply and demand can be extended to the consolidation of economic regimes of varying qualities too.

To prepare the ground for expanding the scope of existing theory along these lines, we first enumerate the most cogent critiques of the consolidation of democracy as it is presently conceived in the literature on comparative politics.

First, critics note that a neat dividing line cannot be drawn between the end of regime transition and the beginning of regime consolidation. As Linz and Stepan recognize, democratic transitions are incomplete if an elected government does not enjoy full authority, both legally and in practice.[49] The persistence of "reserved domains" of political power is germane to countries in Africa where, even after elections, armies lurk in the wings of the political arena and presidents continue to assert excessive executive privilege. In the face of these realities, it is safer to assume that all regime transitions are extended and that the effectiveness of putative new "democracies" is often compromised from the start. As such, we need to make sure that any observed mass expressions of support for democracy are reinforced by popular rejection of military and strongman rule. To truly commit themselves to democracy, people must not only say they prefer it as the best form of government, but they must simultaneously abandon nostalgia for authoritarian alternatives.

Second, the end state of a "consolidated" regime may be difficult to discern. Dahl reminds us that the term "democracy" refers to both ideal and actual forms; in the real world, regimes are never consolidated as perfect models ("polyarchies").[50] All functioning democracies, including mature ones, include hierarchical institutions such as armies, courts, and bureaucracies, whose officials are appointed on the basis of professional merit.[51]

Moreover, in Africa, rulers who wish to govern in outlying rural areas also must come to terms with traditional leaders whose authority derives from heredity, not election.[52] Under these circumstances, political reform almost always leads in the direction of mixed or hybrid polities. In our view, the solution to the end-state problem is to avoid defining democracy in such an elevated fashion that few or no real-world cases can ever qualify. It is far better to portray democracy in realistic terms – warts and all – and to accept pragmatic standards for its achievement. Any indicator of the supply of democracy should therefore allow for the existence of minor exceptions and deviations.

Third, critics argue that consolidation is an encompassing meta process; it refers, in the aggregate, to the evolution of whole regimes. A holistic perspective does not easily permit the possibility that, in practice, political reform unfolds unevenly without overall coordination and that different sectors of the polity liberalize at varying speeds. In Africa, for example, electoral reforms have advanced at a faster pace than the growth of independent legislatures and judiciaries, creating opportunities for elected strongmen to rule without effective checks and balances. Because change is almost always fragmented, we welcome Schmitter's invitation to decompose whole systems and to refocus analysis on subregimes.[53] In this book, we explore the subregime of public opinion, explicitly deriving measures of regime legitimacy and institutionalization from mass perceptions. We invite other researchers – particularly institutionalists – to test whether independent, macrolevel measures of political institutionalization accord with the popular perceptions of the supply of democracy that we report.

Fourth, Przeworski et al. have argued that consolidation has little meaning beyond the sheer durability of a regime.[54] In an econometric analysis of 141 countries between 1950 and 1990, they ask whether the hazard rate – that is, the likelihood that a regime will die in any given year – declines with time. They discover that, once the level of economic development is controlled, older democracies (like, say, Argentina) are as likely to die as younger ones. Because the risk of democratic breakdown is independent of the age of the regime, they conclude that consolidation is an empty term. Although we confirm that time is unrelated to the probabilities of democratic decline or reversal in Africa (for example, Zimbabwe and Côte d'Ivoire have recently slid back), we think it is a mistake to conclude that regimes do not consolidate. On the contrary, the legitimization and institutionalization of rules and procedures – which increase the probability that a regime will not break down – is precisely what most scholars are referring to when they use the word "consolidation."

Finally, and most importantly, the standard paradigm of regime transitions has been indicted with embodying a directional bias. According to this archetype, democratization supposedly unfolds in a fixed teleological sequence – from opening, through breakthrough, to consolidation – with consolidation being "a slow but purposeful process in which democratic forms are transformed into democratic substance."[55] Carothers makes a strong case for abandoning the transition paradigm altogether because countries that exit from dictatorial rule do not automatically move in a democratic direction. As previously argued, most African political regimes are hybrids. Within an intermediate zone, new political regimes have emerged in Africa that have some democratic characteristics (notably elections), but which are marred by shifting party loyalties or by one-party dominance. Whichever direction is taken, these emergent regimes constitute *alternatives* to democracy. The time has therefore come, or so goes the argument, to discard a paradigm that assumes the inevitability of democratic outcomes in favor of a framework that allows the systematic comparison of a wide tableau of regimes.

We propose such a framework here. All political leaders seek to consolidate power. Because the most efficient way to exercise power is to win voluntary compliance from followers, leaders in every type of regime endeavor to legitimize their rule. Otherwise, they must resort to coercion – an unsustainable option for staying very long in public office – or to material incentives, which invariably dwindle under economic crisis. What distinguishes democracy ("rule by the people") from other regimes, however, is the critical extent to which leaders depend on the voluntary consent of citizens. Whereas autocratic or hybrid systems can survive for extended periods on the basis of enforced popular acquiescence or the distribution of rewards, democratic regimes depend centrally on the creation and constant renewal of popular legitimacy.

We further argue that the consolidation of political regimes requires that citizens do more than endorse model political arrangements. It is quite easy, after all, for respondents to sample surveys to say that they prefer democracy in the abstract, just as they might approve of motherhood. To ensure that any such ideal preferences are anchored in the reality of citizens' circumstances, it is also necessary to elicit opinions on how much political institutionalization is actually underway. Only if citizens perceive that democratic institutions are being supplied (also at a high level), can we infer that their country's regime is consolidating as a democracy. A common regime scenario in Africa is that ordinary people demand more democracy than political elites are willing or able to supply. To the extent that there are such institutional deficits, democracy's consolidation will be impaired.

Notwithstanding the critics, we therefore regard the concept of regime consolidation as innately appealing, especially if it can encompass other arrangements as well as democracy. We can imagine, and are interested in, a range of situations where regimes stabilize.[56] In these settings, political practices become regular and routine and cannot be disturbed easily by external shocks like war, political scandal, economic recession, or natural catastrophe. Of course, no political regime (including democracy) can ever be completely consolidated in the sense of always withstanding disturbances and never risking collapse. As such, consolidation is best conceived in contingent and probabilistic terms. In terms of a formal definition, consolidation is the probability of the avoidance of regime breakdown. In short, the consolidation of a regime is a prognosis about its survival prospects.[57]

To summarize, we wish to expand the rubric of "the consolidation of democracy." We extract a useful part – "consolidation" – and apply it to a range of political regimes. We even hold out the possibility that others might apply it to economic regimes. A shift to a more generic language of "regime consolidation" avoids the deterministic view that democratization is universal, and allows that political regimes may solidify in various autocratic or hybrid forms. What matters is whether mass populations endorse the arrangements for governance that are actually supplied. Stated differently, is there equilibrium between the level of demand for a regime and the level of the supply of its institutions? While leaving the door open to the possibility that some contemporary African regimes might consolidate as democracies (at a high level of both supply and demand), we expect that only a small minority will succeed in doing so. Thus, we retain the concept of the consolidation of democracy, but grant it a much more modest and conditional status than it has enjoyed in the literature to date.

DERIVING PUBLIC OPINION

To conclude this chapter, we suppose that incomplete reforms and hybrid regimes give rise to distinctive profiles of public opinion and participation. In so doing, we begin to shift gears from the macro level of whole-system reforms to the micro level of mass attitudes and behaviors. We infer from the features of existing, half-formed regimes a few general propositions about the expected nature of mass support for democracy and markets in Africa.

First, if regime change is partial, then popular awareness of reform programs will be rudimentary. We expect that ordinary people will find it hard to recognize concepts like democracy or policies like structural adjustment if they have never come into contact with fully developed examplars of these arrangements. How, for example, could Africans have attained a sophisticated attachment to democracy when they have only ever experienced traditional rule or colonial and postcolonial repression? Nor are brief, recent experiences with liberalized autocracy likely to generate deep understandings of democratic values and procedures. Popular awareness is likely to be even more limited with regard to economic reforms, which are often technically complex, even counterintuitive. It is not immediately obvious to most people (or even to some leaders!), for example, that administrative price controls lead to shortages, black markets, and, thereby, unintentionally to higher prices. Even if people have heard about liberalization, they may have trouble attaching to it much meaning or relevance. In short, where political and (especially) economic literacy are low, attitude formation will hinge critically on popular learning about the content and implications of reform.

Second, we still expect to find a considerable measure of popular support for something called "democracy" and high levels of rejection of failed political systems from the past. This is so because ordinary people joined mass movements calling for the ouster of dictators in the 1990s, thus revealing an indigenous demand for political reform. They were primed to prefer principles like free speech and multiparty competition that embody the political changes they desire. By contrast, we anticipate that popular support for a market economy will be limited, in large part because the initiative for economic liberalization has come from above. State elites who reluctantly accepted IMF-led reforms had little incentive to inform the mass public of harsh fiscal targets and aid conditions. Moreover, because economic reforms began a decade earlier than political reforms, more time has since elapsed for popular expectations to dissipate. Thus, whereas mass euphoria engendered by recent political transitions may persist, "adjustment fatigue" has set in wherever economic reforms have not resulted in broad-based recovery.

Third, we expect Africans to distinguish between the ideal regimes they prefer and the real (but imperfect) systems with which they must "make do." Stated differently, we expect significant gaps between popular demands for change and perceptions of the amount of reform actually supplied. Much depends on the (often stratospheric) altitude of mass expectations, for example about the accountability of elected leaders. If ordinary people become disillusioned with the performance of the leaders for whom they voted, then the latter will face ongoing pressures for reform. Even though, at the time of transition, economic hopes were inflated, the desire for improved living standards did not commonly take the form of demands for a market economy. We suspect that most Africans prefer to retain a significant economic role for the state. If this turns out to be true, then demands for, and the perceived supply of, markets will stabilize at much lower levels than the equilibrium for democracy. In short, we expect to find that economic reform has been partial in Africa in large part because producers and consumers have not insisted upon it.

Finally, we expect the contradictions of market capitalism to undermine the acceptability of all reform agendas. We confidently predict that mass publics in African countries will display an aversion to any inequalities in income, assets, and wealth that result from market-based economic reforms. Indeed, we expect that increasing economic inequality will prove to be the Achilles' heel of economic reform in Africa, at least insofar as winning popular support for these reforms is concerned. The big question is whether mass anxiety about widening rich-poor fissures spills over from economic to political regimes, thus undermining support for, and satisfaction with, democracy. Two scenarios are possible. One is that the market defames democracy in the popular imagination by associating elected regimes with unfair austerity measures. The other is that ordinary people, recognizing that corrupt political elites are keeping the benefits of economic reform to themselves, deepen their commitments to democracy, if only to secure the mechanisms for removing such leaders from power. On the basis of empirical analysis of public opinion, this book seeks to discover which of these outcomes is more likely.

2

Studying Public Opinion in Africa

During the 1990s, Africans voted for new leaders because they were tired of economic mismanagement by despotic presidents. They went to the polls with high expectations that improvements in the quality of life would follow from competitive elections. Before long, however, citizens began to feel that politicians' promises about the benefits of political and economic reform were not being met. In a focus group discussion in Zambia's rural Southern Province just one year after the country's historic founding election, a peasant farmer asked: "Why should I vote (again) when I didn't get what I expected?" As another participant in Lusaka put it: "People hoped for miracles after the elections. Now they blame democracy."[1]

How common is this line of reasoning? Do Africans generally make connections between their life satisfactions and support for new political regimes? Or do they tend to fall back on deep-seated cultural values in deciding whether democracy and markets are right for them? Do they make well-informed judgments when deciding whether to support a new regime or participate in it? Or do they reflexively lapse into old habits, such as loyally voting for the ruling party and continuing to trade through government-controlled marketing agencies, regardless of institutional performance?

This chapter introduces our argument that attitudes to reform in Africa derive from popular learning. It makes a case that Africans learn about reform by gaining awareness of the issues at stake and choosing among alternative courses of action. In so doing, we summarize the principal theoretical approaches from the recent literature on the mass popularity (or otherwise) of democratic and market transitions in postcommunist Europe, Latin America, and East Asia. As for research methods, we ask whether well-established techniques of sample surveys can be applied with success under the challenging field conditions of sub-Saharan Africa and, if so, with what essential modifications. In so doing, we introduce the Afrobarometer, the data set on which our analysis is based.

Public opinion is broadly conceived here. Our definition encompasses not only values and attitudes, but also related behaviors. After all, new political and economic regimes are unlikely to thrive unless their supporters act on the courage of their convictions. That is, the legitimation of democracy and markets necessarily involves participation in daily political and economic life and standing up to defend new regimes should the need arise. We will always try to be clear about the particular dimension of attitudes and behavior that we are seeking to explain. Moreover, it is safe to assume that a phenomenon as complex as public opinion can never be encapsulated by any single factor. Defensible explanations will necessarily be multivariate, drawing upon a combination of theoretical strands. Thus, even as we settle on a theory of popular learning, we prefer to place competing theories in the order of relative influence rather than to definitively accept one and reject all others.

COMPETING THEORIES, RIVAL HYPOTHESES

This chapter reviews five families of possible explanation for regime support and popular participation. The first approach is *sociological*, locating the sources of public opinion in the structure of society as measured initially by the demographic characteristics of survey respondents. A second possibility is *cultural*, in which public opinion emanates from the norms and values inherited from an indigenous past and is expressed through habitual behaviors. A third approach is *institutional*, whereby a contemporary superstructure of legal rules, associational memberships, and formal activities shapes people's preferences. As we will show, scholars who have studied mass orientations in transitional societies around the world have found merit in each of these schemes and we anticipate that each will contribute to our understanding of public opinion in African countries too.

But we are predisposed to favor two alternate lines of explanation. We propose that, in the first instance, individual orientations toward national-level regimes in Africa will depend heavily on ordinary people's *awareness of public affairs*. We expect that Africans will form basic attitudes according to their levels of political and economic knowledge, including whether they can attribute a meaning to the notion of democracy, have heard about their country's structural adjustment program, and other, related, cognitive considerations. It seems to us that, for people to demand the introduction of reforms, they must first become aware of their political and economic surroundings. We also anticipate that people in Africa will develop their attitudes toward democracy and markets on the basis of *performance evaluations*. We posit that, far from being driven primarily by identity, ideology, or institutions, Africans know their individual and collective interests, on which they act pragmatically and instrumentally. Simply stated, if people see leaders and governments as effective at delivering desired goods and services, then they will give backing to liberalized regimes. If not, people will withhold their endorsement, finding the new arrangements deficient in important respects.

To reiterate: various explanations of public opinion in Africa are plausible; and different explanations may account for its various facets, especially its behavioral ramifications. But the unifying question is "why?" *Why* do Africans think and act as they do about democracy and markets?

We start by reviewing the answers proposed by competing theories.

Social Structure

Social scientists routinely assume that demography – measured by qualities like *gender, age*, and *residential location*[2] – shapes the ways in which individuals reason and behave. Indeed, modernization theory posits that upwardly mobile individuals – such as those who migrate to towns and enter nonagricultural occupations – are agents of change. Accordingly, people located in the modern parts of society would seem likely to become supporters of reform and to undertake various acts of political and economic participation.[3]

Along these lines, one would expect to find differences in regime preferences between generations who grew up before, during, or after the old order reached its peak, with newer generations being more open to change. Finifter and Mickiewicz found in the then USSR that supporters of reform were drawn predominantly from "the young (who) have derived both psychic gratification from (new) policies and are looking for distinct career advantages."[4] A negative relationship between age and reformism – with older people being more resistant to change, especially the introduction of a market-based economy – was confirmed by Miller, Hesli, and Reisinger in subsequent studies in Russia, Ukraine, and Lithuania in 1990–92.[5] While these authors agree on little else, they confirm each others' findings about the effects of social structure: characteristics such as youth, male gender, and urban residence incline citizens of the former Soviet Union to support reform initiatives.

Interestingly, other studies fail to replicate these demographic effects. In a nine-country, crossnational study in Eastern and Central Europe, Rose and colleagues discover that age does not discriminate between supporters and opponents of the current political regime, especially when controls are introduced for education.[6] Similarly, gender and residential location do not predict whether an individual will adopt reform orientations, though women are slightly more likely to harbor nostalgia for previous one-party political systems. Likewise, Shin finds in Korea that age is the least effective demographic predictor of support for a democratic regime, even though students and young workers played leading roles in the mass protests that precipitated an end to military rule. Moreover, the slight tendency for men and urban dwellers to express support for democracy again fails to hold up when education is brought into the equation.[7]

New urban-rural divisions may emerge, however, as a consequence of structural adjustment programs that aim to correct urban bias in the allocation of public investments.[8] These reforms create economic winners and losers by extending incentives (like higher farm-gate prices) to rural producers of food and export crops and reducing public services (like food and fuel subsidies) to consumers based in towns. Moreover, while a simple "urban versus rural" comparison is adequate as a first cut, a finer-grained social analysis may be even more desirable. In some rural areas, for example, subsistence producers or consumers of imported fertilizers who do not benefit from price liberalization will not automatically jump on the economic-reform bandwagon. And the imposition of school fees hurts the urban and rural poor alike. Nevertheless, the main point stands: one can expect variations in support for economic reform according to the location of actors in the social structure.

Our instinct is to suppose that modernizing middle classes are the natural constituency for reform movements, but that contextual conditions offset this tendency. As noted earlier, the middle class is very small in Africa and is inclined to defend gains made under old regimes. Moreover, the promise of modernization has failed many ordinary Africans – especially those who are educated but unemployed – thus hindering their natural advocacy of democracy and markets. It remains an open question, which we hope to resolve empirically, as to how urbanization and other modernizing trends have affected the formation of public opinion in Africa. We anticipate that other features of the social structure – especially poverty and ethnicity, but possibly also race and religion – will come into play. Since these elements have been understudied in the modernization literature, we will explicitly test them here.

Cultural Values

Alternatively, public opinion may be shaped by indigenous cultures. This school of thought assumes that deeply embedded values invest social situations with distinctive meanings that regulate individual attitudes and behavior.[9] For example, agrarian societies usually promote communal ethics, according to which the welfare of the group takes precedence over the personal interests of any individual. In the past, communitarian cultures ensured the survival of families and clans during times of environmental stress or external threat. But it is unclear whether values like kinship obligation or loyalty to a patron are also well suited to democratic politics or economic growth. Existing normative orders may inhibit the expression of political dissent or business entrepreneurship. And obligations to kin may come into conflict with the laws of a bureaucratic state, which mandate equal treatment for all citizens.

Reviving the concept of political culture,[10] Inglehart argues that, "the publics of different societies are characterized by durable cultural orientations that have major political and economic consequences."[11] He finds that a syndrome of values – including interpersonal trust, life satisfaction, and support for the existing social order – is, in the aggregate, strongly linked to the number of years that democratic institutions have functioned, a claim based on data from seventy countries on five continents that cover "almost 80 percent of the world's population."[12] Controlling for the effects of economic development and social structure, "over half the variance in the persistence of democratic institutions can be attributed to the effects of political culture alone."[13] In similar vein, Putnam argues that a tradition of civic engagement – reflecting interest in politics and values of political equality and compromise – essentially displaces the influence of economic development on democratic performance.[14] This pattern of norms generates social capital, a moral resource that enables coordinated action.[15]

To test such claims at the individual level in Africa, we will examine whether three core cultural values shape orientations to political and economic reform. The first is *interpersonal trust*, which measures the extent that individuals are predisposed to be open in their relations with other people. Democratization requires, in Inglehart's words, that "one must view one's political opponents as a loyal opposition who will not imprison or execute you if you surrender political power to them, but can be relied on to govern within the laws, and to surrender power if your side wins the next election."[16] Another key norm is *individual responsibility*. Do people believe that, at root, they are personally liable for ensuring their own well-being? Or do they wait passively for deliverance, relying on outside interventions from the community, a powerful patron, or a beneficent welfare state?[17] We suspect that individualism is a precondition for asserting political rights, debating policy alternatives, and acting as a political or economic entrepreneur. Finally, we wish to know about people's *tolerance for risk*, which reflects not only their comfort level with market economics but also their willingness to try an untested political regime like democracy. An innovative study of popular economic values in the Soviet Union and the United States found few differences in the opinions of the two publics regarding the desirability of incentives and rewards for hard work.[18] This leads us to expect that, even in societies where norms of collective responsibility purportedly prevail, individuals still wish to seize opportunities to improve their lot.

For various reasons, we avoid the term "political culture" here. We do not find it helpful to characterize whole civilizations, countries, or groups according to homogenous syndromes of values.[19] Rather, we see cultural orientations as attributes of individuals, who flexibly adopt diverse combinations of norms, including mixtures of tradition and modernity, materialism and postmaterialism, and indigenous and Western values. Moreover, the introduction of radical reform agendas (such as democratization or structural adjustment) disturbs the prevailing cultural order and causes normative disorientation among the general public. As Eckstein has predicted, "changes in political cultures that occur in response to social discontinuity should initially exhibit considerable formlessness."[20] We therefore suspect that cultural values will be fairly incoherent, having less influence on public opinion in African countries than theories of political culture would have us believe.

Institutional Influences

A third theoretical approach traces individual action to rules and organizations. Hadenius argues that the emergence of a civic culture "depends in a high degree on the institutional setting, that is, the structure of the state."[21] All forms of organization embody rules. Rules, in turn, provide signals to individuals about the rewards and punishments to be expected from various courses of action. As Grofman puts it, "preferences can be understood only in the context of institutionally generated incentives and institutionally available options that structure choice."[22]

Adopting a narrow notion of institutions, we report on three ways in which they impinge directly on public opinion. First, an individual's *identification with a political party* surely shapes his or her view of the world. In industrial societies, people tend to adopt partisan alignments on the basis of affinities with party positions on a "left-right" ideological scale. In agrarian societies, however, party loyalties tend to accrete around hometown solidarities and familiar patrons. What matters most in either setting, though, is the success of one's preferred party at the polls – in other words, whether one sees oneself as a political *winner* or *loser*. It can be expected that adherents of winning political parties will hold a rosier view of the legitimacy of the political regime than those who lost the last elections. Especially in systems based on patronage, and in countries where political office is one of the only reliable routes to personal wealth, partisan identification with a governing party is critical to one's life chances. Anderson and Guillory have shown that the winners of electoral contests in Western Europe are more likely than the losing side to express satisfaction with democracy.[23] And, importantly for Africa's winner-take-all politics, Norris confirms that, "winners have higher confidence in governing institutions than losers."[24]

Second, individuals who belong to *voluntary organizations* take cues from these institutions. According to Cohen and Rogers, voluntary organizations "shape the beliefs, preferences, self-understandings and habits of thought and action that individuals bring to more encompassing political arenas."[25] From Tocqueville onward, voluntary associations and interest groups have been seen as training grounds for democratic citizenship and as way stations on the road to broader forms of political participation. The comparative empirical record tends to confirm this. As Nie and colleagues first observed, an individual's "organizational involvement is the predictive variable with the most strength."[26] Latterly, McDonough and colleagues note for contemporary Spain that "membership in voluntary associations is convertible, after some slippage, into political participation."[27] One wonders precisely how associational life is conducive to democratic citizenship. Brady, Verba, and Schlozman propose a resource model of participation in which civic skills are honed in voluntary associations. They find that involvement in organized religion is especially conducive to political activism, especially if it is organized congregationally rather than hierarchically.[28]

Finally, institutions influence attitudes when citizens take part in *formal participatory procedures*. The guiding assumption of the new institutionalism is that rules shape behavior; the logical extension of this chain of causality is that behaviors then shape attitudes. Muller and Seligson pose the possibility that mass attitudes are "an effect rather than a cause of democracy... a learned response to the experience of living in a country that has a stable democratic regime."[29] The mechanisms of such mass political learning have not been well explored. An emerging literature on the effects of civic education in new democracies hints that the act of voting, especially for people for whom it is a novel experience, can build support for democracy.[30] While it stands to reason, for example, that an engaged and politically confident person who is interested in public affairs is likely to vote, it is also plausible that such participatory experience in turn enhances interest and efficacy.[31] We fully expect that, in transitional countries where the majority of the population has only recently won the right to make an unfettered choice at the polls, the experience of voting is itself formative in building regime support.

Cognitive Awareness

Theorists generally agree that public opinion has a cognitive element and, accordingly, that democracy and markets operate best when "the people" are well informed.[32] For example, to hold political leaders accountable, citizens require information. The quality of citizenship improves as they learn to identify their leaders, understand how the political system works, and become exposed to contemporary policy debates. Cognitive engagement with political and economic environments also enables citizens to form opinions about the pros and cons of reform. Yet, especially in poor countries, many people continue to lead parochial lives, absorbed in the day-to-day economic routines of household survival. Under these circumstances, low levels of information and a generalized lack of popular awareness about public affairs can constitute major obstacles to reform.

It stands to reason that individuals become aware of public affairs in good part as a function of *formal education*. Education increases a wide range of relevant skills: how to read, write, and calculate and how to critically evaluate information provided by the mass media. Education also increases popular knowledge on a range of relevant topics, including procedures for navigating through the complex requirements of modern life. Finally, education helps to dispel superstition and fatalism, boosting people's confidence that they can influence events. As a vast literature confirms, to the extent that education diffuses values of freedom, equality, and competition, it is also conducive to democratization.[33] Indeed, researchers have found that education consistently shapes opinion about new political regimes across the various nations that have recently undergone transitions; net of other modernizing influences, education significantly increases the likelihood that individuals will support liberalization.[34]

Beyond education, however, effective citizenship would seem to require *cognitive engagement* in public affairs. People must evince an *interest in politics*, engage in *discussion* of current events and policy issues, and possess an internal sense of *personal efficacy*. As Dahl reminds us, a "good citizen is concerned about public affairs and political life; well-informed about issues, candidates, and parties; (and) engaged often with fellow citizens in deliberations on public matters."[35] Few people ever live up to these lofty standards; in most countries, only a minority is deeply interested in public affairs or actively engaged in debates over economic policy. In Korea, although very few people say they are "very interested" in politics, these attentive individuals prefer democracy in the present and future.[36] Individuals also require the confidence to act, for example to approach policy elites and to make their preferences known.[37] Research in Costa Rica has shown that a subjective sense of self-confidence propels people to join voluntary organizations, contribute to community development projects, and to vote in national and local government elections.[38]

Finally, effective citizenship rests on the acquisition by individuals of relevant political and policy knowledge. John Zaller has proposed the term *political awareness* to refer to "the extent to which an individual pays attention to politics *and* understands what he or she has encountered."[39] He notes that people vary greatly in their attentiveness to politics and that average overall levels of information are quite low. For example, less than half of eligible adult voters in the United States can name their congressional representative and many Americans are ignorant of international affairs and their own country's foreign policies.[40] The observation that many citizens are underinformed provides a basis for modeling the formation of public opinion in Africa. We fully expect that Africans are "able to react critically to the arguments they encounter only to the extent that they are knowledgeable about political affairs."[41] Any model of public opinion in Africa must therefore include measures of factual information, such as citizen knowledge of the identity of elected leaders and the content of concepts like democracy and economic structural adjustment.

Performance Evaluations

Performance evaluations are based on rational choice. People compute the costs and benefits associated with different regimes and align themselves with arrangements that best serve their interests. If average citizens see that politicians are fulfilling campaign promises of peace and prosperity, then support will increase, not only for the government of the day, but also for democracy. If, however, people suffer repression or unemployment, then they are prone to turn against new political or economic systems. As such, regime support based on performance evaluations is conditional: it depends on what regimes actually do, and whether this performance lives up to popular expectations. The ever-present dangers are that ineffective governments fail to deliver desired goods, expectations dwindle into disillusionment and, in the process, democracy is discredited. In Elster's blunt words, "democracy will be undermined if it cannot deliver goods in the economic sphere."[42] Such predictions resonate well with prevailing perspectives on Africa's "politics of the belly."[43]

But performance evaluations cover at least two baskets of public goods. In one basket are *economic goods*, like jobs, incomes, assets (for example, land), consumer products, and an array of basic social services; in the other basket are *political goods* including political order, civil liberties, electoral rights, human dignity, and equality before the law. Generally, governments find it easier to deliver political goods. Provided there is a modicum of political order (no small requirement in Africa), the authorities can provide civil liberties and electoral rights virtually at the stroke of a pen, achieving immediate and broad benefit at low economic cost. The restoration of economic growth and full employment are much more difficult long-term projects that inevitably involve severe short-term dislocations. Evaluations of regime performance, especially during dual transitions, therefore hinge on the delivery of *both* kinds of public goods. In the short run, the provision of political freedoms may buy time for market reforms to take effect; and in the long run, improved performance of the economy may help to legitimate democracy. But this ideal outcome depends on citizens making "separate and correct" distinctions between "a basket of economic goods (which may be deteriorating) and a basket of political goods (which may be improving)."[44]

As Norris has noted "theories of political economy commonly focus on how system support relates to public evaluations of government performance, particularly concerning the economy."[45] Studies of North America and Western Europe have confirmed the formative influence on regime support of individuals' present, past, and future assessments of economic conditions.[46] Similar findings have recently emerged from countries undergoing dual transitions, notably in Eastern and Central Europe. Kitschelt connects the public's subjective perception of its own and the country's economic situation to support for democracy in this region.[47] And Dalton discovers that positive evaluations of the West German national economy, as well as negative evaluations of the former East German national economy, lead East German survey respondents to express democratic values.[48]

Beyond expectations of economic growth, the general public often also insists on distributive justice. In Spain, an economic boom helped to build support for the socialist government of Felipe González and legitimacy for the regime of democracy. Spaniards supported the new regime because, across social classes, it generated "an impression of fairness – with a sense of relative justice."[49] In East Germany, too, feelings about whether one has received a fair share financially are strongly related to support for democratic norms.[50] In an insightful study in Central America, Anderson demonstrates that "people may find non-economic reasons for taking political action even when their problems of material insecurity have not yet been resolved."[51] Peasants in Nicaragua and Costa Rica rarely act for economic reasons alone and often impute moral meaning to their participation in politics; they do not "separate economic insecurity from injustice but view them as one and the same problem."[52]

This brings us to political goods. In an influential article, Evans and Whitefield introduce the idea that "citizens' commitment to democracy may be less a function of how the market is perceived to work than of how democracy itself is experienced."[53] From this perspective, the proper criterion for judging democracy is not so much the delivery of economic growth or material welfare, but the provision of peace, freedom, and accountability. Rose, Mishler, and Haerpfer ask whether people feel freer under postcommunist regimes "to say what they think, to choose their own religion, to join any organization, to take an interest or not in politics, and to travel where they want."[54] Three quarters of the survey respondents across nine former Eastern bloc countries say they feel freer in these ways. And, importantly, 65 percent of these lovers of freedom also express support for the new political regime, compared to a "deviant few" (16 percent) who do not feel freer on any count.

Thus, we endorse the caution against "taking at face value reductionist economic theories that treat all political attitudes as if they were simply derivative of economic conditions."[55] Numerous researchers have explored the effects of adding institutional trust and political goods to multivariate statistical models of support for democracy. They consistently find stronger impacts from political than economic evaluations.[56] They generally conclude that a complete model of support for democracy requires *both* economic and political predictors, but that "politics matter more."[57] In Gibson's terms, "attitudes towards democratic institutions have a greater influence over economic attitudes than economic attitudes have over attitudes to democracy."[58] In the words of Evans and Whitefield, "people support democracies because they are seen to work ... rather than on the basis of a simple 'cash nexus.'"[59] Thus, we cannot automatically conclude that citizens will blame democracy if political transition is not immediately followed by economic recovery.

TOWARD A LEARNING APPROACH

If scholars of Africa consider public opinion at all, they usually depict it as a product of entrenched social conditions or enduring cultural identities. While the fixed features of society and culture may tell part of the story, however, structural analyses do not allow that adults may also flexibly adopt attitudes as agents in their own right. We think that the evolution of public opinion depends to a large degree on certain key individual qualities that, taken together, describe how people orient themselves toward public affairs.

On one hand, we draw attention to emerging popular understandings of what a democracy or a market actually *is*. For people to arrive at a judgment about any new regime, especially an unfamiliar one, they require information about its content. On the other hand, we also emphasize mass perceptions of what, in practice, democracy and markets actually *do*. In this instance, people establish opinions by checking their own reactions to the concrete consequences of new political and economic arrangements. The content and consequences of new regimes lead us to focus on knowledge and experience as the key determinants of public opinion. Indeed, we think that *cognitive awareness* (of what a new regime *is*) and *performance evaluations* (of what a new regime *does*) together constitute the foundation for what we call *learning about reform*.

The notion of popular learning is hardly new because it is implicit in theories of political socialization. In a classic statement, David Easton identified "diffuse support" as a deep-seated set of values that provide legitimacy to a political system.[60] These values are learned early in life, being imbibed during childhood from family and school. Diffuse support is inculcated with little conscious choice, leads to prevailing regimes being largely taken for granted, and is relatively impervious to change. As numerous authors have argued, the historical context in which individuals are raised has a significant impact on their outlooks, leading to congruence between prevailing regimes and mass cultures.[61] But because democratic or market regimes have rarely existed before at the national level in Africa, these regimes are novel. Thus, people must learn about them largely from scratch.

Rose and colleagues amend the classic socialization thesis by arguing that people arrive at their attitudes and values by combining youthful learning with current experience.[62] They note the practical payoffs that adults (do or do not) derive from the performance of the regimes they have lived under in the immediate past and present.[63] A full account of the formation of public opinion therefore requires the amalgamation of deep and recent occurrences into a "lifetime learning model."[64] The important point is that:

Although socialization and performance theories are often presented as rival, the theoretical distinction between them is overdrawn. Both approaches conceive support as a product of experience. They differ principally in the time frames and the types of experience they regard as most relevant.... (If these theories are) integrated into a developmental model of lifetime political learning ... support for the regime is initially shaped by early socialization and then evolves continuously through adult life as initial beliefs are reinforced or challenged by later experiences.[65]

Others complement these insights. Eckstein identifies "a postulate of cumulative socialization," according to which "learning is continuous throughout life" and "the bits and pieces of cognitive, affective, and evaluative learning form a consistent whole."[66] Bermeo submits that, "the concept of political learning is based on the premise that beliefs are not immutably fixed in childhood and that they can be affected by political events such as the replacement of one regime with another."[67] She cites approvingly Axelrod's trial-and-error approach to norms, *viz* that, "what works out well ... is likely to be used again while what turns out poorly is likely to be discarded."[68] We take these views to be consistent with Diamond's position that political culture is not eternal:

Three decades of research since *The Civic Culture* have shown that the cognitive, attitudinal, and evaluational dimensions of political culture are fairly 'plastic' and can change quite dramatically in response to regime performance, historical experience, and political socialization. ... Recent survey data suggest that even the deeper, normative layer of mass political culture may respond fairly rapidly to major changes in a country's political system, making it possible to entrench democracy even when a country has little if any prior historical experience of it.[69]

Our approach pushes these observations to a logical conclusion, namely that learning about reform is a recent phenomenon that occurs primarily in adulthood. A process of learning about reform is initiated by regime transition. In Africa, it reflects popular efforts to establish and come to grips with the new rules to the political and economic game that were introduced via liberalization in the 1980s and 1990s. These regime changes call upon adult Africans to make use of all their cognitive and rational faculties to arrive at decisions about whether democracy and markets are right for them.

If we are correct that the formation of public opinion is largely a function of contemporary learning, then the following propositions should hold. First, in terms of cognitive awareness, support for liberalization will be stronger among those who understand the features of the reform agenda and weaker among those who – for lack of education, interest, or information – do not fully comprehend the issues at hand. Second, in terms of rational evaluation, support for liberalization will be higher among people who think that democratization and market reforms have served their interests and lower among those who fear that they are losing out.

Low levels of formal education and the limited spread of mass media on the African continent make cognitive considerations especially important in the formation of public opinion, depressing the proportion of the population that has arrived at informed attitudes. And the authoritarian legacies of strongman government and central economic planning limit the numbers of people who find it safe to think for themselves about political and economic affairs. But even people who are relatively isolated and uninformed can engage in "low information reasoning" from everyday observations in their community.[70] They can comprehend trends in the wider political economy from rising or falling prices, the availability of consumer goods, the frequency of formal or informal housing starts, the number of beggars or job seekers on the street, and the nature of their interactions with police and other public officials. Others gain valuable additional information by talking to friends and neighbors about the pressing political and economic issues of the day. Thus, even citizens with low levels of information have grounds for arriving at performance evaluations of leaders, governments, and regimes.

In addition, even if African leaders often repeat the mistakes of their predecessors, ordinary citizens can still learn from experience. Against a backdrop of economic and political crisis – which is manifest at the popular level in poverty and powerlessness – people harbor great expectations that any change to the status quo will appreciably improve the quality of life. At the same time, they doubt that the powers that be will ever share authority or make a good faith effort to pursue a societal project aimed at a common good. Under these conditions, evaluations of the performance of leaders and institutions are likely to profoundly influence public opinion about whole regimes. With the introduction of democracy and markets, the supposed beneficiaries of reform gain the opportunity to challenge governments with the query: "How exactly have I benefited?" By monitoring their gains and losses, especially compared to the status quo ante, people learn whether or not liberalization is in their interest.

On a more speculative note, we suppose that popular learning will apply asymmetrically to the demand and supply sides of reform process. We propose that *cognitive awareness* of public affairs will best illuminate *demand* for new regimes. This is so because understanding of the nature of democracy or a market economy is necessary for the expression of an authentic popular demand for such a regime. While some people may go along with reforms that they do not fully comprehend, we expect that active support for democracy and adjustment will be strongest among those who have the firmest knowledge of the precepts of these regimes. On the other hand, we expect that popular *performance evaluations* will lead the way in explaining the perceived *supply* of reform. In this instance, people will use pragmatic criteria to judge the extent to which new regimes have been installed and are generating satisfactory outputs. They will refer to their own perceptions of elite performance in determining whether their country is achieving political liberty and economic growth.

For the moment, we leave open the question of which actually comes first: demand or supply. On one hand, people might need prior knowledge of the content of a regime before arriving at assessments of its performance. On the other hand, in a low information environment, people might glean their knowledge from observations of regime consequences. We suspect that, in public opinion, demand and supply are related reciprocally, with each partly shaping the other. In this way, public attitudes behave at the micro level in parallel fashion to whole regimes at the macro level, whose consolidation, we have argued, is marked by equilibrium between aggregate demand and supply (see Chapter 1). Much depends, of course, on whether people grasp what democracy and markets fully entail, or whether they are content to accept imperfect, hybrid forms.

Above all, a learning approach allows us to address several interesting puzzles.

First: What Sort of Understanding?

The central concepts in this study – democracy and markets – are not written on a blank slate, but are freighted with meanings derived from the contexts, largely Western, in which they were conceived. How do Africans regard these big ideas? What if they attach their own meanings, or ascribe different meanings across countries, or can give no meanings at all? The best approach is to ask Africans themselves what they understand about liberalization reforms, allowing them to answer in their own words. Once survey results are assembled, we will be able to say whether Africans think about reform in universal or parochial terms.

If there is a shared, universal core to popular understandings of reforms, then we are on firm ground in making cross-national comparisons within Africa and to other countries in the world. If our respondents evince variant and distinctive understandings of the meanings of key concepts, however, then we must be careful to interpret results accordingly. In this instance, public opinion may reside partly within the eye of the beholder. For example, people who have a minimalist view of democracy – as, say a set of *political procedures* like elections – may be more easily satisfied than those who regard it expansively – for example, by expecting democracy to deliver outcomes with *socioeconomic substance*, such as employment or income equality.

Second: Whose Performance?

When ordinary people state their opinions on the delivery of desired goods and services, are they referring to the performance of leaders, institutions, governments, or regimes? By paying close attention to the objects of performance evaluation, we try to sort out the referents that people have in mind. In Africa's neo-patrimonial regimes, where personal relationships loom large in all transactions, one would expect that people would use the easy cue of leadership performance. They may project their feelings about a sitting president onto their assessments of the performance of public institutions, whole governments, or even democracy and markets writ large. Indeed, we anticipate the *personalization* of performance evaluations. We will explore the consequences of this expected tendency on regime survival and consolidation. Do Africans distinguish individual leaders from political and policy regimes? Can they use democratic means (like elections) to effect an alternation of political power? Or will they throw the baby (democracy) out with the bathwater (an underperforming president)?

Third: What Kind of Support?

We assume that people will extend tentative support to new regimes if only because democracy and markets promise change from failed formulae of the past. But what is the nature of such support? Is it *intrinsic*, based on an appreciation of liberal principles like freedom, rule-governed procedures, and uncertain outcomes? Or do expressions of regime support reflect a more *instrumental* calculus, in which, say, democratization is a means to other ends, such as the alleviation of poverty and the improvement of living standards. The resolution of this puzzle also has direct implications for regime consolidation. Intrinsic support is a long-term commitment "for better or worse"; as such, it has the potential to sustain a fragile regime even in the face of economic downturn or social upheaval. By contrast, instrumental support is conditional. If citizens evaluate democracy mainly in terms of its capacity to "deliver the goods," then they may succumb to the siren song of populist leaders who argue that economic development requires the sacrifice of political liberties.

The status of political goods is critical here. If popular satisfaction with the delivery of political goods (including civil liberties, free and fair elections, and trustworthy political institutions) leads to support for democracy, is such support intrinsic or instrumental? In this study, we treat the satisfaction of a desire for *any* good or service, whether political or economic, as evidence of instrumentalism. This is so because people are supporting the regime not for what it *is*, but for what it *does* for them. We are establishing a strict standard to be sure, but one that avoids a potential problem of circular reasoning whereby political procedures and demand for democracy may be measured in an overly similar fashion. Whereas we impute mainly instrumental reasoning to the supply of reforms (partly defined, for example as "the way democracy works"), we expect demand for reforms (ideal preferences, defined in the respondent's own words) to signify more intrinsic commitments.

Fourth: What Kind of Reformers?

A transition to democracy does not necessarily require "democrats" or "free marketeers," in the sense of leaders and followers fully committed to liberal norms. Even diehard autocrats or central planners can sometimes conclude that compromise is an acceptable way forward. By contrast, the consolidation of new regimes would seem to depend on a widespread cultural change in which elites and masses come to believe in core democratic and market values. For example, *consolidated* democracy seems to need "democrats."

But does it? While Dahl and his followers define democrats in terms of value commitments, Rose and his colleagues have drawn attention to Winston Churchill's much more practical benchmark. A Dahlian democrat is "one who believes in individual liberty and who is politically tolerant, who holds a certain amount of distrust of political authority but at the same time is trustful of fellow citizens (and)... who views the state as constrained by legality."[71] By contrast, Churchill defined democracy in 1947 as "the worst form of government, except all those forms that have been tried from time to time."[72] Thus, a Churchillian democrat need only judge the current regime to be "better than the alternatives... if the alternative is an evil regime, then a democracy with many faults is preferable."[73]

While we sometimes refer to ideal regimes in this study, we do not expect to discover full-blown democratic or market cultures in any African country. Far from it; we explicitly allow that Africans can learn to appreciate democracy and markets simply as imperfect real-world advancements over systems previously determined to be unacceptable. This realistic perspective is implicit in an approach that asks citizens to arrive at performance evaluations by comparing old regimes with new. For us, therefore, citizens do not have to accept and embody a full set of liberal values in order to prefer the hybrid systems that currently prevail in their countries.

Finally: What Mode of Learning?

To grasp how people learn about reform, we apply a time perspective to the development of cognitive and rational faculties. We envisage several phases of learning that distinguish subgroups within African populations. A standard rational choice perspective is deficient insofar as it accounts only for people's short-term economic evaluations, which fluctuate with the public mood of the day and depend on how well leaders, governments, and regimes are seen to be coping with crises. It applies best to young people who have short time horizons.

To get a fuller picture of the process of learning, however, we entertain three possibilities, each of which involves learning in adulthood. The first is *generational* learning: it assumes that enduring lessons about political regimes are learned during formative periods of late adolescence and early adulthood – lessons that then structure or filter subsequent political learning. If true, we should expect to find significant and considerable differences in regime preferences between cohorts, or generations, who came of age politically under different types of regimes. The second possibility is *lifetime* learning, by which people constantly acquire new information as they get older. Whereas a theory of short-term rationality implies that new information drives out old, a lifetime model assumes that opinions gradually accrete over long time periods. If true, the lessons learned about authoritarian or democratic regimes should differ not by generation, but according to cumulative individual experience with a range of differing regimes. Finally, learning may occur on a *collective* basis. This mode of learning leaves room for historical period effects that impart a set of common lessons, regardless of age or generation. What matters is a country's distinctive political legacy. For example, the dramatic events of political transition (such as the breakdown of old regimes or the founding election of a new regime) might lead to collective resocialization and a society-wide transfer of regime loyalties.

Finally, we leave open the possibility that certain individuals with high levels of education, information, and awareness will come to see democracy and markets as open-ended regimes with no time horizons. This group will shift their benchmarks for assessing regimes from the outcomes of the game (an instrumental and substantive outlook) to appreciation of the way the game is played (an intrinsic and procedural understanding). Of all groups, they are least likely to defect from the reform agenda in reaction to adverse payoffs because they learn that, if the game goes on, they stand a chance of benefiting at some time in the future.

SURVEY RESEARCH IN AFRICA

To test competing explanations of attitudes to reform in sub-Saharan Africa, one would need a comprehensive set of public opinion data, preferably for a range of countries. But, since Africa remains an understudied continent, such data are scarce, spotty, or entirely nonexistent.

Under previous dispensations, political leaders and technocrats thought that they knew best what "the people" wanted. With the exception of periodic national censuses and occasional household production or consumption surveys – which were essential for planning purposes – little systematic evidence was collected about living conditions, let alone mass preferences. Nor were official population counts always reliable. Ironically, ambitious national development plans were therefore launched in African countries without the benefit of relevant facts, a defect that surely contributed to spectacular policy failures.[74] Governments that sought to control all major transactions in the economy by restricting private enterprise and foreign investment also tended to hold the reins tight against the emergence of popular movements, independent mass media, and opposition political parties. These authorities therefore discouraged or prohibited public opinion surveys, which threatened to reveal that ordinary people were less than fully content with the strategy and performance of the governments of the day.

Creative survey researchers nevertheless found ways around these restrictions, particularly in the early years of independence before authoritarian regimes clamped down completely. A modest literature began to chronicle what Africans in selected countries were thinking during the 1970s. Among Nigerians, for example, Peil discovered that a majority wanted military leaders to include civilians in their ruling coalitions and that a plurality favored a return to civilian multiparty democracy.[75] Barkan concluded that both rural and urban dwellers in Kenya were better informed about politics than Americans, at least in terms of being able to identify their elected representatives.[76] And Hayward found by 1975 in Ghana that an individual's "sense of well-being was negatively associated with confidence in government and satisfaction with government policy."[77] In this case, cocoa farmers in the south and central regions of the country, while better off than their compatriots, had begun to complain about the low prices and inefficient marketing services offered by the state.

Although this first burst of survey research in Africa laid down useful baseline findings, it suffered key theoretical and methodological weaknesses. Like most social science at the time, survey design was guided by modernization theory, from which themes and hypotheses were uncritically derived. Once modernization came under broadside attack from dependency ideas and neo-Marxism, the survey research tradition abruptly vanished from African studies. Moreover, one never knew how safe it was to draw generalizations from early survey results. Nationally representative samples were rarely employed and, even through the 1990s, too many studies relied on local or specialized sets of respondents. For example, Becket and Alli's otherwise fascinating finding – that between 1973 and 1995 in Nigeria popular priorities shifted from favoring economic development to favoring democracy – is marred by the limitation that it refers only to elite samples of university students.[78] And while this and other studies occasionally made comparisons across time, the scope of surveys was almost always confined to a single country as in Botswana or Zambia.[79] Systematic cross-national comparisons of public opinion were not introduced to Africa until the World Values Survey was extended to Nigeria and South Africa in 1993.[80] In this case, however, the research instrument was derived from advanced industrial settings and applied only to urban populations.

Since the mid-1980s, the winds of liberalization have warmed the climate for survey research in Africa. The introduction of policy reforms aimed at economic growth stimulated an urgent need to monitor the supply responses of African producers. Arrangements for gathering data on economic production, productivity, and exports have been included in the stabilization and adjustment loan agreements that governments sign with donors. Alongside regular demographic health surveys and household budget studies in numerous countries, the World Bank has sponsored cross-national investigations of official corruption and explorations of social capital in places like Tanzania.[81] And new series of microeconomic data – such as household panel surveys from rural Ethiopia and rural Zimbabwe, plus crossnational studies of manufacturing firms for Ghana, Ethiopia, Tanzania, Kenya, and Nigeria – are now becoming available.[82] Often missing from these otherwise valuable resources, however, is systematic attention to popular attitudes toward economic reform programs.

Liberalization has even enabled survey researchers to break the taboo on asking sensitive political questions about elections, partisan preferences, and government performance. As a rapid response to Africa's round of founding elections in the early 1990s, researchers implemented focus group interviews to gauge popular reactions to sudden transitions. While limited in scope, this type of qualitative research nonetheless produced indicative results. For example, six months after political transition in 1994, South African participants expressed fervent hopes for significant improvements in living standards but already expressed disillusionment with the pace of change. Importantly, however, South Africans were "considerably more aware of the limits facing the new government, more realistic in its expectations, and more patient and hopeful about the future than conventional wisdom holds."[83] One year after Malawi's founding election of 1994, focus group participants continued to believe that "the advent of multiparty democracy has produced tangible rights and freedoms never before enjoyed in this country."[84] In both countries, satisfaction with the new regimes was sufficiently widespread that "people want to prod the system, not to smash it."[85]

As political space appeared in Africa's electoral democracies, survey researchers jumped at the opportunity to measure public opinion. Surveys conducted by international nongovernmental organizations (NGOs) reveal, for example, that Ghanaians are dissatisfied with their personal financial situations and that Kenyans want constitutional reforms to reduce the powers of the executive presidency.[86] The "Nigerbus" survey conducted quarterly by a Lagos research firm shows that approval ratings for the president of Nigeria swung widely during the transition period, from 39 percent for Sani Abacha in April 1998 to 84 percent for Olusegun Obasanjo in December 1999.[87] A Congolese firm reports that 51 percent of Kinshasa residents said they would have voted for the neophyte Joseph Kabila if a presidential election had been held in April 2001, about double the proportion that apparently would have voted for his father, Laurent Kabila, at a similar early stage in the latter's administration.[88]

In general, African survey researchers seem most interested in monitoring changes in the pulse of public opinion, emphasizing volatility in the performance of presidents and popularity of election candidates. Despite some overlap with this agenda, international researchers lean more toward measuring more stable underlying values and attitudes and focusing on the governance issues (like constitutional reform and corruption control) favored by external donors. As long as surveys are conducted with scientific precision and cultural sensitivity, however, then both kinds of research are welcome additions to the existing stock of social science knowledge about Africa.

Rarely, however, have opinion researchers exhibited cross-national ambition. To our knowledge, the only recent exception is R. W. Johnson's *The Condition of Democracy in Southern Africa*, which reviews mass political attitudes in six countries in 1997.[89] On the economy, he found a downbeat popular mood regarding "a hard, even depressing period in which only the political triumph in South Africa has enlightened a considerable economic gloom."[90] For example, fully 70 percent of survey respondents in Lesotho thought that their financial situation had worsened over the past five years, although black South Africans saw improvements. With regard to politics, Johnson reported "a distinctly deferential political culture in which an exaggerated fear or respect for government is common."[91] To be sure, 70 percent of Swazis said that they had to be careful about expressing their political views; but this kind of caution was offset by the 63 percent in Namibia who said they felt free to criticize the authorities. Ground breaking though it was in its cross-national design, the Johnson study was based on small national samples and, to our taste, offered overly bleak interpretations.[92]

THE AFROBAROMETER

Thus, despite recent progress, the collection of data on African public opinion has barely begun. An empirical record must be generated largely from scratch. Hence, the Afrobarometer.

The Afrobarometer is a comparative series of national mass attitude surveys on democracy, markets, and civil society. The project is implemented by an international network of researchers in universities and nongovernmental research institutes, primarily based in Africa.[93] Between mid-1999 and mid-2001, the Afrobarometer Network conducted surveys in twelve countries: Botswana, Ghana, Lesotho, Malawi, Mali, Namibia, Nigeria, South Africa, Tanzania, Uganda, Zambia, and Zimbabwe. Known collectively as Afrobarometer Round 1, these surveys cover about 45 percent of the sub-Saharan population and form the empirical foundation for this book.

Because the survey instrument asks a standard set of identical or equivalent questions (see Appendix A), countries can be systematically compared. The topics covered include:

Democracy. Popular understanding of, support for, and satisfaction with democracy, as well as any desire to return to, or experiment with, authoritarian alternatives;

Governance. The demand for, and satisfaction with, effective, accountable, and clean government; judgments of overall governance performance;

Livelihoods. How do individuals and families survive? What variety of formal and informal means do they use to gain access to food, shelter, water, health, employment, and money?

Macroeconomics and Markets. Citizen understandings of market principles
and market reforms and their assessments of economic conditions and
government performance at economic management;

Social Capital. Whom do people trust? To what extent do they rely on informal networks and associations? What are their evaluations of the trustworthiness of various governmental and nongovernmental institutions?

Conflict and Crime. How safe do people feel? What has been their experience with crime and violence? Which mechanisms do they prefer for
the resolution of violent disputes?

Participation. The extent to which ordinary folks say they join in development efforts, comply with the laws of the land, vote in elections, contact
elected representatives, and engage in protest;

National Identity. How do people see themselves in relation to ethnic and
class identities? Does a shared sense of national identity exist?

Data are gathered through face-to-face interviews by teams of trained interviewers in the language of the respondent's choice. Special care is taken
to ensure the accurate and equivalent translation of concepts into local languages and to control the quality of data collected in the field. The questionnaire is applied to a representative cross section of voting age citizens in each
country with the object of giving every adult an equal chance of selection
for interview. The size of the national sample varies from about 1,200 in
six countries[94] to more than 2,000 in Ghana, Mali, South Africa, Tanzania,
and Uganda, to some 3,600 in Nigeria. Because sampling units are selected
randomly at every stage (census area, starting point, household, and individual), Afrobarometer results can be generalized to national populations
within known levels of sampling error.[95] A detailed sampling protocol is
provided in Appendix B.

For purposes of analysis, Round 1 data from the twelve Afrobarometer
countries was pooled into a single data set. Because a few questions were not
asked in all countries or because interviewers sometimes failed to capture a
full set of responses from the field, certain missing values were imputed (see
Appendix C). Most country samples are self-weighting; but weights were
applied to correct for intentional or inadvertent over- or undersampling in
five instances.[96] To correct for variations in the size of national samples,
the data were weighted to standardize each country at n = 1200. When we
report descriptive statistics, the mean figures for each country and the full
Afrobarometer sample (sometimes labeled as the "Afro" mean) reflect this
adjustment.[97]

The reader should also be alert to a major caveat: the results of the Afrobarometer should not be generalized to sub-Saharan Africa as a whole! Our
unrepresentative selection of countries is intentionally biased toward liberalizing regimes, as shown by their distribution toward the top left corner of
Table 2.1. Survey research on popular support for reforms can be conducted

TABLE 2.1. *Political and Economic Reforms in Afrobarometer Countries*

		Economic Reform		
		Good Compliance	Weak Compliance	Poor Compliance
Political Reform	Liberal Democracy	Botswana* South Africa*		
	Electoral Democracy	Ghana Mali Malawi Namibia*		
	Ambiguous		Tanzania Zambia	Nigeria
	Liberalized Autocracy		Lesotho* Uganda Zimbabwe	
	Unreformed Autocracy			

Note: An asterisk (*) marks countries without a World Bank program that have developed their own orthodox economic policies
Sources: Tables 1.1 and 1.2

meaningfully and reliably only in countries that have attempted to install democracy, a market economy, or both. Thus, we do not pretend that Afrobarometer findings can be extended to the continent's remaining authoritarian regimes, to its controlled economies, or to the substantial number of African states that are imploding through civil war. Moreover, ten of the twelve Round 1 survey countries use English as an official language, with only Tanzania adopting Swahili, and Mali, French. Until returns are received from Portuguese- and additional French-speaking countries in Round 2, we limit our general claims to liberalizing regimes in former British colonies. If and when we refer to "Africans," which we often do throughout the book, we have this restricted population in mind.

AN APPROPRIATE METHOD?

Cross-national survey research on public opinion has been attempted only rarely in sub-Saharan Africa for numerous good reasons. It is expensive; it is technically complex; it is logistically difficult; and – the main objection that we address here – it may give rise to misleading results. The gist of the last critique is that probability sample surveys are an alien methodology. It is hardly appropriate, so goes the argument, to transplant a research technology developed in mass industrial society into Africa's characteristic rural areas. Any effort to employ survey methods under these conditions will threaten conceptual validity and measurement reliability. We list several core objections. For each legitimate concern we offer proposed resolutions which, when taken together, amount to a defense of our decision to adopt the survey research method for this book.

First, some might argue that Africans have distinctive ways of seeing the world that cannot be uncovered using standard survey instruments. The conceptual categories preferred by respondents may differ in important ways from the theoretical frameworks and questionnaire items that survey researchers conventionally employ. Thus, unwittingly or not, researchers cannot help but impose their own intellectual templates onto the interview discourse, thus casting responses into preformed molds.

To address this concern, we took the following steps. Before designing the questionnaire, we convened focus groups to discuss core concepts with prospective respondents in Zambia and South Africa.[98] The draft instrument was then reviewed and amended by the African scholars in the Afrobarometer Network. For key concepts such as "democracy" and "structural adjustment" we designed open-ended questions that allow survey respondents to offer definitions in their own words. For closed-ended questions we made liberal use of the category of "other," which always allows respondents to answer outside the straitjacket of precoded responses. And after the first national survey was complete we convened another series of focus groups (this time in Ghana), encouraging participants to help us interpret results.[99] Of these various techniques, we consider open-ended questions to be the most important. Take just one example: researchers can grasp the nature of the popular development agenda only after asking people, in an entirely unconstrained format, "in your view, what are the most important problems facing this country?"

Second, survey researchers have long acknowledged that ordinary people do not hold coherent or consistent opinions on political or policy matters.[100] Far from being firmly established and remaining stable over time, public opinion is ephemeral. Indeed, most people do not think deeply or regularly about the issues that preoccupy scholars, instead answering questionnaire items by saying the first thing that pops into their mind. Survey questions about abstract concepts (including democracy and markets) are especially likely to elicit half-baked responses, all the more so if the respondents are not literate, do not live in cosmopolitan locations, or if they are otherwise unfamiliar with the concepts at hand. Under these circumstances, researchers must be careful not to record "nonattitudes" as if they were hard and fast facts.

Our general solution to this persistent dilemma is to ask concrete questions. We resist the assumption that nonliterate, poorly educated, or parochial respondents lack opinions on matters that are important to their own livelihoods and sense of well being. We fully expect that ordinary people feel strongly and can think clearly about salient issues of economic survival and political authority. The challenge is to find ways to cast these existential concerns in terms that are meaningful to the respondent and that can prompt reliable responses. Hence, we refrain from asking in the abstract: "Do you support market reforms?" Instead we paint a more vivid scenario that working people and peasant farmers might actually have encountered. And we pose a balanced choice, thereby reducing the risk of merely obtaining passive acquiescence.[101] For example, we ask people which they prefer: to have low prices in the market even if there are shortages of goods; or to have plentiful goods in the market, even if prices are high? Moreover, wherever possible, we measure our major analytic building blocks (like demand for democracy and a market economy) with indices constructed from several such concrete questionnaire items, the better to confirm that we have dependable indicators.

Third, opinion surveys are an unfamiliar research tool in Africa, rarely encountered in everyday life. Respondents can therefore be excused for wondering about the purpose of the exercise, the source of its sponsorship, and the possibility of risks to themselves. Given uncertainty about such consequential matters, is it not sensible for respondents to be cautious, self-censorious, or even deceptive? In some cases, individuals may be too afraid to answer honestly, fearing retaliation from authorities. A related concern in many African countries is the government's monopoly control of the mass media, especially radio, from which most people glean the bulk of their political and policy information. According to a fashionable interpretation, public opinion is little more than a socially constructed echo of agendas set by elites and disseminated over the airwaves, an argument that becomes all the more persuasive in the absence of media independence.[102] Thus, even if people do not parrot the government line out of fear, they may do so because they have never been exposed to alternate points of view. How, then, can survey researchers feel confident that survey responses reflect true individual preferences?

We try to minimize the unavoidable problem of respondent self-censorship in various ways. We conduct Afrobarometer surveys only in countries that have undergone political liberalization and which allow a good measure of free speech.[103] Accordingly, these tend to be countries that also permit pluralism in the mass media and the circulation of nonofficial ideas. Whenever feasible, we avoid scheduling fieldwork during election or referendum campaigns when political passions are inflamed and when contenders for power are eager to hear expressions of partisan loyalty. And, when interviewers randomly select a household for inclusion in the survey, they introduce themselves as representing a politically independent, nongovernmental entity.[104] They assure prospective respondents that participation in the survey is voluntary and that results will be kept confidential.

Internal to the survey itself, we then run several checks. The logic is as follows: if respondents do not dare to reveal their true opinions, they can refuse to answer questions, feign ignorance by saying they "don't know," or intentionally give false answers. Testing for these possibilities, we find relatively few serious threats to the reliability of Afrobarometer responses.

First, the refusal rate for Round 1 Afrobarometer surveys is gratifyingly low, with a cross-national average of only 5 percent of respondents declining to participate in a face-to-face interview, in a range from 11 percent in Zimbabwe to less than 1 percent in Tanzania.[105] These figures compare very favorably with far higher refusal rates in Western industrial countries where the general public is jaded about ubiquitous telephone, mail, Internet, and in-person surveys.[106] By contrast, many African interlocutors spontaneously thank our interviewers at the end of the interview for eliciting their views, mention that no one has bothered to ask before, and urge that their opinions – including criticisms – are conveyed to the national government.

Second, the frequency of "don't know" responses in Afrobarometer surveys is not disproportionately large for rural populations with low levels of literacy. For example, with reference to questions just cited, only 1 percent could not name an important problem facing the country and only 3 percent could not choose between market and controlled prices. To be sure, more people say they "don't know" about abstract concepts like democracy and structural adjustment, but we surmise that these responses arise as much from lack of knowledge as from residual political fear.

Finally, to measure political fear, we ask people to agree or disagree whether, "in this country, you must be very careful of what you say or do with regard to politics." To all appearances, Africans do not yet feel fully free: on average, twice as many people express wariness of engaging in open expression and behavior (59 percent) as assert a lack of caution (29 percent). Some respondents react negatively to the very notion of politics, which they regard as a realm of lies and violence. Cross-national variation is substantial, ranging from the 89 percent in Tanzania to the 33 percent in Malawi who say that, "you must be careful."[107] These findings nicely encapsulate the incompleteness of political reforms across various African countries, where overt politicking is still seen by many to involve a measure of personal risk. But anxiety about repercussions constitutes a hazard to public opinion research only if nervous respondents purposely censor their survey responses in a bid to appear politically correct.

To test this conjecture, we search for correlations between the above indicator of political fear and an array of core questions in the Afrobarometer (see Table 2.2). The results are mixed. On one hand, "careful" people tend to slightly inflate reports of their participation in the last election, their loyalty to the winning party, and their evaluations of the performance in office of the incumbent president. In short, on highly visible partisan issues, they tend to toe an official line in order to protect themselves.[108] On the other hand, self-censorship does not appear to undermine honest opinions about the performance of the macro economy and the trajectory of popular living standards. Indeed, people seem consciously to throw caution to the wind

TABLE 2.2. *Effects of Political Fear on Public Opinion*

	Thinking that "you must be very careful of what you say or do with regard to politics" makes Africans:	Pearson's r	Significance
Positive Effects			
	More likely to say that they voted in the last election	.015	.033
	More likely to say that they identify with the ruling party	.023	.001
	More likely to positively evaluate the president's performance	.036	.000
Negative Effects			
	Less likely to approve of macroeconomic performance	−.014	.038
	Less likely to see recent improvements in standard of living	−.038	.000
No Effects			
	No more or less likely to express trust in government institutions	−.009	.164
	No more or less likely to express national pride	.006	.401
	No more or less likely to positively evaluate the government's policy performance	−.001	.827

on these matters because being fearful actually makes them *less* likely to approve of economic performance. Perhaps because they feel constrained about speaking out on political issues, they pour their hearts out about any economic miseries. Further reflecting such mixed impacts, we find *no self-censorship effects* on numerous other manifestations of public opinion. For example, people who are politically fearful are no more or less likely than people who feel politically free to express trust in government institutions, to evince national pride, or to positively evaluate the incumbent government's policy performance. In other words, on such important matters, the answers of respondents are apparently uninflected by anxiety and constitute reliable representations of public opinion.

The reader is urged to bear in mind these selective effects of self-censorship when reading the results reported by survey respondents in the rest of this book.

A QUEST FOR COMPARISON

The dichotomy between explanatory and interpretive forms of social science is inevitably overdrawn. All good research uses eclectic methods to triangulate on its subject matter from a mix of perspectives. While this book proceeds by reporting the quantitative results of microlevel survey interviews and relies heavily on statistical forms of explanation, we do not stand on this single methodological leg. At the beginning and end, we dissect our findings from macro-political and macro-economic perspectives. We occasionally cite qualitative interpretations offered by focus group participants. And we interrogate our findings in the light of rich historical and anthropological heritage of African studies. Sometimes we find the conventional wisdom wanting in this field but, more often than not, we glean insights that illuminate, or cause us to be cautious about, our survey results.

Moreover, we attempt to situate survey findings, not only within the local contexts from which they are drawn, but also comparatively. Three forms of cross-sectional comparison are attempted in the analysis that follows: across countries, within societies, and between reforms. Let us illustrate with a key finding: in twelve African countries, an average of more than two thirds of all adults (70 percent) say that they "find democracy preferable to any other form of government" (see Chapter 3). But is this a high level of support for democracy? Or is it low? Comparisons provide a point of reference. By design, the Afrobarometer measures popular support for democracy in very similar form to the Eurobarometer, the Latinobarometro, and the New Democracies Barometer, thus enabling comparisons across continents. The mean score on support for democracy for the African countries falls squarely between the mean scores for Western Europe (80 percent in the 1990s) and Latin America (59 percent in 2000).[109] By this standard, the populations of selected Africa countries do not lag behind the rest of the world because they enjoy moderate levels of expressed democratic commitments.

Other forms of cross-sectional comparison, for example, between different types of liberalization reforms, can also be revealing. Again anticipating findings, we report that barely half (49 percent) of the twelve-country Afrobarometer population supports any single market reform policy and only 7 percent support a full package of reforms (see Chapter 4).[110] A comparison with democratic preferences (at 70 percent), suggests that popular acceptance of a market system is therefore quite low. This comparison constitutes a first piece of evidence to substantiate our claim, inferred earlier, that political reforms have put down deeper popular roots in Africa than have economic reforms.

To the extent that sample size allows, cross-sectional comparisons are also possible within societies, for example among subnational regions or particular social or opinion groups. It is common knowledge that people from different parts of African countries ("northerners," "southerners") often have been differentially incorporated into the polity and economy. At least, Africans commonly express this perception. It should come as no surprise, therefore, that support for democracy is higher in southern Nigeria than in northern Nigeria. Indeed, subnational comparisons open the door to a full range of analyses based on demography and social structure (see Chapter 6).

Having, at the time of writing, completed only one round of the Afrobarometer, most of the comparisons in this book are cross-sectional, that is, based on measurements in several countries at a similar time. Yet perhaps the most relevant point of comparison for assessing reform processes is a country's *own* history. According to this criterion, change is calibrated against the country's previous condition, thus allowing judgments about progress, stasis, or decline. So far we have accumulated time-series data for just five countries: Ghana, Namibia and Nigeria (two surveys), Zambia (three), and South Africa (five). Thus, any trends that we project will be tentative at best. But, since these sparse data represent a significant advance over what is otherwise available, we occasionally present the odd cross-temporal comparison. And our questions often explicitly ask survey respondents to compare old and new regimes. The hints their answers contain about directions in the evolution of mass support and participation in African countries can be treated as hypotheses for future research.

PART II

POPULAR ATTITUDES TO REFORM

3

Attitudes to Democracy

Noting that "blatant reversions to military or one-party authoritarianism" were rare in Africa in the 1990s, Richard Sandbrook ventures that, among Africans today, "democracy...(is) widely perceived as the only legitimate form of government."[1] The present chapter tests empirically the reliability of this seasoned scholar's informed intuition. We confirm from survey research that popular support for democracy is indeed widespread among the general public, at least in almost all African countries where governments have attempted political reforms. For ease of presentation, support for democracy (along with satisfaction with democracy, and perceptions of the extent of democracy) is initially discussed as if political sentiments were aggregate attributes of whole "countries." We reserve explorations of variations among social and opinion groups within countries until Part III. Having established that support for democracy is widespread, however, we issue a warning that it is also shallow.

UNDERSTANDINGS OF DEMOCRACY

Some see democracy in Africa as a "unique case."[2] Many writers distinguish indigenous conceptions of popular rule from liberal democracy, which is portrayed as an alien form of government derived from Western political experience.[3] Along these lines, Claude Ake proposes that, rather than placing emphasis on "abstract political rights," Africans "will insist on the democratization of economic opportunities, the social betterment of people, and a strong social welfare system."[4] Similarly, Osabu-Kle considers that an alternative "culturally compatible" model of democracy can be reconstructed in Africa from consensual modes of decision making practiced in the precolonial past and applied in the present by an "encompassing coalition capable of enjoying the support of all sections of society."[5] Schaffer captures these various currents when he summarizes Wolof conceptions of democracy in Senegal as "embedded in popular culture" and therefore connoting "communality and harmony... (and) a wide distribution of material benefits."[6]

Based on evidence from systematic social surveys, we take issue with the supposed uniqueness of African conceptions of democracy. We side with Amartya Sen, who argues that "development can be seen as a process of expanding the real freedoms that people enjoy," that "freedoms are not only the primary ends of development, they are also among its primary means," and that "political liberty and civil freedoms are directly important on their own, and do not have to be justified indirectly in terms of their effect on the economy."[7] Consistent with Sen, we find that Africans value democracy both as an end in itself and as a means to improved governance and welfare. For the Africans we interviewed, the core meanings of democracy are – perhaps surprisingly – relatively liberal, even procedural. While certain popular interpretations have distinctive cultural flavors, ordinary people embrace a vision of democracy that is more universal than particular.

As a contested term, democracy means different things to different people. To open up the definitional debate, the Afrobarometer asks: "What, if anything, does 'democracy' mean to you?" Although the question was posed in the local language of the respondents' choice, interviewers were instructed to present the "d-word" in the official language, that is, English, French, or Swahili.[8] All survey respondents who could offer any sort of meaning were held to possess a basic awareness of democracy. Across our twelve countries, more than three quarters of all respondents (78 percent) were able to volunteer a definition. By this criterion, the concept of democracy is recognizable to most Africans interviewed. Because it is a compound concept, some 14 percent could come up with two meanings and 5 percent with three. On this basis, awareness of democracy is apparently more widespread in these African countries than in Indonesia, where only 39 percent could devise an answer to a similar question.[9]

For the moment, we do not enquire into the content of popular definitions, but simply note that clear majorities in every country have some conception of a regime called democracy (see Figure 3.1). Interesting cross-national variations nonetheless exist. Public awareness ranges from a high of 94 percent in Nigeria to a low of 58 percent in Lesotho, a contrast that implies that the diffusion of political ideas occurs most easily in relatively urbanized countries with well-educated populations. For these reasons, South Africans are much more likely than other nationalities to be able to offer multiple definitions of the meaning of democracy. But the fact that Malawians are also well aware of democracy (92 percent) suggests that low literacy levels and rural populations do not necessarily act as barriers to basic political consciousness.

Over one person in five (22 percent), however, is unable to say what democracy means. For some, a lack of understanding is due to never having heard of democracy, while others have heard of the concept but feel that it means "nothing," is "meaningless," or that its meaning "doesn't matter."

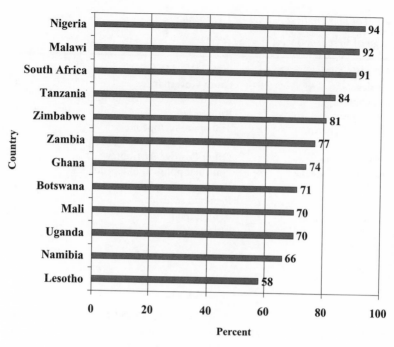

Question: "What, if anything, does 'democracy' mean to you?"

Note: Figures are percentages who can offer any definition of the term.

FIGURE 3.1. Awareness of Democracy

Thus, even though a majority of the Africans interviewed seems cognizant of democracy, a sizeable minority still admits to blissful ignorance. The fact that "don't know" was the second most frequent response overall, and the *most* common response in Lesotho (42 percent), Uganda (30 percent), and Botswana (26 percent), indicates that familiarity with democracy is still nascent in many parts of the continent. Presumably, democracy has not fully entered public consciousness in the last two countries for somewhat different reasons: whereas Ugandans vigorously debate the merits of Museveni's "movement system" versus multiparty rule, the discourse is not always cast in terms of democratization; and Batswana may have become so accustomed to their system of peaceful multiparty elections that the fate of democracy writ large is not a pressing issue of public concern.

Beyond simply recognizing the term, what do people think "democracy" means? Our open-ended question ("What, if anything, does democracy mean to you?") encourages respondents to answer in their own words. We ask for free associations to avoid imposing an imported framework on the results and to capture any distinctive meanings that Africans might wish to attach. A summary of the full range of answers is given in Table 3.1.[10]

TABLE 3.1. *Popular Understandings of Democracy*

(Percentage of first responses, n = 21,531)

POSITIVE MEANINGS	73	POSITIVE MEANINGS (cont.)	
Civil Liberties	28	**Good Governance**	2
Freedom (general)	13	Effective and efficient government	2
Freedom of speech	12	Rule of law	<1
Other individual liberties	2	Transparency/openness	<1
Group rights	1		
Popular Participation	15	**Other Positive Attributes**	4
Government by, for, of the people	9	National political independence	1
		Personal responsibility	1
Power sharing	2	Personal security	<1
Listening to/informing the people	2	Telling the truth	<1
		Other	1
Political accountability	1		
Deliberation and discussion	1		
Political Rights	9		
Electoral choice	3		
The right to vote	2	NEUTRAL MEANINGS	4
Multiparty competition/rule	2	Civilian government	3
Majority rule	2	Change of government	<1
Peace and Unity	7	Other (e.g., government)	1
Social peace	3		
National unity	2		
Political consensus	1	NEGATIVE MEANINGS	1
Mutual understanding and respect	1	Social and political conflict	<1
Equality and Justice	5	Economic hardship	<1
Political equality	2	Corruption	<1
Social equality	2	Neo-colonialism/democracy is foreign	<1
Social justice	1	Bad governance	<1
Legal justice	<1	Other	<1
Socioeconomic Development	3	DON'T KNOW, ETC.	22
Developing the country	1	Don't know/never heard of democracy	20
Improving living standards	1	Nothing/meaningless/doesn't matter	2
Ensuring economic independence	<1	Refused to answer	<1
Providing education	<1		

Question: "What, if anything, does 'democracy' mean to you?"

Note: The option to give three responses was offered in only ten of the twelve countries surveyed. Thus, for purposes of comparability, only first responses are presented.

Three features stand out. First, with few exceptions, the survey respondents attach a *positive* value to democracy. Most people (73 percent overall, rising to 93 percent among people aware of the concept) volunteer a laudatory connotation: democracy is a public good that in some way makes conditions better. This is consistent with public opinion in posttransition situations elsewhere in the world: for example, democracy was judged negatively by only about 1 percent in Hungary in 1990, rising to about 4 percent by 1993.[11] In several African countries (Ghana, Namibia, Nigeria, South Africa, and Tanzania), positive views of democracy are so widespread that almost no politically aware person came up with a negative definition. The danger with overwhelmingly favorable associations, however, is that democracy has become ideologically unassailable, a symbol that nobody wishes to openly oppose. People may conveniently pay lip service to a fashionable idea, without at the same time knowing precisely what it means.

Only 1 percent overall said democracy was bad in any way. This small minority thinks that democratic reforms bring elite corruption, social and economic hardship, or violent political conflicts. Several respondents in Nigeria and Zambia described democracy as a "government of the rich." Such negative views were most widespread in Mali, where multiparty competition was seen to lead to incivility (*"manque de respect," "synonyme anarchie"*) and Lesotho, where democracy was linked to unwanted modernization and political violence ("disruption of the Basotho way of life," "building mortuaries"). Almost nobody identified democracy as an alien import by linking it with foreign or neocolonial rule; indeed, this connotation arose in only three of the twelve countries surveyed and was perceptible statistically only in Namibia, a country only recently decolonized. At minimum, the fact that few Africans presently see downsides to democracy helps to give lie to those – not only excolonials but also contemporary African strongmen[12] – who claim that democratization is too risky because it will inevitably incur ethnic strife and political disorder.

The remainder of the Africans interviewed saw democracy in neutral terms (4 percent), usually as a "change of government" or as "civilian politics" without implying that a new political regime would be better or worse than its predecessor. We suspect that some people, not really knowing what democracy connotes, took refuge in such noncommittal responses. Indeed, uncertainty about the meaning of the "d-word" is testament to a certain superficiality of popular understandings.

Second, respondents regard democracy in *procedural* as well as *substantive* terms. A procedural view of democracy refers to the political processes for arriving at decisions, whereas substantive interpretations refer to concrete outcomes. A procedural perspective includes guarantees of civil rights and rules for elections, under which uncertain policy outcomes arise from the interplay of contending political forces. By contrast, a substantive view prescribes a specific content to policy, such as a wealthier or more equal society. Much of the literature paints democratization in Africa as a quest for social and economic justice, a portrayal often accompanied by a critique of procedures like constitutional guarantees and multiparty elections as mere formalities.[13] We find otherwise. When asked to define democracy for themselves, a majority of Africans interviewed (54 percent) regard it in procedural terms by referring to the protection of civil liberties, participation in decision making, voting in elections, and governance reforms (see Table 3.1). Many fewer (22 percent at most) elect substantive outcomes like peace and unity, equality and justice, and social and economic development.[14] Thus, when left unprompted, the majority of Africans interviewed expect democracy to provide a rather minimal set of guarantees of political participation rather than to herald a sweeping transformation of economy and society.

Moreover, the rank order of substantive interpretations is revealing: more respondents associate democracy with *political* goods (such as peace, unity, justice, national independence, or personal security, which together account for 14 percent of responses) than with *economic* goods (material gains or hardships, which account for just 4 percent).[15] The "peace and unity" response is twice as prevalent in Uganda as in most other countries studied, probably reflecting popular revulsion against the brutalities of the Obote and Amin eras. A strong connection between democracy and a desire for political order is also evident in Zimbabwe and Nigeria, countries that have recently experienced violent internal unrest. One would expect an even closer connection in countries emerging from civil or liberation wars in which democratic elections have been employed to implement peace agreements, though we find no such evidence from Namibia or South Africa.[16] But the main point stands: when the Africans we interviewed consider the substantive benefits of democratization, they think first of a peace dividend rather than of democracy's impact on socioeconomic development.

Third, popular African conceptions of democracy are unexpectedly *liberal*. People cite civil liberties and personal freedoms more frequently – 28 percent as a first response and 41 percent overall[17] – than any other meanings of democracy (see Table 3.1). These responses represent an image of democracy based on individual rights that stands in marked contrast to the conventional view that Africans operate in a largely communal context.[18] In fact, only 1 percent of the survey respondents across twelve countries cite group rights, mostly from just four places (Malawi, Nigeria, South Africa, and Uganda) where ethnic and regional cleavages have been especially salient to national politics.[19] Otherwise, we find almost no evidence either that Africans regard human rights in collective terms or that individual rights, universally conceived, are alien to indigenous cultural traditions.[20] The Africans we interviewed seem to understand freedom in much the same way as people in other parts of the world, that is, as a fundamental personal entitlement. And they resemble the citizens of other posttransition societies, such as Hungary in 1990 and Indonesia in 1998, where similar proportions associated democracy with civil liberties.[21]

When African respondents do distinguish specific rights, they overwhelmingly define democracy in terms of free expression, including the freedoms of conscience, speech, and press. Explicit mention of free speech is made most often in Ghana and Malawi, both countries where the former regime suppressed independent thinking and instilled a culture of silence. Before 1994, Malawi under Hastings Banda was notorious for its draconian laws against criticism of the country's life president and for the "muzzling, harassment, intimidation, detention, and even murder of journalists."[22] In Ghana, Jerry Rawlings forced independent opinion underground by closing down newspapers and using intelligence services and popular militias to threatened dissenters.[23] The most palpable benefit of political opening in both these countries is that citizens no longer have to look over their shoulders before expressing political views in public. As several respondents from Malawi put it, no doubt with a liberating sense of relief, democracy means "being able to criticize government."[24]

Even citizens who do not define democracy in terms of free speech say that they value this universal liberty, including recognizing its collateral obligations. Across the four countries where we explored this issue, more than three quarters agreed that "if people have different views than I do, they should be allowed to express them" and less than one quarter considered that "it is dangerous to allow the expression of too many different points of view."[25] This choice was designed to tap into any fears that lifting controls on political expression will destabilize the state. The proportion of people supporting free speech was highest in Tanzania and lowest in Mali; within Tanzania, support was almost universal on the Zanzibar islands, where the residents of this politically excluded region apparently see free speech as a weapon to defend minority interests.[26] Even if people fail to act in accordance with these stated values, a strong majority in every country at least expresses a predisposition to tolerate dissenting opinions. As might be expected, such tolerance is high among those who define democracy in terms of civil liberties and low among those who lack social trust (see Chapter 7).

After civil liberties, the populations of the survey countries were most likely to conceive of democracy as *popular* democracy. Aspects of popular participation appeared in 15 percent of all definitions (see Table 3.1). The most common formulation was "government by the people," followed by "government by, for, and of the people." These wordings, which echo classical Greek notions of *demokratia* or Lincoln's Gettysburg Address, imply a learned response that people may have picked up during schooling. Indeed, there is a strong, positive relationship between an individual's level of education and a preference for participatory democracy.[27] We detect a genuine demand for decentralized forms of government, whereby citizens seek opportunities to influence collective decisions. In the words of Ugandans, democracy is "allowing anyone to join in the political affairs of the country," "fair play: the government does not force issues on the community," and "returning power in the people's hands." As expressed in the surveys, popular participation also embraces ideas of power sharing (both vertically between elites and masses and horizontally across communities), political consultation ("listening to/informing the people"), along with a healthy dose of debate and discussion. In Ghana, numerous respondents referred to a deliberative process in which "you say some and let me say some," a popular Akan phrase for democracy.

Fewer respondents associated democracy with voting in multiparty elections, though one in ten made this connection (9 percent, see Table 3.1). Elections, competing parties, and related political rights are most prominent in the hierarchy of popular images of democracy in Nigeria (14 percent), perhaps because the survey was conducted there just six months after a historic electoral transition. But, even in Nigeria, electoral rights do not displace free speech (also 14 percent) or, especially, popular participation (38 percent). These findings demonstrate that, while election procedures contribute to an emerging mass consensus about the meaning of democracy, they are relatively less important than citizen involvement between elections.[28] Perhaps people who have grown up knowing elections mainly in the context of a one-party system are skeptical that electoral procedures can ever provide unfettered political choices. Alternatively, elections may well have distinct functions in Africa's new democracies: instead of providing opportunities for choice among competing candidates, they may allow communities to express solidarity around a single leader and to assert claims on that leader's patronage.[29]

To summarize: in seeking a suitable form of government, the Africans we interviewed seem to conceive of democracy as a system based on a mixture of liberal and participatory norms.[30] They envision a sort of open, direct, and decentralized form of democracy rather than a model that hinges mainly on the intermittent election of political representatives to national governmental office.[31] That many Africans associate democracy with direct contact with leaders and personal participation in decision making does not come as a major surprise since these elements recur in much discussion about culturally apt political institutions for Africa. The unexpected element in the popular political imagination is civil liberties. Perhaps it derives from a deep history of popular resistance to repression, whether against internal slavery, the international slave trade, colonialism, or white settler rule. But previous analyses of African politics seem to have missed the intense feelings of resentment among ordinary Africans about the political constrictions imposed by indigenous military and one-party authorities in the period after independence.[32] If nothing else, democracy in Africa has come to symbolize the freedom to speak one's mind. In our view, the longing for this basic individual right renders contemporary African conceptions of democracy more universal than particular.

SUPPORT FOR DEMOCRACY

The tension between Africa's political legacy of autocracy and a mass contemporary yearning for liberty gives rise to an interesting question. Do ordinary Africans therefore support democracy as a preferred political system? How committed, if at all, are the denizens of African countries to this largely unfamiliar form of political regime? And further, are any such commitments transitory or permanent?

We estimate popular support for democracy by means of a standard question that has been posed in scores of countries on several continents.[33] It asks, "Which of these statements is closest to your own opinion? a. Democracy is preferable to any other form of government; b. In certain situations, a nondemocratic government can be preferable; c. To people like me, it doesn't matter what form of government we have." Those persons who find democracy always to be the best form of government (option a) are deemed to support democracy.

By this measure, democracy enjoys a wide base of popular support, at least in those parts of Africa that have recently undergone multiparty electoral transitions. On average, across the twelve Afrobarometer countries, two out of three survey respondents (70 percent) say that they prefer democracy above other forms of government. The rest are equally divided between those who remain attached to nondemocratic alternatives (12 percent) and those who are indifferent about the form of government practiced in their country (13 percent).

As in Latin America, however, variance in country scores is wider than in Western Europe, revealing a continent whose populace has yet to reach a consensus about democracy's virtues or vices (see Figure 3.2). At the top end of the scale are countries like Botswana, Tanzania, and Nigeria, where more

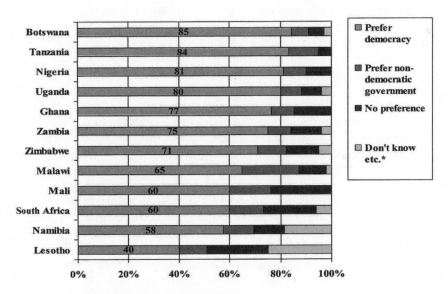

For question wording, see text and Appendix A.
Note: * "Don't knows" include refusals to answer but exclude missing data

FIGURE 3.2. Support for Democracy

than 80 percent of adults regard democracy as the best form of government, though for diverse reasons. In Botswana, citizens have grown supportive of multiparty competition and participatory government through forty unbroken years of experience with such institutions. Although the country has yet to experience an electoral alternation of power between political parties, it is widely acknowledged as one of Africa's most stable, open, and well-governed regimes. On mainland Tanzania, a dominant political party has promoted a model of democracy based on a restricted scope of political competition that has apparently won widespread support. On the Zanzibar islands, fraud and violence in recent elections have served only to strengthen the popular appetite for a more honest form of democracy. And in Nigeria, the survey was conducted in January 2000, when popular attitudes were inflated by transition euphoria; but support for democracy at this time also surely reflects a genuine outburst of jubilation over the death of a corrupt military dictatorship and the restoration of civilian rule.

Moreover, there is no gainsaying that, in eleven out of twelve countries surveyed, a majority of respondents say that they prefer democracy. Populations expressing an above-average level of support for democracy (71 percent or more) include Ghanaians, Zambians, and Zimbabweans, whose recent struggles for regime change have led to very different results. At the time of this writing, democracy in Ghana was consolidating: the country had undergone a gradual, phased transition from military rule through a series of progressively fairer elections, peaking in an alternation of leaders and ruling parties in December 2000. In Zambia, progress on democratization had stalled. After an early landmark transition to multiparty politics in 1991, the new government conducted a series of increasingly questionable polls culminating in a disputed general election and the installation of a minority government in December 2001. And in Zimbabwe, democracy was dying. Although formally a multiparty regime since independence, the country descended into an abyss of political intimidation and violence at the hands of a dictator who openly flouted the rule of law and brazenly stole the presidential election of April 2002. Under such divergent circumstances, it is perhaps surprising that the electorates of these countries would express such similar (and high) levels of commitment to democracy. But this finding demonstrates that Africans can demand democracy, in spite of (or because of) the poor quality of governance actually supplied by governments of the day.

The pattern of widespread support for democracy is interrupted only by the exception of Lesotho. A survey in August 2000 revealed that only a minority of the adult population (40 percent) opted for democratic rule. Instead, Basotho expressed considerable cynicism about political arrangements, with one quarter saying that the form of government "doesn't matter" and a further one quarter (25 percent, higher than in any other country) saying they "don't know" their own regime preferences. Such detachment is directly attributable to a controversial general election held in May 1998. A winner-take-all electoral law led to lopsided election results, which in turn sparked opposition protests, military preparations for a coup, armed intervention by South Africa, and the destruction of the central business district in the capital city.[34] These chaotic events created an atmosphere of instability that is reflected in a profile of public opinion that is clearly skeptical of democracy.

Critics of our principal generalization – that support for democracy is widespread across and within a selected group of African countries – might raise various objections. First, reported levels of support for democracy may be inflated because people who fail to understand the meaning of democracy give acquiescent responses. To test for this possibility, we apply what we learned earlier about popular consciousness: does an individual's awareness of democracy increase support for this political regime? We find that, while a small minority does express uninformed support for democracy (11 percent), the vast majority bases regime preferences on recognition of some positive quality of democracy (81 percent). People who cannot give meaning to the concept of democracy are significantly more likely to say they prefer a nondemocratic system or that the type of regime doesn't matter to them.[35]

Second, some readers may wonder whether individual responses to survey questions about democracy are colored by local context. Could Tanzanians have a distinctive understanding of the meaning of democracy? And do attitudes to democracy on Zanzibar differ from those on the Tanzanian mainland because the islanders support a pro-Islamic opposition party that would probably win a fair election, with their so-called "support for democracy" going no deeper than that?[36] We do not deny that democracy in Africa is subject to multiple cultural and ideological interpretations and we try to acknowledge the most important of these as they inflect the survey results. But we stand by our finding that, among African variations on democracy, one hears common themes of liberties and participation. It is this shared conceptual core that enables the comparison of support for democracy and other attitudes to reform across communities and countries.

Third, the term "democracy" in the standard barometer question may be so overloaded with acclamatory connotations that respondents are loath to reject it. To guard against this possibility, we avoid the "d-word" altogether in an alternate item that asks respondents to rate the "present system of government with regular elections and many parties." On a scale of zero to ten, people gave this "present system" a mean score of 6.7, compared to the "previous system" (whether colonial, one-party, or military), which received only 3.9. In other words, two thirds of respondents scored the posttransition political regime at 6 or higher and one quarter gave it a 10! We interpret these figures to represent a solid expression of support for new multiparty electoral regimes across the eight African countries where this question was asked.[37] Moreover, this alternate measure of support was strongly, positively, and significantly correlated with regime preferences when measured explicitly as support for "democracy."[38]

Finally, a related objection is that support for democracy, as measured by the standard barometer question, is overly abstract. Because it refers to ideal regimes, there is nothing of import at stake in respondents' answers. To test whether support for democracy is rooted in the real world, we examine whether it links to indicators measuring popular commitments to concrete democratic institutions. Data collected in Ghana, Namibia, Nigeria, and South Africa in 2001 and 2002 show that support for democracy is positively correlated with mass attachments to competitive elections, multiple political parties, presidential term limits, and legislative checks on the executive. But, while the correlation coefficients run in the right direction and are always statistically significant, they are not always strong.[39] For example, while supporters of democracy clearly think that, "we should choose our leaders in this country through regular open and honest elections,"[40] they are more cautious about asserting that, "many political parties are needed to make sure that (people) have real choices in who governs them."[41] Thus, while we can again confirm that support for democracy is widespread – 85 percent endorse elections as the best way to choose leaders – we acknowledge that further investigation is required about the depth of such commitments.

REJECTION OF ALTERNATIVE REGIMES

One of the shortcomings of political transitions in Africa during the 1990s was that political protesters knew what they were against, but did not have a clear vision of what they were for. They were against dictatorship, with all its attendant repression, mismanagement, and corruption. They said they were for democracy, but more as a slogan than as a comprehensive system of institutions for dividing and balancing power and for ensuring accountability. In fact, people seemed ready to accept mere political change, however defined, provided it led away from the political status quo, long deemed unacceptable. As such, mass movements for political transition were generally antiauthoritarian rather than specifically prodemocratic.

The Afrobarometer provides strong evidence that antiauthoritarianism persists. Respondents were asked to approve or reject various ways in which their country could be governed. These alternatives included military rule ("the army should come in to govern the country"), one-man rule ("we should abolish elections and parliament so that the president can decide everything"),[42] and one-party rule ("candidates from only one political party should be allowed to stand for elections and hold office"). Figure 3.3 indicates that survey respondents reject all three authoritarian alternatives, often resoundingly.[43] Table 3.2 shows that Zambians emerge with the highest overall mean score for rejection of authoritarian rule, a profile of public

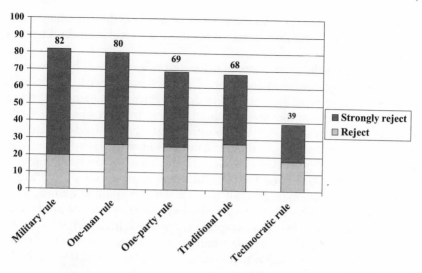

Question: Some people say we would be better off if the country was governed differently. What do you think about the following options: (a) the army should come in to govern the country, (b) we should get rid of elections and parliament so that the president can decide everything, (c) candidates from only one political party should be allowed to stand for election and hold office, (d) all decisions should be made by a council of traditional elders, (e) the most important decisions, for example on the economy, should be left to experts?

FIGURE 3.3. Rejection of Alternative Regimes

TABLE 3.2. *Rejection of Authoritarian Rule, by Country*

	Reject Military Rule	Reject One-Man Rule	Reject One-Party Rule	Reject Authoritarian Rule (Mean Score)
Zambia	95	91	80	89
Nigeria	90	83	88	87
Ghana	88	86	78	84
Botswana	85	88	78	84
Tanzania	96	92	60	83
Malawi	83	87	76	82
Zimbabwe	80	78	74	77
Uganda	89	84	53	75
Mali	70	73	73	72
South Africa	75	67	56	66
Lesotho	70	69	51	63
Namibia	59	57	63	60

Note: For question wordings see Figure 3.3 and Appendix A.

opinion that is consistent with their ouster of a nationalist founding father at the polls in 1991 and their denial of his successor's bid for a third term in 2001.

Military rule is the most unpopular form of rule in Africa, being repudiated by an overwhelming majority of all persons interviewed (82 percent). When people dismiss military rule, they do so vehemently: 62 percent reject it "strongly." The view that soldiers should stay in the barracks is especially pervasive in Tanzania and Zambia, countries that have retained civilian governments since independence, though Zambians may be reacting against an aborted coup attempt in 1997. Armies are also widely spurned as rulers in Ghana and Nigeria, here on the basis of harsh experience with repressive modes of armed governance. In all but one African country studied, anti-coup sentiment is even more widespread than the average level of prodemocracy support (70 percent). The exception is Namibia: because just over half (59 percent) of the population reject military rule, there would appear to be a sizeable constituency there who might hail – or at least tolerate – a military takeover.

Almost as many Africans say that they reject presidential dictatorship (one-man rule), which is disavowed by 80 percent of those interviewed. Tanzania and Zambia again lead the pack (92 and 91 percent respectively), a somewhat surprising finding given that Julius Nyerere and Kenneth Kaunda, as well as their less charismatic successors, have practiced relatively benign styles of personal rule. But one-man rule is not convincingly rejected everywhere. We already know that many Namibians are willing to countenance the concentration of power in the hands of the president, which suggests extremely fragile democratic commitments. Similarly, South Africa suffers a low ranking in antistrongman sentiments, which mars its reputation as a leading force for democracy in the region. According to our survey in June 2000, a rump of one third of South Africans felt that the country would be better off if electoral institutions were abolished and a strong leader was allowed to "decide everything."

Compared to one-man rule, fewer people, though still a clear majority (69 percent), reject one-party rule. The size of this segment matches the proportion of the electorate that says it supports democracy, though the makeup of these opinion groups does not perfectly overlap.[44] A country may or may not have experienced one-party rule in the past for its population to reject it as an alternative in the present. Neither Nigeria nor Botswana, for example, has ever been a de jure one-party state, but the adult population of each country roundly rejects this mode of rule. Yet the populace in Zambia and Malawi, which went through periods when only one political organization was legally allowed to exist, now also widely rejects a one-party system. Similarly, direct previous experience with a one-man show or a military junta is not a necessary prerequisite for current popular rejection of these regimes. Taken together, it would seem that a country's prior institutional history cannot alone account for the contemporary profile of its public opinion (but see Chapter 13).

Importantly, a one-party regime retains a measure of appeal for some Africans. In four countries, citizens barely reject this form of government: Lesotho (51 percent), Uganda (53 percent), South Africa (56 percent), and Tanzania (61 percent). One-party rule remains a viable alternative in Lesotho and Uganda because multiparty competition in these places is presumed to give rise to political violence, against which rule by a paramount entity seems to promise greater stability. In Tanzania, many people have bought into Nyerere's original vision of a vanguard party regime, as they have for Yoweri Museveni's "Movement system" in Uganda, itself a variation on the one-party theme. And South Africans are willing to flirt with one-party government perhaps because it comes close to what they already have: the African National Congress (ANC) has adopted a controlling style of governance reminiscent of other former liberation movements, yet still retains overwhelming electoral support.[45]

To recapitulate: several decades after political independence, citizens in many parts of Africa appear to have concluded that government by military or civilian strongmen is no longer acceptable. In several countries, the general public is close to unanimous in rejecting the intervention of the army into politics. As mass sentiment presently stands, almost nobody in these countries would dance in the streets if a colonel invaded the national radio station to announce a coup. The Africans we interviewed also express severe misgivings about one-man rule, suggesting that ordinary people are no longer willing (if they ever really were) to extend blind allegiance to arbitrary dictators. In fact, in nine out of twelve countries, more people reject one-man rule than reject one-party rule, suggesting that they welcome the imposition of some kind of institutional constraints on the whims of leaders. And, in seven out of the twelve countries, more than two thirds of the population also opposes the institutional arrangements of the single-party state. Overall, these findings suggest that most citizens have dismissed all the authoritarian models of governance that have been attempted in postcolonial Africa. Instead, they seek a stronger set of constraints on executive power than any of these models provide.

Before changing subjects, let us acknowledge a couple of other regime alternatives that are not necessarily authoritarian, but which have ambiguous relationships to democracy. To the extent that precolonial political systems may have allowed procedures for holding leaders accountable and even replacing them, they are not incompatible with contemporary forms of democracy. One wonders, however, how widely political accountability was practiced in the past and whether it continues to apply in the fragmented and compromised forms of traditional rule that survive today.[46] In addition, because administrative power is delegated to technical experts in all modern governments, technocracy and democracy can also coexist in African countries. To the extent that African bureaucracies depart from Weberian ideals, however, expert rule may reinforce corruption rather than legal decision making.

For research purposes, the Afrobarometer questionnaire refers to traditional rule as a system in which "all decisions are made by a council of elders, traditional leaders or chiefs" and technocratic rule as a system where "all important decisions, for example on the economy, are left to experts." As before, we asked survey respondents to say whether or not they approved of these alternative regimes, and how strongly.

Most Africans interviewed do not wish, even if it were possible, to return to a traditional system of governance. Two out of three reject the idea of decision making at the national level by a council of chiefs or elders, especially insofar as this form of government might replace elected representative institutions (see Figure 3.3). Again, the opponents of traditional rule (68 percent) are as numerous as supporters of democracy (70 percent), but the memberships of these two opinion groups do not directly coincide.[47] Part of the reason is that there is considerable cross-national variance on this item, ranging from a high of 89 percent rejection of traditional rule in Tanzania to a low of 48 percent rejection in Mali.[48] The Tanzanian result is understandable in terms of the central government's systematic campaign to discredit the indigenous authority structure and replace it with a network of ten-house cells and party cadres. Chieftaincy survives in more viable and legitimate forms in Mali, where the weak penetrative capacity of the central government and an underdeveloped communications system has left many rural communities to their own devices. And support for traditional models of rule is consistent with Malian proclivities to define democracy in terms of familiar cultural models of mutual aid and respect.

More generally, opposition to traditional rule is weakest where rural dwellers are geographically and administratively isolated, as in Namibia (55 percent reject) and Lesotho (59 percent reject). Chiefs retain popularity here, even if they enjoy few real powers. By contrast, resistance to the traditional option is strong in places where chiefs have retained or regained authority, as in Ghana (71 percent reject), Botswana (74 percent reject), and Uganda (80 percent reject). This seems to signify that, where traditional rule has persisted or been restored, people have concluded that it is not appropriate to their contemporary needs. A slight variation is observable within Uganda: support for traditional rule is higher in districts encompassing the old Buganda kingdom than it is in the rest of the country. But, consistent with cross-national trends, it is lower than average in districts comprising other historic kingdoms (for example, Ankole and Busoga), perhaps reflecting popular doubts about the efficacy of monarchy in addressing modern problems of socioeconomic development, or the marginalization of these areas compared with a resurgent Buganda.[49]

Apart from democracy, the only other political regime favored by a majority of Afrobarometer respondents was rule by experts. In nine out of twelve countries, more people accepted technocratic governance than rejected it. Interestingly, expert rule met with least resistance in the continent's two largest industrial economies: Nigeria (only 24 percent reject) and South Africa (26 percent reject). The results come as something of a surprise since expert management of the economy can imply control of key economic decisions by outsiders, for example by the IMF or foreign oil companies in the case of Nigeria. Indeed, majority rejection of technocracy tends to occur in contexts of dependence on expatriate personnel, where rule by experts is interpreted as foreign control, as in Botswana (52 percent reject) and Zambia (60 percent reject).[50]

Overall, though, these findings suggest that African citizens do not feel confident in their understandings of the operation of the national economy (see Chapter 4), a realm of endeavor they would rather delegate to other nationals whom they deem more competent. They seem willing to surrender their rights to participate in major decisions about the direction of the macro economy.[51] We therefore surmise that national leaders who choose to pursue an orthodox economic management strategy that requires the insulation of technical decisions from popular pressures will encounter little mass objection.

By way of conclusion, we reiterate that most Africans interviewed support democracy and roundly reject regimes run by soldiers and strongmen. One-party and traditional models of governance are also shunned, but remain viable regime alternatives in certain countries. And, generally speaking, Africans are less resistant to hierarchical political regimes (like traditional and technocratic rule) than to overtly authoritarian ones.

SATISFACTION WITH DEMOCRACY

If Africans prefer democracy in the abstract, do they also endorse it in practice? Actual political regimes rarely live up to citizens' ideal preferences anywhere in the world and are perhaps least likely to do so in poor countries. Much depends on the yardstick that individuals use to judge the accomplishments of the new order. If measured against recollections of the previous regime's record, democracy may appear as the lesser of two evils. But if counterposed against dreams of a perfect future, democracy is destined to always fall short.

To clarify: we draw a sharp distinction between *support* for democracy and *satisfaction* with democracy. The former refers to an abstract normative preference, absent constraints, of one's favorite political system. The latter refers to an empirical assessment of the concrete performance of an actual elected regime. Because satisfaction with democracy is the more exacting standard, it almost inevitably lags behind support for democracy.

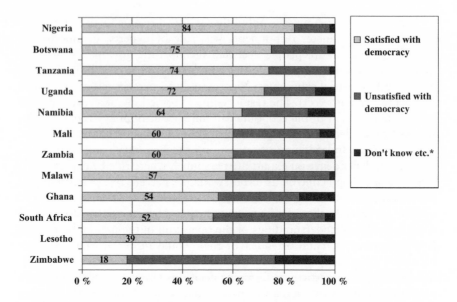

For question wording see text and Appendix A. *Note:* Figures are percentages who are "satisfied with the way democracy works in this country." *"Don't knows" include neutral, and "this country is not a democracy."

FIGURE 3.4. Satisfaction with Democracy

The Afrobarometer surveys trace satisfaction with democracy by asking a standard question: "Generally, how satisfied are you with the way that democracy works in (your country)?" The name of the country is inserted and respondents are offered the options of "very satisfied," "fairly satisfied," "fairly unsatisfied," and "very unsatisfied." In Figure 3.4 and the discussion that follows, we describe as "satisfied" all those who answered either "fairly satisfied" or "very satisfied."

Overall, more than half of all African respondents (59 percent) said they were satisfied with democracy in the period between late 1999 and early 2001. An absolute majority was satisfied in ten out of the twelve countries surveyed, and more people were satisfied than dissatisfied in eleven countries. The Afrobarometer mean score at this time was on a par with the Eurobarometer mean score on the same item in 1996 (56 percent), and much higher than Eastern Europe in 1996 (34 percent) or Latin America in 2000 (just 30 percent). We propose several possible interpretations of this unexpectedly positive result. Perhaps African citizens are starting from a very low base of satisfaction with previous regimes. Or maybe they are generally accepting of the governance their leaders provide. Alternatively, they may not yet have had enough experience with new political regimes to develop mature and balanced assessments. Or all of the above may apply.[52] We note, however, that the quality of satisfaction is strained: more people are only "fairly" satisfied (38 percent) than are "very satisfied" (21 percent).

These results also reveal the widest cross-national variation in public attitudes found so far. At one extreme was Nigeria in January 2000, where 84 percent of adults interviewed said they were satisfied with the way democracy was working; at the other end stood Zimbabwe, where only 18 percent were satisfied in September 1999. This stark departure is best interpreted as a contrast between a Nigerian populace caught up in the thrill of liberation from military rule and a Zimbabwean citizenry bemoaning an intransigent civilian autocracy. Yet these conditions are not fixed in perpetuity. As we will show, the astronomical level of satisfaction in Nigeria readily erodes once the Obasanjo administration fails to live up to optimistic popular expectations. And if and when Mugabe allows a change of government via transparent elections, then Zimbabweans will surely express higher levels of democratic satisfaction.

Other countries are arrayed between these extremes. In terms of people professing to be "very satisfied" with democracy, Botswana (32 percent, the highest in the sample) actually exceeds Nigeria, once again reflecting a populace whose attitudes are based upon an accumulated set of generally positive experiences. Yet Ghana scored lower on satisfaction than its relatively high scores on support for democracy might lead one to expect. Conducted in July 1999, the Ghana survey captured a popular mood that tempered satisfaction with recent political reforms and advances with the fact that Jerry Rawlings had not yet completely loosened his grip on power. The highest levels of dissatisfaction with democracy were recorded in South Africa (44 percent), Malawi (41 percent), and Zambia (37 percent).[53] In these countries, significant minorities expressed creeping disillusionment, apparently feeling that political transition had not brought them everything they had expected.

Some scholars have recently challenged the theoretical validity of satisfaction with democracy.[54] The concept does not specify whether survey respondents are referring to satisfaction with a political regime (democracy), a set of institutions (the state), or an incumbent group of policymakers (a government). Believing that this argument has merit, we replicated some of the critics' analyses with African data. Table 3.3 shows that, when Afrobarometer respondents report on satisfaction with democracy, they are thinking simultaneously about all three of these political objects. Almost every coefficient is statistically significant, suggesting that regimes, states, and governments figure jointly in popular conceptions of regime satisfaction, even after being controlled for one another. But it is also apparent from the size of the coefficients that satisfaction with democracy is influenced principally by evaluations of government performance (see shaded cells). Indeed, the wording of the standard question – which asks about satisfaction with "the way government works" – invites such evaluations.

Moreover, the relationship between satisfaction with democracy and the evaluation of government performance is consistently strong across all countries.[55] Even where satisfaction with democracy mainly reflects regime

TABLE 3.3. *Multivariate Correlates of Satisfaction with Democracy*

	Support for Democratic Regime[a]	Trust in State Institutions[b]	Evaluation of Government Performance[c]
Botswana	0.146***	0.179***	0.246***
Ghana	0.149***	0.205***	0.243***
Lesotho	0.216***	0.131**	0.371***
Malawi	0.248***	0.311***	0.295***
Mali	0.241***	0.211***	0.223***
Namibia	0.090*	0.244***	0.174***
Nigeria	0.101*	0.118***	0.233***
South Africa	0.235***	0.155***	0.331***
Tanzania	0.110***	0.373***	0.201***
Uganda	0.205***	0.089***	0.321***
Zambia	0.161***	0.056 (not sig.)	0.249***
Zimbabwe	−0.056 (not sig.)	0.082*	0.255***

Notes: Values are standardized ordinary least squares regression coefficients (betas). Shading indicates strongest relationship for each country.

[a] Measured using the standard barometer item on support for democracy.

[b] Measured as an *index of trust in state institutions* (electoral commission, courts of law, the army and the police). For question wordings, see Appendix A.

[c] Measured as an *index of government policy performance* (at managing job creation, inflation, education, health care, and crime control). For question wordings, see Appendix A.

*p = <.05
**p = <.01
***p = <.001

support (as in Mali) or trust in state institutions (as in, say, Malawi), popular assessments of the government's performance still plays a formative role in determining mass satisfaction. Because the results for all African countries lean in one direction, that is, toward a pragmatic conception of satisfaction with democracy, we think it justifiable to engage in cross-national comparisons about this important popular attitude. And we take this finding as a strong initial signal that the popularity of democracy across the full range of reformist African countries will be determined in good part by performance considerations.

WIDE BUT SHALLOW

We have established that, in a range of important African countries – including regional powers like South Africa and Nigeria and influential models like Botswana and Ghana – ordinary people say they support democracy. Those Africans who live in countries undergoing political reform at the turn of the twenty-first century basically welcome the demise of *ancien regimes*. In place of military and one-party monopolies they regard some set of open and participatory arrangements – which they associate with the term "democracy" – as preferable to other forms of government they have known or could reasonably imagine.

Though wide, however, support for democracy may well be shallow. Robert Dahl asks a penetrating question: "might what is called 'democracy' become both broader in reach and shallower in depth, extending to more and more countries as its democratic qualities grow ever more feeble?"[56] In Africa, prodemocracy sentiments may be a veneer beneath which lasting democratic commitments, behaviors, and habits have yet to take root. For reasons analyzed as follows, we urge caution about assuming depth to expressed democratic commitments. Widespread popular support for democracy is loose, sometimes contradictory, formative, perhaps temporary, and based on experience with hybrid regimes that have not completed the process of democratization. These arguments are made with reference to five claims, each supported with survey and other evidence:

Liberalization Does Not Equal Democratization

Liberal democrats will welcome the discovery that many Africans define democracy in terms of universal human rights. But, since the notion of popular liberalism runs against the grain of the conventional wisdom about political culture on the continent, it requires further interrogation. For example, if Africans think democracy amounts to little more than freedom of speech – a problem we call the fallacy of liberalization – then it is not difficult to understand why democratization on the continent is incomplete.

While many Africans interviewed conceive of democracy in terms of civil liberties, they do not do so everywhere. In the twelve countries surveyed, this liberal definition ranked first alone in only nine. In Nigeria, Lesotho, and Botswana, people were just as likely to opt for populist and participatory visions. In African contexts, "government by, for and of the people" may reflect collectivist interpretations that run counter to standard liberal accounts. Such meanings are consistent with Jerry Rawlings' populist cry of "power to the people" or Julius Nyerere's communitarian recollections of "talking until we agree."[57] And in Mali, where many respondents draw on traditional values when reading democracy as "mutual respect," contrasting interpretations are possible. On one hand, norms of respect and reciprocity may enhance deliberations, smoothing the way to decision making and peace building at the community level. On the other hand, these values can also require deference to a consensus enforced by a traditional power hierarchy, which makes one doubt whether patrimonial and democratic rule can be easily reconciled.[58]

Moreover, Africans use hazy terms when speaking of political freedoms, for example referring to "freedom of choice," "freedom as a birthright," "the right to everything," and "control over one's own life." These vague connotations – expressed by almost half of those citing civil liberties (see Table 3.1) – suggest that popular conceptions of human rights remain highly undifferentiated. Civil liberties are regarded in especially encompassing terms in South Africa, perhaps as a reaction against the totalizing ambitions of the former regime. Because apartheid forced its way into every cranny of people's lives, South Africans seem to have adopted unusually holistic views of democracy. For example, many respondents there said it means "living freely," and that "people should always be free." While these formulations surely capture essential truths and reflect genuine aversion to oppression,[59] they also underestimate the importance of specific liberties – from religious freedom to the right to legal representation – that are codified in international human rights treaties.

Indeed, apart from freedom of speech, the Africans interviewed locate few other specific liberties at the heart of democracy. Together, the right to personal security and the freedoms of conscience, religion, movement, assembly, and association were mentioned by only 2 percent of respondents (see Table 3.1). Such rights have low salience despite the frequency of religious-based conflicts in countries like Nigeria and the denial of free movement and rights of organization under authoritarian regimes everywhere in Africa. Individual privacy and property rights were hardly mentioned; nor were socioeconomic rights like claims to employment, education, or healthcare. Thus, Africans conceive human rights rather narrowly, focusing on a particular civil liberty (freedom of expression) as opposed to a broader gamut of political and socioeconomic rights.

This last point has theoretical implications. Democratization requires more than political liberalization. Even if free speech were restored and upheld – and even if other constitutional guarantees were somehow put in place – democracy would still not necessarily be secured. A full range of institutions is required that only barely enter into current African conceptions of democracy. Our survey respondents have told us that regular, competitive, multiparty elections are not especially important, and almost nobody mentioned the rule of law and civilian control of the military. Thus, it is far from clear that, beyond demanding the right to criticize despotic presidents, African citizens have dedicated themselves to the long-term tasks of building democratic institutions. We detect a *fallacy of liberalization* in which ordinary people seem to think that free speech will be enough and that movements for political reform need go no further than wringing political openings from authoritarian governors. Unless wide popular commitments are substantially deepened beyond a preoccupation with expressive liberties, democratization in Africa could easily stall at the stage of the liberalization of authoritarian regimes.

Popular Understandings of Democracy Are Malleable

Earlier in this chapter, we showed that African understandings of democracy were both procedural and substantive, but that procedural interpretations predominated. This finding was based on an open-ended question that allowed respondents to define democracy in their own words. But an alternate, structured question gives rise to dissonant results. Because "people associate democracy with many diverse meanings," respondents were asked to say which items on a list of political and economic attributes were "essential . . . for a society to be called democratic." The precoded list included procedural political elements – like majority rule, freedom to criticize the government, regular elections, and multiple political parties – that derive from a minimal and liberal version of democracy. The list also added substantive socioeconomic elements – like satisfying basic needs, jobs for all, equal access to education, and a small income gap between rich and poor – that are often cited by proponents of social democracy.

Only in Zimbabwe do respondents rate political procedures and socioeconomic substance as equally essential to their conception of democracy, though they come close in Botswana and Zambia (see Table 3.4). In seven other countries, and especially in Tanzania and South Africa (but also Mali and Nigeria), respondents report that substantive features are significantly more essential than procedural ones.

At minimum, therefore, expectations of what democracy should do also include material components of economic delivery and social equity. Factor and reliability analyses of this item reveal two dimensions underlying popular conceptions of democracy, each of which is internally coherent, and which can be labeled "procedural" and "substantive."[60] Partly artifacts of question wording, these dimensions point to the distinction between recall versus recognition in mass surveys: once prompted to scan substantive considerations, respondents elevate them above procedural ones.[61] Individuals with low levels of formal education and limited media access are particularly likely to latch onto conceptions of a democratic society that include universal access to basic material needs. By contrast, as individuals gain education and media exposure, they increasingly conceive of democracy as a set of political procedures.[62]

We infer that popular understandings of democracy are susceptible to manipulation, especially among less-educated segments of the population or in countries that have limited exposure to regime alternatives. In one plausible scenario, political elites offer the electorate a trade-off: in return for limitations on individual political liberties, leaders will deliver socioeconomic development. We know that this deal can be attractive because many citizens accepted it in the years following national independence. And the Afrobarometer data contain a test case of a country in which a bargain of this sort has been struck in contemporary times. In Uganda, the National Resistance Movement (NRM) installed a so-called "no-party system," which allows competition for office among individual candidates but outlaws campaigning by political parties. As a government, the NRM undertook an extensive and sustained program of economic reform, which contributed to a

TABLE 3.4. *Essential Features of Democracy*

(Percentage saying "essential")

	Bot	Les	Mwi	Mali	Nam	Nig	Saf	Tan	Zam	Zim	Afro Mean
Political Procedures											
Majority rule	47	41	66	46	42	48	38	29	47	67	47
Freedom to criticize the government	41	39	58	39	26	46	35	45	40	60	43
Regular elections	46	32	47	46	37	45	37	30	36	61	42
At least two parties competing	45	35	45	33	22	53	29	38	38	58	40
Socioecon Substance											
Everyone has access to basic necessities	52	60	77	60	51	70	67	71	57	69	64
Jobs for everyone	49	64	55	63	53	73	73	54	45	67	60
Equal access to education	51	56	68	65	56	74	66	72	44	62	62
A small rich-poor income gap	34	37	50	50	26	57	35	47	29	51	42
Mean, Political Procedures	45	37	54	41	32	48	35	36	40	62	43
Mean, Socioecon Substance	47	54	63	65	47	69	60	61	44	62	57
Procedural – Substantive Gap	-2	-17	-9	-24	-15	-21	-25	-25	-4	-	-14

Question: "People associate democracy with many diverse meanings. In order for a society to be called democratic, how important is each of these?"

Note: This question was not asked in Ghana or Uganda.

decade-long expansion of the economy at rates well above the level of population increase. In a context of limited political rights but a growing economy, most Ugandans pronounce themselves both supportive of democracy (80 percent) and satisfied with democracy (72 percent).

Paradoxically, therefore, citizens in Uganda associate democracy with a regime that clearly violates core democratic principles, such as the right to form associations for the purposes of running for electoral office. And, as in neighboring Tanzania, citizens express similarly high levels of democratic support and satisfaction for a regime in which the Chama Cha Mapinduzi (CCM) continues to exploit its dominance in the electoral commission and other state institutions as if opposition politics had never been relegalized. Citizens in both countries say they understand democracy in terms of civil liberties (26 percent in Uganda, 39 percent in Tanzania), yet their standards for such liberties are apparently low.[63] The danger, of course, is that the concept of democracy has become so flexible that it means all things to all people, thus losing any core content.

Pockets of Authoritarian Nostalgia Remain

Prodemocratic sentiments have not everywhere won the day. Apart from Lesotho, where only a minority supports democracy, pockets of authoritarian nostalgia remain even in countries where majorities support democracy. And enclaves of vestigial authoritarianism coexist even alongside widespread antiauthoritarian sentiments.

For example, more than one out of five Malawians (22 percent), consider that "in certain situations, a non-democratic government can be preferable." Compared to other Africans, Malawians do not draw sharp distinctions between support for the present multiparty electoral system and the previous authoritarian regime (6.1 versus 5.4 on a scale of zero to ten). These opinions appear to be carefully considered, occurring as they do in a context of high political literacy: 92 percent of Malawians, second only to Nigerians, can offer a meaning for democracy. Authoritarian nostalgia in Malawi is most prevalent (30 percent) in the Central Region, the political base of Dr. Banda, the country's former strongman. In South Africa, willingness to entertain authoritarian alternatives is also above average, especially among whites.[64] In both these countries, support for nondemocratic alternatives appears to be an expression of regret for an old regime among persons who previously possessed – but who have now lost – access to the levers and spoils of power.

In other countries, political disengagement is more widespread than authoritarian nostalgia. In Mali, almost one-quarter (24 percent) of its largely rural and poorly educated population withdraws from tendering an opinion when asked to compare political regimes. A further 16 percent flirts with the idea of a nondemocratic alternative, perhaps recalling that the army served as a midwife to democracy: installed at the head of a transitional government of 1991, General Amadou Toumani Touré (A.T.T.) convened a national conference of popular forces, supervised an open election, and, by 1992, voluntarily ceded power to a civilian regime. And by 2002, A.T.T. proved that he could run successfully for the civilian presidency even as a former military head of state.[65] In South Africa too, more people say that "it doesn't matter to people like me what form of government we have" (21 percent) than long for strong authoritarian rule (13 percent). In this instance, however, disengagement is concentrated more among Coloureds (27 percent) and Indians (36 percent) than among whites and blacks. Yet blacks in the Eastern Cape Province – the homeland of both Mandela and Mbeki – also express indifference about various political regimes, perhaps because they live in the poorest and most neglected region of South Africa.

To further probe the depth of democratic commitments, Southern Africans were also asked to weigh the relative virtues of democracy and "a strong leader who does not have to bother with elections."[66] When the question was posed this way, more Namibians actually agreed that "a strong leader is sometimes needed who does not have to bother with elections" (50 percent), than insisted that "democracy is always best" (43 percent). This authoritarian majority was huge in the four stronghold regions of the ruling South West African Peoples' Organization (SWAPO): Kavango (68 percent), Oshana (83 percent), Omusati (86 percent), and Ohangwena (91 percent). SWAPO swept the 1999 presidential and national assembly elections in these predominantly rural regions with similar proportions of the overall vote. Given high levels of expressed trust and popularity for President Nujoma in these regions, it seems likely that those who prefer strong leadership had the incumbent in mind.[67]

Rejection of Authoritarianism Does Not Amount to Support for Democracy

We have ascertained that rejection of authoritarian regimes is even more widespread than support for democracy. In fact, almost all Afrobarometer respondents (fully 93 percent) reject *at least one* form of autocracy, that is, *either* military rule *or* one-man rule *or* one-party rule (see Figure 3.5). But the proportions quickly decline for those who simultaneously dispel more than one form. Fewer people (83 percent) reject two forms and, importantly, *just over half* of all respondents, whom we might call "committed antiauthoritarians," reject all three forms (that is, military, one-man, and one-party rule).[68] In other words, even if people turn their backs on one form of autocracy, they do not always discard all its manifestations.

If rejection of authoritarian rule were evolving into support for democracy, we would expect these negative and positive sentiments to be strongly correlated. The relationships between antiauthoritarianism and prodemocracy run in the predicted direction and are statistically significant, but the

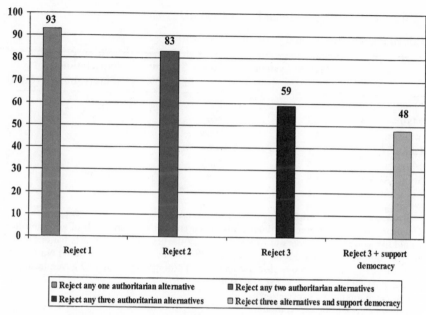

FIGURE 3.5. Depth of Democratic Commitments

correlations are not particularly strong.[69] In other words, African opposition to dictatorship has yet to fully deepen into an unshakeable commitment to democracy. Indeed, only a minority of the people we interviewed (48 percent) can be described as "committed democrats" in that they consistently say that they *both* reject all three authoritarian alternatives *and* support democracy (see Figure 3.5). Later in this book we use an *index of commitment to democracy* derived from these indicators to measure popular *demand for democracy* (see Chapters 6 to 13). Others express discordant views, simultaneously saying that they support democracy and that they harbor nostalgic feelings for more forceful forms of rule. These people, who can be thought of as "proto-democrats," amount to almost one third (32 percent) of all survey respondents and presumably constitute a reserve army of the undecided who, in the face of democratic failures, might be tempted to revert to nondemocratic options.

Because popular rejection of authoritarian rule is therefore incomplete, sober assessments are warranted about the depth of democratic attachments in sub-Saharan Africa. Not only is support for democracy apparently shallow, but even the degree of antiauthoritarianism can be easily overstated.

Attachments to Democracy May Decay Over Time

Will popular attitudes to democracy prove durable? Or does the Afrobarometer capture only a fleeting snapshot of fickle public opinions that are destined

TABLE 3.5. *Expectations About Future Political Regimes*

(Mean regime ratings on a scale of zero to ten)

	Present System	Future System	Expectation (Future minus Present)
Nigeria	7.53	8.96	+1.53
Mali	6.68	6.97	+0.29
Tanzania	6.84	7.03	+0.19
Ghana	6.71	6.66	−0.05
Malawi	6.08	5.87	−0.21
South Africa	6.08	5.80	−0.28
Lesotho	5.85	4.56	−1.29
Zambia	5.98	4.28	−1.70

Question: "We are now going to discuss how much you like different kinds of government. I would like you to give marks out of ten. Let us say the best government gets ten out of ten and the form of governing gets no marks at all. What mark would you give to (a) our present system of government with free elections and many parties (b) the system of government you expect (this) country to have in five years time?"

+ signifies an optimistic expectation

− signifies a pessimistic expectation

soon to change? While a definitive answer is impossible at the present stage of our research, we can offer some early indications by comparing a few countries over time.

To start, we juxtapose people's assessments of multiparty electoral systems with their expectations about future political regimes. As with the "present system," we asked respondents to rate, on a scale of zero to ten, "the system of government you expect (this) country to have in five years time."[70] As Table 3.5 shows, citizens themselves are unsure of whether they will remain satisfied with the political regime. In only three of eight countries do respondents expect the quality of governance to be better under a "future system" (see plus signs). Only Nigerians in 2000 had very optimistic political expectations. By contrast, the general public in five African countries thought that future political regimes would be less desirable than ones currently in place (see minus signs). To people in Lesotho and Zambia, the political future looked especially bleak. Popular pessimism in Lesotho is readily understandable given the fact that the survey was conducted during a period when the country's democratic experiment was suspended and citizens were questioning the viability of multiparty elections. In Zambia, however, pessimism about the political future was expressed against a background of widespread public commitment to democracy and an outright rejection of all authoritarian options. Unlike Basotho, therefore, Zambians know they want democracy; but like Basotho, they fear they may not achieve it in the future.

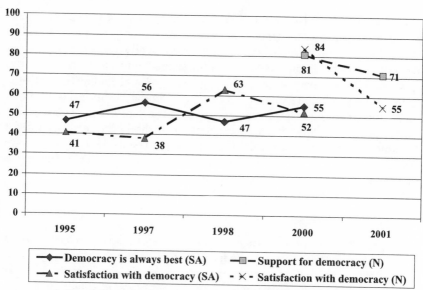

FIGURE 3.6. Trends in Attitudes to Democracy, South Africa and Nigeria

Beyond forward expectations, which are hypothetical, we have begun to measure change in selected democratic attitudes in two major countries. In South Africa between 1995 and 2000, the proportion that thinks that democracy is "always best" has remained relatively stable, hovering either just above or just below 50 percent (see Figure 3.6).[71] Satisfaction with "the way democracy works in South Africa" has also fluctuated, but shown gradual gain over time, from 41 percent in 1995 to 52 percent in 2000 (but down from a high of 63 percent in 1998). This seems to suggest that, while prodemocratic sentiments were mixed at the time of the political transition in South Africa, the regime has gradually won over new adherents. The Nigeria data tell a quite different story. The 1999 transition was followed by an upsurge of hope of such inflated proportions that it was not sustainable. From January 2000 to September 2001, Nigerians came back down to earth: support for democracy sagged by ten percentage points (from 81 to 71 percent) and satisfaction with democracy eroded even more precipitously, plunging from 84 percent to 57 percent in eighteen short months. In the process, Nigeria dropped from first to eighth place among Afrobarometer countries in terms of the level of satisfaction.

Because trends in attitudes to democracy have diverged in South Africa and Nigeria, it is not yet possible to generalize about the temporal evolution of African public opinion. All we can venture is the working hypothesis that support for democracy is likely to prove more stable and less volatile than satisfaction with democracy. The former tends to embody deeply held political values, while the latter reacts to the political exigencies of the day.

The direction of trends in democratic attitudes in Africa also depends on the level of euphoria after the transition. Where expectations for the new regime are moderate, as they were when the views of all racial groups were taken into account in South Africa, there is room for support and satisfaction to move upward. Where expectations are overly buoyant and perhaps unrealistic, as in Nigeria, a rapid collapse can occur in initial enthusiasms. If Latin America is anything to go by, where support for democracy experienced a gradual secular decline during the 1990s, then the Nigerian scenario, not the South African one, may point the way for the rest of Africa.[72] Before we can be sure, however, we need to collect more data on identical items across additional countries and for longer time periods.

THE EXTENT OF DEMOCRACY

From a popular perspective, then, democracy in Africa is seen as a work in progress. Many Africans acknowledge that, when it comes to building democratic institutions, many tasks remain unfinished. We conclude this chapter by reporting on public perceptions of the extent of democracy that has actually been achieved in various countries.[73] Later in this book, we combine the extent of democracy with satisfaction with democracy to develop a composite measure of the popularly perceived *supply of democracy*.

Nowhere across twelve countries does a simple majority of respondents think that the current regime in their country is a full democracy (see Figure 3.7). An average of just 30 percent holds this view overall. Only in Botswana does a plurality of citizens (46 percent) consider that their democracy has come to fruition and, in this opinion, Batswana lead other nationalities by a considerable margin. By contrast, a similar proportion in Nigeria (47 percent in both 2000 and 2001) sees democracy facing "major problems," which we think accurately reflects the tremendous challenges faced by untested political institutions in this deeply divided society. Finally, a plurality of Zimbabweans (38 percent) considers that their country is not a democracy, a figure more than twice as high as in any other country.

How well do Afrobarometer indicators match up with other standard measures of democracy's extent? Freedom House provides annual estimates of the attainment of civil liberties and political rights for over 190 countries in the world, including our twelve African cases.[74] The methodologies for constructing Freedom House (FH) and Afrobarometer (AB) indicators differ markedly. Whereas the FH estimates are expert judgments by a small number of qualified country specialists, the AB data are based on the everyday opinions of a large number of citizens in each country. The opportunity thus arises to test whether measures of the extent of democracy derived by different methods validate one another.

The extent of democracy as measured by the Afrobarometer turns out to be strongly and significantly correlated with status of freedom as estimated by

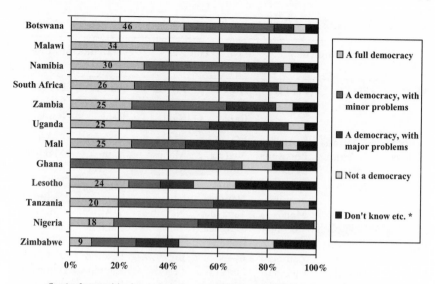

Botswana
Malawi
Namibia
South Africa
Zambia
Uganda
Mali
Ghana
Lesotho
Tanzania
Nigeria
Zimbabwe

□ A full democracy

■ A democracy, with minor problems

■ A democracy, with major problems

□ Not a democracy

■ Don't know etc. *

Question: In your opinion, how much of a democracy is (this country) today?
Note: "Don't knows" include refusals to answer but exclude missing data.
In Ghana, respondents were only offered the choice of "yes, it is a democracy" or "no, it is not a democracy."

FIGURE 3.7. Extent of Democracy

Freedom House in 2000–01.[75] It is even more strongly associated with the FH civil liberties score which, incidentally, helps verify our claim that Africans interpret democracy in rather liberal terms.[76] Consider a couple of cases: Botswana places first on ranked country lists for both the Afrobarometer indicator of the extent of democracy and the Freedom House measure of civil liberties (see Table 3.6). And Zimbabwe in 2000 consistently ranks dead last. These findings suggest that Western academic specialists and lay African citizens arrive at roughly similar judgments about the level of democracy in any given country.[77]

We can push the analysis even further by examining *processes* like political liberalization and democratization.[78] Do AB indicators match FH scores when the object of inquiry is political change over time? Again, the answer is affirmative. AB indicators of political liberalization and democratization are strongly and significantly correlated with the respective FH indicators.[79] The rank order distribution of countries is very similar: five countries share rankings on liberalization and four share rankings on democratization (see Table 3.6). Most remaining countries differ across measurement methods by only a rank or two.

Moreover, the same two countries are responsible for all major rank deviations: Nigeria and South Africa. Interestingly, the discrepancy between popular and expert opinion runs in opposite directions for these two African giants. In AB surveys, Nigerians perceive more political liberalization than do

TABLE 3.6. *Comparison of Popular and Expert Democracy Rankings, circa 2000*

Extent of Democracy			Political Liberalization		Democratization	
AB Rank	FH CL Rank	FH PR Rank	AB CL Change Rank	FH CL Change Rank	AB PR Change Rank	FH PR Change Rank
Botswana	Botswana	S. Africa	Malawi	S. Africa	Malawi	S. Africa
Malawi	S. Africa	Botswana	Nigeria	Malawi	Mali	Malawi
Namibia	Malawi	Malawi	Mali	Mali	Nigeria	Mali
S. Africa	Namibia	Lesotho	Ghana	Nigeria	Ghana	Ghana
Zambia	Mali	Namibia	Namibia	Ghana	Namibia	Namibia
Mali	Zambia	Mali	Tanzania	Namibia	S. Africa	Tanzania
Lesotho	Lesotho	Tanzania	S. Africa	Tanzania	Zambia	Lesotho
Uganda	Tanzania	Nigeria	Zambia	Zambia	Tanzania	Nigeria
Tanzania	Nigeria	Zambia	Botswana	Botswana	Lesotho	Zambia
Nigeria	Uganda	Uganda	Lesotho	Lesotho	Zimbabwe	Zimbabwe
Zimbabwe	Zimbabwe	Zimbabwe	Zimbabwe	Zimbabwe	Botswana	Botswana

Notes:
AB = Afrobarometer
FH = Freedom House
CL = Civil Liberties
PR = Political Rights
Shading indicates shared rank.

experts on FH panels. The mass public in Nigeria sees more political change than do foreign-based Afro-pessimists, who tend to project onto Nigeria their worst fears for the African continent. By contrast, South Africans think that less political liberalization has occurred in their country than do FH experts. In South Africa, racial minorities pull down the country's scores on the perceived degrees of liberalization and democratization. In this instance, outsiders are prone to celebrate the political progress made by South Africa in the 1990s and to project onto that country their highest hopes for the continent as a whole.

Where measurements differ, we are inclined to place greater reliance on Afrobarometer results, which reflect indigenous voices. As this chapter has shown, many Africans demand democracy, which they define in liberal and participatory terms, even as the citizens of some countries express lingering nostalgia for one-party rule. Whether they think governments can supply democracy, and the material improvements that they associate with a democratic society, however, are open questions that this book will continue to explore and explain.

4

Attitudes to a Market Economy

We live in an age of shrinking states and expanding markets. The idea has diffused globally that market incentives are more likely than administrative commands to encourage economic production, distribution, and exchange. In Africa, as elsewhere in the developing world, a neoliberal intellectual and policy paradigm has influenced and redirected official development strategies. Since the early 1980s, governments in the sub-Saharan subcontinent have embarked, more or less voluntarily but sometimes with heavy-handed encouragement from international financial institutions, on programs to relax controlled economies.[1] A broad consensus has emerged among scholars and policy analysts about the desirability of stabilizing public expenditures and liberalizing market prices, but debates continue about the pace of reform, its sequencing, and institutional arrangements. At issue is the size of the state. And the impacts of adjustment on poverty and inequality remain matters of intense dispute.[2]

Since professional economists cannot agree, it would be startling if the inhabitants of African countries spoke with one clear voice on the subject of a market economy. We find that Africans who live in countries undergoing neoliberal reforms express ambivalent and contradictory views about these developments. On one hand, they assert personal self-reliance and tolerance of risk but, on the other, they insist that the state retain a preeminent presence in economic life. They are dissatisfied with the past and present performance of the economy, but optimistic (often unrealistically so) about the future. They support some elements in the structural adjustment package, but not others. On balance, Afrobarometer respondents offer only lukewarm support for market reforms and are singularly critical of the performance to date of official stabilization and adjustment programs.

All told, while Africans show considerable accord on a preferred political system, they are divided over the shape the economy should take. They feel most comfortable with a mixed (or hybrid) economy, preferring to steer a middle course between state and market. Above all, any tentative support for the conversion of state-run economies into competitive market regimes is offset by a deep popular concern with emerging economic inequalities.

THE POPULAR DEVELOPMENT AGENDA

To provide context for discussing economic policy reform, we start by examining Africans' own priorities for national development. After all, it is likely that ordinary people will support a policy regime only to the extent that it addresses concerns central to their own lives. Axiomatic among students and practitioners of planned development is the belief that the chances of success for any policy, program, or project hinges critically on whether local people – from state elites to ordinary villagers – take ownership of the development effort. Yet, in the past, international donors and lenders have usually taken the lead in setting the agenda for development.

To detect popular perceptions of developmental priorities, the Afrobarometer asks a commonplace question: "In your opinion, what are the most important problems facing (your) country that the government should address?" Since respondents volunteer spontaneous answers to this open-ended inquiry in their own words, we sorted replies into categories after the fact. The results, presented in Table 4.1, can be thought of as a "people's agenda" for development.

This agenda is headed by economic and social concerns, which together account for over nine tenths of all problems cited. About half the time, people allude to economic problems (51 percent), closely followed by social issues, including service delivery (42 percent). Whereas economic concerns are most likely to be voiced by Nigerians, Zimbabweans, Basotho, and Malians (over 60 percent of all responses), social issues like education and health are more likely to command the attention of South Africans, Namibians, and Tanzanians (almost half of total responses). Compared to economic and social affairs, political problems attain low salience in the worldviews of our African interlocutors, being cited just 8 percent of the time. For example, less than one out of a hundred respondents mentions democracy as an important problem facing the country, either because people regard democracy as more of a solution than a problem (see Chapter 3), or because, compared to critical economic and social needs, political affairs apparently do not loom large in the public consciousness.

A key exception is Uganda where political problems were mentioned more than twice as often as elsewhere (19 percent), often with reference to violent conflicts, both within the country and with neighboring territories. Given that Uganda was deeply involved in internal and international conflicts at the time of the Afrobarometer survey in May 2000, this is hardly surprising. Most concerns about political violence arose in Uganda's northern region, where more than half of the respondents saw political insecurity as the nation's top problem. Since coming to power in 1986, the National Resistance

TABLE 4.1. *Most Important Development Problems*

(Percentage of total responses, n = 28,795)

Economic Problems	51	**Political Problems**	8
Unemployment	17	Corruption	2
Macroeconomic conditions	8	Political violence	1
Poverty or destitution	6	Political tensions	1
Famine or food shortages	6	Discrimination or inequality	1
Agriculture	4	Democracy	<1
Infrastructure	4	Other political problems	2
Loans and credit	2		
Wages	1		
Rates and taxes	1		
Other economic problems	2		
Social Issues and Services	42	**Other**	4
Health	9	No problems	1
Education	9	Don't know	1
Crime and security	7	Other	2
Water	4		
AIDS	3		
Services (general)	3		
Transportation	1		
Housing	2		
Other social/services problems	4		

Question: "In your opinion, what are the most important problems facing (your) country that the government should address?"

Note: The number of responses exceeds the number of respondents because up to two responses were allowed and counted. Since the question was not asked in Ghana or Nigeria, the results refer to ten countries only. Total percentage exceeds one hundred due to rounding.

Movement has never been able to fully extend governmental authority over the North, prompting President Museveni to temporarily move his national headquarters there in 2002. The region remains a redoubt of support for the Uganda Peoples' Congress and other opposition groupings, as well as a site of persistent banditry and politically motivated insurgencies. Two general observations can be drawn from this case. On one hand, political problems in conflict zones are all consuming, so much so that they ascend to the top of the "people's agenda," preempting other developmental concerns. On the other hand, violent conflicts tend to be localized and, contrary to impressions too often conveyed in the international media, rarely engulf whole countries or dominate the attention of entire national populations.

Instead, the Africans we interviewed loudly demand government attention to the work-day problem of unemployment. At 17 percent of all responses, the creation of jobs is mentioned almost twice as often as any other single development need. Employment is variously conceived, for example, as a "way to get money for my family," according to a thirty-year-old unemployed laborer in Dar es Salaam, and as a "chance to use my education" by a school leaver in Accra. The fact that only 1 percent of all responses concern the low level of wages seems to suggest that any job, even if poorly paid, is regarded as better than no job at all. We confirmed this hunch in Nigeria, where over 80 percent of survey respondents said that, "it is better for everyone to have a job, even if wages are low" and fewer than 15 percent agreed that "it is better to have high wages, even if some people have to go without a job."[3] Nobody mentioned underemployment as a problem, perhaps because people commonly engage in subsidiary economic activities in addition to their primary occupation.

Concern about unemployment is hardly universal, however. It gains highest priority in Lesotho (36 percent), whose economy depends on the remission of wages from the mines and other industries of neighboring South Africa. Unemployment also tops the development agenda in South Africa itself (31 percent) and in Botswana and Namibia (30 and 29 percent respectively), all countries that are integrated into the region's industrial complex. At the other end of the scale are Mali, Tanzania, and Uganda, where job creation receives much lower priority as an economic problem (all 5 percent). In these countries, individuals apparently continue to look mainly to self-employment in agriculture and a variety of nonfarm activities, rather than expecting to base livelihood on a paid wage from the industrial or service sectors of the formal economy. Interestingly, Malawians, once avid participants in Southern African labor circuits, now look inward to self-generated occupations within their own communities. More like Tanzanians than Basotho, only 4 percent of Malawians cite unemployment as a most important problem requiring government attention.[4]

Instead, people in countries with large agrarian populations most commonly mention poverty (as in Mali and Uganda), and food shortages, hunger, and even famine (as in Mali and Malawi). The specter of hunger is prevalent in ecological zones where droughts are common: in Mali, people are acutely aware of the uncertainty of the annual Sahelian rains and, in Malawi, expressed early warnings about the likelihood of upcoming crop failures.[5] Reflecting the geographical and sociological diversity of their country, Nigerians frequently cite *all three* problems: unemployment (26 percent) *and* poverty (15 percent) *and* hunger (10 percent).[6] As expected, unemployment is a bigger worry for city folk than for rural dwellers in Nigeria. But, less obviously, urban Nigerians are also significantly more likely than their country cousins to be anxious about food shortages; indeed, concerns about hunger are just as frequently expressed in the capital city of Lagos as in the semiarid northeastern zone.

After unemployment, people's economic anxieties center on the condition of the national economy and the quality of government's macroeconomic management. Included in this category are concerns about slow or negative economic growth, government budget deficits, the sinking value of the national currency, and the increasing costs of basic consumer goods. For example, a thirty-six-year-old trader in Kano complained that "the naira (the Nigerian currency) is no longer worth anything," a white-collar professional in South Africa ventured that "the government is spending too much," and more than a few Zimbabweans pointed to "the high price of mealie-meal." Indeed, economic mismanagement is a fixation among Zimbabweans, being mentioned one third of the time (32 percent of all responses) no doubt reflecting concern about a multifaceted economic crisis – combining economic contraction with accelerating deficits, devaluation, inflation, and latterly, food shortages – in that country.

As for social services, people predictably see the provision of education and health care as the most pressing national challenges. African families have long valued education as a passport to economic mobility and it continues to be the leading social demand in Namibia (21 percent), where adequate access to quality schooling was long denied, and in Mali (12 percent), where the availability of schooling, especially for girls, continues to lag behind other parts of the continent. But the quest for education may have peaked and is now diminishing. In most African countries, where educational services have been readily available for at least a generation, people have learned that a school certificate no longer automatically guarantees a job.[7] Hence, in Tanzania, Uganda, Zambia, and Zimbabwe, among other places, health care has displaced education as people's premier social priority.[8] When people mention health as a problem, many must be thinking about HIV-AIDS.[9] Zambians now cite health care as their very top need, above even employment, reflecting the recent uncontrolled spread in this country, not only of HIV-AIDS, but also malaria and tuberculosis. They are also reacting against the annual outbreaks of cholera that strike the crowded informal settlements of Lusaka and the Copperbelt during the annual rainy season.

Another prominent social issue is crime, at least in some countries. In South Africa, fear of crime far outpaces any other social concern (at 22 percent of all responses) and is perceived second only to unemployment as the top overall national problem.[10] Mentioned by more than half of all respondents, concern about becoming a crime victim is widespread across all of South Africa's racial groups; but it is more heavily concentrated among Indians and whites (75 and 69 percent respectively) than among Coloureds or blacks (55 and 48 percent respectively). Crime has also become a leading popular issue in Malawi and Lesotho, though less because of high absolute crime levels and more due to recent increases of theft and violence in previously tranquil countries. By contrast, crime barely registers in the litany of development concerns listed by Namibians, Tanzanians, and Ugandans and, in Ghana in 1999, significantly more people said they felt safer from crime than they had five years earlier. These results raise the intriguing question of why the mass public becomes preoccupied with crime in some democratizing countries but not in others.

The public's development agenda is interesting as much for what is left out as for what is included. On several key problems, Afrobarometer respondents were either silent or much quieter than expected. Take HIV-AIDS. The disease was cited as the leading social problem only in Botswana (12 percent), the country with the highest estimated HIV prevalence rate in Africa in 2000.[11] It also attracted a modicum of attention in Namibia, South Africa, and Zimbabwe where deaths from the scourge are now prevalent and rising. But it is striking that, in every other country studied, only 1 percent or fewer of all respondents considered that the pandemic was a major problem of national importance. Not one Zambian actually mentioned HIV-AIDS, yet two-thirds said they knew someone who had died of the disease. Perhaps the threat of AIDS has yet to fully penetrate popular consciousness, especially in West Africa where HIV infection rates are estimated to be lower.[12] Or maybe people see AIDS as a matter of private responsibility rather than a public problem, or wish the government to devote its energy to addressing other development challenges.

People also gave short shrift to other seemingly important issues. For example, despite escalating consumer prices in Zambia (averaging 70 percent per year during the 1990s, the highest rate in the Afrobarometer),[13] only 3 percent of Zambians pointed to inflation as an important national problem. We take this as a signal of the wide reach of informal markets in which ever larger numbers of people provide for their own needs, engage in barter, or otherwise operate outside the cash economy. And, in Zimbabwe, where Robert Mugabe made the forced acquisition and redistribution of agricultural land the centerpiece of his bid to maintain political power, we found that the land issue did not resonate in public opinion. In a context where people were preoccupied with the management of the economy and the lack of job opportunities, a mere 1 percent of Zimbabweans volunteered that they were concerned about "a fair distribution of land."

Across all countries, few people spontaneously complained about discrimination, inequality, or minority rights (just 1 percent). Similarly, gender politics and women's concerns hardly appeared. And, while official corruption was mentioned as the most common political problem, it arose less frequently than standard critiques of governance practices in Africa might lead one to expect. Overall, just two percent of total responses made reference to corruption, ranging from a high of five percent in Nigeria to just one percent in Botswana, Lesotho, Mali, Namibia, Zambia and Zimbabwe. As such, we are led to believe that ordinary Africans regard official corruption as a less salient national problem than do investigative journalists and international donors and lenders.

By way of summary, we explore whether there is any coincidence between popular agendas for development and donor aid priorities. Table 4.2 presents

TABLE 4.2. *Donor and Popular Priorities for Development*

Rank	Donor Priorities[a]		Popular Priorities[b]
	DAC Bilateral	Multilateral	
1	Transport/ Communications	Public sector	Employment
2	Education	Transport/ Communications	Health
3	Action relating to debt	Agriculture	Education
4	Emergency aid	Energy	Economic management
5	Program assistance	Education	Crime control
6	Water supply	Water supply	Poverty alleviation
7	Agriculture	Health	Food security
8	Public sector	Program assistance	Water supply
9	Health	Industry/Construction	Transport/ Communications
10	Energy	Emergency aid	Agriculture

Sources:
[a] Organization of Economic Cooperation and Development/ Development Assistance Committee (OECD/DAC), "Aid by Major Purposes, 2000," *Development Cooperation Report, 2001* (*www.oecd.org*), Statistical Annex, Table 19.
[b] Afrobarometer, Round 1, 1999–2001. See Table 4.1.

the major purposes of development assistance as represented by the expenditure of bilateral and multilateral donor funds. The entries in the table are donor priorities ranked in order of total aid flows allocated to particular activities in 2000.[14] Several interesting findings emerge. Ignoring rankings for the moment, we first notice a measure of overlap in the purposes of official aid and the developmental preoccupations of Afrobarometer respondents: five topics – transport, education, water, education, and health – appear on all three lists. Moreover, if emergency aid helps to ensure food security, and if program assistance is conditioned on improved economic management, then internal and external agendas can be seen to address a rather similar scope of activities.

But, donors and recipients then go different ways. First, the various parties assign markedly different priorities to the range of development tasks. For example, international donors see transport and communications infrastructure as being far more central to the project of national development than do Africans themselves. It may well be that improved road networks and state-of-the-art cell-phone services will help to promote transactions in African economies, but apparently there is less popular demand for these infrastructural services than donors stand ready to supply. Conversely, the Africans we interviewed place much greater emphasis on health services, including access to basic preventive care, than is reflected in donor budgetary allocations. While health care ranked second overall on the popular agenda, it comes in seventh on the multilateral donor list and ninth for the bilateral agencies. In this case, demand for basic health services seems to run well ahead of the will and capacity of financiers to respond, perhaps because they know that African governments have squandered past investments in basic health care, for example, by allowing clinics to operate without adequate staff or supplies.

In addition, certain priorities are ignored – or, at best, are differently conceptualized – by donors and recipients. The most glaring anomaly regards public sector governance reform, which is the top priority of multilateral donors (and important too for bilateral donors), but which nowhere appears on the public agenda. Indeed, while the donor community calls for improvements in the effectiveness and efficiency of state bureaucracies, which often entails civil service job cuts, ordinary people insist that they want expanded employment opportunities, presumably including jobs provided by the state, usually the largest employer in African countries. Other differences include the following: while donors emphasize the provision of energy, including electricity, ordinary people prefer crime control and the alleviation of poverty. One could argue of course, that donor programs to upgrade water supplies, agriculture, and energy have clear antipoverty objectives, but public opinion appears to hold that these efforts are neither well targeted nor nearly extensive enough.

BETWEEN STATE AND MARKET

If unemployment is the main development problem, how will it be addressed? Whom do people hold responsible for the provision of jobs and, more broadly, for guaranteeing public welfare? Is it the state, the private sector, or the individual? By exploring these topics, the Afrobarometer generates a preliminary profile of the economic values held by respondents in twelve sub-Saharan countries that are transitioning between economic regimes. In so doing, we reveal African perspectives on the great debate of our time, namely, whether development is best pursued via state or market, or by some judicious mix of strategies.

We start by asking whether people perceive themselves as autonomous economic agents, responsible for their own and their family's advancement, or whether, in order to get ahead, they prefer to look to assistance from the government. Specifically, the survey question was posed as a choice: who should be responsible for ensuring the success and well-being of people: individuals or government? In general, the Africans we interviewed in 1999–2001 are split down the middle on this matter: whereas 51 percent opted for self-reliance, some 46 percent placed the onus for their personal and family prospects on the government. Interestingly, these figures resemble responses in seven former Soviet republics in 1989, save that a bare majority there and

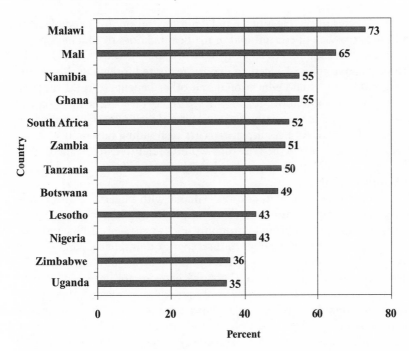

Question: "Choose A or B: A: People should look after themselves and be responsible for their own success in life. B: The government should bear the main responsibility for ensuring the well-being of people."

Note: Figures are percentages who choose A, the self-reliant option.

FIGURE 4.1. Economic Self-Reliance

then favored government provision over individual responsibility (51 versus 49 percent).[15]

Representing the Afrobarometer norm on this score are countries like Botswana, Tanzania, Zambia, and South Africa, where populations are essentially divided about the locus of responsibility for popular well being (see Figure 4.1). One half would look to own resources; the other half would turn to the state. Otherwise, sharp national differences are evident. Self-reliance is reportedly highest in Malawi, where more than seven out of ten people (73 percent) say they prefer to put faith in their own initiative, and some 64 percent feel this way "strongly." It is also high in Mali. Reported self-reliance is lowest in Zimbabwe and Uganda, where over six in ten respondents regard the government as responsible for public welfare.

These cross-country distinctions reflect the prevailing policy regimes and the fiscal health of governments. In Malawi and Mali, governments with meager export revenues have lacked budgetary capacity to deliver production and social services to mass populations and their stance toward the rural sector has historically been more extractive than distributive. The minimalist economic policies of the Hastings Banda administration, for example, provided little in the way of educational or medical facilities to Malawi's population of self-provisioning peasants. By contrast, in Zimbabwe and Uganda, governments have enjoyed access to export-generated foreign exchange and were committed to extend educational and other benefits to rural supporters. After 1980 in Zimbabwe, for instance, ZANU-PF solidified its political base in the countryside by distributing agricultural credit, marketing services, and, eventually, land. As a result, citizens are responding rationally – on the basis of experience – when they say they would prefer to fend for themselves in Malawi and Mali but that they would rather make claims on the state in Uganda and Zimbabwe.

To reinforce this argument, contrast Ghana with Nigeria. These neighboring countries display different profiles of public opinion, with 56 percent of Ghanaians stressing personal autonomy and 57 percent of Nigerians favoring governmental responsibility, a discrepancy that reflects the divergent paths of the two economies and resultant public policies in recent years. The Ghanaian economy, including much of the state sector, largely collapsed in the early 1980s and the country subsequently experienced almost two decades of reasonably consistent market-oriented reforms. This sequence of events has, by necessity, tended to bring individuals around to an independent economic outlook. Nigeria's oil economy, while battered by low export prices and grievous mismanagement, nonetheless sustained many government services, subsidies, and institutions. As described in the introduction, market reforms were erratic and failed to distract people from the common knowledge that the government sits atop a reservoir of oil revenues. As a consequence, Nigerians have comparatively less confidence in self-help in the marketplace and a greater propensity to seek perquisites from the state.

Apart from attitudes of self-reliance, we detect other signs of economic individualism. Even in Nigeria, for example, slightly more people agree that "everybody should be free to pursue what is best for themselves as individuals" (53 percent) rather than putting "the well-being of the community ahead of their own interests" (43 percent).[16] To be sure, there are notable differences in the degree of expressed economic individualism between the largely Yoruba residents of the southwest region (58 percent) and the predominantly Hausa-Fulani northwest region (48 percent). Two thirds of all Nigerians also feel a measure of personal economic efficacy, stating that, "I always try to plan ahead because I feel I can make my plans work." They are joined in this sentiment, and in the rejection of the fatalistic notion that "it is not wise to plan too far ahead because many things turn out to be a matter of luck," by 77 percent of Tanzanians, 70 percent of Zambians,[17] and even 53 percent of Malians, whose orientations otherwise tend to be relatively passive.

The more we probed economic values, the more that individualistic and entrepreneurial attitudes were revealed. Across the twelve countries, a slim majority considers that "the best way to create jobs is to encourage people to start their own businesses" (53 percent), whereas fewer think that "the government should provide employment for everyone who wants to work" (44 percent). A higher level of support was recorded for the idea that, "people should be free to earn as much money as they can, even if this leads to differences in income among people" (63 percent), as opposed to the alternative proposition that "the government should place limits on how much the rich can earn, even if this discourages some people from working hard" (32 percent). The strongest entrepreneurial response emerged when a significant majority agreed that, "if a person has a good idea for a business, they should invest their own savings or borrow money to try to make it succeed" (76 percent). Only a small minority feared that "there is no sense in trying to start a new business because many enterprises lose money" (18 percent). Self-reliance and personal responsibility for job creation hang together in a syndrome of individualism.[18]

Notably, however, majorities in every country in the Afrobarometer believe that personal risk taking is required to make a business succeed. In some cases – see Nigeria, Ghana, and Malawi – overwhelming majorities (over 80 percent) say they feel this way. In contexts where poor and vulnerable populations are supposed to be averse to uncertainty,[19] it is unexpected to find such a remarkably high tolerance for risk. On one hand, perhaps the choice to invest personal savings is too hypothetical for many respondents to envisage. Or they might take a relaxed attitude to borrowing capital, thinking that it only jeopardizes someone else's money.[20] On the other hand, tolerance for risk may be more widespread than usually thought among Africans, many of whom apparently wish to take advantage of new opportunities to start businesses, especially in small-scale production and the retail and wholesale trades, that have arisen as economies have become liberalized.

Moreover, the institutions of private enterprise are held in high public esteem. The Afrobarometer asks how much trust people place in a range of institutions, including governmental agencies (in all twelve countries) and private sector and nongovernmental entities (in four countries). As Table 4.3 shows, Africans in Ghana, Nigeria, Mali, and Tanzania generally find market-based institutions like banks and businesses to be more worthy of trust (averaging 72 percent) than government institutions like parliament and the police (averaging 58 percent). Of course, some respondents may not possess enough first-hand knowledge of businesses, and especially banks, to arrive at an informed assessment. Another possible objection is that a comparison with government institutions is not entirely fair since the police are the least trusted of all government institutions in most African countries. But police officers represent the frontlines of government service and they have as much regular contact with the populace as do local businesspeople (like traders and transporters); thus, it is reasonable to ask people to compare

TABLE 4.3. *Popular Trust in Institutions*

	Ghana 1999	Nigeria 2000	Mali 2001	Tanzania 2001	Mean
Government					57.9
Parliament/Assembly	70	58	55	92	
Police	49	29	48	62	
Nongovernment					71.9
Churches	84	73	39	88	
Mosques	52	67	92	80	
Private					72.1
Banks	84	76	67	87	
Businesses	74	72	39	78	

Question: "How much do you trust the following institutions?"
Note: Figures are percentages saying they trust these institutions "somewhat" or "a lot."

the two groups. However, it is worth noting that private sector institutions are not as highly regarded as the dominant religious organization in each country: for example, trust in businesses is lower than for churches in Ghana, and trust in banks is lower than for mosques in Mali. All told, though, people say they have higher regard for market (and nongovernmental) entities than they do for the official institutions of the nation–state.

Finally, a popular constituency has developed in some parts of Africa for a private-sector approach to development, as evidenced by tantalizing snippets of information from Nigeria and Ghana. In follow-up surveys in 2001 and 2002, the Afrobarometer for the first time explicitly inquired about popular preferences for various macroeconomic regimes. Informed that "there are many ways to manage an economy," Nigerians were asked to approve or disapprove of various alternative economic arrangements. Substantial minority-indicated approval of a regime in which "the government plans the production and distribution of all goods and services" (43 percent in Nigeria, 49 percent in Ghana). Tellingly, however, a clear majority preferred a system whereby "individuals decide for themselves what to produce and what to buy and sell" (65 percent in both countries). At this stage, we do not know whether this result will be reproduced in other countries, but, when the question is posed this way, almost two thirds of these West Africans say they prefer a market regime.

None of the evidence presented previously should be taken to mean that Africans have undergone a wholesale conversion to a neoliberal vision of a market economy. While being titillated by promises of new market opportunities, people also express a strong strain of economic statism. We detect clear demands for the state to intervene to manage the macro economy, to provide for basic social needs, and to regulate the uncertainties and inequalities that accompany market reform.

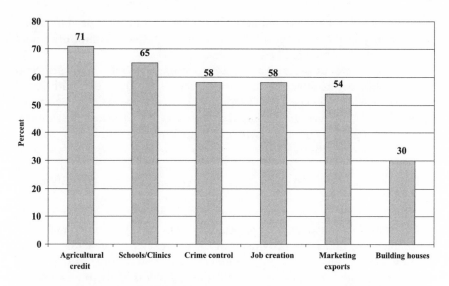

Question: "I am going to read out a list of things that are important for the development of our country. In your opinion, who is responsible for providing these things? The government, private businesses, or the people themselves? Or some combination of these providers?"

Note: Figures are percentages saying they prefer government to deliver these services.

FIGURE 4.2. Preference for Government Provision

As Figure 4.2 shows, people expect the state to assert itself in a national project of socioeconomic development. Respondents were asked their opinion regarding who should take charge of performing half a dozen basic development functions: government, the private sector (including both businesses and private individuals), or some combination of providers? The results reveal that government is the favored provider for five out of the six activities.

First, most Africans interviewed (71 percent) think that government should shoulder responsibility for providing agricultural credit. They were of a single mind on this subject because agricultural credit is the only development function for which majorities in all countries call for government leadership.[21] Such demand is very high in Tanzania (87 percent), where people still see the partially privatized Cooperative and Rural Development Bank as a public enterprise. It is lowest in Namibia (54 percent), where smallholder cropping is prevalent mainly in the North, where the government has distributed free inputs such as hybrid seed, fertilizer, and plowing services, thus vitiating some of the demand for seasonal credit.[22] The universal claim for agricultural finance does not represent special pleading on the part of rural areas because aggregate support for a government role does not vary significantly by an African country's level of urbanization. On average, across all countries, a mere 6 percent prefers private solutions. Apparently, popular trust of banks does not stretch so far as to give people confidence that these institutions will make seasonal agricultural loans to small-scale cultivators. Because they lack legal title to land, this class of farmers cannot offer land as collateral for commercial bank credits.

Second, people (65 percent) also want government to remain the principal dispenser of basic health and education services. They know that faith-based agencies provide only specialized services (like Koranic learning centers) or reduced levels of coverage compared to the past (like Christian mission stations). In urbanized countries, where private schooling and health care are available only for the wealthy, the general populace is firmly committed to public provision. Indeed, majorities of citizens consistently identify state delivery of education and medicine as the preferred modality virtually everywhere. The only exceptions are Tanzania and Malawi, where people seem to have lost faith in the quality of public services, because almost half the respondents (47 and 44 percent respectively) stand ready to experiment with a combination of service providers. In the aggregate, the general public is slightly more willing to try nongovernmental educational and health services in countries with large Christian populations, and less likely to do so where Muslims are in the majority.[23]

Third, Africans also prefer that the government take the lead in controlling crime, a conventional function of states. Oddly, this preference is weaker (58 percent) than for more demanding tasks like delivering agricultural credit and social services. Perhaps existing criminal justice systems are seen as less than fully reliable in providing for public safety and security. Our interviewers certainly heard many doubts expressed about the capacity of the police and the courts to arrest, prosecute, and punish criminals. There is considerable variance in the extent to which Africans want their governments to take charge of crime control, from 82 percent in Mali to just 32 percent in Botswana. Indeed, the general public in parts of Southern Africa – like Botswana, Namibia, and South Africa – is likely to regard crime control as a shared responsibility that should involve the private security agencies that are now growing rapidly in these countries.[24] But, in Nigeria, where vigilante groups have sometimes taken upon themselves the duties of an ineffective police force,[25] most people still think that crime control should be a government function.

Fourth is the vexed topic of jobs. Having previously stated (by a slight majority) that job creation was more of a personal than a public obligation, respondents reverse themselves, with six out of ten now stating that the government should take prime responsibility. The volatility of public opinion on this topic (which varies according to the way the question is asked) nicely captures the ambiguity that Africans feel about how best to address unemployment, the problem they have identified as being most central to national development. In this instance, citizens in eight countries want the government to take the lead in generating jobs, with Basotho and Malians (79 and 75 percent respectively) leading the pack. The domestic private sector is underdeveloped in both places and, because it creates few jobs, many citizens are forced to emigrate in search of paid employment. But Botswana, Namibia, and South Africa each have a sizeable private sector led by major mining companies. Accordingly, at least half of all respondents in these countries think that a mixture of public and private initiatives is the best approach to job creation.

Fifth, Africans even prefer that governments direct the marketing of the country's main export commodity, though now by only a slim and questionable edge (54 percent). The commodity varies by country,[26] as does the level of popular preference for government control. In fact, majorities preferred an outright public monopsony in only five countries, opting instead for competition between private traders and official marketing boards in six countries. These conflicting results can be understood in the light of the mixed, but generally inefficient and often corrupt performance of parastatal marketing boards at turning a profit in the sagging crop and mineral markets of the 1980s.

The general public wants the government to retain control of export marketing if the commodity in question is a strategic mineral whose revenues are central to the government budget. Hence, support for governmental involvement in marketing arrangements is highest in Botswana (81 percent) and Zambia (78 percent), though for different reasons and perhaps based on an overestimation of the real extent of government control. The Botswana government sells diamonds through the Debswana Diamond Company, a fifty-fifty joint enterprise with the De Beers Corporation that has provided reliable revenue flows into state coffers even in the face of rising threats from synthetic and illegal sources of diamonds. At the time of the survey, the Zambian government produced and sold copper through Zambia Consolidated Copper Mines; despite constituting a net drain on the national treasury due to dwindling copper reserves and falling world commodity prices, a clear majority of Zambians wanted to retain a firm government hand in mineral marketing.

Other Africans, especially those living in economies based on smallholder agriculture, showed greater openness to private trading, as well as to economic competition in the trade of farm commodities. For example, only about a third of Malians and Malawians (32 and 38 percent respectively) insisted that the state retain its marketing monopoly on export crops. In Malawi, many farmers have welcomed the opportunity to sell their burley tobacco to private merchants at improved prices, especially after the financial collapse of the official Agricultural Development and Marketing Corporation (ADMARC) in the mid-1980s.[27] Many of their counterparts in Mali, notably in the cotton zone, accept the advantages of a marketing partnership between the governmental Compagnie Malienne pour le Dévellopement des Textiles (CMDT) and the farmer-controlled Syndicat des Producteurs de Coton et de Cultures Vivrièrs (SYCOV).[28]

Finally, the sole economic function broadly seen as a private affair is the construction of housing. On average across the Afrobarometer countries, only three in ten survey respondents think that the state has a duty to provide families with a roof over their heads. South Africa is the only exception, where a majority (63 percent), many themselves shack dwellers, perceives a state obligation. This orientation reflects both the policy legacy of apartheid, in which public construction projects were a cornerstone of residential segregation, and the posttransition policy innovations of the African National Congress (ANC), whose Reconstruction and Development Program (RDP) in 1994 introduced a crash program to build a million low-cost houses in five years.[29] Apart from South Africans, the people we interviewed generally agree that individuals operating in an open market are best placed to provide their own housing. Certainly in Ghana and Tanzania – where just 10 and 2 percent respectively regard housing as a state function – there is no widespread expectation that the state will step in to bestow shelter.

Let us summarize what we have learned about basic economic values. On one hand, the people we interviewed see themselves as autonomous economic agents who wish to decide for themselves what to produce, buy, and sell. On the other hand, they demand state intervention to provide an array of services, including financial loans to farmers and the construction and operation of schools and clinics. To reconcile these divergent preferences, several interpretations are possible. The most positive view is that, in a mixed economy, there is no trade-off between state provision and individual enterprise; the state builds a foundation of social and economic infrastructure, but thereafter leaves individuals and families alone to pursue their own interests. A less-generous rendering would emphasize the tension, perhaps even contradiction, between reliance on the state and the quest for economic autonomy. This antithesis is captured in the acute popular ambiguity about the locus of responsibility for the provision of employment. Depending how the subject of employment is framed, people oscillate – often quite wildly,[30] – between proposing approaches to job creation that are either strongly prostate, strongly promarket, or somewhere in between.[31] In short, on the core issue on the popular development agenda (employment), Africans seem to feel caught between state and market.

AWARENESS OF ECONOMIC REFORMS

We now consider how people evaluate the economic reform programs introduced in African countries over the past couple of decades. Prescribed by international financial institutions as an antidote to economic crisis, stabilization and structural adjustment programs have sharply reduced state services, instead introducing market transactions into economic policy. To date, the literature on this subject has focused heavily on the process of elite bargaining over loans and on government compliance in implementing policy conditions. To the extent that popular attitudes to economic reform have been considered at all, they have usually been portrayed in all-or-nothing terms. Without benefit of much evidence, commentators assert that Africans are either "for" or "against" (usually "against") the entire stabilization and adjustment package. For example, Mkandawire and Olukoshi refer to the "sheer unpopularity of the programme," Tati to "the absence of social support for structural adjustment," and Domingo to "a public reaction against the SAP *per se*."[32]

Have ordinary people heard much about the official economic reform program adopted in their countries? Loan agreements are usually negotiated in private – sometimes in distant donor capitals like Paris or Washington – and little information is published about terms and conditions. In Tanzania in 1986, for example, the prime minister reportedly refused to answer parliamentary questions about dealings with the IMF, arguing that the executive enjoyed the sole prerogative to negotiate international agreements.[33] Thus, we expect that popular awareness of adjustment, and knowledge of its content, will be quite limited. Instead, mass opinions about economic reform will be based on personal experiences with particular policy measures, for example, the removal of price controls on staple foodstuffs or the layoff of workers from state enterprises. Do people generally view the orthodox market reform package as a bitter pill that must be swallowed whole? More likely, we think, they draw distinctions about the acceptability (or not) of a reform program's various component policies. If, as we have shown, the general public has mixed economic values, it would be surprising if the stabilization and adjustment package was accepted or rejected in its totality. As Africans with various interests grope to find for themselves a zone of comfort between expanding markets and shrinking states, different groups are likely to extend support to some parts of the reform program but to reject others. Indeed, we find that public opinion on policy issues varies widely and cannot be neatly characterized as simply proreform or antireform.

To test popular awareness of official national programs of economic reform, the Afrobarometer asks: "have you ever heard anything about (the government's structural adjustment program [SAP]) or haven't you had a chance to hear about this yet?"[34] The approved name and acronym for this program – for example, the Economic Recovery Program (ERP) in Ghana, or the Economic Structural Adjustment Program (ESAP) in Zimbabwe – was inserted for each country. If the respondent seemed uncertain, a prompt was added: "you know, the reforms to the economy introduced in the 1980s/1990s." Because there was no identifiable adjustment program in Botswana, Lesotho, and Namibia, this and related questions were not asked there.

On average, across the nine remaining countries, we found rather low levels of awareness of the official economic reform program. Fewer than half of all respondents (43 percent) said that they had ever heard of their country's SAP, even when prompted and when reference was made to the program's local name. Some policymakers will see this as a setback: after two decades of sustained international effort to induce governments to reorient their economies toward the market, more than half of the intended beneficiaries are ignorant that such a strategy even exists. On the other hand, other policy elites will discover a blessing: if an economic stabilization or adjustment agreement signals a government's impotence in the face of international pressure, then low public awareness will shield leaders from a loss of political legitimacy and allow them to undertake reform by stealth. Beyond these elite calculations, it is never easy for ordinary people to grasp the abstruse content of technical reforms like exchange rate flotation, international tariff liberalization, and the recalibration of the rural-urban terms of trade. Low levels of name recognition may also reflect the shifting and cryptic acronyms assigned to policy programs – such as the switch from ERP to SAP in Ghana, with a detour into a social safety net called PAMSCAD. Above all, lack of mass familiarity is also probably due to the fact that many African governments only partially adopted market reforms, promoted them half-heartedly, or implemented them inconsistently.

It is therefore not surprising that people have scant understanding of the purpose of economic reform programs. In four countries – Ghana, Mali, Nigeria, and Uganda – we asked, "in your opinion, what is (the SAP) supposed to do?" Overall, less than one third of respondents (29 percent) could venture an answer, and even persons who claimed to have heard of SAPs often did not know. This low level of economic literacy stands in marked contrast to the more than three quarters that can attach a meaning to democracy (See Chapter 3).

Like democracy, however, economic reform is viewed positively. Among the minority who are aware of SAPs, only one out of a hundred made reference to negative purposes (see Table 4.4). Admittedly, a handful of people thought that the reform program aimed at "bringing hardship and difficulties," "benefiting the rich," or "domination étrangère." But almost 99 percent cited positive goals, a remarkable finding in the light of the emotional claims in the literature about the inappropriateness and unacceptability of market reforms in Africa. Contrary to conventional wisdom that "the people" regard SAPs in a derogatory light, we find that most knowledgeable respondents in four countries seem to associate economic reform programs with affirmative economic objectives. We do not know, however, how many people are simply parroting official propaganda in this respect.

What are these objectives? As Table 4.4 shows, two purposes stand out: to improve the macroeconomy and to raise mass living conditions. In countries with sustained economic reform programs – Ghana, Uganda, and Mali – people tend to refer first and foremost to the growth and revitalization of the overall economy, whereas Nigerians think the main objective is to improve the living standards of common people. These responses suggest that

TABLE 4.4. *Popular Understandings of Economic Reform Programs*

	Ghana 1999	Nigeria 2000	Uganda 2000	Mali 2001	Mean
Improve the economy	46	25	32	39	35.4
Improve living conditions	31	29	21	18	24.8
Stabilize the economy	7	12	3	2	6.1
Restructure economic institutions	5	9	9	1	5.8
Increase jobs	3	4	11	1	4.7
Give grants and loans	0	0	0	16	4.0
Encourage self-reliance*	<1	9	5	0	3.4
Provide social services	4	1	2	<1	1.9
Other, good	4	10	17	20	12.8
Other, bad	0	<1	<1	4	1.1

Question: "In your opinion, what is the (structural adjustment program; specific name inserted here) supposed to do?"

Note: Figures are percentages of those persons who can attach a purpose to SAP (n = 2,981) (excludes "don't know" and "not applicable"; the question was not asked of persons who had never heard of their country's SAP).

* Includes "hard work."

most well-informed citizens consider that, even if the medicine of adjustment is bitter, SAPs are designed to bring about economic recovery and a reduction in poverty. At the same time, popular comprehension of the purposes of the orthodox reform package is loose at best. Very few respondents associate economic reform with its principal goals: first to stabilize the economy, for example, by shaving budget and trade deficits, cutting inflation, and putting the national currency on a sound and sustainable footing (together just 6 percent); and then to adjust the structure of the economy by reducing the role of state, not only in setting prices and tariffs, but including institutional reforms to sell off public enterprises and to streamline the civil service (jointly only another 6 percent). In short, and not surprisingly, issues of monetary policy and trade liberalization do not loom large among popular preoccupations.

Instead, the general public describes the purposes of economic reform in terms that are even sketchier than their elementary interpretations of democracy. In Mali, survey respondents interpreted SAPs more in terms of a windfall of international grants and loans than in terms of tough policy conditions. Common responses included "to aid poor people," "to help poor countries" and "to finance the government." Because, in Mali, economic reforms were introduced from abroad in the context of programs of food relief and budgetary support, popular economic thinking is imbued with an ethos of aid dependence. In other places, though, people are beginning to regard economic reform programs as instruments for advancing preferred economic

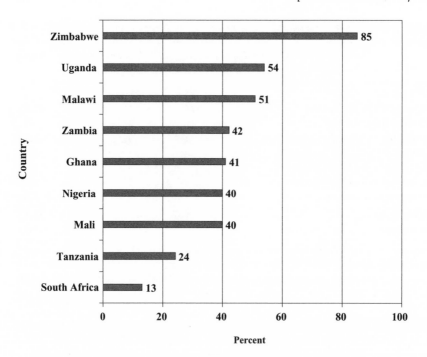

Question: "Have you ever heard anything about the government's (structural adjustment program; specific name inserted here), or haven't you had a chance to hear about this yet?"
Note: Figures are percentages who have heard of their country's SAP.

FIGURE 4.3. Awareness of Structural Adjustment Programs

values and for addressing national development priorities. In Nigeria, for example, a sliver of opinion holds that SAPs aim to encourage individual "self-reliance" and "hard work" (9 percent) and in Uganda, a slice of the population thinks that SAPS aim at job creation (11 percent).

There is more cross-national variation in awareness of adjustment than on any other attitude we studied (see Figure 4.3). At one extreme, 85 percent of Zimbabweans claim to have heard of the country's Economic Structural Adjustment Program, known colloquially as ESAP. Introduced in 1991, ESAP aimed at liberalizing trade by reducing import tariffs and providing incentives to promote exports. But widespread drought and uncontrolled budget deficits meant that reform was followed by recession and inflation, notably in food prices.[35] The government repeatedly tried to blame these consequences on the World Bank and IMF, at whose instigation the adjustment programs had been introduced. As such, ESAP terminology entered public discourse and popular culture ("Elastic Stomach Adjustment Program!," "Eat Sadza And Perish!"[36]), including pop songs.[37] Thus, many Zimbabweans learned about the program, usually attaching to it a negative connotation.

At the other extreme, only 13 percent of South Africans recognize their government's Growth, Employment, and Redistribution Policy, commonly known as GEAR. This stands in stark contrast to the program's prominence in elite debate. Launched in 1996 to replace the Reconstruction and Development Program (RDP), GEAR was a homegrown, macroeconomic strategy that was consistent with the preferences of international financial institutions, foreign investors, and the local business community. It aimed to create a competitive platform for export-led growth, a fiscally disciplined public budget, a flexible labor market, and the full or partial privatization of public agencies.[38] It has consistently drawn the ire of the alliance partners of the governing African National Congress: the South African Congress of Trade Unions and the South African Communist Party. Perhaps because it downplayed social redistribution in favor of economic growth, GEAR never gained the public currency of the RDP. Indeed, by claiming that GEAR was simply a means to implement redistribution, the government never actively publicized the adjustment program. It is in this context that South Africans' stunningly low public awareness of GEAR must be understood.

Nigeria and Zambia are more representative of the Afrobarometer in that about four out of ten adults have heard of the national economic structural adjustment program.[39] It is surprising that public awareness of SAPs is not more widespread because, in both countries, the issue of market reform was debated in civil society and electoral campaigns. In Nigeria in 1986, the government of Ibrahim Babangida broke with the IMF over the conditions it imposed on its loans, invited the public to express their own views on economic policy in a series of public forums, and then announced its own "home-grown" macroeconomic strategy, which differed little in principle from the IMF demands. In the founding elections in Zambia in 1991, the opposition Movement for Multiparty Democracy campaigned against the Kaunda government's economic mismanagement and promised radical reforms to reduce the role of the state in the economy. It therefore came as no surprise to the electorate when the new MMD government quickly halved, and then later eliminated, the subsidy on maize-meal, the country's staple food. Indeed, this politically sensitive reform, which Kaunda was never able to implement, was accepted with apparent public equanimity when implemented by a legitimately elected government.

SUPPORT FOR ECONOMIC REFORMS

Perhaps, as suggested previously, citizens develop their general attitudes to economic adjustment with reference to specific constituent elements of the reform program. They stake out positions, one by one, to sectoral policy measures – such as subsidy reductions on consumer goods or job reductions in the civil service – that they encounter in their daily lives. To explore this proposition, we break down the standard economic reform package by

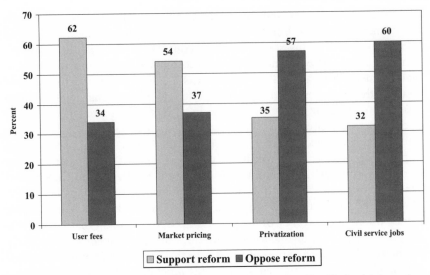

FIGURE 4.4. Support for Economic Reform Policies

asking people whether they support or reject four of its component policies. The findings are summarized in Figure 4.4. and in an additive *index of support for market reform.*[40]

We begin with user fees. As a means of controlling runaway public expenditures, governments search for ways to share the costs of providing social services, for example by asking consumers to make payments to offset the real costs of service delivery.[41] Across sub-Saharan Africa, governments have had little choice but to introduce charges for basic health care services, which require patients to contribute to the costs of medical consultations and prescription drugs. Similarly, many African governments have been forced to retreat from policies of free, universal, primary education by reintroducing fees at the elementary level and to steeply increase the costs to families who wish to send their children to secondary school or university.[42]

We asked respondents to choose: "Is it better to get health care (or education) for free, even if standards of service are low? Or is it better to raise health care (and educational) standards, even if you have to pay fees?" Unexpectedly, in all twelve Afrobarometer countries, more people preferred the reform option (impose fees, raise standards) to the status quo ante (no fees, low standards). And they did so by a factor of almost two to one (62 percent versus 34 percent). In some cases, the reform constituency was far larger than the antireform faction (see Tanzania, Ghana, and Nigeria) but in other places the reform majority was slim (as in Malawi and Namibia).[43] But majority support for user fees was evident even in countries where the government had recently introduced free universal primary education, as in Malawi in 1994 and Uganda in 1997. Since we asked about medical fees in Southern Africa and school fees in East and West Africa, apparent differences across countries may also reflect variance between services. If so, then people display greater willingness to lay out their own resources for health care than education, which accords with what we found earlier about the declining salience of education and rising importance of medical services as national problems. But the key finding is this: despite the fact that people grumble about the burden of paying user fees for social services, they are nonetheless willing to do so.[44] In return, however, they insist that standards of services must rise.

Second, we looked at attitudes toward market pricing for consumer goods. In many African countries in the 1980s, subsidies for staple foodstuffs and other basic commodities ballooned to the largest item in the government budget. Economic stabilization required the removal of subsidies, allowing prices to find their own levels in the marketplace. One happy side effect of "getting the prices right" is that supplies of consumer goods usually expand to meet demand, thus putting an end to policy-induced shortages. Commodities flood onto once-empty supermarket shelves. While consumers may have to pay higher prices for these goods – and some may be unable to afford them – they no longer have to queue up in the early hours of the morning, as urban Zambians did just to buy bread.

The survey choice was: "Is it better to have a variety of goods available in the market, even if prices are high? Or is it better to have low prices, even if there are shortages of goods?" In this instance, we again find support for market-oriented reform (at 54 percent), but less resoundingly than for user fees. In nine out of twelve countries, people prefer to allow the market to set prices for consumer goods rather than to receive price subsidies and risk facing shortages. Support for market pricing is strongest in Ghana (72 percent), Tanzania (70 percent), and Uganda (69 percent). In these countries, proreform sentiments can be traced to popular memories of severe policy-induced consumer goods shortages during the 1980s, leading consumers to reject the hardships associated with the old economic regime. Support for market pricing is weakest in Lesotho (38 percent), Malawi (41 percent), and Zimbabwe (43 percent), where more people prefer subsidized prices. Up to the time of the surveys in these countries, state intervention had never induced shortages of staple foods; as a result, people remained confident that the state could reliably smooth out imperfections in the market. And while a balance of South Africans prefer market pricing, the large minority supporting price controls in this country is also probably connected to the bounty of its supermarkets.

Third, we turn to public opinion on privatization.[45] We asked: "Should the government sell its factories, businesses, and farms to private companies and individuals? Or should it retain ownership of these enterprises?" In this instance, the Afrobarometer responses amount to a strong antireform reaction. In contrast to support for basic efforts to stabilize public budgets, we find little popular support for the institutional reforms associated with economic structural adjustment. There is little mass enthusiasm for the state to divest itself of public corporations since, in none of the countries surveyed does a majority favor the sale of public assets and, in many places, this reform policy is rejected by a large margin. In Zambia, for example, where the survey took place shortly before the government finalized the sale of the copper mines in 1999, two out of three citizens opposed the divestment of public companies. No doubt many people feared job losses, which had occurred as other industries had been sold to cost-cutting multinational corporations and as previously protected industries were shut down, having failed to compete in a liberalized trade regime. In Tanzania too, where support for reform policies is otherwise very strong, a majority opposed privatization, even though the sale of state assets has not undermined state revenues or led to labor unrest.[46] Only in Botswana did more people prefer than oppose privatization (49 versus 36 percent).

Fourth, and finally, we examine attitudes to public sector reform. Many economists now acknowledge that political accountability and managerial reorganization within the civil service are necessary in order to restore growth to African economies. Washington-based international financial institutions have come to include good governance initiatives in their adjustment and poverty alleviation programs.[47] A core element in these initiatives is the rehabilitation of run-down state bureaucracies by reducing the size of the personnel establishment and improving professionalism and efficiency. Unavoidably, some public employees lose their jobs in the process, even as others become better trained, paid, and motivated.

To get at popular attitudes to public sector reform, we asked respondents to choose between the following statements. Either "The government cannot afford so many public employees, so it should lay some of them off"; or "All civil servants should keep their jobs, even if paying their salaries is costly to the country." The results show that there is even less support for civil service retrenchment (32 percent) than for privatization (35 percent), with barely one out of five people in four countries supporting this policy.[48] We expected that people who depend on the wage or salary of a government worker – including employees of local government authorities and the public teaching service – would be especially resistant to job cutbacks in the public service. But when we singled out these groups in second surveys, we found no significant link in Nigeria and South Africa, which suggests that, far from being a narrow interest of patronage beneficiaries, resistance to cutbacks in public employment permeates society. Perhaps people assume (as prompted by our question) that the costs of a bloated civil service are not born personally by taxpayers, but collectively by "the country." Or, given the high priority that people attach to job creation, they are predisposed to resist any reduction in the capacity of the state, the economy's largest employer, to generate and distribute jobs.

At the country level, there are only two exceptions to the antireform consensus that opposes the institutional restructuring of the civil service: Zimbabwe and Tanzania. Against the continental grain, just over half of all adults in these countries (51 and 59 percent respectively) actually approve of retrenchment in public employment. We suspect that, among Zimbabweans, even erstwhile supporters of ZANU-PF react against the abusive patronage practices of the ruling party, which have stuffed government bodies with unqualified political appointees and closed public employment to those deemed disloyal. In Tanzania, where support for all economic reform measures is unusually high and awareness of the official SAP is extremely low, some respondents uncritically follow the government's line.[49] Alternatively, civil servants had already developed various sideline businesses (*miradi midogo midogo*) that cushioned them, not only from severely eroded salaries, but from layoffs too. Other Tanzanians who were not civil servants had also migrated into the informal sector, where they found little point in criticizing job cutbacks long after they had ceased to derive much benefit from collapsed public services.[50]

A comment is in order about the intensity of public opinion on issues of economic reform. We know that the Africans interviewed are not broadly aware of the existence of official stabilization and adjustment programs and have little intimate knowledge about their objectives. But they have no difficulty in recognizing policies that have a direct impact on their own lives. Most respondents were able to express an opinion when faced with the range of practical policy choices listed above; only a few said they "didn't know" (between five and ten, depending on the question). Instead, respondents felt strongly about adjustment as evidenced by the clustering of responses (whether "pro" or "con") toward the "strongly agree" ends of the spectrum.

To close this section, we summarize the bifurcated nature of mass attitudes toward economic reform. Far from being wholly for or against market-oriented policies, most Africans interviewed express discriminating views. For example, they generally *support*, or at least tolerate, *getting the prices right*. African citizens place a lofty value on education and (especially) health care, to the point of being willing to pay school and clinic fees to obtain these services. To a lesser extent, most citizens accept market pricing for consumer goods perhaps because, under adjustment policies, so many more of them have become private traders, especially in the informal economy.

By contrast, we also note a strong streak of resistance to other parts of the orthodox structural adjustment package: the Africans we interviewed generally *oppose the restructuring of economic institutions*. By saying "no!" to privatization and public service retrenchments, people express strong attachments to the role of the state as the principal provider of employment.[51]

Even if public sector salaries are in decline, the rents and perquisites associated with public office are apparently still attractive. For example, even if
civil servants cannot earn a living wage, they still value the houses, vehicles,
telephones, and contacts that often come with an official job, and which can
be exploited to piece together a livelihood. By contrast, people doubt that
the private sector, whether driven by international investment or small-scale
enterprise, can deliver a reliable supply of remunerative positions.

SATISFACTION WITH ECONOMIC REFORMS

How, then, do Africans judge the impact of economic reform programs?[52]
Most interviewees say they are not satisfied with the changes that they attribute to stabilization and adjustment. In every country bar Uganda, more
people express dissatisfaction than satisfaction with SAPs (see Figure 1.2).[53]
In Mali, where a plurality expresses contentment, the results are clouded by
economic illiteracy; one third of the Malians who claim to be aware of the
SAP say they do not know enough about its operations to judge whether
the SAP is working to their gratification. All told, in 1999–2001, there was
no country in the Afrobarometer in which an absolute majority of economically aware citizens expressed pleasure with the changes wrought by the
introduction of a regime of market-friendly policies.

This indictment compares very unfavorably with popular assessments of
democracy's performance. Whereas more than half of the Africans interviewed say they are satisfied with the way democracy works in their country
(see Chapter 3), less than one quarter (just 21 percent) expresses satisfaction
with the marketplace as it presently operates. Even in Tanzania, where more
people feel more at ease with the official adjustment program than anywhere
else (41 percent), an equal or greater number of people (44 percent) are disgruntled. Indeed, market liberalization as currently implemented has clearly
failed to create popular contentment – even in countries like Tanzania, Mali,
Uganda, and Ghana – where governments have implemented the most far-
reaching and sustained policy reforms. And in countries where compliance
with IMF and World Bank strategies has been weak or inconsistent, people
can barely muster a kind word about the performance of the new economic
regime. For example, as Figure 1.2 shows, some two thirds of economically
aware Nigerians are dissatisfied with the track record of SAPs, as are fully
nine out of ten of their counterparts with ESAP in Zimbabwe.

On a cautionary note, we wonder whether mass discomfort with the
performance of SAPs is a case of mistaken identity. Are people conflating
economic reform with economic crisis, thereby blaming the medicine for
the disease? We therefore asked people: "Who is responsible for current
economic conditions?" Almost everyone attributed custody for the country's economic circumstances to an indigenous, national government, as did
83 percent in Ghana and 76 percent in Nigeria. More people blamed a current

government than a previous government (for example, 52 versus 6 percent in Tanzania, and 43 versus 13 percent in Mali). Across these four countries, only a handful of economically informed respondents identified SAPs as the cause of their country's current developmental difficulties (just 1 percent). People may express dissatisfaction with the effects of SAPs on their quality of life, but they do not confuse these programs of market reform with the underlying causes of stalled macroeconomic growth. We therefore conclude that ordinary people can distinguish economic crisis from policy response and that they blame the former on economic and fiscal mismanagement by their own previous and (especially) incumbent political leaders.

Moreover, the survey results demonstrate the failure of efforts by some African leaders to transfer onus for people's hardships to the IMF and the World Bank. In Kenya, for example, President Moi proved to be an extremely reluctant economic reformer, readily sacrificing the policy conditions attached to foreign assistance at the altar of the patronage or electoral requirements of his ruling clique. The South African government has made a case to its people that, in a world of mobile capital, a country cannot attract investments unless its economic policies conform to prevailing global standards, attributing the country's economic slowdown of the late 1990s to the Asian financial crisis of 1997. Attempts of this sort to turn public opinion against international influences have fallen on stony ground: very few people accept that international financial institutions or other "international economic forces" are responsible for the current condition of national economies, ranging from just 1 percent in Nigeria to 6 percent in Tanzania. Indeed, in Mali, more respondents believe that economic conditions are "the will of God" or the result of other supernatural forces!

Nonetheless, adjustment is seen to foster uneven social effects. When asked whether the government's economic policies have "helped" or "hurt" most people, a majority of respondents see increased inequality (see Figure 4.5).[54] On average, 66 percent of those able to offer a valid answer agree that structural adjustment has disadvantaged most people and benefited few. In no African country did a majority of respondents think that stabilization and adjustment reforms had assisted most folk. The largest vote of confidence in SAPs was mustered in Mali where 41 percent saw broad-based benefits, perhaps because price liberalization has led to improved profits for livestock herders and institutional reforms have restored the timely payment of public salaries. Ghana and South Africa, where only about one in three respondents think that most people have gained, represent the Afrobarometer norm. These results suggest that most ordinary people are concerned that prosperity is not trickling down in countries where market-based strategies have been tried.

Is there a causal connection between perceptions of unequal social effects and dissatisfaction with SAPs? The apparently similar distributions of opinion in Figures 1.2 and 4.5 would suggest so. A simple bivariate test,

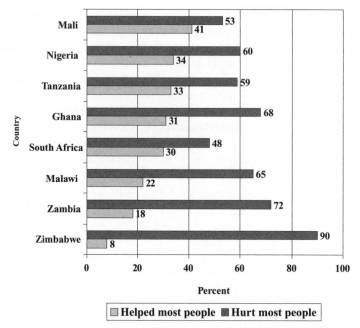

Question: "Choose A or B. A. The government's economic policies have helped most people; only a few have suffered
B. The government's economic policies have hurt most people and only benefited a few. Percentages who 'agree' or
'agree strongly.' "

FIGURE 4.5. Perceptions of SAPs' Effects on Inequality

which reveals a strong and statistically significant positive relationship between these two opinions, lends credence to this idea.[55] Fully 71 percent
of the people who think that SAPs increase inequality are also dissatisfied
with the performance of the economic reform program. This stands in stark
contrast to the 39 percent dissatisfaction rate among those who think that
SAPs have benefited most people.[56] The relationship between perceived inequality and dissatisfaction with SAP is especially strong in countries like
Malawi, Zambia, and Zimbabwe where large majorities suspect that the
benefits of policy reform are accumulating to an elite few. Indeed, in Malawi,
the connection is close to perfect.[57] And the relationship is even statistically
significant for Nigeria, the country where perceived inequality is apparently
least influential in driving dissatisfaction with SAPs.[58] On the face of it, growing social inequalities tend to undermine the reputation of economic reform
programs across African countries, but the problem is especially severe in
Southern Africa.

On a related point, respondents think that, across a range of developmental tasks, reformist governments do worst at "narrowing the income gaps
between the rich and the poor." For example, even though 64 percent saw
the Obasanjo government in Nigeria doing "well" at combating corruption,

only 39 percent said the same about its performance at closing income gaps. In Ghana, even fewer (30 percent) praised the Rawlings government's handling of income distribution in a context where 56 percent gave it a good grade for controlling crime. And two thirds or more of the electorate think that their government is doing poorly at narrowing income gaps in Mali, Tanzania, and South Africa. At minimum, these widespread concerns about growing social inequality indicate that people want offsetting policy actions to ensure that the least advantaged members of society are not impoverished by the impact of adjustment. To date, however, national governments and international donors alike have granted low priority to social safety net programs, attaching them to SAPs, if at all, as last-minute afterthoughts.

Public opinion clearly identifies winners from economic reform. Asked "which group has benefited most from the government's economic policies?," overwhelming majorities report that the fruits of adjustment accrue to "people close to government." Among those mentioned are the state president, cabinet ministers, senior officers in the party, regional barons appointed by the top leadership, and individuals in the informal circles of power around such leaders. Many Africans seem to agree with Hibou that these political elites organize an "economy of plunder" built on "the acquisition, the creation, or the conquest of markets by various means by persons linked to those in power but operating in a private capacity ... (such) procedures for privatization are concentrated in the hands of those close to the head of state."[59] In this crony form of capitalism, faction leaders struggle to control state resources in order to provide patronage favors and build political support. A top bureaucratic stratum engages in insider trading for personal advantage, obtaining advanced or privileged knowledge about policy reforms, whether these involve incentives to engage in export production, the availability of early retirement packages from the civil service, or the sale of public corporations or other state assets.

As Table 4.5 demonstrates, three quarters or more of Ghanaians, Nigerians, Malians, and Tanzanians blame top political cronies. No other category of supposed beneficiary comes close; for example, foreign business interests are cited by just 6 percent of respondents, though Tanzanians are more prone than other Africans to suspect gains by outsiders. Moreover, people do not automatically blame ethnic or regional groupings for grasping more than a fair share of the returns from reform; consistently across countries, only 4 percent said that subnationalities were benefiting unfairly. When they rarely mentioned a region, Ghanaians cited Volta (the homeland of then President Jerry Rawlings), Malians spoke of Sikasso (the cotton heartland), and Nigerians pointed to Hausaland (or, more generically, "the north.")

Thus, Afrobarometer respondents tend to interpret the social impact of economic reform in terms of class rather than community. But the social classes they have in mind are not the classic formations of a property-owning bourgeoisie (fewer than 1 percent cited "the rich" or "the upper class") or

TABLE 4.5. *Perceived Beneficiaries of Economic Reform*

	Ghana 1999	Nigeria 2000	Mali 2001	Tanzania 2001	Mean
People close to government	74	86	84	77	80.4
Foreign business interests	4	3	2	13	5.6
Particular subnational regions	4	4	5	3	4.1
Rural areas	3	1	2	<1	1.6
Other	14	6	6	7	8.4

Question: "In your opinion, which group has benefited most (from the government's economic policies)?"

Note: Figures are percentages volunteering these responses. Figures may not add up to one hundred due to rounding.

a market-oriented peasantry (fewer than two percent named "les paysans"). The latter finding undercuts the common expectation that price liberalization, by raising the earnings of cash crop farmers and cutting food subsidies, would benefit rural producers at the expense of urban consumers. Instead, the popular discourse about the consequences of SAPs identifies as beneficiaries a political class who gain access to economic opportunities by occupying the offices of the state. Ordinary people are convinced that government officials have designed economic reform policies to benefit themselves. On this basis, we propose that the key weakness of a market-oriented development strategy in Africa is its strong association in the popular imagination with the intensification of politically based social inequalities, an issue which we explore again later in this book.

ECONOMIC PATIENCE?

To conclude our description of African attitudes to markets, we speculate about the durability of any support for, and satisfaction with, programs of economic reform. How patient are African jobseekers and consumers? How long are they willing to wait for expected economic benefits to materialize?

As is well known, market reforms tend to make economic conditions worse before they get better. The returns from economic liberalization conventionally require actors to endure sacrifices in the short run in order to realize the promise of future gains.[60] During the 1990s, only four Afrobarometer countries made meaningful economic progress, in the sense that their economic growth rates outstripped population growth rates by more than 1 percent (Uganda, Botswana, Namibia, and Ghana). Elsewhere, per capita incomes either remained stagnant (Malawi, Mali, Nigeria, Tanzania, and Zimbabwe) or declined (Lesotho, South Africa, and Zambia). In other words, the curve of contraction had yet to hit bottom and growth had yet to

TABLE 4.6. *Economic Patience*

	Ghana 1999	Nigeria 2000	Uganda 2000	Mali 2001	Tanzania 2001	Mean
The costs of reforming the economy are too high; the government should therefore change its economic policies.	62	49	35	38	37	44.3
In order for the economy to get better in the future, it is necessary for us to accept some hardships now.	38	45	47	49	53	46.1
Do not agree with either	0	3	4	6	7	3.3
Don't know	0	3	15	7	3	5.5

Note: Figures are percentages who agree ("somewhat" or "strongly"). In Ghana, the last two response options were not offered. Figures may not add up to one hundred due to rounding.

turn upward. Under such circumstances, popular support for a market economy depends heavily on whether people are willing to defer gratification.

We endeavoured to measure economic patience by posing the following choice to respondents in five countries: either "the costs of reforming the economy are too high; the government should therefore change its economic policies now"; or "in order for the economy to get better in the future, it is necessary for us to accept some hardships now." We had expected that, following euphoric political transitions, economic expectations would be sky-high and therefore easily dashed. We did not think that people would show much forbearance for economic reform programs whose benefits keep disappearing over an ever-vanishing horizon.

Yet the results revealed a modicum of economic patience (see Table 4.6). Slightly more people are willing to shoulder hardships for the moment than to insist that the government immediately overhaul its policies.[61] And in three countries (Uganda, Mali, and Tanzania), the constituency willing to wait for rewards was larger than the economically restless group by statistically significant margins. In Tanzania, an absolute majority volunteered a tolerance for economic hardship, whose limits, even after years of grinding privation, have apparently not yet been reached. In Ghana, by contrast, a vein of adjustment fatigue lay close to the surface in 1999, with more than six out of ten respondents called for immediate relief from the economic policies of the Rawlings administration. Underlining the intensity of this sentiment, four out of ten Ghanaians felt this way "strongly."

At first glance, Africans profess more economic patience than political patience.[62] In Southern Africa, respondents were asked whether the present "system of government" would "take many years...to deal with inherited problems" or whether it "ought to be able to deal with problems right now." When the question is asked this way, respondents appear to lack political patience, with an average of only 25 percent across seven Southern African countries thinking that democratic political arrangements are adequate to tackling their nations' problems. In East and West Africa, we posed the second option differently: "if the present system of government cannot produce results soon, we should try another form of government." Once it became clear that democracy might be at risk, the frequency of expressed political patience increased greatly: 73 percent of respondents across these five countries wished to grant more time for new political institutions to address socioeconomic problems. By this measure, political patience appears to be a more deeply held conviction than economic patience. In a direct comparison across the countries for which we have obtained measurements of both kinds of patience, more people wish to retain a reformed political regime (73 percent) than to stick with a liberalized economy (47 percent).

Thus, while the Africans we interviewed are more patient than expected with economic reform, their perseverance has limits and is less fulsomely granted than their willingness to tolerate experiments with democracy. By way of conclusion, we simply note that distribution of economic patience appears to bear no relationship to the ratio of benefits gained to costs incurred by a market reform program. Popular patience to allow time for the market to perform its "magic" is granted both in countries where growth has taken off (as in Uganda) and in countries where expansion remains stalled (as in Tanzania). And people withhold economic patience where the economy is volatile (as in South Africa) as well as under conditions of halting economic recovery (as in Ghana).

The lack of obvious pattern to these results reflects the ambivalence felt by folk who are trying to figure out where they stand between shrinking states and expanding markets. At one and the same time, they tentatively support some of the principles of a market economy but question the way that governments have implemented adjustment policies in practice. They simultaneously say that they trust the private sector more than the public sector, but they continue to prefer the delivery of needed services by government institutions. Our main conclusion is that popular attitudes on economic policy are barely formed. Because people may be thinking systematically about economic reform for the first time, many may draw their responses unreflectively out of thin air, lending a randomness to public opinion about market economies that will prove difficult to explain (see Chapter 11).

To be sure, some Africans are attracted by the opportunities for personal gain that arise with the loosening of government controls. At the same time, however, others are repelled by the uncertainties associated with economic liberalization, evincing loyalty to state services and public employment. On the face of it, such attachments seem illogical, since the capacity of African states to provide jobs and services has been in decline for several decades. But, since a viable, large-scale private sector does not exist anywhere outside of Southern Africa, there is a defensive logic to this position. In reality, the main existing alternative to a state-run economy is a ramshackle, semilegal, small-scale, informal economy that can aid in survival but which holds few promising opportunities for significantly improving livelihoods over the long run.[63] Until such time as private businesses create employment and services at the same level as even a hollowed-out state, many Africans apparently prefer to stick with the devil they know.

5

Economic and Political Behavior

So far, we have established that the denizens of a dozen leading countries in Africa express support for democracy but harbor decidedly uncertain feelings about a market economy. We wonder whether these facets of public opinion have tangible consequences for day-to-day behavior. When trying to meet basic human needs, for example, do people act on their expressed preferences for public provision of social services by turning for help to state agencies? Or do they rather make use of the marketplace, the community, or the family? And on the political front, do they convert their declared conviction that democracy is the best form of government into concrete acts of political participation such as voting, attending community meetings, and contacting elected officials? Or do they opt out of – or work around – official channels?

The consolidation of new regimes, especially those based on principles of citizen or consumer sovereignty, hinges critically on broad popular participation. Beyond simply being humans bearing rights, people incur duties from belonging to a political community, including obligations to contribute to group decision making and to the expansion of the collective economic pie. If, however, people elect to withdraw from public life and to suffer in silence, then they obtain the governments and economies that they deserve. Absent mass participation, the door is open for autocrats or embezzlers to seize power or, at best, for nonelected technocrats to assume responsibility for governance and economic management. If, however, people are willing to stand up and assert themselves – for example, by resisting attempts by leaders to undermine constitutional guarantees or steal state resources – then prospects for a brighter political economy are enhanced. In truth, the institutions of democracy and markets are likely to flourish only if people actually use them.

In this chapter, we examine the self-reported economic and political behavior of Afrobarometer respondents, noting that people sometimes exaggerate their involvement in activities that they deem to be socially approved or politically correct and to minimize their roles in activities that violate community standards or are punishable under the law. Even so, we find that people's actions generally speak louder than their words. Whereas people say that the government ought to be the main provider of goods and services, they actually rely on kinship and market networks far more frequently than they turn to agencies of the state. Similarly, although people profess commitment to the principles of electoral democracy, they solve the problems of everyday life by turning to religious leaders or private patrons rather than by activating their connections to elected representatives in central and local governments. In both cases, people tend to vote with their feet by avoiding the official channels of the state and migrating to the informal sectors of the economy and polity.

LIVING STANDARDS

To set the scene for discussing economic behavior, we first provide some contextual information about sources of livelihood and standards of living. By what means do Africans put food in the family pot?

Table 5.1 presents a picture of the main economic occupations reported by Afrobarometer respondents. The largest group says "none" (29 percent), by which they mean that they do no work outside of the home. This group is composed of self-described "housewives" (11 percent of all respondents), students (6 percent), or persons who have never held a job (7 percent). Their preponderance reflects the overall shortage of career opportunities in these economies and echoes the popular preoccupation with job shortages. The proportions reporting no occupation outside the home are high in all countries, inordinately so in Namibia, where the harsh natural environment offers few opportunities for viable livelihoods based on agricultural smallholding. It is lowest in Tanzania, where most people engage in self-employment in agriculture and few consider themselves entirely without an occupation.

Many African economies remain agrarian, with one third to one half of the population saying that they earn a living off the land in Tanzania, Uganda, Mali, Malawi, and Ghana. Most of these people have taken the "peasant option" by seeking to combine food production for home consumption with varying amounts of crop or livestock sales.[1] Also included in agricultural occupations are small numbers of commercial farmers and farm workers, mostly in Southern Africa. In Nigeria, people prefer to pursue livelihoods centered on commerce, including buying and selling goods that others produce, with one out of four Nigerians reporting being a businessperson, shopkeeper, or (most commonly) a trader in informal markets. As economies have liberalized, small-scale trading has begun to provide a ready alternative or supplement to farming, with substantial proportions now seeing themselves mainly as traders even in agrarian Tanzania, Ghana, and Uganda. Alternatively, in the industrialized economies, people have attained

TABLE 5.1. *Self-Reported Occupations, by Country*

	Bot	Gha	Les	Mwi	Mali	Nam	Nig	Saf	Tan	Uga	Zam	Zim	Afro Mean
None	30	19	40	27	35	46	35	31	11	23	25	29	29
Agriculture	4	33	9	39	40	16	13	6	54	43	23	9	26
Commerce	1	16	1	<1	8	1	25	2	17	14	1	1	10
Skilled trade	12	11	19	5	5	7	13	16	4	4	7	11	9
Unskilled trade	12	<1	15	14	0	6	0	19	0	0	13	13	6
Professional	11	5	5	12	5	12	2	12	1	1	15	12	6
Government	2	9	1	1	3	2	8	2	8	9	2	2	5
Services	5	6	6	3	2	5	2	10	1	3	3	6	4
Other	0	1	0	0	1	>1	1	0	4	2	0	0	1
No answer	24	0	6	>1	0	6	0	3	<1	0	12	19	4

Question: "What is your main occupation?"

Note: Figures are percentages of respondents reporting an occupation in this category (n = 21,511).
Totals may not add up to one hundred due to rounding.

technical skills or taken up unskilled manual labor, most notably in South Africa, Lesotho, Botswana, and Zambia. Only in Southern Africa do sizeable segments of the population describe themselves as professionals (like lawyers and accountants) or service providers (like clerks, nurses, and domestic or security workers).

The government provides more employment in Ghana and Uganda (9 percent) than anywhere else, but across all Afrobarometer countries the civil service accounts for an average of only one out of twenty occupations, including positions for teachers, soldiers, and police officers. Measured by this achievement, the public sector is an insufficiently powerful engine to create the large number of jobs demanded by Africans. Even where people profess an occupation, they may not always be employed, especially where jobs are temporary. Remarkably, across all twelve countries, almost half of all respondents (47 percent) – including those both with and without an occupation – reported being unemployed at some time during the previous year. Thus, a major reason that people worry most about employment is that jobs are not only scarce, but the supply is also unreliable, intermittent, or seasonal.

We probed the nature and extent of employment most fully in Southern Africa. Defining it rigorously as "a job that pays a weekly or monthly cash income" (now excluding self-employment) we discovered extraordinarily high levels of reported joblessness. As Table 5.2 shows, the unemployment thus defined ranges between 33 percent in Zimbabwe to 45 percent in Botswana. Lesotho lies outside this band at an astounding 76 percent, reflecting the fact that most wage and salary earners are resident beyond the country's borders. We have confidence in these figures because our estimate of the unemployment rate in South Africa in 2002 (36 percent) is virtually identical to an official labor force survey result for the same year (37 percent).[2] As well as being temporary, employment is all too often part time, as with one third of available jobs in Lesotho, Zimbabwe, and South Africa. Needless to say,

TABLE 5.2. *Self-Reported Employment, Southern Africa, 1999–2000*

	Bot	Les	Mwi	Nam	Saf	Zam	Zim
Unemployed (not looking)	29	30	65	36	26	43	42
Unemployed (looking)	32	53	15	30	27	21	19
Employed, part-time (not looking)	2	1	2	2	4	2	6
Employed, part-time (looking)	7	4	2	5	10	5	7
Employed, full-time (not looking)	18	7	12	19	22	17	18
Employed, full-time (looking)	11	4	4	7	10	10	7
Don't know, refused, etc.	1	1	0	1	1	2	1
Unemployment Rate	**45**	**76**	**42**	**47**	**36**	**38**	**33**

Questions: "Do you have a job that pays a weekly or monthly cash income? Is it full-time or part-time? And are you looking for a cash job (or looking for another one if you are presently working)?"

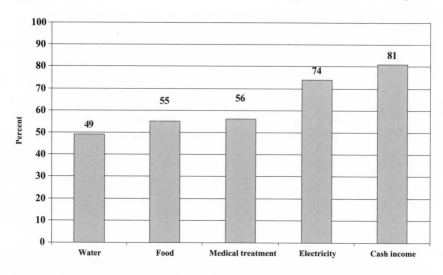

Notes: For question wording, see text and Appendix A. Figures are percentages saying that their household "occasionally," "frequently," or "always" went without these basic goods and services.

FIGURE 5.1. Shortages of Basic Human Needs

part-time jobs do not provide full salaries and usually lack benefits. Finally, many people who are employed full time are dissatisfied with their jobs, as evidenced by the one out of three permanent employees in Botswana and Zambia who continue to look for a better job even while they are working.

At root, people take up occupations and seek jobs in order to avoid poverty.[3] In order to appraise the extent of poverty, the Afrobarometer has developed a *lived poverty index* based on existential standards.[4] Presenting a list of basic human needs, we ask, "over the past year, how often have you or your family gone without . . . water, food, medical treatment, electricity, or a cash income?" Figure 5.1 displays the proportions of respondents who say they "occasionally," "frequently," or "always" go without each of these things. Overall, over one half of all Africans interviewed report at least occasional shortages of basic goods and services. People are most likely to be able to find a reliable source of water (though half say they cannot) but are most likely to forego a regular flow of cash income (which affects four out of five). Thus, in order to make ends meet, people supplement the family cash budget with other resources, either through self-provisioning, noncash barter transactions, or turning to others for help.

Cross-nationally, clear patterns of difference exist in the satisfaction of basic human needs. Take water. Despite an arid climate, Botswana's government has made considerable strides in providing its population with access to household water supplies; relatively few Batswana report occasional or frequent shortages (29 percent). Yet in neighboring Zambia, which has a more favorable rainfall regime but a less effective development bureaucracy, many more people report that they lack a reliable supply of water for household use (61 percent). As for food, Ghanaians report the least paucity (33 percent) and Namibians much greater needs (70 percent). Food shortages occur seasonally, usually before the food crop harvest, and the severity of the need can be traced partly to differences in demographic and agro-ecological conditions between and within countries: food shortages are most common in Ghana's arid northeast and in Namibia's heavily populated northern region. Although electricity is hardly a basic need, it does make an important contribution to easing hardship on a continent where fuel sources are meager. Electricity is in extremely short supply in Lesotho (where 95 percent report they "always" do without), but is relatively widespread in South Africa (where 50 percent "never" do without, including one third of blacks).[5]

Consistent with what we have learned about unemployment, people most often run short of cash income. There is much less variation across countries in this fundamental need because everywhere, including in the cash-based economies of Southern Africa, some two out of three Africans say they are short of income at least occasionally. South Africans enjoy the most reliable access to a wage or a salary; 35 percent are "never" short of a cash income. But the situation is less rosy for blacks in South Africa: the 79 percent that report insufficiencies of cash match the norm elsewhere in the Afrobarometer. Again, Zambia is worst off: fully 88 percent of the population complains about encountering deficits in their household budgets at least occasionally, if not frequently.

One would expect that poverty would be a function of unemployment. To be sure, individuals who lack jobs are more likely to report frequent shortages of cash income. But, because the positive relationship between these variables is not especially strong,[6] we can confirm two earlier observations. First, given the temporary nature of so many jobs, formal employment does not generate a reliable cash flow into the household. Second, some individuals manage to obtain cash even though they do not have a job of any kind because they draw upon sources of income other than formal employment. It is also true that joblessness is associated with shortages of food, clean water, and health care services. But, again, while this relationship runs in the predicted direction, it is weak,[7] implying that people have developed multistranded strategies for gaining access to essential goods and services. It is to popular strategies for securing survival, escaping poverty, and achieving welfare that we now turn.

SECURING ECONOMIC LIVELIHOODS

As is well known, Africans respond to economic crisis and personal hardship by diversifying their livelihoods. Rural dwellers, who face bureaucratic hurdles and dwindling returns when marketing crops through official channels, seek supplementary off-farm employment. Urban dwellers, for whom the cost of living has long exceeded the purchasing power of devalued official wages, take on various income-generating projects on the side. In short, individuals avidly participate in, and thus help to create, "that part of the economy variously referred to as the second, parallel, informal, underground, black or irregular economy."[8] The informal economy runs the gamut from backyard farmers, small-scale artisans, and street vendors to organized smuggling rings that span international frontiers.[9] Their activities take place beyond official jurisdictions and, by depriving the state of tax revenues and diverting the attention of public employees from official responsibilities, contribute to the fiscal crisis and weakening capacity of the state.

We possess only rough estimates of the scope of the informal sector in Africa. By 1970, the value of the illicit export trade in coffee and peanuts in Zaire and Senegal respectively was thought to exceed the annual net turnover of the central marketing boards. By 1980 in Ghana and Uganda, the second economy approached, if not exceeded, the size of the official national gross domestic product. By the 1990s in Tanzania, Tripp reports that, "for urban dwellers, employed and self-employed alike, the informal economy accounts for what the majority of people do to make most of their income."[10] To help document these estimates and with a view to cross-national comparison, the Afrobarometer systematically records the involvement of individuals in various informal economic activities.

Table 5.3 presents data for four countries in East and West Africa. It lends credence to the image of Africa as a continent of traders because an average of 37 percent of all respondents in Ghana, Mali, Nigeria, and Tanzania say they "buy and sell goods" as one activity among the various "things you do to earn money." Approximately half of this number in these countries state their main occupation as a trader, which implies that the other half are engaged in trade circuits as a secondary or sideline enterprise. Just as Nigeria leads the Afrobarometer in the proportion of people in trading occupations, so too Nigerians surpass other Africans interviewed in supplementing their household incomes by buying wholesale commodities and selling them at the

TABLE 5.3. *Supplementary Economic Activities*

	Ghana	Nigeria	Mali	Tanzania	Mean
Buy and sell goods	36	46	35	33	37
Sell skills or services	36	34	20	16	26
Operate a bank account	31	24	10	15	20
Employ others	24	19	16	16	19
Owe borrowed money	10	9	18	4	10

Question: "Considering all your economic activities (that is, your main occupation plus other things you do to earn money), Do you currently . . . :"
Note: Figures are percentages saying they engage in these economic activities.

retail level, either in public places or from their own homes. In all countries, many such enterprises are small scale, eking profits from mass consumer markets, including by unbundling packaged goods – like cigarettes, sweets, or soft drinks – into units that consumers can afford. In rural areas, and especially among women, beer brewing and buying and selling chickens are common commercial ventures. Some urban enterprises are larger in scale and trade in bulkier products or goods with higher markups, for example real estate and construction materials, or furniture and electronic appliances.

Larger enterprises often generate jobs, as reflected in the average of 19 percent of respondents (24 percent in Ghana) who say they "employ other people to work for (them)." For example, a civil servant will commonly employ relatives or acquaintances to operate a business – say a taxi vehicle or fleet – as a way to compensate for the shrinking value of an official wage or salary. But much of this employment takes the form of domestic service.

Other people will become employees in the informal sector by "selling (their) skills or services to other people" in the form of casual labor or the provision of on-call services. About one quarter of our interviewees indicated that they take on supplementary paid work in addition to their main occupation, as when formal sector workers undertake home or vehicle repairs on their own time. These practices are most prevalent in Ghana and Nigeria, where more opportunities exist for outside work for pay than in the poorer economies of Mali and Tanzania. Even so, rural dwellers can sometimes earn money by hiring themselves out as field laborers during peak periods in the agricultural cycle or by taking care of the livestock of absentee owners who live in towns.

As Kasfir notes, *magendo* (the parallel market) is not entirely segregated from the formal sector of the economy or even from the operations of the state.[11] Some 20 percent of respondents say they operate an account in a commercial bank and 10 percent report that they currently owe money that they have borrowed for business purposes, including from the state agricultural finance company. Indeed, the formal and informal sectors of the economy have become thoroughly interpenetrated, not only by the multiple activities that constitute individual livelihoods, but by the circulation of money, skills, and other resources from one sector to another.

A good indicator of the diversified nature of African livelihoods is the number giving more than one answer to questions like, "how do you currently obtain food?" or "in what ways do you normally obtain cash income?" Across seven Southern African countries, almost everyone (99 percent for food, 94 percent for cash) could identify at least one means to lay their hands on these necessities. The most common means of getting food was to purchase it (71 percent) and the most common source of cash was a paid job or self-employment. For some people, however, the *primary* method of meeting basic needs is to rely on a family network of parents, spouses, children, other relatives, neighbors or friends, to whom 13 percent turn for food and 17 percent to cover their needs for cash. A marginal minority reports no visible means of support: they say they "go to sleep without food" or "collect (food) from the forest" (less than 1 percent); or, with regard to cash, they admit that there is "nothing I can do" or "I would give up" (6 percent). Still others have no choice but to resort to uncertain methods like begging, living "from hand to mouth," and "praying to God."

Nonetheless, livelihoods are diverse. Some 39 percent of Southern Africans named an alternate method for ensuring personal food security, most commonly by "farming," usually on a household plot. Moreover, 29 percent had a second means of obtaining cash income, either by counting on regular contributions from kin or from "buying and selling goods." On the other side of this coin, however, the majority of people were *un*able to identify any alternate sources of livelihood, either because they did not need them, or because such sources were not available. And thereafter, options disappear quickly. Only 7 percent of Southern Africans say they draw upon three different sources of food, and just 5 percent enjoy three different methods for raising cash; almost no one had four options for securing these necessities. Thus, while Africans are highly resourceful at piecing together livelihoods, the economic environment actually offers rather scarce opportunities for diversification. Indeed, the main role of the informal sector is to serve as a temporary refuge when formal public and private institutions fail to generate enough employment. But, like the straitened African state, the second economy does not generate enough reliable and remunerative jobs to lift large numbers of people permanently out of poverty.

When people have exhausted their normal sources of livelihood, what sort of survival strategies do they employ? We asked a subset of respondents, "to whom do you usually turn when you are unable to get . . . food, water, schooling, and medical treatment . . . for your family?" The aggregate results from four countries are reported in Table 5.4.

TABLE 5.4. *Survival Strategies*

	Food	Water	Education	Health	All
No one	36	38	38	32	36
Kin	36	13	33	37	30
Market	21	25	12	15	18
Community	7	16	8	7	9
Government	1	7	10	10	7
Illicit	<1	1	<1	<1	<1

For question wording, see text.
Notes: Figures are percentages saying they turn to these sources of assistance when they encounter shortages of various basic necessities. The data are means for four countries: Ghana, Mali, Nigeria, and Tanzania.

Many Africans express a sense of economic vulnerability, with more than a third of interviewees saying that they have "no one" to turn to in times of need. This segment of the population is most likely to consume water from an unimproved source or to keep children out of school because they cannot afford to pay fees for education. Unable to withstand external shocks like drought or famine, these potentially destitute households are the first candidates for emergency food aid. According to the Afrobarometer, they outnumber those who can find comfort and support from members of their extended families.

Nevertheless, kinship provides the most readily available safety net. Three in ten respondents say that, when stressed, they turn for help to relatives in their nuclear or extended families. In the absence of reliable baseline data, it is difficult to say whether this figure represents a continuation, an increase, or a decline in the importance of kinship ties from an earlier time. However, we are inclined to think that kin-based mutual aid was probably more prevalent in the past.

People are most likely to rely on kin for food (36 percent), which includes eating meals at the homes of relatives or receiving gifts of produce and health care (37 percent), for example, by having family members provide home nursing services for someone who is sick.[12] Older siblings, aunts and uncles also routinely step forward to pay school fees for young relatives or to make loans for other domestic purposes.[13] These networks of mutual support are essential to the survival strategies of needy households, but they are relatively ineffective in addressing all contingencies of modern life. For example, only 13 percent of respondents say they turn to their relatives when they have difficulty in obtaining clean household water. To the extent that kinship networks are localized, then all the members who live in the same village or urban neighborhood are likely to face the same shortages and do not have the wherewithal to help one another.

Nor is the reliability of kinship ties uniform across the continent. To compare countries, we calculated a score of the extent to which people reported activating their family networks in times of need. Considering the four countries for which we have data, we found that Tanzanians tended to make much more recourse to kin (43 percent) than did Nigerians (25 percent). They did so consistently for resolving food, water, schooling, and health care needs, though the gap between national populations was widest for health care (58 versus 26 percent). To all appearances, the effects of urbanization, internal migration, and industrialization have been far more corrosive of traditional social solidarities in Nigeria than Tanzania.

What do needy Africans do if they cannot rely on kin? We are particularly interested in comparing how people behave in relation to the available institutions of the state and the market economy. The results in Table 5.4 show that survey respondents are twice as likely to enter markets as a way of meeting unfulfilled basic wants than they are to seek assistance from agencies of the state. Whereas 18 percent say they seek market solutions, just 7 percent say that they turn to the government. Notably and consistently, markets were favored over the state in *every* country studied.

The extent of the market edge, however, depends on the commodity in question. People are twenty times more likely to address unmet needs for food by purchasing produce from a vendor or in a marketplace than they are to petition a government agency. This probably reflects a combination of factors: the preferences of householders to rely on their own resourcefulness in securing a critical commodity like food, the dearth in normal times of official programs like food-for-work or emergency relief, and a lack of public confidence in the accessibility or fairness of any such programs that do exist. With regard to health and education services, however, a significant minority (10 percent) still turns to government ministries, often because there are no private enterprises that offer similar services. But, comparing education and health care, it is worth noting that people are more market oriented in their search for medical services, often being willing to pay considerable amounts for the professional services of private doctors or the homegrown remedies of traditional healers. Finally, we notice that commercialized behavior is most pronounced with regard to water supplies. When facing a household water crisis, 25 percent of people say they buy water from a private vendor compared to just 7 percent who turn to the government ministry responsible for water affairs. All told, these results point to a profound crisis of public confidence in the services of the local and central state that is manifest in the actions of ordinary people in opting to use nongovernmental alternatives.

Of four nationalities that we compared, Nigerians are most apt to turn to the market economy for solving shortages of basic needs. Remarkably, more than half reported that, if faced with a water shortage, they would purchase a supply from a private vendor (53 percent). This reflects the emergence in Nigeria (among other West African countries) of private services that use tanker trucks to make door-to-door deliveries of water, often at extortionate prices. Overall, an average of 38 percent of Nigerians opted for market solutions across four basic needs, which stands in marked contrast to the 7 percent of Malians who do so. Therefore, market-based behavior has spread differentially, not only by commodity, but also, importantly, by country. Alongside Nigeria, where well-developed markets have penetrated even the intimate corners of family life including basic supplies of food and water, markets for basic commodities in Mali remain relatively undeveloped, and therefore unused.

Of course, private markets are not the only nongovernmental alternative. People may also find relief by approaching community-based and nonprofit organizations that operate within civil society. The evidence suggests, however, that voluntary associations are thin on the ground in the twelve African countries surveyed; overall, community-based projects reportedly serve as providers of last resort for only 9 percent of respondents. As with the market-oriented behavior, people are most likely to make use of community-based organizations in their quest to obtain supplies of clean household water. A sizeable minority reports depending in emergencies on a communal source (16 percent), which might take the form of a natural spring protected by a chief, headman, or village committee to a reticulated water system installed by a foreign-funded NGO. To be sure, community-based initiatives make an extremely modest contribution, especially in relation to the enormous challenges of fulfilling basic human needs in African countries. But in seeking to address food and water emergencies, more Africans say that they now turn to NGOs than approach their own governments.

To summarize, the economic behavior of ordinary Africans bespeaks vulnerable populations, many of whose members teeter on the edge of poverty. Apart from the small minority who do not wish to work, almost all adults are engaged in a constant search for more and better jobs. In trying to find reliable flows of cash income, people have diversified their portfolios of economic activities by adding a supplementary array of informal projects, schemes, and enterprises. Even so, individuals regularly encounter shortages of basic household necessities that cannot always or easily be overcome. In the kinship-based African societies we have studied, people continue to obtain emergency relief principally from relatives, though reliable family support is available to only one out of three persons and may be in decline. The most striking finding is how few people – under one in ten – turn to governmental agencies and programs when seeking to satisfy unmet basic human needs. They are slightly more likely to present themselves to community-based institutions or NGOs, and twice as likely to try to purchase their own goods and services in a marketplace.

COMPLIANCE WITH THE LAW

When personal or family survival is at stake, Africans sometimes face fundamental moral dilemmas: at the extreme, for example, is it justifiable to steal food to feed hungry children? We wondered whether, as shortages of basic needs are incurred, people calculate that it becomes worthwhile to engage in illicit, or even illegal, behavior. If so, insight may be gained into why the rule of law proves so difficult to establish in poor countries. If not, we may discover the importance of inherited cultural codes in regulating antisocial behavior.

Some respondents mention main occupations that lie outside the law, like sex worker or brewer of *kachasu* (moonshine liquor). But only a handful of people (less than 1 percent) were willing to admit that they engaged in illegal activity to address food shortages. The most common of these rare responses were "I would steal it," "I would bribe a government official," or "I would pretend to be eligible for government assistance." A few more people (2 percent) conceded that they used such methods to get electricity or water. And the figures rose further for particular commodities in certain countries, for example, 4 percent for electricity in South Africa and 3 percent for water in Ghana. But these modest levels of reported malfeasance cannot be squared with the reality that many more households in South Africa's urban townships have hooked up unlawfully to the electricity grid or have boycotted the payment of electricity bills. Indeed, noncompliance rises if black, urban township dwellers are considered alone.

Of course, we surmise that people underreport behaviors that carry negative social or legal sanctions. As a way of counterbalancing this tendency, respondents in Southern Africa were asked to clarify whether they would "never" break particular laws or whether "I would do this if I had the chance."[14] Would they, for example, consume public services like electricity or water without paying for them if they thought they could get away with it? More than one out of ten (11 percent) Southern Africans now said they would. A similar proportion would evade income tax, property tax, or head tax ("development levy") if the opportunity ever presented itself. And almost twice as many (18 percent across the region) would "claim a government benefit to which you are not entitled, like a pension, maintenance, or unemployment payment." Willingness to circumvent the law was most marked in Lesotho, where more than half said they would fraudulently claim an unearned pension and, in Namibia, where almost a fifth would withhold payment for a household service. Similarly, disregard for the law by political elites in Zimbabwe has spread to the popular level where, by 1999, 15 percent said they stood ready to evade the payment of income taxes.

We pushed our inquiry into popular compliance with the law in a slightly different direction in West Africa, achieving even starker results. Absolving respondents entirely from the risk of implicating themselves, we probed whether respondents thought their fellow citizens were respectful of the law. Advised that, "some people obey the law and others do not," interviewees were asked: "in your opinion, how often do (others, naming their nationality) break the law by . . . not paying for services like piped water?" When the question was asked this way, perceptions suddenly reversed: a large majority (72 percent) was held to be delinquent in paying for household water services. The same applied to other activities like "evading income taxes" (80 percent) and "selling goods without a trader's licence" (84 percent).

How reliable are such heady estimates? Based on observable public behavior in Africa's crowded cities, we tend to think that our respondents are roughly accurate when they judge that eight out of ten of their fellow citizens "disregard traffic signs" and that nine out of ten "throw rubbish in public places." If they are right about these minor infractions, then we assume that they can guess the order of magnitude of more serious offenses such as illegal petty trading and income tax evasion. In an atmosphere in which the formal laws of a weak state are easily evaded, citizens have plentiful opportunities to duck legal obligations. A culture of impunity may even develop, in which "everyone" – leaders first – is assumed to be undermining the law. And, anyway, ripping off the government can easily be interpreted as a victimless crime. Under these circumstances noncompliance is easily justified as normal.

The West Africa data reveal patterns of the rule of law that seem proportionally correct. For every violation – from discarding garbage to unlicensed trading – Nigerians judge themselves as the least law-abiding nation in the region. Malians are much less likely to indict their fellow citizens as tax dodgers, and Ghanaians are much less likely to accuse each other of failing to pay water fees. Yet we were surprised to learn that Nigerians doubt that it is easy to evade the long arm of the law. Three out of four of them think that it is "likely" (40 percent "very likely") that "a person like you" would be caught if he "obtained household services (like water and electricity) without paying" or failed to "pay a tax on some of the income you earned." These responses indicate that Nigerians attribute to state authorities a stronger capacity for law enforcement than analysts usually assume. As such, people apparently restrain themselves from law breaking, perhaps with reference to inculcated social norms. While they think that others are breaking the law and getting away with it, they are unwilling to take such a risk themselves because they fear that, by doing something wrong, there is a good chance that they will be caught.

VARIETIES OF POLITICAL PARTICIPATION

Turning from economic behavior, we now describe the patterns of political participation adopted by Africans in recently democratized regimes. We again assume that people behave pragmatically, that is, they take political actions and choose channels of representation on the basis of what works best. In so doing, we cast light on an informal sector of the polity that mirrors in important respects the scope and functions of the informal sector of the economy. In characterizing political participation in African countries in all its conventional and vernacular varieties, we consider whether it amounts to an expression of citizenship or whether it is better understood as a form of clientelism.[15]

Conventionally defined, political participation consists of "legal activities by private citizens that are more or less directly aimed at influencing the selection of government personnel and the actions they take."[16] Given the recent proliferation of multiparty elections in Africa, there is urgent need to study voting behavior on the continent in the context of what is already known comparatively.[17] As a multidimensional concept, however, political participation encompasses far more than voting in elections. It includes, among other things, collective action around policy issues, contacting political representatives, and outbursts of street protest.[18] And because, like economic activity, key aspects of political behavior in Africa take place informally, we expand the definition of political participation to make room for individuals' engagement in community affairs and their contacts with patrons – like traditional leaders, religious figures, or business leaders – who do not necessarily hold offices in the formal hierarchy of the state.

Since elections are the most fundamental democratic institution, the best starting point is voting behavior. Chapter 3 noted that African worldviews of democracy include voting rights, but that Africans grant elections less centrality as building blocks of democratic governance than do Western donors. Because the Africans we interviewed conceive of democracy primarily as free speech and direct participation rather than in terms of electoral choice and representative government, one might anticipate that voters may not bother to turn out for multiparty presidential and parliamentary elections. In line with this expectation, voter turnout in posttransition elections generally has been lower in new democracies in Africa than in Eastern Europe and (especially) Latin America. Moreover, voter turnout has declined across sub-Saharan Africa between founding and subsequent elections.[19]

To explore electoral participation at the individual level, we asked Afrobarometer respondents: "Did you vote in the last (presidential/ parliamentary/ general) election?" To clarify the point of reference, the type of election and its date were provided. Table 5.5 presents these estimates of voter turnout for twelve countries in the last national election prior to the survey.

The data illustrate how difficult it is to make reliable statements about mass participation in Africa's multiparty elections. Rates of voter turnout vary markedly, not only from country to country, but also according to the method of measurement. When national electoral authorities calculate voter turnout in standard fashion – as the proportion of registered voters who cast a valid ballot – the figures range widely between a high of 92 percent in Malawi's general election of June 1999 and a low of 22 percent in Mali's presidential election of May 1997.[20] These extremes of officially reported voter turnout are among the highest and lowest in the world.[21] They point to a contrast between countries (like Malawi, South Africa, Tanzania, Ghana, and Botswana) where a mobilized population is apparently primed to take advantage of new opportunities for electoral action, and countries (like Mali, Zimbabwe, Nigeria, and Zambia), where the electorate is seriously disengaged from politics, prompting concern about citizen apathy and fear for the future of democracy.

Depending on the quality of electoral registers, however, official election statistics in some African countries rest on shaky foundations. When reported voter turnout is recalculated as a proportion of eligible voters (that is, the number of adults eighteen years and older projected from the last national census[22]), we discover numerous anomalies. In half of the countries studied, registers are apparently swollen with phantom voters, to the point that the

TABLE 5.5. *Voter Turnout, by Country, 1996–2000*

	Type and Date of Election	Officially Reported Voter Turnout[a] (as percentage of registered voters)	Officially Reported Voter Turnout[a] (as percentage of eligible voters)	Differences (percentage registered minus percentage eligible)	Self-Reported Voter Turnout[b] (as percentage of eligible voters)	Differences (self-reported minus official voters)
Malawi	General, 1999	91.9	97.3	−5.4	90	−7.3
South Africa	Parliamentary, 1999	87.3	66.2	21.1	82	15.8
Tanzania	General, 2000	81.0	55.8	25.2	87	31.2
Ghana	General, 1996	77.9	86.2	−8.3	89	2.8
Botswana	Parliamentary, 1999	77.1	47.0	30.1	54	7.0
Uganda	Presidential, 1996	72.3	79.3	−7.0	79	−0.3
Lesotho	Parliamentary, 1998	71.2	58.7	12.5	69	10.3
Namibia	Presidential, 1999	61.3	64.8	−3.5	65	0.2
Zambia	General, 1996	58.4	31.4	27.0	50	17.6
Nigeria	Presidential, 1999	49.7*	52.1*	−2.4	66	13.9*
Zimbabwe	Presidential, 1996	31.5	27.5	4.0	46	18.5
Mali	Presidential, 1997	21.6	28.3	−6.7	71	42.7
AFRO MEAN		65.1	57.9	7.2	71	13.1

Notes:

[a] Calculated on the basis of total valid votes cast (except Ghana, Lesotho, and Mali, where data was available only for total votes, that is, including invalid votes).

[b] *Question:* "Understanding that some of (your fellow citizens) choose not to vote, let me ask you: did you vote in the last (presidential/ parliamentary/ general) election of (month, year)?"

* estimates

Sources: Dieter Nohlen, Michael Krennerich, and Bernhard Thibaut (eds.), *Elections in Africa: A Data Handbook* (Oxford: Oxford University Press, 1999); "Elections Around the World" (www.electionsworld.org); "Election Watch" (www.cnn.com/world/electionwatch); and World Bank, "Age Structure of the Population," *African Development Indicators, 2001,* p. 308.

proportion voting is higher among those eligible than among those registered. Our calculations suggest that voter registers were inflated in Ghana and Uganda in 1996, Mali in 1997, Malawi and Namibia in 1999, and Nigeria in 2000. Indeed, to accept official figures, one would have to believe that almost every eligible adult actually voted in the 1999 general elections in Malawi! In the remaining six countries, the figures look more plausible, with a smaller proportion of eligible adults than registered voters having cast a ballot.

Survey estimates of voter turnout have their own shortcomings. As is common in other parts of the world for political acts considered obligatory, Africans overreport their involvement in voting, with some 71 percent alleging that they voted in the last election. Apart from censoring their responses out of fear of the ruling party (see Chapter 2), the Africans we interviewed clearly feel a need to associate themselves with the act of voting. They claim they are active in electoral politics whether or not they actually voted and regardless of the quality of elections in terms of being open, free, fair, or otherwise democratic. Like democracy itself, voting is infused with a positive aura that has escalated professed political behavior. But fear may also play a part. Self-reported voter turnout is especially exaggerated in Mali and Tanzania, where political cultures put an extraordinarily high premium on conformity with prevailing social norms or partisan loyalties.[23] If these two countries are excluded, then overreporting of voter turnout drops to an average of eight percentage points, which brings Afrobarometer countries more into line with margins observed from surveys elsewhere in the world. In Namibia, Uganda, and Ghana, we found a close correspondence between officially and popularly reported levels of voter participation, allowing us to put confidence in the figures for these countries.

A great deal of caution is warranted, nevertheless, when analyzing voting behavior in Africa (see Chapter 11). Afrobarometer survey respondents claim figures for turnout that, on average, are thirteen points higher than the 58 percent for eligible voters reported by African election authorities (see Table 5.5). We enter self-reported claims into our analyses on the assumption that they are rough proportional values, but in full recognition that, for future studies, we need better data.

In order to cast ballots, citizens must be registered voters. Yet people regularly encounter difficulty in complying with procedures for voter registration, which can be demanding. In Zambia, for example, would-be voters must visit an often distant registration center several times – to apply, verify the roll, and collect a voter's card – before finally returning to vote. And ruling elites do not hesitate to close the registration gate to their political opponents. In recent elections in Zimbabwe, for instance, the ZANU-PF government made available many fewer registration centers per capita in urban areas and on commercial farms than in the communal (peasant farming) areas.[24] To get a sense of the nature of such obstacles, we asked those in five countries who had not registered why they had failed to do so. First, people miss the registration period, usually because the government does not disseminate information in good time, or available information never reaches them (21 percent overall, 41 percent in Ghana).[25] Second, where voter rolls are out of date or where registration is conducted well before elections, younger prospective voters cannot get on the electoral lists because they are not old enough (17 percent overall, 29 percent in Nigeria). Third, since many people work away from home, they are absent from their electoral district at the time that registration is conducted (16 percent overall, 22 percent in Tanzania). Others report being ill (15 percent overall, 29 percent in Tanzania). Finally, some people simply state that they are "not interested in voting" (14 percent overall, 26 percent in Mali).

In East and West Africa, we heard more complaints about administrative incapacity or statements of voter indifference than about deliberate manipulations of voter registration by ruling elites. Across five countries, just one in ten persons mentioned that they were denied registration because they could not produce the right documents or because a government or party official placed some other administrative obstacle in their path. And fewer than one in twenty persons voluntarily withdrew from the electoral process because they doubted the sincerity, credibility, or fairness of the official registration drive. It is very likely, however, that some of those who reported being "not interested in voting" or "otherwise engaged" during registration did so because they felt that the electoral playing field was tilted against them. By the same token, lack of registration was a surmountable barrier to electoral involvement in some places. One in ten respondents, including both supporters and opponents of the incumbent government, reported being able to cast a ballot in the last election even though they were not currently registered as voters.

To cast further light on electoral abstention, we posed a choice to the nonvoting respondents in the seven Southern African countries: did you *decide* not to vote? Or were you *unable* to vote? In this region, nonvoting was less a product of voluntary choice (41 percent of nonvoters) than of unwelcome prohibition (59 percent). Residents of Namibia, Zambia, and Botswana were particularly likely to say that they were unable to vote (25 percent), in part because rural voters faced long hikes in order to reach the nearest polling station. In Zimbabwe, by contrast, where self-reported voter turnout is lowest among Afrobarometer countries, slightly more people said they chose not to vote (23 percent) than claimed to encounter an impediment (21 percent unable). In this case, abstention includes conscious acts of political resistance.

People also report engaging in other forms of electoral behavior. As Figure 5.2 shows, 44 percent across twelve countries say that they attended a campaign rally in connection with the last election. The mobilization of prospective voters at mass rallies is common in Tanzania and Uganda, where a dominant national party continues to exercise control over local politics.[26]

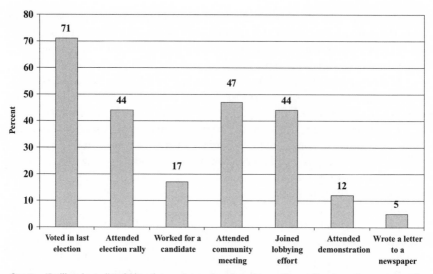

Question: "I will read out a list of things that people sometimes do as citizens. Please tell me how often you, personally, have done any of these things during the last five years?" Apart from voting, figures are percentages saying they have "sometimes" or "often" done these things.

FIGURE 5.2. Varieties of Political Participation

Election rallies attract even more participation in Malawi (71 percent), where three main political parties each dominate a region: the United Democratic Front (UDF) in the south, the Malawi Congress Party (MCP) in the central region, and the Alliance for Democracy (AFORD) in the north. This pattern seems to suggest that, even under multiparty rules, mass electoral mobilization in Africa continues to be a response to official stimuli from powerful political centers rather than an opportunity for open-minded voters to "shop around" among the platforms of various contending parties. In countries with meaningful party competition – as in Botswana, Ghana, and Zambia – we find levels of participation in election rallies close to the Afrobarometer norm. Finally, where political parties are extremely weak – such as in Mali (where the winning candidate in the 2002 presidential election ran without party affiliation), Lesotho (where the ruling party split and changed its name before the 1998 election), and Nigeria (where only three loose partisan groups were permitted in the 2000 contests) – fewer than one in five respondents reported attending an election rally.

Equally small proportions of people engage in canvassing for candidates running for political office. The 17 percent who claim to have done so may be distorted upward by the vague wording of the question, which asked loosely about "working" for a candidate.[27] Interestingly, Ugandans are more likely than other Africans to say that they have done this sort of electioneering (43 percent), presumably by spreading the word on behalf of individual candidates (or on behalf of the official "Movement") in a context where campaigning by political parties is explicitly banned. In South Africa, where party functions have been professionalized and where voters cast ballots for an electoral list, few volunteers donate time to working for candidates (just 7 percent).

Figure 5.2 also summarizes selected aspects of political behavior between elections. Activities other than voting may well be more important than voting itself in terms of building sustainable democratic institutions. Interelectoral interludes provide occasions to test in practice the forms of democracy that Africans have told us they want, namely models featuring free expression and popular direct rule. Indeed, most politics in Africa, especially nonelite political exchanges, take place via oral communication and in parochial settings. What levels of popular participation prevail in these contexts?

After voting, the most commonly reported activity is attending a "community meeting" or a meeting of "a group that does things for the community."[28] Afrobarometer respondents seem to have interpreted these questions to mean meetings of either voluntary associations or village or ward development committees at the lowest levels of local government. Almost half of all respondents say they have recently attended a meeting of this sort (47 percent). Attendance is reportedly highest in Uganda (81 percent) where, since 1993, the government has gradually devolved basic public functions and provided block grants to a pyramid of elected local councils starting at the village level.[29] According to Uganda's constitution, local councils should meet monthly, though few stick to this schedule and popular involvement declines as one ascends the tiers of the council system.[30] Turnout in community forums was reportedly lowest in Botswana (23 percent) and Lesotho (24 percent). Since these countries anchor either end of the distribution of popular support for democracy in the Afrobarometer (with Botswana at the top and Lesotho at the bottom), there is apparently no relationship between the extent of community participation and the degree of mass attachment to democracy. Botswana's low ranking on community participation is surprising since its government recognizes "the pivotal role that traditional institutions such as ... the *kgotla* (traditional assembly) could play in democratic political order."[31] We find, however, that, unlike Ugandans, Batswana take little advantage of the opportunities afforded by community-based institutions to debate local developments and to petition their government.

If Africans have yet to breathe life into the local organs created by the state, then perhaps they participate more readily in spontaneously organized self-help activities. We asked whether people had ever "joined with others to raise an issue ... affecting the community or nation?" Overall, slightly fewer people had joined a single-issue lobbying effort (44 percent) than had attended official community meetings. But, in half the countries surveyed – including Botswana – people were more likely to opt for spontaneous modes of collective action. In Zambia in the 1990s, almost twice as many people said they formed ad hoc pressure groups rather than attending planned meetings (39 versus 21 percent), due no doubt to the collapse of local-level party structures (and with them, village and ward development committees) in the wake of the transition to multiparty rule.[32] In Zimbabwe, 56 percent reported taking part in a self-organized lobby as opposed to the 21 percent who said they attended community meetings. By avoiding party indoctrination, Zimbabweans freed themselves to press for political liberalization, for example by rejecting government efforts to block constitutional reform in a referendum in February 2000.[33]

If conventional forms of participation fail to make popular voices heard, citizens in a democracy are within their rights to resort to boycotts, strikes, or demonstrations. Relatively few Africans interviewed had exercised the protest option (12 percent). Political demonstrations were extremely uncommon in Lesotho (3 percent) suggesting that only a small minority joined in the mob violence that torched Maseru in 1998. The twelve-nation average for unconventional participation was pulled up sharply by a couple of countries where political protest was common: South Africa and Zimbabwe (both 24 percent).[34] These figures capture the boycotts and demonstrations that made the urban townships ungovernable under apartheid in South Africa in the early 1990s, and which have since inhibited tax collection by elected local governments. And they document the mounting public resistance to the rising cost of living and dissipating rule of law in Zimbabwe in the late 1990s. When faced with political misrule or economic mismanagement, a critical minority of activists is apparently inclined, not only to associate independently in nongovernmental and oppositional groupings, but to undertake explicitly antigovernmental mass actions.

Indeed, there may be greater latent pressure for good governance than actual behavior reveals. In the Southern African countries, we asked respondents who had never attempted impromptu political conduct whether they would do so "if you had the chance." Interestingly, under the right conditions, quite a few can envisage becoming activists: 35 percent would join a lobbying effort and 25 percent said they would attend a demonstration. In Botswana, where almost half would join with others to raise a development issue, people apparently long for more such opportunities. And, in South Africa, where 30 percent would join a demonstration, a culture of protest has taken root at the heart of popular politics. In 2001 and 2002 mass demonstrations were mounted in the streets of Pretoria, Johannesburg, and Cape Town against international pharmaceutical companies and the national government over the price and availability of anti-AIDS drugs.

Beyond assembling in groups, citizens also take individual initiatives, for example, by contacting public officials (14 percent) or other influential leaders (27 percent). Such contacts serve to address either private-cum-familial problems or to air collective public grievances. But, the relationships are dyadic, that is one-on-one interactions between a petitioner and a power

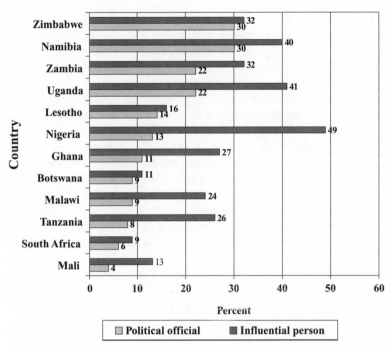

Question: "During the past five years, how often have you contacted any of the following persons for help to solve a problem?" Figures are percentages who say they have personally contacted a leader "sometimes" or "often."

FIGURE 5.3. Contacts with Leaders

broker. And, consistent with Africa's oral heritage, political communication is spoken rather than written, with no more than a handful of political actors ever having signed a petition or written a letter to a newspaper (5 percent each).[35] In Africa's neo-patrimonial political cultures, such face-to-face personal ties between patrons and clients constitute the very stuff of parochial politics.

As Figure 5.3 graphically shows, the Africans we interviewed are much more likely to take their problems to influential people in the community rather than to approach public officials associated with the state (27 versus 14 percent). In other words, we found an analogue in the political realm for patterns of behavior that we observed in the economy. When faced with a problem requiring a political solution, people rely on social networks (and, to a lesser extent, on market exchanges) rather than on official state institutions. And this tendency is remarkably consistent: in *every* country in the Afrobarometer, the frequency of informal political contacts exceeds formal ones.[36]

Figure 5.3 illustrates the dearth of formal connections between political officials and their constituents, which we call the representation gap. In many parts of the continent, the state remains a remote and distant entity, whose agents and structures barely interact with the multitudes. In Mali, for example, fewer than one out of twenty persons had "sometimes" or "often" contacted an official of a government ministry over the course of the previous five years. If the inhabitants of countries with agrarian economies and underinstitutionalized states choose to live their lives outside the ambit of officialdom, then they are largely able to do so. Remarkably, people can even evade the grasp of a well-endowed central state in urbanized and industrial environments, as evidenced by the case of South Africa. Hardly more South Africans than Malians report contacting a public official (6 versus 4 percent). The only places in Afrobarometer countries where people frequently turn for help to official channels are the dominant-party states of Zimbabwe and Namibia (30 percent each).[37] Through conscious strategies to build mass movements that suffuse the grassroots, leaders in these countries have seemingly convinced a core of loyal constituents to work through the official network of a party state.

Generally speaking, opportunities for contact with public functionaries decay with distance from the capital city. In Mali, only 2 percent report making official contacts in upcountry regions like Segou and Mopti, as compared to 11 percent in Bamako. Even if the state has established a grassroots presence, rural dwellers may elect to go it alone: in Mali's cotton belt, where agricultural services have been extended to smallholders, only 3 percent report turning for help to agents of the state. In South Africa, people choose to avoid state agents both in the townships of the Gauteng megalopolis and the rural homesteads of Kwa-Zulu Natal. Yet, when political contact occasionally occurs, it happens mainly through local structures: 70 percent of formal petitioners in South Africa approach the state via elected local councilors or local government administrators, compared to 22 percent who go directly to an official of a national institution and just 7 percent who reach out to a provincial government official. Tellingly, more South Africans say they meet officials of a national political party (15 percent) or a national government ministry (5 percent) than communicate with an elected parliamentary representative (just 3 percent). When calculated as a percentage of all South African respondents, only an infinitesimal proportion (0.2 percent) says that they have ever contacted an MP.

How typical is this representation gap? The phenomenon is present in all countries studied, with an average of only 6 percent of all respondents ever having interacted with a national legislator. People everywhere were least likely to report a face-to-face encounter with an MP (or national assembly deputy), and most likely to say they had approached a local government councilor. This is hardly surprising since local government representatives serve small geographical areas and, unlike MPs, almost always live in the locality. After South Africa, constituents say they contact their MPs least frequently in Namibia (1 percent), Botswana (2 percent), and Nigeria

(2 percent), records that seriously call into question the ability of "the people" to project their voices into the national legislative arena. Reported contact rates are somewhat higher in Ghana (12 percent), Tanzania (12 percent), and Uganda (16 percent) though even here, the vast majority of citizens are out of touch with their elected representatives.

We have yet to settle on a systematic explanation for the representation gap. For example, the physical size of countries is not a reliable guide. Predictably, several large countries (like Namibia and Nigeria) have poor rates of MP-constituency contact, presumably partly because of the difficulty that MPs face in traveling to their far-flung districts. By the same token, however, some constituents and MPs in certain large countries (like Tanzania and Zambia) have apparently found ways to begin to close this part of the representation gap.

Alternatively, one might suspect the institutional design of the electoral system.[38] Contacts with elected representatives are especially low under a list system of proportional representation (which is used in South Africa and Namibia). The incentives in this institutional arrangement lead MPs to respond to the party leaders who nominate them rather than to any constituents.[39] At the other extreme, the countries with the highest MP-constituent contacts have all adopted electoral systems based on the geographical delimitation of electoral districts and first-past-the-post electoral races. The evidence suggests that constituents are more easily able to seek accountability from MPs who are chosen to represent particular geographical districts. At the same time, however, we also find very low levels of MP-constituency contacts in certain countries that have adopted such plurality rules (like Botswana and Nigeria). So institutional effects are hardly consistent.

If elected and other state officials are hard to reach, what alternative strategies do citizens use for solving problems? Figure 5.3 exhibits the frequency of informal contacts with "influential persons." These intermediaries occupy nongovernmental positions but usually have established political connections, both inside and outside the state, that enable them to get things done. We take the level of these informal contacts as an indication of the extent to which individuals behave as clients by relying on the interventions of patrons more powerful than themselves. South Africans are least likely to try to solve problems by calling on someone with political clout to step in on their behalf (9 percent), but they are still more likely to do so than to make a formal overture to a public official. Similarly, Batswana tend to play by the official rules of the citizenship game; only one in ten (11 percent) feels the need to put their faith in patrons perhaps because they can rely on relatively equal treatment before the law. By contrast, and by a clear margin, Nigerians live in an unruly society where law enforcement is unreliable and access to public services is capricious. As such, they are very likely to try to get a "big man" to exert personal influence, with fully 49 percent of all respondents in this country saying they have tried this strategy. And four out of ten Ugandans and Namibians have also behaved as clients, probably because, in dominant party systems, one can best attain political advantage by attaching oneself to a faction leader with ties to the ruling monolith.

When approaching notables, people turn most readily to religious leaders. They apparently consider that priests and imams can offer sage advice, or even material assistance, to resolve problems that people cannot handle on their own. In addition, these leaders possess the social standing to intervene with political authorities in cases where lay petitioners cannot get a hearing. People frequently turn to Christian leaders for just such assistance in Uganda (52 percent), Tanzania (44 percent), Nigeria (43 percent), Ghana (35 percent), and Zambia (25 percent). And Malians and Zanzibaris routinely enlist the political assistance of the local leaders of Muslim brotherhoods (20 and 23 percent respectively), some of whom double as merchants and business entrepreneurs.[40] On average, people across the twelve-nation Afrobarometer are twice as likely to seek a religious patron as a traditional one.[41] Traditional leaders are still regularly sought out in Mali (22 percent), Ghana (19 percent), and Uganda (17 percent), usually to resolve civil disputes around marriage, inheritance, and land, and especially in regions like Ashanti and Buganda where kings and chiefs retain prestige and authority. But they are almost entirely bypassed in Zambia and South Africa, where traditional leaders have been sidelined and are now, at best, minor players in the politics of resource allocation.

What motivates nonelectoral political participation? We wondered how Africans themselves rationalize their engagement in collective action or their efforts to contact leaders. We therefore asked a question to this effect in three countries and classified the results into three main categories: self-interested, civic, and social motivations.[42] Most respondents said that they got involved politically for reasons of self-interest, that is, predominantly "to get help for a personal or family matter" but also "to get a job or advance my career" (together 44 percent). In some cases the objective was material gain, but in others it was less tangible, as when people asked leaders to help resolve domestic disputes. Professed civic motivations, however, were also common, for example "to help bring services or opportunities to our community" but also "to do my duty as a citizen" (36 percent). Finally, others sought out social interaction, saying that they wanted "to have a chance to work with others" or "to help unify our community" (18 percent). We note a clear difference between Ugandans, who put personal self-interest well ahead of other motivations, and Tanzanians, who claimed to put civic duty first. Thus, while the individualistic values associated with market reform have apparently diffused widely in Uganda, the collectivist ideology of *ujamaa* continues to resonate in Tanzania.

In Uganda, we also asked abstainers why they chose *not* to participate in political life between elections. More than half the open-ended responses

(51 percent) made mention of competing obligations – "I have too much work" or "I do not have enough time" – that are entirely consistent with popular struggles to piece together multiple streams of livelihood. Interestingly, numerous respondents said they lacked certain qualifications – "I don't have the resources" or "I am not educated enough" – perceived as necessary to participation (15 percent). In African politics, participants apparently feel that they require economic or social standing in order to join efforts of collective action or, especially, to approach an officeholder for a favor. Given pervasive inequalities, individuals who feel politically insecure are prone to turn to patrons to represent them. Others do not participate because "I have no problem to solve" (11 percent), because "I am prohibited by a relative" (5 percent), or because "I am not interested in politics" (also 5 percent).

DEFENDING DEMOCRACY?

What are the implications of mass political behavior for the survival and consolidation of democracy? Are ordinary people willing to stand up to protect the political regime should it ever come under attack? Ideally, one would prefer to observe actual instances of resistance. On one hand, we detect healthy signs of popular opposition in countries where incumbent leaders have sought to rig elections (for example, Zimbabwe and Nigeria) or rewrite constitutions (for example, Zambia and Malawi). On the other hand, we have recorded minimal levels of mass involvement in protest, suggesting that active champions of democracy may be few and far between.

Because political threats have not arisen uniformly everywhere, we posed to respondents a set of political scenarios that could plausibly come to pass in any hybrid political regime. The following official violations were mooted: "shutting down opposition newspapers that criticize the government"; "dismissing judges who rule against the government"; and "suspending parliament and canceling the next elections." We asked people "what would you do?" in the face of such provocations: support the government, oppose it, or do nothing? While the situations were hypothetical, and the behavior intended, we think that insight can be gleaned about what citizens might (or might not) actually do to defend democracy.

Some respondents had difficulty imagining scenarios of democratic breakdown, with one out of six saying they didn't know, couldn't answer, or otherwise refused.[43] Thereafter, a clear and consistent pattern emerged: some 6 percent said they would support the government, some 35 percent said they would do nothing, and some 51 percent said they would take countervailing action. These average figures were virtually constant regardless of the type of threat; for instance, almost identical proportions opposed the shutdown of a single opposition newspaper and a wholesale ban on electoral and legislative institutions. Thus, while about half of African electorates say they are predisposed to defend democracy,

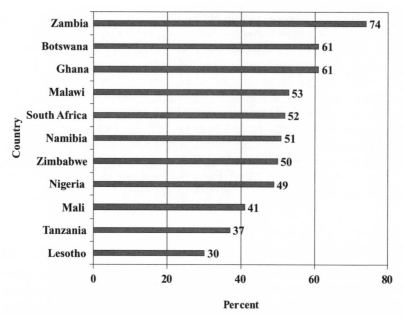

Notes: For question wordings, see text and Appendix A. Figures are average percentages of persons saying they are willing to "do something" to oppose shutdowns of opposition newspapers, dismissal of judges, and cancellation of elections.

FIGURE 5.4. Willingness to Defend Democracy

they do not calibrate their professed resistance according to the severity of attacks.

As illustrated in Figure 5.4, the strongest would-be defenders of democracy are found in Zambia, where fully 74 percent claimed that they would "do something" to oppose political abuses by a powerful president. Citizens of Botswana and Ghana are also determined to protect their emergent democratic systems, with an average 61 percent saying they would back independent newspapers, judges, and legislators against an overreaching executive. By comparison, Tanzanians and Basotho seem politically passive: for example, only 30 percent of Basotho would ever actively resist arbitrary rule and fully 14 percent of Tanzanians would actually support a shutdown of opposition newspapers. Reflecting widespread distrust of judicial benches that still contain appointees from the old apartheid regime, even more South Africans and Namibians (16 and 22 percent respectively) would support the dismissal of judges who do not toe the official line.

To defend democracy, what steps would its advocates actually take? Probing this question in Southern Africa, we found that most people would merely "speak to others" (36 percent of those who would "do something") presumably to alert them about an impending political crisis, but with unclear further intent. Zambians were most likely to stop short by only spreading the word to their neighbors, so their resistance would not necessarily have much impact. Otherwise, roughly equal proportions of Southern Africans would either "join a march or a demonstration," or "contact a government official" to protest a government crackdown (23 and 22 percent respectively). Again, South Africans were most likely to say they would take to the streets. Finally, about one in five (and even more Namibians) would contact the media in order to publicize their opposition via newspapers, radio, or television.

Consistent with the shallowness of mass democratic commitments, however, many Africans clearly have higher priorities than the defense of democracy. In East and West Africa, we also asked people what they would do if "the government told you what religion you must follow." Across the four countries where this question was asked, fully 80 percent would "do something" to protect freedom of religion, versus just half that number who would do the same if elections and parliament were threatened (40 percent).[44] Nigerians are most likely to actively oppose restrictions on religion, but, in both Nigeria and Mali, Christians (who perhaps see themselves as embattled faiths) are more likely than Muslims to say they would join a religious protest. The main point, however, is that the Africans we interviewed are twice as likely to rush to the defense of their religion than of key democratic institutions. In a hierarchy of popular values, and as a basis for mass mobilization, religion clearly trumps democracy.

FROM ATTITUDES TO BEHAVIOR

The defense of democracy and markets rests critically on whether the individuals who support these regimes convert their preferences into action. We end this chapter by reiterating the queries with which we began: Does regime support beget active participation? While we open this discussion here, we conclude it toward the end of the book (see Chapter 12).

First, are supporters of democracy primed to participate politically? In the aggregate, we find that more Africans make verbal commitments to democracy than actually take part in political life. A larger proportion of the eligible electorate expresses support for democracy (70 percent, see Chapter 3) than actually voted in their country's last election (58 percent, according to official returns, see Table 5.5). And even fewer people report engaging in participatory acts between elections. These findings tend to confirm our earlier thesis that democratic commitments, while wide, may be shallow. Of course, what matters is whether self-professed democrats are more likely to become politically active than authoritarians and politically uncommitted people. Simple bivariate tests confirm that supporters of democracy are slightly more likely to report voting in the last election and attending a community meeting.[45] Importantly, though, they are somewhat more likely to join with others to lobby on behalf of an issue of community or national importance.[46] But more compelling evidence is required before we can conclude that

Africans engage in political life as a matter of democratic conviction (see Chapter 12).

Second, do supporters of an open economy exhibit market-oriented behavior? In the aggregate, we find that fewer Southern Africans support market pricing for consumer goods (47 percent, calculated from Chapter 4) than make purchases in the marketplace as their primary source of food (71 percent, see previous discussion). In other words, more people depend on a cash nexus for key parts of their livelihood than believe in the magic of the market. For this reason, market-oriented behaviors are much more widespread in Africa than low levels of popular support for market reform would lead one to expect. We confirm this disconnection in East and West Africa where, across four countries, individuals who support market pricing for consumer goods are no more likely than anyone else to actually engage in trade as either a primary or secondary activity.[47] Similarly, there is no observable difference between supporters and opponents of market pricing in the likelihood that, when faced with a household water shortage, they will purchase water from a private vendor.[48] In other words, Africans turn to the market as a matter of need, not as an act of conviction.

Finally, are there any connections between economic and political behavior? We have made a case that, in Africa, informal modes of action are ubiquitous within the economy and polity alike. It seems possible, therefore, that cross-fertilization may have occurred across these arenas. Do participants in the second economy also tend to make use of political patrons? And, conversely, are the clients of political big men inclined to become informal economic entrepreneurs?

We confirm that relationships of this sort exist both across countries and among individuals. At the macro level, we find a strong, positive relationship between countries where people enter occupations in trade and commerce and countries where people rely on political ties to men of influence.[49] The contrast between Nigeria and South Africa is instructive here: Nigeria ranks first in the Afrobarometer for both trading occupations and contacts with patrons; and South Africa ranks last or next to last on both dimensions. A similar contrast can be made between Uganda, where informal modes of action prevail in both polity and economy, and Botswana, where people routinely rely on the officials and agencies of the state. At the micro level, too, we discover that people in trading occupations are more likely than almost all others to make use of informal patronage ties (37 percent versus 28 percent).[50] The main exception is that persons employed by government are even more likely to rely on patrons (43 percent).

We interpret these connections as follows. An informal economy and an informal polity can be found in all African countries, but these sectors are larger and more important in West and East Africa than in Southern Africa. In these settings, Africans survive – and occasionally even thrive – by developing a repertoire of practical survival and livelihood skills. These now include sidestepping the official agents and formal programs of the central state, which no longer operate as effectively or as generously as they once did. In place of officialdom, people rely on a combination of personal initiatives, schemes, and contacts that maximize their access to whatever public and private resources happen to be available. The political economy of informal behavior in Africa increasingly emphasizes a combination of private trading in liberalized markets with patronage ties to notables within and around a shrinking state. As such, state and market are conjoined, with benefits accruing to those who can operate simultaneously in both arenas.

PART III

COMPETING EXPLANATIONS

6

The Structure of Society

It is one thing to describe the features of public opinion, but quite another to explain the mechanisms of its formation. To test competing explanations, we shift from description to analysis. Parts III and IV of this book are designed, through a gradual process of accretion, to build comprehensive accounts of the sources of public opinion across Afrobarometer countries. To simplify the task, Part III focuses on just two paired objects of inquiry. On *political reform*, we seek to understand the sources of popular commitment to democracy and mass perceptions of democracy's extent. With reference to *economic reform*, we examine popular support for, and satisfaction with, the core policies that comprise structural adjustment programs. Later, in Part IV, we turn separately to behavior, endeavoring to understand why some people participate in the political arena and economic marketplace, whereas others do not.

The first question is whether the structure of society has any bearing on the ways that Africans approach the reform agenda. Just because people support democracy and oppose economic restructuring in many African countries does not mean that regime preferences are evenly distributed throughout the population. An individual's position in prevailing social hierarchies – of age, gender, occupation, or social class – are liable to strongly shape his or her opinions on the important issues of the day. For example, Afrobarometer results can arbitrate a dispute from other world regions about the role of young urbanites: are they the vanguards or the laggards of political and economic liberalization? As well as examining standard facets of demography, we also emphasize subnationalism (in its various ethnic, racial, and religious guises) and the lived experience of poverty (as captured by shortages of basic needs), social features that are important in Africa but which to date have received limited attention in new democracies.

A structural interpretation portends immutability in social values and mental orientations. It ordains that individuals adopt opinions according to their ascribed station in life and that mass attitudes and behaviors are thereby largely fixed and unchanging. We do not deny that accidents of birth have profound effects on the life chances and outlooks of individuals, granting advantage to some and blocking the ambitions of others. But birth is not always destiny. African societies are caught up in rapid and wrenching transformations, which mean that life chances are fluid and that individuals have prospects for mobility – both upward and downward. As such, social structure may frame public opinion, but it is unlikely to fully determine it. Instead, we anticipate that an individual's position in society will tell part of the story about popular support for reforms, but perhaps only a small part.

DEMOGRAPHIC DETERMINANTS

The topography of a society follows the profile of its population. By global standards, African countries have high birth rates, young populations, and flat age pyramids. Rural residents outnumber town dwellers though, with the highest rates of urbanization in the world and the emergence of megalopolises like Lagos (Nigeria) and Gauteng (South Africa), Africa is fast losing its agrarian character. Unlike parts of Asia, Africa does not contain pockets of females who are "missing" from the population; instead, women in Africa slightly outnumber men, mainly among older age groups and especially in the countryside. This section explores the implications of these demographic distributions for public opinion.

Gender

Do African men and women hold distinctive opinions on political and economic affairs? Given that many African societies are organized along lines of matriarchal descent, one wonders if women ever serve as opinion leaders. Or, conversely, given what we know about actual practices of patriarchy, women may be inclined to take their cues from men.[1] By alternating respondents within households, the Afrobarometer interviews equal numbers of men and women.[2] This distribution, which closely mirrors official census breakdowns, facilitates comparisons by gender.

While women's political opinions and behaviors look much like men's, we do find, at the margins, observable gender gaps. Take a simple, bivariate analysis of support for democracy. Across all twelve Afrobarometer countries, men are more likely than women to regard democracy as the best political system, by agreeing that "democracy is preferable to other forms of government" (74 percent versus 66 percent).[3] This gender divide is widest in countries with large Muslim populations – Ghana, Mali, Nigeria, and Tanzania – a fact that suggests that religion or other factors might also be at work alongside gender. The gap is also wide in Lesotho, where women's relative exclusion from formal education and disproportionate confinement to rural areas probably influence their political views. As we proceed, we will weigh gender alongside such other influential social factors.

Just because fewer women than men support democracy does not automatically mean that they prefer authoritarian alternatives. Instead, women tend to be indifferent about political regimes, being more likely to agree that, "to people like me, it doesn't matter what form of government we have." However, women are markedly less skeptical than men about the well-worn political arrangements of the African one-party state.[4] Wherever a women's wing of a ruling party has invested in campaigns of political mobilization – as in Tanzania, Uganda, and Zimbabwe – political leaders have been especially successful in persuading female followers to endorse the virtues of single-party rule. Indeed, male party activists explicitly target women, especially less educated rural women, because they perceive them as "easier to organize."[5]

The sexes also part company on support for economic reform. Men are somewhat more likely than women to embrace an orthodox package of stabilization and adjustment policies.[6] The gender gap is narrowest on user fees for social services, which attract support from both men and women, especially in South Africa where clear majorities are equally insistent that, "it is better to raise health care standards, even if we have to pay medical fees." Women's concern with family welfare, especially in a country where the cash economy is king, probably helps explain this tolerance of cost sharing. The gender gap is widest on policies of privatization, notably in Uganda where only half as many women as men strongly agree that, "it is better for the government to sell its businesses to private companies and individuals." Despite attaining considerable equality of opportunity in recent years,[7] Ugandan women seemingly still think that men have unfair advantages in competitive markets.

Accordingly, African women are also generally less satisfied than men with the performance of SAPs. This stands to reason if one accepts that the burden of marketization has fallen most heavily on women, for example, raising costs for household staples and by increasing the hours of unpaid work they must undertake to ensure family welfare.[8] But the relationship is unstable; in four of the nine countries measured – Mali, Nigeria, Tanzania, and Zimbabwe – slightly more women than men express support for SAPs. We therefore await multivariate analysis to see whether other social factors – such as rural residence or lack of education – dilute this apparent gender effect.

Age

Do younger Africans differ in their attitudes and behaviors from those who are middle aged or older? Given social change, one would expect recent generations to have had singular life experiences and thus to express distinctive profiles of opinion. The literature suggests that younger people are likely to form student political associations to spark prodemocracy protests, but also to enlist with partisan militias and radical rebel movements.[9] And there is anecdotal evidence that younger generations are motivated to oppose policy measures that dissolve their dreams of paid university places and guaranteed public jobs.[10]

Because the Afrobarometer concerns adult citizens, that is, persons eligible to vote, we interviewed only those who were eighteen years or older on the day of each survey. Since our samples reflect the age profile of national populations, the largest cohorts are under the age of thirty and the mean age of all adults is just thirty-six years. Among the Africans interviewed, age alone has little impact on attitudes to economic and political reform. If anything, the relationship is curvilinear: middle-aged people (aged thirty to forty-four) are more likely than both their elders and their juniors to say they support democracy.[11] And all age groups tend to agree on rejection of authoritarian rule and the extent of democracy that has been achieved in their countries. Moreover, we find no significant differences by age on either support for economic reform or satisfaction with the implementation of reform policies. We certainly cannot confirm that young people lead the way in demanding change.

There is some evidence that age influences political attitudes at the country level but, even so, it pulls in contradictory directions. In Ghana, middle-aged and older people are significantly more likely to consider that democracy is the best form of government, whereas youngsters tend to entertain the acceptability of authoritarian rule.[12] Yet it is young people in Mali who are the strongest supporters of democracy and most vocal opponents of its alternatives. Perhaps this contrast can be traced to the mode of political transition in each country, which in Ghana was a gradual process controlled from above by the military, and which in Mali was more convulsive, including a catalytic mass movement of university and high school students.[13] As for the perceived extent of democracy, we find that South African youth, whether through zeal or inexperience, are unusually quick to jump to the conclusion that their country has attained a "full democracy."[14]

Age also helps define economic attitudes in a few countries but, again, hardly consistently. In countries where adjustment programs were introduced some time ago, as in Ghana in 1983, young people are less likely to know about SAPs because they do not remember what, for them, are historical events.[15] By contrast, where adjustment is a more recent innovation, as in Zimbabwe from 1991 onward, youngsters recognize ESAP more readily than their elders, though educational attainments also surely help.[16] Other age-based distinctions emerge between countries in relation to popular support for economic reform. Young people back user fees for medical services in Zambia and middle-aged and older people lend support to the privatization of public corporations in Tanzania. Although the reasons for such divergent attitudes are not entirely clear, we speculate as follows: perhaps younger Zambians are expressing concern about the need for improvements in the availability of health care for their under-five children; and maybe mature Tanzanians possess a long-term perspective on the persistent decline in the performance of state-owned companies, which now leads them to favor policy change.[17]

In general, chronological age seems to matter less than political generation.[18] In other words, people may form policy preferences on the basis of a shared historical experience of the regime prevailing at the time they first become voters. We regrouped the age data according to the period during which individuals turned eighteen: under colonial rule, under an indigenous authoritarian system, or under a current multiparty regime.[19] Again in curvilinear fashion, the "postcolonial" generation is significantly more supportive of democracy (74 percent) than either the old "colonial" generation (62 percent) or the new "multiparty" generation (69 percent). It seems that, for Africans, suffering political repression at the hands of an indigenous autocrat is a formative learning experience, especially about which forms of government to avoid.[20] To be sure, youngsters of the "multiparty" generation are more committed to democracy than their grandparents of the "colonial" generation, who are sometimes prone to cling to past models of governance. But young people who, during their adult lives in the 1990s, have only experienced a new multiparty dispensation are more blasé than their parents about the dangers of autocracy.

Rural-Urban Location

It is an article of faith in African studies that urbanization amounts to a profound disruption of the rhythms and relationships of social life. Africa's cities have long been recognized as crucibles of new political and economic ideas and the source of novel forms of organization. Accordingly, like nationalist movements in the independence era, the antiausterity protests of the 1980s and the democracy movements of the 1990s were largely urban phenomena. And analysts have long argued that development policy in Africa was infected with "urban bias," which skewed benefits in favor of town dwellers and disadvantaged their country cousins.[21] One would therefore expect that a person's residence, whether rural or urban, would have structural effects on his or her politico-economic orientations.

The overall urban:rural ratio in the Afrobarometer sample is 42:58 percent, ranging from 70 percent urban in South Africa to 85 percent rural in Uganda.[22] Because rural populations are disproportionately female and elderly, observed differences in public opinion between urban and rural areas may also embody distinctions of gender and age. Age considerations are especially pertinent in Lesotho, Mali, Zambia, and Zimbabwe, where rural areas have been largely abandoned by young adults and serve mainly as a refuge for older people, including those whose urban working days are over. Only in South Africa, where apartheid-era policies of population removal and influx control still exert long-term effects, do our surveys record slightly more young people than older people in rural areas.

Against conventional wisdom, we find no significant difference in expressed support for democracy between the residents of urban and rural areas. This unexpected generalization holds true overall and within nine out of the twelve African nations studied. Only in Zambia and Zimbabwe do urbanites express greater support for democracy, and only in Uganda do rural residents do so. In the first two countries, however, some 73 percent of rural respondents regard democracy as preferable to other forms of government. Thus, even though democratic ideas may have originated in towns, they have since also gained wide currency in the countryside. Population movements and other trends – such as the regular circulation of people between urban and rural areas, occasional reverse migration by those who can no longer afford the costs of living in town, and the ubiquitous reach of communications technology, especially radio – are contributing to social homogenization.[23] Because urban and rural areas are no longer as socially distinct as they once were, residential location hardly influences the formation of political attitudes.

But attachments to democracy may be particularly shallow in rural areas. As evidence, we note that people who live in the countryside (including professed supporters of democracy) are somewhat less likely than their urban relatives to reject certain forms of authoritarian rule. One-man rule is roundly renounced everywhere, but urbanites are distinctly more dismissive of one-party rule than rural dwellers.[24] The tendency for rural people to remain attached to a single-party system is especially marked in Malawi, Namibia, and Zimbabwe – all countries where hegemonic political parties have constructed a political base among a peasantry. More curiously, one-party rule is even considered a plausible alternative by some rural dwellers in countries – like Nigeria and South Africa – that have little institutional experience with this form of government. Perhaps they regard the single-party's ideology of unity and consensus as compatible with traditional or liberation movement values. Or perhaps rural South Africans and Nigerians are unaware of the loss of liberties that have accompanied the implementation of one-party rule elsewhere on the continent. Whatever the reason, the fact remains that, in nine out of twelve African countries, rural folk are significantly more sympathetic to a single-party monopoly. This suggests that, if one-party rule ever makes a comeback, it will probably be on a rural foundation.

On economic reform, we turn up unexpected results. The standard argument is that structural adjustment favors the countryside, by enabling farmers to capture world market prices for their produce and by eliminating subsidies on urban consumer goods. We find no such general outcome in Afrobarometer opinion. If anything, urban dwellers display a slight tendency to favor an orthodox policy package, though the relationship is hardly strong.[25] Perhaps because this group has better access to cash income, they are more likely to buy into a policy that charges market prices for consumer goods and user fees for improved social services. Yet, despite sometimes deriving income from public sector jobs, urbanites are also markedly more likely to advocate privatization.[26] This distinctive set of urban policy preferences is most evident in Namibia, which has a particularly dualistic economy that combines urban industrial and service enclaves with a vast rural hinterland.[27]

Why might the residents of Africa's rural areas fail to become convinced about the virtues of economic reform? We identify several tenable interpretations. First, agricultural price reforms are directed at firms and households that produce crop and livestock surpluses for sale. Yet many rural households in most African countries continue to operate on a subsistence basis, or to enter into monetary exchanges only in local markets. To the extent that these households do not participate in national or international exchange, they are poorly positioned to take advantage of reforms. Second, the removal of price supports may undermine the budgets of rural as well as urban households, especially as subsidy cuts lead to price increases for seed, fuel, and fertilizer. Under these circumstances, market-oriented farmers may find that escalating costs of production exceed any additional returns that can be gained from higher producer prices.[28] And, contrary to convention, many rural households now also purchase food. Finally, agricultural producers face an especially uncertain environment of economic institutions. There is no guarantee that, if national marketing boards are shorn of their monopoly powers, that private traders will step in to fill the void. Farmers who live at points distant from central communications networks are especially vulnerable; they often discover that privatization has left them entirely without suppliers of inputs or buyers for their crops.[29] Under these circumstances, it is hardly surprising that rural dwellers are less supportive of economic reform than urban dwellers, a group that is conventionally thought to have borne the brunt of the costs of reform.

VARIETIES OF SUBNATIONALISM

Having inherited arbitrary colonial boundaries, African governments preside over unusually diverse societies. Only a handful of African countries are socially homogenous; most are culturally plural; and several are very deeply divided. Few observers would dispute Africa's cultural diversity, even as they debate the essential nature of social cleavages (are these ethnic, religious, or based on social class?) and the character of communal groups (are these primordial attachments or artificial social constructs?).[30] Whatever position one adopts in these debates, we take it as given that "communal identities are not a residue of the past, but are a live force in today's politics."[31] We also subscribe to the view that "all people have multiple identities ... which identity is salient depends on the situation."[32] In this section, however, we defer discussion of subjective identities (to Chapter 7) in favor of objective indicators that individuals use to locate themselves – and, especially, groups of "others" – within the structure of society.

We ask whether membership in subnational communities – of ethnicity, race, and religion – is related to popular support for reforms. One expects individuals to opt for policies that will promote the interests of their own group. Wherever resources are scarce, support for reforms should be strongest among groups who feel capable of competing successfully with others. But the relationship between social pluralism and reform does not run in only one direction; liberalization itself is likely to lead to increased levels of competition and conflict in society. As political reforms relax the control of the state over society, so subnational splinter groups will find new latitude to express particularistic demands. As market reforms introduce requirements of efficiency, so competition will intensify between local communities over nonrenewable assets or limited supplies of goods and services. Thus, various communal groups support or oppose reform depending on whether they gain or lose in an increasingly competitive environment.

Ethnicity

As a more or less objective indicator of ethnicity, we asked Afrobarometer respondents to name their home language, meaning their mother tongue, first language, or language of origin.[33] According to the distribution of responses, we then classified each language group as "major," "secondary," or "minor."[34] This classification reveals very diverse profiles of ethnic pluralism across African countries (see Table 6.1). At one extreme, Lesotho and Botswana are socially homogenous, with 99 and 97 percent of respondents respectively naming Sesotho or Setswana as their mother tongue. At the opposite pole, Nigeria and South Africa are deeply divided along ethnic lines, with 42 and 68 percent of the population respectively saying they belong to secondary groups.

Does the status of one's ethnic group shape one's political and economic attitudes? It is not immediately clear, for example, whether ethnic minorities are likely to be more or less supportive of democracy. Perhaps minorities fear that a political system based on the principle of majority rule would consign them to the margins of the political arena and permanently exclude them from decision making. Alternatively, minorities may embrace democracy because they consider that its constitutional guarantees of civil liberties will provide the protections they seek from domination by others.

Overall, across twelve African countries, the evidence tilts toward the second conjecture. In other words, ethnic minorities generally express higher

TABLE 6.1. *Ethnic Pluralism, by Country*

	Bot	Gha	Les	Mwi	Mali	Nam	Nig	Saf	Tan	Uga	Zam	Zim	Afro Mean
Major Ethnic Group	97	60	99	70	48	50	32	25	44	26	32	78	55
Secondary Ethnic Group	0	17	0	15	38	33	42	68	10	35	39	15	26
Minor Ethnic Group	3	23	1	16	14	17	26	7	46	39	29	6	19

Question: "What is your home language?"
Note: Figures are percentages of respondents. Totals may not add up to one hundred due to rounding.

levels of support for democracy than do the members of each country's largest ethnic group.[35] The tendency for minorities to advocate democracy is most clearly evident in Mali and Zimbabwe.[36] In Mali, over three quarters (77 percent) of the formerly rebellious Touareg express support for this form of government, compared with just over half (53 percent) of the much larger heartland population of Bambara speakers. To all appearances, the Touareg have developed a stake in the political regime from the National Pact of 1992, which granted special representation to northern regions, and the Flame of Peace agreement of 1996, which decommissioned weapons and integrated armies.[37] In Zimbabwe, attachments to democracy are noticeably stronger among the marginalized minority of Sindebele speakers (84 percent) than among the majority who speak dialects of Chishona (69 percent). In this case, however, a truce between ethnic rivals has yet to be hammered out. Thus, as well as supporting democracy, Sindebele-speaking voters affiliate themselves with the Movement for Democratic Change (MDC), the country's main opposition political party.[38]

Ethnic minorities are also vigorous in their rejection of various forms of authoritarian rule, especially rule by a strongman.[39] They are prone to personalize the political regime, being most resistant to authoritarianism when the ethnicity of the head of state is different from their own. Take the examples of Nigeria and Namibia.[40] In Nigeria, members of secondary ethnic groups are distinctly more resistant to strongman rule than the more populous Hausa speakers.[41] Probably convinced that a narrow "Hausa mafia" has long dominated Nigerian national politics, almost all Yorubas (87 percent) and Ibos (92 percent) declare themselves opposed to a presidential monopoly of decision making. And, in Namibia, most members of ethnic minority groups (whether they speak Oshiherero, Nama, Afrikaans, English, or German) reject the concentration of political powers in the hands of a strong president (68 percent). By contrast, fewer than half of all Ovambos reject this personal form of government (44 percent), which they associate with their own favorite son, incumbent president Sam Nujoma. Indeed, it is the political loyalty of the Ovambo ethnic majority that provides Nujoma with much of the leeway he has needed for manipulating the constitution.

Ethnicity has mixed effects, however, on popular judgments about the supply of democracy. In some countries, ethnic majorities are most likely to perceive that democracy is taking root; in other countries, ethnic minorities are more likely to express this optimistic opinion. In Malawi, for example, the members of the major Chewa-speaking ethnic constellation are much more likely than minority Tumbuka speakers to think that the task of building democracy is "complete" (37 percent versus 4 percent). This result no doubt reflects the perception by northern ethnic groups that, even under a multiparty dispensation, they remain excluded from power at the political center. In Ghana, by contrast, the Akan-speaking majority, which includes the Ashanti ethnic group, was twice as likely as the Ewe-speaking minority to think that Ghana was "not a democracy" in 1999. This difference derives in good part from the resentment then felt by Ashantis at their exclusion from national affairs by a president (Rawlings) who hailed from Eweland. What matters for popular perceptions of democratic consolidation, therefore, is less the relative size or status of any given ethnic group, but whether its members feel they possess a share of state power.

Economic attitudes are also influenced by ethnic considerations. In general, minority ethnic groups tend to be supportive of policy measures to liberalize African economies. This is especially true for reforms that allow consumer goods to trade at market prices and that streamline the operations of the civil service.[42] Take just two prominent examples. In Mali, certain secondary and minor ethnic groups are much more likely than core Bambara-phones to favor the decontrol of market prices (60 percent versus 43 percent). It is no accident that these minorities include speakers of Sonrhai, Soninké, Maure, Arabic, and Tamasheq, who, unlike Bambara farmers, are among Mali's key trading groups.[43] In Zimbabwe, the unusually high level of public support for civil service retrenchment derives in significant part from the attitudes of minorities: whereas less than half of Shona respondents favor job cutbacks, almost six out of ten Ndebele respondents do so. We suspect that the latter are reacting in part to perceived job discriminations against speakers of non-Shona languages, whose opportunities for public employment in a politicized civil service are limited by their allegiances with opposition parties.[44]

Race

But do these considerations also apply to the special case of racial minorities? What stances are taken by white, Asian, and mixed race populations in

Southern Africa on issues of regime reform?[45] It would be reasonable to expect that wealth and other advantages enjoyed by these groups in former settler colonies would lead them to endorse a market system based on economic competition. But it is much less obvious that racial minorities would also welcome democracy, since the principle of "one person, one vote" threatens to limit seriously the ability of small segments to exert political influence.

Both propositions are confirmed. Whites and Indians (and, to a lesser extent, those Southern Africans who refer to themselves as "Coloureds") support economic reform.[46] Strikingly, whites are more than twice as likely as blacks to support at least three policies on a four-point *index of support for economic reform* (59 versus 23 percent). The races are especially polarized when it comes to institutional adjustments like restructuring the civil service and the sale of public corporations.[47] For such policies, the distinction is most marked in South Africa,[48] where three quarters of whites advocate privatization, but just one third of blacks do so. Indeed, at the time of writing, the Congress of South African Trade Unions had called a general strike to protest job losses, which black protesters attributed to the government's privatization policies ("privatization is apartheid!").

We interpret these outcomes in light of the dissolution of settler colonialism and the attainment of majority self-government in the region, most recently in South Africa but also previously in Zimbabwe and Namibia. Once black majorities gain control of the state, they promote the Africanization of the civil service and widen the distribution of public housing, education, and health care to previously excluded populations. Naturally, these gains have led blacks to defend state-centered policies and to turn to the state as a provider of jobs. Whites, by contrast, are no longer able to rely on race-based policies for special access to public employment or state services. To the extent that the civil service and public corporations cease to grant privilege to racial minorities, whites (especially Afrikaners) have become latter-day converts to the gospel of free markets, which they expect will reward their inherited advantages of education and purchasing power.

Compared to their warm embrace of markets, racial minorities are tepid toward democracy.[49] In this instance, and although most people of both races prefer democratic rule, blacks in Southern Africa are significantly more positive than whites (64 percent versus 56 percent).[50] Of greatest interest, however, are the political attitudes of those who are historically located between the two largest groups. In terms of supporting democracy, Coloureds predictably adopt opinions squarely between blacks and whites. Surprisingly, however, persons of Indian extraction are, by a large margin, very unsupportive of democracy (33 percent).[51] This pattern of alienation from the prevailing political regime reappears with respect to the perceived extent of democracy, with three times as many Indians as other racial groups considering that their country is "not a democracy."[52] To all appearances, and notwithstanding the prominence of Indians in the leadership of South

Africa's ruling ANC, ordinary members of this racial minority feel that the recent political transitions have failed to address their exclusion from political life in both South Africa and the wider Southern Africa region.

Religion

Whereas subnationalism takes on racial overtones in Southern Africa, religion is an increasingly important basis of group solidarity and conflict in East and West Africa.[53] Especially in countries where Christians and Muslims live side by side, we wonder whether religious attachments shape people's dispositions to reform. Does Islam, for example, act as a brake on the formation of democratic sentiments? Does Protestantism, especially in new evangelical versions, imbue Africans with a spirit of capitalism?

Some influential observers allege that Islam and democracy are incompatible. For example, Huntington argues that, because the Koran rejects the distinction between religious and political authority, Islamic civilization cannot easily coexist with democracy.[54] And Kedourie holds that mass suffrage, elections, and representation are "profoundly alien to the Muslim political tradition."[55] Others disagree. Esposito and Voll stress the diverse spectrum of conservative and progressive tendencies within Islam, including new movements that seek to reconcile religious resurgence and democratization.[56] Filali-Ansary goes even further, claiming that values of freedom and accountability, normally identified as Western concepts, can be found in early Islam.[57]

We find that, across four African countries studied, Muslims are about as supportive of democracy as non-Muslims. Regardless of religious orientation, an average of more than seven out of ten people say they support democracy: some 71 percent of Muslims and 76 percent of non-Muslims agree that, "democracy is preferable to any other form of government."[58] The slight gap derives from Nigeria, where commitments to democracy among African Muslims are weakest. At the country level, Muslims in Uganda and Mali actually express *more* support for democracy than non-Muslims. And the two religious communities are *equally* supportive of democracy in Tanzania. Moreover, responses to the alternate question about support for "our present system of government with free elections and many parties" show Muslims generally – now including Nigerians – to be just as positive as non-Muslims. On balance, therefore, Muslims and non-Muslims are hard to distinguish with regard to their support for a competitive multiparty electoral system, otherwise commonly known as democracy.[59]

So far, we have treated Muslims as a homogenous group, as if all believers were equally observant of the Prophet's faith. Yet, as with other broad creeds, Islam accommodates a broad cross-section of adherents, from the very casual to the extremely fanatic. The intensity of religious commitment – otherwise known as religiosity – might actually be more important than nominal religion to the formation of political attitudes and the activation of political participation.

The Afrobarometer measured religiosity for the first time in Nigeria in 2001 by asking, "apart from weddings and funerals, how often do you attend religious services?" Among nominal Muslims, we detect a clear, strong, and positive relationship between religiosity and support for democracy. In other words, the more often that Muslims attend organized Friday prayer meetings, the more likely they are to support democracy. This important result calls into question any effort to stereotype all mosques as hotbeds of antidemocratic rhetoric or to portray fervent Islamists as automatically opposed to democracy. Instead, at least among Nigerian Muslims, religious practice is likely to deepen rather than undermine commitments to a democratic form of government. We also find hints that religiosity may increase political tolerance. For example, attending weekly prayer services makes Nigerian Muslims significantly more likely to concur that, "since we will never agree on everything, we must learn to accept differences of opinion within our community." Similarly, religiosity *reduces* dogmatic commitments to *sharia* law. Some 63 percent of nonpracticing Nigerian Muslims think that northern states should be governed by their own religious legal system, a view that is shared by only 52 percent of weekly mosque goers. Almost as many of this group of highly observant Muslims (45 percent) think that "Nigeria is a secular state: it should have one, nonreligious legal system that applies to all people."

Does membership in a Christian faith affect public opinion?[60] Perhaps because church leaders often figured prominently in prodemocratic protest movements or national constitutional conferences,[61] it is not surprising that mainstream Catholics and Protestants are virtually unanimous in rejecting strongman and military rule at levels higher than the adherents of other faiths.[62] More unexpectedly, evangelical Protestants, who are often stereotyped as politically conservative, are especially vociferous in rejecting one-party rule, perhaps because born-again beliefs emphasize individual salvation and the evils of misused secular power.[63]

Along these lines, we expect that adherents of evangelical or pentecostal movements will also respond positively to the opportunities presented by market reforms, since they are told from the pulpit that individual salvation is manifest in conspicuous success in the material world.[64] Conversely, since Jesuit intellectuals have drawn attention to the negative social impacts of structural adjustment, we expect that Catholics show less favor for economic reforms.[65] In fact, neither of these hypotheses can be confirmed. In terms of the number of reform policies supported, we find no difference between evangelical Protestants and the followers of other religions. And, if anything, Catholics actually tend to support *more* reform policies.[66] Christian fundamentalists stand out from other religionists, including Catholics, only in their above-average acceptance of user fees for educational and health services.[67] Evangelicals in Tanzania are especially willing to invest personal cash resources in the health and education of their families (87 percent) and in this respect they stand in stark contrast to Muslims in Nigeria (59 percent). Otherwise, we discern no distinctive appetite for capitalism among Africa's born-again Christians.

THE BURDEN OF POVERTY

What about the poor? A large literature asserts that structural adjustment in Africa has worsened the plight of people in poverty.[68] If this observation is correct, one would expect poor people to reject policy changes that increase the competitiveness of the economic environment. Moreover, because poverty forces individuals to preoccupy themselves with daily survival, poor people may be relatively unconcerned with debates about democratization. In the memorable words of Nelson Mandela, "democracy is an empty shell if people do not put food in their stomachs."[69] With the caveat that a majority of poor people nonetheless prefers democracy, this section finds some support for these claims.

As indicated in Chapter 5, the Afrobarometer's *index of lived poverty* measures poverty in terms of consumption, or lack thereof. We ask how often households experience shortages of basic human needs during the previous year, from which data we construct an index based on the frequency of shortages of food, water, and medical treatment.[70] Four social strata can be discerned along this index: the "nonpoor" (who never suffer shortages of basic goods and services: 22 percent), the "poor" (who suffer occasional shortages: 55 percent), the "very poor" (who suffer regular shortages: 18 percent), and the "destitute" (who report frequent or permanent shortages: 5 percent). By this standard, Lesotho has the most people in the poorest strata and the citizens of Botswana suffer the least destitution (see Table 6.2).

TABLE 6.2. *Poverty, by Country*

	Bot	Gha	Les	Mwi	Mali	Nam	Nig	Saf	Tan	Zam	Zim	Afro Mean
Nonpoor	35	37	11	12	30	12	27	29	27	7	15	22
Poor	57	48	49	65	50	66	57	59	47	58	54	55
Very poor	7	10	30	20	16	20	13	11	21	28	24	18
Destitute	1	5	10	4	4	3	3	2	6	7	8	5

Question: "Over the past year, how often have you or your family gone without ... water, food, medical treatment, electricity, or a cash income?"

Note: Percentages are based on an *index of lived poverty* based on reported shortages of food, water, and medical treatment. See Appendix A. Totals may not add up to one hundred due to rounding.

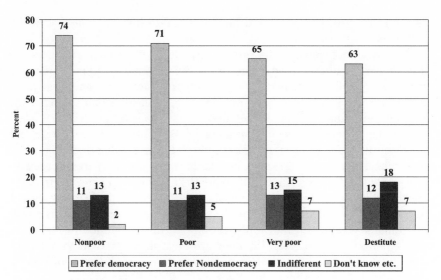

FIGURE 6.1. Support for Democracy, by Poverty

In a simple two-way analysis, we find that, as poverty increases, support for democracy declines.[71] The data describe a gradual but steady secular trend: dropping from 74 percent of the nonpoor who support democracy to 63 percent of the destitute (see Figure 6.1). Lower levels of democratic commitment among the victims of poverty are accompanied by higher levels of indifference to all political regimes, rising to 18 percent for the destitute. Poor people may be undecided about their political regime preferences because they do not fully understand what is at stake; we find, for example, that the destitute are twice as likely as the nonpoor to say that they "don't know" what democracy means.[72] Thus, it will be necessary to use multivariate techniques to check whether lower levels of support for democracy among the poor are due to the adversities of poverty itself or to some other educational or informational disadvantage (see Chapters 8 and 11).

It is noteworthy that poverty's negative effect on support for democracy is consistent across all but one of the twelve Afrobarometer countries. The relationship is strongest in Malawi, where *less than half* of those who frequently lack food express support for democracy and over one third think that, "nondemocratic government can be preferable."[73] Of all the elements in our poverty index, shortage of food is most corrosive of democratic commitments, which suggests that the deepening of drought and famine in Southern Africa after 2000 will weaken fledgling democracies in that region. Only in Nigeria in 2000 was there an odd, positive, but statistically insignificant relationship between poverty and support for democracy. By 2001, however, as the poor in Nigeria saw that a transition to multiparty civilian rule alone was unlikely to alleviate their material deprivations, the relationship turned negative and Nigeria fell into line with the rest of the continent.

At first glance, poverty appears to have little effect on preferences for nondemocratic alternatives (Figure 6.1). But distinctions appear once we separately examine particular types of former regimes. For example, all poor people are equally likely to reject military rule, confirming that soldiers with political ambitions can no longer find a mass following anywhere, even among the most economically marginalized. By contrast, the very poor and the destitute remain especially susceptible to the siren song of civilian one-man rule. The two poorest strata are significantly less likely to reject excessive presidentialism (67 percent) than are the nonpoor (79 percent). In other words, while two out of three of society's most impoverished citizens would oppose the abolition of democratic elections and a representative legislature, a strongman could still find followers among the remainder. In Namibia, where, among all countries, the poor are most likely to yield to one-man rule,[74] extreme poverty and destitution are concentrated disproportionally among the Ovambo ethnic majority.[75]

As might be expected, poverty makes an even deeper impression on economic attitudes. After all, market economies operate on principles of natural selection in which only the fittest survive. Poor people quickly recognize that they stand at a disadvantage because of their lack of assets, meager incomes, and shortages of basic necessities and services. Accordingly, we expect the poor, even more than other Africans interviewed, to withhold support from economic reform policies.

As Figure 6.2 shows, the likelihood that an individual will fail to endorse all reform policies (whether market pricing, user fees, civil service cutbacks,

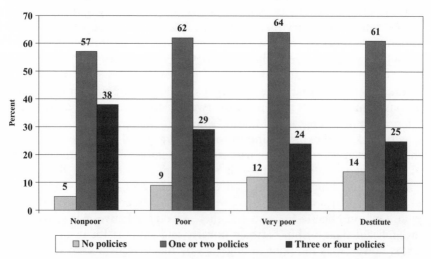

FIGURE 6.2. Number of Economic Reform Policies Supported, by Poverty

or privatization) rises steadily with poverty.[76] And conversely, the likelihood of supporting a package of three or four reform policies declines with poverty, with the proviso that the very poor and destitute groups show equally low levels of enthusiasm. The negative connection between poverty and market commitments holds true without exception within *every* Afrobarometer country. The connection is especially strong in the former settler colonies of South Africa, Namibia, and Zimbabwe, probably reflecting the coincidence there of race and poverty. In South Africa, for example, the region's most unequal society, the wealthy (that is, nonpoor) are five times as likely as the destitute to support a full package of reforms.[77] But poverty also drags down support for economic reform in Botswana, Zambia, and Ghana, suggesting that, even in the absence of large racial minorities, poverty has its own powerful effects on economic opinion.[78]

Poor people resist all elements in the economic reform package. They disapprove of the liberalization of prices on consumer goods, especially in Zimbabwe where rampant inflation (caused, ironically, by administrative price controls) has plunged the mass of the population, including wage earners, into poverty. Also reflecting shortages of cash income, the poor show even greater disapproval for fees on educational and medical services, especially in Botswana where users have grown accustomed to high levels of government subsidy. Only the nonpoor, notably in Namibia and South Africa, stand firmly behind policies of civil service retrenchment, perhaps because they hold secure jobs or expect employment opportunities in the private sector. And, when it comes to privatization, the same pattern of opinion holds across the various consumption groups in these two countries. We also now discover that the unusually high level of support for privatization previously reported for Tanzania does not extend to its poor people: instead, whereas just over half of better-off (that is, nonpoor) Tanzanians want the government to sell its farms and factories, merely one third of their destitute compatriots feel the same way.[79]

This section ends with an examination of the effects of poverty on popular satisfaction with prevailing regimes. Consistent with results reported previously, we find that poverty is an influential factor, but again more so in relation to economic rather than political attitudes. To be sure, poverty depresses satisfaction with democracy; but it has an even bigger negative effect on satisfaction with SAPs.[80] As Figure 6.3 shows, Africans are much less satisfied with adjustment than democracy, but both kinds of satisfaction generally decline with poverty.[81] Since satisfaction is measured on the same scale in each case, it is possible to compare standardized scores, for instance as variations around a mean (of 60 percent satisfied with democracy and 21 percent satisfied with adjustment).[82] As Figure 6.4 shows, variations are far greater for satisfaction with adjustment. And both figures illustrate that the very poor derive least satisfaction from market-oriented policies.

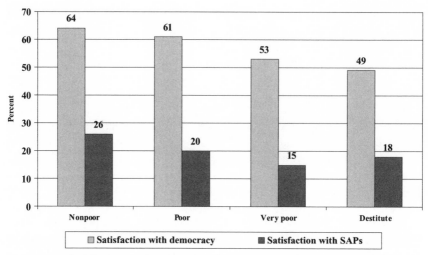

FIGURE 6.3. Satisfaction with Political and Economic Regimes, by Poverty

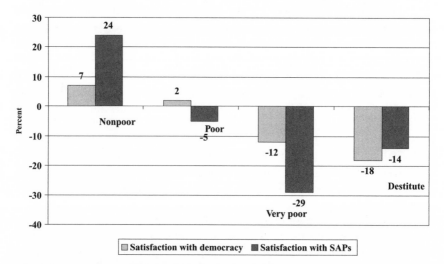

Note: Scores are percentage deviations from mean levels of satisfaction.

FIGURE 6.4. Variations in Regime Satisfaction, by Poverty (Standardized Scores)

Finally, we also uncover hints that destitution has particularly pernicious effects for satisfaction with democracy. Not only are less than half of the destitute satisfied with democracy (the only consumption group to sink below this critical threshold, see Figure 6.3), but extreme poverty apparently has more impact on satisfaction with democracy than on satisfaction with economic reform (see Figure 6.4).[83] Together, these findings suggest that the destitute are especially prone to blame democracy for their economic dissatisfaction.

Before closing, we wish to comment on the possible contribution of the impact of poverty to a class analysis of social structure. It has always been difficult, without substantial adaptation, to retrofit classical Marxist class categories to the study of African societies. Our findings reinforce this point anew. Using data on stated occupation, we classified respondents into social classes: either as "middle class," "working class," "peasantry," or (the reserve army of the) "unemployed." While we find, predictably, that a middle-class occupation inclines individuals to support economic reform, we also note that there is limited overlap between class and poverty. Both of these structural predictors should be present in any overall model of the unpopularity of adjustment. The existential implications are considerable. In Africa, economic crisis has become so pervasive that it has caused a trickling up of poverty into the ranks of previously privileged groups. As a consequence, a middle-class occupation no longer provides individuals with any guarantee their families will not suffer deprivations of food, water, and health care.

STRUCTURAL MODELS

To summarize: we have shown that, in isolation, various aspects of African societies – from gender to social class – impinge, in varying degrees, on public attitudes to reform. To move toward more definitive conclusions, we now merge all such factors into unified, multivariate statistical models.[84] In so doing, we weigh the relative explanatory power of every element (simultaneously controlling each for all others) and observe how much variance societal factors together explain. In short, we distinguish the most important dimensions of social structure and estimate the extent to which they collectively shape attitude formation.

In pursuit of parsimony, we also construct a streamlined, composite *index of commitment to democracy*, which we henceforth employ in all multivariate analyses. So far, we have treated support for democracy and rejection of authoritarian rule (which is itself an index of rejection of presidential, one-party, and military rule) as if these were separate attitudes. But what if, together, these attitudes represent a larger construct? We tested this idea statistically: factor analysis confirms that the responses to these items provide a valid and reliable representation of a single, underlying dimension.[85] We name it the *index of commitment to democracy* because it plumbs the shallowness or depth of attachments to this political regime. In our view, people are committed to democracy to the degree that they *both* support democracy *and* reject all forms of authoritarian rule.[86] Starting with this chapter, a key object of this book is to explain the emergence of such deep (that is, nonshallow) commitments.

As Column 1 of Table 6.3 shows, all the attributes of social structure that correlate simply with commitment to democracy retain the same signs and remain significant in a multivariate model. By introducing mutual statistical

TABLE 6.3. *The Effects of Social Structure on Attitudes to Reform*

	Commitment to Democracy	Perceived Extent of Democracy	Support for Economic Reform	Satisfaction with Adjustment Program
Constant	1.403^{***}	2.348^{***}	2.322^{***}	2.660^{***}
Female	$-.112^{***}$	.004	$-.063^{***}$	.013
Age	$.068^{***}$	$-.003$	$-.004$	$-.028^{**}$
Postcolonial generation	$.267^{***}$	.044	$.051^{***}$	.011
Multiparty generation	$.192^{***}$	.006	$.032^{*}$	$-.033^{*}$
Rural	$-.064^{***}$	$.045^{***}$	$-.043^{***}$	$.061^{***}$
Major ethnic group	$-.026^{***}$	$.021^{**}$	$-.031^{***}$	.016
Poverty	$-.064^{***}$	$-.102^{***}$	$-.115^{***}$	$-.112^{***}$
Middle class	$.073^{***}$	.008	$.100^{***}$	$-.025^{**}$
Working class	$.026^{***}$	.008	.012	$-.011$
Peasant class	$.040^{***}$	$.055^{**}$	$.045^{***}$	$.063^{***}$
Standard error	.535	1.159	1.065	1.198
Adjusted r squared	.068	.019	.036	.024

Note: Unless otherwise indicated, entries are standardized regression coefficients (beta).
N = 21,531
***p = <.001
**p = <.01
*p = <.05

controls, however, the most influential social factors now stand out in bold relief. Other things being equal, considerations of political generation would seem to be paramount. Coming of age under an old authoritarian regime has the greatest impact on an individual's commitment to democracy. Belonging to the first postcolonial political generation moves an individual up the three-point index of commitment to democracy by about a third of a point.[87] Perhaps the shared experience of homegrown autocracy induces conversion in the regime preferences of this cohort of Africans: those who would otherwise be committed authoritarians encounter a crisis of doubt; those who would otherwise be undecided, begin to convert to democracy; and those who harbor even shallow commitments to democracy, deepen these commitments.

This notable structural effect seems to suggest that political learning occurs by generation and by negative example. In other words, Africans of the postcolonial cohort become democrats by aversion, that is, they react against the unwelcome (and generation-specific) experience of being initiated into politics under the restrictions of one-party or military rule. We cannot yet rule out an alternate hypothesis, however, namely that learning is a collective experience that cuts across several generations. We notice, for example, that members of the multiparty generation – who came of age politically since recent transitions to democracy – are also substantially more committed to democracy than the norm. As we proceed, we will explore whether these respondents have benefited from political learning based on a positive set of experiences with open politics. In addition, since age is now related to reformism, we infer that the longer a person experiences the effects of living within a given political generation, the more they make commitments to democracy, which suggests that learning also accretes gradually over the course of a lifetime. Finally, gender must remain a topic of active investigation since, once other social factors are controlled, women emerge as consistently less committed to democracy than men.

Second, we find that social structure has few meaningful impacts on public judgments about the extent of democracy (see Table 6.3, Column 2). The only social groups who perceive that democracy is taking root are relatively well-to-do rural peasants who belong to their country's major ethnic group. To begin with, this finding highlights the fact that, even though the poor remain unsatisfied, most social segments remain agnostic about democracy's consolidation. Note, however, that popular judgments about the extent of democracy may be unreliable, concentrated as they are among those elements in society who, either through ignorance about the content of the new regime or loyalty to the political status quo, are least likely to arrive at an informed opinion. As such, we expect education and related indicators of political awareness to eclipse these weak structural effects in later analyses.

Third, opposition for economic reform is propelled more by poverty than by any other social factor. As Africans slide down the slippery slope of poverty, each notch – whether from "nonpoor" to "poor," or from "very poor" to "destitute" – increases resistance to structural adjustment policies by about four percentage points.[88] While poverty has trickled up through societies in economic crisis, it has not entirely obliterated the consequences of social class. Middle-class occupations, with their attendant salaries and perquisites, are also a powerful structural influence. But their influence is positive, with middle-class Africans being significantly more likely to support economic reform than those in the working classes. And other findings are reconfirmed even under controlled conditions: women remain more resistant to adjustment than men, as do rural dwellers compared to city dwellers.

Fourth, poverty is also the only meaningful social determinant of satisfaction with adjustment. Once all elements of social structure are controlled for, however, being a peasant producer has, on balance, a positive effect on both support for and satisfaction with economic reform. We suspect that the control for poverty is eliminating the influence of the poorest rural households and revealing that commercially oriented agricultural producers tend to back adjustment reforms and to be satisfied with their effects. On the other side of the coin, we see that the poor are united – across generations and in both urban and rural locations – in a groundswell against adjustment.

Finally, we acknowledge that, overall, social structure does not explain a great deal about any of the political or economic attitudes studied here.

Together, structural considerations never account for more than 7 percent of total variance and are sometimes virtually invisible. This important finding is good news for leaders and activists who aim to build democracy in Africa. It confirms (as proposed in Chapter 3) that support for democracy has diffused quite widely throughout African societies. Key social groups who, if organized politically, might constitute a threat to democracy – such as young generations, urban dwellers, and ethnic minorities – actually favor a democratic form of government. Any pockets of outright opposition to democracy – or, more likely, redoubts of political indifference – tend to be concentrated among social groups – such as women, the older "colonial" generation, and the rural poor – who are among the least well-organized segments of society. The poor may be united against adjustment, but they are not cohesive in any opposition to democracy. At this stage, therefore, we are unable to identify any organized base of social resistance that is poised to call into question the project of democratization.

7

Cultural Values

If the structure of African societies is changing, then cultural values assuredly are also adapting and evolving. Etounga-Manguelle summarizes the conventional starting point for understanding cultural values on the continent: "African thought rejects any view of the individual as an autonomous and responsible being... the African can only bloom and develop through social and family life."[1] According to this familiar formula, members of kin groups are encouraged, from childhood onward, to define their identities and behaviors in terms of obligations to a community. Goran Hyden gives pride of place to such indigenous norms when he depicts traditional rural life in terms of an "economy of affection,"[2] which is based on "the principle of reciprocity embedded in customary rules."[3]

Against this background, however, Africans have been thrust into a modern world where, starting with formal education and extending through wage employment, they perform as individuals. It would be a mistake to assume that socialization into indigenous norms leaves people entirely unprepared for such challenges. With reference to child-rearing practices, Weisner notes that "individualism, autonomy, self-reliance, and self-expression are also encouraged... there are children and families throughout Africa ready to engage in new forms of market activity and civic life."[4] In deconstructing the idea of an "economy of affection," Lemarchand makes a powerful case that reciprocity and cooperation are based as much on self-interest as on altruism.[5] When calculating the costs and benefits of cooperation, he argues, individuals weigh the risk of penalties from fearsome neighbors as much as the expectations of reward from trusted friends and kinfolk. Moreover, as peasants are incorporated into larger systems of authority and exchange, "the demise of the moral economy (is) replaced with a highly individuated petty commodity system in which households increasingly confront the market as individuals."[6]

In this chapter, we explore the tension between attachments to indigenous norms – especially compelling duties to community – and an emergent individualism, often expressed as economic ambition. We begin by asking about identities – that is, whether people feel subjective attachments to ethnic, religious, or class groups, or to no group at all – and whether these subnational ties can coexist with a sense of national unity. The chapter also takes up the issue of social capital. We measure the extent of interpersonal trust expressed by the Africans we interviewed in the expectation that it will help us understand the prospects for economic cooperation and political institution building in present-day Africa. By examining the self-described roles of individuals and groups within society, we hope to illuminate the current status of cultural values.

Cultural values are subjects of innate interest, since their distributions help us interrogate the validity of clichés about Africans as wedded to tradition, divided by ethnicity, and deficient in national unity. Mostly, we find such typecasting unwarranted. Importantly for the project at hand, however, we also wish to appraise the impact of cultural values on attitudes to reform. We propose that individualists are more likely than communitarians to endorse the goals of democracy and adjustment and to welcome the achievements to date of actual reform programs. We are less certain about other potential effects. Is ethnic or class identity more corrosive of preferences for liberalization? Is interpersonal trust an essential building block in the construction of open societies? In short, we want to know whether, and in which directions, cultural values propel attitudes toward democracy and economic reform.

SELF-DEFINED IDENTITIES

In the previous chapter, we examined various outward manifestations of group identity such as home language or nominal religion. But these objective markers – which help determine how one is seen by others – do not necessarily coincide with subjective group identity – that is, how one sees oneself. Thus, in this chapter, we examine Africans' self-defined identities, in the belief that such intimate personal qualities offer insight into the cultural values that people hold dear. If individuals define their group loyalties primarily in terms of communal ties, then it is reasonable to suppose that they will draw their cultural values from traditional sources. If, however, they see themselves as having achieved entry into new occupational groups or classes, then they are implicitly switching allegiance to a more modern culture.

To introduce the topic of self-defined group identity, survey interviewers presented a preamble: "We have spoken to many (Namibians/ Nigerians/Malawians, etc.)[7] and they have all described themselves in different ways. Some people describe themselves in terms of their language, ethnic group, race, religion, or gender, whereas others describe themselves in economic terms, such as working class, middle class, or a farmer." We then asked: "Besides being a (the name of a nationality is inserted here,

TABLE 7.1. *Self-Defined Group Identities*

Occupational identities	40	Occupation (e.g., farmer, trader)	27
		Social class (e.g., worker)	13
Ethnic identities	32	Ethnicity (including clan, tribe, language)	25
		Race (e.g., black, white)	5
		Region (e.g., northerner)	2
Religious identities	17	Religion (e.g., Muslim)	17
Other identities	11	National (e.g., Batswana)	3
		Gender	2
		Individual (i.e., nongroup)	2
		Continental (including African)	1
		Other	3

Note: For question wording, see text. Figures are percentages who choose this identity "first and foremost."

e.g., Namibian), which specific group do you feel you belong to first and foremost?" The answers that people gave in their own words were coded into the categories displayed in Table 7.1.

We expected that Africans would declare primary allegiance to ethnic identities. A vast literature has created the powerful impression that Africans remain embedded in solidarities of kinship and language and that these ethnic identities constitute the principal obstacle to nation building.[8] Against the grain, we find diverse patterns of subjective group attachments in which ethnicity is not uppermost. And we discover that many types of group loyalty – including ethnic identity – readily coexist with nationalism.

Most commonly, the Africans we interviewed derive a sense of who they are from their economic occupations (27 percent). In other words, the labor that Africans do each day is central, not only to their economic survival, but also to the development of their social and political personae. Farmers, teachers, miners, shopkeepers, and transporters are most likely to declare occupational identities, as are East Africans. For example, some 76 percent of Tanzanians and 62 percent of Ugandans cite an economic identity, with most saying they are farmers. We interpret such high proportions in these countries to reflect both the spread of market-based opportunities for agricultural pursuits and active campaigns by the public authorities to shift the bases of social identity away from ethnicity and religion, including banning associations or political parties that organize along these lines.

A further 13 percent of respondents identify with social classes, mainly as "workers" or "peasants," but also self-described "poor" and "unemployed" persons and the odd self-declared "professional" or "intellectual." Because Africans commonly use class terms to signify occupation – "*paysan*" in Mali can mean farmer, "worker" in Southern Africa can mean government employee – we feel justified for purposes of analysis in subsuming class under occupation. By this expanded definition, occupations account for the self-defined identity of four out of ten Africans interviewed (see Table 7.1).[9]

Ethnicity – which we first define narrowly as a sense of belonging to a clan, tribe, hometown, or group based on language or dialect – forms the basis of about one quarter of responses (25 percent). These types of ethnic identity are especially strong in Nigeria, being cited by almost half of all Nigerians (48 percent), the highest proportion in the twelve countries. Across Nigeria's main cultural divide, Yoruba are considerably more likely than Hausa or Fulani to define themselves in ethnic terms (46 percent versus 30 percent), suggesting that the former are more likely to respond to communal appeals, including for political mobilization. Ethnic identities are almost as strong in Namibia as in Nigeria, where Ovambo are particularly prone to adhere to a shared solidarity along linguistic lines. Ethnicity also retains above-average importance as a basis of self-ascription in Malawi, Mali, and Zimbabwe, where it bests other modes of subjective solidarity. Thus, while many East Africans say they eschew ethnicity, many Africans in West and Southern African countries continue to cling to family, clan, and language as key aspects of identity.

One would expect that ethnic minorities, who risk being sidelined by a dominant culture, would be especially protective of communal identities. To our surprise, however, we find no overall difference in the prevalence of ethnic identities between members of majority or minority ethnic groups. Any such effects are country specific. In Nigeria, for instance, Ijaw-speaking minorities from the Niger delta and Tiv and Igbo speakers from the Eastern zone express an intense sense of ethnic awareness. These groups are liable, more so even than Yoruba speakers, to cluster defensively around cultural identities (79 percent). By contrast, ethnic minorities in Namibia are less likely than the majority Oshivambo speakers to fall back on the expression of kin-based connections. Most members of the Silozi minority on Namibia's northeast border with Zambia, for example, describe themselves in terms of their occupations as farmers (70 percent). Perhaps what matters most is whether ethnic minorities feel discriminated against economically in their relations with others, as do Nigeria's Ijaw over oil revenues, Tiv over land, and Igbo over opportunities for trading. Adding to this economic interpretation, we note that, for all Afrobarometer countries, individuals who are unemployed are almost twice as likely as others to define themselves in ethnic terms.[10] We take this as evidence that ethnic attachments are often constructed, situational, and derivative of economic distress.

In addition to kinship and language, ethnic feelings arise from other sources. As indicated in Table 7.1, race and subnational region can be grouped within a broader definition of ethnicity. As expected, race is important to identity formation only in Southern Africa, with one in five South Africans describing their primary affinity in terms of being black, white,

Indian, or Coloured. Region is most important in Botswana mainly because, in this linguistically homogenous country, few salient cultural divisions exist apart from the homelands of the various Batswana clans. In most of the African countries we studied, however, new regional identities (for example, "northerner," "southerner") have not superseded more primordial ethnic attachments. And, even when identities based on race and regionalism are counted together with those derived from language and tribe, only one third of all Africans interviewed express ethnic identities broadly defined, a proportion significantly smaller than the proportion who express occupational outlooks. In this respect, we find prima facie evidence that modern identities have overtaken traditional ones.

Nonetheless, account must still be taken of religious and other identities. Almost one in five Africans claim, first and foremost, an identity with a community of faith, either Muslim, Christian, or traditional (for a total of 17 percent of all respondents). Adherents of Islam are between two and four times as likely as the followers of other faiths to see themselves primarily in terms of their religion.[11] Across countries, however, religious identity is most widespread in Zambia, where 36 percent make this claim, more even than feel themselves members of an occupation or class (25 and 23 percent respectively). Almost all these Zambians profess a Christian soul – whether Protestant, Catholic, African independent, evangelical, or Jehovah's Witness – though a handful are Muslim or Hindu. Expressions of religious identity are above average also in Lesotho and Malawi (principally for Christians) and in Mali and Nigeria (mainly for Muslims). Indeed, residents of Nigeria's northern zone are more likely to declare Islam than ethnicity as the primary basis for self-organization, potentially also in politics. Hence, even as ethnic tensions in Nigeria derive largely from the south, the country's religious disputes would seem to originate mainly in the north.

The last row of Table 7.1 records the distribution of other identities. In one country, Botswana, many people refused to draw a distinction between their citizenship and any group identity, insisting instead on seeing themselves as nationals. Since one out of three Batswana take this stance, their responses account for almost all of the fictitious "average" displayed for "all" countries (3 percent). Despite offering the option of gender identity in the preamble to the question, very few people define their group identity in this way (2 percent), almost all of them women, most commonly in Tanzania and Uganda. A similarly small fraction rejects all group labels, defining their identities instead in individualistic, and usually flattering, terms (for example, "an honest person," "a good Samaritan"). Finally, one out of every hundred saw himself or herself from a continent-wide perspective as a pan-territorial "African."[12]

Just because Africans express a sense of belonging to a subnational group does not necessarily condemn them to intergroup conflict. Clashes between groups occur mainly if group identities turn chauvinistic, for example when

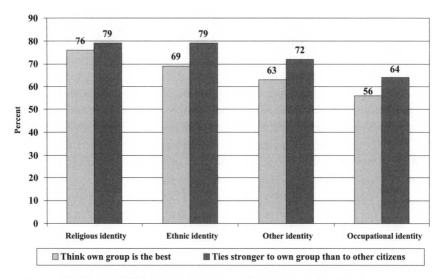

Question 1: (Agree/disagree) "Of all the groups in this country (your identity group, insert name) is the best?"
Question 2: (Agree/disagree) "You feel much stronger ties to (your identity group) than to other (people of your nationality)."

FIGURE 7.1. Group Chauvinism, by Identity

members of one group claim superiority over another. But the potential for aggression and conflict are ever present in Africa, as evidenced by the six out of ten respondents who think that their own identity group is "the best."[13] This sort of group chauvinism is most prevalent in Nigeria (82 percent), where, in a surefire recipe for mutual misunderstanding, speakers of the three main languages all strongly believe that their group is superior to the rest.[14] By comparison, Malawians are much more self-effacing; fewer than half (49 percent) assert the exceptional merit of their own group.

The type of subnational group also matters (see Figure 7.1). Africans who profess a religious identity are most likely to be chauvinistic, whereas those who express an occupational identity are least likely to lord it over others.[15] All these findings, taken together, reinforce differences earlier observed between the Afrobarometer's West and East African cases: whereas religious and ethnic communities in Nigeria are primed to clash, cross-cutting occupational groups in places like Tanzania help to soothe and ameliorate conflict.

Do Africans also possess a sense of national identity? To all appearances, they definitely do: fully 95 percent of Afrobarometer respondents agree that they feel pride in being a national of their country, and 70 percent agree strongly.[16] The same overwhelming majority also wants their children to think of themselves as national citizens. Across the continent, there is remarkable unanimity on the topic of national pride, from a "low" of 87 percent among Malawians to a high of 98 percent among Malians. The residents of Lesotho, whose embattled country is surrounded by a powerful neighbor, express the most intense nationalism, with 87 percent agreeing strongly. By contrast, South Africans (especially ethnic minorities)[17] lend fainter endorsement, with only 54 percent expressing pride in the new "rainbow nation."

It is intriguing to note that national and group identities are not mutually exclusive. Instead, they easily coexist. Africans apparently find no difficulty in expressing a sense of belonging, at one and the same time, to both nation-state and a subnational community. In other words, people possess a repertoire of multiple collective identities, which they activate selectively depending on the situation. Moreover, Africans who feel strong affinities with special interest groups tend to be the self-same people who are the strongest proponents of national pride.[18] We therefore conclude that the dichotomy between group and national identities is false.[19] Just because Africans feel strong identifications with their local occupational, ethnic, and religious communities, they are not thereby inhibited from also learning to love their country. In fact, we are struck by the almost universal extent to which nationality – that is, a cultural value represented by symbols of the state like flags, boundaries, and citizenship – has been internalized by the Africans we interviewed, including those who profess identity with a primary group.

But what happens if country and community clash? Which proves the stronger temperament: one's clan or one's nationality? When we asked people directly whether their ties were stronger to their own group or to other national citizens, we received skewed responses: 70 percent agreed that they felt closer ties to their own group. In this instance, identifications with ethnic groups were just as insular and inward looking as ties to religious groups (see Figure 7.1). But, again, occupational identities were associated with a more open and broad-minded view of the world that allowed for associations with people different from oneself.[20] At the extremes, almost all Nigerians put their own clan ahead of other Nigerians (89 percent), as compared to just over half of Zambians (57 percent). On one hand, this contrast starkly illustrates the social distances that Nigerians must traverse before they can reach a lasting national accommodation. On the other hand, it shows that Zambians have already achieved a good measure of social consensus. For all his policy failures, former president Kenneth Kaunda did succeed in balancing ethnic and other sectional claims and bequeathed to his countrymen a strong sense of national unity.

A caveat, however, is in order here about the survey question: it asked whether people agreed with a statement that in-group ties *were* stronger, and it named other citizens rather than the nation as an entity; thus it may be leading, even biased. When the question is rephrased, we unearth a streak of nationalism even among Nigerians. In a second survey in 2001 we asked: "Let us suppose that you had to choose between being a Nigerian and being a (member of your own identity group).[21] Which of these two groups do you feel most strongly attached to?" The sample was split down the middle: half named Nigeria (49 percent) and half said their subnational identity group (50 percent). We also asked whether Nigeria should remain united or, because of persistent group conflicts, the nation should break apart. Perhaps chastened by traumatic memories of devastating civil war (1967–70), a clear majority emerges in favor of national unity (74 percent). We take this result as an initial indication that, even in the African countries most deeply rent by social division, citizens have become attached to a larger civic entity. If African nation-states were once artificial, they are no more.

Does a sense of national identity affect attitudes to reform? Following Rustow's classic insight, we assume that a preexisting, consensually accepted, political community is essential, not only for political stability, but also for the smooth operations of a democratic polity and a market economy.[22] Does this macrolevel cultural precondition also hold at the micro level of public opinion? We find that it does. The stronger an individual's sense of national identity, the more likely he or she is to support democracy and reject author-itarian rule.[23] Perhaps by identifying with a nation writ large, individuals come to appreciate the enormity of the stakes involved in political experi-ments, thus strengthening their commitments to democratic reform.[24] To an even greater extent, a sense of national identity is associated with height-ened satisfaction among Africans with the workings of both democracy and markets.[25] In this regard, the attainment of nationhood appears to be nec-essary accompaniment to the free flow of goods and services, though we cannot be certain whether it is a cause, effect, or both.

In order to explore the connections, if any, between subnational group identities and attitudes to reform, we roughly classify each type of identity group according to its modernity. At issue is whether individuals adopt tra-ditional or modern values as a result of the group identities they choose for themselves. We classify as "traditionalists" all those who express ethnic iden-tities (broadly defined), plus people who see themselves first and foremost as traditional leaders or part of an age set (for example, elder). We classify as "modernizers" all those who claim occupational identities, plus people that self-identify as individuals, nationalists, or members of political parties. At first we were torn about the classification of new religious identities in African contexts, but ultimately scored them as "traditional" on the logic that religions promote mystification rather than rationality. According to this simple (and admittedly crude) classification, the Afrobarometer sample is evenly split between 52 percent traditionalists and 48 percent modernizers. It is hard to imagine a more vivid illustration of Africa as a continent caught between two cultures.

We posit that Africans who identify with modern values are predisposed to embrace reforms. While this hypothesis is confirmed, the results, with one major exception, are not especially compelling. To be sure, a modern identity everywhere pushes support for democracy and rejection of authoritarian rule in a positive direction, but the results are statistically significant in only half the countries.[26] Reassuringly for the thesis, though, "traditionalists" are everywhere more likely to approve the restoration of rule by chiefs or a council of elders.[27] Compared to weak connections between group values and democratic reforms, however, stronger links are evident to support for economic reforms. "Modernizers," especially those who profess occupational identities, are almost twice as likely as "traditionalists" to support a full package of economic reforms.[28] And modern values are especially likely to induce support for radically restructuring the civil service in places like Namibia, Tanzania, and South Africa.[29] Thus, while support for democracy has diffused quite widely among both modernizers and traditionalists, support for economic reform is a much more modern attitude.

INTERPERSONAL TRUST

How do Africans relate to one another? Are they generally trusting or suspicious? Is trust a prerequisite for reform? Among other indicators, the amount of generalized trust expressed by members of a society signifies its reserves of social capital.[30] Because trust lubricates interpersonal relations, people who place confidence in others find it easier to join political associations, to enter economic transactions, and thus, to build the large-scale institutions of representative democracy and a national economy. By this logic, theorists like Putnam argue that networks of social cooperation foster economic growth and institutional performance.[31] Others, like Inglehart, suggest that the total amount of interpersonal trust in a society is one of the most powerful cultural factors explaining both economic development and the stability of democracy.[32]

Social capital is usually treated as an attribute of whole communities, regions, or countries. But it can also be observed at the individual level, at least in preliminary and proximate fashion, by measuring the extent of interpersonal trust expressed by survey respondents. The Afrobarometer adopts a standard formula that has been employed in cross-national research for several decades: "Generally speaking, would you say that most people can be trusted or that you must be very careful in dealing with people?" The answers to this question speak to a person's beliefs about the benevolence or selfishness of human nature. The distribution of answers across African countries is displayed in Figure 7.2.

Overall, reported levels of interpersonal trust are low on the sub-Saharan subcontinent. On average, just 18 percent of the Africans we interviewed think that most people can be trusted, whereas fully 79 percent consider that it pays to be cautious in interpersonal affairs. In response to the same question posed in 1990, six out of ten Scandinavians and over four out of ten Japanese said that they generally trust others.[33] And about half of the

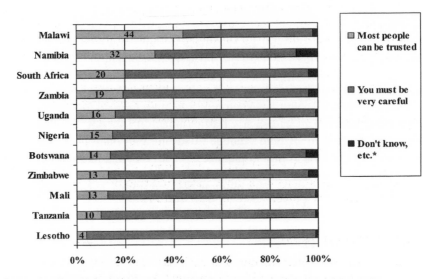

Question: "Generally speaking, would you say that most people can be trusted or that you must be very careful in dealing with people?"
Note: "Don't knows" include refusals to answer but exclude missing data.

FIGURE 7.2. Interpersonal Trust

respondents from five Central European countries in 1998 expressed a sense of "personal trust" in "most people (they) meet."[34] Unlike these Northern hemisphere countries, where a foundation of generalized trust has apparently been laid, the African cases more closely resemble Latin America. In 1996, just 19 percent of the respondents in eleven Latinobarometer countries answered the standard question positively, leading Lagos to infer "a common regional heritage of distrust."[35]

While social capital seems to be scarce in Africa, its availability varies across countries. Trust in other persons is most lacking in Lesotho, where some families live alone in upland homesteads under isolated conditions that afford few opportunities for mingling. Trust is also in short supply in Tanzania, a country whose settlement patterns were disrupted during the last generation by programs of rural collectivization that thrust unrelated strangers into close residential proximity. The low level of interpersonal trust in Tanzania is an anomaly in a country whose citizens otherwise express the highest levels of institutional trust on the continent (see Chapter 10). Perhaps Tanzanians feel free to express honest opinions about their fellow citizens but are constrained to follow the party line when appraising the trustworthiness of government agencies.[36] At the other end of the spectrum, however, interpersonal trust is most prevalent in Malawi. As rural dwellers in densely populated, kin-based villages, most Malawians face strong incentives to maintain social harmony by cooperating with relatives and neighbors. In addition, interpersonal trust is higher in South Africa and Namibia than their histories of racial strife would dare one to predict. But this may well be due to high levels of solidarity *within* subnational groups.

Because distrust is widespread, it affects all manner of folk. Faith in one's fellows is found wanting to a similar degree among both women and men, both old and young, and more surprisingly, both urban and rural dwellers. One might have expected, for example, that urban residents, who are thrust into the multicultural environment of an anonymous throng, would have developed more caution than rural folk. But the Afrobarometer data say otherwise. Apparently, in Africa's rural villages, familiarity breeds contempt, if not for one's own kinsmen, then at least for others with whom villagers come into contact. Nor is low trust a characteristic only of ethnic minorities or the poor. In short, we found no meaningful demographic limits to the common cultural value of wariness in interpersonal affairs.

As intimated previously, however, distrust may hinge on the perceived identity of the "other." Trust can be expected to decay with social distance from the respondent, with people expressing more confidence in the members of their own inner circles than in unfamiliar outsiders. We find exactly this pattern in the six countries where we inquired into this issue (see Table 7.2).[37] Interpersonal trust declines in step-by-step fashion from a high level for one's relatives, to progressively lower levels for neighbors, the members of one's own ethnic group, and fellow nationals of other ethnic groups. The only exception to this trend is Zambia, where people trust their own ethnic group more than their neighbors. Because of their country's high rates of migration and urbanization, Zambians are more likely than most Africans to have a person of a different ethnic group as a coresident. As a result, urban Zambians are twice as likely to distrust their neighbors as rural Zambians. As a general pattern, the Africans we interviewed had much more confidence in their own families than in the members of other ethnic groups (54 percent versus 16 percent). The low level of the last figure suggests that most respondents are mentally picturing ethnic strangers when they answer the general question about interpersonal trust (which refers to "most people"). Once the object of trust is specified, and especially if the object is close to home, then levels of reported trust rise substantially.

TABLE 7.2. *Interpersonal Trust, by Identity of "Other"*

	Ghana	Mali	Nigeria	Tanzania	Uganda	Zambia
Family	65	40	44	50	–	69
Neighbors	39	35	25	20	–	38
Your own ethnic group	35	39	17	15	29	44
Other ethnic groups	19	15	11	11	14	24

Note: The figures are percentages saying this group can be trusted. The Zambia data are from 1996.

Does interpersonal trust also vary by the respondent's own self-defined identity? We speculate, for example, that defining one's identity in ethnic terms would inflame distrust. And we guess, given the message of tolerance preached by most religions, that a religious identity could help to overcome such suspicions. In fact, neither proposition can be confirmed. There is no observable difference among our African respondents in levels of interpersonal trust between the adherents of ethnic and religious identities. But traditional value orientations (as represented by ethnic and religious identities combined) do incline people to be more trusting than those with modern (that is, occupational or individualistic) identities. So, one adjunct of modernization is that, at least initially, it induces Africans to become more distrustful of the society around them.

We now turn from causes to consequences. To date, the few efforts to study the effects of social capital in Africa have produced mixed results. Based on survey research in Botswana and Uganda, for example, Widner and Mundt found that "the elements of social capital, as typically defined, do not cohere the way they do in other parts of the world." Moreover, although "levels of trust exert independent influence on some forms of political participation," there is – contra Putnam – "no clear relationship between social capital and the performance of institutions."[38] As for economic impacts, Narayan and Pritchett show that, in rural Tanzania, "a village's social capital has an effect on the incomes of the households in that village, an effect that is empirically large, definitely social, and plausibly causal."[39] They also contend – in this case pro Putnam – that trust and cooperation enable villagers to monitor the performance of government and, thus, indirectly, improve the effectiveness of public services.

Although we cannot settle these disputes definitively here, we can push the discussion forward. We find that interpersonal trust modestly influences mass perceptions of political and policy performance; but its effects are not the ones so far reported in the literature. The Afrobarometer results suggest that Africans who are generally trustful are more likely to be satisfied with the way democracy works and to perceive that democratic institutions have been installed.[40] In other words, unlike Widner, we detect trace evidence of a positive linkage between social capital and popular perceptions of democratic performance. But we also notice that interpersonal trust has no bearing on satisfaction with SAPs, which include policies to raise the quality of health and education services.[41] For this reason, our data cannot confirm Narayan and Pritchett's conjecture that social capital enables citizens to collectively hold the government accountable for improving service delivery. Until such time as researchers can agree on comprehensive standards for measuring social capital and institutional performance, however, all such results will inevitably remain tentative.

Our main interest here is in whether values of interpersonal trust build popular support for political and economic reform. In this case, we can make a more authoritative certification: at the individual level, Inglehart's thesis that interpersonal trust is a core democratic value is not confirmed.[42] In the microlevel Afrobarometer data, there is no observable linkage between a person's willingness to trust others and his or her expressed support for democracy.[43] Stated differently, Africans who are socially wary are just as likely as those who are generally trusting to consider democracy the best form of government (both 70 percent). In a statistically rare event, the two values are actually perfectly uncorrelated in Zambia.[44]

Moreover, this neutral relationship turns negative for rejection of authoritarian regimes. Again counter to Inglehart, Africans who trust others are somewhat *more* likely to accept a reversion to authoritarian rule.[45] In our view, this finding is plausible since individuals who view the world innocently are easy targets for political strongmen. Indeed, we notice that Africans who place their faith in others are especially likely to welcome interventions by soldiers into African politics.[46] Such hopeful subjects are especially likely to dream of military rule in Zimbabwe, or be nostalgic for its return in Nigeria.[47] These popular sentiments give rise to little cause for concern about democratization in Zimbabwe and Nigeria, however, since in both countries the group of trusting persons is only a small minority (see Figure 7.2). The main point, however, is that a population that is cautiously skeptical, rather than blindly trusting, is the most conducive to democracy.

AN EMERGENT INDIVIDUALISM

This chapter now returns to the core issue in the debate over cultural values in Africa. What is the balance between inherited community values and any new trends of individualism? A 1993 pilot survey in Zambia seemed to reveal a powerful communitarian undertow: seven out of ten Zambians said they "do better working with a group" rather than "working alone." Yet a 2002 survey in Namibia seemed to suggest the opposite. Asked whether "each person should put the well-being of the community ahead of their own interests" or whether "everyone should be free to pursue what is best for themselves," seven out of ten chose the latter option. These responses are so antithetical that, for the moment, the safest general conclusion is that individualistic and communitarian values are pitted against each other in an unresolved contest.

Interestingly, this is exactly what we found when we asked (in Chapter 4) who was responsible for popular well-being: the individual or the state? As reported earlier, Afrobarometer respondents are split on the issue: 51 percent express self-reliance, while 46 percent prefer the government to guarantee welfare; and 53 percent think that people should create their own jobs versus 44 percent who see employment creation as a government responsibility. Because these indicators are correlated, we use an *index of individualism* to capture the cultural divide between "individualists" and "communitarians."[48]

Exactly who are the emergent individualists? We find that gender, age and political generation have little influence on whether a person professes self-reliance: younger females of the multiparty generation, for examples are just as likely to say that they prefer to stand on their own feet as older males of the colonial generation. Interestingly, rural dwellers express more self-reliance than urban residents, perhaps because their experience tells them that it is often futile to rely on the ineffective machinery of a distant central government. Offsetting this rural slant, however, people who have been exposed to education and the mass media – groups who tend to live in towns – also express a sense of individual responsibility for their own advancement (see Chapter 8).

As expected, individualists are more likely than communitarians to support democracy and reject authoritarian rule. But, while the statistical signs are predictably positive, the connection is only moderate for democracy and weak and insignificant for authoritarianism.[49] Cultural values appear to have a big political impact mainly in Malawi, where proponents of personal initiative are especially likely to both support democracy and reject one-party rule.[50] Malawi stands out because individuals required exemplary courage to embark on a campaign of resistance to the old one-party regime. As indicated earlier, the former supremo constructed a hegemonic state apparatus based upon networks of secret informers and the ritual invocation of traditional symbols, including witchcraft.[51] Thus, to become a democrat in Malawi, individuals were required to shrug off not only the very real risks of arrest or disappearance, but also a prevailing set of occult cultural symbols that the leader had appropriated to buttress his power.[52]

In general, people who are attached to individualistic values are more likely to think that democracy is being achieved in their countries.[53] This relationship holds for all Afrobarometer sites except Zimbabwe, where communitarians see a greater extent of democracy. In this instance, ZANU-PF's strategy for political survival – which includes purchasing the allegiance of key chiefs and headmen, mainly in the Shona heartland – has apparently succeeded among the most conservative elements in society.[54] The more common effect (of individualism encouraging perceptions of democratic consolidation) is especially strong in Uganda,[55] reflecting a quite different political strategy on the part of Yoweri Museveni. While allowing the restoration of traditional kings, the government of Uganda has carefully excluded them from politics and restricted them to the cultural realm. At the same time, the ruling National Resistance Movement has apparently managed to convince even independent-minded and forward-thinking citizens that its no-party system is a form of democracy.

That said about democracy, individualism has a far greater impact on attitudes to economic reform. People who value personal economic autonomy tend consistently to support more components in the adjustment policy package.[56] This relationship holds across all countries studied, with the exception of Uganda and Lesotho, where support for economic reform is diffuse, albeit at much higher levels in Uganda than in Lesotho. Individual values are most influential in Zimbabwe, where support for the ESAP package is heavily concentrated among those who, to achieve personal welfare, prefer to rely on their own efforts.[57] This individualist streak among the supporters of economic reform is most marked among racial minorities in Zimbabwe; but it is also present among black African respondents in Ghana, Malawi and Zambia.

When economic reform policies are compared, we find that groups with different values part company over price policies. Individualists are significantly more likely to prefer to have plentiful goods in the marketplace even if these are costly, while communitarians want to keep prices down, even if shortages occur.[58] We also find a sharp cleavage of economic attitudes between risk takers and those who are averse to gambling with their welfare. For example, people who say they would invest their own money to start a business are also strong supporters of user fees for health or education.[59] This relationship is exceptionally strong in Nigeria, where a widespread entrepreneurial culture apparently reinforces the strong commitments of parents to purchase for their children the best education that their money can buy.[60]

By using an alternate measure, we discover that economic individualism shapes popular support, not just for simple price reforms, but also for more complex and far-reaching reforms to economic institutions. The measure is an *index of support for private provision* that taps the respondent's preference for private sector delivery of development goods and services, including by both firms and individuals.[61] Not surprisingly, the more that Africans think that development should be a private sector affair, the more likely they are to support SAPs.[62] From this perspective, we can identify who is most deeply committed to adjustment; in other words, who lends most support to institutional reforms like privatization and civil service retrenchment. In four countries in particular – Ghana, Tanzania, Zambia, and Zimbabwe – individualists who sympathize with a private sector approach to development make their presence felt in the economic reform debate by supporting these far-reaching institutional changes.[63]

Importantly, the effects of cultural values appear to carry forward from policy preferences to evaluations of regime performance, and in interesting ways. As predicted at the outset, Africans who adopt an individualistic outlook are likely to be more satisfied – or, at least, less dissatisfied – with the practical performance of SAPs.[64] Whereas two thirds of communitarians express a lack of satisfaction with their government's current economic policies, only about one half of individualists say the same (67 versus 53 percent). Moreover, among Ghanaians, Malians, and Ugandans – who all live under regimes that have shown compliance with orthodox reform recommendations – only a minority of self-reliant individualists is dissatisfied with the SAP (45 percent).[65] Granted, these findings hardly amount to a ringing endorsement of the achievements of economic liberalization. But new values of individual self-reliance would appear to prime the pump for at least a measure of popular satisfaction with reform policies.

By the same token, those who are most committed to adjustment – that is, the private sector sympathizers who favor institutional reforms – clearly recognize that adjustment programs are not performing well. Because these individualists harbor high hopes that reform will bring about economic transformation, they are disappointed when efforts to revive the civil service or privatize public companies are implemented only halfheartedly. Thus, we find that the people who want the most radical economic reforms are least likely to be satisfied with partial programs that governments deliver in practice.[66]

CULTURAL MODELS

To all appearances, Africa is a culturally contested continent. Its people are buffeted by conflicting values. Africans respond to these tensions by adopting multiple, shifting identities. At the same time as they declare pride in their nation-states, for example, they also express strong allegiances to a rich variety of parochial groupings. Ethnicity and religion remain important bases for cultural identity, but such communal ties are being superseded by new solidarities based on economic occupation and a modern social class structure. Perhaps partly due to clashes over culture, Africans are unsure whether they can place much trust in their fellow citizens, especially "others" whose values depart from those of their own reference group. And, in settings where social capital is scarce – or limited to those who share identities – people may have little choice but to devise individualistic strategies for finding their way in the world.

Following our approach from the last chapter, we conclude by exploring the lone and joint effects of sundry cultural values (see Table 7.3). As before, we combine variables wherever possible, including measuring the key dependent variable of commitment to democracy as an amalgam of support for democracy and rejection of several types of authoritarian rule. On the predictor side of the regression equation, we employ the index of private provision and the construct of individualism that were introduced in the previous sections.

Of the values that matter, which are uppermost? All else being equal, we find that tolerance for economic risk has the largest effect on commitment to democracy. As individuals move from being strongly risk averse to strongly profit seeking they gain one third of a point on the three-point commitment to democracy scale.[67] Presumably, people who feel ready to compete with other producers in a market also feel comfortable with the cut and thrust of competition among interest groups and political parties in a multiparty democracy. Given that they strongly reject authoritarian rule, risk takers are

TABLE 7.3. *The Effects of Cultural Values on Attitudes to Reform*

	Commitment to Democracy	Perceived Extent of Democracy	Support for Economic Reform	Satisfaction with Adjustment Program
Constant	.507***	1.432***	.949***	2.101***
Modern identity	.053***	.015*	.098***	.024
National pride	.084***	.100***	−.042***	.075***
Interpersonal trust	−.061***	.067***	−.075***	.023*
Individualism	.056***	.081***	.120***	.147***
Risk tolerance	.177***	.004	.093***	−.015
Prefer private provision	.072***	−.022**	.099***	−.084***
Standard error	.538	1.157	1.053	1.193
Adjusted r squared	.057	.022	.057	.033

Note: Unless otherwise indicated, entries are standardized regression coefficients (beta).
N = 21,531
***p = <.001
**p = <.01
*p = <.05

clearly willing to take a chance on untested political arrangements, as long as these mark a sharp break with failed political formulae of the past.

Additionally, when all other factors are controlled, national pride continues to be an asset for democracy. The regression model shows that people's feelings of belonging to a nationwide political community have positive, reinforcing effects on popular commitments to a democratic political regime. This result lends support to the thesis that "rule by the people" depends initially on agreement among "the people" themselves that they share a common political destiny. In linking national pride to commitment to democracy, would-be democrats in Africa apparently have developed a system of cultural values that resolves the paradox of unity in diversity. At the same time as celebrating their membership in a unified nation, they are willing to risk open competition between organized forces within it. Here is at least some evidence, therefore, to counter the conventional view that Africans are too divided among themselves to ever make democracy work.

Cultural values have least impact on the perceived extent of democracy. National pride and economic individualism continue to have slight positive effects. But interpersonal trust, which was negative for support for democracy, now turns positive. Apparently the relationship between trust and democracy is not consistent: trust does not need to be generally present in society for people to decide that they prefer democracy, but its presence does help to convince people that democracy is being attained. Thus, democracy can be installed in the absence of generalized trust, for example as a second-best compromise between leery political combatants. But for people to believe that democracy is being consolidated, they need confidence and assurance that all participants in the political process will abide by the rules of the game. From our microlevel perspective, social trust therefore appears to be a product of democratization, rather than, as Inglehart would have it, a prerequisite.

Among cultural values, an emergent individualism underpins support for economic reform. Africans who prefer to rely on their own efforts, who adopt modern (mainly occupational) identities, who embrace risk, and who think that the private sector should lead development are most likely to back an orthodox package of economic adjustment policies. Individualistic values are also the best cultural predictor of whether Africans will be satisfied with the performance of SAPs. All things considered, however, we continue to find that support for SAPs and satisfaction with their consequences are minority sentiments within African populations. In this regard, the true adherents of a private sector development strategy ("prefer private provision") are sorely disappointed by the underperformance of economic reform programs as actually implemented.

Overall, then, are mass orientations to reform shaped by cultural values? As Table 7.3 shows, cultural values never explain more than 6 percent of the variation in reform attitudes, suggesting a modest impact at best. We take this as evidence that public opinion in Africa evolves partly as a consequence of the modernization of traditional values, but that these cultural dynamics are only a subplot in the story. To be sure, modern individualists are more likely than those who are guided by community obligations to develop commitments to democracy and adjustment. But traditional values are not an insurmountable obstacle to becoming a democrat and modern individualism is no watertight guarantee of market preferences. Instead, where cultures clash and people adopt multiple identities, competing values tend to offset one another, reducing the impact of each. In such polyvalent settings, we tend to think that factors other than cultural values will prove to be more important in explaining the nature of public opinion in African countries.

8

Awareness of Public Affairs

As people become ever more aware of the world around them, they gain the ability to form opinions on the political and economic issues of the day. They learn about the large-scale systems in which their villages and neighborhoods are embedded and begin to comprehend the manifold ways in which their lives are affected by decisions made by distant powerholders. In an effort to exercise agency in these larger arenas they sometimes try to get political leaders and economic markets to respond to their needs. In this chapter, we explore various aspects of cognitive awareness because we expect that an individual's education, media exposure, information, interest, and personal efficacy will have important effects on the expression of public opinion.

Once disparaged as a dark continent, Africa came late to the Western Enlightenment. Until recent years, opportunities for formal education have been scarce and, after independence, the quality of expanding school systems has been undercut by economic crisis. Given the large geographical size of African countries and the weak capacity of central institutions, large numbers of Africans remain beyond the reach of world markets and administrative authorities. Many peasants understandably prefer to avoid capture by extractive markets and repressive states.[1] Nor does active agency come easily in patron-client cultures because ordinary individuals usually lack the educational standing, level of knowledge, and personal self-confidence to engage power holders on an equal footing. In short, one might suppose that many Africans will be too poorly informed about public affairs to engage in effective demand making on their own behalf.

We have already presented evidence that popular awareness of public affairs is incomplete in sub-Saharan Africa. For example, we showed earlier that fewer than one half of the people we interviewed had ever heard of their country's structural adjustment program (see Chapter 4). To be sure, more people are knowledgeable about democracy, since just over three quarters can attach a meaning to the concept (see Chapter 3). But the very incompleteness of public consciousness on both these topics offers opportunities for analysis, enabling us to compare attitudes to reform among people with various levels of political and economic information. At face value, one would expect that low levels of information would decrease people's ability to connect their interests with political and economic reforms. One would also suppose that people who are best informed about public affairs are the strongest reform advocates.

The Afrobarometer results generally confirm these standard expectations. For the most part, sub-Saharan Africa remains a low-information environment in which ambitious elites can easily take advantage of mass ignorance. But, we also uncover some interesting, offsetting quirks. In some countries, Africans display high levels of knowledge about national leaders. In many countries, they express intense interest in political and policy matters. And across the board, access to education and exposure to the mass media make Africans much more skeptical about the quality of democracy and economic performance that governments deliver. Thus, there is evidence that, even where mass populations are inclined to passively accept whatever their leaders offer, pockets of critical citizenship are beginning to emerge.

THE SPARK OF EDUCATION

Education is a catalyst of social change; formal schooling informs people about the way things work in the world; and it creates awareness of public affairs. We fully expect to confirm these conventional impacts of education, finding among the graduates of Africa's schools and universities the continent's most ardent citizens and entrepreneurs.

But these positive connections are not automatic. Organized along the elitist lines of colonial public education, official school systems in Africa have obvious authoritarian features.[2] Standardized by a bureaucratic Ministry of Education, the classic model of instruction is rote academic memorization, with little emphasis on practical skills or independent thought. African school systems, therefore, can be expected to produce individuals who are submissive, wary of risk, and respectful of authority. Alternative attributes, essential for maintaining liberal regimes, are usually absent from the classroom: open-mindedness, reliance on evidence, discussion of ambiguity, tolerance of dissent, and willingness to bargain and compromise. Thus, if we find that education ignites support for democracy and free markets, then it will do so despite formal schooling, not only because of it. Or, the spark of education will induce people to think for themselves at least in part as an unintended consequence of the objectives of schooling.

For ease of presentation, we discuss four levels of education, which are distributed among Afrobarometer respondents as follows: no formal schooling (19 percent), primary education (35 percent), secondary education (36 percent), and postsecondary education (11 percent). There is a cavernous gulf in the availability of education across countries: whereas only 4 percent

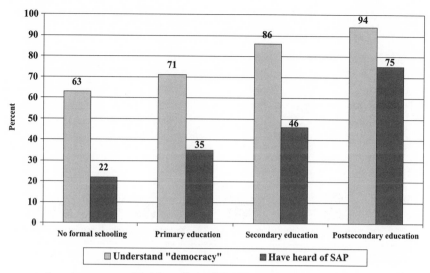

FIGURE 8.1. Awareness of Public Affairs, by Education

of sampled South Africans report no formal schooling and 78 percent say they have received at least some secondary education, the proportions are inverted for Malians: 71 percent have never been to an official, non-Koranic school and just 9 percent have proceeded to the secondary level.

We can confirm that education increases popular awareness of public affairs. For example, every additional level of schooling greatly enhances an individual's ability to attribute a meaning to the term "democracy."[3] Whereas almost all Africans with a postsecondary education express an understanding of the concept, less than two thirds can do so if they have never been to school (see Figure 8.1). Just as potently, awareness of structural adjustment programs is a function of education.[4] In this instance, three quarters of those with postsecondary qualifications claim to have heard of their country's SAP, but three quarters of those without education admit to being uninformed about it.

Moreover, as presented in Figure 8.2, education induces support for democracy, and it does so mainly at the expense of attachments to non-democratic alternatives.[5] As individuals gain formal education, they disengage from allegiances to old political regimes and become adherents of rule by the people. These positive effects are evident in every country in the Afrobarometer, and are especially marked in countries where education is thinly spread, as in Mali and Tanzania. In these situations, we suspect that educated people serve as opinion leaders, who diffuse vital information to their neighbors about civil liberties, political rights, and the operations of a multiparty system. The democratizing effect of education holds even for Lesotho where schooling is a scarce commodity but where,

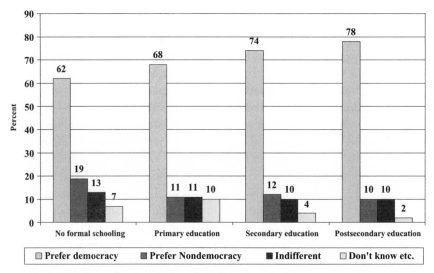

FIGURE 8.2. Support for Democracy, by Education

compared to other countries, educated people are unusually dubious about democracy.

While formal education is a solvent of attachments to all types of previous regime – including traditional authority, one-party government, and a strongman system – it is especially caustic in dissolving popular support for military rule.[6] Notably in countries emerging from military dictatorship, educated people lead the way in opposing the restoration of rule by soldiers.[7] In a dramatic display of unanimity, some 95 percent of Nigerians and Ghanaians who have attended college or university oppose military rule. During past periods of military government, students, educators, clerics, and professionals tried to preserve autonomous realms of free speech in their own corners of society and joined forces to seek to restore civilian democracy in these countries. Even today, educated groups remain the principal indigenous source of advocacy for constitutional rule and the domestication of armed power.[8]

As opinion leaders, educated people are also the first to criticize the imperfect quality of Africa's hybrid democracies. Thus, importantly, the relationship between education and political attitudes now turns negative. Even under hierarchical styles of schooling, education apparently sharpens critical faculties, which leads to a sense of dissatisfaction with the way democracy actually works and to recognition that fully functioning liberal democracies are rarely being realized in African countries.[9] For example, respondents with postsecondary qualifications are only half as likely as those with primary or no education to consider that their country has attained a "full" or "complete" democracy.[10] In Tanzania, where most citizens are uncritical of

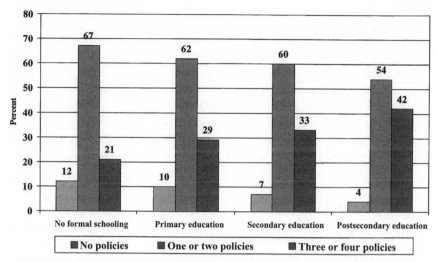

FIGURE 8.3. Number of Economic Reform Policies Supported, by Education

the regime supplied by a dominant party-state, it is noteworthy that a healthy political skepticism has emerged within a small intelligentsia. At least one out of ten Tanzanians with secondary education insists that Tanzania is "not a democracy." In Uganda, by contrast, a similar form of regime appears to have won adherents among citizens of all educational attainments.

Turning to support for economic reform, we again find strong associations with education. Schooling increases the number of economic reform policies that respondents accept, to the point that the most-educated group is twice as likely as the least-educated group to support a full package of reforms (see Figure 8.3).[11] This positive relationship holds in every Afrobarometer country except Lesotho, where, perhaps due to a preemptive political crisis, issues of economic reform do not feature prominently on the public policy agenda. By contrast, education clearly shapes support for adjustment in Botswana where, among persons with secondary education or above, a majority actually supports privatization. Even larger educational effects are observable in Uganda, where a Presidential Economic Council invited opinion leaders to debate the pros and cons of an initial Economic Reform Program in 1987 and a second round of adjustment in 1994.[12] Perhaps because of local involvement in the policy design process, the educated elite in Uganda is three times as likely as those without education to embrace a full package of reforms. Interestingly, they are particularly supportive of reforms to educational policy itself.[13] Whereas three quarters of the most educated people agree that they would pay school fees in return for quality education, just over one third of the least educated are willing – or able – to do so.[14]

To draw this section to a close, we record education's effects on satisfaction with economic reform. Does an educated person's endorsement of SAP objectives extend to expressions of satisfaction with actual policy outcomes? Or, as with reduced levels of satisfaction with democracy, does education make respondents more critical of the way that market regimes really work? We find the latter.[15] Overall, fewer than one quarter of those with secondary education are satisfied with SAPs. But this relationship is not especially strong and it is uneven across countries. In Tanzania, where moderate levels of satisfaction with SAPs prevail, education reduces this contentment. But in Zimbabwe, where satisfaction with SAPs is extremely low, education helps at the margins to raise contentment. This seems to confirm that the intellectual elite in Tanzania hold more critical views about the government's policy performance than does a broadly accepting populace. But the opposite is true in Zimbabwe, where educated people concede that ESAP may have brought more positive benefits than the utterly disaffected masses will allow.

Ironically, educated people are unable to completely shed their socialization in postcolonial school systems. When the subject turns to political equality, elitist preferences peek through. In four Afrobarometer countries we asked respondents to choose between two statements: either, "all people should be permitted to vote, even if they do not understand all the issues in an election"; or, "only those who are sufficiently well educated should be allowed to vote." Overall, just over three quarters prefer a universal franchise, which constitutes further evidence of the wide spread of prodemocratic sentiments. But this generalized preference for political equality *declines* with education, from 83 percent of those with primary education to 68 percent of those with postsecondary education. Educated Ghanaians, who benefited from the most sophisticated school system in Africa at the time of independence, are most likely to favor restrictions on the franchise: almost twice as many postsecondary graduates do so than those without education (30 percent versus 16 percent). Just below the surface of democratic commitments, therefore, educated Africans seem to harbor doubts that their fellow citizens are wise enough to be trusted with full political rights.

EXPOSURE TO MASS MEDIA

Whatever their level of education, Africans enjoy unprecedented opportunities for awareness of a wider world as a consequence of the global communications revolution. The electronic mass media now penetrate even remote parts of the African continent, and urban areas are slowly but surely becoming connected to the Internet.[16] During the 1990s, the liberalization of media controls led to a flowering of daily and weekly publications in African capital cities and the privatization of media houses permitted the emergence of a flock of independent FM stations, sometimes controlled by rural communities. While these media outlets provide heavy doses of music, sports, and religious programming, they also sponsor independent news analysis and interactive forums for discussion of public affairs, such as letters to the editor and radio call-in shows. Such recent trends in the mass media have "been at the forefront of creating political space for other actors in the public arena," thereby "enhancing civic consciousness."[17]

The mass media expose ordinary people to vicarious experiences beyond their immediate environment, which then are fed into public opinion. News bulletins and other public affairs programs play several roles in this regard, including: making people aware of the issues confronting government, both at home and in its dealings with international agencies; helping to set an agenda for national development by raising the salience of particular policy issues; priming the general public to lean one way or another on these issues; increasing or reducing the perception of risks, say from crime or corruption; and aiding mass political learning about the operations of state and market institutions. In short, the news media expand the range of considerations that people bring to bear in forming their political and economic attitudes.[18]

Africans get their information about public affairs principally by listening to news broadcasts on the radio. Across the twelve Afrobarometer countries, radio listening exceeds other forms of media usage by a large margin: more than half of the people we interviewed say they listen to news on the radio every day, compared to only one quarter who see a television news bulletin daily, and about one in eight who report reading a daily newspaper (see Table 8.1). As with the school system, there are tremendous cross-national discrepancies in access to the mass media. South Africa again leads the way in terms of day-to-day exposure to all three media, with over 70 percent listening to radio news, more than 60 percent seeing TV news, and 24 percent reading a newspaper. Mali lags furthest behind on daily newspaper readership (2 percent), Malawi on daily TV news viewing (6 percent), and Lesotho on tuning in to radio news (37 percent daily).

Regardless of country, urban residents consistently enjoy greater access to news media than do rural dwellers. Some 44 percent of urban residents see daily TV newscasts, compared to only 8 percent of rural dwellers; and although 23 percent of urban residents report reading a daily newspaper,

TABLE 8.1. *Exposure to News Media*

	Radio	Television	Newspapers
Use every day	54	22	13
Use less frequently	33	22	35
Never use	14	55	51
Don't know	<1	1	1

Question: "How often do you get news from radio/television/newspapers?"
Note: Figures are percentages of respondents who say they obtain news from these sources. Television usage was not asked in Ghana.

only 6 percent of rural dwellers do so.[19] Reflecting recent declines in the circulation of newspapers (which many people cannot afford) and an accompanying spread of electronic communications, residents of African cities are now almost twice as likely to obtain their daily news from television rather than from a newspaper! African governments generally find it easier to control television, for instance by monopolizing the airwaves with a single official TV station than the often unruly print press. Thus, unless urban news consumers read an independent newspaper or listen to a private FM radio station, they are likely to face a restricted diet of information.

Like educated people everywhere, the graduates of Africa's schools and universities actively seek out news reports. Indeed, there is an exceptionally strong correlation in the Afrobarometer data between formal schooling and an *index of mass media exposure* to radio, television, and newspapers.[20] Whereas only 1 percent of people with no schooling consume all three media on a daily basis, some 28 percent of postsecondary graduates do so. Conversely, only 1 percent of postsecondary graduates never receive public affairs messages via the media, compared to 23 percent of persons without education. In this section we establish that media exposure acts on public opinion much the same way as education. At the end of this chapter, we will try to unravel whether awareness of public affairs gained informally through the mass media simply reinforces, or sometimes substitutes for, formal education.

We find that, like education, regular consumption of news reports is associated with popular awareness of both democracy and adjustment.[21] And, as people gain access to news media, so they come to support democracy and reject authoritarian rule. Among the three popular forms of media, listening to the radio is most likely to increase support for democracy, which helps us understand how democratic political sentiments spread to the countryside. As might be expected, reading newspapers (which can include independent newspapers) has more impact on democratic attachments than watching TV news (which is disproportionately government controlled). Newspapers, which offer a plurality of perspectives, also have greatest impact in inducing an audience to reject authoritarian rule, especially one-party rule. Moreover, like education, media exposure reduces satisfaction with democracy and popular estimates of the extent of democracy. Stated differently, consuming news from the mass media makes people more likely to criticize the quality of government, though these effects of media exposure are not particularly strong.

Again like education, consumption of news reports is associated with higher popular support for economic reform programs and lower satisfaction with the way such programs have been implemented.[22] Individuals who rely on the news media, especially those who regularly read newspapers, are especially likely to have heard of their country's SAP. They are also more inclined than others to support privatization policies. And finally, they tend to be vociferous in their expressions of dissatisfaction with the performance of SAPs. Thus, newspaper readership is a good point of media entry for Africans who seek to educate themselves about the ramifications of market reform processes currently unfolding in their countries. But, because newspapers have the smallest audience studied here, the prospects for large increases in economic literacy via this medium would appear to be slim.

COGNITIVE ENGAGEMENT

Apart from attending to public affairs as a result of education or the media, individuals may gain such awareness by virtue of internal mental processes. They may possess an inherent *interest* in current events, regularly *discuss* hot topics with others, or feel competent to *understand* governmental procedures and policy debates. We discuss this set of psychological orientations under the rubric of "cognitive engagement."

To begin, we ask directly: "How interested are you in politics and government?" Afrobarometer respondents split into three groups: 23 percent say they are "very interested," 46 percent "somewhat interested," and 28 percent "not interested." Self-expressed interest in public affairs is highest in Uganda, where 45 percent claim high attentiveness, a figure undoubtedly swollen by the conduct of the survey during the run-up to a national referendum in 2000 on the no-party system. Public curiosity is lowest in Mali, where fully two thirds of the populace said they are *not* interested, which again confirms the extraordinary detachment of Malians from national political and economic affairs. Unexpectedly, only half as many Batswana as Basotho say they are very interested in politics and government (15 versus 31 percent). This result is the opposite of what democratic attachments would lead one to expect in these two countries. But this cross-country contrast illustrates the impact of political stability in lulling public opinion into a sense of security (as in Botswana) and of political crisis in awakening and alarming the populace (as in Lesotho).

Political and policy discussions follow similar patterns: 20 percent of Afrobarometer respondents say they "often" enter into discussions with other people, with 41 and 38 saying "sometimes" or "never" respectively. Discussions among friends and neighbors are an especially important medium of communication in Africa's predominantly oral cultures. The rumor mill – known in francophone Africa as *radio trottoir* (sidewalk radio) – along with jokes, slogans, graffiti, flyers, and audiocassettes, together constitute a veritable "alternative sphere of communication."[23] Through everyday interactions, Africans share with others their commentaries on the quality of life and attribute blame for its shortcomings. In lively wordplay, they borrow and parody official slogans, tuning them back as critiques of the prevailing order.[24] In these ways, informal communication supplements the organized mass media as a device for informing and mobilizing the public.

Reportedly, Ugandans again lead the way in discussing public affairs with others, though Tanzanians are active too. Residents of Lesotho, however, do not follow through on their interest in politics to engage one another in policy discussion. Surprisingly, South Africans are least likely to often discuss public affairs (just 11 percent in 2000, down from 17 percent in 1995), though over half do so sometimes. After a period of furious political mobilization before 1994, many South Africans are apparently now content to take a break from public debate and to let the government make major policy decisions.

Turning to the respondents' sense of internal efficacy – sometimes known as subjective competence – we find it in short supply. Overall, twice as many Africans interviewed concede that, "the way government operates sometimes seems so complicated that I cannot really understand what is going on" (64 percent) as express confidence that "I can usually understand the way that government works" (28 percent). Amazingly, there is no Afrobarometer country in which a majority (or even a plurality) of the adult population declares assurance in understanding public affairs. Even in Uganda, just 47 percent claims understanding, and in South Africa, just 12 percent do so (10 percent among blacks!). The South African results must be understood against the background of a long history of black exclusion from national civic life, as well as the complexity of the country's new semifederal governmental system and advanced and diversified industrial economy. But low levels of expressed personal political competence are worrisome flaws when it comes to fully involving all South Africans in democratic decision making and modern economic production.

Does cognitive engagement form a coherent syndrome? Yes and no. We find that, while political interest and policy discussion are strongly correlated, internal efficacy stands alone.[25] Thus, henceforth, we combine interest and discussion in an *index of cognitive engagement*, but analyze efficacy separately. These psychological considerations are distinct dimensions of public awareness, separable from education and media exposure.

Does cognitive engagement affect an individual's views of political reform? Indeed it does. The more that our interviewees are intellectually immersed in the world around them, the more likely they are to support democracy and disassociate themselves from authoritarian rule.[26] For example, Namibians who take an interest in public affairs are especially likely to support democracy, offsetting their country's otherwise relatively low levels of this attitude. By the same token, when Zimbabweans discuss politics with friends, their opposition to military rule – an imaginable possibility in a country where the civilian government has bought the allegiance of the top brass with awards of land and contracts and appointed soldiers to senior government posts – shifts from below the Afrobarometer average to above it. In short, people who engage the wider world are exposed to ideas that are unavailable to persons who are isolated; in the process, they come to embrace reform.

Similar patterns prevail for economic adjustment. Individuals who are primed to enter public arenas are stronger supporters of an orthodox policy package.[27] Among the inhabitants of Botswana, for example, those who show interest in public affairs and discuss public policy with others are very much more likely to support market pricing of consumer goods. Among South Africans, by contrast, low levels of cognitive engagement help to explain why so few people have heard of GEAR (the country's official SAP) and why – in South Africa among all countries – political interest and policy discussion have the weakest impact on support for privatization in any country.

Finally we note that, unlike education and media exposure, cognitive engagement does not make Africans more critical of ineffective performance by their governments. Instead, people who are interested in politics and who discuss policy regularly tend to express higher levels of satisfaction with democracy and SAPs.[28] Moreover, they judge the process of building democracy in their country to be more complete. Thus, while education and media exposure breed critical citizens, the pursuit of free speech prompts satisfaction. The mere ability to follow an interest in politics or to express one's policy opinions seems to convince people that they are being supplied with democracy.

POLITICAL AND ECONOMIC KNOWLEDGE

Cognitive engagement also enables the acquisition of basic political and economic knowledge. In an innovative study in Benin, Duch proposes that the availability of information to eligible voters determines not only "the ability of citizens to monitor their (elected) agents" but even "the payoffs associated with the adoption of democratic institutions."[29] The logic of the argument is that gaps in knowledge about public affairs impede citizens from forming stable opinions on policy issues, arriving at rational evaluations of the performance of leaders, and resisting the manipulations of propaganda. If so, then low levels of information about public affairs should reduce support for political and economic reforms; stated with a positive spin, we expect that better-informed citizens will be more committed reformers.

In a test for knowledge of public affairs, the Afrobarometer asked respondents to recall the names of four leaders: the vice president of the country, the minister of finance, their parliamentary or national assembly representative, and their local government councilor.[30] While other, more advanced probes are possible, we think that the identity of leaders is an appropriate starting point in Africa's personalized political and economic systems.[31] Information about elected leaders creates a point of vicarious contact between voters

Competing Explanations

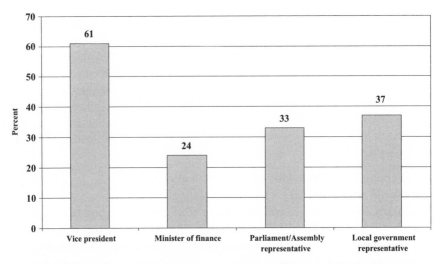

Question:*"Can you tell me the name(s) of (a) your local government councilor/mayor, (b) the Member of Parliament/ Deputy to the National Assembly for this area, (c) the Minister of Finance, and (d) the Vice President of (this country)?"* Note: Figures are percentages of respondents who can recall the names of these leaders.

FIGURE 8.4. Knowledge of Leaders

and the political system, along with a cognitive hook for grasping the game of democratic politics. Respondents' recollections of incumbents' names are tallied in Figure 8.4. In the analysis that follows, those who could name no leaders, or just one leader, are described as having "low information"; those who could name two or three leaders are described as having "medium information"; and those who could name all four leaders are described as having "high information." Tellingly, more than half of the Africans interviewed fall into the low information group, and just 6 percent of the sample evinces high levels of information.

The identity of the national vice president is common knowledge, with a majority of adults recalling the incumbent's name in every country.[32] The vice president is best known in Botswana (by 84 percent), perhaps because Seretse Ian Khama is the son of the country's founding father and serves as the king of the core Bamangwato clan. The vice president is least known in Tanzania (though still by 51 percent), maybe because the occupant of this low-key ceremonial position always comes from offshore Zanzibar and is regularly overshadowed by the president. By contrast, far fewer people in all countries know the identity of the minister of finance (24 percent), even though the budget and policy decisions of this leading economic official have substantial impacts on their lives. Whereas fewer than one in ten can name the finance minister in Mali and Lesotho, at least a third of all adults can do so in Ghana, Namibia, and Zimbabwe. Interestingly, even though South Africans are unfamiliar with the government's signature economic strategy (GEAR), some 38 percent are able to name Trevor Manuel (South Africa's first black finance minister, a prominent ANC spokesman on economic affairs, and one of GEAR's main architects). Can this be interpreted to mean that Africans attend more to personalities than policies? Undoubtedly they do, but not for this reason. In all countries – especially Ghana and Nigeria, and including South Africa – knowledge of the identity of the finance minister is a good predictor of an individual's awareness of the country's SAP.[33]

People display intermediate levels of knowledge about elected officials who are closer to home. On average, only about one in three can name their own member of parliament (MP) or deputy to the national assembly, a proportion similar to the United States.[34] But we discover considerable cross-country variation on this item: whereas a startling 85 percent can give a correct answer in Malawi, fewer than 1 percent can do so in Lesotho.[35] We attribute this chasm mainly to high levels of mass mobilization by competing political parties in the various regions of Malawi as compared to the circulation of elite factions across fluid party boundaries in Lesotho.

Slightly more respondents (almost four in ten) can name the person who represents them in a local, district, or town council. Knowledge of elected local government leaders is impressively diffuse in several countries: in Botswana, Ghana, Mali, and Zimbabwe, well over half of all respondents can name their local councilor or mayor, a minimal precondition for holding such officials accountable and a record that Westerners would find hard to emulate. And there is less cross-national variation in knowledge of local than national leaders. Note, however, that South Africans now trail, with less than 1 percent in 2000 being able to name their local government representative. In the rural areas of South Africa, struggles for power between traditional leaders and newly elected councilors have caused genuine popular confusion about the limits and legitimacy of different local authorities.[36] And in South Africa's urban townships, where local councils were long resisted as a hated instrument of political control – and where councils still encounter difficulty in collecting property rates and service fees – people have yet to embrace local government leaders as their own.

Generally speaking, one would expect that public awareness would be an asset to reform but that public ignorance would constitute a serious obstacle. By way of confirmation, we find that an *index of political knowledge* based on the ability of individuals to name leaders is positively related to support for democracy.[37] This finding is robust within every Afrobarometer country. In addition, as Figure 8.5 shows, the acquisition of information about political leaders also intensifies an individual's rejection of authoritarianism.[38] This relationship holds in a clear stepwise pattern for every form of nondemocratic rule: people with high information are consistently more opposed to every authoritarian alternative – and at very high levels – than people with medium information; and, in turn, people with medium information are more strongly opposed to returning to all old political regimes than persons with

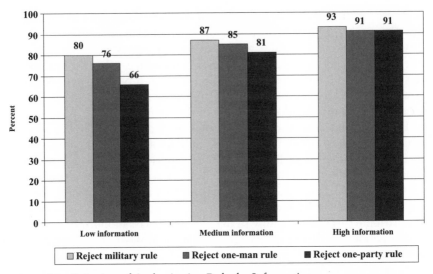

FIGURE 8.5. Rejection of Authoritarian Rule, by Information

low information. The acquisition of information is most effective at undermining support for one-party rule, as illustrated by a twenty-five-point difference between those with low and high levels. We think that this relationship is thoroughly recursive: the more vigilant one is about the identity of elected representatives, the more one strongly opposes antidemocratic abuses, and vice versa.

Knowledge is also a factor, both across and within countries, in marshalling support for economic reform.[39] Africans with high information are nearly three times as likely as those with low information to back a full adjustment package.[40] And the economically attentive, defined as those who can recall the identity of the minister of finance, are especially likely to support reforms, most notably privatization. But, because the minister of finance is not well known by most people, and because very few Africans fall into the high information category, the impact of economic knowledge, while strong, remains marginal. Rather, the predominance of low-information actors in our survey populations helps to explain why the constituency for economic reform in African countries is really rather small.

THE EYE OF THE BEHOLDER

This chapter now turns from the quantity to the quality of the prevailing popular wisdom. To do so, we reintroduce observations made earlier about how democracy and adjustment are viewed through African eyes. Chapter 3 established that, while Africans define democracy as a set of political procedures, they also find that social and economic equality are essential attributes of a good society. And Chapter 4 showed that, while the purposes of adjustment are poorly understood, slightly more respondents think that economic reforms aim at reviving the macro economy than at lifting their own living standards. We now explore whether, ultimately, such popular expectations have any bearing on the acceptability of reforms. In short, do attitudes to reform reside partly in the eye of the beholder?

We start with an individual's awareness of democracy in the sense that he or she can attach a meaning to this key concept. Recall from Chapter 3 that an individual's awareness of democracy was a good predictor of his or her support for democracy. Only a small minority said they supported something called democracy without knowing what it meant. We now confirm that those Africans who profess to know nothing about democracy are predominantly rural people with limited education and scant exposure to media. Cognitively disengaged, they possess low levels of information.[41] The same applies to being conscious of the existence of one's country's SAP, with the proviso that those who say they have never heard about the adjustment program are common in urban areas too.[42] In short, individuals who lack awareness about public affairs are also very likely to be oblivious to the meaning of democracy and the purposes of adjustment.

Let us focus on the majority who say they understand what democracy means. Do their mental images of the qualities of democracy affect their orientations to various political regimes? In other words, we want to know which group of beholders is more strongly committed to change. Is it primarily the *proceduralists*, who see democracy in political terms, that is, as a matter of rights and elections? Or is commitment to change stronger among *substantivists*, who see democracy as manifest in a just society and economy?

We first briefly identify the kinds of people who comprise these categories. Proceduralists are drawn disproportionally from among elites: they tend to be urban dwellers with higher levels of education; moreover, they are both well informed and cognitively engaged with the world around them. Substantivists are distributed throughout the general population: they live in both urban and rural areas and have attained less education;[43] and, while they enjoy some exposure to the news media and know their leaders, they tend to hold back from engagement in public life. Importantly, though, substantivists are not as isolated as people who cannot attribute *any* meaning to democracy. These profiles strongly suggest that African elites and masses tend to conceive of democracy distinctively, with the latter being more prone to blur the line between political and economic regimes.

We now present a key finding: democratic commitments increase if citizens conceive of regime change in procedural terms. For example, 76 percent of those who think that multiparty competition is "essential" to a democratic society also name it as the best form of government; the comparable figure is 59 percent for those who see it as unimportant. And support for democracy

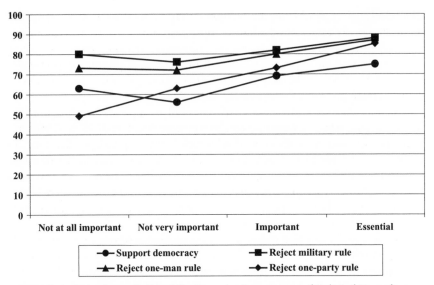

FIGURE 8.6. Attitudes to Political Regimes, by Importance of Political Procedures

is very low among those who conceive democracy as meaning "social and economic hardship" (53 percent). Moreover, persons who think of democracy as a minimal regime of civil liberties are more likely to express satisfaction than those who hope that democracy will foster maximum gains like equality and justice (70 versus 61 percent). We conclude that people who have modest procedural expectations – namely that democracy will enable them to freely choose their own leaders (and not much more!) – are likely to become reliably committed to new multiparty regimes. By contrast, persons who believe that democracy will transform the socioeconomic order – in which everyone will be provided with jobs, incomes, and safety – are setting themselves up for disillusionment. South Africans, as hardcore substantivists, are particularly susceptible to this fate.

The influence of political and procedural thinking is confirmed visually in Figure 8.6. Respondents were divided into groups depending on the importance they attach to procedural qualities like free speech, regular elections, multiparty competition, and majority rule. The ascending lines in the chart indicate that, as individuals come to value such guarantees, the more likely they are to both support democracy and reject all authoritarian alternatives, especially one-party rule.[44] For example, well over eight out of ten strong proceduralists (that is, those who find political procedures "essential" to democracy) disavow all three forms of authoritarianism. By contrast, those who think that rights protection and competitive elections are "not at all important" continue to flirt with authoritarian alternatives. Strikingly, only a minority (49 percent) of these nonproceduralists actually opposes the one-party state. If nothing else, these findings constitute evidence that struggles to democratize civilian political regimes in Africa hinge in important part on disputes over a rule of law.

Does the eye of the beholder also matter for economic reform? Is the unpopularity of adjustment shaped by mass ignorance of SAPs and popular misunderstandings of adjustment's purposes? Let us first establish that there is a positive relationship between a basic awareness of SAP – in the sense of having heard about this program in one's own country – and support for economic reform.[45] Furthermore, one might expect that people with a wide worldview who think that SAPs aim at restoring *macroeconomic* growth would be more inclined to back reform policies. Conversely, one might predict that individuals who take a narrower, egocentric, *microeconomic* view, expecting from SAPs immediate improvements in their own and others' informal sector incomes, would be more easily alienated from the reform process. In practice, however, we find no noteworthy differences.[46] If anything, the people who see economic reform programs simply as a delivery mechanism for foreign aid are SAP's strongest supporters and most satisfied customers, a viewpoint that helps us understand the relatively high level of approval of these programs in Mali.

COGNITIVE MODELS

Are there common threads to the various aspects of cognitive awareness discussed in this chapter? We can point to several mutually reinforcing effects: for example, education sparks a person's sense of internal efficacy; and exposure to mass media prompts policy discussion. But which aspects of cognition are determinative? This last section weighs their relative influences in a sequence of multivariate models. Following precedents from previous chapters, we separately enter all independent variables into a multivariate model (see Table 8.2).

All cognitive considerations, even when mutually controlled, continue to contribute significantly to the development of democratic commitments. But awareness of democracy and knowledge of leaders have greater impact on democratic commitments than formal education (which is significant but weak) and exposure to media (the impact of which is both weak and negative). Indeed, perhaps unexpectedly, education and media tend to reinforce rather than substitute for each other. In other words, educated people enjoy extensive exposure to news media but uneducated people are rarely able to use the media to overcome their lack of schooling.

Importantly, however, basic knowledge about democracy, including understandings of its content and limitations, is not the private preserve of educated elites. To a degree, ordinary Africans can compensate for low levels of formal education by learning, probably from discussions among themselves rather than via the radio, about the virtues of a set of procedures like free speech and open elections that point to a regime called "democracy." To the

TABLE 8.2. *The Effects of Cognitive Awareness on Attitudes to Reform*

	Commitment to Democracy	Perceived Extent of Democracy	Support for Economic Reform	Satisfaction with Adjustment Program
Constant	.311***	2.073***	1.264***	3.225***
Education	.050***	−.062***	.054***	−.103***
Media exposure	−.020*	−.004	.136***	.023
Cognitive engagement	.100***	.084***	.053***	.029**
Internal efficacy	.013*	.102***	.049***	.098***
Knowledge of leaders	.134***	.010	.032***	−.030*
Awareness of democracy	.135***	.065***	.065***	.067***
Awareness of SAP	.097***	−.111***	.045***	−.179***
Political understanding	.185***	.034***	−.017	−.106***
Substantive understanding	.074***	−.021*	−.002	−.006
Standard error of estimate	.502	1.501	1.047	1.662
Adjusted r squared	.179	.034	.068	.075

Note: Unless otherwise indicated, entries are standardized regression coefficients (beta).
N = 21,531
***$p = <.001$
**$p = <.01$
*$p = <.05$

extent that, in the process of discourse and deliberation, they also gain information about the identities of political representatives, and thus associate known faces with elected offices, they begin to put their faith in democratic institutions.

Yet individual cognition explains very little about the perceived extent of democracy (Table 8.2, Column 2). Internal efficacy is the only element to make much of a positive contribution. Extrapolating from a personal sense of competence in public affairs perhaps Africans feel that, if they can understand the way government works, then democracy must surely be under construction. Conversely, there is a striking negative relationship between awareness of SAPs and perceptions that democracy is being built. In other words, people who are economically illiterate are unable to offer a critical political judgment; stuck in the dark about adjustment, they blindly accept that democracy is being built without asking too many hard questions.

Cognitive awareness is somewhat more important in forming attitudes about economic reform. In this instance (Table 8.2, Column 3) support for economic reform is driven by media exposure. Africans who regularly attend to media news outlets (especially newspapers) have learned about the existence of their government's macroeconomic recovery program and have decided to hitch themselves to its bandwagon. At minimum, this result should alert policy practitioners to the effectiveness of mass (especially print) media in raising economic literacy and inducing popular demand for market-based reforms, both of which currently languish at low levels. In these tasks, formal education also helps to a degree.

Finally, we note that awareness of SAPs is the major cognitive factor affecting satisfaction with economic reform. But, again, the relationship is strongly negative (Table 8.2, Column 4). The more that Africans actually know about SAPs the less likely they are to think they are being implemented! This finding is reinforced by the effect of education, which also runs in a negative direction. Our interpretation is that education sharpens techniques of critical thinking, enabling people to understand that, in most African countries, adjustment has failed to live up to its promise of restoring economic growth. In this instance, mass media do not impart enough of the skill or information necessary for uneducated people to arrive at this reasoned conclusion.

Theorists assert that democracy and markets work best when citizens have relatively equal amounts of information.[47] We have shown that, in some African countries, a few items of basic information – like the identity of certain leaders – are quite broadly distributed. This sort of knowledge helps to buttress efforts at reform. But pockets of cognitive capability in African societies cannot offset the overall impression that many in the populace are handicapped by limited awareness of public affairs. A majority of Africans lack one or more key cognitive attributes – whether secondary education, daily contact with media outlets, a sense of political efficacy, or understanding of the content of adjustment policies – that are important in shaping reform constituencies. Instead, African societies are divided between a small elite who are aware of public affairs and much larger pluralities that are barely conscious of such niceties.

9

Performance Evaluations

Regardless of whether or not Africans are well informed, they pass judgments on public affairs. They evaluate the suitability of prevailing regimes to their own personal or national circumstances. Against benchmarks of great expectations – often born in the enthusiasm of regime transition – people offer appraisals of the performance of policies and governments. The state of the beleaguered nation is a topic of constant discussion in public places, from minibuses to marketplaces, and from workstations to watering holes. Animated debates about institutional performance engage all manner of people, whether in the opinion pages of daily newspapers or in the *palaver* shelters of village elders. In irreverent style, jokesters wickedly mock any less-than-satisfactory performance by states and markets.

At the core of popular concerns lies what South Africans refer to as the "delivery" of development.[1] People want proof that democratization and market reform beget tangible benefits whose consumption improves the quality of daily life. In the public imagination, political representation involves "more than talking . . . leaders must act."[2] Individuals judge the performance of officials – as well as the governments, regimes, and institutions for which they stand, and the economies which they manage – by practical tests of personal and collective self-interest. As such, performance evaluations are instrumental and utilitarian. Even if faced with incomplete information, people nonetheless weigh perceived costs and benefits. And, because evaluations occur under conditions of regime transition, performance is often judged relatively by means of before-and-after comparisons between the present and the past.

Long excluded from the study of political economy in Africa, theories of rational choice have now made a mark. Since Robert Bates first demonstrated that peasants are motivated to migrate out of rural areas by opportunities to earn income in towns, commentators have been less inclined to interpret behavior in terms of cultural mores rather than economic logic.[3] A rational calculus has since been profitably applied in studies of land rights in colonial Ghana and wildlife resources in Zambia, Zimbabwe, and Kenya.[4] In this chapter, we test the applicability of a soft version of rationality – by which ordinary people make approximate, qualitative judgments about political as well as economic conditions – to the analysis of public opinion in Afrobarometer countries. We assume that Africans have well-defined personal goals, can weigh the potential impacts of alternate courses of action, and will choose strategies that lead to preferred outcomes. In this way, Africans estimate whether democratic and market institutions are living up to expectations.

As outlined earlier, "delivery" may refer to distinct "baskets" of development goods – both economic and political. Moreover, Africans place special emphasis on distributive goals and egalitarian outcomes (see Chapter 2). We also try to discern the objects of credit or blame for institutional performance. At issue here is whether ordinary folk attribute responsibility for institutional performance to individual elected representatives, to the incumbent government of the day, or to regimes of democracy and structural adjustment. As sovereign citizens and consumers, do they routinely draw distinctions between individual providers and whole systems? Or, like clients in patrimonial networks, do they blur these borders by judging institutional performance on the basis of their feelings about personal patrons? This enigma has profound implications for the consolidation of liberal regimes because it speaks to whether Africans are able to replace nonperforming suppliers without, at the same time, overturning the institutional rules of democracy or markets.

EVALUATING THE ECONOMY

As things fall apart, daily survival has become increasingly difficult. Over the years, many African families have been forced to drastically reduce consumption of essential commodities like meat, fish, beans, sugar, cooking oil, soap, and fuel. The poorest people cannot afford to buy staple grains (especially when marketed in large sacks); instead they spend each day trying to scrape together just enough money to buy a small quantity sufficient for an evening meal (say a one liter scoop from a market stand). As a last resort, people simply eat fewer meals each day, especially during lean seasons. In a reversal of past practices, parents are finding ways to limit the number of children they produce because large families are proving too expensive to feed, clothe, and educate. And there is a widespread loss of confidence in national currencies, the purchasing power of which is locked in a seemingly endless downward spiral.[5]

Reflecting economic insecurity, Africans are generally unhappy about material life. In the period 1999 to 2001, fewer than one in three Afrobarometer respondents (28 percent) expressed any degree of satisfaction with the current state of their national economy.[6] In addition, people feel that "things ain't what they used to be": more of them thought that economic conditions

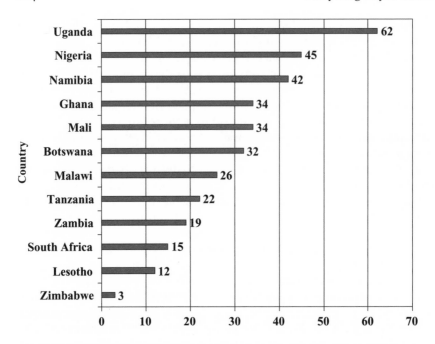

Question: "How satisfied are you with the condition of the (national) economy today?"
Note: Figures are percentages "fairly" or "very" satisfied with the national economy circa 2000.

FIGURE 9.1. Satisfaction with the National Economy

had worsened over the previous year than saw improvements (46 percent versus 31 percent).[7] This grim picture brightens a little when people begin to think about the future: slightly more allowed that economic conditions would advance rather than decline in the year ahead (37 percent versus 30 percent).[8] Future expectations outpace past evaluations in most countries. But in certain places – notably Mali and Nigeria – hopes for the economic future run well ahead of past experiences.[9]

At the time of the surveys, Uganda was the main exception to the continent's mood of economic malaise (see Figure 9.1). Well over half of all adult Ugandans were satisfied in 2000 and a similar proportion judged that economic conditions improved during the year prior to the survey. By contrast, only a tiny minority of Zimbabweans was satisfied with the performance of their economy, which shrank rapidly during the previous year. Africans thus seem to derive their current and anticipated satisfaction with the economy in good part on the basis of knowledge about its performance in the immediate past.[10] A process of experiential learning can induce a downward spiral in mass opinion, however, since a recent history of economic stagnation or contraction tends to depress popular evaluations about present conditions and reduce optimism about the future.

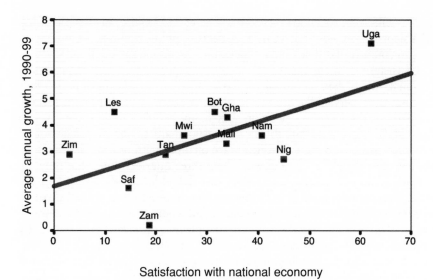

FIGURE 9.2. Satisfaction with Economic Conditions, by Economic Growth

Figure 9.2 shows a strong, positive association between the growth rate of a country's gross domestic product in the 1990s and the aggregate level of expressed popular satisfaction with the national economy circa 2000.[11] Ugandans enjoyed the fastest growing economy in our sample of countries and also expressed the highest overall economic satisfaction. By the same token, subpar national economic growth rates in the 1990s helped to reduce economic contentment among Zambians and South Africans in 2000.[12] The close correspondence between objective performance and subjective perceptions suggests that the Africans we interviewed have enough basic awareness of macroeconomic trends to arrive at reasonably well-informed evaluations.

Because views of the past strongly influence current and prospective perceptions, we can summarize each person's evaluations with a composite *index of the performance of the economy*.[13] We use this index, which also includes perceptions of relative deprivation, in analyses that follow at the end of this chapter.

In arriving at economic evaluations, we assume that people compare themselves to others. To measure whether individual Africans harbor a sense of relative deprivation we ask: "would you say that your own economic conditions are worse, the same as, or better than other Batswana/Ghanaians/Basotho?" (the relevant nationality was inserted for each country). To capture any economic discrimination felt by various subnational groups, we asked: "are (your identity group's) economic conditions worse, the same as, or better than other groups in this country?" Given that Africans purportedly prefer egalitarian social arrangements, one would expect that a sense of relative deprivation would drive other aspects of public opinion. At minimum, we can confirm that it strongly undermines economic satisfaction.[14]

Consistent with emergent individualism, deprivation is experienced on a personal, rather than a communal, basis. Whereas 45 percent of individuals feel that they, personally, are worse off than others, just 33 percent feel the same about their group's position, but many people situate themselves in the middle, with about one third of all respondents saying that their household and group economic conditions are on a par with others. Deprivations are felt most widely in Zimbabwe, where three quarters think that they are personally disadvantaged, and where one half thinks their group lags behind. These results portray a Zimbabwean population that is shell shocked by rapid contractions in living standards and where gross economic disparities have opened up between ordinary people and privileged party elites. By contrast, very few Nigerians – about one in ten – feel either kind of deprivation. In this regard, the self-confidence and group chauvinism that we noted earlier among Nigerians (see Chapters 7 and 8) seem to immunize them, realistically or not, from feeling less well off than others.

As expected, a sense of relative deprivation rises with poverty and declines with wealth.[15] Surprisingly, however, ethnic minorities are not generally likely to feel the sting of economic discrimination, perhaps because they actually enjoy material advantages in many countries. Compare Nigeria to Malawi. Minority groups like Ijaw speakers in the Niger Delta, who have been stripped of their area's oil wealth, understandably tend to feel relatively deprived; by contrast, in southern Malawi, speakers of Yao, a minority group with ethnic ties to incumbent President Bakili Muluzi, say they feel relatively better off. Nor do people who define their group identities in tribal, linguistic, or regional terms feel especially maltreated. Instead, a sense of economic abandonment is most prevalent among those who adopt racial or class identities: fully half of those who see themselves through these lenses think that their group is worse off than others. Thus, when it comes to the formation of popular perceptions of economic discrimination, we find race and class to be more fundamental than ethnicity.

But puzzles arise about relative deprivation in South Africa, the African country in which race and class are most closely intertwined. Even though South Africans live in one of the most unequal societies in the world, fully one third say they are doing "about the same as others," the highest proportion in the Southern Africa region.[16] And almost half of South Africans think that the economic condition of their self-defined identity group is holding steady with other groups.[17] Against all intuition, however, wealthy South Africans express a deeper sense of deprivation than objectively poor groups. Fully 61 percent of whites and Indians in South Africa feel that their group suffers from inferior economic conditions, in contrast to just 36 percent of blacks and Coloureds. This startling inversion suggests that apartheid continues to segregate popular consciousness. Different groups of South Africans are so socially isolated from one another that they apparently calculate their relative deprivation largely with reference to their *own* group. In short, whites compare themselves to other whites, blacks with other blacks.[18] In addition, poor whites may be feeling, under majority rule, that the shoe of discrimination is now uncomfortably on the other foot.

At the same time, however, the proportion of South Africans, especially blacks, who feel a sense of relative deprivation has increased sharply since 1997.[19] One possible explanation is that the government's economic reform package and the accelerated development of a black middle class have exacerbated intraracial inequalities.[20] In absolute terms, there are now more blacks than whites in the top two categories in the country's official Living Standards Measure.[21] And, by most estimates, the gap between poor and wealthy blacks is now wider than between the two main race groups as a whole. Accordingly, the increased visibility of income inequalities among blacks may well have begun to generate a sense of frustration among those left behind.

We can now pose three queries critical to this study. First, does economic dissatisfaction undermine support for policies of structural adjustment? A simple correlation test finds no significant impact.[22] The same small proportion of the adult population (about 9 percent) supports a full package of adjustment reforms *regardless* of whether they are extremely satisfied or extremely dissatisfied with overall (that is, past, present, and future) economic conditions. This interesting finding can be interpreted in one of two ways. Either African supporters of economic reform correctly recognize that, under an adjustment regime, economic conditions often worsen before they get better; accordingly, they are willing to wait patiently for eventual economic recovery. Or, alternatively, most Africans are ideologically opposed to market reforms and will stick to their guns even in the face of evidence that reforms lead to improvements in economic conditions. Given what we have discovered about the pragmatism of our respondents, their willingness to experiment with price reforms, and their economic patience, we tend to favor the former, wait-and-see interpretation.[23]

Second, are the outcomes of adjustment unpopular because of perceived effects on economic conditions? In this instance, bivariate estimates point to a strong and positive relationship between satisfaction with the condition of the macro economy and contentment with SAP performance.[24] This relationship holds across the board in all nine countries for which data are available. Ghanaians are most likely to appraise SAP outcomes in terms of macroeconomic performance, but the same powerful current also runs through public opinion in other parts of the continent.[25] Economic performance elevates SAP satisfaction for some Africans (like Malians, Tanzanians, and Ugandans) but pulls it down for others (like Nigerians, South Africans, and Zimbabweans). These results extend and generalize the case histories presented in the introduction to this book and strongly suggest that Africans everywhere – not only in Mali and Nigeria – make rational calculations about the performance of economic reform by judging whether the program has delivered improved economic conditions.

Third, and most importantly, does economic dissatisfaction dampen demand for democracy? At first sight, two-way tests reveal contradictory results. On one hand, our index of macroeconomic evaluations is positively related to support for democracy.[26] In eleven out of twelve Afrobarometer countries, but especially in South Africa, support for democracy rests upon mass satisfaction with a range of past, present, and future economic conditions.[27] On the other hand, economic satisfaction is negatively related to preferences for authoritarian alternatives, particularly one-man rule.[28] In ten out of twelve Afrobarometer countries, but demonstrably so in Zimbabwe, citizens who are economically distressed are strong opponents of personal dictatorship.[29]

We therefore arrive at a higher-order generalization. Economic dissatisfaction undermines regime support under democracy, but generates demand for democratization under dictatorship. In Africa's hybrid political regimes – which mix democratic and authoritarian features – the overall relationship between popular economic evaluations and mass democratic commitments is therefore rather weak.[30]

Nevertheless, if people's concerns about economic conditions arise from perceptions of unequal distribution, then democracy remains at risk. Relative deprivation – especially between individuals, but also among groups – is more strongly correlated to democratic commitments than mere economic dissatisfaction.[31] Even in South Africa, where people estimate inequalities primarily on the basis of the perceived prospects of their own racial groups, those who feel relatively deprived are quickly turned off to democracy. Indeed, growing economic inequalities among blacks in South Africa are especially corrosive to popular support for democracy there, though such perceptions undermine democratic support also in Mali, Malawi, and Zambia.[32] As this chapter proceeds, we will continue to explore the impacts of perceived economic inequalities on the support base for various reforms.

THE CORRUPTION OF THE STATE?

How do Africans regard the state? Do they trust its institutions? Do they consider its officials corrupt?

Reflecting the mood of the literature, Englebert paints a bleak picture of the performance of African states. Given imported origins, they are:

...not the endogenous creations of local history. They lack legitimacy....By substituting patron-client links for its lack of moral foundations...the modern state is reduced to a merely instrumental role...Bureaucracies turn into ghostly institutions. Eventually the rule of law vacillates, as does the trust of citizens in their institutions. As respect for institutions diminishes, corruption spreads...(and) the very logic of the system makes it resistant to reform.[33]

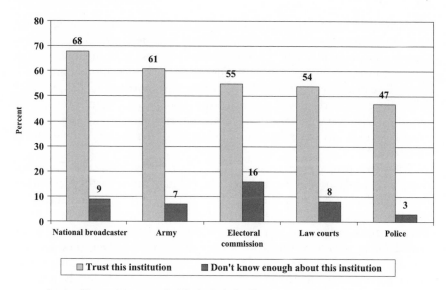

Question: "How much do you trust the following institutions?"
Notes: In Southern Africa the phrase "to do what is right" was added to the question.
Figures are percentages who say they trust these institutions "somewhat" or "a lot."
Figures do not add up to one hundred because distrust is not shown.

FIGURE 9.3. Trust in State Institutions

Our surveys reveal that ordinary people hold somewhat less gloomy views of African states. We asked whether respondents "trust" a range of public institutions "to do what is right." The aggregate responses for five institutions are shown in Figure 9.3. More than half the respondents made positive assessments of four institutions, with a trustful average of 57 percent for all five.[34] This global figure matches the levels of confidence expressed by West Europeans toward a similar array of political institutions, which averaged 59 percent in 1980–81 and 53 percent in 1990–91.[35] In the absence of data over time, we do not know whether institutional trust is in long-term decline in Africa as it has been for several decades in the OECD countries.[36] But these figures suggest that Africans are no more or less skeptical of the performance of state institutions than are the residents of the advanced industrial democracies. But, given that the institutions in question often perform abysmally in Africa, one is forced to consider whether Africans are perhaps *too* trusting, or whether they lack the experience or information necessary to arrive at more critical judgments.

On average, Africans extend most trust to national broadcasting services, with two thirds of the population across twelve countries indicating that they find official news pronouncements reliable. This finding comes as a surprise to opposition elites in capital cities, who condemn national broadcasters for their lack of editorial independence.[37] Unquestioning trust in official media is extremely high in Mali, where fully 88 percent place faith in L'Office de Radiodiffusion et Television du Mali (ORTM), though some respondents may have confused this national provider with now ubiquitous private or community FM stations. Trust is lowest in Zimbabwe where, in 1999, just 40 percent placed confidence in the information aired by the Zimbabwe Broadcasting Corporation (ZBC), a proportion that has probably fallen since the government converted the ZBC into a blatant propaganda mouthpiece. Given wide variation across countries, state broadcasters attract more trust than any other institution in just six of the twelve Afrobarometer countries.[38]

Elsewhere, people place greatest trust in the national army, as in Tanzania, Botswana, Malawi, and Zimbabwe. The military forces of these countries have been deployed mainly in external conflicts, as with Tanzania's incursion into Uganda in the late 1970s and the Zimbabwe army's involvement from 1998 to 2002 in the civil war in the Democratic Republic Congo.[39] If the armed forces have intervened in politics at home, however, they are less warmly embraced. If, for example, soldiers have illegally seized state power under previous regimes, as in Nigeria, or became covertly involved in the repression of domestic dissent, as in South Africa, popular trust in the army is much lower today (37 and 44 percent respectively). We therefore assume that popular trust in the army, where it is expressed, signifies acceptance of the performance of this institution only in its constitutionally defined role as the protector of the national territory against foreign threats. We do not interpret high average levels of trust in the armed forces to mean that Africans are ready to abandon civilian control of the military and to welcome soldiers as governors (see Chapter 3).

In arriving at reasoned judgments about other state institutions, Africans appear to rely on factual information. For instance, trust in the electoral commission is high in countries where successive elections have been increasingly well administered (for example, 63 percent in Ghana) but plummets in countries where elections have been botched (32 percent trust in Lesotho) or rigged (26 percent in Zimbabwe). The importance of institutional performance is reinforced by a comparison over time in Uganda: prior to that country's 2000 referendum, the Electoral Commission of Uganda was broadly trusted (by three quarters of the adult population); after the 2001 presidential elections, which were marred by intimidation and violence, and accusations of corruption against the commission, trust dropped precipitously (to just one quarter). Note, however, that of all institutions surveyed, Africans are least familiar with the electoral commission, whose prominence – if not its provenance – dates to the recent multiparty era. Fully one in seven of our survey respondents had not heard enough about their country's electoral commission to feel comfortable in forming an opinion about its probity.

Since Africans are able to offer reasonably reliable estimates of the performance of state institutions, it is troubling to learn about the low public esteem in which they hold the agencies of the law. Barely half think that the national court system can be trusted and, in four out of twelve countries, more people express distrust than trust.[40] In no country are the courts the most trusted institution, though they rank second in Zambia and Uganda, where they have occasionally challenged incumbent governments. Instead, a majority of South Africans expresses distrust in the court system, no doubt because blacks consider the judicial bench and the legal profession to be untransformed holdovers from the previous apartheid regime. Malians are also leery of involvements with the formal legal system, here because they regard it as an arcane and culturally inappropriate vestige of French colonial rule. To back up this result, we note that 28 percent of Malians have never personally encountered a judge or a lawyer, 17 percent do not know enough about their functions to form an opinion, and that more than half of the remainder are unsatisfied with their dealings with these representatives of the legal system.

Most importantly, Africans express wariness of the police. On average, a bare majority actually distrusts them (50 percent). We presume this assessment to be reliable since police officers, as uniformed agents in front-line contact with the populace, are well-known representatives of the state.[41] The police force is least trusted in Nigeria (29 percent) and South Africa (35 percent), both countries where law and order is a central rather than local responsibility, and where an overstretched national police force is widely regarded as ineffective, corrupt, and even violent. Nigerians are sick and tired of being stopped at roadblocks set up by the federal Nigeria Police Force (NPF) or accosted on the street by wayward NPF officers who extort money for real or imagined offenses.[42] And South Africans lack confidence that the South African Police Service (SAPS) is capable of containing the country's wave of violent crime, either by apprehending wrongdoers or ensuring that they are convicted by the criminal justice system.[43] Among all institutions studied, the police force attracts the least trust in seven out of the twelve Afrobarometer countries, where absolute majorities of the adult population give them a vote of no confidence.

These findings can be summarized in a single *index of trust in state institutions* that represents all five institutions.[44] Individuals who trust one public body are also likely to trust others – and vice versa. Thus, the state, which is often construed in the political theory literature as an overly abstract construct, has a tangible existence in the African collective imagination. Moreover, the state's performance can be observed through the lens of public opinion.

Where does trust in the state come from? We can dispel the notion that it arises from structures of gender or age since older women place no more confidence in state institutions than younger men. But rural dwellers are twice as likely as urban residents to say they have faith in the full range of state institutions.[45] And, as with interpersonal trust, education and media exposure reduce institutional trust.[46] Thus, unschooled peasant populations tend to display above-average levels of confidence in public institutions. But this common form of trust is essentially blind, since it is rarely based on first-hand knowledge of the day-to-day performance of the agencies of the state. Because rural folk possess inadequate amounts of information about how well its institutions actually work, they sometimes gullibly grant a distant state the benefit of the doubt, a predilection most common among Tanzania's uncritical citizens. By contrast, educated town dwellers – especially those who have attained secondary education or more – are both better informed and less trustful of the state, as evidenced by the opinions of Zimbabwe's so-phisticated urbanites. Because educated urban elites interact more regularly with public officials and understand what state agencies are supposed to do, they are better placed to reliably assess institutional performance.

The best overall predictor of institutional trust is whether people think that state officials are corrupt. Among the Africans we interviewed, trust in the state is strongly – and, as expected, negatively – associated with an *index of perceived official corruption*.[47] In other words, the greater the perceived frequency of official corruption, the more likely are respondents to say that they distrust state institutions. As Figure 9.4 illustrates, this individual-level relationship holds also when scores for corruption and trust are summed at the country level.[48] Tanzania is now revealed as an anomaly: even though people in this country perceive considerable official corruption, they nonetheless

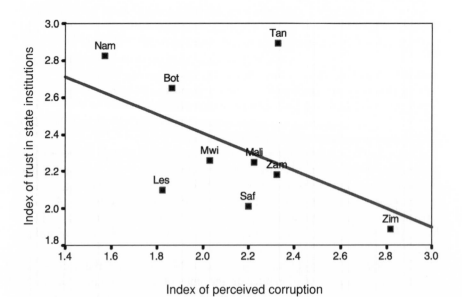

FIGURE 9.4. Trust in State Institutions, by Perceived Corruption

express extremely high levels of institutional trust. While Tanzanians resemble other Africans in their perceptions of corruption, they register sentiments of institutional trust that are twenty percentage points above the Afrobarometer mean. Everywhere else, the more normal condition is that popular perceptions of official corruption undermine trust in the state.[49]

This important general finding lends credence to the claim that "corruption can undermine political legitimacy...by alienating the citizenry from its political leadership and making effective government more difficult."[50] Africans clearly base their judgments about the trustworthiness of state institutions in good part on whether they expect to receive honest treatment from public officials. There is a direct connection between perceptions of corruption in the police, courts, and electoral commission and the relatively low levels of popular trust enjoyed by these institutions.[51] In Mali, for example, perceptions of corruption alone account for about one fifth of the variance in popular trust in judges and police officers.[52]

Corruption is not endemic, however, to all African states. Generally speaking, people perceive the largest and most entrenched problem in West Africa, where 85 percent of Ghanaians and 73 percent of Nigerians agree that, "bribery is common among public officials." Some Southern Africans, however, recognize that they live within islands of relative rectitude: only 25 percent of Namibians and 28 percent of Basotho think that, "most (or)...almost all...government officials...take money or gifts from the people and use these for themselves." A clean bill of health may reflect recent initiatives by the government of Namibia to establish an independent anticorruption unit and the government of Lesotho to prosecute foreign companies that offered bribes to win contracts on the Lesotho Highlands Water Project.[53] It is nonetheless true that, on average, about half of our survey respondents think that all or most government officials are corrupt (52 percent). But it is important to distinguish whether the informants are Nigerians or Namibians, since these populations have widely opposed views on the extent of corruption in their respective countries.

Citizens also draw distinctions about corruption between various branches and levels of government. Asked to choose among officials, people generally regard elected representatives as having a better reputation for honesty than civil servants, though differences are small, as well as being inconsistent across countries.[54] In Lesotho, for instance, more people see malfeasance among civil servants than among local government leaders (30 percent versus 11 percent). But the police are almost everywhere ranked as the most corrupt public officials, followed by customs agents and judges.[55] These variations should be understood partly in terms of the scale of offenses. Whereas people see local government leaders dealing – if at all – in petty corruption, they guess that national officeholders secretly enjoy all manner of opportunity for larceny on a grand scale.

Yet perceptions of corruption are only tenuously linked to actual experience. Remarkably, relatively few people state that they have ever had to offer a bribe, a tip, a gift, or a favor in return for a public good or service to which they were entitled. On an undergoverned continent where contact with officials is low, the opportunities for offering a bribe may actually be few and far between.[56] And since all parties to petty corruption understand what is expected and exchanges of favors are conducted wordlessly as a matter of course, corruption may not always be recognized as such. Finally, citizens surely interpret corruption, a catch-all term, to include not only open-side payments, but also subtle sins like nepotism or embezzlement.

Tanzanians are more likely to report making illegal payments (40 percent) than are Nigerians and Malians (28 and 25 percent respectively). In response to a more narrowly framed question, however, only 5 percent of Southern Africans report offering bribes in return for a job, a house or a plot, or an electricity or water connection. In this region, the highest incidence of victimization occurs in Zimbabwe, where 12 percent report direct personal experience with these petty forms of corruption.

Thus, Africans routinely imagine a more ubiquitous official graft than they ever encounter in practice. At the low end (in Tanzania), perceptions of government corruption are almost twice as high as actual experience; at the other extreme (in Botswana), perceptions are fully forty times higher! These discrepancies suggest that the general public derives its estimates of overall corruption from assumptions about the prevalence of vice among top political and economic elites. Because the misdeeds of leaders are hidden from public view, people extrapolate their estimates of such corruption from information gleaned from press reports about a small number of high-profile incidents. As evidence, the consumption of all types of news media – notably newspapers, and especially in combination with TV and radio – increases the extent to which people perceive corruption.[57] The media have the clearest such impact in agrarian societies – like Mali, Tanzania, and Uganda – where urban news consumers have access to investigative journalism but rural dwellers mostly do not.[58]

Where reliable information is not available, people thrive on unsubstantiated gossip. To be sure, they are often justified in suspecting shady dealings behind the closed doors of the upper levels of African governments.[59] By the same token, the possibility exists that popular perceptions of official corruption are sometimes inflated. That said, we acknowledge that perceptions matter; they shape attitudes and action; and, as we will test, perceptions may matter even more than first-hand experience. Toward this end, we confirm here that the Africans we interviewed base their evaluations of institutional performance on unflattering estimates of pervasive leadership corruption.

Thus, we arrive at the mission of the moment, which is to discover whether popular perceptions of the state – such as institutional trust and concerns about official corruption – help determine attitudes to reform. One plausible scenario is that people who distrust state institutions become advocates of reform as a means of combating corruption. Certainly, prodemocracy protesters commonly demand an end to official graft and improvements in public sector transparency. But the opposite is also tenable. Africans may consider that the state has decayed and corruption has deepened as the *upshot* of democratic and market reforms. In this alternative scenario, the loosening of state controls over society results in criminality and other deleterious effects that, in turn, undermine support for liberalization. This section ends with an examination of these possibilities.

We find that popular trust in state institutions has a mixed relationship to popular political attitudes. On one hand, people who place confidence in a range of state institutions are likely to say that they support democracy.[60] On the other hand, trustful people also display a proclivity to cling to one-party rule.[61] We interpret this paradox to mean that democracy's "shallow" supporters – many of whom are poorly educated peasants who offer lip service to a political regime they hardly understand – see no contradiction between democracy and the single-party state. Instead, uncritically, they put blinkered trust in any institution that a ruling party presents to them, say in the name of some cultural version of consensual democracy. Remarkably, they are even willing to trust the single-party state in the face of evidence that its officials are corrupt, for example in Tanzania. Because such myopic faith prohibits the rejection of authoritarian alternatives, it does not deepen support for democracy. It therefore comes as no surprise that, in a bivariate test, institutional trust bears no relationship whatsoever to our composite index of commitment to democracy.

By contrast, however, we find that Africans look for clean institutions as evidence that democracy and markets are actually being constructed. Popular perceptions of the extent of democracy are underwritten by powerful connections to indices of institutional trust (in a positive relationship) and perceived corruption (in a negative relationship).[62] The same patterns of association apply to mass satisfaction with SAP outcomes.[63] These relationships are so strong and statistically significant that we expect them to survive controls for alternate performance evaluations and other competing predictors of the supply of reforms. In short, Afrobarometer respondents clearly recognize that democracies and markets function best via honest agents and legitimate institutions. Indeed, Africans take the trustworthiness of institutions as confirmation of the success of programs of political and economic reform, but the presence of corruption as evidence that such reforms are failing.

ASSESSING REGIME PERFORMANCE

In the next three sections we distinguish among mass attitudes to phenomena other than the permanent institutions of the state. How do Africans evaluate the performance of more ephemeral entities like regimes, governments, and leaders?

To get at popular judgments about the performance of democratic regimes, we ask people to compare the present governmental system with the previous one, be it a colonial administration, a one-party state, or a military dictatorship. Do they think that the availability of desired goods and services is better or worse since the transition to democracy? To measure *the delivery of political rights*, we compile an index of three basic freedoms – of speech, of association, and of voting for candidates of one's choice – plus political equality.[64] To measure the *delivery of economic welfare*, we ask the same before-and-after comparison about whether "people have an adequate standard of living." Because, to a greater or lesser extent, economic reform programs were in place in all Afrobarometer countries at the time of the political transition, we take this latter evaluation to refer also to the performance of adjustment.

As Figure 9.5 shows, the Africans we interviewed clearly consider that democratization has delivered political rights. About four out of five respondents say that climate of freedom – for speaking one's mind, associating with others, voting in elections, and obtaining equal treatment before the law – has improved since their country's transition to multiparty rule. Only one out

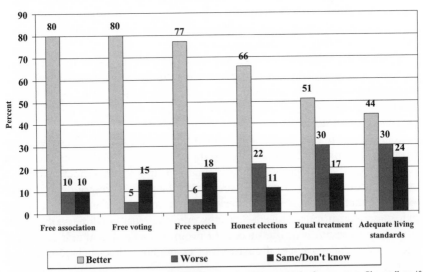

Question 1: "We are now going to compare our present system of government with the former system. Please tell me if the following things are better or worse now than they used to be: (a) people can join any organization they want, (b) each person can freely choose who to vote for without feeling pressured, (c) people are free to say what they think, (d) everybody is treated equally and fairly by the government, and (e) people have an adequate standard of living?"
Question 2: "In your opinion, how free and fair were the last national elections, held on (date)?"
Note: Figures are percentages who indicate "better/free and fair" or "worse/unfree and unfair."

FIGURE 9.5. Performance of Democratic Regimes

of twenty sees worse conditions for the expression of political views and for choice among electoral candidates. These substantial and positive changes must be regarded as major achievements of Africa's recent democracy wave.

Nevertheless, there is room for further improvement in the political atmosphere, especially in the honesty of elections. Reflecting the contrasting quality of parliamentary contests across countries, many more South Africans accept the validity of the smoothly administered 1999 elections in their country than do Basotho their problematic 1998 polls.[65] Moreover, only half of all respondents consider that, under democracy, gains have been registered in "everyone (being) treated equally and fairly by the government." In the wake of arbitrary rule by Abacha's army, which was accompanied by the militarization of both civilian administration and social life, Nigerians see the greatest gains in equal treatment. Their neighbors, the Ghanaians, still worry about unequal treatment, however, since, at the time of the first Afrobarometer survey, Jerry Rawlings was still in power with his rough-and-ready style of rule.[66]

In contrast to the majorities who welcome political freedoms, only a minority regards new regimes as having delivered economic welfare. Just 44 percent think that democracy and adjustment have heralded higher standards of living and 32 percent think that such standards have actually dropped. The remainder sees the quality of life remaining much the same despite a change of political regimes. Malians make the most positive assessment of regime performance – 61 percent think that living standards are better – at a time when wages were being paid and goods were plentiful in the marketplace. Zambians remain the most gloomy – only 28 percent think that economic life is better in their inflation-sapped economy, with 57 percent seeing it as worse than under the old order – to the point where some people have given up hope that any political or policy regime can bring about a recovery in living standards.

The attainment of political freedoms appears to trump the delivery of economic welfare, at least in forming public commitments to democracy. Africans support democracy more because it liberates their thoughts and actions than because it puts grain in the family pot.[67] Along these lines, the provision of economic goods in the present has no effect whatsoever on popular rejection of past authoritarian systems: regardless of recent economic gains or losses, people reject dictatorship anyway![68] They prefer democracy above previous systems mainly because it provides civil liberties and political rights, an orientation that is highly consistent with their own understandings of the nature of democracy. And, looking back on the ways they used to be ruled, Africans explicitly reject authoritarian alternatives (especially military rule) because of the restrictions these systems placed on self-expression and freedom of political choice.

The delivery of economic goods becomes important, however, when the general public considers how democratic and market regimes work in practice. Concerning satisfaction with democracy, the delivery of material welfare initially appears to have a greater impact than the provision of political freedoms, though both are influential.[69] It is clear that mass expectations about democracy's performance include, not only continued guarantees that freedom will be protected, but also that material life will improve for ordinary people. Thus, over the long run, satisfaction with democracy cannot withstand a persistent and seemingly endless decline in living standards.

The same holds true for structural adjustment. People want to experience economic benefits. Interestingly, though, both kinds of goods – political and economic – seem to be equally important in kindling satisfaction with SAPs.[70] Thus, where it exists, the minority sentiment of satisfaction with structural adjustment among Africans is apparently based as much on an appreciation of free choice, in this case as producers and consumers in the economic marketplace, as on the limited material improvements that SAPs actually deliver.

GRADING THE GOVERNMENT

Governments, defined as corporate political groups temporarily elected to state office, generally come and go more regularly than regimes. After all, some semblance of a structural adjustment regime has remained in place across most African countries even during the tumult of transitions to democracy, with almost all incumbent and opposition parties now basing their electoral campaigns on market-friendly principles. Moreover, the advent of democracy has been accompanied in a few countries (such as Ghana and Mali in our sample) by the peaceful alternation of governments according to rules of multiparty election. We therefore now ask: How do Africans evaluate the performance of governments? And do they distinguish governments from regimes?

The Afrobarometer measures government performance along various policy dimensions. The question asks: "How well would you say the current government is handling the following problems?" We then list the eight policy issues displayed in Figure 9.6. Four of these policies form a single dimension that can be summarized in an *index of government policy performance.*[71]

Clearly, African populations think that their governments are doing a better job at implementing social policy than at managing the macro economy. On average, well over half of those interviewed give the government credit for improving health and education services, including preventing the spread of HIV-AIDS. These are surprising findings in light of collapsing social services and declining public health standards in many countries. Perhaps these results can be understood in the context of low popular expectations about the capacity of governments to deliver services, marginal recent improvements in the quality of some fee-paid services, incomplete public awareness about AIDS, and the early stages of the AIDS pandemic in West Africa. Con-

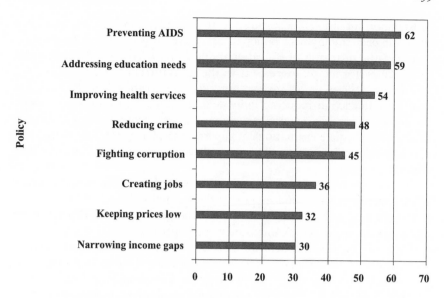

Question: "How well would you say the current government is handling the following problems?"
Note: Figures are percentages saying "fairly well" or "very well."

FIGURE 9.6. Policy Performance of the Current Government

sistent with economic crisis, however, fewer adults assign passing grades to their government for the implementation of economic policy: only about one in three says that governments are doing well at job creation, controlling inflation, and narrowing income gaps between the rich and the poor. These assessments accord much more closely with what people told us earlier about the unfulfilled delivery of economic welfare. Finally, the public generally has, at best, mixed feelings about government's performance in the management of basic state functions like crime and corruption control.

Some governments are deemed to be performing better than others. Among all Africans interviewed, South Africans are the most critical of their government's policy record. A mere one out of ten thinks that the ANC administration is creating enough jobs, and less than one out of five is satisfied with its measures for controlling crime. At the other end of the spectrum, Ugandans give good grades to their NRM government. Remarkably, almost nine out of ten say it is doing well at improving education, a resounding vote of confidence in the policy of free universal primary education. Additionally, over seven out of ten Ugandans endorse their government's handling of the AIDS crisis, in this case applauding its pioneering public education campaign that succeeded in bringing down what was once the highest sero-positivity rate on the continent.[72]

Which goods and services are most critical to opinions about government performance? Given what people said earlier about unemployment as the most important problem requiring government attention (see Chapter 4), one would expect employment policy to drive overall perceptions. In practice, however, the provision of educational opportunities is pivotal to the index of policy performance, more so than the official record at delivering jobs. Of all the policies under review, however, job creation has the strongest positive influence in inducing individuals to think that economic welfare has been delivered.[73] As such, we propose that education policy is directly salient to immediate evaluations of governments, but that public delivery of jobs has indirect impacts (via living standards) on the acceptability of whole regimes.

Do Africans make use of current assessments of government performance to calculate whether to lend support to democracy and markets? Or do they resist allowing any disillusionment with the government-of-the-day from undermining longer-term commitments to larger regimes?

We come to mixed conclusions on this matter. On one hand, there is some evidence that ordinary Africans cannot draw the fine, but important, distinction between governments and regimes. For example, individuals who consider that their governments are doing a good job at implementing policies are more likely to support democracy, though the relationship is not overly strong.[74] On the other hand, present policy performance has a negative bearing on rejection of authoritarian regimes. In other words, people reject old dictatorships *even if* new, elected governments perform poorly.[75] Especially when we isolate the evaluations of the minority of committed democrats (that is, those who simultaneously support democracy and reject autocracy), we find the weakest residual link from government to regime.[76] One can feel reassured, therefore, that committed democrats are unlikely to throw out the baby (the democratic regime) with the bathwater (an underperforming government). More likely, committed democrats will use newfound electoral rights to change governments while retaining, and reinforcing, the procedures of democracy.

Discriminating judgments are even more common in relation to economic reform. Stated differently, popular views of the government's policy performance have no observable effects on support for the structural adjustment regime.[77] This is the same disassociation that we noted earlier with regard to popular views of the condition of the economy. In other words, survey respondents adopt attitudes about adjustment policies (the most common pattern is to support price reforms and reject institutional reforms) *regardless* of how well they think government is implementing its official development policies.[78] We take this as initial evidence that, especially for economic reform, Africans make a mental separation between the government-of-the-day and the larger regime. One interpretation is that people understand that Africans governments unwillingly endorse structural adjustment policies mainly to meet conditions imposed by international lending agencies.

Thus, people cut their leaders some slack for their performance in the implementation of macroeconomic policies that are not indigenously owned.

But we do not wish to push this argument too far. Support for democracy (which is widespread) clearly is more vulnerable to downturns in government policy performance than support for market reforms (which has a narrower base). Persons who have a shallow commitment to democracy are especially likely to conflate government and regime in their own minds. Accordingly, the grades that Africans give their governments on policy performance remain a reliable (if partial) guide to popular satisfaction with the way that hybrid regimes actually work in African countries.[79] Because proto- (that is, less than fully committed) democrats can still be tempted by the appeals of strongmen, however, they may fail to defend the regime of democracy against the failures of particular governments. Some significant risk therefore remains that dissatisfaction with government performance could lead a majority of Africans to abandon democracy.

A REPRESENTATION GAP?

Finally, how do people view the performance of elected leaders? In settings where "big men" continue to stride the political stage, we would expect evaluations of individual leaders to infuse the formation of public opinion. It is therefore with some concern for the consolidation of democracy that we further examine the representation gap, that is, the dearth of formal contacts between the electorate and their chosen leaders (see Chapter 5).

Only about half of the Africans we interviewed approve of the performance of their elected leaders in the legislature (49 percent) and in local government (53 percent). This modest level of satisfaction with grassroots representatives compares unfavorably with average popular evaluations of the job performance of national presidents (64 percent), which range from a low of 21 percent for Mugabe in Zimbabwe in October 1999 to a high of 93 percent for Museveni in Uganda in June 2000.[80] In East and West Africa, people consistently consider that their local councilor is doing a better job than their MP or deputy, suggesting the beginnings of relatively effective local governments in places like Mali and Uganda. But in Southern Africa the opposite is true, a fact that points to the greater effectiveness of parliaments in this region, notably in Botswana, where many people praise their MPs (64 percent). But in all other Afrobarometer countries, people give higher marks to the incumbent head of government (the president or prime minister) than to either local councilors or national legislators.

In several countries, people express considerable disappointment with elected leaders. In South Africa in 2000, for instance, only 32 percent approved of the performance of local councilors and just 44 percent were satisfied with MPs. In good part, such popular disquiet is due to the inexperience of councilors and the immaturity of council structures, which have been in place in rural South Africa only since 1995. Fewer even than South Africans, just 34 percent of Zimbabweans approve of the performance of local government councilors and just 19 percent are happy with MPs. We suspect that Zimbabweans are also reacting against the heavy-handed style of representation practiced by ZANU-PF officials, which includes pressure to vote for the ruling party and sanctions for failing to carry a party card. At the time of the survey, and before the opposition MDC made electoral gains, the parliament of Zimbabwe and the Harare municipal council – whose performance was approved by only 15 percent of the adult residents – were wholly in the grip of ZANU-PF, which depressed evaluations of elected representatives.

Thus, voters in almost all countries see a representation gap. They complain that parliamentary deputies do not visit the locality, fail to deliver development benefits, and return only when seeking reelection. And they connect these shortcomings to impressions that elected representatives are engaged in self-enrichment in a context where ordinary people are sinking into deeper deprivation. About members of parliament, participants in focus groups in Zambia said: "they don't attend to pressing national problems but only to issues concerning themselves"; "they have granted themselves hefty salaries and big new (Toyota) Land Cruisers"; "most MPs don't go there (to the National Assembly) for charity reasons but to help themselves to a good standard of living"; and, "while asking us to sacrifice they are displaying choking (sic) luxury." One man, who felt unappreciated for the campaign work he had done for the Movement for Multiparty Democracy, coined a bitter metaphor: "they treat us like matchsticks; they light their cigarettes, then throw us away."

To close the representation gap, African voters want ease of contact with their political agents. A popular solution is for leaders to live in the locality: hence, local government councilors receive higher ratings than legislators, who usually reside in the capital city. People are especially resentful of dominant ruling parties that impose unknown urban candidates on "safe" parliamentary seats in the rural periphery. National presidents may thereby succeed in composing a parliament or cabinet of their choosing, but such arrogant practices only deepen a sense among the electorate that they are being exploited for elite political purposes. In addition to being able to obtain attention when they need it, people seem to expect face-to-face relationships with their representatives in which they can make oral demands in person. Moreover, they value a shared sense of identity based on a common place of origin, for it is widely felt that only residents have an authentic appreciation for the problems of the hometown.

Ironically, it may be rational for elected leaders to avoid their constituents, thus explaining the representation gap. The discipline demanded by parliamentary whips in dominant party systems creates a disincentive for MPs to attend to their constituents' opinions, which might conflict with the party line. Moreover, in settings where legislators represent large populations of poor constituents, they face many more demands than they can ever conceivably address. Many of these demands are highly personal – that is, to help a particular individual, family, or village – and almost all require the delivery of material resources. Quite apart from the excessive amounts of time required to attend to all supplicants, there are never enough resources to go around. Especially where governments are bankrupt or aid-funded development programs are scarce, elected leaders may be expected to contribute personal funds to such diverse causes as weddings and funerals, the education of AIDS orphans, the provision of relief supplies, and sundry community self-help projects.[81] Overwhelmed by the sheer magnitude of local needs, the representative finds it impolitic to keep saying "no" and, instead, finds it easier to stay away. Of course, some members of parliament may fail to visit their constituencies for more self-serving reasons, but even the most dedicated representatives ultimately choose to put some distance between themselves and the people who vote them into office.

In support of these conjectures, we find that poverty has a consistently negative effect on evaluations of the performance of elected leaders.[82] In other words, the most needy people grant the lowest job approval ratings, presumably in part because they feel that leaders have failed to solve their personal, material problems. In Ghana, we asked: "when deciding whom to vote for," would you prefer to vote for "a candidate that lives in your area" or "a political party, (without) worry(ing) about where the candidate lives." As expected, more people would vote for a favorite son (or daughter) from the locality than for unknown candidates put up by a central political party (48 percent versus 41 percent). And, also as expected, these hometown boosters are consistently less satisfied with leadership performance. At this stage, however, we do not know whether resident representatives actually perform better or worse than outsiders.[83]

Performance evaluations also hinge on what citizens expect leaders to do. In four countries we asked an open-ended inquiry: "in your opinion, what are the most important responsibilities of your member of parliament/your deputy to the National Assembly?" People commonly offered instrumental responses that amounted to "the delivery of development" or referred to representational functions like "speaking about our needs" and "listening to the people." Very few mentioned legislative tasks such as "to make laws," "to approve budgets," or "to check the executive branch." An interpretation of political representation as a mechanism for delivering political and economic goods fits especially well in Mali and Tanzania. In these countries, people who expected a direct payoff from voting were above average in their disapproval of MP performance.

But a small measure of political responsiveness will go a long way to closing the representation gap. In an interesting twist, the delivery of concrete development benefits is less important to Nigerians; instead, those who expect the MP to "listen to the people" are most disapproving of MP performance.[84] Moreover, across the seven countries in Southern Africa, people's estimates of their representatives' interest in their well-being are critical to performance evaluations. Those Southern Africans who believe that leaders are "interested in what happens to you" and "hearing what people like you think" are very much more likely to approve of leadership performance.[85] If nothing else, these results suggest that Africans insist that leaders care about them and consult them on decisions that affect their lives. And, because responsive representatives gain higher performance evaluations, it seems that MPs can gain considerable credit simply by making themselves available to lend an ear to constituent concerns.

We conclude this section by reporting another clear result: evaluations of the performance of elected leaders have powerful effects on attitudes to democratic and market reforms. To pursue this analysis, we employ two constructs.

The first combines evaluations of the performance of local councilors and national legislators, which we call *representatives' performance*.[86] Evaluations of all elected leaders, including the president, are highly correlated. We interpret these connections to mean that ordinary Africans – less than one fifth of whom can name *both* their councilor *and* their MP – use limited information about one type of representative to make inferences about the performance of others. MPs in Uganda therefore benefit from being associated in the public imagination with the popular President Museveni, but MPs in Zimbabwe are dragged down by perceptions that they are agents of the unpopular Mugabe. Moreover, many Africans remain puzzled about the separate responsibilities of different levels of government: half of all Ghanaians and Zambians, for example, think that central and local government are "the same thing." This perception is especially widespread in former one-party states. And it persists in multiparty systems with dominant parties where legislators continue to make use of local government councilors as their agents in the locality.

The second construct combines trust in the national president and his current job approval rating.[87] *President's performance* is strongly and positively related to institutional trust, which suggests that Africans infer their trust in public institutions partly from their evaluations about the national president, whom they feel they know better than the various agencies of the state.[88] And trust in institutions is boosted to the extent that most people feel that the president is doing an acceptable job, which two thirds do. But presidential popularity is strongly and negatively related to perceptions of corruption.[89] Predictably, perceived corruption among elected leaders – including the biggest of the big men – is more toxic to the popularity of presidents than to, say, civil servants.[90] People feel betrayed if elected leaders become infected by the graft that they assume already exists among the state's permanent administrative staff. This is especially so if presidents, legislators, and councilors run for office as new brooms that promise to sweep clean.

To close this section, all that now remains is to trace the magnitude of the bivariate connections between leadership popularity and attitudes to political and policy reform. We find that the perceived performance of all types of leaders is positively linked to mass support for democracy.[91] And leadership popularity is an extremely strong predictor of mass satisfaction with both democracy and SAPs.[92] Presidential performance alone explains fully one quarter of the variance in satisfaction with democracy and more than one fifth of the variance in satisfaction with economic reform.[93] These are among the strongest correlates we have yet found to reformist attitudes among the general public. And the effects of leadership evaluations hold powerfully and consistently in every single African country for which we have collected data.

Across the board, presidential performance is consistently more important than the reputation of other elected representatives in increasing attachments to reform, though both matter. It shows up most starkly in countries like Malawi and Tanzania where formidable past presidents stamped a personal touch on the political apparatus and economic strategy of their countries.[94] Even when presidential popularity is summed at the country level, it shows a markedly linear relationship with aggregate rates of satisfaction with democracy (see Figure 9.7).[95] In short, the Africans we interviewed tend to personalize their judgments about democracy and markets

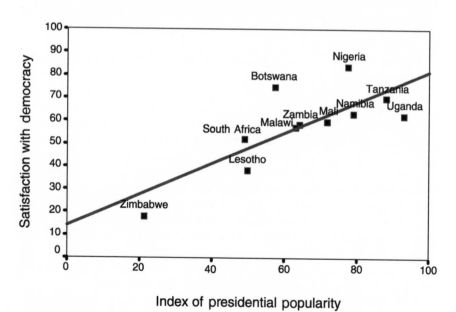

FIGURE 9.7. Satisfaction with Democracy, by Presidential Popularity

by deriving their support and satisfaction with these regimes from their evaluations of the performance of individual elected leaders, especially national presidents. The president provides less-informed voters with a salient, easy cue from which they may infer the performance of the larger political regime. In this respect, public opinion reflects a political economy whose viability hinges in critical respects on the behavior of key patrons as viewed through the eyes of their clients.

PERFORMANCE MODELS

Africans demand the delivery of development. And they judge institutional performance in this light. This chapter has reviewed a sequence of popular performance evaluations, beginning with public views about the condition of African economies. We then examined a nested set of assessments about African polities, starting with state institutions, and then turning to the regime of democracy, the current government, and incumbent leaders. Because these forms of evaluation overlap, it becomes necessary to isolate their relative effects. By statistically controlling each for all others, we aim to discern the key performance considerations that lie behind constituencies for and against reform.

Multivariate performance models are displayed in Table 9.1. In general, rational calculations by African citizens explain a considerable amount about popular contentment with reform programs. On their own, performance evaluations account for 34 percent of the variance in the perceived extent of democracy and 21 percent of the variance in satisfaction with adjustment programs.

The first column of Table 9.1 shows that, other things equalized, commitment to democracy depends mainly on the delivery of political rights, especially basic liberties. In other words: if citizens acknowledge that democratization has expanded certain core freedoms, support for democracy grows. Africans therefore express a political rationale for becoming democrats in much the same way as people celebrate liberation from repressive autocracies in other parts of the world. Indeed, evidence begins to emerge that mass democratic orientations do not depend on calculations of economic performance. The negative sign on the delivery of economic welfare confirms that popular democratic commitments can survive the failure of elected regimes to raise living standards, at least in the short term over which we have made measurements. We also discover that responsive leadership is central to building mass commitments to democracy; in other words, Africans prefer democracy because they think it will produce accountable leaders who will listen to them and who will help them address their needs.

With reference to the second column of Table 9.1, we inquire: which aspects of performance drive the perceived extent of democracy? For the first time, free and fair elections now stand out. Even though Africans do

TABLE 9.1. *The Effects of Performance Evaluations on Attitudes to Reform*

	Commitment to Democracy	Perceived Extent of Democracy	Support for Economic Reform	Satisfaction with Adjustment Program
Constant	.541***	−.417***	1.379***	1.323***
Economy				
Performance of the economy	.011	.084***	021*	.130***
State				
Trust in state institutions	−.037***	.080***	−.047***	.052***
Perceived corruption	.083***	−.083***	.074***	−.061***
Regime				
Delivery of political rights	.195***	.083***	.021*	.070***
Free and fair elections	.016*	.167***	−.001	.036***
Availability of free speech	.009	.047***	−.054***	−.029*
Delivery of economic welfare	−.062***	.029***	−.055***	.010
SAP creates inequality	.051***	−.049***	−.023*	−.201***
Corruption worse	−.023**	.013*	.052***	.081****
Government				
Government policy performance	−.023**	.102***	.038***	.032**
Identity group treated fairly	.012	.061***	.017*	.067***
Leaders				
Representative's performance	−.018*	.038***	−.015	.030**
President's performance	.042***	.164***	.044***	.105***
Leadership responsiveness	.159***	.036***	.100***	−.024
Standard error of estimate	.534	.950	1.070	1.079
Adjusted r squared	.073	.340	.027	.208

Note: Unless otherwise indicated, entries are standardized regression coefficients (beta).
$N = 21,531$
***$p = <.001$
**$p = <.01$
*$p = <.05$

not define democracy primarily in electoral terms (being more concerned with civil rights and direct participation), they use the quality of national electoral contests as a cue to judging whether democracy is being attained in their countries. In this respect, the general public resembles the international donor community in finding electoral quality a quick and reliable indicator of the maintenance of basic democratic standards. Africans also demand honesty in the performance of state institutions, as indicated by the strong negative weight that perceptions of corruption impose on popular estimates of the extent of democracy. When everything else is controlled for, trust in the president and in state institutions are central components in the popular calculus of how much democracy has been achieved. And these political considerations are even more important than economic considerations. Instead, people look to the overall performance of government in implementing a range of economic, political, and social policies when judging the distance their own country has traveled toward "full" democracy.

Turning to support for economic reform, the third column points again to the centrality of perceived leadership responsiveness: only if people think leaders are serving a common interest will they extend support to government economic policies. It seems that a great deal of goodwill could be generated if leaders would consult their constituents in advance of the introduction of austerity or adjustment measures. And strikingly, political considerations (like the availability of free speech) are just as important as economic ones (the delivery of improved living standards), even when the object of evaluation is the economic reform program.

Interestingly, however, ordinary people do not seem to insist that responsive leaders are incorruptible, perhaps because they perceive opportunities for sharing in the proceeds of ill-gotten gains. Given the hard choice, people apparently prefer a dubious patron with plentiful largesse to a clean leader who fails to widely distribute development goods.

Finally, the last column of Table 9.1 highlights the dynamics of satisfaction with SAPs. Only here do economic calculations take center stage. Popular evaluations of economic conditions strongly shape satisfaction with this reform attitude. But, even more importantly, SAP satisfaction is propelled by considerations of economic equity, in this case whether adjustment has "helped" more people than it has "hurt." The large, negative coefficient in the regression table indicates that, in practice, Afrobarometer respondents are dissatisfied with SAPs because they perceive that these programs lead to economic inequalities. Recall that, from a popular perspective, the spoils of adjustment are broadly seen as accruing politically to "people close to government" (see Chapter 4). As Ackerman puts it: "corruption . . . tends to distort the allocation of economic benefits, favoring the haves over the have-nots and leading to a less equitable income distribution."[96] So, while ordinary Africans welcome being invited to participate in networks of patronage – indeed, they actively seek inclusion – they become disillusioned when leaders systematically leave them out. Thus, potential popular support for economic reform is squandered, being converted instead into dissatisfaction with widening wealth gaps.

Taken together, these results signify that ordinary Africans employ a straightforward logic – that is, a rational calculus based on their felt best interests – in positioning themselves toward regimes of reform. They weigh the anticipated costs of new political and economic arrangements against the benefits they expect to receive. In this way, instrumental evaluations of institutional performance play a powerful role in the formation of public opinion, especially popular satisfaction with the way democracy and markets actually work.

But, because regime alternatives are often vague and information about them is usually scarce, people cannot grasp the full gamut of relevant considerations. They therefore look for shortcuts in arriving at performance evaluations. On the basis of the evidence presented in this chapter, we argue that the performance of the national president plays this role in African countries. Along with leadership responsiveness, it is the most robust predictor across various multivariate models, positively shaping support and satisfaction alike for both democratic and market regimes. Because of its pervasive and consistent influence, we think that the perceived performance of the national president is a convenient touchstone for many Africans in deciding where they stand on larger, regime-level issues. If they approve and trust the president, they project these positive sentiments onto democracy and markets. And the opposite holds for negative sentiments about the president, which can pull whole regimes into popular disrepute. As such, the African public employs a highly personalized form of rationality in which the popularity of larger systems in Africa continues to depend upon people's feelings about the top leader who heads the state and economy.

10

Institutional Influences

Even if Africans wish to make rational decisions about reform, the available choices are far from infinite. Public opinion is forged within a framework of political and economic institutions. Some institutions open up opportunities for individuals to adopt novel attitudes. Churches and trade unions that run civic education programs, for example, may help participants to develop healthy skepticism about the trustworthiness of leaders. And, by reducing the costs of obtaining information, farmer associations may aid agricultural producers in learning about commodity prices and marketing channels. But other institutions foreclose options. A dominant political party may, in the name of loyalty, require its members to stifle their freedom of expression or suspend their critical faculties. Or glutted markets may induce private traders to refuse to purchase farm products at the peak of the season, thus inducing economic dissatisfaction.

Our eyes are open in full recognition that the term "institution" has been abusively overstretched into one of the loosest in the social science lexicon. It has been deployed variously to refer to the rules of the political and economic game (like constitutions and contracts) to organizations that link individuals into larger systems (like bureaucracies and firms) or even to "stable, valued, and recurring patterns of behavior."[1] Hence, we wish to be explicit about the way we use this contested term. In this chapter, we intentionally employ a narrow definition of institutions as the organizational affiliations and routine behaviors of individual political and economic actors. Included under this rubric are people's memberships in voluntary associations, their identifications with political parties, and acts of participation in the rituals of political and economic life, like voting and trading. In looking for institutional influences at this micro level, we acknowledge that African institutions are generally underdeveloped and that informal institutions are often more pervasive than formal ones.

ASSOCIATIONAL LIFE

Faced with falling economies and failing states, ordinary Africans have created institutions of their own. The literature abounds with examples. Trager draws attention to local associations that "bring community members home to celebrate their town while also raising money for community projects."[2] Woods reports that, as the state withdraws from cooperatives in the countryside, a plurality of rural clubs spring up to "provide transport and financial support ... to purchase crops ... (and) to represent rural producers."[3] And Kraus finds that, "organized private capital, in the form of business associations" has "become more active in public life" including "develop(ing) influence in public policy formation and implementation."[4] In villages and towns across the continent, ordinary people pursue collective goals by contributing personal resources to burial societies, parent-teachers' associations, and – especially among women's groups – small-scale enterprises.

Analysts usually assume that these stirrings of associational life signal a vibrant civil society.[5] Other commentators warn that voluntary associations are not always autonomous from the state and may lack the necessary capabilities and dispositions to effect real regime change.[6] To help adjudicate this debate, we wish to know whether individuals who engage in associational life are supportive of programs of democratic and market reform. Moreover, leading theorists propose that voluntary associations – like rotating credit groups that pool members' savings – can only operate successfully in the presence of "generalized reciprocity and mutual trust."[7] Yet exploratory research in Uganda and Botswana suggests that, "neither membership of social clubs or other voluntary associations nor frequency of participation in meetings of such groups account(s) for the levels of generalized trust."[8] Again, to mediate these disagreements, we explore whether connections exist between associational life and other dimensions of social capital.

According to the Afrobarometer, associational life is alive and well in Africa, and high by world standards. Almost three quarters of the Africans we interviewed (74 percent) claim that they belong to, or are active in, a voluntary association of some kind. The median respondent belongs to only one association, though about one third of the sample belongs to two or more organized groups. By this measure, ordinary Africans are most fully integrated into civil society in Uganda, where local organizations thrive, though one can question the independence of groups sponsored in this country by the ruling elite, traditional kingdoms, and local government. People are more cut off from one another in Lesotho, Botswana, and South Africa, where social relations have been disrupted by labor migration and a money economy (see Figure 10.1).[9] In searching below for effects of associational life, we use an additive *index of group membership* based on the number of associations to which people belong.[10]

Question: "I am going to read out a list of voluntary organizations. For each one, could you tell me if you are an official leader, an active member, an inactive member, or not a member of that type of organization?"

FIGURE 10.1. Voluntary Associations, Mean Number of Memberships

Africans associate mainly in religious groups, in which 65 percent of respondents claim to be active members. Most report involvement in an established church or mosque, but others affiliate with a revival movement, an indigenous or syncretic sect, or some other community of faith. Participation in organized religious activities is most common among evangelical Protestants (92 percent) especially when compared to followers of traditional African beliefs (21 percent). Muslims fall in between: about two thirds report attachment to a mosque or regularly attending festivals and prayer meetings, but another one third of African Muslims pursue their professed spiritual beliefs on their own. Women and rural dwellers are slightly more likely to claim affiliation with religious groups, but they do not diverge widely from men and urban residents in this respect. A better predictor is poverty, with religious association rising as people become poorer.[11] Indeed, as prospects for individual prosperity worsen under economic recessions, Africans – most markedly in Ghana, Tanzania, Zambia, and Nigeria[12] – turn to associations that promise salvation in the afterlife.

Other, secular forms of voluntary association attract far smaller followings. Just one quarter of respondents reports involvement in local-level development associations like agricultural marketing groups or hometown improvement societies. And fewer still claim that they belong to, or attend meetings of, nationally federated groups like professional or business associations (19 percent) or labor or farmers' unions (17 percent). These findings are consistent with our earlier observation that, in times of need, Africans rarely turn for assistance to community-based organizations, instead preferring to rely on family ties or, under duress, the marketplace. Compared to their limited presence in towns, development associations draw more participants from the countryside, where kinship ties continue to provide a foundation for collective action. Not surprisingly, business associations and trade unions are more commonplace in urban areas, especially among people who define their identities in occupational terms. Somewhat offsetting the prevalence of religious groups, associations based on the workplace are gaining strength in the relatively industrialized economies of Namibia, Zambia, and Zimbabwe, though many respondents also claim allegiance to farmer associations in Mali.[13]

Whatever form associations take, the voluntary arena allows the expression of subnational solidarities. As might be expected, Africans who adopt collective identities ("Muslim," "worker," "southerner") are more likely than self-professed individualists to join organized groups. Moreover, we find a slight positive relationship between the index of group membership and the likelihood that an individual will express a sense of generalized trust in other people.[14] This suggests one of two things: either individuals feel the need to develop confidence in prospective fellow members before making a commitment to collective action or, by belonging to a group, people learn to trust one another. Either way – whether groups are the products or the catalysts of trust – we take this positive relationship as prima facie evidence that associational life is part of a syndrome of social capital. To bolster this weak association, we note that group membership is even more strongly connected to newspaper readership and to turnout in elections, which others take as components of social capital.[15]

But what sort of social capital results from collective association? Is it the "bridging" sort that builds crosscutting ties within society, for instance by bringing together people of different backgrounds? Or is it the "bonding" kind that is internal to identity groups and reinforces social cleavages, for example along lines of language and place of origin?[16]

It is hard to find evidence that associational life eases social tensions in Africa. To be sure, people who assert occupational identities are slightly more likely to join a voluntary association than people who see themselves ethnically. But the difference is small (79 percent versus 74 percent), implying that ethnicity remains a viable basis of organization and mobilization.[17] Moreover, even members of urban-based professional associations often wish to cultivate a beneficent reputation with their communal group, for example, by contributing generously to projects in their ethnic hometowns. While some

analysts conclude that, on balance, the benefits of such kinship-based association are positive for local development, others express concerns about the
"ethnicization" of civil society.[18] Moreover, the emergence of new religious
identities often reinforces existing ethnic, linguistic, and regional divisions
rather than dissolving them.[19] In Nigeria, for example, many northerners
have used the idiom of Islam and the infrastructure of the mosques to react
against the 1999 shift of political power to the south. We interpret the introduction of *sharia* law in northern states as one tactic in this political strategy.
Finally, we find no evidence that group memberships boost national pride.[20]
In these respects, the formation of voluntary associations in African settings
is almost as likely to deepen existing divisions within society as to bridge
them.

Do voluntary associations help develop the habits of the heart that
Tocqueville saw as essential to democracy? We defer discussion of whether,
as schools of democracy, voluntary associations teach the practical skills
necessary for active citizenship (see Chapter 12), instead confining our inquiry in this chapter to attitudes rather than actions. Does an individual's
involvement in associational life shape his or her opinion about various
liberalization reforms?

As an intermediate step, we test whether membership in voluntary associations is connected to cultural values and cognitive orientations already
found to be conducive to democratic and market attitudes. For example,
we have shown earlier that individuals who are willing to tolerate economic
risk are more likely to support both democracy and markets (see Chapter 7).
Does risk tolerance arise from associational life, for example, as business
and professional groups bring would-be entrepreneurs into mutual contact?
At minimum, we can confirm that members of voluntary associations are
significantly more likely to risk personal capital on a business venture.[21] As
another example, we have shown previously that individuals who possess
a sense of internal efficacy are more likely to be satisfied with democratic
and adjustment reforms (see Chapter 8). Can the development of personal
self-confidence be attributed to the experience of associating with others in
an institutional setting? We think so, at least in one limited respect: our data
indicate that members of associations are significantly more likely to express
an efficacious understanding of the way that government works.[22]

At this time, however, we do not know whether these cultural values
and cognitive attributes are consequences of associational life. The causal
logic may run in reverse, with people who are already self-confident and
risk tolerant choosing to join organized groups. Whatever the mechanism,
however, (and, for the moment, we suspect two-way effects) there is clearly an
affinity between associational life and a syndrome of open-minded attitudes.

An individual's experience in voluntary associations should therefore
presage support for, and satisfaction with, regimes of reform. When all
types of group membership are considered jointly, we can confirm that

associational life is positive for reform attitudes.[23] The relationship is only moderate, however, because some such attitudes are widespread (for example, three quarters of respondents say they support democracy), whereas most associations – especially secular groups (which involve, at most, one quarter of respondents) – are much less so. Firmer connections are only revealed when religious affiliations, which are also distributed generously among Africans, are considered separately. In a simple, two-way test, an individual's attachment to an organized church, mosque or spiritual movement boosts support for democracy by more than ten percentage points.[24] People who attend religious assemblies seem to gain their democratic preferences in part from sermons, readings, and discussions about the moral content of good government. Religious congregants are also less likely to say that they "don't care" about the form of government,[25] suggesting that religious institutions play a vital part in educating people about the implications of various regimes and the obligations of citizenship.

Religious association has most impact on support for democracy in Uganda, Tanzania, Mali, and Nigeria. But different denominations are at work in East and West Africa. Being an active member of a Protestant congregation boosts one's support for democracy by fifteen percentage points in Uganda, and by almost twice as much in Tanzania.[26] In these countries, association with the Roman Catholic church apparently has fewer benefits for democracy.[27] And in Tanzania, membership in an Islamic mosque has no discernible effect whatever. Islamic associations do have an impact in West Africa, however, where a slight increment in support for democracy – six percentage points – is visible among members in both Nigeria and Mali.[28] Overall, in the African countries we have studied, the institutions of the Protestant church have had the greatest success in attracting or developing a membership that supports democracy, a finding that runs counter to Huntington's thesis about Vatican II catholicism as the major religious force for democratization in the late-twentieth century.[29]

As for popular attitudes to old political regimes, one would expect that participants in civic life – who, after all, depend on free association – would reject one-party states. Indeed they do, but not as roundly as they reject other forms of autocratic rule.[30] People apparently feel that it is better to have a restricted choice of association under a one-party state than to have no associations at all. Affiliation with religious groups again intensifies these political attitudes, sometimes in interesting ways. In Nigeria, Muslims who belong to Islamic associations are much more likely than nonmembers – by an eighteen percentage-point margin – to reject military rule.[31] Hence, it would be quite wrong to conclude that Nigerian Muslims uniformly mourn the passing of General Sani Abacha and long for the return of an army government. And in both Zambia and Namibia, Christians are more likely than other religionists to reject presidential rule by a dominant strongman.[32] Indeed, churchgoers are among the only segments in Namibian society to register resistance to the personalized style of governance favored by Sam Nujoma.

To close this section, we comment on connections between associational life and attitudes to economic adjustment reforms. The more groups that a person joins, the more likely he or she is to endorse a standard reform package, but again the tendency is hardly strong.[33] Among the various types of association, only memberships in business groups and trade unions lead to increased support for adjustment.[34] Belonging to a business association marginally increases support for privatization.[35] Trade unionists, perhaps because they represent a privileged group within the working class, are somewhat more inclined to accept user fees for social services and market prices for consumer goods. Surprisingly, though, since public sector workers are usually unionized, members of labor unions are also more likely to back job retrenchment in the civil service.[36] Finally, members of development associations constitute a solid antiadjustment bloc, being consistently more likely than nonmembers to reject every policy in the economic reform portfolio.

PARTY IDENTIFICATION

After being suppressed for decades, multiparty competition has flowered in Africa during the 1990s. In all but a handful of countries, opposition political parties are now legally permitted to form, organize, and compete in elections. Responding to these political openings, politicians moved quickly to register new political parties, often as vehicles to promote personal bids for power.[37]

As a result, party systems in Africa are fragmented.[38] The political arena is populated with a plethora of personal and ethno-regional political structures with vague programs and weak organizations. Reflecting these characteristics, an emergent literature on African party systems points to low levels of party institutionalization, high levels of electoral volatility, and the revival of dominant parties. For example, Kuenzi and Lambright draw attention to the brief life spans of political parties in Africa and their tendency to collapse when they fail to win elections.[39] Van de Walle observes that, "the modal party system that is emerging across much of the region is a system with a large dominant party surrounded by a bevy of small, highly volatile parties."[40] This distinctive pattern is encouraged by the concentration of powers in the hands of presidents and the predisposition of politicians to use patronage to build support among clients. Under these circumstances – where winners take all – the incentive for leaders and followers alike is to claim allegiance to the winning party.

Largely missing from the literature on African political parties is evidence on their linkages to the mass public. In this section, we examine how African populations respond to the expanded range of potential institutional affiliations presented by party competition. Do people throw in their lot with dominant parties, including those led by old incumbents? Or, conversely, do they commit themselves to insurgent oppositions? Or do they cast a plague on both houses, preferring instead to remain strictly nonpartisan? Critical in this investigation is whether people identify with the winning or losing side in the last election. As forecast earlier, we anticipate that an individual's partisan status (as a "winner" or a "loser") will have profound effects on his or her attitudes to reform.[41] We expect winners to be forgiving toward reform programs that are associated with the party in power. Supporters of this party will tend to discount negative information about institutional performance in favor of unconditional loyalty. By contrast, we think losers are prone to pounce on negative information about performance. In other words, they are predisposed to blame their own exclusion on the machinations of winners and, by extension, on the shortcomings of current political and policy regimes.

At this stage in the continent's political evolution, the Africans we interviewed have yet to embrace political parties. Admittedly, a small majority says that they "feel close" to a political party (57 percent); but a large minority insists on remaining nonpartisan (43 percent). Given the importance of political loyalties to the distribution of patronage rewards, one might have expected more people to jump on a party bandwagon, especially on the winners'. Furthermore, we cannot confirm that new political parties in Africa are forming primarily along ethnic lines. As we saw for associational life, party identification is actually slightly more common among people who evince occupational rather than ethnic identities.[42] This is true even among those who feel that their group is discriminated against ("treated unfairly"). Thus, while we do not deny that ethnic identities and grievances constitute an important basis of party affiliation, we suspect that African political parties are forming along more pluralistic lines than concerns about ethnic fragmentation would have one believe.

Respondents echo their ambivalence toward parties by also expressing low levels of trust in these institutions. Just over half of the respondents in five countries say that they trust parties either "somewhat" or "a lot" (51 percent).[43] Compared to other institutions, political parties consistently receive lower trust ratings than any government or political agency except the bottom-ranked police. Indeed, among people who think that corruption is common among elected leaders, trust in political parties is just as low as trust in the police.[44] Popular suspicions about dishonesty among party officials help us understand why many Africans have yet to identify with partisan institutions.

According to Figure 10.2, partisan identification varies amply across countries. Oddly, these differences seem to be entirely unconnected to the degree of political competition in the party system, as measured by the numbers of parties that contest elections or win representation in parliament. Party identification is highest in Malawi's three-party system. Each party has successfully mobilized support in its own region, a factor that we have

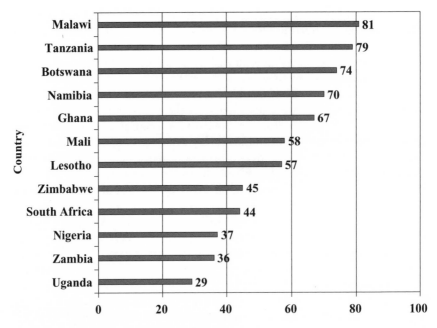

Question: "Do you feel close to any political party?"
Note: Figures are percentages who answer "yes."

FIGURE 10.2. Party Identification

used to explain why Malawians are knowledgeable about their leaders. But identification with political parties is also high under the dominant party system that has long prevailed in Tanzania.[45] In this case, the overwhelming majority of mainland Tanzanians identify with the ruling organization, with small opposition redoubts appearing only on the Pemba and Zanzibar islands and among selected residents of Dar es Salaam. At the other end of the spectrum, party identification trails in Nigeria. Even though three parties ran in the 1999 elections, the total number of these entities was restricted, all were artificially and hastily assembled, and none had a history of deep ties to the electorate.[46] Yet party identification is also low in Zambia, a country that traded a de jure one-party monopoly for a de facto dominant party system in 1991. Zambians – who resent having been forced, under the old regime, to buy party cards in order to receive government services – now choose to remain independent of *all* political factions.

The issue of party identification is especially germane in Uganda. Since coming to power in 1986, President Yoweri Museveni and the National Resistance Movement have tried to blame multiparty competition for political violence. Ugandans are not yet ready for open party competition – or so goes the argument – because social relations are rooted in the divisive identities of ethnicity and religion, which parties reproduce and entrench.[47] In the place of multiparty competition, Museveni promotes a "no-party" version of democracy: Uganda's "Movement system" is a hierarchy of elected organizations that stretches from village to national levels. Political parties are permitted to exist but are prohibited from electoral campaigning.[48] Yet Uganda has a long tradition of partisanship based on rivalry between the Democratic Party (DP) and the Uganda Peoples' Congress (UPC). Joined by a host of newer and smaller parties, these groups chafe under the restrictions of the Movement system and actively seek to restore multiparty elections.

Yet the Afrobarometer indicates that Ugandans remain deeply suspicious of political parties. Only 29 percent are willing to admit that they feel close to a party – and four out of five of these say they identify with the Movement, whose leaders claim (disingenuously, in our view) that their organization is not a political party. Asked about a battery of statements concerning political parties and multiparty competition, Ugandans never muster a proparty majority.[49] For example, a majority of Ugandans thinks that "political party competition undermines national unity by causing conflict and confusion" (62 percent), a statement with which only a minority of neighboring Kenyans agrees (46 percent).[50] Thus, Museveni seems to have struck a deep popular chord in linking multiparty competition with political instability. Accordingly, even more than Zambians, Ugandans prefer to remain nonpartisan.

Of those Africans surveyed who identify with a political party, twice as many profess to have sided with winning candidates in the last national election as admit to being losers. Of course, some respondents may rewrite their personal histories by reporting voting records deemed politically correct. Despite the possibility that we were sometimes intentionally misled, we still expect that being a self-proclaimed "winner" increases one's loyalty to incumbent leaders and reduces one's willingness to criticize their performance.

Two quick tests, illustrated in Figure 10.3, strongly confirm these conjectures. First, winners are more likely than losers to turn a blind eye to corruption. They consistently report that they perceive fewer abuses of office among civil servants and (especially) among elected officials.[51] A generous interpretation of these findings is that political loyalists receive priority treatment from their representatives and therefore have less need to resort to bribery. A more cynical rendition is that winners expect to be rewarded for their votes by subsequently sharing in the proceeds of illegal favors, rents, and prebends. Second, winners are very much more likely than losers to offer positive appraisals of the performance in office of elected leaders. For example, by a margin of eighteen percentage points, they give higher job performance ratings to members of parliament and local government councilors.[52] Even more strikingly – now by a margin of thirty-nine percentage points – winners are more than twice as likely as losers to approve the job performance of the national president.[53] This relationship is so strong that, in predicting how a person will rate the performance of the big man,

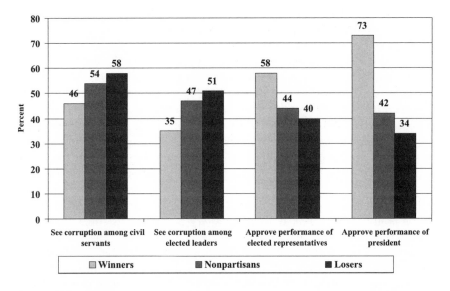

Note: "Winners" are individuals who say they "feel close" to the political party that won the last national elections.

FIGURE 10.3. Winners and Losers

one needs to know little more than how that individual voted in the last presidential election. Such is the overwhelming strength of personal loyalties in African politics.

All that remains in this section is to check whether winners and losers part company on matters of democratic and market reform.

We find that an individual's partisan status affects support for political reforms, but in contrary directions. As expected, those who feel close to an incumbent party are inclined to favor current democratic arrangements.[54] This is especially true for supporters of parties – like the African National Congress in South Africa and the Movement for Multiparty Democracy in Zambia – that rose to power at the head of mass movements for democracy. But it also holds for dominant parties that managed to stay in office by introducing their own minimal, preemptive reforms – like the National Democratic Congress in Ghana and the Chama Cha Mapinduzi in Tanzania. Precisely because many contemporary winners are long-time loyalists of historically dominant parties, however, their commitments to democracy are often shallow. Accordingly, winning is negatively related to rejection of authoritarian rule.[55] As such, Africans who are driven primarily by party loyalties are likely to pay lip service to democracy, but to indulge in ongoing nostalgia for stronger forms of government in the back of their minds.

Moreover, partisan loyalties extend only so far. While attachments to incumbents inflate support for political reforms, they do not pump up support for economic policy change. We find absolutely no relationship between a person's affiliation with a winning party and his or her support for economic adjustment reforms, either individually or as a package.[56] Moreover, the warm glow of being a political winner is insufficient to offset any negative feelings about being an economic victim. To the contrary, Africans who base their attitudes mainly upon loyalty to a victorious political party are particularly likely to become disillusioned with economic reforms. We find that political winners are prone to consider that their government's economic policies have hurt more people than they have helped,[57] especially where governing parties have not taken ownership of reforms imposed by external donors and lenders.

Finally, partisan affiliations propel people to arrive at conclusions about how well democracies and markets work. Whereas three quarters of political winners express satisfaction with democracy (74 percent), less than half of political losers do so (47 percent).[58] And, despite their disappointment with adjustment's inequalities, winners are still twice as likely as losers to be satisfied with SAPs (29 percent versus 14 percent).[59] We saw previously that mass satisfaction with reforms was shaped in important respects by the public's levels of knowledge and awareness and their rational evaluations of institutional performance (see Chapters 8 and 9). We are now discovering that attitudes to reforms-in-practice also depend on subjective fealties of a highly partisan nature. As the analysis proceeds, we will wish to examine whether such loyalties – which can be automatic and unthinking – are a stronger or weaker force than cognitive rationality.

POLITICAL PARTICIPATION

To express partisan preferences, Africans vote. They also engage in other forms of political participation before and between elections. The incidence with which people turn out at the polls and contact various types of leaders was documented in Chapter 5 and does not require repetition here. Instead, we simply note that many commonplace political behaviors are governed by formal rules and are channeled through formal organizations. Voters are mobilized, for example, not only by political parties and voluntary associations, but also by campaigns of protest, lobbying, and voter registration. Do such organized forms of participation impart patterns to public opinion? The logic of this inquiry is that people learn by doing.

Take voting. For several decades before the 1990s, voting in African elections had become a meaningless ritual since voters could only affirm official incumbents – rather than choose challengers – at the polls. Even when opposition candidates were eventually permitted to compete, ordinary people continued to doubt that entrenched rulers, who controlled the resources for running elections, would permit free and fair contests. Under these circumstances, it was perfectly reasonable for citizens to withhold judgment about the feasibility of democracy until they received corroborating evidence that opposition candidates stood a reasonable chance of winning. Of course, the strongest proof that political change was afoot was when, against the odds, voters managed to pull off an upset by electing an outsider. We suspect that, by participating in elections that allow real choice, Africans begin to believe that freer forms of political regime are possible. By using electoral procedures to occasionally achieve political alternation, voters gradually gain confidence in democracy.

Adult blacks in South Africa are especially likely to have learned by doing. Denied the franchise under apartheid, they were never socialized into democratic values. Thus, the attainment of the vote in 1994 was a life-changing experience. The founding election, which extended to black voters new feelings of human dignity and political equality, emphasized political inclusion above administrative rigor. Almost anyone who wished to vote was permitted to do so and the polls were kept open for four days to ensure that nobody was turned away. By 1999, the electoral process had become more institutionalized: voters were now required to obtain a national identification document, to register to vote, and to queue up on a single appointed election day.[60] One would expect that the introduction of such regular procedures for casting ballots would lead voters to learn about citizenship; they would gain, among other things, improved knowledge of political leaders, enhanced political efficacy, and deeper awareness of democracy. In fact, we can confirm that voting is positively associated with all these political attitudes, not only among South Africans, but also among Afrobarometer respondents in general.[61]

At issue, once again, is whether public attitudes are a cause or a consequence of institutionalized participation. According to Brady, Verba, and Schlozman, "political interest and political efficacy, for example, certainly facilitate political activity, but activity presumably enhances interest and efficacy as well."[62] The problem with the latter line of argument, of course, is that it is hard to prove that the arrow of attribution runs from behavior to attitudes. As most analysts acknowledge, an equally plausible case can be made that attitude change comes first (doing comes from learning). Thus, individuals who are already knowledgeable, efficacious, and aware are likely to turn out to vote on the day of elections. For the moment, perhaps the safest conclusion is that attitudes and behaviors interact reciprocally. We later make a systematic effort to disentangle such mutual effects (see Chapter 12).

At the present time, we address this conundrum by examining a form of political behavior that, in African politics, usually precedes rather than follows transitions to democracy. Political protests and demonstrations are much more common in the twilight of old autocracies than in the early morning of new democracies. While it might be argued that only committed democratic activists take to the streets, we think this is true mainly for protest leaders; the shock troops of street demonstrations are usually young people with ill-formed political attitudes. The relative naiveté of demonstrators ("they know what they are against but they don't know what they are for") combines with the temporal precedence of protests to make a good test case of the effects of behavior on attitude formation. We propose that acts of political protest build awareness, solidarity, and commitment among participants that are manifest in higher levels of political information, political efficacy, and understanding of democracy. Again, we find support for all of these suppositions among Afrobarometer respondents.[63]

If participation in organized political activities sometimes changes attitudes, we need an efficient way to review these effects. Theorists have long recognized that political participation is a multifaceted concept that embraces a variety of forms, including voting, campaigning for candidates, lobbying, and contacting leaders, and (when all else fails) protesting.[64] We find that political participation among Africans is structured along these lines, much as it is in other parts of the world. As Table 10.1 shows, factor analysis reduces nine participatory acts into three main dimensions, which we label "voting," "contacting," and "communing." The same clusters tend to emerge even when this statistical procedure is performed separately for each African country, suggesting a consistent underlying shape to political participation across the continent.[65]

But political participation takes on distinctive features in Africa. First, the most conventional form of political participation – that is, voting – coheres with the least conventional form – namely attending protest demonstrations. This unusual conjunction draws attention to the reality that, in many Afrobarometer countries, open elections were secured as a consequence of

TABLE 10.1. *Dimensions of Political Participation*

Type of Activity	Voting/ Protesting	Communing	Contacting
Voted in last elections	−.624	.288	.141
Attended protest demonstration	.537	.396	.393
Wrote a letter to a newspaper	.428	.379	.347
Attended campaign rally	−.234	.669	.300
Worked for a political candidate or party	.005	.653	.253
Attended community meeting	−.362	.587	−.163
Got together with others to raise an issue	.099	.714	−.127
Contacted public officials	.305	.484	−.444
Contacted influential person	.210	.458	−.639
Eigenvalue	1.194	2.555	1.097
Percentage of variance explained	13.3	28.4	12.2

Note: Factors are derived from principal components analysis. The coefficients are the loadings of each variable on each factor.

mass protest. But there is a negative sign on the coefficient for voting in Table 10.1. In other words, individuals who took to the streets to demand democracy did not always follow up by exercising the right to vote. Our data confirms that young people in their late teens and early twenties, who were overrepresented in the protest crowds, have since lagged behind in electoral turnout. In Mali, for example, where youth were active in prodemocracy protests in 1991–92, many fewer persons under thirty years old in 2002 (the "multiparty generation") were registered to vote than those aged forty-five and above (64 percent versus 84 percent). And, even in South Africa, the under thirties were ten percentage points less likely to have voted in 1999 than the oldest cohort.[66] Because protesting and voting are inversely related in the factor analysis, it is therefore advisable to consider each as a separate dimension of participation, as researchers usually do for non-African countries.

Second, in the African countries studied here, popular involvement in electoral campaigns does not cohere with voting. In other words, many Africans who attend political party rallies, and even those who say that they "work" for a candidate or party,[67] do not later cast a ballot. Perhaps when joining in political campaigns, these participants have motives other than voting. Maybe they wish to gain access to the handouts (food, clothing, or money) distributed by candidates intent on buying votes. Or maybe people attend partisan forums mainly for purposes of social interaction with friends and neighbors. These interpretations are strengthened once we realize that, in the factor analysis, campaigning hangs together with attending community meetings and getting together with others to raise a personal, policy, or development issue. Thus, political campaigning plays similar roles to collective social action, including affirming personal goals, shared identities, and agendas for community development. We attach the label of "communing" to this distinctive dimension of political participation. It reflects a cultural expectation that formal political institutions like campaign rallies and development meetings are also moments of informal social and economic exchange.

Third, like citizens everywhere, Africans seek contact with leaders between elections. On the theme of informal politics, we showed earlier that people enjoy more frequent contacts with influential notables – like traditional, business, and religious leaders – than with elected officials or civil servants (see Chapter 5). We now confirm that informal contacts are central to African constructs of political participation since they constitute the main element in the dimension of action that we call "contacting." In some countries – like Tanzania, Zambia, and Zimbabwe – participants appear to have given up trying to work through public officials because contacts with "some other influential person" stand alone as the sole element in the contacting dimension. It is even plausible that the more thoroughly a single party dominates a multiparty arena, the more likely that citizens – especially the "losers" in the last election – find it necessary to work around it.

Because "communing" accounts for twice as much variance in overall political participation as voting or any other dimension,[68] it is the core element in political participation in Africa. While Africans value elections and other forms of representation – such as writing letters to a newspaper – they do not regard these conventions as being central to the way they want to practice democracy in their countries. Instead, Africans expend their political energies in pursuit of deliberation in local level forums and involvement in decision making. In short, rather than seeking representation, people want a direct form of democracy.

Do institutionalized forms of participation – whether voting, contacting, or communing – help build popular support for reform? We report affirmatively that an *index of communing and contacting* is associated with support for democracy and rejection of authoritarian rule.[69] Specifically, people who often get together with others to raise an issue are twelve percentage points more likely to support democracy.[70] And this sort of collective action is associated with a seventeen percent increment in ardent rejection of military rule.[71] The link to support for democracy is strongest in Lesotho,[72] which suggests that "communing" helps to overcome the political isolation that we have previously noted among Basotho. And collectively raising issues is most strongly connected to rejection of military rule in Nigeria,[73] reflecting a groundswell of antimilitary sentiments in that country during the 1990s.

ECONOMIC PARTICIPATION

To conclude our exploration of institutional influences, we inquire whether the experience of participating in economic markets also affects mass attitudes to popular reform. It seems plausible that entrepreneurial experiences – like trading goods and services, employing others, or taking the risk of borrowing money for a business[74] – lead people to support adjustment reforms. By contrast, we expect that more passive economic actors, such as those whose livelihoods depend on kinship relations rather than market institutions, are likely to oppose adjustment.

Interestingly, we cannot confirm these hypotheses. In the countries we studied in East and West Africa,[75] a popular form of entrepreneurship has been born out of sheer economic necessity. Almost all classes of people have been forced to resort to petty trade ("buying and selling goods") and moonlighting at second jobs ("selling your skills to others"). And these widespread forms of participation in the informal economy have no detectable effect on the likelihood that a person will support or oppose adjustment. Nor, in Southern Africa, has the commonplace experience of integration into formal markets resulted in the emergence of a popular constituency for economic reform. People in this region who purchase their food supply, for example, are no more likely to support a full adjustment package than those who rely mainly on kin for their daily bread. Perhaps behavior and attitudes are disconnected in the economic realm because, unlike democratic participation, market participation is a necessity, not a choice.

Indeed, for most of the Africans interviewed, market-based exchange has been an unhappy experience. As currently configured, formal markets in African countries do not generate enough well-paid positions to satisfy mass demands for employment or to sustain the standards of living desired by jobholders. And the informal sector is broadly regarded as a second-best, stop-gap solution. People engage in sideline jobs and petty trading not because they are converts to the values of entrepreneurship, but because they have no other way of making economic ends meet. As a consequence, market participants are slightly less satisfied with SAPs than those who operate largely within an "affectionate" economy of family ties and mutual aid.[76] In short, for most people, participation in markets has not induced support for reform and has actually reduced their economic satisfaction.

Only with reference to a small class of genuine entrepreneurs who engage in more specialized business practices do we find evidence of reformism. First, people who have actually taken financial risks ("borrowing money for business purposes") are barely, but significantly, more likely to support a package of adjustment reforms.[77] Second, people who manage enterprises that create jobs ("employ others to work for you") are somewhat more likely to endorse reform.[78] Third and finally, people who institutionalize their economic activities by participating in the formal banking system ("operate a bank or a savings account") are reliable advocates of adjustment.[79] But all these groups are small minorities. And, again, even market champions are inclined to disapprove of the way their preferred economic system actually works in practice.[80]

INSTITUTIONAL MODELS

This chapter has asked whether an individual's organizational affiliations and routine behaviors are forces for reform. We have considered the potential impacts of membership in voluntary associations, identification with political parties, and acts of political and economic participation. To approach closure, we now weigh these various influences with a view to determining how much each contributes to an institutional explanation of public opinion.

Table 10.2 summarizes institutional influences on reform attitudes. Because observable effects are negligible, the results need not detain us long. Regression analysis reveals that institutional influences never account for more than about 6 percent of the variance in reform attitudes and often even less. Close-to-null findings are not surprising on a continent where political and economic institutions remain weak. We should expect that fledgling associations, parties, and procedures – many of which (like opposition parties) are novel products of regime change – have yet to exert a formative hold on

TABLE 10.2. *The Effects of Institutional Influences on Attitudes to Reform*

	Commitment to Democracy	Perceived Extent of Democracy	Support for Economic Reform	Satisfaction with Adjustment Program
Constant	1.187***	1.730***	1.670***	2.427***
Member of religious group	.126***	.045***	.065***	−.025*
Member of other associations	−.079***	−.017*	−.042***	.007
Identifies with political party	.056***	−.019**	−.013	.008
Identifies with winning party	−.051***	.226***	.002	.133***
Voted in last elections	.040***	.050***	.017*	.050***
Participated in demonstration	−.038***	−.030***	.014	−.006
Contacted influential person	.048***	−.009	.014*	−.023*
Communing and contacting	.149***	.031***	.098***	.011*
Standard error of estimate	.537	1.132	1.075	1.198
Adjusted r squared	.060	.065	.017	.024

Note: Unless otherwise indicated, entries are standardized regression coefficients (beta).
N = 21,531
***p = <.001
**p = <.01
*p = <.05

African attitudes. Most Africans continue to live their lives – and form their opinions – beyond the reach and control of formal institutions.

That being said, we can still discern which institutions are more or less influential for the inception of public opinion. Take commitment to democracy. All the institutional predictors of this key democratic attitude remain statistically significant even after being mutually controlled. But two influences now jump out. First, political participation between elections (as measured by the index of communing and contacting) is the strongest factor in the model. In other words, the more fully that Africans involve themselves in everyday political procedures – from attending community meetings to contacting officials – the deeper their commitments to democracy. At minimum, therefore, Africans are consistent in their actions and attitudes; maximally, they learn to love democracy by practicing its procedures. Second, active membership in a religious association is a gateway to democratic commitments. While it is well known that the members of certain Christian churches were advocates of transition to democracy in several African countries, our data suggest that, less overtly, membership in Islamic movements and other religious associations also induces quiet commitment to democracy.

Popular perceptions of the extent of democracy are driven by quite different dynamics. When people appraise democratic attainments, what matters most is loyalty to a winning political party. Other things being equal, people who regard themselves as winners in the last election are 20 percent more likely to think that democracy is being attained in their country.[81] To this considerable extent, they are willing to endorse the institutional performance of their party – right or wrong – and to deem it "democratic." A similar pattern prevails for satisfaction with SAPs. Once all else is controlled, self-proclaimed winners are 9 percent more likely to express satisfaction with their country's economic reform program in a context where no other institutional predictor explains half as much variance.[82] Thus, wearing winner's glasses imparts a rose-colored glow to the world. As indicated earlier, we still want to know whether this institutional affiliation is powerful enough to induce citizens to suspend their faculties of rational evaluation. Or, in the final analysis, will winners require their party to deliver the goods (see Chapter 11)?

Lastly, institutional influences are anemic with regard to support for economic reform. To be sure, people who participate politically are more likely to be persuaded by the doctrine of adjustment, as are the members of all kinds of associations. But being a "winner" has no effect here. And the model explains so little variance that we feel certain that noninstitutional factors – reviewed collectively in the next chapter – will tell a more compelling story.

Overall, formal institutions lend shape to the consciousness of ordinary Africans only at the margins. This reflects, we believe, the early stage of institutional development in Africa's hybrid political and economic systems. But, before we dismiss institutions entirely, we leave open two important possibilities. First, even if rules and organizations do not forge the contours of public attitudes, they may still be influential in guiding actual behavior. We examine this possibility in Chapter 12. Moreover, even if institutional influences are hard to detect at the individual level, the prospects for African countries writ large may still be conditioned by political legacies inherited from the past. In Chapter 13 we use aggregate data to investigate these historical paths.

PART IV

EXPLAINING REFORM CONSTITUENCIES

II

Modeling Attitudes to Reform

The last part of this book aims at synthesis. It offers general answers to several broad questions about contemporary African realities. How do popular constituencies develop, either for or against reform (see Chapter 11)? What is the nature of mass participation in new multiparty regimes (see Chapter 12)? Are democracies consolidating anywhere on the continent (see Chapter 13)?

The present chapter summarizes lessons learned about the sources of democratic and market attitudes. It integrates the sociological, cultural, cognitive, rational, and institutional approaches reviewed in Part III. Instead of treating each explanatory family separately, we now blend all approaches into exhaustive models. In so doing, we aim to eliminate spurious findings that do not hold up when exposed to a wide array of controls. Our main objective is to derive encompassing explanations that are both statistically powerful and efficient as theory. Above all, we wish to weigh the effectiveness of competing explanations about the origins of African public opinion.

The paths to opinion formation are discussed in broad, theoretical terms. In order to achieve generality, we adopt a universal language about the *demand for* and *supply of* reforms that was first introduced at the beginning of this book. We also use generic terms to sum up the impacts of explanatory families, for instance referring to "social structure" writ large rather than to its component elements like, say, gender. Multivariate regression and path analysis are used to assay which families deserve inclusion in final explanatory models.[1]

Existing results already point to key tests. On the demand side – that is, whether Africans support the goals of liberalization reforms – we know that public opinion depends heavily on whether people are well informed about political and economic affairs. But will demands for democracy and markets still be best explained by a theory of cognition even after the effects of alternate explanations are taken into account? On the supply side – that is, whether people perceive that reforms have actually been implemented – our analysis reveals strong effects of performance evaluations. Once other explanations are simultaneously considered, however, will Africans still base their satisfactions (or dissatisfactions) on calculations about institutional and leadership performance?

To anticipate, we propose that Africans adopt attitudes to reform as the result of a gradual learning process. People arrive at their opinions – however tentative these may be – mainly by making pragmatic judgments based on the acquisition of information. They demand reforms based on what they learn about their content, namely, what democracy *is* and what markets *are*. But they evaluate the supply of reform based on experience of results, that is, what democracy and markets actually *do*.

As such, we contend that *a learning theory of cognitive rationality* goes furthest in explaining the nature of public opinion in Africa. We therefore break with conventional accounts in African studies that base analysis on social structure and cultural values. This is not to say that certain societal factors – like, for example, the political generation in which individuals come of age – lack apparent explanatory power (but see Chapter 13). Nor do we claim that modern cultural values – such as a sense of individual responsibility for one's own welfare – are irrelevant to certain reform orientations. But, on balance, we regard attitude formation as an evaluative mental process, occurring principally in adulthood rather than through deep socialization, through which Africans *learn about reform*. The people we interviewed approach democracy and markets more on the basis of knowledge, reasoning, and experience, than as a function of identities and values ascribed by society and culture.

When focusing on the process of learning, we seek to avoid the standard traps of classical rational choice theories, which assume that citizens are able to know all alternatives, to calculate likely outcomes, and to choose the alternative the best maximizes their own interests. We allow that in Africa's information-poor environment, would-be citizens will always lack enough cognitive awareness to make perfect performance evaluations. But, like non-Africans in other new regimes around the world, they can piece together roughly accurate judgments.

MODELING DEMAND FOR DEMOCRACY

As usual, we begin with attitudes to democracy. The first steps are to construct an explanation of the sources of popular democratic demands and then to account for democracy's perceived supply. The chapter then proceeds with explanations of the demand for – and the observed supply of – a market economy.

Via what routes, then, do Africans arrive at popular demand for democracy? This theoretical concept is represented by the same *index of commitment to democracy* employed in previous chapters. The reader will recall

TABLE 11.1. *Demand for Democracy[a], Explanatory Factors Compared*

	R	B	S.E.	Beta	Adj. R^2 (block)	Adj. R^2 (cumulative)
Constant		$-.330$***	.001			
Cognitive Awareness					.173	.173
See democracy as political procedures	.277	.115	.004	.186***		
Knowledge of leaders	.254	.059	.004	.124***		
Awareness of democracy	.240	.152	.009	.114***		
Cognitive engagement	.202	.073	.006	.086***		
Formal education	.190	.037	.004	.063***		
Awareness of SAP	.227	.064	.008	.055***		
Performance Evaluations					.056	.197
Delivery of political rights	.182	.076	.005	.104***		
Leadership responsiveness	.177	.030	.004	.085***		
Social Structure					.038	.225
Postcolonial generation	.160	.226	.010	.203***		
Multiparty generation	$-.011$	.209	.013	.159***		
Age	$-.044$	.004	.000	.099***		
Cultural Values					.038	.236
Risk tolerance	.186	.039	.003	.094***		
Interpersonal trust	$-.069$	$-.080$	.012	$-.052$***		
Institutional Influences					.026	.247
Member of religious group	.160	.106	.007	.089***		
Member of other associations	$-.000$	$-.047$	.005	$-.074$***		
Full Model		.481				.247

Notes:

N = 21,531

***p = <.001

[a] The dependent variable is the *index of commitment to democracy* (an average score composed of expressed support for democracy plus rejection of military, one-party, and one-man rule).

that that commitment is an average score of expressed support for democracy, plus strong rejection of military, one-party, and one-man rule.

A comprehensive model of demand for democracy is presented in Table 11.1. Using fifteen predictors clustered within five theoretical families, it is possible to account for almost one quarter of the variance in this key attitude. Considering that our findings are based on survey data collected in cultural and institutional contexts traditionally seen as inhospitable to survey research, that democracy is an abstract concept to many Africans, and that individuals may not have directly experienced all authoritarian alternatives, this result must be regarded as a respectable degree of explanation. Our frugal model is at least as powerful as those in other studies of "current regime support" and "support for legislative democratization" in Eastern Europe and South Korea.[2]

Although all five theoretical families contribute to an ecumenical account of demand for democracy, some clearly do more work than others. Whereas a theory of cognitive awareness alone explains about one sixth of the variance in question (17.3 percent), three other theories, each alone, explain less than one twentieth (3.8 percent or less).[3] The contributions of social structure, cultural values, and institutional influences are further reduced when they are entered cumulatively into a model based on cognitive awareness: the last two families then add only about 1 percent change in total variance explained.[4] In other words, much of the apparent explanatory power of these theories is actually the result of their simultaneous association with cognitive factors.

Thus, we find for the Afrobarometer countries that an individual's *cognitive awareness* is the principal source of demand for democracy. Other things being equal, cognitive considerations account for three times as much variance in demand for democracy as any alternative theory.[5] In other words, popular demand for democracy is primarily a product of citizens who are mentally engaged with public affairs. It is noteworthy, however, that more than half of the Africans we interviewed are psychologically withdrawn from politics and a similar proportion possesses low levels of political information. We conclude, accordingly, that shortages of cognitive awareness contribute to the shallowness of democratic commitments among much of the population. But, even those who resort to low-information reasoning can take an interest in the content of reform, talk to others about it, and learn about their leaders. In this process, they begin to develop an appreciation for democracy, including its potentialities, limitations, and suitability to their country's political circumstances.

Information about the meaning of democracy is essential to building popular demand. A central requirement is that people gain some basic comprehension of democracy's content, regardless of whether they see it in terms of constitutional liberties, socioeconomic development, or even – skeletally – as plain old civilian (that is, nonmilitary) government. For some people, simply regarding a new multiparty regime in a vaguely positive light is apparently sufficient to induce them to conclude that democracy is the best form of government. More critically, popular demand for democracy is driven by a knowledgeable core of opinion leaders within the populace who regard democracy as a set of procedures to limit political power. This group sees the content of democracy in terms of freedom of speech, regular multiparty elections, and majority rule. Indeed, when all other factors are controlled, a procedural understanding of democracy is a top-ranked element explaining why some Africans demand democracy and others do not.

Procedural understandings even trickle down to low-information citizens. Whereas only 43 percent of the people we interviewed think that rules to ensure that powerholders are held politically accountable are "essential" for a society to be called democratic (see Table 3.4), fully 60 percent find them at least "important." We detect, in this result, evidence of the existence of a mass sentiment favoring checks and balances on would-be dictators. While educated people and those who are active in religious associations may articulate this discourse with a good deal of precision, it is also grasped, at least in its bare essentials, by the man in the street or the woman in the fields. In short, we conclude that an understanding of democracy that includes procedural constraints on the exercise of power is becoming woven into the popular political culture in Afrobarometer countries.

By way of reinforcement, we note that substantive understandings of democracy – as a set of equal socioeconomic outcomes – do not engender demand for democracy. When all explanations are weighed, materialistic interpretations of democracy do not qualify for inclusion in a comprehensive explanatory model. This is not to say that Africans do not think that a democratic society should ensure education and employment for all: some 80 percent find these outcomes either "important" or "essential." But the insight here is that economic substantivists are unlikely to be committed democrats. Indeed, Africans who view democracy in socioeconomic terms are drawn disproportionately from those with low levels of political information.[6] Part of the process of political learning involves realizing what democracy can and cannot do. People may start out expecting that a liberal political regime will guarantee socioeconomic transformation; later, they learn that democracy merely grants them a voice in the political process.

If demand for democracy is at root a mental orientation, and if this orientation is most pronounced among proceduralists, then it is reasonable to suppose that popular demand for democracy is a function of formal education. Perhaps opinion leaders first learn about the principles of political democracy when they are students in a school or university. While our findings allow for a direct path of learning along these lines, they also confirm that formal education is not essential to support for democracy. Education enters our model of demand for democracy only toward the end: while positive, education's impact is relatively slight and does not meaningfully reduce the impact of procedural understandings.[7] And media exposure continues to have no independent effect on demand for democracy.[8] These findings suggest that ordinary Africans obtain political awareness from various sources – including informal sources like word of mouth – and that they do not depend on transmission of information only from formal institutions.

Indeed, as already established, *institutional influences* have less effect on demand for democracy than any other family of explanation, and considerably less than a theory of cognitive awareness. Religious organizations are the only institutions that seem to play a role in increasing demand for democracy but, even so, their influence is relatively attenuated. Viewed from a broader perspective, political party identifications or active engagement in a range of participatory behaviors are no longer critical to the formation of democratic commitments. In this respect at least, popular demands for democracy emerge more from civil society than from political society, and more as a consequence of association in churches and mosques than from the influences of other institutions.

While we are addressing this issue, let us note that *cultural values* are also quite marginal to a comprehensive explanation of democratic demand. Feelings of national pride are no longer essential to the development of democratic commitments because their effects are overridden by cognitive factors. Importantly, interpersonal trust remains inversely related to demand for democracy. This finding constitutes further confirmation that, at the individual level, a reservoir of trust is not a prerequisite for people to become democrats. On the contrary, democratic procedures may provide exactly the sort of legal constraints on arbitrary behavior that makes governance possible in distrustful societies.

Performance evaluations add a measure of additional explanation. When comparing democracy to its authoritarian alternatives, Africans choose democracy as the best form of government in part for instrumental reasons. They opt for democracy because it improves welfare by delivering desired goods and services. But the nature of the anticipated basket of benefits gives lie to the conventional wisdom that Africans demand democracy only because they expect it to raise material living standards.

Two observations substantiate this important point. First, the delivery of economic welfare – measured as perceived improvements in mass standards of living since the transition to a multiparty regime – is absent from our final model of demand for democracy. For that matter, economic goods of all kinds fail to appear in *any* explanatory model of the demand for democracy that we have tested.[9] We can only conclude that, in the African countries we have studied, considerations of economic instrumentalism are entirely independent of popular demands for democracy. Second, people are especially eager for a government that is respectful of their civil rights and politically responsive to their needs. These are the performance standards that are uppermost in the public mind as Africans develop demands for democracy. Our model clearly indicates that the delivery of political rights – measured as the freedoms of speech, association, and voting – is the most potent performance consideration in building commitments to democracy. In other words, committed democrats are political – not economic – instrumentalists. They demand democracy, at least in part, because they see it as delivering the freedoms they long for.

Who, precisely, longs for such freedoms? We find that, while a theory based on social structure tells us little overall, an individual's *political generation* is apparently central to popular demands for democracy.

Most demographic factors – gender, ethnicity, social class, or rural-urban residence – do not reliably discern who will want democracy. But the postcolonial generation – that is, those who achieved voting age between independence and the advent of recent liberalization reforms – place a high value on democracy today. This group is even more likely to be committed democrats than a younger multiparty generation who attained political maturity during Africa's recent round of regime transitions. Indeed, in the present model, being a member of the postcolonial political generation is the single best overall predictor of demand for democracy.

If this result holds, then we will have uncovered evidence that learning about reform occurs on a generational basis. Africa's postcolonial cohort bore the brunt of the oppression and deprivation meted out by indigenous one-party and military regimes in the two or three decades preceding 1990. By this interpretation, a whole generation learned the hard way to reject authoritarian forms of government. Moreover, as indicated by the independent effect of age, the longer people lived through such negative experiences, the more likely they are to be democrats today. In this regard, demand for democracy also seems to depend on a lifetime of accumulated experience. Whether learning about reform is a lifelong journey – and whether it is concentrated among particular generations – will be further tested as we proceed.

MODELING THE SUPPLY OF DEMOCRACY

Having seen whence demands for democracy arise, we now trace the determinants of democracy's perceived supply. What leads Africans to consider that democratization is – or is not – underway in their countries?

For a political regime to take root, the general public must assent that a constitutionally defined set of institutions and procedures are firmly installed and working smoothly. Hence, to arrive at the *supply of democracy*, we combine two familiar public attitudes: the perceived extent of democracy and popular satisfaction with democracy.[10] Strongly correlated, an average of these indicators constitutes a valid construct of democratic supply.[11] This construct has the advantage of reducing the impact of the attitudes of uncritical citizens. Numerous in Tanzania, Uganda, Nigeria, and Namibia, uncritical citizens are dubious that democracy is being attained in their country, but nonetheless still say they are satisfied with democracy. In sum, this composite measure of the supply of democracy moderates the tendency of some citizens to settle for a political regime that actually falls well short of democracy.

Table 11.2 presents an inclusive yet efficient model of the supply of democracy. It reveals a simple theoretical profile. Only twelve predictors are required, clustered in just three explanatory families. In accounting for the perceived supply of democracy, *performance evaluations* of one kind or another do all the heavy theoretical lifting. Indeed, a very lean explanation that

TABLE 11.2. *Supply of Democracy[a], Explanatory Factors Compared*

	R	B	S.E.	Beta	Adj. R² (block)	Adj. R² (cumulative)
Constant		−.363***	.062			
Performance Evaluations					.337	.337
President's performance	.465	.155	.009	.170***		
Free and fair elections	.391	.137	.006	.155***		
Government's policy performance	.379	.116	.008	.107***		
Performance of the economy	.350	.137	.010	.100***		
Delivery of political rights	.294	.144	.011	.093***		
Perceived corruption	−.297	−.098	.008	−.085***		
Trust in state institutions	.352	.095	.008	.084***		
Identity group treated fairly	.270	.054	.007	.059***		
SAP creates inequality	−.226	−.037	.006	−.050***		
Availability of free speech	.052	.039	.007	.045***		
Institutional Influences					.057	.340
Identifies with winning party	.238	.090	.010	.054***		
Cognitive Awareness					.008	.340
Knowledge of leaders	.011	.061	.007	.060***		
Awareness of SAP	−.084	−.109	.015	−.044***		
Full Model			.948			.344

Notes:

N = 21,531

***p = <.001

[a] The dependent variable is a construct of *satisfaction with democracy* and the perceived *extent of democracy* (average score). See Appendix A.

accounts for fully one third of the variance in the supply of democracy can be constructed using performance evaluations alone! No other conceptual schema is essential to explaining assessments of democratic supply. But to round out the account, and to add an iota of additional resolution and interpretation, we choose to include certain institutional and cognitive influences. One cannot escape the conclusion, however, that mass opinion about the supply of democracy in Africa is driven by the public's calculations about performance. Indeed, performance evaluations play such a formative role that their effects are projected with little perturbation from a single theory model (see Chapter 9) to the multitheory test conducted here.

But we discover that, with other considerations now held constant, the deeds in office of the elected national president become decisive.[12] Reflecting the concentration of political power at the top of the executive branch in most African countries – including even parliamentary regimes like Lesotho and semipresidential systems like Botswana and South Africa – the behavior of the country's big man dominates public opinion. This tendency is especially marked in countries where powerful executive presidents – whether popular (like Museveni in Uganda) or unpopular (like Mugabe in Zimbabwe) – loom over the political scene. In calculating the supply of democracy in their countries, the Africans we interviewed take no account of the performance of those they apparently consider to be small fry, including legislative representatives and local government councilors.[13] Instead, people take their cues from the president, whose decisions about whether to play by the rules of the game are critical to the fate of democracy. As a key expression of the big man syndrome in African politics, the performance of the president is much more important to democracy building than the performance of the macro economy.[14] Indeed, so complete is the personalization of politics that, for many Africans, the man and the system are fused.

Offsetting this neo-patrimonial worldview, we detect the stirrings of political institutionalization. The convocation of free and fair elections is the second most important consideration overall in popular perceptions of the supply of democracy. The Africans we interviewed seem to agree with liberal democratic theorists that a solid democracy requires a strong electoral foundation. Unless citizens consider that the last multiparty elections in their country were free and fair, they are unlikely to perceive that democracy is actually under construction. It is interesting that ordinary people arrive at this conclusion even as they stress that preelectoral freedoms (like speech, conscience, and association) and postelectoral participation ("government by the people") are more central to their personal definitions of democracy. Moreover, elections prove to be almost twice as important to democratization as the trustworthiness of state institutions generally.[15] Admittedly, voters are often less well informed and laxer in their standards than official election observers, leading – in Nigeria, Tanzania, and Zambia, among other places – to injudicious popular endorsement of dubious voting contests. Notwithstanding these lapses, however, ordinary Africans make a clear connection between the quality of elections and the nature of the resultant political regime.

The electorate also insists on public policy performance. We can now confirm that, all else being equal, the perceived supply of democracy depends in good part on overall popular evaluations of the current government's record at addressing important socioeconomic issues like employment, inflation, education, and health care. An aggregate index of government performance in these policy areas is the third most important consideration when explaining whether ordinary people think that their country is getting to democracy. At the same time, people make independent judgments about the performance of the macro economy, which they regard as primarily a government responsibility. And, when people assess the concrete achievements of democratic regimes in Africa, they again attribute progress to the delivery of civil rights ahead of the delivery of improved living standards, indicating that political goods remain pivotal.[16]

Our African respondents reconfirm the corrosive impact of official state corruption. In fact, the negative effect of corruption on the democratic project is so powerful that it undercuts much of the satisfaction arising from economic growth and entirely counteracts all reassurance arising from trust in state institutions![17]

People also insist on equity. In estimating the supply of democracy, they weigh whether the government treats their own identity group in a fair and equal manner. They also judge whether the prevailing policy regime of economic adjustment has hurt or helped most people. The greater the perceived levels of these political and economic equalities, the more likely people are to think that democracy is being attained. It must be remembered, however, that despite the advent of new political rights, only about one half of the Africans interviewed think that newly elected governments actually mete out equal treatment to all citizens. And, following the introduction of SAPs, fully two thirds of the Africans interviewed think that economic policy has deepened economic inequalities ("hurt most people and helped only a few"). Thus, concerns about persistent inequalities – mainly economic, but also political – remain a key point of vulnerability for democratic performance in Africa.

To complete the present discussion, we try to resolve two debates from earlier chapters. First, when evaluating performance, do Africans distinguish between individual leaders, incumbent governments, and political regimes? Or do they attribute credit and blame indiscriminately, blurring these realms? Table 11.3 parses out the explanatory power of various dimensions of a

TABLE 11.3. *Supply of Democracy, Dimensions of Performance Compared*

	R	S.E.E.	Adj. R^2 (block)
All performance evaluations	.581	.952	.337
Performance of regime[a]	.463	1.037	.215
Performance of government[b]	.422	1.061	.178
Performance of state[c]	.414	1.065	.171
Performance of leaders[d]	.373	1.084	.141
Performance of economy[e]	.350	1.096	.123
All except performance of leaders	.565	.965	.320

Notes: The dimensions of performance are composed from Table 11.2 as follows:
[a] Free and fair elections, Delivery of political rights, Availability of free speech, SAP creates inequality
[b] Government policy performance, Identity group treated fairly
[c] Perceived corruption, Trust in state institutions
[d] President's performance
[e] Performance of the economy

theory based on performance evaluations. To be sure, it reconfirms that the record in office of the top leader is an eminent part of the mix. But the performance of political regimes, governments, and states is each more decisive. As a consequence, it is possible to construct a credible account of the supply of democracy, explaining almost one third of the variance, without reference to *any* leader's performance (see Table 11.3, last row).

We therefore moderate our earlier concern that the rule of men and the rule of laws are thoroughly fused in the African public imagination. While the big man's job record is critical, it is not paramount when all aspects of regime performance are considered as an ensemble. In a complete explanation of the supply of democracy, the performance of the supreme patron is counterbalanced by the overall performance of new regimes writ large. And the big man's dominant place in performance evaluations is offset to a degree by the policy performance of incumbent governments and the institutional performance of the permanent bodies of the state. We find in this reanalysis a modicum of evidence that African politics are beginning to shift, albeit incompletely and haltingly, from personalities to institutions.

Second, since performance evaluations presume that people make pragmatic calculations of costs and benefits, can we therefore conclude that Africa's protocitizens are reasoning rationally? If clients blindly follow presidential patrons for reasons of ethnic or partisan loyalty, we concede that they probably judge performance viscerally, that is, on the basis more of fellow feeling than rational forethought. Under these circumstances, people who identify with the national president will tend to judge his performance favorably, an affective trait that infects public opinion also in advanced democracies. But we are struck that our final model of the supply of democracy depends in no meaningful way on mass feelings of ethnic identity, shared culture, or political partisanship.

In the first place, for all twelve countries combined, the perceived supply of democracy does not depend on *any* element of *social structure*, including the key cleavage of ethnicity. For example, members of majority and minority ethnic groups are equally likely to perceive that democracy is being supplied.[18] Moreover, a theory of *cultural values* also fails to appear in the overall model. In other words, satisfaction with democracy and visions of full democracy do not arise because individuals identify with modern identities or because they trust their fellow citizens.

Finally, we are ready to test whether rationality or loyalty is the more important source of democratic attitudes. The answer is clear. According to Table 11.2, the only *institutional influence* that helps explain the perceived supply of democracy is an individual's identification with the winning party in the last election. Considered in isolation, being a "winner" does indeed inflate perceptions of the achievement of democracy (see Chapter 10), in good part because loyalists are inclined, deservedly or not, to give their own party full credit for any achievements.[19] But once a statistical control is introduced for performance evaluations, this institutional effect disappears almost entirely.[20] In short, and contrary to the conventional wisdom, Africans are much more likely to rely on reasoning rather than loyalty when assessing the extent of democracy. This major finding has profound implications for political incumbents. It means that they cannot rely indefinitely on unconditional support from the followers who voted them into office. Sooner or later – and probably fairly soon – even the most loyal adherents of governing parties begin to ask the holders of elected office: "how, exactly, have I benefited?"

MODELING DEMAND FOR A MARKET ECONOMY

Turning to economic reforms, we begin by searching for the sources of popular demands. Why do some Africans become advocates of free markets? And what leads the vast majority of the population to shun this orientation? As before, we measure demand for a market economy with an additive index – the *index of support for economic reforms* – that counts whether individuals support user fees, market prices for consumer goods, the privatization of public corporations, and job retrenchment in the civil service.

A summary model of popular demand for a market economy appears in Table 11.4. It shows that public attitudes of free markets are barely formed, especially when compared with demand for democracy. We are able to explain little more than one tenth of the largely random variance, confirming once again that Africans remain disturbingly unfamiliar with the principles of economic liberalization. As we have just shown, people embrace democracy for reasons both cognitive and rational. But they are still figuring out where they stand in relation to economic adjustment. And to the extent that Africans come reluctantly to tolerate market reforms, they do so via routes that are far less clearly charted than the road to democratic commitments.

An explanation of mass economic demands does, however, decisively exclude one theory. We find no evidence of *institutional influences*, all of which fail to appear in our final model. We cannot confirm, for example, that individuals who feel close to a ruling party – including parties that have sponsored adjustment programs – are swayed by partisan attachments to support unpopular market policies. Once again, political loyalty is insufficient to overrule other considerations. Active involvement in a religious group has a slight positive influence on market preferences, but not enough to warrant inclusion in an efficient model.[21] The same applies to participation in formal political procedures: whereas political activism was seen to help build support for economic reforms when institutional factors were considered on their own (see Chapter 10), its influence largely disappears when controls are introduced for alternate explanations. In other words, to the scant extent that Africans have arrived at demands for economic reform, they seem to have done so on informal or idiosyncratic bases, that is, outside of the boundaries of formal institutions or procedures.

TABLE 11.4. *Demand for a Market Economy*[a], *Explanatory Factors Compared*

	R	B	S.E.	Beta	Adj. R^2 (block)	Adj. R^2 (cumulative)
Constant		.427***	.054			
Cognitive Awareness					.061	.061
Media exposure	.214	.093	.006	.132***		
Formal education	.177	.084	.009	073***		
Awareness of democracy	.140	.160	.018	.061***		
Internal efficacy	.084	.040	.006	.053***		
Cultural Values					.055	.099
Individualism	.136	.073	.005	.097***		
Modern identity	.113	.192	.015	.089***		
Prefers private provision	.130	.178	.019	.071***		
Risk tolerance	.096	.047	.007	.058***		
Interpersonal trust	−.081	−.166	.022	−.057***		
Social Structure					.017	.106
Lived poverty	−.130	−.109	.013	−.058***		
Peasant class	.013	.121	.016	.053***		
Performance Evaluations					.013	.114
Availability of free speech	−.058	−.062	.010	−.078***		
Leadership responsiveness	.097	.036	.005	.052***		
Full Model		1.021				.114

Notes:
N = 21,531
***p = <.001
[a] The dependent variable is an additive *index of support for economic reform*, including support for user fees, market pricing for consumer goods, privatization of public corporations, and retrenchments of civil service jobs. See Appendix A.

Our model also demonstrates the limited explanatory power of two other theories. First, *performance evaluations*, whether alone or as a supplement to other theories, explain only marginal amounts of variance in the demand for a market economy.[22] Contrary to expectations, demands for a market economy are not driven primarily by concerns about macroeconomic decline, government corruption, shrinking living standards, and growing social inequality. Perhaps the advocates of adjustment understand that market-conforming measures have been incompletely or weakly implemented to date. Instead, political evaluations seemingly matter more. For example, as people become confident that elected governments will do their bidding, only then are they likely to call for economic reforms. One interpretation is that governments have to prove their democratic credentials before people are willing to risk supporting their policy programs, including an agenda of economic reform.

Second, poverty is one of the only elements of *social structure* that qualifies for inclusion in an efficient model. To be sure, demands for market reforms emanate from people in agrarian occupations, but are offset by the suppressive effects of poverty. Poor urban classes – whether workers or unemployed – as well as poor people in the countryside, are predisposed to oppose economic restructuring. In this regard, we corroborate the common observation that those who bear the brunt of the price inflation and job losses associated with adjustment are likely to form a blocking coalition. But our argument does not stop short at structural analysis. After all, poverty alone explains just 2 percent of the variance in demand for a market economy and almost disappears when included in a multivariate equation.[23] Other things being equal, therefore, we expect nonstructural theories to hold more explanatory promise. We emphasize two such theories.

According to Table 11.4, popular demands for a market economy are a battleground between cultural values and cognitive awareness. Each of these theoretical families contributes an equal amount of explanation to the final regression model. We think that this result neatly captures the tension in public opinion over the highly controversial subject of economic adjustment. On one hand, many Africans remain wedded to a set of economic values that are based on communitarian traditions that served them well in the past. As kin-based economies of affection have eroded, however, people first transferred their hopes for collective welfare onto the institutions of the postcolonial state. They later watched with alarm as state institutions lost capacity to direct and deliver development and, in some cases, collapsed entirely. Gradually realizing that only the strong survive in a global market economy, they have learned to fend for themselves, not only as extended family groups, but also as individuals. So, even as the majority of Africans continue to resist the introduction of alien economic arrangements, the most capable have taken it upon themselves to fashion new entrepreneurial livelihoods. And, even as large proportions of their compatriots are left behind, a small but cognitively aware minority has chosen a market economy as the best option for their own and their country's future.

Without implying theoretical primacy, we first consider the effects of *cultural values* on economic demands. Take, in order of importance, a few key elements. People who define themselves with a modern identity – that is, an occupation, social class, or nationality – are more likely to subscribe to a neo-liberal economic reform agenda. Traditionalists – whose identities derive from ethnic, language, or religious roots – are much more resistant to such reforms. The experience of identity change, by which people leave behind the ascriptions of birth in favor of their own achievements, apparently has a liberating effect on the formation of public opinion. Consistent with the above argument, people who value individualism – as a sense of responsibility for one's own work and welfare – are primed for conversion to a free market ideology. By contrast, people attached to a collective ethic – seeing the state or the community as the guarantor of social and economic advancement – resist this transformation.

Along with identity change, value change (which we have summarized as a shift from communitarianism to individualism) lies at the heart of an explanation of demand for a market economy. In our final model, individualism and modernism occupy second and third place in an overall explanation of the emergence of market-oriented demands. In short, economic reform appeals mainly to those Africans who have undergone prior processes of value change leading to a sense of personal autonomy. Indeed, the market economy proves attractive precisely because it is more conducive to individual self-realization than either a socially controlled moral economy or a legally regulated command economy. And it offers a measure of hope in the face of the worst-case scenario: a corrupt and bankrupt patronage economy.

But, it is important to place these findings in context. One must remember that a solid half of all Afrobarometer interviewees continue to espouse traditional identities (48 percent) and communitarian values (47 percent). This rump of respondents is loath to give up the prerogative to claim welfare provision from a collective entity, whether community or state, or both. Indeed, such deep-seated African values are shared even by some individualists, whose numbers are included in the two thirds of the population who continue to demand that the state provide health, education, and agricultural services.

Cultural values therefore play a more central role in explaining economic demands than in accounting for demands for democracy. We interpret this difference to mean that, in Africa, economic reform provokes greater value conflicts than democratization. Embedded in traditional political practices are certain principles that are compatible with modern representative democracy, such as inclusive processes of deliberation and decision making and arrangements for ensuring the accountability and turnover of leaders. It is far harder to find analogous principles in traditional economic practices, whose ethics of collective property ownership, guaranteed livelihood, and equal distribution of wealth are far more consistent with state socialism than neo-liberalism. Thus, getting to a market economy in Africa is bound to be harder than getting to democracy, and to generate along the way far more frequent and heated controversies over the appropriate roles of individual and community.

Where does change in economic values originate? Once again, we unearth answers in *cognitive awareness*. Because this theory accounts for at least as much variance as cultural values, we take it to be just as important (if not more so) in the formation of demands for a market economy. Indeed, it is precisely by informing themselves about public affairs, that cognitively aware individuals learn about forms of economic organization that depart from familiar communitarian prototypes.

The first thing to notice about the elements in the cognitive family is that formal education does not lead the lineup of usual suspects (see Table 11.4). This result stands to reason since school curricula in most African countries make little effort to impart economic literacy.

Instead, the formation of economic demands is driven by the mass media. Exposure to media enables individuals to obtain information about economic policy and economic performance via news coverage on radio and television and in daily newspapers. Accordingly, users of media – above all, newspapers – are more likely to demand economic reform in part because they have learned about the economic issues of the day via these channels. But the quality of economic analysis on the African airwaves is not profound, and the business pages of African newspapers are not widely read. We therefore guess that the mass media have other, more indirect and even insidious impacts: exposure to pop music, sports, and, especially, advertising are critical to the formation of promarket attitudes. The global information revolution has carried images of luxurious mass consumption into most African homes and, in the process, has awakened new appetites and aspirations. These desires – especially in South Africa, where the advertising industry is as sophisticated as any in the Western world – lead to demands for an economy that can produce a plentiful array of consumer goods.

MODELING THE SUPPLY OF ECONOMIC REFORM

Lastly, this section turns to the perceived supply of economic reform. It asks why Africans are so dissatisfied with the implementation of economic adjustment policies. Following the precedent set in earlier chapters, a single item on satisfaction with SAPs is used to capture the perceived supply of economic reform.

As Table 11.5 shows, a final model successfully explains about one quarter of the variance in this key public attitude. Comparing Table 11.5 with Table 11.2, we see that the origins of the perceived supply of economic reform are similar in important respects to the sources of the perceived supply of democracy. Performance evaluations lead the way in both instances, with only two other theories making limited contributions at the margins. Thus, our task here is twofold: first to briefly document the common profiles of political and economic satisfactions; and, second, to draw attention to several interesting differences.

With regard to commonalities, we note that *social structure* plays no essential part in forming public opinion about the supply of any kind of reform. Whereas poverty seemed to undermine economic satisfaction when social structure was considered alone, it washes away when we consider a model that includes other, mainly attitudinal factors. We take this as evidence that

TABLE 11.5. *Supply of Economic Reform[a], Explanatory Factors Compared*

	R	B	S.E.	Beta	Adj. R² (block)	Adj. R² (cumulative)
Constant		1.769***	.153			
Performance Evaluations					.199	.199
SAP creates inequality	−.308	−.148	.007	−.195***		
Performance of the economy	.286	.205	.015	.144***		
President's performance	.329	.113	.026	.120***		
Delivery of political rights	.202	.165	.021	.103***		
Trust institutions	.241	.074	.017	.062***		
Corruption worse under democracy	−.059	.051	.012	.060***		
Identity group treated fairly	.220	.054	.017	.057***		
Cognitive Awareness					.052	.240
Awareness of SAP	−.203	−.401	.029	−.156***		
See democracy as procedures	−.141	−.147	.031	−.109***		
Cultural Values					.026	.251
Individualism	.136	.085	.008	.100***		
Prefer private provision	−.063	−.157	.027	−.056***		
Full Model			1.050			.251

Notes:
N = 21,531
***p = <.001
[a] The dependent variable is satisfaction with SAPs. See Appendix A.

the architecture of society tells us little about the prospects that democracy and markets will take root in the public mind. A more promising line of analysis pays closer attention to the more proximate effects of cognitive awareness and, especially, performance evaluations. Moreover, just as *cultural values* are absent from the explanation of the supply of democracy, *institutional influences* make no appearance in a final model of the supply of economic reform.

Instead, familiar *performance evaluations* recur in both supply models. Citizens hinge their judgments about the extent of democratic and market regimes on the performance of the economy, the performance of the president, the delivery of political rights, and trust in state institutions. In terms of both absolute and relative explanatory power, these aspects of performance play roughly the same roles in explaining the perceived supply of both types of regime. In other words, citizens seem to apply a common core of considerations in determining whether economic and political reforms are meeting their expectations. And, insofar as *cognitive awareness* matters, the critical variable in both instances is awareness of SAPs. From these shared features, we would therefore expect, and will test at the end of this chapter, that popular estimates of the extent of democratization and marketization are mutually reinforcing.

More interesting for the moment are the distinctive determinants of the supply of economic reform. The popular conviction that SAPs create inequality surges to the explanatory forefront. Underlying this trend is a popular recognition that basic economic livelihoods have become harder to attain over recent years, including the period during which SAPs have supposedly been in force. As people notice that SAPs hurt a majority of ordinary consumers, they also suspect that the same policies help an economic elite. As they observe widening benefit gaps, they lose faith in the government's economic policy program. By drawing attention to growing inequalities, respondents reconfirm an earlier finding that the benefits of SAPs are seen to accrue to the advantage of political notables, officeholders, and capitalist cronies who are "close to the government" (see Chapter 4). Inequality persists as the dominant thread of explanation for dissatisfaction with SAPs even after multiple statistical controls have been applied for all other potentially relevant factors. Indeed, the evaluation of inequality is so central to the explanation of the perceived supply of economic reform that it accounts for between one third and one half more variance than standard evaluations of the performance of the economy and the president.

The other new performance element explaining the supply of economic reform is the trajectory of corruption. Unexpectedly, those who see corruption as having worsened since the democratic transition are more – not less – satisfied with SAPs. Based on corruption's previous effects, we had expected the relationship to be negative. A positive connection seems to suggest, however, that those who welcome – and benefit from – a market economy are willing to tolerate an increase in corruption. It is logical that, even as reforms reduce the ready availability of official rents, the loosening of state regulations over the economy creates new opportunities for graft in the private sector. But the emergence of novel forms of corruption reduces support for economic reform, especially among those who see reform as deepening inequality. Thus, there is a contradiction within public opinion that must be resolved before a market economy can take deeper root in African countries. Either the opponents of reform must accept that inequality is an unavoidable consequence of a market-led path to economic growth; or reform beneficiaries must be willing to forego corruption-based privilege.

Finally, we note that, other things being equal, institutional loyalty to the ruling party does not induce people to favorably assess the extent of economic reform. Once the leading cause of favorable economic attitudes when institutional influences were considered alone (see Table 10.2), identifying with a winning party now vanishes from all multivariate models.[24] Even though being a political "winner" is marginally influential in shaping perceptions of the supply of democracy, it ultimately plays no role whatever in explaining the supply of economic reform. It drops out of the theoretical mix once cognitive considerations (for example, awareness of SAPs) and performance considerations (for example, SAP creates inequality) are taken into account. Followers of the ruling party apparently remain highly pragmatic when assessing whether African governments are actually constructing productive market economies. In almost all countries studied (with the possible exception of Uganda), the general public shrewdly concludes that little real economic reform has been supplied. In our opinion, these findings constitute stark evidence that rational calculation is displacing partisan loyalty as the basis of African public opinion.

PATHS TO REFORM: A LEARNING PROCESS

To conclude this chapter, we return to our argument that the route to reform is a learning process. In so doing, we modify the notion that learning takes place over a lifetime by placing special emphasis on learning in adulthood.

Among the African publics studied here, we have found that the effects of childhood socialization are evident to only a limited extent. To be sure, early inculcation into traditional communitarian values predisposes people to reject a market economy. And, as we will show, formal education (during youth) cannot be excluded as a source of the cognitive awareness that underpins support for various kinds of reform. But we think that learning on the basis of adult experiences is a much more powerful force. We have shown, for example, that coming of age under an indigenous authoritarian regime seems to generate demands for democracy among a postcolonial generation. And resistance to market reforms is offset by the consumption of news information from the mass news media, which is mainly an adult activity. Moreover, attitudes about the supply of liberalization reforms have a particularly recent provenance. Africans derive their satisfactions with democracy and their dissatisfactions with adjustment policies almost entirely as a result of immediate popular reactions to the performance of *new* regimes. Thus, while we accept the basic precepts of a lifetime learning model, we place greatest explanatory weight on recent experiences.

To test this late blooming version of a learning process, we now merge all previous analyses.[25] A path model is estimated in Figure 11.1.[26] What value does path analysis add? Among other things, it distinguishes indirect effects that were previously hidden from view and helps to identify the sequences of learning that lead to reform-mindedness. We begin by locating three underlying factors that indirectly impinge upon learning about reform in Africa.

First is political generation.[27] The arrow that runs horizontally across the top of Figure 11.1 reconfirms that spending one's young adulthood under

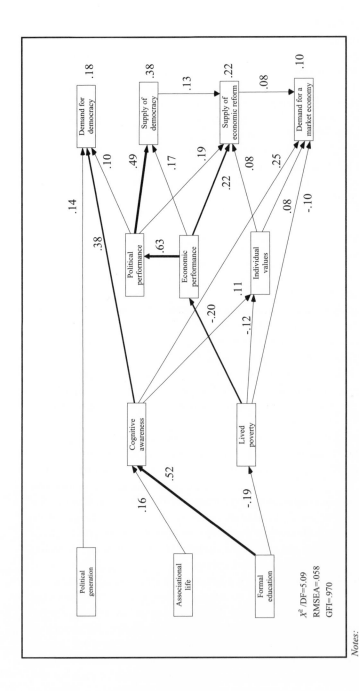

Notes:

1. Structural equation modeling using maximum likelihood estimation. Because some measures of goodness of fit are highly sensitive to large samples (such as X^2 and degrees of freedom), the model was estimated on a randomly selected subsample of N=1,200 (separate subsamples were created from each of the five imputed data sets and the results averaged).

2. Path coefficients are Standardized Regression Estimates. Coefficients attached to the dependent variables are Squared Multiple Correlations and analogous to R^2. X^2 / DF is the ratio of Chi Square to Degrees of Freedom: a good fit indicated by a ratio up to 5 to 1. RMSEA is the Root Mean Squared Error of Approximation: a value up to .05 indicates a close fit, with values of up to .08 representing a reasonable fit. GFI is the Goodness of Fit Index: it estimates the extent to which the hypothesized model fits with the actual data.

FIGURE 11.1. Path Model of Attitudes to Reform

an indigenous authoritarian regime has a direct bearing on demand for democracy. Second is formal education. The path model demonstrates that education has no direct effects on any reform attitude, a somewhat surprising finding in the light of core modernization assumptions. Instead, attending school has hefty indirect effects. Formal education raises cognitive awareness, which in turn leads powerfully to demands for democracy. And, by reducing poverty (people with school qualifications are more likely to earn income), education indirectly helps to lift levels of popular support for a market economy (see the horizontal arrows across the bottom of Figure 11.1).[28]

In our previous analyses, these effects of education were masked in several ways. For one thing, a person's general level of schooling is less immediately relevant to learning deep democratic commitments than his or her specific awareness of public affairs. Although most well-informed Africans are also well educated, not all educated Africans are interested in, engaged in, and informed about debates around politics and the economy. For another thing, even educated people often can't find jobs in collapsing economies: a person's educational background, therefore, is less closely connected to the formation of antiadjustment attitudes than whether he or she is living hand to mouth. Finally, as argued earlier, cognitive awareness also has other important antecedents – note especially the path from associational life – that enable people to learn about democracy and economic reform from other sources. Apart from in the classroom, political and policy information is disseminated via religious, occupational, and development groups. Although many Africans attend a church or a mosque, far fewer join secular associations, which helps to explain why levels of cognitive awareness are generally quite low in Africa and why, in turn, shortages of political and economic information constitute powerful inhibitions on support for reforms.

Third is the lived experience of poverty. We already know from earlier analysis that poverty directly undermines demands for a market economy, no doubt because poor people are acutely aware that they stand at a disadvantage in a competitive economic environment. The path model now shows that poverty also reduces popular evaluations of economic performance. And by suppressing individualism, poverty also indirectly reduces satisfaction with the implementation of structural adjustment programs. These linkages are based on learning from the lived experience of poverty and the attendant difficulties of piecing together livelihoods. The main path of learning runs sequentially from mass shortages of basic needs, through judgments about the performance of the economy, to perceptions that economic reform is not being supplied.

The path model also casts light on critical intermediary roles played by popular evaluations of political and economic performance.[29] As we already know, performance theories – which assume that citizens make instrumental calculations based on their own best interests – are central to explanation of reform attitudes in Africa. The location of popular performance evaluations at the heart of the path model – alongside, and multiply linked to, reform attitudes – is eloquent visual testament to their importance. Little further evidence is required that reform attitudes in African countries are powered by a heavy dose of instrumentalism.

We have argued that Africans expect their governments to deliver both political and economic goods, but that political performance takes priority. In the strongest linkage in the path model, we now see that assessments of economic performance apparently underpin judgments about political performance. Stated concretely, Africans who think that the economy is de-livering material goods are also likely to consider that the polity is providing political rights. So, even though neither regression nor path analyses reveal an economic logic underlying the formation of democratic attitudes, we find evidence here of certain circuitous economic influences.

For a couple of good reasons, however, the existence of indirect economic effects does not undermine our argument about the primacy of politics in the formation of African public opinion. Even though the path model shows a unidirectional route from economic performance to political performance, in actuality the relationship is thoroughly reciprocal. An almost equally efficient and plausible model can be constructed with the arrow running in the oppo-site direction, that is, from political performance to economic performance.[30] Moreover, the linkages to reform attitudes from political performance are always stronger than from economic performance. Not only does political performance do more than twice as well in explaining perceptions of the sup-ply of democracy but, remarkably, it even does slightly better at explaining assessments of the supply of economic reform. All other things considered, people's sense that they have obtained political rights and free elections still lead the way in influencing their economic satisfactions. It is therefore safe to conclude that a basic political logic runs through the process of learning about *all* types of reform.

We have proposed that performance considerations are more likely to drive contentment with the existing *supply* of reforms than to prompt new *demands* for change. The path analysis allows us to come to closure on this matter. Take demand for democracy. This key attitude is directly influenced only by political performance and the weak path from economic performance bears a negative sign.[31] Thus, these two aspects of performance tend to cancel each other out: whereas good political performance raises demand for democracy, good economic performance lowers it. The net consequence is that performance considerations – the hallmark of instrumental reasoning – begin to disappear from the explanatory mix. In their place, we are left with a parsimonious account of demand for democracy that depends principally on a direct path from cognitive awareness. This very strong relationship implies that demand for democracy is primarily a learned attitude. And, in the absence of strong influence from performance evaluations, we cannot make a case that people learn to prefer democracy mainly on *instrumental* grounds.

Instead the Africans in our study appear to value democracy *intrinsically*, that is, as an end that is worth attaining in and of itself.

This path to learning about reform raises a broader, final inquiry. Do simultaneous effects exist *between and among* attitudes to reform? Does one attitude to democracy or markets help to cause another? And, if so, in what direction do the arrows of causality run? Answers to these questions are easily apprehended with reference to the vertical paths described on the far right side of Figure 11.1.

The first thing to notice is that demand for democracy is unconnected to any other reform attitude. The model definitively confirms that Africans commit themselves to democracy as a preferred form of government without necessarily also concluding that the hybrid regimes that political elites supply in African countries resemble a democratic ideal. Indeed, as we will explore in the last chapter, ordinary Africans regularly demand more democracy than political elites supply. In addition, demand for democracy does not lead to support for other neo-liberal reforms (and vice versa); the path model shows demand for democracy to be *independent* of demand for a market economy. The main reason is that liberal attitudes are distributed asymmetrically throughout the population: while the small number of free market advocates in African societies usually claim to be democrats, most converts to democracy are strongly opposed to an orthodox package of economic adjustment reforms.

A causal path can be observed, nonetheless, from the perceived supply of democracy to the perceived supply of economic reform. We call this connection the *democratic dividend*. It measures the extent to which satisfied democrats (who see working democracies being built in their countries) tend to accept SAP implementation. This linkage constitutes another important instance in which political attitudes shape economic attitudes, rather than the reverse.

The democratic dividend accrues as follows. Among the many reasons SAPs quickly gained a bad reputation among African publics was that they were first introduced under the illegitimate and heavy-handed governments of the 1980s. The general public was rarely, if at all, consulted about the content of economic policies: strict austerity or adjustment programs were simply announced as faits accomplis. During the 1990s, new governments were formed as a result of democratic transitions. While these governments have hardly been more consultative on economic policy, the winning party's platform usually paid obeisance to a market reform agenda. But the very fact that leaders were elected in open, multiparty contests infused legitimacy into official policy pronouncements. Compared to predecessor administrations, elected governments therefore have found it easier to implement unpopular economic reform policies without stirring up protest. We attribute this change to a groundswell of popular goodwill, not least from satisfied democrats. We do not know how long such honeymoons last. But a democratic divided was plainly evident in the Afrobarometer data circa 2000, that is, up to a decade after Africa's first democratic transitions.

Lastly, a causal path connects the perceived supply of economic reform to demands for a market economy. The point we made earlier about this linkage bears repeating because it contributes to our argument about instrumentalism. Not only for individualists, but now for all Africans, including those who closely monitor the economy and its managers, performance matters. Before people will lend their allegiance to a market economy, they want evidence that it can provide desired goods and services and address the most important problems facing African countries. Given what we know about popular development priorities, Africans are most concerned to discover whether market economies will generate enough well paid jobs to broadly go around.

In conclusion, we have shown in this chapter that there are various paths to reform in African countries. To a greater or lesser extent, all are based on processes of learning by which adult Africans adapt to the political and economic circumstances in which they find themselves. The Africans we interviewed have learned from their own experiences that they no longer want to be ruled by aging big men who know not when to step aside. Ideas about democracy and market reform, while not deeply appreciated, are beginning to catch on among people who have become aware of public affairs, either through exposure to schools, the mass media, or voluntary associations. Above all, adult experiences of evaluating the performance of regime experiments against standards of self-interest have been central to the formation of public opinion. In short, Africans are learning through trial and error to make up their own minds about the desirability of competing political and economic regimes. For reasons both intrinsic and instrumental, they have staked out clear positions in relation to democracy and markets.

12

Predicting Political Participation

We have argued that, far from emanating from the deep structures and cultures of African societies, public opinion about liberalization springs mainly from recent political and economic learning. Mass attitudes about regime changes are primarily the product of acquired knowledge and instrumental calculation. But a critic might reasonably interject: "so what?" Does it really matter what ordinary Africans think and feel about public affairs? Don't the prospects for democratization and economic reform depend more critically on what these actors actually *do*? Surely public opinion can only be taken seriously if attitudes are converted into action?

We happen to think that attitude change is central to processes of regime consolidation and thus is worth studying in its own right. But, to address valid concerns about practical consequences, this chapter explores whether attitude change results in active citizenship. The focus is on political participation in all its variegated dimensions, from voting and protesting to what we all have called communing and contacting. These topics were broached earlier. On the extent of participation, we showed that the Africans we interviewed are politically busy during elections but less so between elections (see Chapter 5). Yet we found that people who contact their leaders and engage in collective action are also early adopters of democratic and market reforms (see Chapter 10). In this chapter we search for the underlying determinants of political participation and try to settle whether such behaviors are best regarded as a cause or an effect of reform.

There are important theoretical and policy stakes to this inquiry. From a practical angle, the health of fragile new regimes depends in good part on whether citizens give them life. What is the point of convening a multiparty, founding election if citizens subsequently fail to take advantage of novel opportunities to participate? Why is it, in some African countries, that voter turnout rates are low or in decline? And, why do many Africans continue to hold back from wholehearted involvement in democratic procedures between elections? With the survival and consolidation of real-world regimes in the balance, we now assess whether emerging reform preferences motivate individuals to become politically active. To cut a long story short, we find that commitment to democracy sometimes inspires citizen action, especially with regard to willingness to stand up in defense of political liberties. But other reform attitudes have limited action effects.

From a theoretical standpoint, we also aim to illuminate the chicken-and-egg debate over which comes first: attitudes or action? Stated differently, we intend to test whether political participation performs better as a product of learning about reform or as a predictor of reform attitudes (as in Chapter 10). The answer will help us characterize mass political participation in Africa's new democracies: Is it entered into autonomously from below by free-thinking citizens? Or is it institutionally mobilized from above by political elites? To anticipate results, we find that – with few notable exceptions, like the just-mentioned effects of demand for democracy – political participation in Africa continues to be more mobilized than autonomous. One implication is that, at the individual level, Africans have yet to complete a transition from clientelism to citizenship.

VOTING

Who votes in African elections? Why do they do so? And does voting behavior grow from the same roots as attitudes to reform?

Table 12.1 displays a thrifty model of voter turnout for the twelve Afrobarometer countries. The model explains an individual's self-reported claim to have cast a ballot in the last presidential or parliamentary election.[1] Some 19 percent of the variance in voting is explained using just two main theoretical approaches. One is immediately struck, however, that the explanatory profile for voting behavior is very different to that of reform attitudes. Instead of cognition and rationality, the driving forces are social and institutional structures.

Take the impact of social structure on voter turnout. Other things being equal, young Africans who have achieved voting age since the democratic transition are *least* likely to vote. Being a member of the multiparty generation reduces an individual's probability of voting by over 24 percent.[2] And, while each year of maturity gained after age eighteen improves the chances of voting, it does so only by a minuscule increment of less than 0.2 percent.[3] Young Africans do not voluntarily exclude themselves from voting since they express just as much interest in public affairs as their elders. Instead, they encounter institutional obstacles, especially in registering to vote. In the five countries where we asked about this issue, people under thirty years old were twice as likely to lack a voter's card as those aged forty-five or older.[4] To reinforce this point, we find no evidence that being a member of the older colonial or postcolonial generations either increases or decreases the propensity to vote.

TABLE 12.1. *Political Participation, Explanatory Factors Compared*

	Voting		Protesting		Communing and Contacting[a]	
	Beta	Adj R² (block)	Beta	Adj R² (block)	Beta	Adj R² (block)
Social Structure		.111		.014		.077
Postcolonial generation	–		–.100***		–	
Multiparty generation	–.229***		–		–	
Age	.053***		–.062***		.073***	
Peasant class	.099***		–		.055***	
Working class	.060***		–		–	
Middle class	.056***		–		–	
Rural	.040***		–.048***		.085***	
Gender (female)	–		–		–.061***	
Institutional Influences		.089		.060		.293
Identifies with a political party	.185***		.037***		.092***	
Member of religious group	–		–.039***		.093***	
Member of other association	–		.056***		.188***	
Voted in last election	X		–		.089***	
Joined a protest demonstration	–		X		.153***	
Communing and contacting	.123***		.231***		X	
Contacted influential person	–.045***		–		.199***	
Cognitive Awareness		.000		.041		.177
Exposure to mass media	.057***		.070***		–	
Knowledge of leaders	–		–.034***		.074***	
Cognitive engagement	–		.043***		.181***	
Education	–		.067***		–	
Awareness of SAP	–		–		.085***	
Performance Evaluations		.026		.000		.014
Free and fair elections	.081***		–		–	
Delivery of political rights	.049***		–		–	
President's performance	–		–		.062***	
Cultural Values		.000		.000		.025
Modern identity	–		–		.075***	
Attitudes to Reform		.000		.000		.000
Demand for democracy	–		–.053***		–	
Constant	.221***		.243***		–.490***	
Full Model		.187		.103		.391

Notes: ***p = <.001

An X indicates that the independent variable is also, in whole or part, a dependent variable. Thus, no relationship is calculated. A dash (–) indicates that the relationship is insufficiently strong and significant to include the independent variable in a final, reduced model.

[a] A five-item *index of communing and contacting* is composed of (a) joining with others to raise an issue, (b) attending a campaign rally, (c) promoting an electoral candidate, (d) attending a community meeting, and (e) contacting a government official. See Appendix A.

In addition, voters in Africa are drawn disproportionately from the ranks of jobholders in the peasant, working, and middle classes. By contrast, those who lack a current source of earned income – including those who are temporarily unemployed, who have never had a job, plus students, housewives, and retirees – are *least* likely to vote. Perhaps because employed or self-employed people feel that they have a stake in electoral outcomes, they are more inclined to vote. If this is correct, then economic policies that respond to mass appeals to create jobs will have the side benefit of boosting voter turnout. And new participants who enter the political system via this route will be drawn not only from emergent middle classes – as modernization theory would have it – but also from among those urban workers and rural peasants who earn income from an occupation.

Above and beyond considerations of employment, there is also a general tendency – significant both in the pooled data set and in eight of the twelve Afrobarometer countries – for rural dwellers to turn out more regularly at the polls than urbanites.[5] This somewhat surprising result lends itself to both positive and negative interpretations. On one hand, electoral participation in the countryside indicates that a broad cross section of the eligible population has embraced basic civic duties; in other words, a narrow urban elite does not monopolize the choice of governmental leaders. On the other hand, the quality of rural voter turnout is as important as its quantity. If, in the countryside, popular understandings of democracy and economic policy are vague and knowledge of leaders is incomplete, then many voters may simply go through the motions of voting without exercising informed choice. Compared to their urban cousins, rural dwellers are disadvantaged in all aspects of cognition.[6] As a result, rural voters may be easily confused by conflicting campaign claims, misled by intentional misinformation, and predisposed to take voting cues from traditional and party patrons. In short, they are susceptible to manipulation and prone to vote as a bloc. To the extent that poorly informed rural dwellers take their lead from others, their electoral participation is more mobilized than autonomous.

Certainly there is little indication in the voting model in Table 12.1 that people decide to participate at the polls on the basis of rational cognition. The only cognitive factor that weighs positively on voter turnout is exposure to news in the mass media.[7] Otherwise, the voting public in Africa is composed of a broad cross section of society that includes both well and badly informed people. The only performance evaluations that enter into the voter turnout decision are political ones: whether the previous election was seen to be free and fair and whether the new regime is seen to have delivered political rights. Otherwise, voters go to the polls in these selected African countries whether they approve or disapprove of the performance of the president, the government, or the economy. To summarize, the standard battery of cognitive and instrumental considerations that drive attitudes to reform plays very little role in an individual's calculus of *whether* to vote.

Instead, institutional influences now join social structure as the engines of explanation. When it comes to voter turnout in Africa, political parties are the strongest institutional link between the political center and the individual voter. People who identify with a political party are almost 17 percent more likely to vote than those who are unaffiliated.[8] Note that partisan identification now refers to both "winners" and "losers," that is, to adherents of either ruling or opposition parties. Individuals who express closeness to *any* political party are likely to be mobilized to vote via get-out-the-vote campaigns. Indeed, there is an established political tradition of mass electoral mobilization in Africa, especially in countries with a legacy of single-party rule. Party agents – or, in extreme cases, gangs from the party youth wing – go door-to-door to urge voters – through persuasion, inducement, or threat – to buy party cards, attend campaign rallies, and to turn out on polling day.

It may seem strange to portray African political parties as mobilization machines when we have asserted they are often weak, underfunded, and disorganized. But, in a context where other mass institutions are even less effectual – note that memberships in religious groups or other voluntary associations have no meaningful influence on voter turnout – parties can seem relatively strong by comparison. Moreover, in the aftermath of regime transition, party identification is not widespread in the population, averaging just 57 percent across the Afrobarometer countries. In an atmosphere of new-found freedoms, the remainder of the populace chooses to eschew affiliation with any party (see Chapter 10). Under these circumstances, low absolute levels of party identification limit the impact of any party mobilizing effects on voter turnout.

To wrap up the explanation of voting behavior, we draw attention to the habituation of individual actors into a constellation of democratic procedures. Voting is not only closely connected to other participatory behaviors, but may be partly encouraged by them. As illustrated in Table 12.1, voting is more common among people who also engage in what we have called "communing" (like attending political rallies and community meetings, events that blur together in countries with dominant political parties) and who contact government officials. Thus, some people appear to be motivated to vote as a consequence of their experiences with collective action and political lobbying. There is reason to believe, therefore, that one democratic behavior begets another and that institutionalized participation develops as a package of related political acts. The upside of this finding is that participatory acts are mutually reinforcing: the simple act of attending a community meeting, for example, lures some citizens into voting. The downside is that those who avoid government officials and shun community meetings are likely to remain completely marginalized from all aspects of political life, even including voting.

Discussion of the effects of reform attitudes on voter turnout and other aspects of political participation is withheld until the last section of this chapter.

PROTESTING

Little needs to be said about the determinants of political protest, an infrequent behavior that resists comprehensive explanation. Only about one in ten Afrobarometer respondents ever participates in a protest demonstration and, so far, we have been able to account for only one tenth of the variance in who does or does not protest. Thus, we simply draw attention to the ways in which patterns of protest deviate from patterns of voter turnout.

Table 12.1 (Columns 4 and 5) presents the relevant results. Within each political generation – whether colonial, postcolonial, or multiparty – protest action is a prerogative of youth. Middle-aged folks in the postcolonial generation show a strong tendency to hold back from street demonstrations, presumably leaving such initiatives to those with less to lose than themselves. Predictably, too, political protesting is an urban phenomenon, though one that our data indicates involves both genders and all social classes.

Whereas a sociological theory does a better job than institutionalism at explaining voting, the reverse is true for protesting. Institutional procedures and structures lead the way in helping us understand who protests and why. To begin with, people who have engaged in communing and contacting are natural recruits for political protest. There is a logical progression from joining with others to raise an issue and taking an intense and theatrical version of such demands into the streets. Indeed, communing and contacting are so closely related to protesting that the latter could legitimately be included in an aggregate index of political participation.[9] To do so, however, would obscure the fact that protesting is a more youthful and urban activity than either collective action or overtures to officials.[10] Hence, we reveal more about the sociological underpinnings of political participation by considering protest separately from other forms of nonvoting behavior.

Moreover, compared to voting, which is largely a function of identification with political parties, protests are precipitated by a wider set of political institutions. True, we find that both ruling and opposition parties sponsor protest marches and in so doing, pull their followers along with them. But greater amounts of protest activity are explained with reference to membership in civic organizations such as trade unions, farmer associations, business forums, and grassroots development groups. Membership in any one of these voluntary bodies increases an individual's propensity to engage in protest by about thirteen percentage points.[11] This relationship makes sense in a context where African trade unions regularly call for work stoppages, boycotts, and mass rallies to protest, among other things, the austerity measures associated with economic structural adjustment reforms. Interestingly, and perhaps counter to intuition, membership in religious communities depresses the impulse to protest. This anomaly does not arise because churches and mosques urge political passivity on their congregations; far from it, many religious leaders often try to raise political consciousness and induce social action. Rather – apart from a minority of zealots – religious folk tend to shun organized confrontation in favor of trying to resolve problems through peaceful discussion and compromise.

To close this section, we note that an individual's cognitive awareness plays a bigger role in prompting protest than it does in encouraging voting. Voters are all-comers: they turn out to cast ballots regardless of their levels of engagement in public affairs or information about the issues in an election. In some respects, protesters are a more select group, being drawn disproportionately from people who are better educated, more media savvy, and more interested and excited by politics. In short, political activists take the lead. But we should be careful not to idealize the role of protest in African politics because, as elsewhere in the world, it brings out a mixed bag of participants. The urban youth who are commonly the shock troops of mass protest are often woefully ill-informed about the issues at stake. To make this point, we note that people who do *not* know the identities of key political leaders (from local government councilors to the national vice president) are likely to show up at street protests.

COMMUNING AND CONTACTING

The Afrobarometer indicates that fewer Africans participate politically between elections than turn out to vote. And, comparing mundane political behaviors, we find that people engage in local varieties of collective action (such as community meetings or self-help development activities) more frequently than they interact with elected or appointed officials of the state. We have summarized these behaviors in an *index of communing and contacting*.

Table 12.1 (last two columns) indicates that this index is readily susceptible to explanation. We are able to untangle more variance in interelectoral forms of participation – some 38 percent – than for any other set of attitudes or behavior in this study. Thus, our conceptual account of participation between elections is much more complete than our effort to theorize about voting.

In contrast to voting, communing and contacting do not derive from an individual's political generation or social class. Once again, the most relevant social characteristic is where one lives, with rural dwellers being more involved than urban residents in organized forms of collective action. For example, perhaps because they live in relatively cohesive communities – or at least in places where they know their neighbors – rural dwellers are twice as likely to often attend civic gatherings.[12] And they are somewhat more likely to regularly get together with others to address an issue of common concern, for example by joining a communal work party for a local development project.[13] Absent close relationships with neighbors or community-based projects, urbanites are more prone to resort to protest.

Although protests attract youth, communing and contacting are the preserves of older people who, over a lifetime, have accumulated the social ties that facilitate participation in a patronage system. To get local demands heard, communities often organize delegations of respected elders to make contact with government officials. And traditional village leaders continue to convene community meetings, even if younger, educated cadres provide technical advice and record the proceedings. The audiences at such gatherings, especially in rural areas, invariably tilt toward older men and women. The negative sign on the coefficient for gender, however, draws attention to apparently lower levels of interelectoral participation among women. While women are just as likely as men to cast a vote in national elections,[14] they report lower levels of communing and contacting across both urban and rural areas. This finding flies in the face of our casual observations at the village level that women often form the backbone of collective action for development. In reality, however, women may be so burdened with family responsibilities that they lack the time to engage in policy debate and political representation. Another possibility, suggested to us by a female researcher in the Afrobarometer Network, is that men lie more than women about the true extent of their participatory behaviors.

To be sure, citizens must show interest in politics and be available for discussion if they are to participate in public life between elections. This much is confirmed by the centrality of cognitive engagement to our model of communing and contacting. It stands to reason that individuals with passionate commitments to policy causes will be more likely to seek out others – whether neighbors or state officials – in search of solutions. And collective forums – including community meetings and campaign rallies – will attract those inquisitive citizens who wish to engage in the public discourse that is so central to democratic decision making. In these ways, cognitive engagement is the leading component of an explanation of participation based on information theory. Of course, other aspects of cognitive awareness matter too. For instance, people who are aware of the existence of structural adjustment programs are better placed than their uninformed brethren to join in policy debates. And those who can readily identify the names and offices of elected leaders possess a resource for establishing productive political contacts. All told, being cognitively aware is an asset to communing and contacting and, in this regard, there is a natural progression from learning about reform to engaging in political action between elections.

Once more, however, institutions loom largest. Remarkably, institutional influences together account for fully 29 percent of the variance in forms of political participation between elections (see Table 12.1, last column).[15] Nonreligious voluntary associations – which are now almost twice as influential as political parties in shaping participation – create arenas for popular assembly and conduits for lobbying leaders. It is common practice in Africa, as elsewhere in the world, for voluntary bodies to convene membership meetings that feature speeches, debates, or question-and-answer sessions with political officeholders. The chamber of commerce hobnobs with the minister of finance and the trade union congress musters with the minister of labor. In this fashion, associations foster direct, formal linkages between policy elites and members of organized groups. The individuals who are most likely to take advantage of these linkages are those activists who already engage in voting and protesting.

The most distinctive feature of interelectoral participation in Africa, however, is informality. Stated simply, the best overall predictor of access to public officials is contact with notables. Ordinary folk who have sought out a business, traditional, or religious leader for advice or assistance are most likely *also* to have interacted with an appointed or elected official of the state. This finding strongly suggests that getting things done politically depends not only on *what* you know (cognitive awareness) but also on *whom* you know (an influential person). The quickest and most effective route of access to top leaders in Africa is through informal patronage hierarchies in which an influential person within or outside the state introduces you to a decision-maker. The fact that both voluntary associations and informal patronage networks are routes to participation suggests that these institutions may be intertwined. If so, then voluntary associations play intermediary roles in a patronage system by facilitating relations between the association's members and top political leaders. The risk is that, far from promoting democratic values, the institutions of civil society thus will tend to reproduce the neo-patrimonial norms of previous political regimes.[16]

Moreover, informal channels of access are narrow, especially toward the upper reaches of the polity, being available only to those with the right connections. Van de Walle has argued persuasively that patronage networks are constricted in Africa: where resources are scarce, only a small elite is able to partake.[17] Thus, if patronage benefits few, its net effect is to curtail, not expand, opportunities for participation. We contend that these limits to patronage help to explain why mass democratic involvements between elections – especially contacts between constituents and their elected leaders – remain stuck at low levels in African countries.

Finally, in an important contrast, we note that patronage does not encourage turnout in elections. In Table 12.1, the sign on the regression coefficient for contacting an influential person is negative for voting. In other words, an individual's dependence on a personal sponsor, including notables connected to political leaders, actually reduces the likelihood that he or she will vote. One implication is that the bargain between clients and patrons – I will follow you if you provide me with material rewards – is breaking down, probably as a consequence of economic crisis. In Uganda's 2000 referendum campaign, we found that efforts by political elites to use local agents to buy votes, distribute development services, or threaten negative consequences had no meaningful consequences. Ugandans were able to resist such pressures or bend them to their own advantage, for example by accepting inducements but voting according to their own desires. Instead, voting in Africa seems to be a genuinely widespread mass activity that takes place beyond the purview of impoverished patronage networks. In this way, elections constitute a unique opportunity for voters to independently reward or punish leaders.

VOTE CHOICE

Do attitudes to reform have behavioral consequences? So far, the shaded section of Table 12.1 seems to suggest not: demand for democracy, for example, has no significant impact on voting or interelectoral participation; and it is negative for protest! Instead, as just demonstrated, popular political participation has less subjective origins. Voting, protesting, communing, and contacting are all shaped by the objective structure of society and the prevailing architecture of its political institutions. Attitudes to reform display only tenuous links with behavior. While attitudes may have changed, behaviors apparently have not.

To apply generally, these conclusions would have to cover a full range of relevant political activities. But we now explore the impact of attitudes to reform on two other important behaviors: vote choice and defending democracy (see Table 12.2). In these cases, each turns out to be a product of attitudinal change.

So far, we have only considered *whether* people vote, not *how* they vote. Beyond turning out, electors in democracies exercise vote choice. Older theories of vote choice in Western Europe had a strong structural bias, as illustrated by classic studies that trace patterns of electoral behavior to social cleavages of class, language, and religion and which emphasize party loyalties that are transmitted across generations.[18] New analyses show, however, that social identities and party cohesion are eroding at the same time as electoral volatility is increasing.[19] In making decisions on how to vote, citizens in Western countries now pay far more attention to the characteristics of individual candidates, the influence of current events, and the nature of media coverage. Are similar processes of behavioral change underway in Africa? In making choices at the polls, do African voters fall back on objective social attachments – especially ethnic ties[20] – or do they subjectively and rationally evaluate the performance of leaders and institutions?[21]

An answer based on Afrobarometer data is displayed in Table 12.2.[22] It shows that social structure plays only a minor role in shaping vote choice.

TABLE 12.2. *Political Participation, Explanatory Factors Compared (continued)*

	Vote Choice[a]		Defending Democracy[b]	
	Beta	Adj R² (block)	Beta	Adj R² (block)
Social Structure		.014		.012
Rural	.069***		–	
Postcolonial generation	−.058***		–	
Peasant class	–		−.036***	
Cognitive Awareness		.000		.114
See democracy as procedures	–		.104***	
Knowledge of leaders	–		.098***	
Education	–		.088***	
Exposure to mass media	–		.084***	
Availability of free speech	–		.066***	
Cognitive engagement	–		.047***	
Performance Evaluations		.154		.026
President's performance	.246***		−.063***	
Free and fair elections	.181***		–	
Performance of the economy	−.071***		.062***	
Delivery of political rights	.043***		–	
Availability of free speech	–		.067***	
Government policy performance	–		−.050***	
Attitudes to Reform		.065		.049
Supply of democracy	.083***		–	
Demand for democracy	−.051***		.131***	
Constant	.204***		1.790***	
Full Model		.170		.139

Notes:
*** p = <.001
A dash (–) indicates that the relationship is insufficiently strong and significant to include the independent variable in a final, reduced model.
[a] Among voters only, those who supported the winning party (N = 15,610).
[b] A three-item *index of defending democracy* is composed of willingness to take action when faced with (a) closure of opposition newspapers, (b) dismissal of independent judges, and (c) shutdown of parliament and cancellation of elections (N = 21,531). See Appendix A.

Alone, a theory based on social structure contributes merely one percent to an explanation of whether an individual cast a ballot for the winning party in the last national election. Strikingly, relevant social considerations do not include ethnicity, at least when this concept is measured as membership in each country's largest language group.[23] Across the Afrobarometer as a whole, winning parties draw electoral support from a broad cross section of majority, minority, and intermediate-sized ethno-linguistic groups.

TABLE 12.3. *Vote Choice by Ethno-Linguistic Group*

Country	Largest Ethno-Linguistic Group	Percentage of this Group who Voted for the Winning Party in Last Election	Correlation, Vote Choice by Ethno-Linguistic Group	Rank, Ethnic Voting
Namibia	Oshivambo	79	.337***	1
Ghana	Akan	32	−.229***	2
Uganda	Luganda	15	−.137***	3
Tanzania	Swahili	56	−.108***	4
Zimbabwe	Shona	45	.104*	5
Malawi	Chewa	51	.095**	6
Nigeria	Hausa	48	.082***	7
Zambia	Bemba	45	.051	8
Botswana	Setswana	53	.047	9
South Africa	Zulu	35	−.043	10
Lesotho	Sesotho	44	.029	11
Mali	Bambara	47	−.014	12

Notes:
Coefficients are bivariate Pearson's r correlations.
$N = 15{,}610$
*$p = {<}.05$
**$p = {<}.01$
***$p = {<}.001$

In general, other social factors perform better than ethnicity at determining how people vote. Across all countries studied, rural dwellers reliably vote for the winning party, whereas members of the postcolonial generation tend to oppose it.

But the importance of ethnic ties emerges once vote choice is broken down by country (see Table 12.3). In some parts of Africa, voters from the largest ethno-linguistic group attach themselves to the ruling party, as do Oshivambo speakers in Namibia and Shona speakers in Zimbabwe. This pattern is most common where the largest group constitutes half or more of the national population, votes as a cohesive bloc in a virtually permanent electoral majority, and projects its own values and symbols onto the larger nation and state. In highly pluralistic societies, however, the speakers of the largest language group lack the sheer numbers to constitute a political majority on their own. In these places, the major ethnic group involves itself in opposition politics, as manifest in its votes for the party that lost the last election. Clear examples are found in Ghana and Uganda, where the speakers of Akan and Luganda lined up behind candidates who were not favored by incumbent authorities in elections in 1996, as did most Zulu voters in South Africa's 1999 elections.

Thus, whether positively or inversely, we find that ethnicity is significantly associated with vote choice in just over half of the Afrobarometer countries. As such, cultural, linguistic, and hometown ties remain critical elements in the calculus used by African electors to choose their leaders. In a separate analysis, we show that the introduction of controls for other aspects of social structure and for performance evaluations does not invalidate this result.[24] It would be mistaken, however, to conclude that elections in contemporary Africa amount to little more than an ethnic census. Ethno-linguistic identity plays no significant role in vote choice in five countries in the Afrobarometer sample, all of which rank low in ethnic voting (see Table 12.3). Either these countries are socially homogenous (Botswana and Lesotho) or they are so socially diverse that aggregated partisan affiliations easily bridge ethnic cleavages (Mali). Alternatively, in other societies where voters are intently focused on the delivery of goods and services by government (South Africa and Zambia), deep ethnic divisions are superseded by mass evaluations of institutional performance.

Indeed, for all countries studied, vote choice is first and foremost a product of popular *performance evaluations* (see Table 12.2). Even in Namibia, the Afrobarometer country that ranks highest in ethnic voting, performance evaluations explain more variance in vote choice than does speaking Oshivambo. What matters most to voting for the winning party is whether people think the national president has been doing a good job. Next in the evaluative tally come popular judgments about the quality of electoral administration, notably whether national polls are generally free and fair. In the tussle for public priorities between political and economic goods, we again find the former are more important, but this time to actual political behavior. The delivery of individual political rights has a positive and significant effect on whether voters side with a winner. Interestingly, however, the performance of the economy is negatively related to vote choice, indicating clearly that voters are even willing to reelect leaders who have accumulated abysmal records at economic management. The proviso, however, is that these leaders must have protected political rights.[25]

Let us be clear about the implications of explaining African voting behavior in terms of a rational theory of performance evaluation. No implication is intended that popular judgments about leadership or regime performance are well informed. Quite the contrary: as Table 12.2 shows, vote choice has no prior requirement of cognitive awareness! In this barren setting, popular performance evaluations may all too easily be swayed by misinformation. For example, people may incorrectly project from the appeal of a well-liked president that the government or economy are performing well. Or voters may be victimized by falsehoods intentionally circulated in the campaign propaganda of political parties that successfully mobilize their followers to turn out at the polls. Indeed, the very absence of cognitive considerations in the formation of voting preferences points to the fact that election campaigns in African countries are conducted, if not in complete isolation from the truth, at least in environments where reliable information is hard to come by.

DEFENDING DEMOCRACY

During the 1990s, young urban Africans poured into the streets to demand political and economic change. Frustrated with the inertia of old regimes, they took matters into their own hands by protesting failed economic policies and voting against corrupt leaders. The question now arises whether these sorts of popular political initiatives have been sustained during a period when the challenge of change has shifted from regime transition to regime consolidation. If the price of freedom is eternal vigilance, then it is legitimate to ask: are African citizens willing to stand up for fragile new democracies when antidemocratic threats inevitably arise? Or will they slip into political quiescence, thus allowing dictators to reemerge?

To recap results from Chapter 5, we found that only about half of the Africans in twelve countries anticipate taking actions to counter government crackdowns. The other half would never mount any form of opposition if the government closed opposition newspapers, dismissed independent judges, or cancelled elections. In Southern Africa, people claim that official violations of the rule of law would trigger fairly tame responses: of those who would "do something," 36 percent would simply "speak to others." And in East and West Africa, people are more eager to protect their religious rights than key democratic institutions like elections and parliaments (80 percent versus 40 percent).

We suspect that even these numbers are optimistically inflated. After all, how many people ever act on their stated intentions? Gibson found that only 10 percent of Soviet citizens reported actually participating in some form of discussion about the Soviet coup attempt of 1991 and only 2 percent claimed to have taken part in anticoup protests (but slightly more in Moscow and Leningrad).[26] Tellingly, he also uncovered a modest correlation between attitudes toward democratic institutions and processes on the one hand and protest participation on the other. Perhaps, therefore, democracy's most attentive watchmen are concentrated in a particular subset of the population. If so, is this vanguard best apprehended as a demographic segment or as a group of opinion leaders? To answer these questions we regress our standard battery of predictors on an *index of defending democracy*, which summarizes popular reactions to government civil rights abuses.[27]

Table 12.2 (last two columns) shows clearly that willingness to defend democracy does not derive from any social, cultural, or institutional structure within society. Theories based on these assumptions contribute no insight on this topic. Democracy's active advocates can be found in all political generations and in both urban and rural settings. They are distributed evenly among members and nonmembers of political parties and voluntary associations. And, remarkably – as with *all* aspects of political participation discussed in this chapter – cultural values *never* determine who stands up for democracy.

Instead, a coherent account of the willingness of individuals to assert themselves as democrats can be constructed using indicators of *cognitive awareness* alone. Defenders of democracy are drawn almost exclusively from Africans who are intellectually engaged in public life and who possess high levels of information. What matters most is that protagonists understand democracy in procedural terms, possess formal education, and have extensive knowledge about political leaders. This pattern of awareness echoes a motif that we first detected when analyzing the sources of demand for democracy. In other words, an individual's willingness to defend an independent press, court system, and parliament seems to be an extension of his or her initial commitment to the *idea* of democracy. In other words, there is prima facie evidence that acts of resistance against antidemocratic violations are underpinned by learned political attitudes.

Of course, the validity of this argument depends in good measure on whether one believes that a professed willingness to oppose government crackdowns is a genuine political behavior. A critic could complain that "willingness" does not capture a real act, but only a predisposition to act. Bluntly stated, willingness to defend democracy may itself be an attitude, which is why it seems to depend so heavily on awareness of public affairs. We concede that an indirect measure of a predisposition is less satisfying than a direct measure of behavior, a problem that only future studies can rectify. But, in mitigation, we note that an individual's expressed willingness to act in the future (when a government suspends liberties) is closely correlated with his or her reported behaviors in the past. For example, Southern Africans who have often attended previous protest demonstrations are four times as likely to say they stand ready to protest any future cancellation of elections.[28] In Uganda in 2000, multiparty sympathizers protested the legitimacy of a referendum on no-party rule by boycotting the polls.[29] And, from 2001 to 2003, Zimbabweans continued to resist the erosion of civil liberties, stolen elections, and security force repressions by participating en masse in work stoppages and stay-aways.[30] Thus, there are some grounds to believe that self-proclaimed "willing" defenders of democracy will in fact follow through to action.

POLITICAL PARTICIPATION: CAUSE OR EFFECT?

We now turn to the chapter's key concerns: is political participation a cause or consequence of attitudinal change? When ordinary Africans get involved in politics, do they take their own initiatives, or does someone else mobilize them? What does the nature of participation – active or passive – imply for the way that popular learning occurs?

Autonomous political participation refers to premeditated action undertaken by "citizens" who know their own minds and make their own political
choices. In other words, people first figure out where they stand on political
and policy issues, then act accordingly. In short, learning motivates agency.
By contrast, "subjects" or "clients" play much more reactive roles in *mobilized political participation* as they respond to organized initiatives by political
elites. At best, people are induced to take part in official events by rewards
of entertainment, food, and transport; at worst, they are rounded up with
heavy-handed threats of negative sanctions. Mobilized participation is not
bereft of benefits; on the contrary, it may have unintended consequences.
Citizens can sometimes learn by doing, gradually adopting new attitudes
as the upshot of practical experience. Given the mixed origins of political participation in Africa, we anticipate that some participatory acts will
be autonomous and others mobilized, the task being to distinguish among
them.

Insights are already available from existing analyses. The shaded rows
at the bottom of Tables 12.1 and 12.2 show the results of regressing various participatory acts on attitudes to reform. Several features stand out. To
begin with, reform attitudes do not have powerful effects on participation,
never explaining much variance and often almost none. While reform attitudes appear to shape some behaviors – notably defending democracy and
vote choice – they have very little influence on protesting and voting. These
findings point away from a conception of political participation in which
individual preferences autonomously shape action.

The main exception is that *demanding* democracy is the single best predictor of *defending* democracy, even after cognitive awareness is controlled
for (see Table 12.2, penultimate column). In other words, what really matters for civic resistance is whether individuals both support democracy and
reject all autocratic alternatives. This finding provides crucial support for
a theory of democratic consolidation via the legitimating effects of attitude
change. Consistent with Gibson, we find that attitudinal commitments to
democracy can prompt mass actions to protect against imminent threats of
authoritarian reversal.[31]

These results help distinguish autonomous actions from those that are
mobilized. Whereas defending democracy and (to a lesser extent) vote choice
are both products of independent decisions by self-reliant individuals, other
aspects of political participation are outgrowths of mass mobilization. The
path model in Figure 12.1 reveals the sequencing of these different types
of political participation. Whereas defending democracy and vote choice
emerge on the right side of the diagram as ultimate *consequences* of attitudinal
change, an index of political participation – including voting, protesting,
and communing and contacting – appears on the left-hand side among many
other *causes* of attitude formation. Although we tested various permutations,
the present path model provides the best fit.

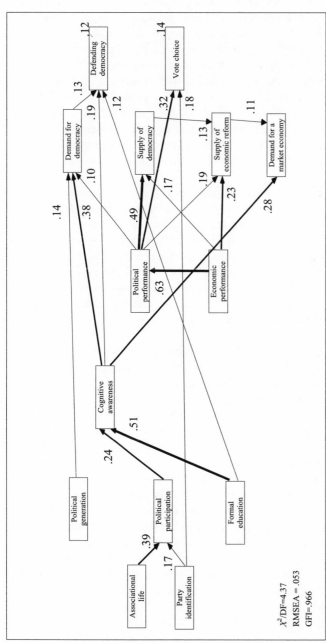

Notes:

1. Structural equation modeling using maximum likelihood estimation. Because some measures of goodness of fit are highly sensitive to large samples (such as X^2 and degrees of freedom), the model was estimated on a randomly selected subsample of N=1,200 (separate subsamples were created from each of the five imputed data sets and the results averaged).

2. Path coefficients are Standardized Regression Estimates. Coefficients attached to the dependent variables are Squared Multiple Correlations and analogous to R^2. X^2 / DF is the ratio of Chi Square to Degrees of Freedom: a good fit is indicated by a ratio up to 5 to 1. RMSEA is the Root Mean Squared Error of Approximation: a value up to .05 indicates a close fit, with values of up to .08 representing a reasonable fit. GFI is the Goodness of Fit Index: it estimates the extent to which the hypothesized model fits with the actual data.

X^2/DF=4.37
RMSEA = .053
GFI=.966

FIGURE 12.1. Path Model of Mobilized Participation

Figure 12.1 confirms that defending democracy is a product – indeed, the only product – of demand for democracy. All things considered, cognitive awareness is an additional determinant of popular willingness to resist authoritarian crackdowns. Somewhat surprisingly, and contrary to expectations raised by the regression analysis (see Table 12.2), there is no direct path from the perceived supply of democracy to vote choice. We had expected to find that people who were satisfied with the extent of democracy in their country would vote for incumbent rulers. Instead, the path analysis reveals that this connection is washed out by a strong direct link from popular evaluations of political performance, especially judgments about the quality of elections and the availability of civil and political rights. Most importantly, however, vote choice remains a consequence of attitude formation.

Treating some aspects of political participation as prerequisites rather than outcomes (by placing them on the left-hand side of the model) yields another important finding: a strong path *from* political participation *to* cognitive awareness. In this formulation, political action precedes and perhaps even provokes attitude change including, eventually, demand for democracy. The behavior of political actors displaces much of the explanation of cognitive awareness that was previously attributed to associational life (see Figure 11.1). And participation becomes an important adjunct to formal education in enabling ordinary people to gain awareness of public affairs. Because cognitive awareness leads to demands for democracy, it is important to recognize that mobilized acts of popular participation, both in and between elections, may have unintended attitudinal effects. The evidence suggests that even rote popular involvement in elections or other forms of collective political action rubs off on mass attitudes, sometimes even catalyzing unexpectedly liberal preferences. In other words, by simply taking part in an election, even novice or uninformed voters learn something about democratic procedures, including that they have a right to vote and that a meaningful vote requires choice.

Finally, we find no substantive linkages between political participation and formal education. Since participation thus does not depend on the ability of individual actors to accumulate personal skills or resources, it can hardly be mainly autonomous. Instead, political participation – or at least voting, communing, and contacting – is predominantly mobilized.

If this is so, how does mobilization actually occur? Which institutions link the state to individuals? Are political parties the main agencies of mobilization? Or have voluntary associations usurped this role?

The path analysis indicates mobilization effects from agencies located in both political society and civil society. In the new era of multiparty politics, political parties – regardless of whether they are incumbent rulers or opposition challengers – remain influential forces for attracting people into politics. But economic interest groups – namely trade union, business, and development associations that recruit members from among the general public – also induce ordinary Africans to get involved in national political processes. The fact that the path from voluntary associations is stronger than the path from political parties should not be misread to mean that the former have displaced the latter, especially when it comes to voting. We reiterate that each of these agencies specializes in particular forms of political mobilization. Parties promote identifications that are central to voting, whereas membership in voluntary associations is critical to communing and contacting (see Table 12.1). According to Norris, this division of labor reflects global patterns in which parties still take the lead in getting out the vote, whereas unions and churches tend to stimulate new forms of lobbying, petitions, and protest.[32]

But the effectiveness of African political institutions is inhibited by organizational weakness and the neo-patrimonial tendencies of their leaders. To illustrate, we refer to Zambia, though we could have chosen almost any African country.

With shrinking memberships, Zambian political parties are withering away. The old dominant party, UNIP, has been reduced to a fragile organizational shell with a narrow regional base; a bevy of minor parties have arisen and fallen over the past decade along with the fortunes of their big man leaders; and the ruling MMD, which never made a complete transition from a social movement to a political party, soon lost followers through leadership splits and ill-advised efforts by party headquarters to impose electoral candidates on local constituencies.[33] Although political parties remain a principal conduit for mobilizing votes and other participatory acts, their capacity is limited. This shortcoming is a major reason for low levels of voter turnout in many African countries (for example, Zambia, Nigeria, and Mali) and low levels of interelectoral participation almost everywhere. As much as political elites might like to reproduce the machine politics of the one-party era, their empty promises of patronage no longer reliably attract votes. Most African political parties barely operate between elections. Thus, levels of participation are low because parties have deteriorated, though not as low as they would be without any parties at all.

Voluntary associations have filled part of this institutional vacuum, while also facing similar impediments. In Zambia, for example, the official agricultural cooperative movement was a mainstay of voter mobilization in the one-party era, and the mineworker and teacher unions helped prompt a shift to multiparty democracy.[34] Since 1991, however, the cooperative movement has collapsed for want of state support and the unions have been sidelined from policy influence, for example from decisions over the privatization of the copper mines.[35] To some degree, religious base communities (especially of the Roman Catholic church) have taken on new mobilization roles by boosting awareness of civil rights and encouraging turnout, notably among voters who avoid identification with any political party. But, because these efforts do not reach large numbers of people or all communities of faith, the potential of civic organizations as agents of political mobilization remains far from fully realized.

Moreover, less savory forms of voluntary organization are emerging, such as the ethnic youth militias of Nigeria and Zimbabwe.[36] These divisive institutions remind us that associational life is not always healthy for society, autonomous from the state, or conducive to democracy.

In sum, political participation in the Afrobarometer countries displays both autonomous and mobilized features. On one hand, as Africans gain awareness of procedures for checking the excesses of autocracy, so they increase their propensity to stand up in democracy's defense. And, as they arrive at critical judgments about the performance in office of elected leaders, so they are more likely to vote against incumbents in multiparty elections. On the other hand, these genuine innovations in African politics are offset by political habits inherited from the past. Partisan elites continue to employ political parties to inculcate regimented attitudes among followers, especially among those rural dwellers who have limited awareness of public affairs and who are ill-prepared to make informed political choices.

A mobilized form of learning – the dominant pattern discovered here – is consistent with the continent's political legacy of overcentralized, top-down, one-man rule, the long-term effects of which are explored in the next chapter. This legacy portends, even within multiparty regimes, the survival of forms of government in which aggrandizing leaders attempt to control the behavior of citizens. However, we also detect a silver lining. Even as dominant parties and local patrons try to mobilize participation by involving poorly informed people in the political process, they unwittingly impart the lesson that ordinary folk have a right to their own self-governance.

13

Deciphering Regime Consolidation

Half a decade after the fall of the Berlin Wall, Linz and Stepan noticed the divergent destinies of new regimes in the postcommunist world. Whereas, in East Central Europe, open politics and free markets were "near to becoming the only game(s) in town," the newly independent states of Central Asia clung to staged elections and economic planning.[1] These distinct paths were all the more intriguing because they emerged against a monolithic background of communist rule. The fact that regime change proceeded smoothly in some parts of the former Soviet empire, yet was derailed in others, draws attention to:

The unanalyzed variation within the region in democratic (or non-democratic) transition *paths*...(which) is explicable in terms of distinctive regime types (or subtypes)...comparative *path-dependent* analysis is called for.[2]

This chapter takes national histories into account. African countries underwent liberalization during much the same period as Eurasia and also embarked on paths of change defined jointly by shared and special legacies.[3] Across the continent, Africans had long endured a debilitating economic crisis, a deep dependence on external finance, and a pervasive culture of neo-patrimonial rule. This common ecology helps to explain why, in every country we have studied, mass satisfactions with regime reforms are heavily influenced by popular impressions of the economic performance of national presidents. As in other world regions, however, national political and economic legacies are not constant across sub-Saharan Africa. Even crisis-ridden African states diverge in their levels of wealth and trajectories of growth. Not only is South Africa rich compared to Mali, but Uganda is recovering as Zambia sinks further into poverty. In addition, the postcolonial political legacies of African countries run the gamut from military, to plebiscitary, to semicompetitive, to multiparty interludes. It is therefore probable that – as in the postcommunist world – inherited characteristics lend weight to the prospects for regime consolidation in contemporary Africa.

The object of interest in this chapter is regime consolidation in general and the consolidation of democracy in particular. We first introduce considerations of "country" into existing explanations of reform. The twelve Afrobarometer countries are then situated spatially within a demand and supply model of regime consolidation. The chapter proceeds by probing which legacies – socioeconomic or political – are more influential in shaping learning about reform. It closes by asking how a country's recent past exerts influence on the prospects for consolidating a high quality democracy in the future.

To do so, we recalibrate the lens of analysis. First, we widen the angle of view from the micro level in order to take account of macrohistorical factors that are common to whole populations. Second, we pull back from the abstract language of explanatory concepts by reentering the proper names of African countries into our accounts of public opinion. Finally, we reach behind the curtain of country names in an effort to decipher the relevant meaning and content of national histories. What does "country" signify? In precisely what ways does it make a difference to grow up as a South African rather than a Nigerian? Does nationality stand for the political or the economic dimension of the learning experience? Is such learning generational, lifetime, or collective? By paying explicit attention to cross-national variations in recent historical legacies, we seek to restore considerations of context to the explanatory schema of this book.

THE EFFECTS OF "COUNTRY"

In earlier chapters, we observed substantial cross-national variations in public opinion across African countries. A couple of brief reminders will suffice. While Batswana say they support democracy, Basotho are undecided (see Chapter 3). And while Tanzanians express some satisfaction with economic reform programs, Zimbabweans clearly do not (see Chapter 4). We wonder whether these and other international differences are adequately explained by the social and attitudinal characteristics of individual respondents. Are Basotho undecided about democracy because of cognitive shortcomings, say their failure to view democracy as a set of political procedures? Are Zimbabweans unsatisfied with SAPs because of attachments to cultural values that discourage taking economic risks?

The alternate hypothesis, of course, is that there is something distinctive about Lesotho or Zimbabwe – that is, about countries as whole entities – that precipitates divergent outcomes. If so, then additional increments of explanation about reform should appear once "country" is entered into analysis. In multivariate regression, significant coefficients for variables representing countries may demonstrate that distinctive legacies – ranging from distant colonial histories to recent patterns of economic growth – are at work in various places.

To test these propositions, we now add dummy variables for Afrobarometer countries to our best regression models of attitudes to reform, with Botswana as the point of comparison.[4] The citizens of Botswana were chosen as the reference group because they surpass most other Africans in levels of support for democracy and markets. Thus, if any country differences appear, we expect the signs on the regression coefficients to be negative, because being a citizen of a country other than Botswana makes Africans less likely to have embraced reform.

Table 13.1 reports country effects on attitudes to democracy and markets. Area specialists will welcome the finding that, even after the attributes of individuals are controlled, the histories of particular countries have substantial impacts on public opinion. When entered into the regression model, the "country" block is the second most important determinant of demand for democracy, supply of democracy, and the supply of economic reform.[5] Only cognitive awareness accounts for more variation in demand for democracy; and only performance evaluations are more powerful in explaining the perceived supply of political and economic reforms. In other words, country legacies displace all individual-level theories of attitude acquisition except the learning theory (of cognitive rationality) on which we have hinged our presentation. While certifying the robustness of explanations derived from cognitive awareness and performance evaluation, the expanded models in Table 13.1 also confirm the secondary or marginal status of explanations based on institutional influences, social structure, and cultural values.

Let us put some contextual meat on these bones. Take demand for democracy (Table 13.1, second column). We can see that, as predicted, living outside Botswana always has a negative effect on democratic commitments, suggesting that this reference country possesses a set of attributes that sets its political development apart from, and ahead of, its neighbors. The contextual environments of Ghana and Zambia also seem conducive to the cultivation of democratic commitments since, once all other things are held constant, Ghanaians and Zambians hardly differ from Batswana in the extensiveness of their demands for democracy. By contrast, the historical legacies of political transition in South Africa and Namibia have constrained the emergence of wholehearted democratic commitments. Whether the democratic cultures of these former settler colonies are poisoned by the disgruntlement of racial minorities or by ideologies of national liberation, the past weighs heavily on present democratic attitudes.

Country legacies even displace social structure. We reported earlier that generational considerations were among the primary determinants of demands for democracy, with members of Africa's postcolonial cohort learning the deepest democratic commitments (see Table 11.1). Now we discover that generational effects are largely a product of country context. Once South Africa and Namibia are entered into the equation, postcolonial generation becomes a weak predictor, and multiparty generation and age turn

TABLE 13.1. *Attitudes to Reform, Country Effects*

	Demand for Democracy		Supply of Democracy		Demand for a Market Economy		Supply of Economic Reform	
	Adj. R² (block)	Adj. R² (cumulative)	Adj. R² (block)	Adj. R² (cumulative)	Adj. R² (block)	Adj. R² (cumulative)	Adj. R² (block)	Adj. R² (cumulative)
Cognitive Awareness	.173		.000		.061		.053	
Performance Evaluations	.056		.337		.013		.195	
Social Structure	–		–		.017		–	
Cultural Values	.038		.057		.055		.026	
Institutional Influences	.026				–		–	
Country[a]	.115	.229	.094	.342	.067	.112	.074	.247
	Beta		Beta		Beta		Beta	
Ghana	–		–		.073***		–	
Lesotho	-.071***		-.103***		–		–	
Malawi	-.044***		-.080***		-.068***		–	
Mali	-.127***		-.168***		-.030***		.050***	
Namibia	-.155***		-.100***		-.056***		–	
Nigeria	-.037***		-.171***		–		-.100***	
South Africa	-.208***		-.083***		.023***		–	
Tanzania	-.060***		-.159***		.194***		–	
Uganda	-.092***		-.146***		.043***		–	
Zambia	–		-.043***		–		–	
Zimbabwe	-.043***		-.162***		.036***		-.069***	
Full Model	.289		.379		.155		.263	

Notes:

N = 21,531

*** p = <.001

[a] Country is measured as a set of dummy variables with Botswana excluded as the point of reference.

– not statistically significant.

318

statistically insignificant. In other words, what previously appeared to be a process of generational learning is in fact a collective experience that affects people of all ages.

Let us elaborate. Having sloughed off colonial rule some thirty years after the rest of the continent, South Africa and Namibia are late political developers. These countries moved directly from settler domination to a multiparty regime without traversing an interlude of indigenous authoritarian rule.[6] Thus, South Africans and Namibians did not share with other Africans the experience of repression and impoverishment at the hands of a majority-rule government. Absent the negative learning experience that independence leaders can be every bit as ruthless and repressive as former European masters, the residents of Africa's southernmost countries are much more willing to flirt with authoritarian alternatives to democracy, especially one-party states. Not having been disappointed – at least not yet – by leaders who stay too long in power, South Africans and Namibians do not insist on procedural guarantees that enable the replacement of failing leaders. Instead, they require that the political regime, whatever its form, deliver long-denied economic benefits. In short, public opinion in South Africa and Namibia is affected by the *collective* learning experience of settler colonialism and a late transition to majority rule.

Country contexts also inform mass perceptions of the supply of economic reform (Table 13.1, last columns). In this respect, South Africa and Namibia (among other countries) now resemble Botswana, but now with regard to rather low levels of satisfaction with market-friendly policies. These countries have never been forced to swallow an externally imposed adjustment program, but their governments have adopted quasi-liberal economic strategies on their own, in all cases without much public discussion or gratitude. Other Afrobarometer countries – even showcase Uganda – also display low levels of public satisfaction with economic policies, indicating the breadth and depths of residual public resistance to markets. Only in Mali – where a government that is compliant to its donors has sustained market reforms for more than a decade – is public satisfaction with economic policy significantly higher than in Botswana.

Most of the substantial "country" effects on satisfaction with SAPs can be attributed to Nigeria and Zimbabwe.[7] The well-educated populations in these countries have engaged in vigorous debates over the legitimacy of adjustment programs, which are popularly understood to originate from conditions required by Washington-based financial institutions. These debates introduced relevant information to the general public, thus reducing the influence of cognitive awareness (that is, the gap between those who are well informed and those who are not) on the perceived supply of economic reforms.[8] Compared to other leaders, Mugabe and Obasanjo were relatively successful at blaming their countries' macroeconomic difficulties on others, whether the British government, previous administrations, ethnic minorities, or international oil companies. But the net effect of leaders' efforts to shift blame and charge economic sabotage is to further undermine support for market-oriented economic policies.

These examples show that country characteristics matter. Remarkably, when it comes to demand for a market economy, a country-based explanation is the most effective of all![9] The single best predictor in Afrobarometer data that an individual will express support for economic reform is being a Tanzanian. Compared with being a Motswana, the probability of supporting economic reform is 70 percent higher among Tanzanians and 30 percent lower among Malawians.[10] We suspect that these differences reflect the vastly different starting points for each country at the time of economic transition. At one time, Tanzania represented the archetype of an African socialist economy and Malawi its African capitalist antithesis. In recent years, however, government policies have been radically transformed in Tanzania, with the result that the market now delivers reliable flows of previously unavailable goods. In Malawi, by contrast, the performance of the market economy has been gradually weakened over time as the country has disengaged from trading ties with South Africa and suffered creeping official corruption and intermittent natural disasters. Thus, comparing the present with the past, Tanzanians are more economically satisfied and Malawians are less so.

All citizens in each country – regardless of their sociocultural background or attitudinal predispositions – experience these countrywide contextual effects. In short, they learn collectively. For this reason, aggregate national characteristics help illuminate demand for a market economy, which previously we found hard to explain. To be sure, no competing theory explains a great deal of variance in support for markets, but an account based on the distinctive historical legacies of African countries is the most convincing. In sum, in understanding why Africans rarely demand free markets, we expect to discover more from divergent country paths than from differences between and among individuals.

DEMAND, SUPPLY, AND REGIME CONSOLIDATION (REVISITED)

The prospects for regime consolidation are also best apprehended from a macrolevel, "country" perspective. After all, consolidation is a characteristic of whole political and economic systems. We argued in Chapter 1 that the concept of consolidation should be broadened beyond democracy alone, because it can refer to the stability of a variety of regimes: whether democratic or nondemocratic, market or nonmarket, or various hybrid forms. Using a simple supply-and-demand model with aggregated Afrobarometer data, we now estimate whether any of the twelve African countries we have studied is likely to consolidate as a democracy.

Our main proposal is that equilibrium between mass demands and institutional supply is the sine qua non for the consolidation of any regime.[11]

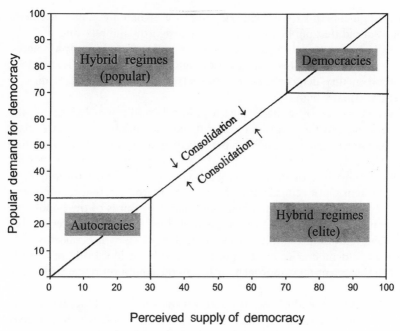

FIGURE 13.1. Demand and Supply for Political Regimes

For example, a high-level political equilibrium connotes the consolidation of democracy; if equilibrium occurs at a low level, then autocracy is becoming consolidated. In graphical terms, the diagonal line in Figure 13.1 represents regime consolidation; it describes the various points at which supply and demand for democracy can potentially come into balance. As the arrows indicate, consolidation occurs to the extent that actual regimes approach the equilibrium line. Regimes that lie elsewhere in the property space, especially far from the line, can be considered *un*consolidated.

This model has a number of innovative features. It treats normative preferences (popular demand for democracy) separately from empirical evaluations (the perceived supply of democracy). As such, it overcomes a common problem of faulty inference that occurs when analysts project consolidation prospects solely from expressed levels of popular support for an ideal regime. The model also corrects the institutional perspective that political elites always determine regime consolidation. We recognize that the arbitrary decisions of leaders often ordain regime outcomes and that African citizens may be powerless to prevent democratic reversals. But we have argued throughout this book that ordinary people are good judges of the quality of leadership; they factor actual or anticipated elite misconduct into their estimates of democratic supply. Moreover, we have shown that estimates of institutional performance based on local knowledge are every bit as reliable as the judgments of external experts; moreover, where these measurements clash, we hold that public opinion is more insightful and relevant.

Finally, our approach recognizes that both demand and supply are necessary conditions for regime consolidation, but that neither alone is sufficient. For good quality democracies to consolidate, for example, *both* must be present at equally high levels.

For *democracies*, how high must a political equilibrium be? Let us initially assume that the consolidation of democracy minimally requires that, for a sustained period of time, 70 percent or more of the adult population wants this type of political regime and a similar proportion thinks they are getting it. This rule of thumb is used for purposes of theorization, without any intention of cementing a universal standard.[12] Actual requirements may vary. But we guess that, when more than two thirds of the population both commit themselves as democrats and think their desired regime has been achieved, the probability is low that democracy will break down. In Figure 13.1, democracies are found in the northeast bloc and are consolidated to the extent they approach, or lie on, the equilibrium line within this space.

At the opposite end of the spectrum (in the southwest bloc) lie *autocracies*. In these regimes, the populace neither demands democracy nor perceives its supply (scoring 30 percent or lower in each case). Because strong initiatives for democratization do not emanate from above or below, the regime is caught in a low-level equilibrium trap. This conjuncture occurs in countries where rulers have resisted political reforms, or made only cosmetic concessions, and where most of the population remains politically dormant. Resultant political regimes are governed by repressive rules, to which all players are acutely attuned. The closer that actual regimes approach the equilibrium line, the more that autocracy is consolidated.

In Africa and other parts of the developing world, the most common conjunctures are hybrid political regimes between autocracy and democracy. To the extent that they lie off the equilibrium line, these regimes are also unconsolidated. Competitive elections may be held but few other features of democracy are present. Using the schema in Figure 13.1, two variants can be distinguished.

Elite hybrid regimes are found to the south and east of political equilibrium. Here, the supply of democracy exceeds the low level of popular demand. Elections have been introduced from the top downward, that is, mainly at the behest of elites. Political reforms are negotiated behind closed doors, where leaders of key factions strike pacts among themselves or with international diplomats, aid agencies, and bankers. Alternatively, leaders encourage the introduction of competitive elections safe in the knowledge that their control of a dominant political party will enable them to easily guarantee electoral victory. Ordinary people play small parts in the process of political change: either they remain passively loyal to a dominant political movement or they allow themselves to be sidelined after a few basic liberalizing reforms have been achieved. In regimes where "the people" do not insist on ruling themselves, the fate of democracy depends on the goodwill of rulers.

Popular hybrid regimes lie to the north and west of the equilibrium line. Mass demands for democracy here exceed the will or capacity of political elites to supply it. Typically, these political regimes first emerge as a result of popular protest, with demonstrators calling for more open and accountable forms of government. Incumbent rulers concede multiparty elections as a way of ending the crisis in the streets, with new governments installed against a backdrop of high popular expectations. Almost inevitably, elected governments fail to live up to the hopes and dreams of the voters. The new leaders forget how they ascended to power at the head of mass movements and, before long, begin to neglect their constituents. Or they discover that the limited resources and machinery of government are inadequate to the task of satisfying mass expectations. Democracy is forestalled because people become disillusioned with the performance of the government and, as a consequence, begin to withhold legitimacy.

Hybrid regimes may consolidate at intermediate levels, lending permanence to forms like electoral democracy, liberalized autocracy, or other semiformed systems. Indeed, the greatest risk to the consolidation of new democracies in Africa is that the architecture of the regime hardens prematurely, that is, before democratic institutions or beliefs have had a chance to take root. In Hellman's terms, regimes arrive at "partial reform equilibrium."[13] Under these circumstances, democratic reforms are compromised by the weight of institutional and cultural continuities inherited from the past.

Commonly, however, unconsolidated hybrid regimes are politically unstable. To the extent that popular preferences and institutional performance are out of balance, semiformed systems embody tensions that portend change, though in various directions. Where leaders supply more democracy than their followers want, as in *elite hybrid regimes*, there are few incentives or pressures to sustain a program of reform, leaving leaders free to manipulate the rules of the political game to their own advantage. Thus, the trajectory of elite hybrid regimes commonly tilts toward the reemergence of authoritarian practices. On the other hand, while *popular hybrid regimes* fall short of democracy, the alignment of political forces is somewhat more favorable for its eventual consolidation. A surplus of popular demand for democracy, if guided into institutional channels, can discipline a poorly performing government, for example, at the polls. The danger, however, is that ordinary people may lower their demands and lapse into disgruntled apathy if they feel that elites fail to listen to them.

In proposing this schema, we intend that consolidation may not be a permanent end state. Rather than accreting gradually over time, a political equilibrium may be attained quite early in the life of a new regime. And this stability may prove to be transient. Indeed, any framework for studying the prospects of new political regimes must explicitly allow for backsliding (from democracy to authoritarianism) and destabilization (when seemingly consolidated regimes begin to unravel). Just as new democracies can emerge, so they can submerge, even after becoming tentatively established. A multivalent framework of this sort is especially helpful when studying new political regimes in world regions like sub-Saharan Africa, where the consolidation of democracy is a low probability event.

THE CONSOLIDATION OF AFRICAN POLITICAL REGIMES

We now apply Afrobarometer data that has been aggregated at a country level to an equilibrium model of the consolidation of political regimes. Where in the two-dimensional space defined by supply and demand for democracy do African countries presently reside?

We predict that the continent contains few, if any, consolidated democracies; thus the northeast bloc will be nearly or completely empty. Numerous entrenched autocracies persist among non-Afrobarometer countries (like Angola, Chad, Ethiopia, Guinea, Mauritania, and Swaziland), where the popular demand for, and perceived supply of, democracy are surmised to be low. In addition, we anticipate a roughly equal proportion of popular and elite hybrid regimes, since some of Africa's democratic experiments were impelled by protest from below and others were pushed by elite splits, realignments, and pacts.[14]

These expectations are borne out in Figure 13.2. For this analysis, the two axes of the model are measured as additive versions of standard constructs. On the Y axis, we measure *demand for democracy* as the percentage who *both* say they support democracy *and* reject three authoritarian alternatives.[15] Accordingly, a mean of 46 percent demands democracy across twelve countries. On the X axis, the *supply of democracy* captures the percentage of the population who are *both* satisfied with the way democracy works *and* perceive their country to be largely or fully democratic.[16] By these stringent criteria, a mean of only 43 percent think that democracy is being supplied. To represent the margin of sampling error inherent in Afrobarometer surveys,[17] the equilibrium line is supplemented with a penumbra of dotted lines. The closer that countries fall to these parameters, the higher the probability that their political regimes will persist in present form.

The reader should notice the absence of consolidated democracies among Afrobarometer countries. Botswana, where 58 percent of adults demand democracy and 70 percent think that democracy is institutionalized, comes closest to this goal. But we discover a hidden flaw in Botswana's political regime, namely that the popular base of democratic commitments is incomplete, a deficit on the demand side that is consistent with critiques about the passivity of the Botswana citizenry.[18] The country's coordinates

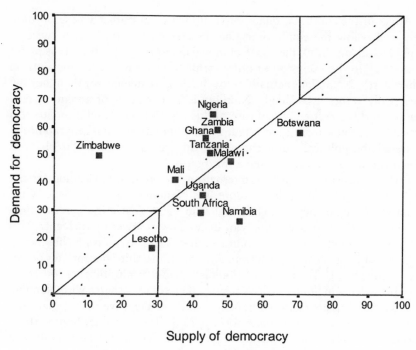

FIGURE 13.2. The Consolidation of Political Regimes, Selected African Countries

approach the equilibrium line, however, implying a relatively low probability of breakdown for this near-democratic regime. By contrast, Lesotho is apparently caught in a low-level trap; in the year 2000, it could even be classified as an autocracy by our standards. Given the paucity of committed democrats in this country (16 percent) and the alienation of almost three quarters of all Basotho from the political institutions existing at that time, one understands why external interventions were required to settle the country's political future.

All other countries possess hybrid political regimes. Democratic demand and the perceived supply of democracy reach intermediate levels in a cluster of countries, including Tanzania, Mali, Malawi, and Uganda. The coordinates for these cases, which constitute the core of Figure 13.2, fall close to the equilibrium line. We infer from this shared spatial location that their regimes are consolidating in a hybrid state that falls well short of democracy. With supply and demand in balance, there is no political force propelling major political changes in the foreseeable future.

Figure 13.2 displays considerable face validity, reinforcing more casual observations about the democratic prospects of many of the aforementioned countries. But the supply-and-demand model also reveals interesting and unexpected findings.

Alone in the southeast quadrant, Namibia is an outlier whose position falls well below the equilibrium line. Its coordinates reveal that twice as many Namibians think they have obtained democracy (53 percent) as prefer democracy to the exclusion of other forms of government (26 percent). In other words, Namibians actually enjoy much more democracy than they say they really want. Accordingly, Namibia is an exemplar of an elite hybrid regime, and the best empirical case of this type we have found to date. An elite-driven regime form is consistent with a population that is geographically scattered and politically disengaged, and an elected president who changed the constitution to allow himself a third term.

Perhaps surprisingly, given its international reputation as a leading African democracy, South Africa looks more like Namibia than Botswana. While demand for democracy is slightly higher in South Africa (29 percent) than in Namibia, the perceived supply of democracy is lower (42 percent). This combination of characteristics indicates that South Africa is an elite hybrid regime, not least because the current national leadership concentrates power in executive hands. Tendencies of administrative centralization are consistent with precedents in South Africa's history. The country shares with Namibia a background of an exclusive franchise and a settler government that used a strong state to try to remake society. And, like Namibia, South Africa effected a transition to an inclusive, nonracial democracy as a result of a series of political, economic, and military pacts that were negotiated among top political elites.[19]

As a different sort of exception, Zimbabwe manifests a huge chasm between the popular demand for democracy (at 50 percent) and the proportion that thinks that Robert Mugabe is supplying it (13 percent). Thus, Zimbabwe contains more frustrated democrats than any other country studied, a constituency that presumably will continue to agitate for political reforms. In other words, despite grim current conditions in Zimbabwe, there is reason to expect redemocratization at sometime in the future. This popular hybrid regime could quickly move to the east in the property space if and when the country achieves an alternation of leaders by means of a free and fair election.

Along with Zambia and Ghana, Nigeria best represents the political tensions inherent in the remaining multiparty regimes in Africa. Demand for democracy in Nigeria (65 percent) greatly exceeds perceived supply (46 percent), suggesting that competition continues between elites and masses over the form of the political regime. While ordinary Nigerians clamor for the opening up of decision making to popular participation, they remain highly dubious that incumbent leaders and existing institutions will respond. In order to predict trends that will emanate from this tension, it would be useful to know whether and how the opinions of thwarted supporters of democracy change over time. Faced with a government that supplies less democracy than they want, do citizens lower or raise their political expectations? A comparison of Nigerian attitudes in January 2000 and September 2001 hints at an answer.[20] Between these dates, the perceived extent of democracy in Nigeria remained much the same (47 percent perceived "a democracy with major problems") but support for democracy dropped by a full ten percentage points (from 81 to 71 percent).[21] Thus, when faced with an underperforming regime, Nigerians are inclined to adjust their expectations downward rather than to maintain pressure for a preferred political regime.

We do not know yet if this finding is peculiar to Nigeria, typical of other populations undergoing decompression from a euphoric transition, or widely applicable to African countries in normal times. But it does suggest that demand for democracy may be difficult to sustain in the face of resurgent authoritarian legacies. In this regard, Ghanaians may have more realistic expectations than Nigerians, and therefore will be less easily disillusioned. And we confirm that Ghanaians display higher levels of both demand and supply as a result of the shift from Jerry Rawlings' liberalized autocracy to John Kufuor's more liberal regime.[22]

THE CORRELATES OF CONSOLIDATION

The spatial placement of African polities in relation to regime consolidation requires further substantiation. In this section, we explore whether Afrobarometer indicators are connected to known correlates of stable democracy. For example, many authors insist that democracy thrives best in rich countries[23] and that regime capacity and durability increases with the passage of time.[24]

In order to express our equilibrium line as a measure of democratic stability, demand and supply are compressed into a single index. We construct a score for *the prospects of the consolidation of democracy* (PCD score), which is an aggregate of demand and supply of democracy, corrected for the current degree of regime consolidation.[25] Table 13.2 displays PCD scores for Afrobarometer countries in the period 1999 to 2001, which run from six for Zimbabwe to ninety-six for Botswana. These raw scores should not be interpreted too literally. The scale simply implies that, in 1999, democracy was far closer to consolidation in Botswana than Zimbabwe. Moreover, a mean PCD score of fifty-four suggests that, at the turn of the century, a "typical" Afrobarometer country – if there is such a thing – stood a slightly better than even chance of becoming a stable democracy.

A critic might object that vital information is lost when independent concepts are collapsed into a common term. For these reasons, we proceed below by conducting analyses of the components of PCD as well as the composite score. But one advantage of using a common currency to measure the degree of democratic consolidation is that countries with different political profiles (for example, Mali, a popular hybrid regime, and Uganda, an elite

TABLE 13.2. *The Prospects for the Consolidation of Democracy*
(PCD), Selected African Countries

Country	Date of Survey	PCD Score
Botswana	(1999)	96
Malawi	(1999)	76
Zambia	(1999)	74
Nigeria	(2000)	72
Tanzania	(2001)	70
Ghana	(1999)	68
Uganda	(2000)	52
Mali	(2001)	50
South Africa	(2000)	38
Namibia	(1999)	32
Lesotho	(2000)	12
Zimbabwe	(1999)	6
Components of PCD		R
Demand for Democracy		.702[*]
Supply of Democracy		.803[**]

Notes:
PCD scores are aggregate country percentages of demand for democracy and
the perceived supply of democracy, adjusted for deviations from the equilibrium
of consolidation.
R values are Pearson correlation coefficients of each component and the PCD
score.
[*]$p = <.05$
[**]$p = <.01$

hybrid regime) may be readily compared. Mali's democracy suffers key institutional deficits (its citizens prefer democracy but the state has yet to establish
acceptable electoral laws),[26] whereas Uganda's democratic shortcomings are
more attitudinal (citizens readily embrace a no-party constitution).[27] While
each country has a distinctive starting point and path to change, their similar PCD scores suggest that both have a roughly equal (and even) chance of
consolidating democracy.

It is noteworthy that the prospects for democracy's consolidation are
shaped more by perceptions of institutional supply than by popular demands, though both are essential to the construct.[28] This formulation is
a useful corrective to the comparative literature, in which overt expressions
of support for democracy are often mistakenly accepted as shorthand for the
consolidation of democracy. If one were forced, reluctantly, to choose just
one simple indicator of consolidation, democracy's perceived extent would
be a more solid proxy than popular support for democracy. We have established that the Afrobarometer's indicator of the extent of democracy is
consistent with the Freedom House "status of freedom" index.[29] Now we

0

TABLE 13.3. *Correlates of Democratization*

	Demand for Democracy	Supply of Democracy	Prospects for the Consolidation of Democracy (PCD Score)
Socioeconomic Legacies			
Urbanization	.341	.278	.239
Adult literacy	−.188	−.120	−.377
Government consumption	−.264	.419	−.102
GNP per capita	−.210	.474	.059
GDP growth (average annual, 1990–1999)	−.289	.073	−.051
Political Legacies			
Previous years of plebiscitary one-party rule	−.360	−.567	−.433
Previous years of military rule	.299	−.083	.147
Previous years of settler rule	−.448	−.172	−.556
Previous years of multiparty rule	.514	.516	.530
Previous years of competitive one-party rule	.283	.139	.397
Number of Previous Elections	.342	−.076	.179
Duration of New Political Regime	.195	.271	.128

Note: Values are bivariate Pearson correlation coefficients. Due to the small sample size (n = twelve countries) significance statistics are not reported. Instead, attention is drawn to the sign and magnitude of coefficients (R = >.250).

report that support for democracy is entirely unrelated to Freedom House scores.[30] We therefore recommend that, if scholars must employ a single indicator to signify consolidation, that they choose the extent of democracy. But, of course, the logic of an equilibrium model is that the intersection of two compound indicators (demand *and* supply) will produce a more valid construct than any simple, one-dimensional metric.

If the PCD score and its components reliably capture democracy's prospects, then they should relate in known ways to socioeconomic conditions. Table 13.3 displays some standard predictors, such as the aggregate level of urbanization, adult literacy, GNP per capita, GDP growth rate, and government consumption for countries covered by the Afrobarometer.[31]

As expected, we find that the prospects for the democracy's consolidation are better in urbanized countries than in countries with agrarian populations. The correlations between urbanization on the one hand, and our indicators of regime consolidation on the other, are consistently large and positive.[32] To illustrate: Botswana, the sample's second most urbanized country, where half the people live in towns, has the highest rates of democratic demand, supply, and consolidation. By contrast, just over a quarter of the population are urban dwellers in Mali, which ranks near the bottom of the country sample on both urbanization and indicators of the stability of the regime. Consistent with modernization predictions, urbanization seems to be conducive to democratization.

Our findings about literacy are less comforting to conventional wisdom, which predicts that democracy is more likely to take root in countries where adults can read and write. At the country level, we find a negative relationship between the proportion of literate adults in 1998 and our indicators of regime consolidation. This result seems to suggest that illiteracy is less of a barrier to democratic citizenship than often thought. And it is consistent with earlier findings that, even without formal schooling, individuals can obtain awareness of public affairs from associational life and practical political participation. Certainly, the Afrobarometer's experience with thousands of survey interviews strongly suggests that people without basic literacy skills are capable of holding political opinions and making political choices.

Another socioeconomic consideration is the size of the state relative to the economy.[33] A conventional measure of state intervention – government consumption as a percentage of gross domestic product[34] – is strongly related to the perceived supply of democracy. Thus, in the popular imagination, the delivery of democracy is a direct function of public spending undertaken by central and local governments. Consistent with popular preferences for a mixed economy, the Africans we interviewed associate the achievement of democracy with a large state that visibly invests resources in basic public functions like political order, economic infrastructure, and social services. Although a large state boosts the way that people judge democracy's supply, it depresses mass demands for democracy. This finding is entirely consistent with microlevel results reported in Chapter 11, namely that while the perceived supply of democracy is based on instrumental calculation, mass commitments to democracy are largely intrinsic.

Lastly, any discussion of democracy's socioeconomic preconditions must include a test of "Lipset's law" that democratic regimes are more likely to stabilize in wealthier than poorer countries.[35] In so doing we append Przeworski's amendment: democracy is no less likely to *emerge* from dictatorship in poorer countries, but, once installed, it is less likely to *endure* there.[36] We find a strong positive relationship between the supply of democracy and a country's per capita wealth and a weaker, but still positive, relationship with its recent economic growth record. Thus, while Africans are more vocal in demanding democracy in poor countries (and where the economy is in decline), they say that democracy is actually delivered only in relatively wealthy countries (that are growing). Very poor countries with stagnant or shrinking economies literally cannot afford democracy, in the sense that their resource-strapped governments lack the financial means to adequately fund the operations of democratic institutions, including regular elections.[37] We are reassured that, even within a narrow band of low- and middle-income African countries, our results tend to confirm the central "law" of democratization studies.

But explanation of democracy's probable prospects cannot stop short at well-worn platitudes about socioeconomic preconditions. The importance of noneconomic considerations, the mechanisms by which wealth promotes democracy, and, indeed, the very direction of the GNP-democracy relationship, are still open to debate. We therefore explore whether supplementary and more proximate factors can throw additional light on the *problematique* of regime consolidation. In so doing, we discover that political institutions, which had little effect at the micro level of individual attitudes (see Chapters 10 and 11), play an essential role at the macro level when the countries are the units of analysis.

Peering into the past, theories of path dependency contend that present regime prospects are molded by inherited institutional legacies.[38] Once countries are launched on a particular trajectory of political change, they become constrained and propelled by it. A common theme in this literature is that the institutional endowment of colonialism conditions the prospects for regime change in independent states, with a British colonial heritage commonly being considered conducive to democracy.[39] Other theorists emphasize rule choices made by political elites in the present. Adherents of the new institutionalism routinely argue that parliamentary constitutions are more beneficial than presidentialism for building democracy.[40]

The Afrobarometer does not contain enough variation across country cases to test for effects of colonial rule and constitutional form. Ten of the twelve countries that we studied are former British colonies or protectorates[41] and eight of the twelve possess constitutions in which a directly elected executive president is endowed with extensive powers.[42] Quite apart from these empirical regularities, we are disinclined to emphasize colonial precedents and institutional engineering for theoretical reasons. As the colonial era recedes into history, Africans have come to shape their own politics and destinies; the institutional innovations of the postcolonial era – notably one-party states and military coups – have long supplanted the political arrangements made at independence. Nor can institutional engineering, which hinges on adherence to rules, be expected to have much impact in settings where the principle of constitutionalism is still profoundly contested.

For sub-Saharan Africa, therefore, we think that *postcolonial political legacies* are the most salient institutional factors. We propose an approach that focuses neither on deep history of colonial rule nor on brand new constitutions, but instead draws attention to the political regimes that emerged in Africa *after* decolonization. In earlier work, Bratton and van de Walle argued that the likelihood, dynamics, and outcomes of recent transitions in sub-Saharan Africa were shaped in systematic fashion by the nature of previous political regimes.[43] They observed, for example, that national constitutional conferences were most common in Africa's *plebiscitary one-party regimes*, where one-candidate elections had been the norm. While national conferences often led to dramatic political openings during the 1990s, these authors predicted that such change would prove hard to sustain. By contrast, *competitive one-party regimes*, which had allowed a modicum of pluralism and competition, encouraged direct movement to multiparty elections and led to incremental, and therefore possibly more durable, political reforms.

We are now in a position to test for any effects of recent institutional heritage on regime consolidation. Table 13.2 introduces indicators of the number of years that Afrobarometer countries spent under various political regimes – military, settler, plebiscitary, competitive, and multiparty – between independence and the year of democratic transition in each country.[44] We wish to know whether, over time, postcolonial political legacies help to determine the probability of the consolidation of democracy. We would expect, for instance, that precedents of plebiscitary rule would provide less encouragement than a recent history of competitive politics, either within, or (especially) between, political parties.

As Table 13.3 shows, the longer that a country spent under plebiscitary institutions after independence, the less likely that its citizens today will demand democracy, or regard it as having been supplied; moreover, the negative political legacy of plebiscitary rule makes it less likely that democracy will consolidate in the future. Among the twelve countries studied, Lesotho had the third longest period of plebiscitary rule and in 2000 enjoyed very poor prospects for consolidation. Basotho lost confidence in elections in good part because of the country's experience under Chief Leabua Jonathan, who installed himself via an annulled contest in 1970 and held only one unopposed voting ritual through 1993. Precedents of settler rule also have consistently negative effects on consolidation and its components. Together, these findings strongly suggest that precedents of various forms of authoritarian rule in the recent past undermine democratic prospects in the present and beyond.

By contrast, a lengthy postcolonial experience with competitive political institutions seems to prime citizens to support democracy today. This finding comes through loud and clear with respect to the number of years that a country experienced *multiparty rule* after independence. Botswana again leads the way with thirty-three uninterrupted years of multiparty rule between 1966 and 1999. Importantly, however, a strong positive relationship between a multiparty legacy and consolidation prospects survives even when Botswana is dropped from the analysis. One reason is that Nigeria's interludes with multiparty competition (totaling ten years between 1960 and 1989) also apparently made a lasting impression on public attitudes by helping to raise the country's ranking to first overall on demand for democracy in 2000.

Even limited political competition within the confines of a *competitive one-party state* can have a salutary effect. Consider the case of Tanzania.

At Julius Nyerere's initiative, Chama Cha Mapinduzi (CCM) institutionalized electoral procedures that encouraged multicandidate competition and allowed debate over policy implementation within the ruling party. This widely copied blueprint allowed the periodic refreshment of the political elite as elected leaders rose and fell within the party and government.[45] Following a brief multiparty interregnum at independence, a competitive one-party system was in place in Tanzania for a period longer than in any other country.[46] This institutional legacy helps to account for Tanzania's simultaneous high rank on support for democracy (where it scores second only to Botswana) and middle rank on rejection of authoritarian rule (because many people still hanker after a one-party option).[47]

Along these lines, frequent elections under *ancien regimes*, including one-party and no-party elections, also help to foster demands for democracy. This is confirmed by the positive signs on the coefficients for the variable for the number of postcolonial elections in Table 13.3.[48] So, as well as prompting prodemocracy protest, a legacy of any kind of electoral activity is an asset to the longevity of new democratic regimes.[49] But, not surprisingly, the number of previous elections in the postcolonial period has no residual effect on the perceived supply of democracy. Precisely because controlled elections did not offer voters a great deal of choice (if any at all), their frequency in the past has no effect on how much democracy citizens think their country has achieved today.

Finally, we estimate the effects of the duration of the new regime. It would seem reasonable that regime consolidation has a temporal dimension; after all, building political institutions takes time. We measured the duration of the new regime as the number of months elapsed from the date of the founding election to the date of the Afrobarometer survey. In Table 13.3, the correlation coefficients for this predictor all run in the expected, positive direction and are strongest in boosting perceptions that democracy is being supplied.[50]

ECONOMIC VERSUS POLITICAL LEGACIES

Among the major correlates of democratic consolidation listed previously, what matters most? For clarity's sake, we boil this inquiry down to its essence: are material legacies – like economic wealth and growth – more or less important than institutional legacies – that is, the nature of previous political regimes? To weigh socioeconomic and political paths, we regress PCD scores on the most important correlates of consolidation.

Table 13.4 reports the results. We find that political legacies, which account for seven times as much variance as socioeconomic legacies, carry most of the load in explaining the consolidation of democracy in the present sample.

To be sure, countries that have accumulated wealth are definitely more likely to consolidate democracy. Indeed, *ceteris paribus*, the size of the

TABLE 13.4. *Regression Estimates of the Prospects for Democratic Consolidation*

	Demand for Democracy		Supply of Democracy		Prospects for the Consolidation of Democracy (PCD)		
	B	beta	B	beta	B	beta	R² (block)
Constant	50.8		31.6		73.3		
Socioeconomic Legacies							.097
GNP per capita	-.011	-.834	.010	.789	.010	.424	
Urbanization	.295	.219	-.397	-.319	-.162	-.066	
Government consumption	-.981	-.424	1.192	.554	-.051	-.012	
Political Legacies							.702
Previous years of multiparty rule	1.091	.698	1.277	.879	2.041	.714	
Previous years of competitive rule	.293	.196	.538	.388	1.214	.444	
Previous years of settler rule	.390	.374	-.337	-.347	-.711	-.373	
Previous years of plebiscitary rule	-.764	-.428	.025	-.015	-.467	-.143	
Time							.016
Duration of new political regime	.037	.260	-.120	-.912	-.131	-.504	
Variance Explained (R²)	.814		.847		.770		

Note: Due to the small sample size (n = twelve countries), significance statistics are not reported. Instead, attention is drawn to the sign and magnitude of (**beta = >.250**).

economy is the only socioeconomic factor that affects democracy's prospects since the effects of urbanization and state intervention are now diminished. But the wealth effect is substantively small: it takes a $100 increment in GNP per capita to buy just one point of democratic consolidation which, for African countries at the bottom of the income scale, is one third of their present average product per head. Note also that wealth has a positive impact only on the perceived supply of democracy; it remains negatively related to demand for democracy, which we again insist is widespread, even in poor countries. Moreover, while important, a country's economic inheritance explains less variance in the prospects for consolidation than certain political legacies. Thus, GNP per capita is not, as Bollen and Jackman would have it, the "dominant explanatory variable," at least in the present Afrobarometer sample.[51]

To explain democracy's prospects, political legacies must be taken into account. To begin with, the number of years previously spent under a multiparty regime has a powerful influence on popular perceptions of democratic prospects. For each additional year of prior multiparty experience, a country's PCD score goes up by two points. Thus, Botswana's democracy gains two thirds of its promising consolidation prospects from an uninterrupted experience of multiparty rule between 1966 and 1999. Note too that while institutional effects are most pronounced on the demand side, they are positive also on the supply side, which suggests a robust connection between past multiparty experience and consolidation in both its main dimensions. To a lesser extent, the same goes for a legacy of competitive one-party rule, which accounts for about half of Tanzania's high PCD score.[52]

In addition, settler and plebiscitary legacies also exert independent effects. In these instances, restrictions on elections under former regimes *inhibit* the legitimation and institutionalization of democracy. For each prior decade in which citizenship and participation were limited to a racial oligarchy (settler rule), a country's PCD score goes down by seven points, thus lessening South Africa's chance of consolidating democracy by some twenty-three points. For each decade that a strongman previously prevailed as a result of one-candidate contests (plebiscitary rule), the PCD drops by over four points. Thus, Mali loses almost ten points on its consolidation prospects because of twenty-one years of prior experience under the plebiscitary regimes of Modibo Keita and Moussa Traore. In countries that experimented with multiple regimes after independence, the potential democratizing effects of multiparty interludes are offset by periods of military or plebiscitary rule, contingencies that continue to hold back the emergence of democracy in Ghana, Nigeria, and Uganda.

If past institutional experience shapes present and future regime prospects, then by what mechanisms does it do so? We again propose processes of popular learning, this time at the level of national populations, who in Africa have collectively endured a variety of postcolonial political regimes. There appear to be at least two modalities of socialization via political regime, namely positive learning and negative learning, which we consider in turn. Positive learning occurs when people encounter modern democratic institutions – such as a free press, competing political parties, and regular and rivalrous elections – which they then come to value, support, and demand. Under the best of circumstances, the exposure of ordinary people to democratic institutions sparks a virtuous circle by which political institutions and mass attitudes become mutually reinforcing. Negative learning takes place when autocracies seek to incorporate citizens into monolithic institutions – like single-party elections, military tribunals, or state-controlled trade unions – which fail to prepare people for democratic citizenship. Over time, this vicious cycle deprives authoritarian institutions of their legitimacy.

Generally speaking, one would expect that positive learning via exposure to open and competitive institutions would be a more effective mechanism for building support for democracy since it provides prototypes of values and behaviors that people can emulate. To the extent that people rely on negative learning, that is, on intimate knowledge of heavy-handed autocratic practices, they will suffer a poverty of political imagination, being hardly aware of the nature of more promising alternatives. Contrary to Bermeo's account, we set store in a path-dependent congruence between institutional forms and political cultures ("like produces like"), with experiences of political competition giving rise to democratic cultures and experiences with autocratic practices doing the opposite.[53] While agreeing that spontaneous popular reactions against authoritarianism may spark political transitions, we find nevertheless that democracy can only be consolidated if ordinary people have an accurate vision of this form of governance clearly in mind.

In practice, past experience with democratic institutions has been extremely scant in Africa. Compared to Latin America and Eastern Europe – where democracy has been an on-again, off-again affair over several generations – Africa has had extremely limited exposure to democracy. The colonial experience, more recent in Africa than elsewhere, remains salient mainly for the *non*democratic precedents that it imparted. In most countries, the multiparty interlude at independence was cut short, only to be soon succeeded by military and civilian monopolies. Today, political elites with dubious commitments to political reform continue to prevent people from learning how democratic institutions are really meant to operate. Thus, most popular learning in Africa has occurred by negative example. As a result, although people know which regimes they *don't* want, they have yet to crystallize ideas about the content of democratic alternatives.

The clearest Afrobarometer example is Mali. Before its founding competitive election of 1992, Mali had *never* experienced an interlude of multiparty politics, even during the independence period when other African countries experimented briefly with open party competition.[54] Its regime history of plebiscitary dictatorships and military governments helps to explain the current low level of popular demand for democracy in Mali and the country's subpar prospects for consolidating democracy.[55] This prognosis arises in good part because, before the late 1990s, Malians had no previous opportunity to learn about, or become attached to, a more pluralistic model for governing their country.

Fortunately, however, a teaspoon of positive learning seems to serve as an antidote to a ladleful of negative learning. Even though Africans have weathered many years of autocratic rule in the recent past, such unfortunate experiences are offset by just a few years of political competition within or among political parties. In Table 13.4, the heavier weight of positive learning is indicated by the larger regression coefficients on the political legacies with positive signs (that is, multiparty and competitive one-party rule) than on the political legacies with negative signs (that is, plebiscitary and settler rule). Thus, at the margins, political learning has a positive bias and dynamic, especially in the few African countries that have accumulated a track record of past multiparty experience.

Even so, it remains true that African publics generally lack the requisite institutional memories on which to base a thorough understanding of democracy and a deep commitment to the preservation of its values and practices. Thus, positive learning about democracy, while apparently essential to democracy's consolidation, has so far been truncated in Africa. Because popular recollections of democratic institutions are largely absent, it becomes easier to understand why so many political regimes in Africa are hybrids (containing autocratic as well as democratic features) and why most popular hybrid regimes remain unstable and largely unconsolidated.

PATHS OF POLITICAL CHANGE

If Africans share political legacies – under predominantly settler, plebiscitary, competitive, or multiparty regimes – then groups of countries may follow generic paths of political development. Most African countries confronted extreme political instability after independence, but one common sequence involved a sequential shift from multiparty to military regimes, followed by plebiscitary one-party systems. Such shared paths can be distinguished according to the type of political regime that survived the longest during the postcolonial era. According to this schema, which is documented in Table 13.5, a legacy of *settler colonial rule* dominates the past of South Africa, Namibia, and Zimbabwe. *Plebiscitary regimes* remained longest in place in Uganda, Mali, and Lesotho. *Competitive one-party states* were the order of the day in Tanzania and Zambia, and to a lesser extent, in Malawi.[56] And *multiparty politics* has been a permanent feature of postcolonial political life only in Botswana, though military regimes in Ghana and Nigeria were interrupted by short-lived multiparty interludes in the late 1970s and early 1980s.

TABLE 13.5. *The Prospects for the Consolidation of Democracy, by Postcolonial Political Legacies*

	Years of Settler Rule	Years of Plebiscitary One-Party Rule	Years of Competitive One-Party Rule	Years of Multiparty Rule	PCD Mean[a]
South Africa	37	0	0	0	25
Namibia	33	0	0	0	
Zimbabwe	23	14	0	7	
Uganda	0	20	4	5	38
Mali	0	18	4	0	
Lesotho	0	16	0	4	
Tanzania	0	0	30	2	73
Zambia	0	0	19	8	
Malawi	0	14	16	0	
Botswana	0	0	0	34	79
Ghana	0	6	0	13	
Nigeria	0	0	0	10	
Afrobarometer					54

Note: Years of military rule are not shown.
[a] Calculated from Table 13.2.
Source: Bratton and van de Walle, *Political Regimes and Regime Transitions* (1996). Revised in 1999.

The prospects for consolidating democracy today depend heavily on these paths of development inherited from the past. The evidence can be found in statistically significant differences in mean PCD scores among regime trajectories (see Table 13.5, last column).[57] From these results, we estimate that countries that sustain multiparty rule after independence – or that successfully reinstall a multiparty regime after an authoritarian episode – are three times as likely to consolidate democracy as countries that emerge directly from settler colonialism. Moreover, former one-party regimes that allowed multicandidate elections have almost twice the chance of consolidating democracy as those that forbade any form of political competition. Indeed, the Afrobarometer sample is cut exactly in half by regime history: on one hand, former settler and plebiscitary regimes face a *less* than even chance of democratic consolidation; on the other hand, former competitive and multiparty regimes enjoy a *better* than even chance of the same outcome (see Table 13.2).

Because these results are especially unflattering to former settler colonies, we are led to reconsider whether Southern Africa deserves to be known as a leading zone of democracy in Africa. To be sure, Botswana's exceptionalism props up the region's affirmative political reputation. But, while our research adds shine to Botswana's image as an African democracy, it signals caution about the quality of democracy in Namibia and South Africa. In these *elite hybrid regimes*, lay populations straggle behind other Africans in demanding democracy, and are even less sanguine about the current supply of democracy than the expert panelists who compile standard democracy indices.[58] Indeed, low PCD scores for South Africa and Namibia cause us to recant the claim made in a previous study, namely that democratization is easier from settler oligarchies (where political competition existed for the racial elite and the main task was to broaden participation) than from neo-patrimonial regimes (where mass participation is encouraged, but competition was restricted).[59] If political legacies matter, then former settler colonies would seem more likely to follow a path defined by Zimbabwe's political deterioration rather than by the consolidation of democracy in Botswana.

Instead, the Afrobarometer directs our attention to bellwether *popular hybrid regimes* in West Africa like Nigeria and Ghana. Because popular demand for democracy far exceeds its perceived supply in Nigeria, we expect the political regime in that country to remain unstable for the foreseeable future. The escalation of sectarian violence since the 1999 political transition and the contested nature and dubious honesty of legislative, gubernatorial, and presidential elections in 2003 testify to the fragility of Nigeria's democracy. More promising is the political trajectory of Ghana. Even before independence, Ghana was the first country in sub-Saharan Africa to establish precedents of mass parties, multiparty elections, and representative government. Despite crackdowns by Nkrumah in the 1960s and Rawlings in the 1980s, Ghana has enjoyed the longest period of multiparty experience of all Afrobarometer countries apart from Botswana. Its recent redemocratization has been gradual, through a sequence of general elections of ever-increasing quality in 1992, 1996, and 2000.[60] And the consolidation deficit – which is measured as the gap between demand for, and supply of, democracy – was narrower for Ghana under Rawlings in 1999 than for Nigeria under Obasanjo in 2000. In these various ways, Ghana's trajectory validates an earlier hunch that "incremental, rather than dramatic gains in levels of democracy are likely . . . to prove most sustainable over time."[61] In our view, recent developments are restoring Ghana to a pan-African leadership position similar to that which it enjoyed in the 1950s.

There are obvious limitations, however, to imputing regime prospects from cross-sectional data. Because consolidation is measured here as equilibrium within public opinion, our predictions should preferably be based on several observations of the changing balance between supply and demand over time. We make a start on this research agenda by reporting on second Afrobarometer surveys for the above four countries, results of which are just becoming available as we are finishing this book. These data reveal an inherent volatility in public opinion, which pushes African countries in diverse directions.

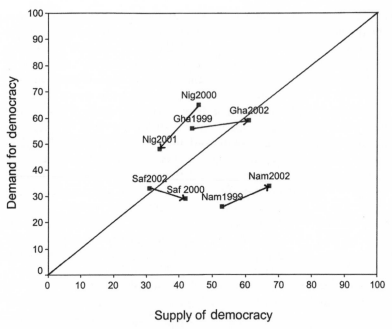

FIGURE 13.3. Paths of Political Change, Selected African Countries, 1999–2002

In South Africa, popular demands for democracy rose between 2000 and 2002 at the same time that fewer citizens came to feel that democracy was being supplied (see Figure 13.3). These trends applied to all races.[62] The combined effect was to move the political regime toward consolidation, but in a form that falls disturbingly short of the ideal democracy promised in the South African constitution. In Namibia, increases were registered in *both* demand and supply between 1999 and 2002. Although more people became aware of democracy and expressed satisfaction with the version provided by SWAPO, this elite hybrid regime became somewhat less stable, as indicated by the drift in public opinion away from equilibrium. Nigeria recorded large declines in popular demand for, and satisfaction with, democracy between January 2000 and September 2001. This plunge in public opinion in a nondemocratic direction indicates that transition euphoria evaporated quickly, bumping Nigerians down to earth. The fact that Nigerian public opinion moved closer to equilibrium suggests, however, the consolidation of a low-quality hybrid regime. Only in Ghana between 1999 and 2002 did we observe an increase in demand, supply, *and* consolidation. Admittedly, and consistent with Ghana's gradual trajectory, some of these gains were incremental. While demand for democracy rose only slightly, more Ghanaians became convinced (perhaps by the peaceful replacement of a former military strongman in the 2000 elections) that democracy was actually being delivered. The fact that opinion settled near the equilibrium line suggests that democracy was consolidating in Ghana, at least in 2002.

In the absence of more comprehensive time-series data, we close this chapter by inferring regime prospects for all twelve Afrobarometer countries using the existing indicator of the duration of new political regimes. We find that, generally, the effects of time on democratization in Africa are ambiguous. If anything, the introduction of controls for institutional and socioeconomic histories stands time on its head. Whereas the duration of new regimes was positively correlated to democratic legitimacy in a simple bivariate test (Table 13.3), the sign turns negative in the regression analysis (Table 13.4). This finding has important theoretical implications since it opens the door to authoritarian backsliding. It is consistent with Przeworski's report that "once the level of development is taken into account...democracies are about equally likely to die at any age."[63] In practice, the Afrobarometer sample is bifurcated, with countries on diverging trajectories of political development: in some cases, the passage of time leads toward democracy; in others it leads away.

Figure 13.4 puts names to these countries and locates their coordinates in a two-dimensional space. The gridlines in the figure represent the median duration and mean PCD scores for the twelve Afrobarometer cases.[64] The five countries in the northeast and southwest quadrants have PCD scores that

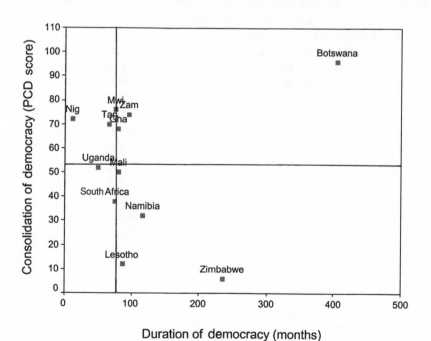

FIGURE 13.4. Consolidation of Democracy by Duration of Political Regime

are positively related to time, a relationship that is consistent with a temporal theory of gradual democratic consolidation. Botswana has the longest standing regime and the highest consolidation score and Uganda and South Africa are low on both counts. All of these countries – including also Ghana and Zambia – have degrees of regime legitimacy and institutionalization that are consistent with the age of their new political systems.

By contrast, the seven countries in the southeast and northwest quadrants have consolidation processes that run against the currents of time. On one hand, Nigeria, Tanzania, and Malawi have PCD scores that are higher than the age of their (relatively new) multiparty systems alone would predict. It is hard to conclude that these scores represent the consolidation of democracy because the regimes themselves are so nascent. After all, Malawi and Tanzania were among the last countries to open up to multiparty elections, especially hesitantly so in Tanzania. Political developments in this group of countries seem to have peaked early. From a public opinion perspective, the PCD score in these places was probably highest immediately after regime transition. The future would seem to portend backsliding, that is, a decline in demand for and perceived supply of democracy over time. As shown previously, these political dynamics are underway with a vengeance in Nigeria.

On the other hand, Mali, Namibia, Lesotho, and Zimbabwe have legitimacy scores that lag behind what one would expect given the age of their political regimes. In particular, the government in Zimbabwe, which held several multiparty elections after independence, should have amassed much more legitimacy than it has in actuality. Where time and regime consolidation are inversely related, we can only conclude that new democracies in Africa are just as likely to decay as to develop. Indeed, within the one dozen countries in the Afrobarometer sample, fewer than half (five) are moving in the direction of democratic consolidation, while the quality of democracy in the remaining seven is deteriorating. Since the Afrobarometer represents countries that are Africa's most aggressive reformers, we can only conclude that the prospects for the consolidation of democracy in other parts of Africa are probably even more austere.

Conclusions

Some say there is little new under the African sun. After all, Africa's semidemocracies and informal economies are actually mixtures of old and new. The family tree of African regimes includes not only colonial rule – which sought to restrict popular politics to a traditional realm and acknowledged minimal state responsibility for public welfare – but also one-party hegemony – which aimed at the opposite: periodic electoral mobilization and planned social transformation. Between these extremes, and overlaid recently with a thin veneer of liberalizing reforms, lie the hybrid systems of Africa today.

Contrary to the view that nothing ever changes in Africa, our study of public opinion challenges sacrosanct assumptions about Africans and their beliefs. We find, for example, that Afrobarometer respondents understand democracy in largely liberal and procedural terms; that popular demand for democracy depends more on the delivery of political rights than on economic performance; that a majority of people extend conditional support to the principle of market pricing for consumer goods and public services; that occupational identities are supplanting ethnic identities in many places; that Muslims are no less supportive of democracy than non-Muslims; that national identity is strong almost everywhere on the continent; and that the Africans we interviewed base their political judgments more on rational calculation than on group loyalty. As their awareness of public affairs increases, and based on their own adult experiences, Africans are learning about reform.

To conclude this book, we summarize the common features of public opinion about democracy and markets in twelve of Africa's most promising countries as revealed by Round 1 of the Afrobarometer. To avoid misunderstanding, we repeat our earlier alert that these countries, which have all undergone a degree of liberalization, may not represent sub-Saharan Africa as a whole. Because our country sample contains not only model reformers (like Botswana), but also liberalized autocracies (like Uganda) and countries in conflict (like Zimbabwe), we need not drop all pretensions to continental generalization. But, to be on the safe side, the reader should remember that the "Africans" we refer to are those who live in countries that have opened up politically and economically in the last couple of decades.

Beyond summarizing the profile of mass attitudes and behavior in these places, we draw implications from our survey results for scholarship in African studies, for selected social science theories, and for public policies of socioeconomic development. To scholars of Africa, we make a case that cultural interpretations of the continent's distinctiveness must be supplemented with systematic comparisons of the ways in which Africans think and act in rather universal fashion. To social theorists, we argue that public opinion is flexible, being shaped mainly by learning in adulthood, and that political and economic attitudes are more loosely and differently coupled than commonly assumed. And, finally, we seek to bring popular demands to the attention of development practitioners: in so doing, we emphasize the need to reconstruct of an effective state apparatus that, beyond helping to stimulate economic growth in Africa, can also attend to heartfelt public concerns about social equity.

THE STUDY OF AFRICA

This book has aimed to establish an empirical foundation for the study of public opinion in Africa. Afrobarometer data have various uses. To gauge mass sentiments, researchers need no longer rely on anecdotal interviews with elites in the capital city or case studies of isolated villages. Using our survey results, scholars can now methodically compare the political and economic views of various social groups within countries and analyze the reasons underlying differences in public opinion across countries.

Our research has ascertained that, at the turn of the twenty-first century, ordinary people in a set of leading African countries express widespread support for democracy. Due partly to a mood of popular elation lingering from a wave of political transitions that occurred up to a decade earlier, they view this political regime in an overwhelmingly positive light. People also warmly welcome the demise of *ancien regimes*. Simply put, misrule by military or civilian strongmen is no longer publicly acceptable. Popular preferences instead lean toward some set of open and participatory arrangements – loosely associated with the term "democracy" – as compared to other forms of government under which Africans have lived.

For people all too familiar with personal dictatorship and racial or ethnic oligarchy, democracy delivers individual dignity, a fundamental human need. While skeptics may retort that it is not possible to eat civil liberties, our data suggest that Africans find these political goods to be central to an individual's overall quality of life. To the extent that even hybrid political regimes can advance peoples' ability to speak their minds without fear, to move around without identity documents, or to conduct business free of extortion, citizens calculate that democracy – or something like it – is in their interest.

Yet mass democratic attachments remain superficial in the African countries we studied. Preferences for "rule by the people" coexist with pockets of authoritarian nostalgia and fewer than half of our respondents can be described as "committed democrats." Although most people say democracy is the best form of government, relatively few are satisfied with the way it actually works in practice. Moreover, many citizens fall prey to a fallacy of liberalization in which they all too readily mistake the availability of a few new freedoms for fully functioning democratic regimes. In terms of political behavior, Africans seem to welcome the opportunity to vote in multiparty elections. But turnout at the polls is still just as likely to reflect rote mass mobilization at the behest of a powerful patron or dominant party as the independent expression of individual choice. And very few people would take meaningful steps to defend democracy if it ever came under threat from a resurgent strongman. In contexts where religious beliefs are held more dearly than democratic values, praying for deliverance is an all too common strategy for trying to bring about social change. As such, democracy in Africa is a work in progress in which the requisite attitudes, actions, and institutions have yet to firmly take root.

While the Africans we interviewed are ready to give democracy a chance, they are much more ambivalent about endorsing a market economy. There is no analogue in Africa to the neo-liberal Washington consensus of the 1990s. Instead, in and around 2000, public opinion is divided on economic reform, including in African countries that have moved quite far down a reformist path. Afrobarometer respondents readily acquiesce to some elements in the structural adjustment package – like budget stabilization – but vigorously oppose others, notably the retreat of the state. While professing an emergent individualism, people continue to demand public interventions in the economy. They also vacillate about job creation – which is the paramount public priority in most countries surveyed – sometimes seeing it as an individual responsibility and at other times as a state obligation. Almost everywhere, though, they are deeply disappointed with official policy performance. Above all, any tentative support for laissez-faire is offset by popular concerns with reform-induced economic inequalities, which are usually attributed to an unseemly scramble for personal wealth within the political class.

Africans thus find themselves trapped between shrinking states and expanding markets, which rarely operate according to a rule of law or at full capacity. Weakened and corrupted public institutions cannot generate employment, deliver services, or regulate the excesses of the market. And a viable, large-scale private sector has yet to emerge anywhere on the continent outside of Southern Africa. Even there, it falls well short of producing the number of jobs that people say they want. Most importantly, where politicians and entrepreneurs seem interested mainly in serving themselves, ordinary people have every reason to wonder whether any leader will sponsor a societal project aimed at a common good.

By dint of necessity, therefore, Africans address their daily needs by coping and hoping. They survive by piecing together eclectic livelihoods from an array of formal and informal economic activities, which – if corruption is involved – blur the distinction between public and private realms. While they would still prefer the state to fulfill core welfare functions, in practice ordinary people reluctantly and increasingly rely on the market for satisfying basic needs. And they bridge the remaining gap between dreams and reality with hope. Faced with public policies that promise more than they deliver, most Africans display remarkable patience in waiting for greater benefits of reform eventually to materialize. As a foil to desperation, they say they feel optimistic about the economic future and believe fervently that their children will live more fulfilling lives than themselves.

For the most part, reform preferences are broadly distributed among Afrobarometer respondents with relatively little regard to their positions in the social structure or their cultural backgrounds. For example, we find that men and women barely differ in their attitudes to reform; surprisingly, the same applies in the aggregate for urban and rural dwellers; and, after extensive analysis, we eventually find that generational differences disappear in the face of collective, society-wide learning. We also confirm that, in the African countries that we studied, interpersonal trust is not a prerequisite to demanding democracy or a market economy. And, while ethnic origin strongly influences vote choice, cultural values play no role whatever in determining the nature or extent of modern forms of political participation. We seek, therefore, to put society and culture in their proper places, which, in our opinion, are at the margins – rather than at the heart – of explanations of public opinion.

But several caveats are needed. First, social context clearly matters. We would not have found meaningful differences in public opinion across African countries unless distinctive historical, economic, and cultural considerations were in play. In searching for the substance of these legacies, we find a large part of the answer in the configuration of previous political regimes – ranging from one-party plebiscites to multiparty electoral systems – the experience of which predisposes people to oppose or support democracy today. While a contextual thesis of this sort can be proposed on the basis of single country case histories, it can only be tested with a systematic cross-national research design such as the one we have employed here.

Second, we do not deny that poverty and traditional cultural values play pivotal roles in shaping demands for a market economy. People who are poor or destitute – as well as those who cling to ethnic identities, or expect others to provide for their personal welfare – are singularly unlikely to demand market reforms. But social deprivation and communitarian values have relatively minor impact on every other reform attitude, including demand for democracy. We therefore conclude that, among ordinary people (and confirming what is already known for whole countries), poverty is not an insuperable obstacle for initiating democracy. We also infer that the indigenous value systems of precolonial Africa are more compatible with contemporary forms of political democracy than with a modern free market economy. A culture clash is less likely to occur as Africans experiment with the former as opposed to the latter.

Third, the conception of democracy described by our African interlocutors, while liberal – valuing, above all, freedom of speech – is also participatory. Perhaps reflecting cultural mores, the Africans we spoke to envision a decentralized form of government that features direct personal contact with leaders and popular involvement in policy deliberation and decision making. In short, Africans want more than intermittent opportunities to vote for distant national leaders; instead, constituents want to close the representation gap that has rapidly emerged within Africa's new electoral democracies.

Otherwise, we break with the custom in African studies of emphasizing the unique contributions of society and culture. In keeping with Chapter 1, we prefer to regard Africa's recent developments from a more global perspective as part of a worldwide wave of political and economic liberalization. We also think it reasonable to suppose that, even if Africans are distinctive in some respects, they respond to international trends in much the same way as other populations undergoing dual transitions. Accordingly, we argue that Africans appraise liberalization reforms both cognitively, using acquired knowledge and information, and rationally, by evaluating whether regime performance is serving their interests. They may be momentarily more captivated by the promise of democracy than most Latin Americans and currently less enamored with the performance of markets than certain East Europeans, but they form their opinions on these matters via similar processes of learning.

THEORIES OF SOCIAL CHANGE

Accordingly, the Afrobarometer speaks to general theoretical concerns. For example, it casts light on the acquisition of popular knowledge and on interactions between political and economic reforms.

Processes of Popular Learning

As well as being materially underdeveloped, sub-Saharan Africa suffers acute scarcities of public information. Especially in rural areas, the everyday lives of ordinary Africans are inward looking, absorbed in community affairs. When information about national and international public affairs is hard to come by, knowledge becomes key. Thus, arguments about Africa's lack of readiness for reform have usually invoked the limited literacy and educational attainments of the continent's populations. Theorists generally agree that democracy and free markets work best where people are literate and well informed. We confirm the importance of education in giving birth to reformist attitudes, but add qualifications to expand the conditions under which reform is possible.

To be sure, we have found that education in a formal school system has systematic positive effects on African public opinion: it dissolves attachments to old regimes; it raises commitments to new ones; it enhances awareness of public affairs generally; and it sharpens critical faculties, making people much more skeptical about the quality of the democratic and economic performance that is actually delivered. The other side of this coin is that rural people who have never been to school know little about democracy. The same applies to economic consciousness, except that ignorance about adjustment programs is common among the undereducated in urban areas too.

But we have uncovered alternate routes to learning. More important and proximate than formal education is cognitive awareness, a mental attribute that is greatly aided by education but does not always depend on it. We have found that even those Africans who possess little or no book learning can be intensely interested in public affairs, know the names of their elected representatives, and sometimes even have an adequate grasp of the core content of reform programs. In learning about structural adjustment, for example, some Africans overcome educational deficits by gaining access to the mass media. And cognitive awareness about democracy develops in the context of associational life as people join voluntary organizations, discuss policy issues with fellow citizens, and partake in participatory rituals such as voting in elections, communing in mass meetings, and contacting leaders. In this regard, organized collective action in Africa is a practical school for political learning.

Adults also learn from direct personal experience, which they use to evaluate the performance of political and economic regimes. This book has identified at least four mechanisms of learning, each distinguished by a time perspective. First, in the short term, Africans infer from their knowledge of current economic and political developments whether the performance of elected governments is meeting their expectations. Second, in the medium term, they show willingness to suspend judgment for a while about the delivery of material welfare to the extent that they receive political goods like peace, liberty, dignity, accountability, and order. Third, people compare the performance of a succession of regimes over the long run: those who suffered through their adult lives under the poorly planned economies of indigenous African dictators are quick to endorse liberalized regimes – even in incomplete hybrid versions – as long as they regard these as perceptibly better than the status quo ante. And, finally, a small cadre of well-informed citizens has learned enough about the content of democracy and markets to demand these regimes for their intrinsic value.

All told, however, pockets of cognitive capability in certain societies cannot dispel the overall impression that African populations are handicapped by limited awareness of public affairs. Only half as many Africans in our surveys find governmental procedures easy to understand as find them hard to fathom. So there is a distinct shallowness even to emerging procedural understandings of democracy. Where information is scarce, politicians can easily take advantage of mass ignorance, especially among nonliterate peasants or unemployed urban youth. These groups are easily mobilized for electoral or other purposes and unlikely to question rulers who manipulate democratic or market rules, exert illegal control over public resources, and seed the popular rumor mill with unreliable information. In these ways, incumbents turn the perquisites of office to their own advantage, even while appearing to be complying with donor requirements for reform. Ordinary people are only just starting to learn about how to counteract such official deceptions; in the meantime, African powerholders can still fool some of the people a good deal of the time.

Relationships between Political and Economic Reforms

In a theme of this book, we have shown that more Africans demand democracy than call for economic reform. Whereas over three quarters of persons surveyed see democracy as the best form of government, less than half support any single element in the orthodox package of economic stabilization or adjustment policies. Almost six in ten express satisfaction with the way Africa's hybrid democracies actually work, but only four in ten say the same about the implementation of SAPs. These polarized sentiments give rise to contrasting levels of public patience: even though Africans evince attachments to certain market principles (like risk taking) and are extraordinarily tolerant of economic hardship (even to a fault), they are nonetheless much more willing to persevere with political reforms than with economic ones.

Given this distribution of public opinion, one can hazard that democratic practices will be easier to consolidate than market-based policies. Recent events tend to bear out this forecast. Consider the party convention of the National Democratic Congress in Ghana in April 2000. On one hand, President Jerry Rawlings officially reconfirmed his intention to step down from office after two elected terms, opening the way for new leaders to contest the December 2000 presidential and parliamentary polls. At the same time, just three days before the party congress, Finance Minister Kwame Prepah announced the reimposition of controls on foreign exchange and international trade, effectively returning these sectors to the status that prevailed before the introduction of Ghana's Economic Reform Program in 1983. So, at the very time that policymakers in Ghana were deepening democracy by abiding by a new set of electoral rules, they turned the clock back on economic reform.

Do political and economic reforms therefore conflict? Or are they compatible? And, to address the question of reform sequencing, which comes first? From the perspective of public opinion, we have found more compatibility than contradiction in this key relationship. In the popular imagination, demand for democracy tends to go together with support for a market economy. And satisfaction with the way democracy works is even more strongly connected to contentment with the implementation of SAP policies. Indeed, it is precisely the coincidence of performance evaluations for both aspects of dual transition that lends African public opinion its defining instrumental character.

Beyond noting the fundamental compatibility of reform processes, however, we nonetheless give primacy to politics, as do other scholars of dual transitions in other parts of the world. As mentioned previously, the frequency of popular demands for democracy is higher than the level of free market preferences. Indeed, the legitimacy of democracy is so widespread across all segments of the population that its positive reputation could conceivably reduce some of the ambivalence people feel about economic reforms. This prospect becomes all the more likely once one realizes that support for liberalization is distributed asymmetrically. On one side, almost all sympathizers of free markets are firmly committed to democracy. On the other, less than one third of all democrats favor the market. Thus, while being a free market advocate is an excellent predictor of being a democrat, the opposite does not hold true. Reform constituencies therefore seem to emerge via a lopsided dynamic: because most supporters of free markets have already opted for democracy, new recruits to laissez-faire can only be drawn from an existing pool of self-professed democrats. In this way, people's prior commitments to political democracy pave the way for the resolution their mixed emotions about economic reform.

The recent evidence from Ghana seems to confirm this sequence. Since being elected in December 2000, the John Kufuor administration has enjoyed a legitimacy bonus born of the country's first peaceful turnover of political leaders. Heir to a center-right tradition in Ghanaian politics, the New Patriotic Party (NPP) government has pursued in a moderately liberal economic strategy. To bring down inflation, it has maintained fiscal discipline at the expense of propoor social spending and granted substantial independence to the Bank of Ghana. Anointing the private sector as the engine of growth, it has sought international debt relief, courted foreign investors, and reached out to representatives of producer groups and other civil society organizations. For their part, members of society have responded positively. Traders of consumer goods and spare parts marked down prices for a short period after the election ("Kufuor prices"). And, in a truly stunning shift, people shrugged off adjustment fatigue: the proportion of adult Ghanaians "willing to endure hardships now" in support of government economic policies doubled from 36 percent in 1999 to 72 percent in 2002. We find it hard to imagine a more striking illustration of a change in economic opinion induced by a deepening of democracy.

Thus, we stake out a clear position in the theoretical debate about sequences of regime consolidation. We reject an economic dynamic, or at least regard it as secondary. Democracy does not consolidate at the popular level because it attracts support from people who have improved their economic situation by taking advantage of open markets, for instance by entering small-scale trade. Given that many Africans think that adjustment has led mainly to unemployment and inequality, economic liberalization hardly encourages people to give credit to the political regime. Rather, the legitimation of reformist regimes proceeds in the opposite direction and according to an essentially political impetus. People who have the chance to choose their own leaders are more likely to see the government as their own. As a result they back its policies, including tolerating the hardships associated with policies of economic stabilization and adjustment.

This concrete manifestation of a democratic dividend indicates at the popular level how political sentiments shape the overall prospects for Africa's reformed regimes. Until such time as new economic policies generate tangible benefits – and unless these benefits are evenly distributed – we do not foresee any great expansion in the promarket constituency. But we remind the reader that this constituency is already larger than what we had expected before this research began. And Africans now have an opportunity to make good use of their electoral and other rights in order to hold leaders accountable for engineering a more broad-based pattern of economic growth in the future. If this eventuality ever comes to pass, then democracy will truly have legitimated the market.

STRATEGIES OF DEVELOPMENT

We have tested various theories of social change for their utility in explaining African realities. But good theory should also contribute to policy and practice. What lessons does this book carry for development practitioners who wish to help Africa escape its multiple crises? By way of conclusion, we briefly propose several ways in which Afrobarometer findings might inform the strategy and tactics of "doing" development.

As a first step, practitioners could help nurture learning about reform. Our survey results suggest that active democratic citizenship is generally enhanced by adult literacy and formal education. Investments in these vehicles of learning should be increased. Specialized items of citizenship training can be imparted via civic education in schools, the independent mass media, and the nonformal education programs of nongovernmental organizations. The content of these courses could inform people about the rules of the democratic game, the identities of principal players, and the functions of various levels and institutions of government. At the same time, civic education should aim to reduce unrealistic expectations about what democratic reforms can deliver. In the countries we have studied, people also need special help in understanding that they can demand political accountability from elected leaders, a right they have only just begun to realize.

Programs to liberalize economic policies should also be sustained. There is nothing in the Afrobarometer findings to indicate that empowering ordinary people will undermine efforts to introduce a measure of market logic into the operations of African economies. At the same time, people must find good jobs if they are to develop a personal stake in the survival of democratic societies. And populations must feel sure they can obtain a fair return on their economic efforts. Under these circumstances, macroeconomic strategies should include measures to temporarily compensate those who incur losses from the reform process. For example, as the state cuts formal sector employment, it must help underwrite the financial needs of small-scale entrepreneurs. And, when donors insist on removing price supports on essential goods and services, they must not fail to provide a safety net for those left behind.

At this juncture, however, we judge that economic miracles are not essential for democracy to survive. Instead, the Afrobarometer respondents tell us that greater immediate progress can be made on democratization and development with an agenda of good governance.

First, ways must be found to encourage elected leaders and policy makers to take public opinion into account. If citizens, for their part, help to formulate economic strategy – for the mixed economy they say they want – they are more likely to participate in its implementation. International donors and African governments could establish forums for open dialogues with African publics to win popular ownership of reforms to reduce the scope of the state-run economy. Conducted in pragmatic terms, these exchanges should confront the hard fact that social welfare depends upon the restoration of economic growth, and that such growth requires a vibrant private sector. In helping ordinary Africans to grasp this imperative, however, the advocates of neo-liberalism will have to abandon their own ideological predisposition that a small state is always and everywhere better.

A second, related requirement is to reverse the declining administrative capacity of the state. Key supervisory, regulatory, and enforcement functions must be strengthened with a view to ensuring public guidance and oversight of newly liberalized markets. It is tempting to interpret the Afrobarometer evidence of popular resistance to privatization and civil service reform to mean that Africans are thoroughly disillusioned with all market-friendly policies. Instead we are struck by a popular mood of economic patience that holds that living conditions will improve in the future. We suspect that people would lend support to the adjustment agenda if institutional reforms were well conducted. Africans presently object to state cutbacks mainly because these occur in an atmosphere of official corruption or lead to the emergence of private monopolies. Thus, the state must be armed with instruments to ensure that liberalization and privatization meet social objectives, including, above all, opportunities for gainful employment.

Third, new incentives are needed to reform the behavior of state officials. African citizens and international donors find themselves in rare agreement that corruption corrodes government performance, undercuts satisfaction with economic growth, and eliminates trust in state institutions. The problem is that, in the absence of institutional alternatives to patronage, ordinary people are themselves too often complicit in corruption. Several approaches are possible in realizing a rule of law: strengthening agencies of restraint within the state; building nongovernmental organizations devoted to watchdog functions; and guaranteeing free and fair elections. There is little doubt that initiatives along these lines would help consolidate fragile new regimes because, even if political transition is not immediately followed by prosperity, democracy can still win popular legitimacy via the delivery of good governance.

In the final analysis, policymakers would also do well to recognize that Africans judge liberalization reforms against standards of social equity. Afrobarometer respondents say they resist free markets mainly because benefits accrue to top political leaders and their cronies. Although ordinary people seem willing to learn about new regimes, and even play by unfamiliar legal rules, they do not trust their leaders to do the same. For their part, the opponents of reform in Africa must learn to accept that a certain amount of social inequality is an unavoidable consequence of a market-led path to economic growth. Perhaps they can find solace in the political equality of one person, one vote. Even for people who are poorly informed, or for individuals who reason instrumentally, this simple democratic principle has powerful intrinsic appeal.

Appendix A

This appendix lists all indicators from the regression and path analyses presented in Chapters 6 through 12.

Three types of indicator are employed. *Single items* are used where a concept is measured with one survey question. We report the verbatim wording of questions along with the frequency distributions of responses. The accuracy (validity and reliability) of single-item indicators is based on the correspondence of the item's wording with the underlying concept (face validity), its association with other theoretically expected correlates (construct validity) or, eventually, test-retest reliability through longitudinal analysis. We also use several *two-item constructs*, the composition of which is reported here. In this case, validity and reliability are established by the methods already mentioned, but also by examining interitem correlation (Pearson's r) and internal consistency (Cronbach's Alpha). Wherever possible, we use *multiitem indices*, again reporting how these are constructed. These indices allow us to establish validity through factor analysis (which measures how each observed item relates to a hypothesized latent construct) and reliability analysis (Cronbach's Alpha).

There are many different combinations of factor analysis. To err on the side of caution, we almost always apply the most stringent methods, that is, maximum likelihood extraction and direct oblimin rotation, guaranteeing that if a factor solution can be found, it will also be found via all other methods. Test statistics from factor and reliability analyses are cited in order to establish the accuracy of all multiitem indices. However, we ultimately calculate simple average index scores and, in specified cases, additive index scores. Since the actual factor weightings of individual items may vary across countries and social groups, it is safest to assume that all items contribute to each index equally.

All statistics are ultimately based on a full, pooled sample of 21,531 interviews (see Appendix C). As in the text, test statistics (correlations, factor loadings, reliability coefficients) are calculated on this unweighted sample.

Descriptive statistics (frequency distributions, means, standard deviations), however, are calculated on a weighted sample of 14,397 that reflects both within-country weights (to correct, if necessary, for any disproportionate subsamples) and across-country weights (to standardize country samples equally at n = 1200). As in the text, all frequency percentages are calculated as proportions of valid responses, that is, after omitting refusals and other forms of nonresponse. However, the actual percentage of missing data is reported in parentheses. Unless otherwise noted, all descriptive and test statistics are calculated after omitting missing data and either excluding don't know answers, or recoding them to theoretically defensible positions on the response scale (see Appendix C).

Attitudes Toward Reform

Support for Democracy

	Don't Know	Doesn't Matter	Nondemocratic Government Sometimes Preferable	Democracy Always Preferable	Missing/ Not Applicable
Which of these three statements is closest to your own opinion? A. Democracy is preferable to any other form of government. B. In certain situations, a nondemocratic government can be preferable. C. To people like me, it doesn't matter what form of government we have.	6	13	12	70	(2)

Rejection of Alternative Political Regimes

		Strongly Support	Support	Neither	Oppose	Strongly Oppose	Don't Know	Refused/ Missing
Reject One-Man Rule	We should abolish elections and parliament so that the president can decide everything.	6	7	4	26	54	3	(1)
Reject Military Rule	The army should come in to govern the country.	5	7	3	20	62	4	(1)
Reject One-Party Rule	Candidates from only one political party should be allowed to stand for elections and hold office.	12	11	3	25	44	4	(<1)
Reject Traditional Rule	All decisions should be made by a council of traditional leaders.	9	13	6	27	41	4	(9)
Reject Expert Rule	The most important decisions, for example on the economy, should be left to experts.	24	23	6	17	22	7	(<1)

Note: Some people say we would be better off if if the country was governed differently. What do you think about the following options?

Rejection of Authoritarian Rule (Index)

	Strongly Support	Support	Don't know/ Neither	Oppose	Strongly Oppose	Mean (1–5)	Standard Deviation	Factor Loadings
Reject One-Man Rule	6	7	7	25	54	4.14	1.194	.74
Reject Military Rule	5	7	7	20	62	4.26	1.156	.57
Reject One-Party Rule	12	11	8	25	44	3.79	1.409	.48

Note: Factor analysis extracted a single unrotated factor (Eigenvalue = 1.45), which explains 48.3 percent of the common variance. Index reliability (Cronbach's Alpha = .61) is acceptable (n = 21,334).

Commitment to Democracy (Index)

	Uncommitted	Partially Committed	Committed	Mean (0–2)	Standard Deviation	Factor Loadings
Reject One-Man Rule	20	26	54	1.34	0.795	0.76
Reject Military Rule	19	20	62	1.43	0.784	0.65
Reject One-Party Rule	31	25	44	1.14	0.855	0.58
Support for Democracy	19	12	70	1.51	0.793	0.30

Notes: Factor analysis extracted a single unrotated factor (Eigenvalue = 2.01), which explains 50.1 percent of the common variance. Index reliability (Cronbach's Alpha = .66) is acceptable (n = 20,887).

Committed democrats are those who say "Democracy is always preferable" and who "strongly oppose" authoritarian alternatives. Partially committed democrats are those who say "In certain situations, a non-democratic government can be preferable" or who merely "oppose" authoritarian alternatives. Uncommitted respondents say "it doesn't matter what form of government we have" and either support, or are noncommittal toward, authoritarian alternatives, or do not express an opinion.

Supply of Democracy (Construct)

		Not a Democracy	Major Problems, But Still a Democracy	Don't Know	Minor Problems, But Still a Democracy	Full Democracy	Missing	Mean (0–4)	Standard Deviation
Extent of Democracy	In your opinion, how much of a democracy is ___ (this country) today?	11	22	9	28	30	(5)	2.44	1.391

		Not At All Satisfied	Not Very Satisfied	Don't Know	Fairly Satisfied	Very Satisfied	Missing	Mean	Standard Deviation
Satisfaction with Democracy	Generally, how satisfied are you with the way democracy works in ___?	17	17	8	38	21	(3)	2.29	1.411

Note: The items measuring extent of democracy and satisfaction with democracy are sufficiently correlated (Pearson's r = .45) and reliable (Cronbach's Alpha = .63) to warrant the creation of a two-item average construct of supply of democracy (n = 20,218).

Support for Market Economy (Index)

	Strongly Disagree	Disagree	Neither/ Don't Know	Agree	Strongly Agree	Missing
Support User Fees	It is better to raise educational standards, even if we have to pay school fees*	22	12	5	15	47	(<1)
Support Market Pricing	It is better to have goods in the market, even if the prices are high**	26	11	10	18	36	(<1)
Support Privatization	It is better for the government to sell its business to private companies and individuals***	42	15	7	11	24	(<1)
Support Retrenchment	The government cannot afford so many public employees and should lay some of them off****	41	19	8	12	20	(<1)

Notes: The opposing statements are as follows:
* It is better to have free schooling for children, even if the quality of education is low.
** It is better to have low prices, even if there are shortages of goods.
*** The government should retain ownership of its factories, businesses, and farms.
**** All civil servants should keep their jobs, even if paying their salaries is costly to the country.

The theory of measurement underlying this index is not based on the concept of covariance. Because the internal consistency of this package of reforms is defined principally by international donor organizations, we do not necessarily expect that agreement with one item among African respondents will necessarily be correlated with agreement with another. Thus, testing for internal consistency with factor or reliability analysis is not appropriate. What we desire is a simple count of the number of reform policies supported. Thus, we collapse each item so that "strongly agree" and "agree" = support (1) and "strongly disagree," "disagree," and "neither/don't know" = not support (0), and sum all reforms supported for a scale ranging from 0 to 4. As with single item constructs, we await test-retest data from longitudinal analysis to assess reliability.

Satisfaction With Market Reform

	Very Dissatisfied	Dissatisfied	Neutral/ Don't Know	Satisfied	Very Satisfied	Missing
How satisfied or unsatisfied are you with the (country's structural adjustment program)?	33	22	25	16	5	(66)

Social Structure

Gender

	Male	Female	Missing
What is the respondent's gender?	50	50	(1)

Age	Percent
18–24	23
25–34	30
35–44	21
45–54	13
55–64	8
65–74	4
75–84	1
85–94	<1
95–100	<1
Missing	(2)

Note: How old were you on your last birthday?

Residential Location

	Urban	Rural	Missing
Type of area in which interview was conducted	42	58	(2)

Class

	Never Employed	Peasant/ Agricultural	Worker	Professional Supervisory	Owner/ Employer	Other	Missing
What is your main occupation?	14	33	23	10	1	20	(7)

Shortages of Basic Human Needs

	Never	Sometimes/ Occasionally	Often	Always/ Not Applicable	Don't Know	Missing Data
Electricity in your home	25	14	16	44	2	(26)
Food for your family	45	37	18	<1	<1	(9)
A cash income	20	41	37	3	<1	(25)
Water for domestic use	51	29	18	2	<1	(9)
Medical treatment for your family	44	36	19	1	<1	(9)

Note: Over the past year, how often, if ever, have you gone without ____?

Lived Poverty (Index)

	Never	Sometimes/ Occasionally	Often/ Always	Mean (0–2)	Standard Deviation	Factor Loadings
Food	45	37	18	.73	.747	.65
Water	51	29	19	.68	.778	.62
Medical Treatment	44	37	20	.76	.760	.42

Notes: Factor analysis extracted a single unrotated factor (Eigenvalue = 1.63), which explains 54.3 percent of the common variance. Index reliability (Cronbach's Alpha = .57) is acceptable (n = 19,067).

Ethnicity

	Minor Language	Secondary Language	Major Language	Missing
What is your home language?	19	26	55	(1)

Note: Respondents whose language constitutes the largest segment of a national population are coded as "major"; respondents whose language is not the largest but is spoken by at least 10 percent of the population are coded as "secondary"; and those whose language is spoken by less than 10 percent are coded as "minor."

Race

	Black/ African	White/ European	"Coloured"/ Mixed Race	Indian/ South Asian	Could Not Tell	Missing
Race of Respondent	95	2	1	1	<1	(1)

Cultural Values

National Identity

	Strongly Disagree	Disagree	Neither/ Don't Know	Agree	Strongly Agree	Missing
It makes you proud to be called a ——.	1	2	2	25	70	(17)

Modern versus Traditional Identities

	Traditional	Modern	Missing
Besides being a ——, which specific group do you feel you belong to first and foremost?	52	48	(14)

Notes: We have spoken to many —— and they have all described themselves in different ways. Some people describe themselves in terms of their language, ethnic group, religion, or gender and others describe themselves in economic terms, such as working class, middle class, or a farmer. Besides being ——, which specific group do you feel you belong to first and foremost?
A full set of responses is presented in Table 7.1. These are coded as "traditional" if respondents express racial, ethnic, religious, regional, or age-based identities. Responses are coded as "modern" if they cite occupation, class, country, political party, or individual identities.

Interpersonal Trust

	Trusts Others	Must Be Careful	Don't Know	Missing
Generally speaking, would you say that most people can be trusted or that you must be very careful in dealing with other people?	18	79	3	(9)

Individualism (Construct)

	Strongly Disagree	Disagree	Neither/Don't Know	Agree	Strongly Agree	Missing	Mean (1–5)	Standard Deviation
People should look after themselves and be responsible for their own success in life.*	35	11	3	15	36	(<1)	3.05	1.756
The best way to create jobs is to encourage people to start their own businesses.**	34	10	3	15	38	(<1)	3.14	1.767

Notes: *Opposing statement: The government should bear the main responsibility for ensuring the well-being of people.
**The government should provide employment for everyone who wants work.
The two items are correlated (Pearson's r = .33) and reliable (Cronbach's Alpha = .50) enough to warrant an average construct of individualism (n = 21,421).

Tolerance for Risk

	Strongly Disagree	Disagree	Neither/ Don't Know	Agree	Strongly Agree	Missing
If a person has a good idea for business, they should invest their own savings or borrow money to try and make it succeed.*	10	8	6	19	57	(25)

Note: *Opposing statement: There is no sense in trying to start a new business, because it might lose money.

Freedom to Earn

	Strongly Disagree	Disagree	Neither/ Don't Know	Agree	Strongly Agree	Missing
People should be free to earn as much as they can.*	21	10	6	18	44	(<1)

Note: *Opposing statement: Government should impose limits on earnings.

Support for Private Provision

	Government	Combination	Businesses	Individuals	Don't Know	Missing
Extending agricultural credit	70	22	3	3	2	(9)
Providing schools and clinics	65	31	1	3	1	(9)
Reducing crime	58	36	1	5	1	(10)
Creating jobs	58	36	2	4	1	(9)
Producing and marketing (major export commodity)	52	28	7	9	4	(9)
Building houses	29	26	3	42	1	(9)

Notes: I am going to read out a list of things that are important for the development of our country. In your opinion, who is responsible for providing these things?

The government, private businesses, or the people themselves? Or some combination of these providers?

Support for Private Provision (Index)

	Government	Both	Individuals/ Businesses	Mean (1–3)	Standard Deviation	Factor Loadings
Creating jobs	58	36	6	1.47	.603	0.65
Reducing crime	58	36	6	1.47	.600	0.58
Providing schools and clinics	65	31	4	1.38	.555	0.55

Notes: Factor analysis extracted a single unrotated factor (Eigenvalue = 1.71), which explains 56.9 percent of the common variance. Index reliability (Cronbach's Alpha = .62) is acceptable (n = 18,861).

Cognitive Awareness

Awareness of Democracy

	Not Aware	Aware
What, if anything, does democracy mean to you?	22	78

Note: Respondents who are unable to supply an answer are coded as "not aware"; respondents who are able to provide any definition are coded as "aware."

Awareness of SAP

	Not Aware	Aware	Missing
Have you ever heard anything about the government's (Structural Adjustment Program*), or haven't you had a chance to hear about this yet?	57	43	(25)

Note: *The popular name or acronym of each country's SAP was inserted here.

Formal Education

	No Formal	Primary Only	Secondary	Postsecondary	Don't Know	Missing
What is the highest level of education you have completed?	19	35	36	11	<1	(<1)

Exposure to News Media (Index)

	Never	Once a Month or Less	Once a Week/Few Times a Month	Few/Several Times a Week	Every Day	Don't Know	Missing Data	Mean (0–5)	Standard Deviation	Factor Loadings
Newspapers	51	11	11	13	13	1	(1)	1.67	1.968	0.76
Television	55	7	6	9	22	1	(9)	1.74	2.160	0.72
Radio	14	5	8	20	54	<1	(<1)	3.77	1.779	0.48

Notes: How often do you get news from ____?
Factor analysis extracted a single unrotated factor (Eigenvalue = 1.84), which explains 61.5 percent of the common variance.
Index reliability (Cronbach's Alpha = .68) is acceptable (n = 19,465).

Internal Efficacy

	Strongly Disagree	Disagree	Don't Know	Agree	Strongly Agree	Missing
I can usually understand the way that government works.*	33	31	8	15	13	(<1)

Note: *Opposing statement: The way the government operates seems so complicated that I cannot really understand what is going on.

Cognitive Engagement (Construct)

	Don't Know	Not Interested	Somewhat Interested	Very Interested	Missing	Mean (0–2)	Standard Deviation
How interested are you in politics and government?	2	28	46	23	(1)	.93	0.727

	Don't Know	Never	Sometimes	Always	Missing	Mean (0–2)	Standard Deviation
How often do you discuss politics and government with other people?	1	38	41	20	(1)	.81	0.741

Note: There is sufficient correlation (Pearson's r = .55) and reliability (Cronbach's Alpha = .71) between items to warrant the creation of a two-item average construct of cognitive engagement (n = 21,391).

Knowledge of Leaders (Index)

	Don't Know	Incorrectly Identified	Can't Determine	Correctly Identified	Missing/ Not Applicable
Your local councilor/mayor	53	5	4	37	(16)
Member of parliament/deputy of the national assembly for this area	61	4	2	33	(13)
The minister of finance	68	6	3	24	(10)
The vice president of (this country)	34	4	1	61	(13)

Notes: Can you tell me the name of the ___?

The theory of measurement underlying this index is not based on the concept of covariance. Because we do not necessarily expect those who know one incumbent to know others, testing for internal consistency with factor or reliability analysis is not appropriate. In order to test for the consequences of awareness, we desire is a simple count of the number of incumbents of which respondents are aware. Thus, we simply sum all correct answers to create an index from 0 to 4. We await test-retest data from longitudinal analysis to assess reliability.

Procedural Understanding of Democracy (Index)

	Not Important At All	Not Important	Don't Know	Important	Essential	Missing	Mean (1–5)	Standard Deviation	Factor Loadings
Elections are held regularly	8	13	6	32	42	(17)	3.88	1.286	0.70
The majority rules	6	10	7	30	47	(17)	4.03	1.210	0.57
At least two political parties compete with each other	8	13	7	32	40	(17)	3.82	1.303	0.55
Anyone is free to criticize government	7	13	6	32	43	(17)	3.91	1.266	0.52

Notes: People associate democracy with many different meanings such as the ones I will mention now. In order for a society to be called democratic, how important is each of these?
Factor analysis extracted a single unrotated factor (Eigenvalue = 2.02), which explains 50.5 percent of the common variance.
Index reliability (Cronbach's Alpha = .67) is acceptable (n = 17,169).

Substantive Understanding of Democracy (Index)

	Not Important At All	Not Important	Don't Know	Important	Essential	Missing	Mean (1–5)	Standard Deviation	Factor Loadings
Education for everyone	2	5	4	27	62	(17)	4.41	.919	0.78
Jobs for everyone	2	7	4	27	60	(17)	4.35	.994	0.77
A small income gap between rich and poor	8	15	7	29	42	(17)	3.81	1.332	0.43
Everyone enjoys basic necessities like shelter, food and water	2	4	4	26	64	(17)	4.45	.909	0.70

Notes: People associate democracy with many different meanings such as the ones I will mention now. In order for a society to be called democratic, how important is each of these?

Factor analysis extracted a single unrotated factor (Eigenvalue = 2.36), which explains 50.1 percent of the common variance.

Index reliability (Cronbach's Alpha = .73) is acceptable (n = 17,155).

Cognitive Awareness (Second Order Factor for Path Analysis)

	Factor Loadings
Political knowledge	0.55
Media exposure	0.52
Awareness of SAP	0.49
Cognitive engagement	0.47
Awareness of democracy	0.40
Procedural understandings of democracy	0.24

Notes: Factor analysis extracted a single unrotated factor (Eigenvalue = 1.98), which explains 33.0 percent of the common variance. Index reliability (Cronbach's Alpha = .52) is low but acceptable for a second order index (n = 13,469).

Evaluations of Economic Performance

Performance of the Economy (Index)

	Very Dissatisfied/ Much Worse	Dissatisfied/ Worse	Don't Know/ Neither/ Same	Satisfied/ Better	Very Satisfied/ Much Better	Missing	Mean (1–5)	Standard Deviation	Factor Loadings
The condition of the —— economy today?*	33	31	7	23	5	(1)	2.37	1.297	0.56
Economic conditions in —— now compared to one year ago?*	22	24	24	24	7	(1)	2.70	1.234	0.74
Economic conditions in one year's time?	18	12	33	22	15	(1)	3.03	1.291	0.69
Would you say that your own living conditions are worse, the same or better than other —s?	19	26	31	21	4	(9)	2.65	1.118	0.66
Are (your group's) economic conditions worse, the same as, or better than other groups in this country?	15	18	42	19	6	(18)	2.84	1.084	0.45

Notes: *How satisfied are you with ____?

Factor analysis extracted a single unrotated factor (Eigenvalue = 2.55), which explains 51.0 percent of the common variance.

Index reliability (Cronbach's Alpha = .76) is very high (n = 16,913).

Government Policy Performance (Index)

	Very Badly	Badly/ Not Very Well	Don't Know	Fairly Well	Very Well	Missing	Mean (1–5)	Standard Deviation	Factor Loadings
Improving health services	21	23	2	38	16	(<1)	3.05	1.445	0.76
Addressing education needs	18	21	3	39	20	(<1)	3.23	1.435	0.73
Creating jobs	32	27	4	27	9	(<1)	2.52	1.401	0.61
Keeping prices low	34	28	6	25	7	(<1)	2.42	1.366	0.56

Notes: How well would you say the current government is handling the following problems?
Factor analysis extracted a single unrotated factor (Eigenvalue = 2.33), which explains 58.3 percent of the common variance.
Index reliability (Cronbach's Alpha = .76) is very high (n = 21,402).

SAPs Create Inequality

	Strongly Disagree	Disagree	Don't Know	Agree	Strongly Agree	Missing
Government economic policies have helped most people, only a few have suffered.*	54	12	6	11	18	(52)

Note: *Opposing statement: The government's economic policies have hurt most people and only benefited a few.

378

Delivery of Economic Welfare

	Much Worse	Worse	Don't Know/ Same	Better	Much Better	Missing
People have an adequate standard of living	15	17	22	29	15	(9)

Note: We are going to compare our present system of government with the former system of __. Please tell me if the following things are better or worse now than they used to be?

Economic Performance (Second Order Factor for Path Analysis)

	Factor Loadings
Government policy performance	0.65
Performance of the economy	0.65
SAP creates inequality	0.32

Notes: Factor analysis extracted a single unrotated factor (Eigenvalue = 1.58), which explains 52.5 percent of the common variance. Index reliability (Cronbach's Alpha = .47) is low but acceptable for a second order index (n = 10,197).

Evaluations of Political Performance

Trust In State Institutions (Index)

	Not At All	Distrust Somewhat	Don't Know	Trust Somewhat	Trust a Lot	Missing	Mean (1–5)	Standard Deviation	Factor Loadings
Courts of law	16	23	8	31	23	(<1)	3.22	1.419	0.72
Police	24	26	3	28	19	(<1)	2.92	1.508	0.70
National election commission	14	15	16	29	26	(1)	3.37	1.388	0.64
National broadcaster	9	14	9	30	38	(17)	3.74	1.329	0.59
Army	15	17	7	27	34	(9)	3.49	1.469	0.58

Notes: How much do you trust the following institutions? (In Southern Africa, " . . . to do what is right.")
Factor analysis extracted a single unrotated factor (Eigenvalue = 2.69), which explains 53.8 percent of the common variance.
Index reliability (Cronbach's Alpha = .79) is very high (n = 15,541).

President's Performance (Construct)

	Not At All	Distrust Somewhat	Don't Know	Trust Somewhat	Trust a Lot	Missing	Mean (1–5)	Standard Deviation
How much do you trust the president?	15	24	7	27	27	(17)	3.28	1.451

	Very Dissatisfied	Dissatisfied	Don't Know	Satisfied	Very Satisfied	Missing	Mean (1–5)	Standard Deviation
What about the way the president has performed his job over the past year? Are you ___?	13	14	8	33	31	(17)	3.54	1.398

Note: The two items are highly correlated (Pearson's r = .70) and reliable (Cronbach's Alpha = .82) enough to warrant a composite construct (n = 13,582).

Representatives' Performance (Construct)

	Very Dissatisfied	Dissatisfied	Don't Know	Satisfied	Very Satisfied	Missing	Mean (1–5)	Standard Deviation
Local councilor performance	15	20	12	36	17	(13)	3.19	1.346
MP performance	18	21	13	35	14	(1)	3.07	1.349

Note: The two items are sufficiently correlated (Pearson's r = .49) and reliable (Cronbach's Alpha = .66) to warrant the creation of a two-item average construct (n = 19,542).

Identity Group Treated Fairly

	Never	Almost Never	Some of the Time	Most of the Time	Always	Don't Know	Missing
In your opinion, how often is__ (your identity group) treated fairly by the government?	10	13	29	16	27	7	(10)

Perceived Official Corruption (Index)

	None	Few/Some	Don't Know	Most	All/Almost All	Missing	Mean (1–5)	Standard Deviation	Factor Loadings
Civil servants	8	28	16	30	19	(17)	2.23	1.262	0.78
Elected leaders	11	29	17	24	16	(17)	2.06	1.266	0.75
Government officials	10	26	13	27	25	(<1)	2.32	1.345	0.46

Notes: What about corruption? (Corruption is where those in government and the civil service take money or gifts from the people and use it for themselves, or expect people to pay extra money or a gift to do their job). How many __ do you think are involved in corruption? Factor analysis extracted a single unrotated factor (Eigenvalue = 1.87), which explains 62.3 percent of the common variance. Index reliability (Cronbach's Alpha = .69) is acceptable (n = 15,744).

Increased Government Corruption

	Much Less	Less	Don't Know/ Same	More	Much More	Missing
How does this (the current level of corruption) compare to the government that this country had under __?	17	20	22	20	20	(9)

Delivery of Political Rights (Index)

	Much Worse	Worse	Don't Know/Same	Better	Much Better	Missing	Mean (1–5)	Standard Deviation	Factor Loadings
People can join any organization they want.	2	3	15	40	40	(9)	4.13	.900	0.83
People are free to say what they think.	4	6	15	40	37	(9)	3.99	1.041	0.75
Each person can freely choose who to vote for without feeling pressured.	2	4	14	38	42	(9)	4.15	.935	0.73
Everybody is treated equally and fairly by the government.	9	13	27	31	20	(9)	3.41	1.204	0.42

Notes: We are going to compare our present system of government with the former system of ___. Please tell me if the following things are better or worse than they used to be?

Factor analysis extracted a single unrotated factor (Eigenvalue = 2.42), which explains 60.4 percent of the common variance.

Index reliability (Cronbach's Alpha =.76) is high (n = 19,102).

Political Fear/Availability of Free Speech

	Strongly Agree	Agree	Don't Know/Neither	Disagree	Strongly Disagree	Missing
In this country, you must be very careful of what you say or do with regard to politics.	30	29	12	16	13	(25)

Free and Fair Elections

	Not Free and Fair	Free and Fair, with Major Problems	Don't Know	Free and Fair, with Minor Problems	Completely Free and Fair	Missing
In your opinion, how free and fair were the last national elections, held on (date)?	11	12	11	27	39	(1)

Leadership Responsiveness

	Strongly Disagree	Disagree	Don't Know/ Neither	Agree	Strongly Agree	Missing
The way you vote could make things better in the future.*	20	10	5	16	49	(17)

Note: *Opposing Statement: No matter how you vote, it won't make things any better in the future.

Political Performance (Second Order Factor for Path Analysis)

	Factor Loadings
President's performance	0.78
Perceived official corruption	0.58
Free and fair elections	0.54
Trust in state institutions	0.53
Delivery of political rights	0.48
Identity group treated fairly	0.47
Leadership responsiveness	0.25

Notes: Factor analysis extracted a single unrotated factor (Eigenvalue = 2.66), which explains 38.0 percent of the common variance. Index reliability (Cronbach's Alpha = .69) is acceptable (n = 8,059).

Institutional Influences

Group Membership (Index)

	Don't Know	Not a Member	Member	Missing
Religious group	<1	35	65	(<1)
Business group	<1	80	19	(9)
Development group	<1	71	29	(9)
Labor union	1	82	17	(9)

Notes: I am going to read you a list of voluntary organizations. For each one, could you tell me whether you are an official leader, an active member, an inactive member, or not a member of that organization?

The theory of measurement underlying this index is not based on the concept of covariance. Because the organizations we ask about vary widely in nature and purpose, we do not necessarily expect those who belong to one group to belong to others. Thus, testing for internal consistency with factor or reliability analysis is not appropriate. We need instead a simple count of the number of memberships. Thus, we simply sum all memberships to create an index from 0 to 4. We await test-retest data from longitudinal analysis to assess reliability. On the basis of significantly different correlates, we sometimes break this index apart and report the consequences of membership in religious groups only.

Identifies with Political Party

	Don't Know	Does Not Feel Close	Feels Close	Missing
Do you feel close to any political party?	<1	43	57	(1)

Identifies with Winning Party ("Winner")

	Don't Know	Losing Party	No Party	Winning Party	Missing
Do you feel close to any political party? If yes, which one?	<1	17	44	39	(3)

Note: Respondents are coded as "winners" if they identify with the party that won the most recent national election, as "losers" if they identified with some other party, and "no party" if they do not identify with any party.

Voted in Last Elections

	Cannot Remember	Did Not Vote	Voted	No Election in My Area	Missing
Understanding that some (people) choose not to vote, let me ask you: Did you vote in the (most recent national election)?	1	27	71	1	(<1)

Participation Between Elections

	Don't Know	Never/Might	Once or Twice	Sometimes	Often	Missing
Joined a demonstration	1	87	5	5	2	(9)
Worked for candidate/party	1	82	4	7	6	(<1)
Got together with others to raise issue	1	57	9	20	15	(9)
Attended campaign rally	1	55	11	18	15	(<1)
Attended community meeting	<1	53	9	20	18	(1)
Wrote a letter to a newspaper	2	84	2	2	1	(9)

Note: I will read out a list of things that people sometimes do as citizens. Please tell me how often you, personally, have done any of these things during the last five years. (In Southern Africa, no time period was set.)

Contacting Leaders

	Don't Know	Never	Once or Twice	Sometimes	Often	Missing
Contact government official	<1	85	6	5	3	(<1)
Contact community leader	<1	73	8	12	7	(<1)

Note: During the past five years, how often have you contacted any of the following persons for help to solve a problem? (In Southern Africa, the specified time period was one year.)

Communing and Contacting (Index)

	Don't Know/ Never	Once or Twice	Sometimes	Often	Mean (0–3)	Standard Deviation	Factor Loadings
Attended campaign rally	56	11	18	15	.92	1.152	.63
Worked for candidate/parties	84	4	7	6	.34	.835	.56
Attended community meetings	54	9	20	18	1.01	1.201	.51
Got together with others to raise issue	57	9	20	15	.93	1.163	.64
Contacted government officials	85	6	5	3	.27	.706	.33

Note: Factor analysis extracted a single unrotated factor (Eigenvalue = 2.16), which explains 42.3 percent of the common variance. Index reliability (Cronbach's Alpha = .66) is acceptable (n = 19,084).

Vote Choice

	Voted for Losing Party	No Information	Voted for Winning Party
Which party do you feel close to? Did you vote in most recent election?	13	57	31

Note: Respondent coded as "voting for losing party" (−1) if respondent reported voting and identify with losing party in the most recent national election; as "no information" (0) if they reported voting and identify with no party; and as voting for winning party (1) if they reported voting and identify with winning party. For path analysis, "did not vote" was scored as 0 rather than missing.

Defending Democracy (Index)

	Support Government	Do Nothing	Don't Know	Take Action to Defend Democracy	Missing	Mean (0–3)	Standard Deviation	Factor Loadings
Dismissed judges who ruled against the government	10	35	6	48	(10)	2.38	.660	0.79
Shut down newspapers that criticized the government	7	35	6	53	(10)	2.46	.616	0.77
Suspended the national assembly and canceled the next elections	7	34	7	53	(10)	2.46	.616	0.70

Notes: What would you do if the government took any of the following actions?
Factor analysis extracted a single unrotated factor (Eigenvalue = 2.14), which explains 71.3 percent of the common variance.
Index reliability (Cronbach's Alpha = .80) is very high (n = 18,647).
The descriptive statistics reported in Chapter 5 include missing values. Persons who cannot say whether they will defend democracy are unlikely to actually do so.

Appendix B

SAMPLING METHOD

Afrobarometer surveys are based on national probability samples representing cross sections of adult citizens in each country. The goal is to give every individual an equal chance of inclusion in the sample via random selection at every stage.

In six countries, a sample of 1,200 individuals allows inferences to national adult populations with a margin of error of no more than plus or minus 2.8 percent with a confidence level of 95 percent. When the sample size is increased to at least 2,000 (in five countries), the confidence interval shrinks to plus or minus 2.2 percent and to 1.6 percent for a sample of 3,600 (in Nigeria).

The sample universe includes all citizens of voting age. Excluded are noncitizens and anyone under the age of eighteen years on the day of the survey. Also left out are people living in institutionalized settings, such as prisons, student dormitories, and hospitals. We also exclude inaccessible areas, such as zones of armed conflict or natural disaster, as well as national parks and game reserves.

The design is a clustered, stratified, multistage, area probability sample. Geographic sampling units of decreasing size are selected in four stages:

Stage One: Selecting Primary Sampling Units (PSUs)

PSU's are the smallest, well-defined areas for which reliable population data are available. Since the Afrobarometer employs the most recent official national census as a sampling frame, PSUs are commonly census enumeration areas. We usually commission a sampling expert from the national census bureau to draw the sample to Afrobarometer specifications.

The sample universe is stratified, first by administrative area (region/province) and then by residential locality (urban or rural). These stratifications increase the likelihood that distinctive ethnic or language groups are included in the sample. The sample is distributed across each locality in each region in proportion to its share in the national population. The total number of PSUs is determined by calculating the maximum acceptable degree of clustering. Because PSUs can be geographically small and socially homogenous, we prefer to accept no more than eight interviews per PSU. A sample of 1,200 therefore contains 150 PSUs; a sample of 2,000 contains 250 PSUs.

PSUs are then sampled within each stratum using random methods. If PSUs have roughly equal populations, then simple random sampling (SRS) is sufficient. If – more commonly – the PSUs have variant populations, then random sampling is conducted with probability proportionate to population size (PPPS), which gives units with larger populations greater probabilities of being chosen. In urban areas with extremely diverse housing patterns, an additional layer of stratification may be added to ensure that the sample does not leave out low-density (especially informal) settlements. Using a street map, a city, or town is divided into high-, medium-, and low-density areas. PSUs within each area are then represented equally (or better yet, in proportion to population sizes, if these are known) within the sample for that city or town.

Once EAs are randomly selected they are plotted on a national map, enabling survey managers to plan travel routes for the fieldwork. In cases where PSUs are inaccessible, substitution is made by randomly drawing another EA. If more than 5 percent of PSUs require substitution, then the entire Stage One sample is discarded and a new one is drawn. If important minority groups are missed or covered too scantily to allow generalizations, then oversampling is introduced, along with post hoc weighting to correct the data.

Stage Two: Selecting Sampling Start Points (SSPs)

Within each PSU, field teams (usually consisting of one field supervisor and four interviewers) travel to a randomly selected start point. The SSP further clusters the sample into manageable areas that are reachable on foot or by a short vehicle ride. One or other of the following methods is used:

If a reliable list of all households is available for every PSU, then this is obtained from the national census bureau or the office of district administrator or local government authority. A random numbers table is used to draw a simple random sample of eight households from the list. A detailed map or description matched to the list is required in order to locate the household. If this method is used, it is not necessary to apply Stage Three: Selection of Households; field teams go straight to Stage Four: Selection of Respondents.

If household lists are not available but the census bureau has provided PSU maps, then the field supervisor chooses a start point using a numbered grid. The coordinates on the grid, which identify the SSP, are drawn from a table of random numbers. The SSP is marked on the map, and given to the field team for that area, who then locate the nearest housing settlement, if necessary seeking directions from local residents. Because actual conditions on the ground can never be known in advance for all PSUs, supervisors randomly choose a second SSP as a substitute.

If neither household lists nor maps are available, the field supervisor contacts a traditional leader, local government councilor, or government official knowledgeable about the area. This person provides information on the number of settlements (for example, villages) in the PSU. These settlements must have identifiable boundaries that do not overlap with one another. They are then listed, numbered, and randomly selected.

The logic of random sampling is to avoid any kind of pattern in the units selected at any stage. Thus, at the start point, the supervisor rotates the place where interviewers begin their walk pattern. If the team starts on a main road at one SSP, they start off the road at the next SSP. If the team starts in a central place (like a school) in one PSU, they start in a peripheral place in the next PSU, and so on.

Stage Three: Selecting Households

Fanning out from the SSP, the field team selects households. The Afrobarometer defines a household as a group of people who presently eat together from the same pot. By this definition, a household does not include persons who are currently living elsewhere for purposes of study or work. And it excludes domestic workers or temporary visitors, even if they ate or slept there on the previous night. In multihousehold dwelling structures (like apartment blocks, housing compounds with multiple spouses, or backyard dwellings for renters, relatives, or household workers), each household is treated as a separate sampling unit.

The method for selecting households is as follows:

In well-populated urban and rural areas, with single-dwelling units: The supervisor chooses any point (like a street corner, a school, or a water source), randomly rotating the choice of such landmarks. The four interviewers on the field team are instructed to walk away from this point in the following directions: interviewer 1 walks toward the sun, interviewer 2 away from the sun, interviewer 3 at a right angle to interviewer 1, interviewer 4 in the opposite direction from interviewer 3. The team applies a day code to randomly establish an interval (n) for household selection. It is calculated by adding together the numbers in the day of the month: on the 5th, 14th, and 23rd of the month the interval is 5, but on the 6th, 15th, and 24th it is 6, and so on. In every case, the interviewer selects the nth house on the right.

In well-populated urban and rural areas, with multiple-dwelling units: If the start point is an apartment block, or if the walk pattern includes such, then the interviewer starts on the top floor and works his/her way downward, stopping at every nth flat on the right. In an exception to the normal walk pattern, which only refers to blocks of flats, the interviewer should only visit *alternate* floors of the block.

In sparsely populated rural areas, with small villages or single-dwelling farms, there may be only a few households around a given start point. We do not wish to overcluster the sample by conducting too many (for example, all eight) interviews in one small village. In these cases, the following guidelines apply: If there are fifteen or fewer households within walking distance of the start point, the field team shall drop only one interviewer there to conduct no more than two interviews. If there are sixteen to thirty households within walking distance of the start point, two interviewers are deployed. If there are more than fifty households, the whole team can operate in the same locality as usual. When only one or two interviewers are deployed, the rest of the team moves to the nearest housing settlement *within the same EA and closest to the SSP*, where fieldwork proceeds according to the above rules.

Each interviewer obtains two interviews per PSU (four interviewers × two interviews = eight interviews, the quota for the PSU). After completing the first interview, he or she follows the same procedure as before. He/she continues walking in the same direction and chooses the nth dwelling on the right (where n = the day code) for the second interview. If the settlement comes to an end and there are no more houses, the interviewer turns at right angles to the right and keeps walking, again looking for the nth dwelling on the right. This procedure is repeated until the interviewer finds an eligible dwelling containing an eligible household.

Stage Four: Selecting Individual Respondents

Once the household is identified, the interviewer randomly selects an individual respondent from within the household. To ensure that women are not underrepresented, the Afrobarometer sets a gender quota of an equal number of men and women in the overall sample, which is accomplished by alternating interviews by gender. First, the interviewer determines from the previous interview whether a male or female respondent is required. The interviewer then lists (in any order) the first names of all the household members of that gender who are at least eighteen years old, even those not presently at home but who will return during that day. From the list, the interviewer randomly selects the person to be interviewed by asking a household member to choose a numbered card from a blind deck of cards.

The interview is conducted only with the selected person and no one else in that household. If an interview is refused, the interviewer substitutes the household by continuing the walk pattern and again selecting the nth dwelling on the right (where n = the day code). Note: in the Afrobarometer, we substitute households, not respondents. It is not acceptable, for example, for the interviewer to substitute a spouse, parent, child, sibling – or domestic worker or visitor – for a selected respondent who happens not to be at home at the time.

If, on the first try, the interviewer finds no one at home in the selected household, he/she makes one return call later in the day. Or, if the designated respondent is not at home, the interviewer makes an appointment to meet them later in the day. Again, a return call will be necessary in order to find the selected respondent and to conduct the interview. It is also acceptable for the interviewer to ascertain the whereabouts of the selected respondent (they may be at work) and, if nearby, to walk to that place to conduct the interview.

If the return call is unsuccessful, say because the respondent has still not come home for the appointment, then, and only then, the interviewer may substitute the household. If the house is still empty or the selected respondent is not at home at the time of the call back, the interviewer is permitted to substitute that household with the very next household in the direction of the walk pattern. This slight change of procedure is necessary under these circumstances since the interviewer may already have had a successful call earlier in the day in the household that is located at the sampling interval.

Appendix C

IMPUTATION OF DATA

Two types of survey responses require special discussion. The first occurs when respondents choose a "don't know" (DK) response. For frequency distributions, DK responses present no difficulty: we simply report the proportion of respondents who choose this option along with those choosing other responses, all as proportions of all valid responses (excluding missing data). For statistical analysis, however – such as calculating means or correlation coefficients – DKs can present special problems. On the questionnaire, these responses are often placed at the end of response scales and numbered accordingly, such as a 5 on a scale that runs from "0 = never" to "4 = every day." However, in this case, computer statistical programs read the DK to signify a substantive value of 5. To prevent this, a standard procedure is to set all DKs as "missing" to make them invisible to statistical analysis. One drawback to this option is that it reduces the number of effective cases, thus limiting our confidence that the results apply across the entire sample, and the population that it represents (more on this below).

Moreover, "don't know" is often a legitimate, substantive answer that should be taken into account rather than discarded.[1] Wherever possible, our preferred alternative is to recode DK to theoretically defensible spots on the response scale. For example, for many of the questions about political participation, we assumed that those who did not know whether they had ever taken a specific course of action had in fact never done so. In other cases, where attitude scales were symmetric (such as five-point scales from "strongly agree" to "strongly disagree") we recoded DK to the middle, neutral category. With regard to other balanced scales with no original middle category (such as a four-point scale that runs from "1 = very badly" to "4 = very well") we created a middle category, and placed the DK responses there, recoding the entire scale to run from 1 to 5 with DK set to 3. In both cases, we presumed that DK is equivalent to some point of zero affect, with other

397

responses measuring positive or negative affect ranging to either side. We resorted to setting DKs to "missing" only when one of the above options was not defensible.

The second type of problematic survey response is the complete absence of data. In some small number of cases, respondents may simply refuse to offer a response (which is different from saying they "don't know"). In an even smaller number of cases, the actual response is irretrievable due to interviewer errors in recording the answer. In this study, however, the bulk of missing data arose from the early evolution of the Afrobarometer Round 1 questionnaire, in which whole questions were not asked in specific surveys. Thus, from time to time, we confront missing data for one or more entire countries.

When trying to assess whether absent cases are likely to differ from fully observed cases in any significant way, analysts distinguish between ignorable and nonignorable missing data. Missing data is nonignorable if there are systematic biases in rates of missingness: for example, where tax cheats are less likely to answer questions about tax compliance, or if lower class respondents are more likely to fail to report an occupation. In such cases, we need to know quite a lot about the data in order to try and fill in the missing information.[2]

When missing data are "ignorable," however, the missingness of data is unrelated to the true value of that variable, as well as to observed values of other known predictors of that variable. For example, the probability of responding to a question on support for democracy should have nothing to do with whether one is a democrat or authoritarian, nor should it relate to levels of education or approval of the president's performance. This condition is known as missing completely at random. Even if authoritarians are less likely to offer an opinion about support for democracy, however, the missing data may be ignorable if that relationship disappears once we control for, say, education. Then it is known as missing at random.

We believe that the vast bulk of our missing data can be regarded as ignorable. While all respondents from a specific country may be missing on a certain variable, this is due to relatively arbitrary factors of the national questionnaire design process, not to any intrinsic quality of citizenship or public opinion in that country. Note that we always leave missing data out of descriptive statistics.

As with DKs, missing data present special problems for statistical analysis, however, which social scientists commonly address by deleting all missing cases (listwise deletion). But given the large number of variables used in our analysis, and the fact that a few of the independent variables were not asked in whole countries, listwise deletion results in the loss of unacceptably large proportions of cases. Moreover, recent analyses have demonstrated that such procedures produce inefficient and biased estimates.[3]

Thus, we use a method known as multiple imputation in order to arrive at a complete data set with valid data for all 21,531 cases.[4] A data management program known as *Amelia* was employed to impute values for all missing data. By randomly deleting responses from fully observed data sets, and then comparing the imputed values to the known real values, King and colleagues demonstrate that *Amelia* performs better than all other known procedures for accurately substituting imputed values.

Imputation procedures use known information on a range of other variables to predict the missing values. However, most imputation procedures assume that the values of missing cases are simply a linear combination of responses across a range of other variables. In other words, they place all missing values directly onto a regression prediction line. However, we know that observed values cluster around a predicted regression line, some closer and some farther away. This uncertainty (or error) must be reflected when imputing missing values. *Amelia* does exactly this. It imputes m values for each missing response, creating m complete data sets where the observed values are all the same, but the missing values differ slightly across the data sets. All statistical procedures are then performed across all data sets and the results combined by taking the average of the m estimates. Ultimately, we created a special data set with the approximately fifty variables that would comprise the regression and path analyses reported in Chapters 6 through 12. *Amelia* then regressed each variable with missing data on all the other variables and through an iterative process filled in the missing data, in this case, producing five data sets across which the imputed values varied reflected the degree of uncertainty with which they were predicted.

Notes

Introduction

1 The trinity of "i's" comes from Mark Lichbach and Alan Zukerman, who neatly summarize recent theoretical approaches to comparative politics in these terms. See their edited volume on *Comparative Politics: Rationality, Culture, and Structure* (Cambridge: Cambridge University Press, 1997), Ch.1.

2 Remember, however, that these figures represent only those individuals who have heard of the SAP. In Tanzania, only 24 percent had done so.

Chapter 1

1 The extensive literature on democratization in Africa includes: John Wiseman (ed.), *Democracy and Political Change in Sub-Saharan Africa* (London: Routledge, 1995); Michael Bratton and Nicolas van de Walle, *Democratic Experiments in Africa: Regime Transitions in Comparative Perspective* (New York: Cambridge University Press, 1997); Jean-Pascal Daloz and Patrick Quantain, *Transitions democratiques africaines* (Paris: Karthala, 1997); John Clarke and David Gardinier (eds.), *Political Reform in Francophone Africa* (Boulder, CO: Westview Press, 1997); Marina Ottaway (ed.), *Democracy in Africa: The Hard Road Ahead* (Boulder, CO: Lynne Rienner Publishers, 1997); Julius Ihonvbere and John Mulum Mbaku, *Multiparty Democracy and Political Change: Constraints to Democratization in Africa* (London: Ashgate, 1998); Richard Joseph (ed.), *State, Conflict, and Democracy in Africa* (Boulder, CO: Lynne Rienner Publishers, 1999); and Stephen Ndegwa, *A Decade of Democracy in Africa* (Boston: Brill, 2001).

2 Thomas Carothers, "The End of the Transition Paradigm," *Journal of Democracy* 13, 1 (2001): 5–21. See also Terry Lynn Karl, "The Hybrid Regimes of Central America," *Journal of Democracy* 6, 3 (1995): 72–86.

3 Larry Diamond, "Thinking About Hybrid Regimes," *Journal of Democracy* 13, 2 (2002): 22. This conjuncture has also been summarized as "pseudo-democracy" or "virtual democracy." See Diamond, *Developing Democracy: Toward Consolidation* (Baltimore, MD: Johns Hopkins University Press, 1999), p. 15. Also Richard Joseph, "Democratisation in Africa After 1989: Comparative and Theoretical Issues," *Comparative Politics* 29, 3 (1997): 363–382.

4   In order, these terms are proposed by Diamond, ibid. (2002), p. 25; Steven
    Levitsky and Lucan Way, "The Rise of Competitive Authoritarianism," *Journal
    of Democracy* 13, 2 (2002): 51–65; and Marina Ottaway, *Democracy Challenged:
    The Rise of Semi-Authoritarianism* (Washington, DC: Carnegie Endowment for
    International Peace, 2003).

5   Michael McFaul, "The Fourth Wave of Democracy *and* Dictatorship: Nonco-
    operative Transitions in the Post-Communist World," *World Politics* 54 (January
    2002): 212–214.

6   Freedom House, *Freedom in the World, 2001* (New York: Freedom House, 2002).

7   By 2001, power alternations had also occurred in three electoral democracies:
    Benin, Senegal, and Ghana.

8   For a classification of African regimes based on press freedoms, see Jeffrey
    Herbst, "Political Liberalization in Africa after Ten Years," *Comparative Poli-
    tics* 33 (April 2001): 357–375. The distribution of countries closely resembles
    Table 1.1.

9   Michael Cowen and Liisa Laakso (eds.), *Multi-Party Elections in Africa* (New
    York: Palgrave, 2002). See also John Daniel, Roger Southall, and Morris Szeftel
    (eds.), *Voting for Democracy: Watershed Elections in Contemporary Anglophone
    Africa* (Aldershot: Ashgate, 1999), plus Jon Abbink and Gerti Hesseling, *Election
    Observation and Democratization in Africa* (New York: St. Martins, 2000).

10 See Bruce Magnusson, "Democratization and Domestic Insecurity: Navigating
    the Transition in Benin," *Comparative Politics* 33, 2 (2001): 222–226. For con-
    trast, see Linda Beck's portrayal of the National Assembly in Senegal as "the
    chamber of applause" in "Democratization and the Hidden Public: The Im-
    pact of Patronage Networks on Senegalese Women," *Comparative Politics* 35, 2
    (2003): 163.

11 Michael Bratton, "Second Elections in Africa," *Journal of Democracy* 9, 3
    (1998): 51–66. For a glass-half-full reinterpretation, see Staffan I. Lindberg,
    "The 'Democraticness' of Multiparty Elections: Participation, Competition and
    Legitimacy in Africa," paper presented at a conference on Diagnosing Democ-
    racy, Santiago, Chile, April 11–13, 2003.

12 See Guillermo O'Donnell, "Delegative Democracy," *Journal of Democracy* 5, 4
    (1994): 55–69.

13 Seminal contributions to the extensive literature on neo-patrimonialism are:
    Samuel Eisenstadt, *Traditional Patrimonialism and Modern Neo-Patrimonialism*
    (London: Sage, 1982); Robin Theobold, "Patrimonialism," *World Politics* 34
    (1982): 548–559; and Christopher Clapham (ed.), *Private Patronage and Public
    Power: Political Clientelism in the Modern State* (London: Frances Pinter, 1982).

14 Richard Rose and Doh Chull Shin, "Democratization Backwards: The Problem
    of Third-Wave Democracies," *British Journal of Political Science* 31 (2001): 331–
    354.

15 The dynamics of the "partial reform syndrome" were first spelled out by Joel
    Hellman, "Winners Take All: The Politics of Partial Reform in Postcommunist
    Transitions," *World Politics* 50 (January 1998): 203–204. For an insightful ex-
    tension with African evidence, see Nicolas van de Walle, *African Economies and
    the Politics of Permanent Crisis, 1979–1999* (Cambridge: Cambridge University
    Press, 2001), pp. 60–63.

16 World Bank, *Adjustment in Africa: Reforms, Results and the Road Ahead* (Oxford: Oxford University Press, 1994), p. 3.

17 A useful overview of the orthodox economic reform package, with references to non-African countries, can be found in Dani Rodrik, "Understanding Economic Policy Reform," *Journal of Economic Literature* 34 (March 1996): 9–41.

18 See Farhad Noorbakhsh and Alberto Paloni, "Structural Adjustment and Growth in Sub-Saharan Africa: The Importance of Complying with Conditionality," *Economic Development and Cultural Change* 49, 3 (2001): 479.

19 Frances Stewart, Sanjaya Lall, and Samuel Wangwe (eds.) *Alternative Development Strategies in Sub-Saharan Africa* (London: Macmillan, 1992); Giovanni Cornia and Gerald Helleiner (eds.), *From Adjustment to Development in Africa: Conflict, Controversy, Convergence, Consensus?* (New York: St. Martin's Press, 1994); and P. Engberg-Pedersen (ed.), *Limits of Adjustment in Africa: The Effects of Economic Liberalization, 1986–1994* (London: James Currey, 1996).

20 The "Washington consensus" between the IMF and the World Bank featured ten policy measures: fiscal discipline, investments in health and education, a broader tax base, market-determined interest rates, competitive exchange rates, liberal trade policies, encouraging foreign investment, privatization of state enterprises, deregulation, and secure property rights. See John Williamson, "Democracy and the 'Washington Consensus,'" *World Development* 21, 8 (1993): 1329–1336.

21 William Easterly, *The Elusive Quest for Growth: Economists' Adventures and Misadventures in the Tropics* (Cambridge: MIT Press, 2002), p. 115.

22 Easterly, ibid.

23 Joseph Stiglitz, *Globalization and Its Discontents* (New York: Norton, 2002), p. 17.

24 *African Economies* (2001), pp. 91–93. On the importance of a capacious state to economic development, see also Robert Wade, *Governing the Market: Economic Theory and the Role of Government in East Asian Industrialization* (Princeton, NJ: Princeton University Press, 1990).

25 Privatization was slow to get off the ground in the 1980s but picked up speed in the 1990s. Van de Walle, *African Economies* (2001), pp. 81–83.

26 World Bank, *Adjustment Lending in Sub-Saharan Africa: An Update* (Washington, DC: World Bank, Operations Evaluation Department, Report No. 16594, 1997).

27 World Bank, *African Development Indicators* (Washington, DC: World Bank, 2001), p. 33. Recent contributions to the literature on economic reform and the challenge of recovery in Africa include: Howard White, "Review Article: Adjustment in Africa," *Development and Change* 27 (1996): 785–815; Jeffrey Sachs and Andrew Warner, "Sources of Slow Growth in African Economies," *Journal of African Economies* 6 (1997): 335–376; William Easterly and Ross Levine, "Africa's Growth Tragedy: Policies and Ethnic Divisions," *Quarterly Journal of Economics* 112 (1997): 1203–1250; and Paul Collier and Jan Willem Gunning, "Explaining African Economic Performance," *Journal of Economic Literature* 37 (1999): 64–111.

28 Qualitative studies of this question include Jennifer Widner (ed.), *Economic Change and Political Liberalization in Sub-Saharan Africa* (Baltimore, MD: Johns Hopkins University Press, 1994) and Richard Sandbrook, *Closing the Circle: Democratization and Development in Africa* (London: Zed Books, 2000).

29 Gamma = .742, p = <.001. For the purposes of this analysis, "ambiguous" democracies were grouped with electoral democracies. For bivariate associations reported in this book, the choice of statistic (whether Cramers V, Eta, Gamma or Pearson's r) is determined by the level of measurement of the variables in question – whether nominal, ordinal, or interval, or some combination thereof.

30 Robert Dahl, *On Democracy* (New Haven, CT: Yale Nota Bene Books, 2000), pp. 58 and 170. For the roots of this argument see Charles Lindblom, *Politics and Markets* (New York, Basic Books, 1977).

31 Philippe Schmitter and Terry Karl, "What Democracy Is . . . and Is Not," *Journal of Democracy* 2, 1 (1991): 75–88.

32 Jean-François Bayart, Stephen Ellis, and Béatrice Hibou, *The Criminalization of the State in Africa* (Oxford: James Curry, 1999), p. 48. See also William Reno, *Corruption and State Politics in Sierra Leone* (Cambridge: Cambridge University Press, 1995) and Patrick Chabal and Jean-Pascal Daloz, *Africa Works: Disorder as Political Instrument* (Oxford: James Curry, 1999).

33 Thandika Mkandawire, "Economic Policy-Making and the Consolidation of Democratic Institutions in Africa" in Kjell Havnevik and Brian van Arkadie (eds.), *Domination or Dialogue: Experiences and Prospects for African Development Cooperation* (Uppsala: Nordic Africa Institute, 1996).

34 Steven Block, "Political Business Cycles, Democratization, and Economic Reform: The Case of Africa," *Journal of Development Economics* 67 (2002): 207.

35 See, for example, John Walton and David Seddon, *Free Markets and Food Riots: The Politics of Global Adjustment* (London: Blackwell, 1994). For a contrary view, see Henry Bienen and Mark Gersovitz, "Consumer Subsidy Cuts, Violence, and Political Stability," *Comparative Politics* 19 (1986): 25–44.

36 Joan Nelson, *Fragile Coalitions: The Politics of Economic Adjustment* (Washington, DC: Overseas Development Council, 1989); Stephan Haggard and Robert Kaufman (eds.), *The Politics of Economic Adjustment* (Princeton, NJ: Princeton University Press, 1992); and Thomas Callaghy and John Ravenhill (eds.), *Hemmed In: Responses to Africa's Economic Decline* (New York: Columbia University Press, 1993).

37 Dahl, *On Democracy* (2000), p. 158.

38 Juan Linz and Alfred Stepan, *Problems of Democratic Transition and Consolidation: Southern Europe, South America, and Post-Communist Europe* (Baltimore, MD: Johns Hopkins University Press, 1996), p. 5. See also Terry Lynn Karl, "Dilemmas of Democratization in Latin America," *Comparative Politics* 23, 1 (1991): 1–21.

39 Samuel Huntington, *The Third Wave: Democratization in the Late Twentieth Century* (Norman: University of Oklahoma Press, 1991).

40 Merilee Grindle, *Audacious Reforms: Institutional Invention and Democracy in Latin America* (Baltimore, MD: Johns Hopkins University Press, 2000).

41 Guillermo O'Donnell, "Delegative Democracy," *Journal of Democracy* 5, 1 (1994): 60–62.

42 John Higley and Richard Gunther (eds.), *Elites and Democratic Consolidation in Latin America and Southern Europe* (New York: Cambridge University Press, 1992).

43 Doh Chull Shin, *Mass Politics and Culture in Democratizing Korea* (New York: Cambridge University Press, 1999).

44 Timothy Colton, *Transitional Citizens: Voters and What Influences Them in the New Russia* (Cambridge, MA: Harvard University Press, 2000).

45 Linz and Stepan, *Problems of Democratic* (1996), p. 5. Richard Gunther, Nikiforos Diamandouros, and Hans-Jurfen Puhle (eds.) use a definition of consolidation that "focuses primarily on political institutions *and* norms of behavior" in *The Politics of Democratic Consolidation: Southern Europe in Comparative Perspective* (Baltimore, MD: Johns Hopkins University Press, 1995), p. 7, emphasis added. For the continuation of this tradition, see Andreas Schedler, "Measuring Democratic Consolidation," *Studies in Comparative International Development* 36, 1 (2001): 66–92.

46 Larry Diamond, *Developing Democracy* (1999), p. 69.

47 Axel Hadenius, *Institutions and Democratic Citizenship* (Oxford: Oxford University Press, 2001), pp. 12–14.

48 Richard Rose, William Mishler, and Christian Haerpfer, *Democracy and Its Alternatives: Understanding Post-Communist Societies* (Baltimore, MD: Johns Hopkins University Press, 1998), p. 14. For an elaboration, see Richard Rose, Doh Chull Shin, and Neil Munro, "Tensions Between the Democratic Ideal and Reality: The Korean Example," in Pippa Norris (ed.), *Critical Citizens: Global Support for Democratic Governance* (Oxford: Oxford University Press, 1999).

49 Linz and Stepan, *Problems of Democratic* (1996), p. 4. On "reserved domains," see p. 67. For Africa, see Joel Barkan, "Protracted Transitions Among Africa's New Democracies," *Democratization* 7, 3 (2000): 227–243.

50 Dahl, *On Democracy* (1998), pp. 26–32.

51 Richard Sklar, "Developmental Democracy," *Comparative Studies in Society and History* 29, 4 (1996): 686–714.

52 For a masterful account of the persistent efforts of central rulers to incorporate outlying provinces in African countries see Jeffrey Herbst, *States and Power in Africa: Comparative Lessons in Authority and Control* (Princeton, NJ: Princeton University Press, 2000), esp. Chs. 5 and 6.

53 Philippe Schmitter, "Interest Systems and the Consolidation of Democracies," in Gary Marks and Larry Diamond (eds.), *Reexamining Democracy: Essays in Honor of Seymour Martin Lipset* (Newbury Park, CA: Sage, 1992), pp. 93–139. See also Herbert Kitschelt, Zdenka Mansfeldova, Radoslaw Markowski, and Gabor Toka, *Post-Communist Party Systems: Competition, Representation, and Interparty Cooperation* (New York: Cambridge University Press, 1999), who argue for shifting the scope of analysis to "specific mechanisms (and) . . . concrete processes" (p. 1).

54 Adam Przeworski, Michael A. Alvarez, José Antonio Chiebub, and Fernando Limongi, *Democracy and Development: Political Institutions and Well-Being in the World, 1950–1990* (New York: Cambridge University Press, 2000).

55 Carothers, "The End of the Transition Paradigm" (2002): 6.

56 As such, we are in accord with Gerardo Munck, "The Regime Question: Theory Building in Democracy Studies," *World Politics* 54, 1 (2001): 119–144.

57 In formulating this approach we have been influenced by Axel Hadenius. See his "Democratic Consolidation: Criteria of Analysis, Explanatory Factors, and Actual Development," paper presented at a conference on Consolidation in New Democracies, Uppsala University, June 8–9, 2002.

Chapter 2

1 Michael Bratton and Beatrice Liatto-Katundu, "A Focus Group Assessment of Political Attitudes in Zambia," *African Affairs* 93, (October 1994): 543 and 545.

2 The concepts in italics represent variables that we operationalize for purpose of analysis (see Appendix A).

3 For a contemporary statement of this thesis see Lucian Pye, "Political Science and the Crisis of Authoritarianism," *American Political Science Review* 84, 1 (1990): 3–19.

4 Ada Finifter and Ellen Mickiewicz, "Redefining the Political System of the USSR: Mass Support for Political Change," *American Political Science Review* 86, 4 (1992): 869.

5 Arthur Miller, Vicki Hesli, and William Reisinger, "Reassessing Mass Support for Political and Economic Change in the Former USSR," *American Political Science Review* 88, 2 (1994): 399–411.

6 Rose et al., *Democracy and Its Alternatives* (1999), pp. 129–130.

7 Shin, *Mass Politics and Culture* (1999), pp. 82–83.

8 One of the best accounts is John Toye, "Interest Group Politics and the Implementation of Adjustment Policies in Sub-Saharan Africa," *Journal of International Development* 4, 2 (1992): 183–197. See also Henry Bienen, "The Politics of Trade Liberalization in Africa," *Economic Development and Cultural Change* 38, 4 (1990): 713–732 and Jeffrey Herbst, "The Structural Adjustment of Politics in Africa," *World Development* 18, 7 (1990): 949–958.

9 Values refer to "general and enduring standards" that are central to belief systems in a way that more transient attitudes are not. See Donald Kinder and David Sears, "Public Opinion and Political Action" in G. Lindzey and E. Aronson (eds.), *Handbook of Social Psychology* (New York, Random House, 1985), pp. 659–741. Tianjian Shi considers that "political culture is the shared values and norms of a society . . . attitudes are excluded." See "Cultural Values and Political Trust: A Comparison of the People's Republic of China and Taiwan," *Comparative Politics* 33 4, (2001): 403.

10 See the pioneering work of Gabriel Almond and Sidney Verba, *The Civic Culture: Political Attitudes and Democracy in Five Nations* (Boston: Little Brown, 1965); also *The Civic Culture Revisited* (Boston: Little Brown, 1980); and Gabriel Almond, *A Discipline Divided: Schools and Sects in Political Science* (Newbury Park, CA: Sage, 1990).

11 Ronald Inglehart, *Culture Shift in Advanced Industrial Countries* (Princeton, NJ: Princeton University Press, 1990), p. 53.

12 Ronald Inglehart, "How Solid Is Mass Support for Democracy Around the World?" University of Michigan, unpublished manuscript, 2001. The dependent variable is level of democracy as measured by mean Freedom House scores, 1981–98.

13 "The Renaissance of Political Culture," *American Political Science Review* 82 (1988): 1220.

14 Robert Putnam, *Making Democracy Work: Civic Traditions in Modern Italy* (Princeton, NJ: Princeton University Press, 1993).

15 Ibid., 169. Putnam also argues that trust helps circumvent problems of imperfect information and enforceability, thus making markets move more smoothly. He cites Timothy Besley, Stephen Coate, and Glenn Loury, "The Economics of Rotating Savings and Credit Associations," *American Economic Review* 83, 4 (1993): 792–810.

16 Inglehart, *Modernization and Post-Modernization: Cultural, Economic and Political Change in 43 Societies* (Princeton, NJ: Princeton University Press, 1997), p. 172.

17 Michael Novak, "Rediscovering Culture," *Journal of Democracy* 12, 2 (2001): 169. See also Lawrence Harrison and Samuel Huntington (eds.), *Culture Matters: How Values Shape Human Progress* (New York: Basic Books, 2000).

18 Robert Shiller, Maxim Boycko, and Vladimir Korobov, "Popular Attitudes to Free Markets: The Soviet Union and the United States Compared," *The American Economic Review* 81, 3 (1991): 385–400.

19 For an influential critique of the universality of Western values, see Samuel Huntington, *The Clash of Civilizations and the Remaking of the World Order* (New York: Simon and Schuster, 1996).

20 Harry Eckstein, "A Culturalist Theory of Political Change," *American Political Science Review* 82, 3 (1988): 796. See also James Alexander, "Surveying Attitudes in Russia: A Representation of Formlessness," *Communist and Post-Communist Studies* 30, 2 (1997): 107–27.

21 Axel Hadenius, *Institutions and Democratic Citizenship* (2001), p. 1.

22 Bernard Grofman and Donald Witman (eds.), *The Federalist Papers and the New Institutionalism* (New York: Agathon Press, 1989), p. 1.

23 Christopher Anderson and Christian Guillory, "Political Institutions and Satisfaction with Democracy: A Cross-National Analysis of Consensus and Majoritarian Systems," *American Political Science Review* 91, 1 (1997), 66–81.

24 Pippa Norris, "Institutional Explanations for Political Support," Ch. 11 in *Critical Citizens* (1999), p. 221.

25 Joshua Cohen and Joel Rogers, "Secondary Associations and Democratic Governance," *Politics and Society* 20, 4 (1992): 393–472.

26 Norman Nie, G. Bingham Powell, and Kenneth Prewitt, "Social Structure and Political Participation," *American Political Science Review* 63, 2 (1969): 365.

27 Peter McDonough, Doh Chull Shin, and Jose Alvaro Moises, "Democratization and Participation: Comparing Spain, Brazil and Korea," *The Journal of Politics* 60, 4 (1998): 926.

28 Henry Brady, Sidney Verba, and Kay Lehmann Schlozman, "Beyond SES: A Resource Model of Political Participation," *American Political Science Review* 89, 2 (1995): 271–294.

29 Edward Muller and Mitchell Seligson, "Civic Culture and Democracy: The Question of Causal Relationships," *American Political Science Review* 88, 3, (1994): 635.

30 For example, Roxana Morduchowicz, "Teaching Political Information and Democratic Values in a New Democracy," *Comparative Politics* 28, 4 (1996): 465–76; Michael Bratton, Philip Alderfer, Georgia Bowser, and Joseph Temba, "The Effects of Civic Education on Political Culture: Evidence from Zambia," *World Development* 27, 5 (1999): 807–824; and Steven Finkel, "Can Democracy Be Taught?" *Journal of Democracy* 14, 4 (2003), 137–151.

31 For observations on this underresearched link see Steven Finkel, "The Effects of Participation on Political Efficacy: A Panel Analysis," *American Journal of Political Science* 29, 4 (1985): 894–913 and "The Effects of Participation of Political Efficacy and Political Support: Evidence from a West German Panel," *Journal of Politics* 49, 2 (1987): 441–464.

32 For an overview, see Miles Simpson, "Informational Inequality and Democracy in the New World Order" in Manus Midlarsky (ed.), *Inequality, Democracy, and Economic Development* (New York: Cambridge University Press, 1997), pp. 156–176.

33 Among many studies, see Norman Nie, Jane Junn, and Kenneth Stehlik-Barry, *Education and Democratic Citizenship in America* (Chicago: University of Chicago Press, 1996) and Mal Leicester, Celia Modgil, and Sohan Modgil (eds.), *Politics, Education, and Citizenship* (New York: Falmer Press, 2000).

34 The literature on this subject is summarized in Diamond, *Developing Democracy* (1999), pp. 199–200.

35 Robert Dahl, "The Problem of Civic Competence," *Journal of Democracy* 3, 4 (1992): 46.

36 Shin, *Mass Politics and Culture* (1999), p. 120.

37 Alan Acock and Harold Clarke, "Alternative Measures of Political Efficacy: Models and Means," *Quality and Quantity* 24 (1990): 100.

38 Mitchell Seligson, "Trust, Efficacy and Modes of Political Participation: A Study of Costa Rican Peasants," *British Journal of Political Science* 10 (1980): 75–98.

39 John Zaller, *The Nature and Origins of Mass Opinion* (New York: Cambridge University Press, 1992), p. 21, emphasis in original.

40 Zaller, ibid., 18–19, 24. See also Michael Delli Carpini and Scott Keeter, *What Americans Know about Politics and Why It Matters* (New Haven, CT: Yale University Press, 1996) and Henry Milner, *Civic Literacy: How Informed Citizens Make Democracy Work* (Hanover, NH: University Press of New England, 2002).

41 Zaller, *The Nature and Orgin of Mass Opinions* (1992), p. 1.

42 Jon Elster, "The Necessity and Impossibility of Simultaneous Economic and Political Reform," in D. Greenberg (ed.), *Constitutional Democracy: Transitions in the Contemporary World* (New York: Oxford University Press, 1993), p. 268.

43 Jean-François Bayart, *L'Etat en Afrique: la politique du ventre* (Paris: Fayard, 1989).

44 Linz and Stepan, *Problems of Democratic Transition* (1996), p. 442.

45 Norris, *Critical Citizens* (1999), p. 218.

46 Among others, Stephen Weatherford, "Economic Stagflation and Public Support for the Political System," *British Journal of Political Science* 14 (1984): 187–205; Michael Lewis-Beck, *Economics and Elections: The Major Western Democracies* (Ann Arbor: University of Michigan Press, 1988); and Christopher Anderson,

Blaming the Government: Citizens and the Economy in Five European Democracies (New York: M.E. Sharpe, 1995). For a dissenting position see Ian McAllister, "The Economic Performance of Governments," in Norris (1999), ibid., pp. 188–203.

47 Herbert Kitschelt, "The Formation of Party Systems in East Central Europe," *Politics and Society* 20 (1992): 7–50.

48 Russell Dalton, "Communists and Democrats: Democratic Attitudes in the Two Germanies," *British Journal of Political Science* 24 (1994): 469–493.

49 Peter McDonough, Samuel Barnes, and Antonio Lopez Pina, "The Nature of Political Support and Legitimacy in Spain," *Comparative Political Studies* 27, 3 (1994): 361.

50 Dalton, "Communists and Democrats" (1994): 486.

51 Leslie Anderson, "Post-Materialism from a Peasant Perspective: Political Motivation in Costa Rica and Nicaragua," *Comparative Political Studies* 23, 1 (1990): 101.

52 Ibid., 103.

53 Geoffrey Evans and Stephen Whitefield, "The Politics and Economics of Democratic Commitment: Support for Democracy in Transition Societies," *British Journal of Political Science* 25 (1995): 485–514.

54 Rose et al., *Democracy and Its Alternatives* (1998), p. 149.

55 Ibid., 157.

56 For example, James Gibson, "Political and Economic Markets: Changes in the Connections Between Attitudes to Political Democracy and a Market Economy within the Mass Culture of Russia and Ukraine," *Journal of Politics* 58, 4 (1996): 961; Rose et al. (1998), ibid., Chs. 7 and 8; Shin, *Mass Politics and Culture* (1999), Ch. 3; Diamond, *Developing Democracy* (1999), Ch. 5; Norris, *Critical Citizens* (1999), Ch. 11.

57 The quotation is from Rose et al., ibid., pp. 176 and 178.

58 "Political and Economic Markets" (1996): 973. The finding refers to Russia, but not Ukraine.

59 "The Politics and Economics of Democratic Commitment" (1995): 501.

60 David Easton, "A Reassessment of the Concept of Political Support," *British Journal of Political Science* 5 (1975): 435–457. See also David Easton and Jack Dennis, *Children in the Political System: Origins of Political Legitimacy* (New York: McGraw Hill, 1969).

61 See the voluminous literature from Almond and Verba, *The Civic Culture* (1963) to Robert Rorshneider, *Learning Democracy: Democratic and Economic Values in a Unified Germany* (Oxford: Oxford University Press, 1998).

62 See Rose et al., *Democracy and Its Alternatives* (1998), p. 118.

63 As an exemplar of performance theory, Rose et al. cite Ronald Rogowski, *Rational Legitimacy: A Theory of Political Support* (Princeton, NJ: Princeton University Press, 1963).

64 Ibid., 116–119, 141–142, 195–198.

65 Rose et al. (1998), pp. 117–118.

66 "A Culturalist Theory" (1988): 791.

67 Nancy Bermeo, "Democracy and the Lessons of Dictatorship," *Comparative Politics* 24, 3, (1992): 275.

68 Robert Axelrod, "An Evolutionary Approach to Norms," *American Political Science Review* 80 (1986): 1097.
69 Larry Diamond, *Developing Democracy* (1999), pp. 164–165.
70 Samuel Popkin, *The Reasoning Voter: Communication and Persuasion in Presidential Elections* (Chicago: University of Chicago Press, 1994).
71 James Gibson, "A Mile Wide But an Inch Deep (?): The Structure of Democratic Commitments in the Former USSR," *American Journal of Political Science* 40, 2 (1996): 396–420. The citation is to Dahl, *Polyarchy* (1971).
72 Rose et al., *Democracy and Its Alternatives* (1998), cited in frontispiece.
73 Ibid., 31.
74 Wolfgang Stolper, *Planning without Facts: Lessons in Resource Allocation from Nigeria's Development* (Cambridge, MA: Harvard University Press, 1966).
75 Margaret Peil, *Nigerian Politics: The People's View* (London: Cassell, 1976).
76 Joel Barkan, "Political Knowledge and Voting Behavior in Rural Kenya," *American Political Science Review* 70, 2 (1976): 452–455.
77 Fred Hayward, "Perceptions of Well-Being in Ghana: 1970 and 1975," *African Studies Review* 22, 1 (1979): 122.
78 Paul Beckett and Warisu Alli, *Democracy and the Elite in Nigeria: Perspectives from Survey Research* (Madison: University of Wisconsin, African Studies Program, 1998).
79 For example, see John Holm and Patrick Molutsi (eds.), *Democracy in Botswana* (Gaberone: The Botswana Society, 1988). Also Patrick Ollawa, *Participatory Democracy in Zambia: The Political Economy of National Development* (Ilfracombe: Stockwell, 1979), Chs. 9 and 10.
80 Paul Abramson and Ronald Inglehart, *Value Change in Global Perspective* (Ann Arbor: University of Michigan Press, 1995).
81 World Bank, *Anticorruption in Transition: A Contribution to the Policy Debate* (Washington, DC, The World Bank, 2000). See also World Bank, *Social Capital: A Multifaceted Perspective* (Washington, DC, The World Bank, 2001).
82 Centre for the Study of African Economies, *Research Summary 2001* (Oxford: University of Oxford: Centre for the Study of African Economies, 2002).
83 For example, Craig Charney, "Voices of a New Democracy: African Expectations in the New South Africa," *CPS Research Reports*, No. 38 (Johannesburg, Centre for Policy Studies, 1995), p. 1. See also Lake Research, "Making Democracy Work: A Report on Focus Groups in South Africa," unpublished manuscript, 1997.
84 National Democratic Institute for International Affairs (NDI), *It Is the People Who Make a Leader: A Report on 14 Focus Groups Conducted in Malawi* (Washington, DC: NDI, 1995). Also Nicholas Wurf, *Imagining Democracy: Focus Groups in Mozambique* (New York, Louis Harris and Associates, 1993). For an overview, try NDI, *Southern Africa: The People's Voices* (Washington, DC, NDI, 1999).
85 Charney, *Voices* (1995), pp. 3–4.
86 International Foundation for Election Systems, *Public Opinion in Ghana, 1997* (Washington, DC: IFES, 1997) and International Republican Institute, *Kenya Political Survey, December 1999* (Washington, DC: IRI, 2000).

87 Research and Marketing Services, *Nigerbus* (Lagos, RMS, quarterly, 1998–present).

88 Bureau d'Etudes, de Recherches et de Consulting International, "Les Cents Jours de Joseph Kabila au Pouvoir," (Kinshasa: BERCI, 2001). See also François Roubaud, *Identités et Transition Démocratique: L'Exception Malgache* (Paris: Harmattan, 2000).

89 R. W. Johnson with Lawrence Schlemmer, *The Condition of Democracy in Southern Africa* (Johannesburg: Helen Suzman Foundation, 1998). Some earlier survey studies were also cross-national: See David Koff and George von der Muhll, "Political Socialization in Kenya and Tanzania," *Journal of Modern African Studies* 5, 1 (1967): 13–51 and Joel Barkan, *An African Dilemma: University Students, Development and Politics* (New York: Oxford University Press, 1975). And one of the authors of this book participated in David McDonald, Lovemore Zinyama, Fion De Vletter, John Gay, and Robert Mattes. "Guess Who's Coming to Dinner? Migration From Lesotho, Mozambique and Zimbabwe to South Africa," *International Migration Review* 34, 3 (2000): 813–841.

90 Johnson and Schlemmer, ibid., 6.

91 Ibid., 9.

92 The average national sample was 629 respondents. At a 95 percent level of confidence, the margin of sampling error approaches plus or minus 4 percent for national populations and plus or minus 8 percent for urban populations.

93 See the Acknowledgments at the front of this book.

94 Botswana, Lesotho, Namibia, Malawi, Zambia, and Zimbabwe.

95 At a 95 percent confidence level, plus or minus 2.8 percent for national samples of 1,200, plus or minus 2.2 percent for samples over 2,000, and plus or minus 1.6 percent for the national sample of 3,600. Subnational samples have larger confidence intervals.

96 To enable generalization about subnational groups, we purposely over sampled ethnic or regional minorities in Mali (among the Touareg), Tanzania (on the Zanzibar islands), and South Africa (whites, Coloureds, and Indians). We unintentionally under sampled women in Ghana (because some males in the Islamic north refused to allow interviews with female household members) and northerners in Uganda (because thirty returns had to be discarded due to interviewer fraud).

97 Pooling is a conventional approach used in other barometer surveys. This weighting scheme overrepresents Lesotho and underrepresents Nigeria in mean scores for Afrobarometer repondents. Researchers who object to this approach are invited to reanalyze the data without weights, or with Nigeria weighted to reflect its large share of the SSA population. The data are available at www.afrobarometer.org.

98 See Bratton and Katundu, "A Focus Group" (1994): 535–563.

99 Kimberly Smiddy and E. Gyimah-Boadi, "Elite Attitudes to Democracy and Market Reforms in Ghana," *CDD Research Paper No. 3* (Accra: Center for Democratic Development, 2000).

100 The magisterial bookends on the shelf of this voluminous debate are Philip Converse, "The Nature of Belief Systems in Mass Publics," in David Apter (ed.), *Ideology and Discontent* (New York: Free Press, 1964), pp. 206–261 and John Zaller, *The Nature and Origins of Mass Opinion* (1992), esp. pp. 28–39

and 76–96. See also Robert Mattes, "The Voice of the People? Presidents, Poll-sters, and the Press" (Ph.D. dissertation, University of Illinois, 1992).

101 On the dangers of respondent acquiesence to agree/disagree items on regime support, see Geoffrey Evans and Anthony Heath, "The Measurement of Core Beliefs and Values: The Development of Balanced Socialist/Laissez-Faire and Libertarian/Authoritarian Scales," *British Journal of Political Science* 24 (1994): 115–132.

102 Justin Lewis, *Constructing Public Opinion: How Political Elites Do What They Like and Why We Seem to Go Along With It* (New York: Columbia University Press, 2001).

103 Hyden's claim that "interview surveys are viewed with suspicion by both au-thorities and potential respondents" has a germ of truth but is less relevant now than before political transitions. See "Africanists' Contributions to Political Sci-ence,'" *PS: Political Science and Politics* 34, 4 (2001): 799.

104 At the end of the encounter in Mali, we asked: "Who do you think sent us to do this interview?" Despite having been clear about our independent status, more than half the respondents thought we had been sent by an agency of government. This misperception led to an increase in the reported levels of expressed trust in government institutions in Mali. But, it had no effects on key objects of study such as demand for, and perceived supply of, democracy and a market economy.

105 The formula for refusal rates (REF1) is drawn from American Association for Public Opinion Research, *Standard Definitions: Final Dispositions of Case Codes and Outcome Rates for Surveys* (Lenexa, Kansas: AAPOR, 2000), p. 39, which is available at www.aapor.org.

106 For mail surveys in the United States, refusal rates over 70 percent are com-mon. Pamela Alreck and Robert Settle, *The Survey Research Handbook* (Chicago: Irwin, 1995) p. 35.

107 Fear of a dominant party is one factor that leads Tanzanians to be unusually *un*critical citizens.

108 The small coefficients indicate, however, that the relationship is hardly strong, being statistically significant mainly by virtue of a large sample size. Moreover, on all these issues, "careful" respondents are no more likely than anyone else to take refuge in "don't know" responses.

109 The Western Europe scores are derived from the Eurobarometer and WVS for 1993–97. See: Russell Dalton, "Political Support in Advanced Industrial Democracies," in Norris, *Critical Citizens* (1999), p. 70. The Latin America scores come from Marta Lagos, "Between Stability and Crisis in Latin America," *Journal of Democracy* 12, 1 (2001): 138 and "An Alarm Call for Latin America's Democrats," *The Economist*, July 28, 2001: 37–8.

110 Measured as an index of support for user fees for social services, market pricing for consumer goods, privatization of public corporations, and cutbacks in civil service employment.

Chapter 3

1 Richard Sandbrook, *Closing the Circle* (2000), p. 25.
2 Claude Ake, "The Unique Case of African Democracy," *International Affairs* 69, 2 (1993): 239–244.

3 Opponents of African independence asserted that Africans, too deeply divided by ethnic identities, were unsuited for multiparty democracy. See, for example, Elspeth Huxley, "Two Revolutions that are Changing Africa," *New York Times Magazine*, May 19, 1957. Later, some scholars defended the one-party state as an authentic African expression of democratic principles. See, for instance, Gwendolen Carter, *African One-Party States* (Ithaca, NY: Cornell University Press, 1964). For a current indictment of international donor efforts to impose Western models of democracy on Africa see M.A. Mohammed Salih, *African Democracies and African Politics* (London: Pluto Press, 2001).

4 Claude Ake, *Democracy and Development in Africa* (Washington, DC: The Brookings Institution, 1996), p. 139. See also *The Feasibility of Democracy* (Dakar: CODESRIA, 2000).

5 Daniel Osabu-Kle, *Compatible Cultural Democracy: The Key to Development in Africa* (Orchard Park, NY: Broadview Press, 2000), p. 9. See also Maxwell Owusu, "Democracy and Africa: A View from the Village," *Journal of Modern African Studies* 30, 3 (1992): 369–396 and Immaculate Kizza, *Africa's Indigenous Institutions in Nation-Building* (Lewiston, NY: Edwin Mellen Press, 1999). For a more skeptical view, try V. Simuyu, "The Democratic Myth in African Traditional Societies" in Walter Oyugi (ed.), *Democratic Theory and Practice in Africa* (London: James Currey, 1988).

6 Frederic Schaffer, *Democracy in Translation: Understanding Politics in An Unfamiliar Culture* (Ithaca, NY: Cornell University Press, 1998), p. 52. For other thoughtful efforts to reveal indigenous theories of democracy see Mikael Kalstrom, "Imagining Democracy: Political Culture and Democratization in Buganda," *Africa* 66, 4 (1996): 485–505 and Dan Ottemoeller, "Popular Perceptions of Democracy: Elections and Attitudes in Uganda," *Comparative Political Studies* 31, 1 (1998): 98–124.

7 Amartya Sen, *Development as Freedom* (Oxford: Oxford University Press, 1999), pp. 3, 10, and 16.

8 There was vigorous debate within the Afrobarometer Network over which languages to use in referring to the concept of democracy. Some vernaculars include indigenous terms for this concept, but these are too often freighted with narrow meanings that predispose idiosyncratic answers. For purposes of consistency and comparability, but also because the "d-word" (or recognizable local derivatives of it like *idemokrasi* in Xhosa and *demokaraasi* in Wolof) have been incorporated into popular discourse, we ultimately decided to use official languages, which refer to "democracy," "démocratie," or "demokrasi."

9 Researchers asked: "if a country is called a democracy, what does that mean to you?" See *The Indonesia National Voter Education Survey* (Djakarta: The Asia Foundation, 1999), p. 68.

10 For other inductive schemas classifying meanings of democracy see: Robert Putnam, *The Beliefs of Politicians: Ideology, Conflict and Democracy in Britain and Italy* (New Haven, CT: Yale University Press, 1973); José Ramón Montero, "Los significados de la democracia en Espana: Un analísis explorativo," *Inguruak* 7 (1992): 61–78; and Janos Simon, "Popular Conceptions of Democracy in Post-Communist Europe," *Studies in Public Policy* No. 273 (Glasgow, University of Strathclyde, Centre for the Study of Public Policy, 1996), esp. pp. 19–42.

11 Simon, ibid., p. 22.

12 Not only Moi of Kenya, but also Kaunda of Zambia and Mobutu of (the then) Zaire, issued warnings that amounted to *après (M)oi, le deluge.* General Kolingba, Former President of the Central African Republic, eerily echoed Elspeth Huxley (see endnote 3), in asserting that Africa "was not ready for multiparty democracy," *Marchés Tropicaux et Meditérranéens,* May 18, 1990.

13 For example, Marina Ottaway, "Should Elections be the Main Criterion of Democratization in Africa?" *CSIS Africa Notes* No. 145 (1998) and Hussein Solomon and Ian Liebenberg (eds.), *Consolidation and Democracy in Africa: A View from the South* (Aldershot: Ashgate, 2000).

14 We classified the following meanings as *procedural*: civil liberties, popular participation, political rights, and good governance. The *substantive* category included peace and unity, equality and justice, socioeconomic development, and other positive attributes and negative meanings. The proportions in each category depend on how one classifies "government by, for, or of the people." Most respondents cast it as "government *by* the people," which together with "government *of* the people," is probably best interpreted in terms of political procedure, as we do here. But even if this response is dropped or reclassified, a plurality of respondents still opt for procedural interpretations. And if "don't knows" are excluded, a majority does so.

15 On the linkages between conflict and economic advancement, see Robert Bates, *Prosperity and Violence: The Political Economy of Development* (London: W.W. Norton, 2001) and Paul Collier and A. Hoeffler "On Economic Causes of Civil War," *Oxford Economic Papers* 50 (2000): 163–173.

16 Stephen Stedman, Donald Rothchild, and Elizabeth Cousens (eds.), *Ending Civil Wars: The Implementation of Peace Agreements* (Boulder, CO: Lynne Rienner Publishers, 2002). In Mozambique, where a dozen Afrobarometer questions were inserted in a survey conducted in August 2001, 12 percent saw democracy in terms of peace and unity, third only to Uganda (19 percent) and Botswana (17 percent).

17 Including second and third responses (where available).

18 For example, Josiah Cobbah, "African Values and the Human Rights Debate: An African Perspective," *Human Rights Quarterly* 9 (August 1987): 309–331. For a more recent exposition on the "primacy of the collective," see Chabal and Daloz, *Africa Works* (1999), p. 130.

19 Johnson and Schlemmer provide corroboration: "In every single (Southern African) state there were majorities who favoured the more pluralist and individualist view of democratic rights over the community consensus version." See *The Condition of Democracy in Southern Africa* (1998), p. 26.

20 On the universality of human dignity and the right of freedom from state repression, see Rhoda Howard, "Group versus Individual Identity in the African Debate on Human Rights," in Abdullah An-Na'im and Francis Deng (eds.), *Human Rights in Africa: Cross-Cultural Perspectives* (Washington, DC: Brookings Institution, 1990), pp. 159–183.

21 Also 28 percent. See Simon, "Popular Conceptions" (1996), p. 23 and Asia Foundation, *The Indonesia National* (1999), p. 68.

22 Steve and Moira Chimombo, *The Culture of Democracy: Language, Literature, the Arts and Politics in Malawi, 1992–94* (Zomba, Malawi: Wasu Publications, 1996), p. 26.

23 Paul Nugent, *Big Men, Small Boys and Politics in Ghana: Power, Ideology and the Burden of History, 1982–1994* (Accra: Asempa Publishers, 1995), pp. 190 and 270.

24 On "the courage to speak out" see Sten Hagberg, "'Enough is Enough': An Ethnography of the Struggle against Impunity in Burkina Faso," *Journal of Modern African Studies* 40, 2 (2002), pp. 217–246.

25 This question was asked in Ghana, Nigeria, Mali, and Tanzania.

26 80 percent in Ghana, 75 percent in Nigeria, 70 percent in Mali, and 81 percent in Tanzania (with 97 percent in Zanzibar).

27 Whereas only 9 percent of people without formal schooling chose this option, over 30 percent of those with postsecondary education did so.

28 This is confirmed in Table 3.4 where, except in Nigeria, "at least two parties competing" in elections was the least essential feature of democracy.

29 Schaffer, *Democracy in Translation* (1998), pp. 93–98. See also Staffan I. Lindberg, "'It's Our Time to Chop': Do Elections in Africa Feed Neo-Patrimonialism?" *Democratization* 10, 2 (2003): 121–140.

30 As such, efforts to sharpen the distinction between liberal and popular conceptions of democracy for purposes of theoretical and political debate seem somewhat misplaced. See John Saul, "Liberal Democracy versus Popular Democracy," *Review of African Political Economy* 73 (1995): 339–353. Also Robin Luckham, "Popular versus Liberal Democracy in Nicaragua and Tanzania?" *Democratization* 5, 3 (1998): 92–126.

31 For an interesting discussion of this issue in Germany see Russell Dalton, Wilhelm Burklin, and Andrew Drummond, "Public Opinion and Direct Democracy," *Journal of Democracy* 12, 4 (2001): 141–153.

32 In similar vein, see Mitchell Seligson and John Booth, "Political Culture and Regime Type: Evidence from Nicaragua and Costa Rica," *Journal of Politics* 55, 3 (1993): 769.

33 In the Eurobarometer, the Latinobarometro, and the World Values Survey. See: Dalton in Norris, *Critical Citizens* (1999) p. 69 ; Marta Lagos, "Between Stability and Crisis" (2001), p. 138; and Hans-Dieter Klingemann, "Mapping Political Support in 1990s: A Global Analysis," in Norris, ibid., 46.

34 The definitive account is Roger Southall and Roddy Fox, "Lesotho's General Election of 1998: Rigged or de Rigueur?" *Journal of Modern African Studies* 37, 4 (1999): 669–696.

35 Eta = .191, p = <.001.

36 We are grateful to Tim Kelsall for helping us acknowledge such possibilities.

37 Ghana, Lesotho, Malawi, Mali, Nigeria, South Africa, Tanzania, and Zambia.

38 At the individual level of analysis, Pearson's r = .213, p = <.001. At the country level of analysis r = .664, p = <.001.

39 For example, in Nigeria, Pearson's r coefficients = .153, .084, .114, and .117 respectively. All p's = <.001.

40 Respondents were offered a choice between agreeing with this statement (85 percent agreed in Nigeria) or "Since elections sometimes produce bad results, we should adopt other methods for choosing our leaders" (13 percent agreed in Nigeria).

41 Respondents were offered a choice between agreeing with this statement (63 percent agreed in Nigeria) or "Political parties create division and confusion;

it is therefore unnecessary to have many political parties" (31 percent agreed in Nigeria).

42 The wording in Western and Eastern Africa was slightly different; it referred to "getting rid of elections so that a strong leader can decide everything."

43 Factor analysis extracts a single unrotated *index of rejection of authoritarian rule*. The composition, extraction, and statistical reliability of all multiitem indices are reported in Appendix A.

44 The correlation between these variables, while positive and significant, is not very strong: r = .128, p = <.001.

45 For a comparative view of South Africa's party system, see Hermann Giliomee and Charles Simkins, *The Awkward Embrace: One-Party Dominance and Democracy* (Cape Town: Tafelberg Publishers, 1999).

46 "There is little evidence that... the primary determination of a (precolonial) state's duration was accountability. Rather, the opposite appears to be true: states rose and fell... in relation to the amount of coercion they were able to broadcast from the center." Herbst, *States and Power in Africa* (2000), p. 52.

47 The correlation between these variables, while positive and significant, is not overly strong: r = .130, p = <.001.

48 Indeed, Malians are exactly split on this question: equal proportions (47 percent) accept or reject the traditional alternative.

49 See Pierre Englebert, "Born-Again Buganda or the Limits of Traditional Resurgence in Africa," *Journal of Modern African Studies* 40, 3 (2002): 345–368.

50 Both factors may be at work in Uganda (51 percent reject).

51 In posttransition Russia, too, "the population appeared willing to remove itself from influencing economic change and (to) allow a small group of leaders to implement policies for them, whatever those policies might be." See James Alexander, "Surveying Attitudes in Russia" (1997), 114.

52 Another possibility is that the twelve-country Afrobarometer mean is biased upwards by the outlying value for Nigeria. Without Nigeria, satisfaction declines to 55 percent.

53 In South Africa in 2000, more than twice as many blacks (59 percent) as whites (26 percent) were satisfied with democracy. Thus, blacks were just as satisfied as people elsewhere on the continent.

54 Damarys Canache, Jeffery Mondak, and Mitchell Seligson, "Meaning and Measurement in Cross-National Research on Satisfaction with Democracy," *Public Opinion Quarterly* 65 (2001): 506–528.

55 The magnitude of the beta coefficients is over .200 in eleven out of twelve cases. There is only one country (Zimbabwe) in which satisfaction with democracy is unrelated to support for democracy, compared to five out of seventeen countries in Latin America in 1997. Ibid., 523.

56 Robert A. Dahl, *On Democracy* (2000), p. 180. For a more optimistic assessment, see Gibson, "A Mile Wide" (1996).

57 *A Revolutionary Journey: Selected Speeches of Flt.-Lt. Jerry John Rawlings* (Accra: Information Services Department, 1983), p. 4. Julius K. Nyerere, *Ujamaa: Essays on Socialism* (Oxford: Oxford University Press, 1977), p. 65.

58 For an insightful discussion, see Claude Fay, "La démocratie au Mali, ou le pouvoir Malien en pâture," *Cahiers' d'Études africaines* 35, 137 (1995): 19–35.

59 Karlstrom finds that the Luganda term for democracy (*eddembe ery'obuntu*) is best translated as human rights, conceived as freedom from oppression. He stresses, however, that "liberty in its most basic sense is...a concomitant of a rightly ordered polity" with a strict hierarchy of authority (1996), p. 487.

60 Maximum likelihood extraction produces two factors. The composition, extraction, and statistical reliability of all multiitem indices are reported in Appendix A.

61 In principle, we are more inclined to put faith in open-ended questions, in which respondents speak in their own words, than in closed-ended questions in which researchers preselect response categories according to outsider views of the world.

62 Education and media exposure are positively related to procedural understandings (Pearson r's = .107 and .090, p = <.001) but not to substantive ones.

63 Ironically, Ugandans and Tanzanians cite civil liberties as the "top" meaning of democracy (26 and 39 percent respectively).

64 Twenty-one percent of whites are nostalgic for authoritarian rule versus 12 percent of blacks. Cramer's V = .226, p = <.001.

65 The two leading contenders for the presidency in Nigeria's 2003 elections were *both* former army generals and military rulers.

66 The question was posed thus: "Sometimes democracy does not work. When this happens, some people say that we need a strong leader who does not have to bother with elections. Others say that even when things don't work, democracy is always best. What do you think?"

67 Christiaan Keulder, "Public Opinion and the Consolidation of Democracy in Namibia," *Afrobarometer Working Paper No. 15* (www.afrobarometer.org), 2001, p. 11.

68 Thanks to Larry Diamond for suggesting this procedure. Note that these calculations do not include hierarchical forms of rule (traditional rule and technocratic rule) since, strictly speaking, these alternatives are neither authoritarian nor necessarily incompatible with democracy.

69 Spearman's rho = .194 (for military rule), .165 (for one-man rule), .102 (for one-party rule), and .094 (for traditional rule). A similar pattern applies when support for democracy is correlated with rejection of multiple alternatives: .156 (for two alternatives), .187 (for three alternatives). All p's = <.001.

70 In Southern Africa the question read: "What grade would you give to the political system of this country as you expect it to be in ten years' time?" Because respondents found difficulty in rating imagined political futures, there were substantial missing data.

71 Using the item that asks respondents whether a strong leadership is needed when democracy fails or whether democracy is always best. See footnote 66.

72 On the basis of an equivalent survey item, the Latinobarometro reports that support for democracy across seventeen Latin American countries dropped from 58 percent in 1995 to 47 percent in 2000. In Brazil, it stood at just 30 percent. See "An Alarm call for Latin America's Democrats," (2001) 37–38. The 2002 Latinobarometro shows an uptick, however, to 56 percent. See Marta Lagos, "A Road With No Return," *The Journal of Democracy* 14, 2 (2003): 163–173.

73 The Afrobarometer asks: "In your opinion, how much of a democracy is (your country) today? Is it not a democracy, a democracy with major problems, a

democracy with minor problems, or a full democracy"? In Southern Africa the wording referred to "exceptions" rather than "problems."

74   Freedom House, *Freedom in the World, 2000–2001* (New York: Freedom House, 2001).

75   Pearson's r = .698. N = 11 because the full Afrobarometer question was not asked in Ghana. Significance statistics are not reported since Afrobarometer countries do not represent a probability sample of some larger population.

76   Pearson's r = .723 (for civil liberties) and .586 (for political rights).

77   Why then go to the trouble of collecting survey data? The Afrobarometer has several advantages: it covers a far wider scope of topics than political freedom, the data can be disaggregated by social and opinion groups within countries, and it enables tests of competing explanations of various public attitudes and behaviors.

78   Political liberalization is measured as follows: by an AB question asking if "things are better or worse" since the political transition in terms of whether "people are free to say what they think" and by the change in FH score on the civil liberties (CL) indicator from 1988 to 2000. Democratization is measured as follows: by an AB question asking if "things are better or worse" since the political transition in terms of whether "people are free to choose who to vote for without feeling pressured" and by the change in FH score on the political rights (PR) indicator from 1988 to 2000.

79   Pearson's r = .862 (for political liberalization) and Pearson's r = .602 (for democratization). N = 11 because the Afrobarometer question was not asked in Uganda.

Chapter 4

1   The opening volley in the market reform debate was *Accelerated Development in Sub-Saharan Africa: An Agenda for Africa* (Washington, DC: World Bank, 1981). Progress was tracked in *Adjustment in Africa: Reforms, Results and the Road Ahead* (New York: Oxford University Press, 1994). The latest bulletin is *Can Africa Claim the 21st Century?* (Washington, DC: World Bank, 2000).

2   For a favorable assessment of the effects of economic reform, including on the poor, see David E. Sahn, Paul A. Dorosh, and Stephen D. Younger, *Structural Adjustment Reconsidered: Economic Policy and Poverty in Africa* (New York: Cambridge University Press, 1997). For more critical reviews, see Adebayo Olukushi (ed.), *The Politics of Structural Adjustment in Nigeria* (Portsmouth, NH: Heinnemann, 1993) and Thandika Mkandawire and Charles Soludo, *Our Continent, Our Future: African Perspectives on Structural Adjustment* (Trenton, NJ: Africa World Press, 1999).

3   See also Nicoli Natrass and Jeremy Seekings in "Democracy and Distribution in Highly Unequal Economies: the Case of South Africa," *Journal of Modern African Studies* 39, 3 (2001): 471–498.

4   For a comprehensive review of diverse livelihood strategies based on production, trade, and transfers, see Deborah Bryceson, "Multiplex Livelihoods in Rural Africa: Recasting the Terms and Conditions of Gainful Employment," *Journal of Modern African Studies* 40, 1 (2002): 1–28.

5 The survey in Malawi was conducted in December at the beginning of the four-month "hungry season" that chronically recurs before every harvest.

6 Note that these data refer to a second survey in Nigeria in September 2001. The figures are percentages of total responses on a question that allowed multiple (up to three) responses.

7 See Cynthia Szymanski Sunal, Dennis Sunal, Ruqayattu Rufai, Ahmed Inuwa, and Mary Haas, "Perceptions of Unequal Access to Primary and Secondary Education: Findings from Nigeria," *African Studies Review* 46, 1 (2003): 97, 105.

8 This finding is confirmed in Andy Norton, Dan Owen, and J. T. Milimo, *Zambia Participatory Poverty Assessment* (Washington, DC: World Bank, 1994).

9 Alan Whiteside, Robert Mattes, Samantha Willan, and Ryan Manning, "Examining HIV-AIDS in Southern Africa Through the Eyes of Ordinary Southern Africans," *Afrobarometer Working Paper No. 21* (2002). See www.afrobarometer.org.

10 South Africa has one of the highest rates of criminal violence in the world. See David Bruce, "Suspect Crime Statistics Cannot Obscure Grim Truth," *Sunday Independent* (Johannesburg), June 10, 2001. See also Institute for Security Studies, "Criminal Justice Monitor," *Crime Index* 1 (January/February 2000).

11 For 1998, HIV prevalence in Botswana was estimated at 43 percent for major urban areas and 30 percent for nonurban areas. See United Nations/World Health Organization, *Epidemiological Fact Sheets* (2000) www.unaids.org.

12 The relevant figures for Nigeria in 1999 were 4.5 percent (urban) and 4.9 percent (nonurban), ibid.

13 World Bank, *African Development Indicators, 2000* (Washington, DC: World Bank, 2000), p. 44.

14 Note that the OECD/DAC data refer to all recipient countries, not just those in sub-Saharan Africa.

15 Finifter and Mickiewicz, "Redefining the Political System of the USSR" (1992), p. 869. The sample covered Russia, Ukraine, Byelorussia, and selected Baltic and Central Asian states.

16 Measured in a second survey in September 2001.

17 Measured in 1993 using a small sample with a confidence interval of plus or minus 4 percent.

18 See Appendix A.

19 See Stephan Dercon, "Income Risk, Coping Strategies and Safety Nets," *Working Paper No. 26* (Oxford, Centre for the Study of African Economies, Oxford University, 2000).

20 John Howell (ed.), *Borrowers and Lenders: Rural Financial Markets and Institutions in Developing Countries* (London: Overseas Development Institute, 1980).

21 This finding is based on data from eleven countries; the question on government, private, or combined responsibility was not asked in Uganda in 2000.

22 We are grateful to Amon Chaligha and Christian Keulder for providing these insights.

23 The results are skewed by Mali, whose population is both uniformly Islamic (99 percent) and least tolerant of nongovernmental arrangements (20 percent).

24 For example, the organization "Business Against Crime" in South Africa works closely with police and civil society. See Mark Shaw, *Crime and Policing in*

Post-Apartheid South Africa: Reforming Under Fire (Cape Town: David Philip Publishers, 2002).

25 Johannes Harnischfeger, "The Bakassi Boys: Fighting Crime in Nigeria," *Journal of Modern African Studies* 41, 1 (2003): 23–49.

26 The question referred to diamonds in Botswana and Namibia, gold in Ghana and South Africa, cotton in Mali and Tanzania, tobacco in Malawi and Zimbabwe, copper in Zambia, oil in Nigeria, and water in Lesotho.

27 See Jane Harrigan, *From Dictatorship to Democracy: Economic Policy in Malawi, 1964–2000* (Aldershot: Ashgate, 2001), esp. Ch. 4.

28 For corroboration and context, see James Bingen, "Cotton, Democracy and Development in Mali," *Journal of Modern African Studies* 36, 2 (1998): 265–285.

29 The South African constitution guarantees a right to shelter.

30 Rather than being ambiguous, public opinion is divided between extreme points of view. One way or another, two thirds of our respondents feel "strongly" about the locus of responsibility for mass welfare.

31 Ugandan opinion is the most divided. Ugandans lead others in thinking that the government should bear the main responsibility for popular well being (61 percent, 47 percent strongly). Yet they are also most likely to think that everyone should be free to earn as much as they can (73 percent, 54 percent strongly).

32 Thandika Mkandawire and Adebayo Olukoshi, "Issues and Perspectives in the Politics of Structural Adjustment in Africa"; Gabriel Tati, "Congo: Social Reactions and the Political Stakes in the Dynamics of Structural Adjustment"; and Etienne Domingo, "Perceptions and Reactions to the Implementation of Structural Adjustment in Benin." All appear in Mkandawire and Olukoshi (eds.), *Between Liberalization and Oppression: The Politics of Structural Adjustment in Africa* (Dakar: CODESRIA, 1995), pp. 3, 367, and 422. To be fair, the editors of this volume do distinguish between pro- and antireform constituencies in rural and urban locations.

33 See Andrew Kiondo, "The Nature of Economic Reforms in Tanzania" in Horace Campbell and Horace Stein (eds.), *Tanzania and the IMF: The Dynamics of Liberalization* (Boulder, CO: Westview Press, 1992), p. 35.

34 Outside of Southern Africa, the question was asked without the option in the last clause.

35 Tor Skalnes, *The Politics of Economic Reform in Zimbabwe: Continuity and Change in Development* (London: Macmillan, 1995), pp. 134–145. Carolyn Jenkins and John Knight, *The Economic Decline of Zimbabwe: Neither Growth Nor Equity* (New York: Palgrave, 2002), pp. 47–51.

36 "Sadza" is the Chishona word for maize-meal porridge, the local staple.

37 Maurice Taonezvi Vambe, "Popular Songs and Social Realities in Post-Independence Zimbabwe," *African Studies Review* 43, 2 (2000): 80–81.

38 Michael Bratton and Chris Landsberg, "South Africa" in Shephard Forman and Stewart Patrick, *Good Intentions: Pledges of Aid for Post-Conflict Recovery* (Boulder, CO: Lynne Rienner Publishers, 2000), 268–269.

39 Forty percent in Nigeria, 42 percent in Zambia.

40 Responses were collapsed: "strongly agree" and "agree" = support (1); and "strongly disagree" and "disagree" = not support (0). All reforms supported were then added on a scale of 0 to 4.

41 See Dennis Anderson, *Public Revenue and Economic Policy in African Countries*, World Bank Discussion Paper No. 19 (Washington, DC: World Bank, 1987), who estimates that revenues could be boosted by up to 30 percent through fees-for-service (p. 18).

42 See Sanjay Reddy and Jan Vandermoortele, *User Financing of Basic Social Services* (New York: United Nations Children's Fund, 1996).

43 For example, 82 percent accepted school fees in Tanzania and 16 percent opposed. In Malawi, however, only 48 percent accepted medical fees versus 44 percent opposed.

44 This finding is confirmed by Paul Mbatia and York Bradshaw, "Responding to Crisis: Patterns of Health Care Utilization in Central Kenya Amid Economic Decline," *African Studies Review* 46, 1 (2003): 85.

45 For an overview, see O. Campbell-White and A. Bhatia, *Privatization in Africa* (Washington, DC: World Bank, 1998).

46 Andrew Temu and Jean Due, "The Business Environment in Tanzania after Socialism: Challenges of Reforming Banks, Parastatals, Taxation and the Civil Service," *Journal of Modern African Studies* 38, 4 (2000): 683–712.

47 For example, World Bank, *Can Africa Claim the 21st Century?* (2000), esp. Ch.2.

48 Namibia (20 percent), Botswana (21 percent), Malawi (21 percent), and Lesotho (23 percent).

49 Although Tanzanians have the highest average proreform score (64 percent over all four items), they are lower than all others apart from South Africans on awareness of SAP (24 percent).

50 We are grateful to Aili Tripp for a personal communication containing these observations. See also Laeticia Mukurasi, *Post-Abolished: One Woman's Struggle for Employment Rights in Tanzania* (Ithaca, NY: ILR Press, 1991).

51 In Herbst's words, "In Africa, the state will continue to have a dominant economic role, given the poverty of most countries' private sectors. The population will thus continue to look to the state as the only organization that can have an immediate impact on their lives ... political demands will inevitably be directed at the state for the foreseeable future, even if politicians no longer have the means to address those demands." See "The Structural Adjustment of Politics" (1990): 955.

52 The question was posed somewhat differently across regions. In East and West Africa, we asked "how satisfied or unsatisfied are you with the (SAP)?"; in Southern Africa we asked "what effect do you think (SAP) has had on your life?" For purposes of comparison, those who thought the SAP had made life worse were scored as "unsatisfied" and those who thought it had made life better as "satisfied." Since these questions were asked only of persons who were aware of SAPs in countries where such programs existed, the sample size was reduced to 7,517 across nine countries. Percentages in the figure do not add up to one hundred because "neutrals" and "don't knows" are not shown.

53 See A. Geske Dijkstra and Jan Kees van Donge, "What Does the 'Show Case' Show? Evidence and Lessons from Adjustment in Uganda," *World Development* 29, 5 (2001): 841–863.

54 The item was posed as follows: "Please tell me which statement you agree with most: A. The government's economic polices have helped most people; only a

few have suffered. B. The government's economic policies have hurt most people and only benefited a few." Percentages in the figure do not add up to one hundred because "neutrals" and "don't knows" are not shown.

55 Gamma = .493, p = <.001.
56 Among this sanguine group, a plurality is satisfied with SAPs (45 percent).
57 For Malawi, gamma = .903; for Zambia, gamma = .628; and for Zimbabwe, gamma = .606. All p's = <.001.
58 Gamma = .099, sig. < .040. Note that Nigerians rank eighth among Afrobarometer populations on satisfaction with SAPs (Figure 4.5), but only second in perceiving policy-induced inequality (Figure 4.6).
59 Béatrice Hibou, "The 'Social Capital' of the State as an Agent of Deception: The Ruses of Economic Intelligence," in Bayart et al., *The Criminalization of the State in Africa* (1999), p. 73.
60 Hellman, "Winners Take All" (1998).
61 The difference between the patient and impatient groups, however, was small enough to be due to sampling or other measurement errors.
62 The seminal contribution on political patience in new democracies is Richard Rose, "How Patient are People in Post-Communist Societies?" *World Affairs* 159, 3 (1997): 130–144.
63 For example, the privatized and deregulated transport system in Dar es Salaam has exposed casual workers to exploitative conditions of employment. See Matteo Rizzo, "Being Taken for a Ride: Privatization of the Dar es Salaam Transport System, 1983–1998," *Journal of Modern African Studies* 40, 1 (2002): 133.

Chapter 5

1 Terence Ranger, *Peasant Consciousness and Guerrilla War in Zimbabwe: A Comparative Study* (Harare: Zimbabwe Publishing House, 1985), p. 25.
2 See Statistics SA, *Labor Force Survey*, September 2000. For a discussion of approaches to measuring unemployment in South Africa, see Liv Torres, Haroon Bhorat, Murray Leibbrandt, and Fuad Cassim, "Poverty and the Labor Market," in Julian May (ed.), *Poverty and Inequality In South Africa: Meeting the Challenge* (Cape Town: David Philip, 2000), pp. 82–84.
3 We hew to Robert Chambers's definition of poverty as "lack of physical necessities, assets, and income. It includes, but is more than, being income-poor. Poverty can be distinguished from other dimensions of deprivation such as physical weakness, isolation, vulnerability and powerlessness with which it interacts." See "Poverty and Livelihoods: Whose Reality Counts?" *IDS Discussion Paper No. 347* (Brighton: University of Sussex, Institute of Development Studies, 1995), p. vi.
4 Robert Mattes, Michael Bratton, and Yul Derek Davids, "Poverty, Survival, and Democracy in Southern Africa," *Afrobarometer Working Paper No. 23* (2002). (See www.afrobarometer.org.)
5 Seventy-four percent of Coloureds, 91 percent of whites, and 93 percent of Indians say they "never" go without electricity in South Africa. Thus cross-racial differences are wide (eta = .409, p = <.001). But cross-national differences in access to electricity are even wider (eta = .986, p = <.001).

6   Pearson's r = .217, p = <.001.

7   Pearson's r = .134, p = <.001. For food, r = .141; for water, r = .062; for health
    care, r = .093. These figures suggest that people rely more on cash income for
    purchasing food than for accessing water.

8   Janet McGaffey, *Entrepreneurs and Parasites: The Struggle for Indigenous Capital-
    ism in Zaire* (New York: Cambridge University Press, 1987), p. 22. Other use-
    ful contributions include T. L. Malyiamkono, *The Second Economy in Tanzania*
    (Athens: Ohio University Press, 1990); Naomi Chazan, "Patterns of State-
    Society Incorporation and Disengagement" and Jane Parpart, "Women and the
    State in Africa" in Naomi Chazan and Donald Rothchild (eds.), *The Precari-
    ous Balance: State and Society in Africa* (Boulder, CO: Lynne Rienner Publishers,
    1988), pp. 121–148 and 208–231. For an update on the international dimen-
    sions see Janet McGaffey and Stephen Ellis, "Research on Sub-Saharan Africa's
    Unrecorded International Trade: Methodological and Conceptual Problems" in
    African Studies Review 39, 2 (1996): 19–41.

9   For detailed insights, try Malongo Mlozi, "Urban Agriculture: Ethnicity, Cattle
    Raising and Some Environmental Implications in the City of Dar es Salaam,
    Tanzania," *African Studies Review* 40, 3 (1997): 1–28 or Margaret Niger-
    Thomas, "Women and the Arts of Smuggling," *African Studies Review* 44, 2
    (2001): 43–70. Donald Mead and Christian Morrison make the valuable point
    that the informal sector is extremely diverse because definitions based on the
    size, capital intensity, or legality of enterprises do not overlap: "The Informal
    Sector Elephant," *World Development* 24, 10 (1996): 1611–1619.

10 Aili Mari Tripp, *Changing the Rules: The Politics of Liberalization and the Urban
    Informal Economy in Tanzania* (Berkeley: University of California Press, 1997).
    Her excellent research shows that urban families in Dar es Salaam with employed
    wage earners derived 90 percent of household incomes from small businesses.

11 Nelson Kasfir, *State and Class in Africa* (London: Frank Cass, 1984), pp. 84–103.

12 Most of those we asked (69 percent in Tanzania and 77 percent in Mali) said
    that, if they fell seriously ill, they could count on help at home from a family
    member.

13 About half of those we asked (46 percent in Tanzania and 53 percent in Mali)
    said they could readily borrow as much as a week's living expenses from a friend
    or a relative.

14 The question was preceded by a reminder that all interview responses were
    confidential.

15 Jonathan Fox, "The Difficult Transition from Clientelism to Citizenship: Lessons
    from Mexico," *World Politics* 46 (1994): 151–184.

16 Sidney Verba, Norman Nie, and Jae-On Kim, *Participation and Political Equality:
    A Seven-Nation Comparison* (New York: Cambridge University Press, 1978),
    p. 46.

17 A start has been made by Robert Mattes and Jessica Piombo, "Opposition Parties
    and the Voters in South Africa's General Election of 1999," *Democratization* 8,
    3 (2001): 101–128 and Daniel Posner and David Simon, "Economic Conditions
    and Incumbent Support in Africa's New Democracies: Evidence from Zambia,"
    Comparative Political Studies 35, 3 (2002): 313–336.

18 Stephen Bennett and Linda Bennett, "Political Participation" in Samuel Long
    (ed.), *Annual Review of Political Science No. 1* (Norwood, NJ: Ablex, 1986),

pp. 85–103. And Joan Nelson, "Political Participation," in Myron Weiner and Samuel Huntington (eds.), *Understanding Political Development* (Boston: Little Brown, 1987), pp. 103–159.

19   In second elections up to 1998, voter turnout as a proportion of registered voters averaged 72 percent in nine new democracies in Eastern and Central Europe and 81 percent in eight Latin American countries. The comparative figure for sixteen African countries was 56 percent, which represents a decline from 64 percent for founding elections. See Bratton, "Second Elections in Africa," (1998). Note, however, that voter turnout in second, third, or subsequent elections in the twelve Afrobarometer countries averages 65 percent (see Table 5.5), which would represent continuity in turnout levels.

20   Mali's low score in 1997 was no anomaly: only 22 percent and 19 percent of voters were mustered in the presidential elections of 1992 and the first round of 2002 respectively. Mali's voter registration system does not require action on the part of would-be voters since all adults are "registered" by virtue of citizenship. Because of migration at various times in the agricultural calendar, many who are resident in urban areas are also counted as resident family members in the home village. The net effects are that registration is really a measure of voter eligibility and that voter rolls contain endemic overcounting. Thanks to Zeric Smith for alerting us to these features.

21   International IDEA, *Voter Turnout from 1945 to 1997: A Global Report on Political Participation* (Stockholm: International Institute for Democracy and Electoral Assistance, 1998). For an update to 2001 see www.idea.int.

22   The base for this calculation was the proportion of the population aged eighteen years and above in the year of the last election. This proportion ranged from a low of 41.8 percent in Uganda in 1996 to a high of 57.3 percent in South Africa in 1999.

23   The residents of these two countries report the highest levels of political fear in the Afrobarometer (see Chapter 2).

24   Liisa Laakso, "When Elections are Just a Formality: Rural-Urban Dynamics in the Dominant-Party System of Zimbabwe," in Cowen and Laakso (eds.), *Multi-Party Elections in Africa* (2002), pp. 324–345.

25   Few African countries have continuous systems of voter registration.

26   Tanzania's Chama Cha Mapinduzi, while no longer a juggernaut, remains the quintessential one-party apparatus on the continent. And Uganda's National Resistance Movement, while claiming to be nonpartisan, operates much like a single or dominant political party.

27   "How often have you, personally, done any of these things . . . worked for a political candidate or party?"

28   The attendance question was worded using the first phrase in East and West Africa and the second phrase in Southern Africa.

29   See Soren Villadsen and Francis Lubanga, *Democratic Decentralization in Uganda: A New Approach to Local Governance* (Kampala: Fountain Publishers, 1996) and Apollo Nsibambi, *Decentralization and Civil Society in Uganda: The Quest for Good Governance* (Kampala: Fountain Publishers, 1998). Care should be taken in comparing figures since the question on attending community meetings referred to a one-year period in Southern Africa and a five-year period elsewhere.

30 Makerere Institute for Social Research, *Study of the Effects of the Decentralization Reform in Uganda*, report prepared for the Danish Agency for Development Assistance (Kampala: MISR, 1997). Also Gina Lambright, "Decentralization and Democratization in Uganda: Opportunities and Constraints," paper presented at a conference on "Consolidation in New Democracies," Uppsala University, Uppsala, Sweden, June 8–9, 2002, pp. 27–32.

31 *Kgotla* is a Tswana word for the place where the adults in a community meet to deliberate about national policy and local matters. Officially, "the *kgotla* has evolved into a consultative machinery through which government policies are explained to the populace. It is also the mechanism through which the people can express their concerns and even reject policies initiated by the Government." Government of Botswana, "The Institutionalization of Governance in Botswana," United Nations System-wide Special Initiative on Africa (UNSIA), www.un.org/depts/eca/sia.

32 Schlyter, Ann. "Urban Community Organization and the Transition to Multiparty Democracy in Zambia," in Lars Rudebeck and Olle Tornquist (eds.), *Democratization in the Third World: Concrete Cases in Comparative and Theoretical Perspective* (Uppsala, Sweden: Uppsala University, 1996), pp. 265–288.

33 Masipula Sithole, "Fighting Authoritarianism in Zimbabwe," *Journal of Democracy* 12, 1 (2001): 160–169. For useful background, read John Makumbe and Daniel Compagnon, *Behind the Smokescreen: The Politics of Zimbabwe's 1995 General Elections* (Harare: University of Zimbabwe Publications, 2000).

34 Whereas only 3 percent engaged in demonstrations "often" in South Africa, 9 percent claimed to do so in Zimbabwe.

35 The latter result is an eleven-country average (without Uganda, where the questions were not asked). The petition result is an average for four countries (Ghana, Mali, Nigeria, and Tanzania).

36 Note, however, that the difference between formal and informal contacts lies within the margin of sampling error in Zimbabwe, Lesotho, and Botswana.

37 In Figure 5.3, Zimbabwe is ranked as having more contacts with state officials than Namibia because more Zimbabweans say they have made such contacts "often."

38 See Dieter Nohlen, *Elections and Electoral Systems* (New Delhi: Macmillan, 1996). The information for the analysis of African electoral systems in this paragraph comes from Andrew Reynolds and Ben Reilly, *Handbook of Electoral System Design* (Stockholm: International IDEA, 1997), Annex A, pp. 139–142. For Africa, see the debate between Joel Barkan and Andrew Reynolds in Timothy Sisk and Andre Reynolds (eds.), *Elections and Conflict Management in Africa* (Washington, DC: United States Institute of Peace Press, 1998), pp. 55–80.

39 In South Africa, the whole country is treated as a single constituency. The African National Congress has had little success in assigning winning candidates to serve specific geographical districts.

40 Leonardo Villalon describes *marabouts* (Muslim religious leaders, usually Sufi) as "absolutely central to people's lives" in *Islamic Society and State Power in Senegal: Disciples and Citizens in Fatick* (New York: Cambridge University Press, 1995), p. 121. See also Catherine Boone, *Merchant Capital and the Roots of State Power in Senegal, 1930–1985* (New York: Cambridge University Press, 1992), esp. Ch. 5.

41 Twenty-three percent (religious) versus 11 percent (traditional).
42 In Mali, Tanzania, and Uganda we asked "on those occasions that you contacted a leader or attended a community meeting, what was your main reason for doing so?" The classification scheme follows Kay Lehman Schlozman, Nancy Burns, Sidney Verba, and Jesse Donahue, "Gender and Citizen Participation: Is There a Different Voice?" *American Journal of Political Science* 39, 2 (1995): 267–293.
43 We therefore chose, in this instance, to include missing values when calculating descriptive statistics. The logic is that people who do not perceive a problem are unlikely to take action to resolve it.
44 Fifty-two percent would protest!
45 The relationships are significant ($p = <.001$) though hardly strong: Pearson's $r = .064$ and $.077$ respectively.
46 Pearson's $r = .121, p = <.001$.
47 Pearson's $r = −.022, p = .146$.
48 Pearson's $r = −.002, p = .844$.
49 Pearson's $r = .540$. Because of the small sample size (twelve countries), however, the relationship is significant only at a relaxed level ($p = .070$).
50 Pearson's $r = .182, p = <.001$.

Chapter 6

1 The weight of opinion in the literature is that women are subordinated. See Ifi Amadiume, "Gender, Political Systems and Social Movements: A West African Experience," in Mahmood Mamdani and Ernest Wamba-dia-Wamba (eds.), *African Studies in Social Movements and Democracy* (Dakar: CODESRIA, 1995), pp. 35–68; and David Hirschmann, "Women and Political Participation in Africa: Broadening the Scope of Research," *World Development* 19, 12 (1991): 1679–1694.
2 The sample contains 50.2 percent males and 49.8 percent females. Apart from a purposive quota to ensure gender equality, Afrobarometer respondents are selected by random methods (see Appendix B).
3 The relationship is significant, but not especially strong: eta $= .071, p = <.001$.
4 Eta $= .095, p = <.001$.
5 The quote was made to one of the authors by a male party official of Zambia's United National Independence Party.
6 Eta $= .060, p = <.001$.
7 Aili Mari Tripp, *Women and Politics in Uganda* (Madison: University of Wisconsin Press, 2000).
8 Ingrid Palmer, *Gender and Population in the Adjustment of African Economies* (Geneva: International Labor Office, 1991). Lourdes Beneria and Shelley Feldman, *Unequal Burden: Unequal Crises, Persistent Poverty, and Women's Work* (Boulder, CO: Westview Press, 1992). And Lynn Brown and Joanna Kerr (eds.), *The Gender Dimensions of Economic Reforms in Ghana, Mali and Zambia* (Ottawa: North-South Institute, 1997).
9 Starting points include William Hanna, *University Students and African Politics* (New York: Africana Publishers, 1975) and Colin Bundy, "Street Sociology and Pavement Politics: Aspects of Youth and Student Resistance in Cape Town,"

Journal of Southern African Studies 13, 3 (1987): 303–330. On recent manifestations, see Ali El-Kenz, "Youth and Violence" in Stephen Ellis (ed.), *Africa Now: People, Policies, Institutions* (London: James Currey, 1996) and Krijn Peters and Paul Richards, "Why We Fight: The Voice of Youth Combatants in Sierra Leone," *Africa* 68, 2 (1998): 183–210.

10   Isaac Albert, "University Students in the Politics of Structural Adjustment in Nigeria," in Mkandawire and Olukoshi (eds.), *Between Liberalization and Oppression* (1995), pp. 374–392.

11   Richard Niemi and Joel Barkan found a similar pattern in "Age and Turnout in New Electorates and Peasant Societies," *American Political Science Review* 81, 2 (1987): 583–588.

12   Gamma = .130, p = .001.

13   Gamma = −.094, p = .006. On the student movement in Mali's democratization, see Zeric Smith, "Building African Democracy: The Role of Civil-Society Based Associations in Strengthening Malian Civic Community," Ph.D. dissertation (University of North Carolina, 1998) and Marie-France Lange and Sekou Oumar Diarrah, "Ecole et démocratie: L'explosion scolaire sous la IIe Republique au Mali," *Politique Africaine* 76 (1999): 164–172.

14   Gamma = −.082, p = .001.

15   Gamma = .157, p = <.001.

16   Gamma = −.210, p = <.001.

17   Perhaps they share William Easterly's opinion that, in Tanzania, government "failed at every big and small development initiative since independence." *The Elusive Quest for Growth* (2001), p. 68.

18   The concept of political generation derives from Karl Mannheim, *Ideology and Utopia: An Introduction to the Sociology of Knowledge* (New York: Harcourt Brace, 1951). An age cohort becomes a political generation when its members develop a common destiny as they face a distinct set of historical challenges.

19   For South Africa and Namibia, "colonial" rule includes the apartheid era. For Uganda, a multicandidate system substitutes for the "multiparty" era. Importantly (see Chapter 11), South Africa, Namibia, and Botswana (where democratization coincided with effective decolonization) are coded as having only "colonial" and "multiparty" generations, whereas all other Afrobarometer countries contain a "postcolonial" generation.

20   Thus, the relationship is curvilinear. Eta = .082, p = <.001.

21   The starting point is Michael Lipton, *Why Poor People Stay Poor: Urban Bias in World Development* (London: Temple Smith, 1977). On Africa, see Robert Bates, *Markets and States in Tropical Africa: The Political Basis of Agricultural Policies* (Berkeley: University of California Press, 1981). For discussion, see Paul Mosley, Jane Harrigan, and John Toye, *Aid and Power: The World Bank and Policy Based Lending in the 1980s* (London: Routledge, 1991), Ch. 1.

22   The designation "urban" was derived from the definition provided by each country's census bureau. It includes rural population centers and peri-urban settlements.

23   For a discussion of the changing nature of urban-rural ties see Josef Gugler (ed.), *Cities in the Developing World: Issues, Theory and Policy* (New York: Oxford University Press, 1997).

24 Eta = .055, p = <.001. Note, however, that this rural-urban distinction occurs at the margins of overall rejection, whereas fully 77 percent of urban dwellers reject one-party rule, some 66 percent of rural dwellers do so.

25 Eta = .051, p = <.001. A two-tailed t-test is also significant at <.001.

26 Eta = .081, p = <.001. Whereas 40 percent support privatization in towns, only 31 percent do so in the countryside.

27 For a full economic reform package, eta = .261, p = <.001. For example, whereas only 47 percent of rural Namibians endorse user fees, fully 64 percent of urban Namibians (including white racial minorities) do so.

28 Alexander Sarris and Hadi Shams, *Ghana Under Structural Adjustment: The Impact on Agriculture and the Rural Poor* (New York: New York University Press, 1991), p. 179.

29 Deborah Bryceson and John Howe, "An Agrarian Continent in Transition" in Stephen Ellis (ed.), *Africa Now: People, Policies and Institutions* (London: James Currey, 1996), p. 182.

30 For the debate, compare Leo Kuper and M. G. Smith (eds.), *Pluralism in Africa* (Berkeley: University of California Press, 1971) or Victor Olorunsola (ed.), *The Politics of Cultural Sub-Nationalism in Africa* (Garden City, NY: Doubleday, 1972) with Leroy Vail (ed.), *The Creation of Tribalism in Southern Africa* (London: James Currey, 1989) or René Lemarchand, *Burundi: Ethnocide as Discourse and Practice* (Washington, DC: Woodrow Wilson Center Press, 1994).

31 Marina Ottaway, "Ethnic Politics in Africa: Change and Continuity," in Richard Joseph (ed.), *State, Conflict, and Democracy in Africa* (Boulder, CO: Lynne Rienner Publishers, 1999), p. 299.

32 Joel Samoff, "Pluralism and Conflict in Africa: Ethnicity, Interests and Class," cited in Naomi Chazan, Peter Lewis, Robert Mortimer, Donald Rothchild, and Stephen Stedman (eds.), *Politics and Society in Contemporary Africa* (Boulder, CO: Lynne Rienner Publishers, 1999), p. 107. For the origins of this insight, see Crawford Young, *The Politics of Cultural Pluralism* (Madison: The University of Wisconsin Press, 1976).

33 We recognize that language and ethnicity are not always completely coterminous. Most commonly, several ethnic groups share a lingua franca and, occasionally, subgroups of the same ethnicity may speak distinct dialects. But language remains the best single marker of cultural identity and is used by Africans themselves as a quick and reliable way to attribute ethnicity. For a discussion of these distinctions, see Daniel Posner, "The Colonial Origins of Ethnic Cleavages: The Case of Linguistic Divisions in Zambia," *Comparative Politics* 35, 2 (2003): 127–145.

34 According to our classification, an ethnic group is "major" if its home language is spoken by the largest segment of the population, "secondary" if not major but is cited by at least 10 percent of respondents, and "minority" if its language is cited by fewer than 10 percent of respondents.

35 Gamma = −.059, p = <.001.

36 Gammas = −.191 for Mali and −.192 for Zimbabwe, p = <.001.

37 See André Bourgeot, *Les sociétés touaregues; nomadisme, identite, resistances* (Paris: Karthala, 1995). Also Robin-Edward Poulton and Ibrahim ag Youssouf, *A Peace of Timbuktu: Democratic Governance, Development and African Peacemaking* (New York: United Nations, 1998).

38 John Makumbe, "Zimbabwe's Hijacked Election" *Journal of Democracy* 13, 4, (September 2002): 87–101.
39 Gamma = −.092, p = <.001.
40 Gammas = −.224 for Nigeria and −.203 for Namibia, p = <.001.
41 On the contested nature of Nigerian population estimates, see Rotimi Suberu, "The Politics of Population Counts," in his *Federalism and Ethnic Conflict in Nigeria* (Washington, DC: United States Institute of Peace, 2001), Ch. 6.
42 For market pricing, gamma = −.096, p = <.001 and, for public service reform, gamma = −.032, p = <.001.
43 We are indebted to Massa Coulibaly for help in arriving at this interpretation.
44 JoAnn MacGregor, "The Politics of Disruption: War Veterans and the Local State in Zimbabwe," *African Affairs* 101 (2002): 9–37.
45 We limit our investigation on this subject to just seven countries in Southern Africa, where racial minorities are substantial. Across the Southern Africa region, 91 percent of respondents were black, 5 percent, 3 percent mixed race/Coloured, and 1 percent Indian/South Asian.
46 Eta = .196, p = <.001.
47 Eta = .172 and .170 respectively, p's = <.001.
48 Eta = .263 and .364 respectively, p's = <.001.
49 This initial finding runs counter to James Gibson, "The Legacy of Apartheid: Racial Differences in the Legitimacy of Democratic Institutions and Processes in the New South Africa," *Comparative Political Studies* 36 (2003): 772–800. On the other hand, because whites are firmer than blacks in their rejection of authoritarian alternatives, their commitments to democracy, while not as widespread, are deeper.
50 Eta = .096, p = <.001.
51 Generalizations about Coloureds and Indians, based on small subsamples, should be handled with care.
52 Thirty-five percent versus 12 percent.
53 This section is based on data from four countries with varying degrees of religious pluralism: Mali, Nigeria, Tanzania, and Uganda. The proportions of Muslims in Afrobarometer samples in these countries (90 percent, 45 percent, 37 percent, and 13 percent respectively) correlates at r = .999 with *The World Factbook*, see www.cia.gov.
54 Huntington, *The Clash of Civilizations* (1996).
55 Elie Kedourie, *Democracy and Arab Political Culture* (London: Frank Cass, 1994), p. 16.
56 John Esposito and John Voll, *Islam and Democracy* (New York: Oxford University Press, 1996).
57 Abdou Filali-Ansary, "Muslims and Democracy," *Journal of Democracy* 10, 3 (1999): 18–31.
58 The difference is statistically significant: Cramer's V = .108, p = <.001.
59 For a fuller account, see Michael Bratton, "Islam, Democracy, and Public Opinion in Africa," *African Affairs* 102 (2003), 493–501.
60 For overviews of the various connections between religion and political power, see Paul Gifford (ed.), *The Christian Churches and the Democratization of Africa* (New York: E.J. Brill, 1995); François Constantin and Christian Coulon (eds.), *Religion et transition démocratique en Afrique* (Paris: Karthala, 1997); and,

especially, Stephen Ellis and Gerrie ter Haar, "Religion and Politics in Sub-Saharan Africa," *Journal of Modern African Studies* 36, 2 (1998): 175–201.

61 For example, see Matembo Nzunda and Kenneth Ross, *Church, Law and Political Transition in Malawi, 1992–94* (Gweru, Zimbabwe: Mambo Press, 1995); Metema M'Nteba, "Les conferences nationals africaines et la figure politique de l'évéque president," *Zaire-Afrique* 276 (1993): 361–372; and Tracy Kuperus, "Building Democracy: An Examination of Religious Associations in South Africa and Zimbabwe," *Journal of Modern African Studies* 37, 4 (1999): 643–668.

62 For both religions, 90 percent reject strongman rule and 95 percent reject military rule.

63 Whereas 79 percent of mainstream Christians reject one-party rule, 89 percent of evangelical Christians do so.

64 On Christian fundamentalism, see Paul Gifford (ed.), *New Dimensions of African Christianity* (Nairobi: All Africa Conference of Churches, 1992); and Kingsley Larbi, "The Development of Ghanaian Pentecostalism," Ph.D. dissertation, (University of Edinburgh, 1995).

65 For example, see Peter Henriot, "Does Zambia Need the IMF?" and the *SAP Monitor*, Catholic Commission for Justice and Peace in Zambia, www.ccjp.org.zm.

66 Eta = .095, p = <.001.

67 Seventy-six percent versus 66 percent.

68 For a sampling, see David Simon (ed.), *Structurally Adjusted Africa: Poverty, Debt and Basic Needs* (London: Pluto Press, 1995) and Kwabena Donkor, *Structural Adjustment and Mass Poverty in Ghana* (Aldershot: Ashgate, 1997).

69 Speech in Melbourne, Australia, September 8, 2000. See www.anc.org.za.

70 For factor and reliability analysis, see Appendix A.

71 Gamma = −.093, p = <.001.

72 Thirty-two percent versus 18 percent. Cramer's V = −.171, p = <.001.

73 The proportions are 49 and 36 percent respectively.

74 Gamma = −.332, p = <.001.

75 Gamma = .199, p = <.001.

76 Gamma = −.163, p = <.001.

77 Gamma = −.293, p = <.001.

78 For example, in Botswana, gamma = −.263, p = <.001.

79 The proportions are 54 and 36 percent respectively. Gamma = −.192, p = <.001.

80 For satisfaction with democracy, gamma = −.083, p = <.001; for satisfaction with adjustment, gamma = −.169, p = <.001.

81 In an apparent anomaly, destitute people appear to be slightly more satisfied with SAPs than very poor people, but this difference is within the range of sampling error for the surveys and is partly attributable to low levels of information about SAPs among the destitute.

82 The mean scores for satisfaction are 60 percent for democracy and 21 percent for adjustment.

83 This finding should be treated with caution due to small subsample sizes and differences that barely exceed the margin of sampling error.

84 We employ ordinary least squares regression models. OLS is preferred to ordered probit because, as the most common analytic technique in social science, it is readily interpretable by most readers. OLS is also ideally suited to the multiitem

indices that we use as dependent variables. Index construction (to reflect underlying scales) and data imputation (which increases N to 21,531) both make for continuous measurement. For a description of the imputation procedure, see Appendix C. Note that, starting with Table 6.3, all regression results are averaged across five imputed data sets.

85 For factor and reliability analyses, see Appendix A.

86 Commitment to democracy is measured on a three-point scale: o = the respondent is indifferent to all forms of government or approves of authoritarian alternatives; 1 = the respondent mildly disapproves of authoritarian forms or accepts that nondemocratic government can sometimes be preferable; and 2 = the respondent always prefers democracy, while also strongly rejects authoritarian alternatives.

87 The unstandardized B coefficient is .320.

88 That is, by about a fifth of a point on a five-point scale. Unstandardized $B = -.214$.

Chapter 7

1 Daniel Etounga-Manguelle, "Does Africa Need a Cultural Adjustment Program?" in Harrison and Huntington, *Culture Matters* (2000), p. 71. For more on the moral economy of traditional African societies see Kwasi Wiredu and Kwame Gyekye, *Person and Community: Ghanaian Philosophical Studies* (Washington, DC: Council for Research in Values and Philosophy, 1992) and Dickson Mungazi, *Gathering Under the Mango Tree: Values in Traditional Culture in Africa* (New York: Peter Lang, 1996).

2 Goran Hyden, *Beyond Ujamaa in Tanzania: Underdevelopment and an Uncaptured Peasantry* (Berkeley: University of California Press, 1980). For discourse on the cultural symbols that bind Africans politically see also Michael Schatzberg, *Political Legitimacy in Middle Africa: Father, Family, Food* (Bloomington: Indiana University Press, 2001).

3 Goran Hyden, *No Shortcuts to Progress: African Development Management in Perspective* (Berkeley: University of California Press, 1983), p. 6.

4 Thomas Weisner, "Culture, Childhood and Progress in sub-Saharan Africa" in Harrison and Huntington, *Culture Matters* (2000), pp. 145–146.

5 See René Lemarchand, "African Peasantries, Reciprocity and the Market," *Cahiers d'Études Africaines* 113 (1989): 33–67. Also Michael Bollig, "Moral Economy and Self-Interest: Kinship, Friendship and Exchange among the Pokot (N.W. Kenya)," in Thomas Schweizer and Douglas White (eds.), *Kinship, Networks, and Exchange* (New York: Cambridge University Press, 1998), pp. 137–157.

6 Michael Watts, "On Peasant Diffidence: Non-Revolt, Resistance, and Hidden Forms of Political Consciousness in Northern Nigeria, 1900–1945" in E. Burke (ed.), *Global Crises and Social Movements* (Boulder, CO: Westview, 1987), p. 140.

7 The relevant nationality was inserted here.

8 In addition to the foundational works cited in Chapter 6, recent contributions include Crawford Young, "Revisiting Nationalism and Ethnicity in Africa," *Coleman Memorial Paper No. 8* (Los Angeles: University of California, 2001) and Cyril Daddieh and Jo Ellen Fair (eds.), *Ethnicity and Recent Democratic Experiments in Africa* (New Brunswick, NJ: African Studies Association Press, 2002).

9 In South Africa, apartheid identities (e.g., race and language) are being gradually displaced by religious and class identities. Robert Mattes, "Uniquely African," in Stephen Burgess (ed.), *SA Tribes: Who We Are, How We Live, and What We Want From Life In South Africa* (Cape Town: David Philip, 2002), pp. 82–98.

10 Compared to 26 percent of all respondents, 44 percent of the unemployed define themselves ethnically.

11 Twenty-five percent of Muslims declare a religious identity, versus 9 percent of Protestants and 6 percent of Catholics. Whereas Islam is central to its followers' lives, Christians profess a wider range of identities.

12 In South Africa, this term became confused with racial labels. We decided to code "black" as a racial response and "African" as a continental one, though different interpretations are possible.

13 This question was asked in just eight countries: seven in Southern Africa, plus Nigeria.

14 Yoruba = 83 percent, Ibo = 80 percent, Hausa = 79 percent.

15 Eta = .219, p = <.001.

16 Depending on the country, the relevant nationality was named in the question.

17 Whereas 62 percent of blacks express intense pride ("agree strongly"), just 33 percent of whites do so.

18 Pearsons' r = .340, p = <.001.

19 Versus Walker Connor, "Ethnonationalism," in Myron Weiner and Samuel Huntington (eds.), *Understanding Political Development* (NY: Harper Collins Publishers, 1987), pp. 196–220.

20 Eta = .219, p = <.001.

21 The respondent's self-defined group identity, as expressed in his or her own words, was inserted here.

22 Dankwart Rustow, "Transitions to Democracy: Towards a Dynamic Model," *Comparative Politics* 2 (1970): 337–363. For an argument that national unity and interethnic peace are preconditions also for economic growth, see Easterly and Levine, "Africa's Growth Tragedy" (1997).

23 These statistically significant relationships are not especially strong, however. Gamma .073 and .119, p = <.001.

24 Note, however, that national identity is negatively related to support for economic reform. Gamma = −.072, p = <.001.

25 Gamma = .174 and .172, p = <.001.

26 Cramer's V = .048 and .066, p = <.001.

27 Cramer's V = .120, p = <.001.

28 Nine percent versus 5 percent.

29 Cramer's V = .218, .163, and .161 respectively (p's = <.001).

30 We recognize that social capital is a multidimensional concept that researchers have operationalized variously with indicators of social contact, associational membership, voluntary activity, optimism about the future, and norms of compromise and cooperation. But generalized trust is central, even essential, to all such constructs. See Diego Gambetta, *Trust: Making and Breaking Cooperative Relations* (Oxford: Oxford University Press, 1988) and Francis Fukuyama, *Trust: The Social Virtues and the Creation of Prosperity* (New York: Simon and Schuster, 1995).

31 Putnam, *Making Democracy Work* (1993), esp. Ch. 6.

32 Inglehart, *Modernization and Postmodernization* (1997), pp. 194, 224. See also his "Trust, Well-Being and Democracy" in Mark Warren (ed.), *Democracy and Trust* (New York: Cambridge University Press, 1999), pp. 88–120.

33 Data are from the 1995–97 World Values Survey. Inglehart, ibid. (1999), p. 91.

34 A 52 percent average for Austria, the Czech Republic, Hungary, Poland, and Slovenia. See Rose and Haerpfer, *New Democracies Barometer V : A 12 Nation Survey* (Glasgow, University of Strathclyde, Studies in Public Policy No. 306, 1998), p. 93.

35 Marta Lagos, "Latin America's Smiling Mask," *Journal of Democracy* 8, 3 (1997): 129.

36 As shown in Chapter 2, however, political fear is unrelated to trust in institutions, even in Tanzania.

37 Ghana, Mali, Nigeria, Tanzania, Uganda, and Zambia. The Zambia data are from 1996.

38 Jennifer Widner and Alexander Mundt, "Researching Social Capital in Africa," *Africa* 68, 1 (1998): 4.

39 Deepa Narayan and Lant Pritchett, "Cents and Sociability: Household Income and Social Capital in Rural Tanzania," *Economic Development and Cultural Change* 47, 4 (1999): 871–878. See also Narayan's "Bonds and Bridges: Social Capital and Poverty," *Policy Research Working Paper No. 2167* (Washington, DC, World Bank, 1999).

40 For satisfaction with democracy, gamma =.133, p = <.001; for extent of democracy, gamma = .155, p = <.001.

41 Gamma = .001, p = .963.

42 For a parallel result see Mitchell Seligson, "The Renaissance of Political Culture or the Renaissance of the Ecological Fallacy," *Comparative Politics* 34, 3 (2002): 273–292.

43 Gamma = −.003, p = .895.

44 Gamma = .000, p = <1.000!

45 Gamma = −.129, p = <.001.

46 Gamma = −.185, p = <.001.

47 Gammas = −.406, −.352, and −.315, respectively, p's = <.001.

48 For strength and reliability of the construct, see Appendix A.

49 For democracy, gamma = .060, p = <.001. For antiauthoritarianism, gamma = .020, p = .074.

50 For democracy in Malawi, gamma = .312, p = <.001. For rejection of one-party rule, gamma = .259, p = <.001.

51 Jan Kees van Donge, "Kamuzu's Legacy: the Democratization of Malawi," *African Affairs* 94 (1995): 227–257 and "The Mwanza Trial as a Search for a Usable African Past," *African Affairs* 97 (1998): 91–118.

52 Simeon Mesaki, "The Evolution and Essence of Witchcraft in Pre-Colonial Africa Societies," *Transafrican Journal of History* 14 (1995): 162–177 and Peter Geschiere, *The Modernity of Witchcraft: Politics and the Occult in Postcolonial Africa* (Charlottesville: University Press of Virginia, 1997).

53 Gamma = .083, p = <.001.

54 Jocelyn Alexander, "State, Peasantry and Resettlement," *Review of African Political Economy* 21 (1994): 325–345. Also her "Chiefs and the State in Independent

Zimbabwe," unpublished paper, workshop on chieftancy in Africa, Oxford University, June 2001.

55 Gamma = .235, p = <.001.
56 Gamma = .113, p = <.001.
57 Gamma = .354, p = <.001.
58 Gamma = .155, p = <.001.
59 Gamma = .244, p = <.001.
60 Gamma = .338, p = <.001.
61 For the components of the index, see Appendix A.
62 Gamma = .139, p = <.001.
63 Gamma = .112 for privatization and .113 for retrenchment, p = <.001.
64 Gamma = .202, p <.001.
65 Fifty-eight percent of individualists in Mali actually express satisfaction with SAPs.
66 Gamma = −.098, p = <.001.
67 The unstandardized B coefficient is .073. A shift from one end to the other on the five-point risk scale is associated with a 0.365 point increase in commitment to democracy.

Chapter 8

1 Goran Hyden, *Beyond Ujamaa* (1980) and *No Shortcuts to Progress* (1983). For revisions, see Donald Rothchild and Naomi Chazan (eds.), *The Precarious Balance* (1988); and Joel Migdal, Atul Kohli, and Vivienne Shue (eds.), *State Power and Social Forces: Domination and Transformation in the Third World* (Princeton, NJ: Princeton University Press, 1994), pp. 231–254.

2 See Clive Harber, *Education, Democracy and Political Development in Africa* (Brighton, Sussex: Academic Press, 1997). Also M. Carnoy and Joel Samoff, *Education and Social Transition in the Third World* (Princeton, NJ: Princeton University Press, 1990) and Robert Serpell, *The Significance of Schooling: Life Journeys in an African Society* (New York: Cambridge University Press, 1993).

3 This relationship is strong: gamma = .456, p = <.001.

4 This relationship is also strong: gamma = .459, p = <.001.

5 Gamma = .150, p = <.001. Education is also positively correlated with an index of rejection of authoritarian rule: gamma = .129, p = <.001.

6 Gamma = .160, p = <.001.

7 For Nigeria, gamma = .332, p = <.001; for Ghana, gamma = .281, p = <.001.

8 See Baffuor Ageyman-Duah, "Civil-Military Relations in Ghana: Survey Report," *CDD-Ghana Research Paper* 9 (2000) and "Civil-Military Relations in Ghana's Fourth Republic," *CDD Critical Perspectives* 9 (2002).

9 For satisfaction with democracy, gamma = −.088, p = <.001; for extent of democracy, gamma = .089, p = <.001.

10 Thirteen percent versus 29 percent.

11 Gamma = .158, p = <.001.

12 Torgny Holmgren, Louis Kasekende, Michael Atingi-Ego, and Daniel Ddamulira, "Uganda" in Shantayanan Deverajan, David Dollar, and Torgny

Holmgren (eds.), *Aid and Reform in Africa: Lessons from Ten Case Studies* (Washington, DC: World Bank, 2001), pp. 101–166.

13 Gamma = .330, p = <.001.

14 In Uganda, "parental contributions continued to increase in real terms despite higher public spending." See Ritva Reinikka, "Recovery in Service Delivery: Evidence from Schools and Health Centers," in Ritva Reinikka and Paul Collier (eds.), *Uganda's Recovery: The Role of Farms, Firms and Government* (Washington, DC: The World Bank, 2001), p. 345.

15 There is a negative relationship between education and satisfaction with SAPs: gamma = −.063, p = <.001.

16 Sally Burnheim, *The Right to Communicate: The Internet in Africa* (London: Article 19, 1999); Jacques Bonjawo, *Internet: une chance pour l'Afrique* (Paris: Karthala, 2002); and United States Congress, House Committee on International Relations, Subcommittee on Africa, *Bridging the Information Technology Divide in Africa* (Washington, DC: U.S. Government Printing Office, 2001).

17 Goran Hyden, Michael Leslie, and Folu Ogundimu (eds.), *Media and Democracy in Africa* (New Brunswick, NJ: Transaction Publishers, 2002), p. vii. See also Louise Bourgault, *Mass Media in Sub-Saharan Africa* (Bloomington: Indiana University Press, 1995) and Peter Takirambudde, "Media Freedom and the Transition to Democracy in Africa," *African Journal of International and Comparative Law* 7, 1 (1995): 18–53.

18 For exploration of these effects see Diana Mutz, *Impersonal Influence: How Perceptions of Mass Collectives Affect Political Attitudes* (New York: Cambridge University Press, 1998), esp. Ch. 3.

19 Eta = .505, p = <.001; eta = .330, p = <.001.

20 Pearson's r = .528, p = <.001. For factor and reliability analyses, see Appendix A.

21 Pearson's r = .264 for democracy and .201 for adjustment (p = <.001).

22 Pearson's r = .212 for support (p = <.001.) and −.030 for adjustment (p = .016).

23 Debra Spitulnik, "Alternative Small Media and Communicative Spaces," in Hyden et al., *Media and Democracy in Africa* (2002), p. 177.

24 Achille Mbembe, "The Banality of Power and the Aesthetics of Vulgarity," *Public Culture* 4, 2 (1992): 1–30; Debra Spitulnik, "Radio Cycles and Recyclings in Zambia: Public Words, Popular Critiques and National Communities," *Passages* 8, 10 (1994); and Allesandro Triulzi, "African Cities, Historical Memory, and Street Buzz," in Iain Chambers and Lidia Curti (eds.), *The Post-Colonial Question* (London: Routledge, 1995).

25 For factor and reliability analyses, see Appendix A.

26 Pearson's r = .180 for support democracy and .125 for reject autocracy (p = <.001).

27 Pearson's r = .133, p = <.001.

28 Although statistically significant, the associations are not overly strong. Pearson's r = .087 (p = <.001) for satisfaction with democracy and .051 (p = .002) for satisfaction with SAPs.

29 Raymond Duch, "How Citizens Decide: Information, Persuasion and Choice in Developing Democracies," paper presented at a conference on Democratic

Performance held at the Center for Democratic Performance, Binghamton University, New York, June 6–7, 2001. For the framework, see Adam Przeworski, Susan Stokes, and Bernard Manin (eds.), *Democracy, Accountability, and Representation* (Cambridge: Cambridge University Press, 1999) and Bruce Bueno de Mesquita and Hilton Root (eds.), *Governing for Prosperity* (New Haven, CT: Yale University Press, 2000).

30 The question was adapted to local circumstances. In Mali, we asked about the identity of the president of the national assembly and the mayor of the commune. Prior to the first local government elections in Malawi in 2000, the question about local councilors was omitted.

31 Della Carpini and Keeter recommend measuring knowledge in terms of the rules of the game, the substance of policy, and the positions of contending parties. *What Americans Know About Politics* (1996), p. 14.

32 But, in Mali, only 24 percent knew the name of the president of the national assembly.

33 Overall, for eight countries, Cramer's $V = .219$ (.333 in Ghana, .283 in Nigeria) ($p = <.001$).

34 See Richard Morin, "Tuned Out, Turned Off," *Washington Post National Weekly Edition* (February 5–11, 1996): 6. Compared to the one third of Americans who recall the identity of their congressional representative, 70 percent of Australians can correctly name their member of the House of Representatives. See Ian McAllister, "Civic Education and Political Knowledge in Australia," *Australian Journal of Political Science* 33 (1998): 7–24.

35 Cramer's $V = .594$, $p = <.001$.

36 T. Maloka, "Populism and the Politics of Chieftaincy and Nation-Building in the New South Africa," *Journal of Contemporary African Studies* 14, 2 (1996): 173–196; I. van Kessell and B. Oomen, "One Chief, One Vote: The Revival of Traditional Authorities in Post-Apartheid South Africa," *African Affairs* 96 (1997): 561–585. See also Somadoda Fikeni, "Conflict and Accommodation: The Politics of Rural Local Government in Post-Apartheid South Africa," Ph.D. dissertation (East Lansing: Michigan State University, 2002).

37 For example, on knowledge of leaders, Pearson's $r = .167$, $p = <.001$. The index is an additive score, ranging between 0 and 4, of the number of leaders an individual can recall.

38 Pearson's $r = .218$, $p = <.001$. The sign is correct for every country; the relationship is significant everywhere but Lesotho.

39 Pearson's $r = .131$, $p = <.001$. The sign is correct for every country; the relationship is significant everywhere but Zambia.

40 Seventeen percent versus 6 percent. The package includes user fees, market prices, civil service cutbacks, and privatization.

41 Logistic regression analysis showed all the variables discussed in this chapter, even when controlled for each other, are significant predictors of awareness of democracy ($p = <.001$).

42 Logistic regression analysis showed that the same variables, even when mutually controlled, significantly predict awareness of SAPs ($p = <.001$).

43 In a logistic regression, education is negatively related to substantive conceptions of democracy.

44 Pearson's r = .178 for support democracy and .240 for reject authoritarianism (p = <.001).

45 Pearson's r = .122, p = <.001.

46 In the four countries where data was available (Ghana, Mali, Nigeria, and Tanzania), all differences in attitudes between people with macroeconomic and microeconomic interpretations of SAPs were within the margin of sampling error for Afrobarometer surveys (i.e., plus or minus 2.8 percent).

47 See Jurgen Habermas, *A Theory of Communicative Action* (Boston: Beacon Press, 1984).

Chapter 9

1 For debates about "delivery," see publications of the Centre for Policy Studies, Johannesburg. For example, Claude Kabemba and Tobias Schmitz, "Understanding Policy Implementation: An Exploration of the Reconstruction and Development Programme," *Research Report, No. 73* (2001) and Tobias Schmitz, "Rethinking Delivery? A Review of the Efforts of the Department of Water Affairs, 1994–9," *Policy Briefing No. 16* (1999). A South African joke asks: "What is the difference between the RDP and a pregnant woman?" Answer: "The woman eventually delivers."

2 The quotation comes from a respondent in a July 2002 Afrobarometer survey in Cape Verde.

3 Robert Bates, *Rural Responses to Industrialization: A Study of Village Zambia* (New Haven, CT: Yale University Press, 1976).

4 See Catherine Firmin-Sellers, *The Transformation of Property Rights in the Gold Coast: An Empirical Analysis Applying Rational Choice Theory* (New York: Cambridge University Press, 1996) and Clark Gibson, *Politicians and Poachers: The Political Economy of Wildlife Policy in Africa* (New York: Cambridge University Press, 1999).

5 For authentic testimonies, sample the African witnesses in Deepa Narayan, *Voices of the Poor: Can Anyone Hear Us?* (Washington, DC: Oxford University Press, 2000), esp. Ch. 2.

6 Just 23 percent were fairly satisfied and a mere 5 percent were very satisfied.

7 Twenty-one percent felt that conditions had stayed about the same.

8 Seventeen percent thought conditions would stay about the same.

9 The interval between satisfaction with past economic performance and future expected performance is thirty percentage points in Mali and nineteen points in Nigeria.

10 Satisfaction with past economic performance is strongly correlated with present and anticipated future satisfaction. Pearson's r = .440 and .497 respectively, p = <.001.

11 Pearson's r = .595, p = <.001. The relationship remains positive (r = .254) but loses statistical significance when Uganda is excluded.

12 While the Ugandan economy grew at an average 7.1 percent between 1990 and 1999, the Zambian and South African economies mustered only 0.2 and 1.6 percent respectively.

13 For the composition of the index, see Appendix A.

14 Pearson's r = −.528, p = <.001.

15 For individual relative deprivation, Pearson's r = .236, p = <.001. For group relative deprivation, Pearson's r = −.353, p = <.001.

16 The 34 percent who see themselves at par, however, cannot match the 44 percent in Tanzania and 65 percent in Mali. The latter countries suffer an egalitarianism born of widespread poverty.

17 The 46 percent who feel this way cannot match Botswana's 69 percent. In terms of group relative deprivation, Batswana see themselves as the most equal society in the Afrobarometer.

18 Note that these findings are unique to South Africa. In other former settler colonies, past policies of racial segregation have not had such profound effects. In Namibia and Zimbabwe, for example, blacks feel more relatively deprived than whites, a much more intuitive result.

19 Nicoli Nattrass and Jeremy Seekings, "'Two Nations'? Race and Economic Inequality in Post-Apartheid South Africa," *Daedalus* 130, 1 (2001): pp. 45–70.

20 Andrew Whiteford and Dirk Van Deventer, *Winners and Losers: South Africa's Changing Income Distribution in the 1990s* (Johannesberg: WEFA, 1999).

21 Jeremy Seekings, "Inequality, Mobility and Politics in South Africa," paper presented to the World Congress of the International Political Science Association, Durban, South Africa, June 30, 2003.

22 Pearson's r = .010, p = .142. The variables in the zero-order correlation are the index of macroeconomic evaluations and the number of structural adjustment programs supported.

23 Notwithstanding a general lack of association, people who are satisfied with economic conditions are likely to support market pricing of consumer goods: Pearson's r = .073, p = <.001.

24 Pearson's r = .314, p = <.001.

25 In Ghana, Pearson's r = .345, p = .001.

26 Pearson's r = .126, p = <.001.

27 In South Africa, Pearson's r = .192, p = <.001.

28 For one-man rule, Pearson's r = −.045, p = <.001.

29 In Zimbabwe, Pearson's r = −.214, p = <.001.

30 Pearson's r = .033, p = <.001.

31 Of course, the correlation is negative: Pearson's r = −.078, p = <.001.

32 In South Africa, Pearson's r = −.219, p = <.001.

33 Pierre Englebert, *State Legitimacy and Development in Africa* (Boulder, CO: Lynne Rienner Publishers, 2000), p. 5. For extreme cases, see William Zartman (ed.), *Collapsed States: The Disintegration and Restoration of Legitimate Authority* (Boulder, CO: Lynne Rienner Publishers, 2000).

34 Thirty-five percent are distrustful and the balance "don't know."

35 As measured by the World Values Survey, the institutions were the civil service, the armed forces, the legal system, the police, and the parliament. Cited in Russell Dalton, "Political Support in Advanced Industrial Democracies" in Norris, *Critical Citizens* (1999), p. 68.

36 In South Africa, trust in parliament fell from 45 percent in 1995 to 31 percent in 2002, but we do not know whether this downward trend applies to other institutions or other African countries. Note, however, that, since September 11, 2001, trust in public institutions has begun to rise again in the United States.

37 An East African said about official news broadcasts, "we (only) listen because we are...interested to hear the funeral announcements at the end." Cited in Hyden et al., *Media and Democracy in Africa* (2002), p. 45.

38 In rank order by degree of public trust: Mali, Namibia, Ghana, South Africa, Zambia, and Lesotho.

39 Trust in the army is twice as high in Mashonaland (61 percent), the heartland of the linguistic majority, than in Matabeleland (30 percent), scene of repression by the army's Fifth Brigade in the early 1980s.

40 In rank order by degree of public distrust: South Africa, Mali, Zimbabwe, and Lesotho.

41 Only 3 percent of survey respondents lack enough information about the police to form an opinion about them (see Figure 9.3).

42 Etannibi Alemika, *Police-Community Violence in Nigeria* (Lagos and Abuja: Centre for Law Enforcement Education and National Human Rights Commission, 2000).

43 See Neville Melville, *The Taming of the Blue: Regulating Police Misconduct in South Africa* (Pretoria: Human Sciences Research Council, 1999) and Antoinette Louw, "Surviving the Transition: Trends and Perceptions of Crime in South Africa," *Social Indicators Research* 41 (1997): 137–168.

44 For factor and reliability analyses, see Appendix A.

45 Pearson's r −.149, p = <.001.

46 Pearson's r = −.140 and −.064, p = <.001. Institutional trust declines with media use. Highest among casual radio listeners, it is lowest among regular consumers of TV news and newspapers.

47 At the individual level, Pearson's r = −.276, p = <.001. The index is based on perceived levels of corruption among elected officials, civil servants, and the government as a whole. For factor and reliability analyses, see Appendix A. The Afrobarometer index correlates quite well with Transparency International's (TI's) corruption perceptions index, which is based on the collective assessments of business leaders and expert risk analysts within each country. Data are available from TI for ten of our African cases, excluding Lesotho and Mali. Pearson's r = −490, p = .015. The sign is negative because the TI index is an inverted scale with 0 being the most corrupt and ten being the least corrupt. See Transparency International, *Global Corruption Report* (London: Profile Books, 2001), pp. 234–236.

48 Ghana, Nigeria, and Uganda are excluded because we did not ask all questions for both indices.

49 With Tanzania, Pearson's r = −.510, p = .160. Without Tanzania, r = −.780, p = .022.

50 Kimberly Ann Elliott, *Corruption and the Global Economy* (Washington, DC: Institute for International Economics, 1997), pp. 1–2. For African applications, see Kempe Hope and Bornwell Chikulo (eds.), *Corruption and Development in Africa: Lessons from Country Case-Studies* (New York: St. Martin's, 2000) and Contance Kanuka and Philliat Matsheza, *Measuring Corruption in Southern Africa* (Harare: Human Rights Trust of Zimbabwe, 2001).

51 Pearson's r = −.239, −.212, and −.215 respectively (p = <.001).

52 In bivariate relationships, Pearson's r = −.475 and −.404 respectively (p = <.001). Thus variance explained (r-squared) = 23 and 16 percent respectively.

53 Penny Dale, "Southern Africa," in *Global Corruption Report* (2001), pp. 57 and 63.
54 Forty-three versus 40 percent cite "most" or "almost all" as corrupt.
55 For example, three quarters or more see corruption as "fairly common" or "very common" among police in Mali, Tanzania, and Uganda.
56 We are grateful to Nic van de Walle for suggesting this interpretation.
57 Pearson's r = .090, p = <.001.
58 Pearson's r = .135, .139, and .188 respectively.
59 There is no better account than William Reno, *Corruption and State Politics in Sierra Leone* (1995). See also Alec Russell, *Big Men, Little People: The Leaders Who Defined Africa* (New York: New York University Press, 2001), esp. Ch. 1 on Mobutu Sese Seko, "the king of kleptocracy."
60 Using the index of trust in state institutions, Pearson's r = .113, p = <.001.
61 Pearson's r = −.110, p = <.001. Note that the index of trust in state institutions is also negatively related to rejection of one-man presidencies and military rule too.
62 Pearson's r = .295 and −.286 respectively, p = <.001.
63 Pearson's r = .321 and −.230 respectively, p = <.001.
64 For question wordings, see Appendix A.
65 Seventy-two percent (South Africa) versus 54 percent (Lesotho).
66 Sixty-five percent (Nigeria) versus 38 percent (Ghana).
67 For political rights, Pearson's r = .157. For economic welfare, Pearson's r = .085. For both, p = <.001.
68 For political rights, Pearson's r = .150, p = <.001. For economic welfare, Pearson's r = .004, p = .587.
69 In a simple, bivariate test, Pearson's r = .309 and .216 for economic and political goods respectively (p = <.001). For the moment, we will wait and see if this balance holds up in multivariate analysis.
70 For political rights, Pearson's r = .207. For economic welfare, Pearson's r = .201. For both, p = <.001.
71 Education, health, employment, and inflation policies form a single factor. For test statistics, see Appendix A.
72 See M. Dombo, *Mitigating the Hetero-Sexual Transmission of HIV/AIDS amongst Women and Children in Uganda* (Milton Keynes: World Vision UK, 1997) and Helen Jackson, *AIDS Africa: Continent in Crisis* (Harare: SAFAIDS, 2002).
73 Pearson's r = .281 for creating jobs versus .259 for improving education. For both, p = <.001.
74 Pearson's r = .107, p = <.001.
75 Pearson's r = −.046, p = <.001.
76 Pearson's r = .022, p = <.010.
77 Pearson's r = −.014, p = <.095.
78 Pearson's r = −.014, p = <.095.
79 For satisfaction with democracy, Pearson's r = .365. For satisfaction with SAPs, Pearson's r = .157. For both, p = <.001.
80 In appraising these figures, the reader should bear in mind that evaluations of presidential job performance are somewhat inflated by political fear (see Chapter 2).
81 Martin Hill, *The Harambee Movement in Kenya: Self-Help, Development and Education among the Kamba of Kitui District* (London: Athlone Press, 1991); Joel

Barkan, Michael McNulty, and M. A. O. Ayeni, "Hometown Voluntary Associations, Local Development and the Emergence of Civil Society in Western Nigeria," *Journal Of Modern African Studies* 29, 3 (1991): 457–480.

82 Though not very strong, the relationships are always significant and all signs run in the "correct" (negative) direction: Pearson's r = −.071 for councilors, −.066 for MPs, and −.066 for presidents (p = <.001).

83 Though not very strong, the relationships are always significant and all signs are run in the "correct" (positive) direction: Pearson's r = .085 for local government officials, .080 for MPs, and .110 for presidents (p = <.001). The data are from a Round 2 Afrobarometer survey conducted in September 2002.

84 The same holds true in Cape Verde, which was added to Round 2 of the Afrobarometer.

85 For MPs, Pearson's r = .628, p = <.001. For local government councilors, r = .601, p = <.001. Questions about leadership responsiveness were asked in this way only in Southern Africa.

86 See Appendix A.

87 See Appendix A.

88 Pearson's r = .483, p = <.001.

89 Pearson's r = −.356, p = <.001.

90 Pearson's r = −.331 and −.247 respectively (p = <.001).

91 Presidential performance predicts support for democracy at r = .189, p = <.001. The only exception is a modest negative link between representatives' performance and support for economic reform.

92 Pearson's r = .512 (p = <.001) for satisfaction with democracy and r = .476 (p = <.001) for satisfaction with SAPs.

93 Calculated by squaring the coefficients in the previous endnotes.

94 On satisfaction with democracy, r = .661 in Malawi and .573 in Tanzania (p = <.001)!

95 In the aggregate, Pearson's r = .776, p = .005. N= 11, since data were unavailable for Ghana. Nigeria data are derived from trust in the president alone.

96 Susan Rose Ackerman, "The Political Economy of Corruption," in Kimberly Ann Elliott (ed.), *Corruption and the Global Economy* (1997), pp. 31–60.

Chapter 10

1 The quote is from Samuel Huntington's classic *Political Order in Changing Societies* (New Haven, CT: Yale University Press, 1968), p. 12.

2 Lillian Trager, *Yoruba Hometowns: Community, Identity, and Development in Nigeria* (Boulder, CO: Lynne Rienner Publishers, 2001).

3 Dwayne Woods, "The Politics of Organizing the Countryside: Rural Cooperatives in Cote d'Ivoire," *Journal of Modern African Studies* 37, 3 (1999): 503–504.

4 Jon Kraus, "Capital, Power and Business Associations in the African Political Economy," *Journal of Modern African Studies* 40, 3 (2002): 395–436.

5 John Harbeson, Donald Rothchild, and Naomi Chazan (eds.), *Civil Society and the State in Africa* (Boulder, CO: Lynne Rienner Publishers, 1994); Stephen Ndegwa, *The Two Faces of Civil Society: NGOs and Politics in Africa* (West Hartford, CT: Kumarian Press, 1996); and Julius Nyang'oro (ed.), *Civil Society and Democratic Development in Africa* (Harare: MWENGO, 1999).

6   E. Gyimah-Boadi, "Associational Life, Civil Society, and Democratization in Ghana," in Harbeson et al., ibid., p. 125. See also Nelson Kasfir (ed.), *Civil Society and Democracy in Africa* (London: Frank Cass, 1998) and John L. and Jean Comaroff (eds.), *Civil Society and the Political Imagination in Africa: Critical Perspectives* (Chicago: University of Chicago Press, 1999).

7   Putnam, *Making Democracy Work* (1993), p. 168. The density of voluntary associations is a central element in his civic community index, pp. 91–92.

8   Widner and Mundt, "Researching Social Capital" (1998), p. 14.

9   More than half of all adults in Lesotho (53 percent) have no voluntary memberships. The comparative figure for Uganda is 12 percent, a country where 9 percent claim to belong to at least four associations.

10 The range of the index is from zero to four associations. For the moment, we acknowledge that expected effects may turn out to be prior causes, with reformers and activists selecting to join associations. We make the case in Chapter 12, however, that causality runs from associational membership to attitudes and actions.

11 Gamma = .064, p = <.001.

12 More than three quarters of all adults claim affiliation with a religious group, ranging from 79 percent in Nigeria to 91 percent in Ghana.

13 See J.-P. Jacob and Ph. Laville Delville (eds.), *Les associations paysannes en Afrique: Organization et dynamiques* (Paris: Karthala, 1994). More specifically, John Davis, "A Single Finger Cannot Lift a Stone: Local Organizations and Democracy in Mali," Ph.D. dissertation (East Lansing: Michigan State University, 1999).

14 Pearson's r = .027, p = <.001.

15 Pearson's r = .107, p = <.001 for newspapers and r = .117, p = <.001 for voting. See Putnam, *Making Democracy Work* (1993), pp. 92–93.

16 Robert Putnam, *Bowling Alone: The Collapse and Revival of American Community* (New York: Simon and Schuster, 2000), pp. 21–24.

17 Cramer's V = .053, p = <.001.

18 Compare Trager, *Hometown Associations* (2001), pp. 260–268 with Francis Nyamanjoh and Michael Rowlands, "Elite Associations and the Politics of Belonging in Cameroon," *Africa* 68, 3 (1998): 320–337.

19 Note that ethnic and religious identities are equally good predictors of whether a person will belong to a voluntary association. Moreover, ethnic identity is almost as good a predictor as religious identity of whether a person will join a *religious* association.

20 A statistical relationship is entirely absent: Pearson's r = .009, p = .558.

21 Whereas 73 percent of nonmembers are risk tolerant, the figure for members is 80 percent. Gamma = .107, p = <.001.

22 Whereas 21 percent of nonmembers say they understand government procedures, the figure for members is 31 percent. Gamma = .112, p = <.001.

23 The index of group membership is positively related to support for democracy (r = .061), rejection of authoritarian rule (r = .038), the perceived extent of democracy (r = .029) and support for economic reform (r = .040). All p's = <.001. The index is positively but insignificantly related to satisfaction with democracy and satisfaction with SAPs.

24 From 64 percent for non-members to 75 percent for adherents of religious groups. Cramer's V = .127, p = <.001.

25 Fourteen percent versus 24 percent.

26 In Uganda, from 68 percent for Protestant nonmembers to 83 percent for Protestant members (V = .146, p = <.001). In Tanzania, from 57 percent for nonmembers to 86 percent for members (V = .195, p = <.001).

27 This general finding contradicts earlier country studies. See Michael Bratton, "Political Participation in a New Democracy: Institutional Considerations from Zambia," *Comparative Political Studies* 32, 5 (1999): 569 and Peter von Doepp, "Liberal Visions and Actual Power: Local Churches and Women's Empowerment in Rural Malawi," *Journal of Modern African Studies* 20, 2 (2002): 273–301.

28 Cramer's V = .078 (p = .008) and .079 (p = .003) respectively.

29 Samuel Huntington, *The Third Wave* (1991), pp. 75–85.

30 The index of group membership is positively related to rejection of one-party rule (V = .090), rejection of military rule (V = .126), and rejection of a one-man regime (r = .108). All p's = <.001.

31 Sixty-four percent versus 46 percent. Cramer's V = .188, p = <.001.

32 Cramer's V = .114 and .128 respectively (p's = <.001).

33 Engagement is measured by the number of group memberships. Pearson's r = .040, p = <.001.

34 For all three groups, r = .054, p = .033.

35 Pearson's r = .016, p = <.001.

36 Pearson r's = .018 (p = .014) for user fees, = .044 (p = <.001) for market prices, and = .030 (p = <.001) for retrenchment.

37 As with political institutions in Africa generally, little has been written about African political parties. Much of what we know derives tangentially from studies of multiparty elections and opposition movements. For instance, see Adebayo Olukoshi (ed.), *The Politics of Opposition in Contemporary Africa* (Uppsala: Nordic Africa Institute, 1998) and Cowen and Laakso (eds.), *Multi-Party Elections in Africa* (2001).

38 For an early statement on this subject that emphasizes the ethnic fragmentation of the party system see Jennifer Widner, "Political Parties and Civil Societies in Sub-Saharan Africa," in Ottaway, *Democracy in Africa* (1997), pp. 65–82. But, as noted by Widner and others, small parties often fail to win elections, leading to parliaments that are no more fragmented than in other world regions.

39 See Michelle Kuenzi and Gina Lambright, "Party System Institutionalization in 30 African Countries," *Party Politics* 7 (2001): 437–468; and "Party Systems and the Consolidation of Democracy in Sub-Saharan Africa's Electoral Regimes," *Party Politics*, forthcoming, 2003. Also V. Randall and L. Svasand, "Party Institutionalization and the New Democracies," *Party Politics* 8, 1 (2002): 5–29.

40 Nicolas van de Walle, "Presidentialism and Clientelism in Africa's Emerging Party Systems," *Journal of Modern African Studies* 41, 2 (2003): 9. A modified account is offered by Peter Burnell in "The Party System and Party Politics in Zambia: Continuities Past, Present and Future," *African Affairs* 100, 399 (2001): 239–263, who argues for reviving the concept of "predominant" party system, first coined by Giovanni Sartori, *Parties and Party Systems* (New York, Cambridge University Press, 1976).

41 "Winners" are those who say they feel close to the party or parties that formed the government following the last election. "Losers" feel close to the party or parties that are in opposition in the legislature or that failed to obtain seats in the last election. Nonpartisans do not feel close to any party.

42 Cramer's $V = .051$, $p = <.001$.

43 The question was only asked in Ghana, Mali, Nigeria, Tanzania, and Uganda.

44 For fuller analysis, see Michael Bratton, "African Views of Political Parties: Some Cross-National Survey Evidence," paper presented at a conference on Network Democracy: Enhancing the Role of Political Parties, organized by the Institute for Multiparty Democracy, The Hague, April 24–5, 2001: 5.

45 See Oda van Cranenbergh, "Tanzania's 1995 Multi-Party Elections: The Emerging Party System," *Party Politics* 2 (1996): 535–547. Other useful country studies are Richard Vengroff, "Governance and the Transition to Democracy: Political Parties and the Party System in Mali," *Journal of Modern African Studies* 31, 4 (1993): 541–562; R. Buijtenhuis, "Les parties politiques Africains ont-ils des projets de société? L'exemple du Tchad," *Politique Africaine* 56 (1994): 119–136; and Kimberly Lanegran, "South Africa's 1999 Election: Consolidating a Dominant Party System," *Africa Today* 48, 2 (2001): 81–102.

46 After the Round 1 Afrobarometer survey in Nigeria, and following a November 2002 ruling from the Supreme Court that the Independent National Electoral Commission could not arbitrarily restrict party registration, more than thirty new parties registered.

47 See Yoweri Museveni, *Sowing the Mustard Seed: The Struggle for Freedom and Democracy in Uganda* (London: Macmillan, 1997) and *What is Africa's Problem?* (Minneapolis: University of Minnesota Press, 2000). For a critique, try Nelson Kasfir "'No-Party Democracy' in Uganda," *Journal of Democracy* 9, 2 (2000): 49–63.

48 *The Constitution of the Republic of Uganda* (Kampala: Government Printer, 1995). Article 269 prohibits political parties from "opening and operating branch offices...holding delegates' conferences...holding public rallies...sponsoring or offering a platform to, or in any way campaigning for or against, a candidate for any public elections...(or) carrying on any activities that may interfere with the movement political system for the time being in force."

49 For the wording of the items – which range from whether parties contribute to "conflict and confusion" or to ensuring that "people in government don't abuse their power" – and the distribution of results, see Bratton and Lambright, "Uganda's Referendum 2000" (2001): 445.

50 The data for Kenya come from *A National Survey of Kenya Voters* (Washington, DC: International Republican Institute, 2001), which replicated the Afrobarometer's battery of political party questions used in Uganda. See www.iri.org.

51 For civil servants, gamma $= -.143$, $p = <.001$. For elected officials, gamma $= -.183$, $p = <.001$.

52 Whereas 58 percent of winners rate positively the performance of elected leaders, only 40 percent of losers do so. Gamma $= .195$, $p = <.001$.

53 Gamma $= .432$, $p = <.001$. This bivariate coefficient of association is one of the strongest so far found among microlevel variables in this study.

54 In a bivariate test, seeing oneself as a winner is positively related to one's support for democracy (Gamma = .138, p = <.001).

55 Gamma = −.083, p = <.001.

56 Gamma = .003, p = .704.

57 Gamma = −.166, p = <.001.

58 Gamma = .235, p = <.001.

59 Gamma = .176, p = <.001.

60 Compare R. W. Johnson and Lawrence Schlemmer (eds.), *Launching Democracy in South Africa: The First Open Election, April 1994* (New Haven, CT: Yale University Press, 1996) with Andrew Reynolds (ed.), *Election '99, South Africa: From Mandela to Mbeki* (New York: St. Martin's Press, 1999).

61 For knowledge of leaders, eta = .073, p = <.001; for understanding of how government works, eta = .048, p = <.001; for ability to attach a meaning to democracy, Cramer's V = .079, p = <.001. All coefficients refer to the full Afrobarometer sample.

62 Brady, Verba, and Schlozman, "Beyond SES," (1995): 271.

63 For knowledge of leaders, eta = .158, p = <.001; for understanding of how government works, eta = .051, p = <.001; for ability to attach a meaning to democracy, Cramer's V = .087, p = <.001.

64 For example, Sidney Verba, Norman Nie, and Jao-On Kim, *Participation and Political Equality: A Seven-Nation Comparison* (New York: Cambridge University Press, 1978), p. 51; Donna Bahry and Brian Silver, "Soviet Citizen Participation on the Eve of Democratization," *American Political Science Review* 84, 3 (1990): 821–827; and Geraint Parry, George Moyser, and Neil Day, *Political Participation and Democracy in Britain* (New York: Cambridge University Press, 1992), p. 50.

65 The same three dimensions emerge in all countries except Ghana and Namibia, where participation can be summarized in two dimensions. In these places, contacting and communing go together.

66 Seventy-six percent for those under thirty years old versus 86 percent for those aged forty-five or more.

67 Given that fully 16 percent of respondents claim to have "worked" for a party or candidate – probably an inflated figure – we think this question was badly phrased and broadly misunderstood. Perhaps people considered the mere expression of a partisan preference during a political discussion as legitimate campaign "work."

68 Of a total of 54 percent of variance in political participation explained overall, "communing" accounts for 29 percent, voting for 13 percent, and contacting leaders for 12 percent. See Table 10.1, bottom line.

69 Pearson' s r = .148 and .105 respectively (p = <.001). The index includes attending a campaign rally, working for a candidate, attending community meetings, getting together to raise an issue, and contacting government officials. For factor and reliability analyses, see Appendix A.

70 Seventy-eight percent versus 66 percent.

71 Seventy-four percent versus 57 percent.

72 Pearson's r = .180, p = <.001.

73 Pearson's r = .186, p = <.001.

74 These items will be considered separately. "Entrepreneurship" explains only one third of shared variance (33 percent) and does not scale reliably enough (alpha = .470) to be aggregated into an index.

75 For the findings in this paragraph, data were available for only four countries: Ghana, Nigeria, Mali, and Tanzania.

76 For example, those who purchase their own food are more dissatisfied with SAPs than those who rely on kin (58 versus 53 percent) (Cramer's V = .054, p = <.001).

77 Pearson's r = .035, p = .016.

78 Pearson's r = .045, p = .001.

79 Pearson's r = .101, p = <.001. Note, however, that holders of bank accounts are especially critical of the way that SAPs are actually implemented (Pearson's r = .141., p = <.001).

80 For example, those who sell their skills on the black market are more dissatisfied with SAPs than those who do not (50 percent versus 44 percent) (Pearson's r = .088, p = <.001).

81 Calculated from the raw regression coefficient, B = .616 on a scale of 0–3.

82 Calculated from the raw regression coefficient, B = .486 on a scale of 1–5.

Chapter 11

1 Final regression models (ordinary least squares, single stage) are derived for four dependent variables: popular demand for democracy, perceived supply of democracy, demand for a market economy, and the perceived supply of economic reform. The following model reduction procedure is used. All the relevant predictors discussed in Chapters 6 through 10 are first assembled into an exhaustive model. Those that are not statistically significant at <.001 are eliminated, if necessary via iterative reductions. Once all predictors are significant at <.001, the model is further trimmed by eliminating variables that make the smallest contribution as determined by their standardized regression score (beta). Thus, we arrive at the most parsimonious version possible that also attains the maximum amount of explained variance (adjusted R^2) and the minimum standard error of the estimate. See William Berry, *Understanding Regression Assumptions* (Thousand Oaks, CA: Sage, 1993), esp. pp. 11–12.

2 Using twenty-three predictors, Rose, Mishler, and Haerpfer explain 28 percent of the variance in support for the current (political) regime in *Democracy and Its Alternatives* (1998), p. 242. Using twelve independent variables, Shin explains 14 percent of the variance in support for legislative democratization in *Mass Politics and Culture* (1999), p. 157.

3 See the first adjusted R^2 column in Table 11.1, which records the variance explained when all variables in one theoretical family are entered as the only block.

4 See the last adjusted R^2 column in Table 11.1, which records the variance explained as theoretical families are entered cumulatively.

5 17.3 percent variance explained by cognitive awareness alone versus 5.6 percent of variance explained by performance evaluations alone.

6 Whereas knowledge of leaders is positively and significantly related to procedural understandings (Pearson's r = .138, p = <.001), it is unrelated to substantive understandings (r = .007, p = .291).

7 Education is the third to last variable to enter the final model, and then accounts for only one third of the variance explained by procedural understandings of democracy.

8 Media exposure is not significant in an exhaustive model that includes all forty-eight predictors.

9 This includes a comprehensive model with thirty-two statistically significant predictors.

10 The construct of the supply of democracy is an average score on two five-point scales. The extent scale is: 0 = not a democracy, 1 = a democracy with major problems, 2 = don't know, 3 = a democracy with minor problems, and 4 = a full democracy. The satisfaction scale is: 1 = very dissatisfied, 2 = dissatisfied, 3 = don't know, 4 = satisfied, and 5 = very satisfied.

11 See Appendix A.

12 While the president's performance was a third-ranked consideration when performance evaluations were weighed alone (see Table 9.1), it is the leading consideration in a fully specified model. Part of this shift occurs because perceptions of corruption decline in explanatory importance when "winning" (feeling close to the ruling party) is entered into the equation.

13 The performance of elected representatives is weakly related to the perceived supply of democracy and fails to qualify for the final cut to thirteen-predictor model (Table 11.2).

14 Compare the beta coefficients for these variables in Table 11.2 (.170 versus .100).

15 Compare the beta coefficients for these variables in Table 11.2 (.155 versus .084).

16 While the delivery of improved living standards is significantly related to the perceived supply of democracy, it is a very weak relationship that fails to qualify for the final cut to a thirteen-predictor model.

17 Compare beta coefficients: perceived corruption = −.085 versus trust in state institutions = .084.

18 None of the major demographic predictors – ethnicity, gender, age, urban-rural location, or even poverty – are statistically significant in an elaborate model with forty-eight variables, so all were dropped during model reduction.

19 Alone, identifying with a winning party accounts for 5.7 percent of the variance in perceived extent of democracy.

20 The cumulative impact of adding "winners" to a performance-driven model is to increase variance explained in the supply of democracy by only 0.3 of a percentage point.

21 Whereas religious group membership is significant in a twenty-one-predictor model, it does not survive the cut to the final model.

22 Performance evaluations account for just over 1 percent of variance on their own; and they account for just under 1 percent of variance in conjunction with other theoretical families.

23 The change in R^2 when poverty is entered into the final model is just 0.4 of a percentage point.

24 In an exhaustive model with forty-eight predictors, identification with the win-
    ning party shows no significant association with the perceived supply of eco-
    nomic reform (beta = .004, p = .552).
25 In the words of Herbert Asher, "Path analysis allows one to examine the causal
    processes underlying the observed relationships and to estimate the relative im-
    portance of alternative paths of influence." See *Causal Modeling* (Beverly Hills,
    CA: Sage, 1983) 2nd ed., p. 37. We also benefited from reading James Davis,
    The Logic of Causal Order (Thousand Hills, CA: Sage, 1985) and James Arbuckle
    and Werner Wothke, *Amos 4.0 User's Guide* (Chicago: Smallwaters Corporation,
    1999).
26 For clarity's sake, Figure 11.1 only displays paths with partial regression coef-
    ficients above beta = >.10. The broad arrows distinguish paths where beta =
    >.20 or beta = >.40. The error terms for the observed variables, which are
    assumed to be zero, are not displayed.
27 This concept is collapsed into a single variable scored +1 for postcolonial gen-
    eration, 0 for multiparty generation, and −1 for colonial generation. The scale
    measures the extent to which individuals were oppressed by an indigenous au-
    thoritarian regime.
28 See David Card, "The Causal Effect of Education on Earnings" in Orley
    Ashenfelter and David Card (eds.), *Handbook of Labour Economics* (Amsterdam,
    Elsevier, 1999), pp. 1801–1863, and Malcolm Keswell and Laura Poswell, "How
    Important is Education for Getting Ahead in South Africa?" *CSSR Working
    Paper No. 22*, University of Cape Town, Centre for Social Science Research,
    2002.
29 For indices of political and economic performance, see Appendix A.
30 Reversing the arrow produces an almost identical result (beta = .62).
31 Not shown in Figure 11.1, but see delivery of economic welfare in Table 9.1.

Chapter 12

1   Voting is measured on a three-point scale: I voted, I wanted to vote but was
    unable to do so, and I chose not to vote. Along with the imputation of fractional
    scores for missing values, this construction allowed us to treat voting as a con-
    tinuous variable for purposes of OLS.
2   Calculated from B = −.243 on a generation scale of 0–1.
3   Calculated from B = .016 for age in years.
4   On average (in Ghana, Nigeria, Uganda, Mali, and Tanzania) 23 percent of
    youths were unregistered compared to 11 percent of elders. The problem was
    greatest in Mali (a twenty-point gap) and slightest in Tanzania (an eight-point
    gap).
5   The exceptions are Botswana, Ghana, Malawi, and Nigeria, where there is no
    significant difference between urban and rural patterns of voter turnout. In the
    remaining countries rural dwellers are more likely to vote.
6   For example, rural folk are twice as likely as urbanites to be unable to give a
    meaning for "democracy" (28 percent versus 14 percent).
7   We already know that rural dwellers are less likely to gain media access, espe-
    cially to newspapers and television (see Chapter 8).
8   Calculated from B = .166 on a party identification scale of 0–1.

9 To do so, however, would obscure the contrasting signs on the items of social structure in Table 12.1. Hence, we reveal more by considering protesting separately from other forms of nonvoting behavior.

10 See the contrasting signs on these items in Table 12.1.

11 Calculated from B = .040 on an associational life scale of 0–3.

12 Twenty-four percent versus 12 percent.

13 Seventeen percent versus 11 percent.

14 Indeed, other things equal, women are slightly more likely to vote than men. But the effect of gender is too weak to warrant inclusion in a final explanatory model (beta = .017, p = .013).

15 On interelectoral participation, institutional influences account for four times as much variance as social structure.

16 See Michael Bratton, "Micro-Democracy? The Merger of Farmer Unions in Zimbabwe," *African Studies Review* 37, 1 (1994): 9–38.

17 Nicolas van de Walle, "'Meet the New Boss, Same as the Old Boss'? The Evolution of Political Clientelism in Africa," paper presented at a Conference on Consolidation in New Democracies, Uppsala University, Uppsala, Sweden, June 8–9, 2002.

18 See Seymour Martin Lipset and Stein Rokkan, *Party Systems and Voter Alignments* (New York: Free Press, 1967) and David Butler and Donald Stokes, *Political Change in Britain* (London: Macmillan, 1974).

19 Mark Franklin, Tom Mackie, and Henry Valen, *Electoral Change: Responses to Evolving Social and Attitudinal Structures in Western Countries* (New York: Cambridge University Press, 1992). Also Geoffrey Evans, *The Decline of Class Politics?* (Oxford: Oxford University Press, 1999). And Terry Clark Nichols and Seymour Martin Lipset, *The Breakdown of Class Politics* (Baltimore, MD: Johns Hopkins University Press, 2001).

20 Donald Horowitz, *A Democratic South Africa? Constitutional Engineering in a Divided Society* (Berkeley: University of California Press, 1991).

21 An alternate literature, based on assumptions of economic voting, argues that elections in Africa hinge on performance considerations. See Mattes and Piombo, "Opposition Parties" (2001) and Posner and Simon, "Economic Conditions" (2002). See also Leonard Wantchekon, "Clientelism and Voting Behavior: Evidence from a Field Experiment in Benin," *World Politics*, 55, 3 (2003): 399–422.

22 Absent a survey question on "who did you vote for?" we coded vote choice as follows: 1 if the person voted and identifies with the winning party, −1 if the person voted and identifies with a losing party, and 0 if the person does not identify with a party. With nonvoters excluded from analysis, N = 15,610.

23 Membership in a majority ethnic group is entirely unrelated to vote choice. In an exhaustive forty-six-predictor model, beta = .001, p = .874.

24 Pippa Norris and Robert Mattes, "Does Ethnicity Determine Support for the Governing Party?" *Afrobarometer Working Paper No. 26* (2003), www. afrobarometer.org.

25 Consistent with our findings, a recent study suggests that at least some voters in young democracies use their vote to choose, not only between political parties, but also between political regimes. See Stephen White, Richard Rose, and Ian McAllister, *How Russia Votes* (Chatham, NJ: Chatham House, 1997).

26 James Gibson, "Mass Opposition to the Soviet Putsch of August 1991: Collective Action, Rational Choice and Democratic Values," *American Political Science Review* 91, 3 (1997): 671–684.

27 See Appendix A.

28 Whereas 29 percent of previous protesters would take to the streets again, only 7 percent of nonprotesters expect to do so in the future.

29 Bratton and Lambright, "Uganda's Referendum 2000" (2001), 429–452.

30 John Makumbe, "Zimbabwe's Hijacked Election," (2002).

31 "Mass Opposition" (1997).

32 Pippa Norris, *Democratic Phoenix: Reinventing Political Activism* (New York: Cambridge University Press, 2002), pp. 96–97 and Chs. 7 and 8.

33 An evaluation report on Zambian political parties says it all: "the level of organization is weak or almost non-existent . . . there are major internal party communications difficulties . . . (and) internal democracy, party procedures, political tolerance and ethical standards of conduct remain important issues to be addressed." National Democratic Institute, *Zambia: Strengthening Political Parties* (Washington, DC: NDI, 1996), pp. 1–2.

34 On the past political and patronage roles of cooperatives see Steven Quick, "Bureaucracy and Rural Socialism in Zambia," *Journal of Modern African Studies* 15, 4 (1977): 379–400 and Bonard Mwape, "Farmers Organizations in Africa: the Case of the Zambia Cooperative Federation," *African Rural and Urban Studies* 1, 1 (1994): 91–110. On the trades union congress during the transition, see Per Nordlund, "Organizing the Political Agora: Domination and Democratization in Zambia and Zimbabwe" Ph.D. dissertation (Uppsala, Sweden: Uppsala University, 1996) and Michael Bratton, "Civil Society and Political Transitions in Africa" in Harbeson, Rothchild, and Chazan (eds.), *Civil Society and State in Africa>* (Boulder, CO: Lynne Rienner Press, 1994), pp. 83–102.

35 See Kimberly Ludwig, "Prospects for Pluralism: Economic Interest Groups and Dual Transition in Zambia's Third Republic" Ph.D. dissertation (East Lansing: Michigan State University, 2001).

36 For example, Norumitsu Onishi, "Nigerian Militias Wield Power Through Intimidation," *New York Times*, October 6, 2002 and Ginger Thompson, "Zimbabwe's Recruits Flee Brutal Zimbabwean Past," *New York Times*, April 15, 2003.

Chapter 13

1 *Problems of Democratic Transition* (1996), pp. 253–254, 434. See also McFaul, "The Fourth Wave" (2002): 212–244.

2 Ibid., p. 253, emphasis in original.

3 For comparisons bridging these seemingly disparate world regions, see Mark Beissinger and Crawford Young (eds.), *Beyond State Crisis: Postcolonial Africa and Post-Soviet Eurasia in Comparative Perspective* (Baltimore, MD: Johns Hopkins University Press, 2002).

4 The dummy variables are binary: $1 =$ the country in question; $0 =$ any other country. If all countries were entered, the set would be perfectly collinear, thus violating a key assumption for regression. In any event, eleven dummies capture all categorical variation across the twelve countries. Hence, Botswana is

excluded. See Melissa Hardy, *Regression with Dummy Variables* (Beverly Hills, CA: Sage, 1993).

5 On their own, "country" considerations account for 11.5 percent, 9.4 percent, and 7.4 percent respectively of total explained variance on these three key attitudes. Collectively, however, individual-level considerations (which cut across countries) *always* explain much more variance (22.9, 34.2, and 24.7 percent respectively). Their overarching effects help validate our decision to pool the data.

6 Of course, Botswana followed a similar trajectory, directly from a British protectorate to a multiparty system. But Botswana's sustained experience with multipartism puts it in a category all its own.

7 Apart from Mali, these are the only countries significantly different from Botswana at p = <.001.

8 Unlike social structure, however, the effects of cognitive awareness are merely reduced, not eliminated.

9 While "country" may edge out cognitive awareness in this case, it does not displace individual level characteristics generally, which still explain almost twice as much variance (11.2 percent).

10 Calculated from raw B coefficients of .695 and −.321 respectively.

11 Note: We measure equilibrium as an aggregate balance of supply and demand, fully recognizing that these concepts do not always fully refer to the same group of individuals.

12 In this regard, we endorse Diamond's proposal that "at the level of the mass public, consolidation is indicated when the overwhelming majority of citizens believe that democracy is the best form of government ... both logic and empirical evidence suggest that two-thirds is a minimum threshold, and 70–75 percent is a more compelling indicator ... but only when two other conditions are met: when this level is sustained consistently over some period of time and when ... rejecting the legitimacy of democracy ... is held by only a small minority." See *Developing Democracy* (1999), p. 68.

13 Joel Hellman, "Winners Take All" (1998): 203–204.

14 Barbara Geddes, "What Do We Know About Democratization After Twenty Years," *Annual Review of Political Science* 2 (1999): 115–144.

15 Military, one-party, and one-man rule.

16 Satisfaction with democracy includes those who are "somewhat satisfied" and "very satisfied." The extent of democracy includes those who perceive either "a full democracy" or "a democracy with minor problems."

17 Plus or minus three percentage points.

18 See John Holm, "Botswana: A Paternalistic Democracy" in Larry Diamond, *Democracy in Developing Countries, Vol. 2, Africa* (Boulder, CO: Lynne Rienner Publishers, 1988), pp. 179–215.

19 On transitional pacts in South Africa see Timothy Sisk, *Democratization in South Africa: The Elusive Social Contract* (Princeton, NJ: Princeton University Press, 1995). For a contrary perspective, try Elisabeth Jean Wood, *Forging Democracy from Below: Insurgent Transitions in South Africa and El Salvador* (New York: Cambridge University Press, 2000).

20 Even though based on carefully drawn national probability samples, these results should be treated with caution. It is not possible to reliably infer trends in newly

formed public attitudes, especially across two observations on nonpanel data that are barely separated in time.

21 Satisfaction with "the way democracy works in Nigeria" dropped even further, from 84 percent to 55 percent.

22 Support for democracy in Ghana rose from 70 to 82 percent between 1999 and 2002. Rejection of all authoritarian alternatives remained high over the same period. The perceived extent of democracy was also up, as was satisfaction with democracy (from 54 percent to 72 percent). However, differences between Round 1 and 2 surveys in the way questions were implemented in the field mean that these figures are not precisely comparable. But we believe the general trends to be correct.

23 Seymour Martin Lipset, "Some Social Requisites of Democracy: Economic Development and Political Legitimacy," *American Political Science Review* 53, 1 (1959): 69–105. For confirmations, see also Gary Marks and Larry Diamond (eds.), *Reexamining Democracy: Essays in Honor of Seymour Martin Lipset* (Newbury Park, CA: Sage Publications, 1992).

24 On the "chronological age of institutions," see Robert Jackman, *Power Without Force: The Political Capacity of Nation-States* (Ann Arbor: University of Michigan Press, 1993), pp. 124–131. On "regime duration" see Mark Gasiorowski, "Economic Crisis and Political Regime Change: An Event History Analysis," *American Political Science Review* 89, 4 (1995): 882–897.

25 The formula is $PCD = a + b - c - d$, where a = demand for democracy (country percent on additive index), b = supply of democracy (country percent on additive index), and c = consolidation deficit, regardless of regime type (deviation from the equilibrium line, calculated as $a - b$ or $b - a$), and d is a constant (20) to standardize the range of values between 0 and 100.

26 The Constitutional Court annulled the first round of the 1997 presidential elections in Mali. Opposition election boycotts followed. See M-F. Lange, "Elections in Mali (1992–7): Civil Society Confronted with the Rule of Democracy," in Abbink and Hesseling, *Election Observation and Democratization in Africa* (2000), pp. 228–254.

27 Peter Bouckaert, *Hostile to Democracy: The Movement System and Political Repression in Uganda* (New York: Human Rights Watch, 1999) and Justus Mugaju and J. Oloka-Onyango, *No-Party Democracy in Uganda: Myths and Realities* (Kampala: Fountain Publishers, 2000).

28 The supply of democracy is a more central component of the PCD score (Pearson's r = .803) than is demand for democracy (r = .702).

29 To repeat, Pearson's r = .616, p = .033.

30 Pearson's r = .248, p = .437.

31 World Bank, *African Development Indicators 2001* (Washington, DC: World Bank, 2001).

32 With a small sample of just twelve countries, correlation and regression results will normally fall short of statistical significance. Hence, for the rest of this chapter, we emphasize the sign and the size of coefficients. In any event, since the Afrobarometer does not represent the continent as a whole, regularities across the existing twelve countries are of greater interest than generalizations to a wider population.

33 While size of the state's economic role does not fully represent Linz and Stepan's idea of "stateness" – which refers more to territorial integrity and administrative coherence – it surely captures a part of it.

34 Annual average 1990–99. See World Bank, *African Development Indicators* (2001), p. 21. This indicator includes all current expenditure for purchases of goods and services by all levels of government, including capital expenditure on national defense and security.

35 Seymour Martin Lipset, "Some Social Requisites of Democracy" (1959) *op. cit.* See also Ross Burkhart and Michael Lewis-Beck, "Comparative Democracy: The Economic Development Thesis," *American Political Science Review* 88, 4 (1994): 903–910; John Londregan and Keith Poole, "Does High Income Promote Democracy?" *World Politics* 49, 1 (1996): 1–30.

36 Przeworski et al., *Democracy and Development* (2000), p. 78.

37 Botswana anchors the top end of these distributions, ranking first in both wealth and perceived democratic supply; and Uganda scores near the bottom, ranking eighth on both dimensions. This is not to say that national wealth is political destiny or that there are no African exceptions to Lipset's law. Malawi, with the lowest income per capita in the sample, ranks third in the extent of democracy that its population perceives. But the existence of a general statistical relationship only underlines the exceptionality of this case and the fact that Malawians, lacking experience with democracy, may be easily satisfied.

38 Douglass North, *Institutions, Institutional Change, and Economic Performance* (New York: Cambridge University Press, 1990) and Terry Lynn Karl, "Dilemmas of Democratization" (1990): 1–20. See also the special issue on Leninist political legacies in *Comparative Political Studies* 28, 2 (1995). Kitshchelt et al., *Post-Communist Party Systems* (1999) and Juliet Johnson, "Path Contingency in Postcommunist Transformations," *Comparative Politics* 33, 3 (2001): 253–274, leaven path determinacy with a healthy dose of agency and choice.

39 For example, see Axel Hadenius, *Democracy and Development* (New York, Cambridge University Press, 1992). Without endorsing British colonial legacies, but indicting Belgian ones, Crawford Young articulates the premise of path dependency as follows: "a regime develops a logic of its own, whose ultimate aim is the reproduction over time of its particular configuration of institutional arrangements and dominant ideas." *The African Colonial State in Comparative Perspective* (New Haven, CT: Yale University Press, 1994), p. 41.

40 For accounts of the presumed advantages of parliamentary systems, see Juan Linz, "Presidential or Parliamentary Democracy: Does it Make a Difference?" in Juan Linz and Arturo Valenzuela (eds.), *The Failure of Presidential Democracy* (Baltimore, MD: Johns Hopkins University Press, 1994). Also Alfred Stepan and Cindy Skatch, "Constitutional Frameworks and Democratic Consolidation: Parliamentarism versus Presidentialism," *World Politics* 46 (1993): 1–22. On this understudied topic in Africa, Andrew Reynolds, *Electoral Systems and Democratization in Southern Africa* (Oxford, Oxford University Press, 1999), esp. pp. 69–70, 83–88, 125–129 is the best current source.

41 The French and Germans colonized Mali and Namibia respectively. Note, however, that British colonialism did not have consistent effects, as evidenced by the divergent regime trajectories of neighboring Zambia and Zimbabwe.

42 There is only one pure parliamentary system among the Afrobarometer countries (Lesotho). South Africa, Namibia, and Botswana have mixed systems with strong parliamentary features, in which the president is indirectly elected by the legislature and removable by a parliamentary vote of no confidence. Ironically, Lesotho is the Afrobarometer's democratic laggard, a finding that does not augur well for a confirmation in Africa of the emerging consensus in the comparative literature that parliamentary arrangements best promote democratic consolidation.

43 Bratton and van de Walle, *Democratic Experiments in Africa* (1997).

44 Data are updated from Michael Bratton and Nicolas van de Walle, *Political Regimes and Regime Transitions in Africa: A Comparative Handbook* (East Lansing, MI: MSU Working Paper on Political Reform in Africa, No. 14, 1996). Instead of ending in 1989, all figures are extended to the year of each country's transition to a multiparty regime. For the latecomers to majority rule – Zimbabwe, Namibia, and South Africa – the starting point is 1957, the year of Ghana's independence. For Botswana and Zimbabwe, formally multiparty regimes since independence, the end date is set at 1999. And Zimbabwe is recoded from a multiparty regime to de facto plebiscitary one-party regime after the merger of the two main parties in 1987. For justification, see Masipula Sithole and John Makumbe, "Elections in Zimbabwe: The ZANU (PF) Hegemony and Its Incipient Decline," *African Journal of Political Science* 2, 1 (1997): 122–139.

45 Joel Barkan (ed.), *Politics and Public Policy in Kenya and Tanzania* (New York: Praeger, 1984). For an update see *Beyond Capitalism versus Socialism in Kenya and Tanzania* (Boulder, CO: Lynne Rienner Publishers, 1994).

46 Twenty-five uninterrupted years until 1989, plus a further six years until the country's 1995 transition.

47 In Tanzania, competition within a single party (rather than between multiple parties) has fundamentally shaped the very conception of democracy that people hold. Many Tanzanians now support "democracy," at least in the unitary and semicompetitive terms in which they define it.

48 The inclusion of controlled contests, including not only competitive but also plebiscitary varieties, lowers the significance of this relationship below conventional levels. But, again, we do not seek to make inferences beyond the Afrobarometer countries themselves.

49 The first finding was reported by Bratton and van de Walle (1997), pp. 140–144. The second was implied in Chapters 7 and 8 of this volume.

50 Note, however, that the coefficients turn negative when Botswana is dropped. For further discussion of the connection between time and consolidation, see the last section of this chapter.

51 Kenneth Bollen and Robert Jackman, "Political Democracy and the Size Distribution of Income," *American Sociological Review* 50 (1985): 438–457. A fuller test would have to include Africa's oil producers, which are disinclined to democracy: see Michael Ross, "Does Oil Hinder Democracy?" *World Politics* 53, 3 (2001): 325–361.

52 Tanzania's legacy of thirty years of competitive one-party rule account for thirty-six of its seventy PCD points.

53 "Democracy and the Lessons of Dictatorship" (1992): 283.

54 Modibo Keita's Union Soudanais – Rassemblement Démocratique Africain (US-RDA) controlled all seats in the National Assembly at the time of Mali's independence in 1960. Thus, there was never a viable opposition.
55 PCD = 50. See Table 13.2.
56 As well as sixteen years of competitive one-party rule, Malawi also had fourteen years of plebiscitary rule.
57 Eta = .865 and eta squared = .749. Hence, the dominant postcolonial path accounts for 75 percent of the variance in the PCD score.
58 For example, Freedom House, *Freedom in the World* (annual) (www. freedomhouse.org) and Monty Marshall and Keith Jaggers, *Polity IV Project: Political Regime Characteristics and Transitions, 1800–1999* (www.bsos.umd. edu/cidcm/polity).
59 Bratton and van de Walle (1997), p. 179.
60 For generally favorable assessments, see E. Gyimah-Boadi, "A Peaceful Turnover in Ghana," *Journal of Democracy* 12, 2, (2001): 103–117 and Paul Nugent, "Winners Losers and Also Rans: Money, Moral Authority and Voting Patterns in the Ghana 2000 Election," *African Affairs* 100 (2001): 405–428.
61 Bratton and van de Walle, ibid., p. 273.
62 The trends were most marked for blacks, for whom demand for democracy rose from 29 to 35 percent and the perceived supply of democracy fell from 50 percent to 35 percent. For all South Africans, demand rose from 28 to 32 percent and supply fell from 42 to 31 percent (see Figure 13.3).
63 Przeworski et al., *Democracy and Development* (2000), p. 103.
64 Eighty-one months (median duration) and 54 percent (mean PCD score).

Appendix C

1 Gary King, James Honaker, Anne Joseph, and Kenneth Scheve, "Analyzing Incomplete Political Science Data: An Alternative Algorithm for Multiple Imputation," *American Political Science Review* 95, 1 (2001): 49–69.
2 Paul Allison, *Missing Data* (Thousand Oaks, CA: Sage, 2001).
3 King et al., "Analysing Incomplete ... Data" (2001).
4 The procedure is outlined by James Honaker, Anne Joseph, Gary King, Kenneth Scheve, and Nannibal Singh, *Amelia: A Program for Missing Data* (Cambridge, MA: Harvard University, Windows Version, 2000). This program is freely available at http://www.gking.harvard.edu.

Index

Abacha, Sani, 4, 52, 237, 255
acquired immune deficiency syndrome
  (AIDS): *see* HIV-AIDS
Africa
  East, 128, 136, 147, 158, 174, 187,
    241, 255, 265, 308
  West, 128, 136, 142, 147, 158, 174,
    188, 233, 241, 255, 265, 308,
    339
  Southern, 110, 124, 127, 133, 142,
    150, 156, 158, 174, 188, 233, 241,
    243, 265, 308, 337–338
  sub-Saharan, 14, 17, 19, 53, 55, 315,
    324, 331
"Africans," 55, 189, 344
African National Congress (ANC), 7,
  79, 112, 117, 239, 260
African studies, 60, 272, 344
Afrobarometer, 9, 34, 53, 343
  indicators, 94, 96, 324, 355
  Network, 53, 56
age, 36, 165, 183, 231, 264, 296, 302
agriculture, 109, 111
aid, foreign: *see* donors, international
Ake, Claude, 65
Alli, Warisu, 51
Anderson, Christopher, 39
Anderson, Leslie, 43
Angola, 324
Argentina, 29
armed forces (see also military rule),
  19, 20

Asia
  Central, 13, 315
  East, 34
  West: *see* Middle East
associational life (see also voluntary
  organizations), 251, 291, 314, 330,
  348
authoritarianism (see also autocracy),
  319
  backsliding into, 324, 341, 342
  nostalgia for, 89, 260, 345
  rejection of, 76, 77, 90, 171, 175,
    192, 197, 198, 205, 210, 215, 237,
    260, 265, 344
autocracy, 322, 324, 325
  consolidation of, 322
  liberalized, 18, 31, 55, 323
  unreformed, 18, 55
awareness: *see* cognitive awareness
Axelrod, Robert, 45

Babangida, Ibrahim, 4, 117
Banda, Hastings, 6, 71, 89, 106
Barkan, Joel, 51
Bates, Robert, 222
Bayart, Jean-François, 25
Becket, Paul, 51
behavior, political and economic, 130,
  157, 262, 268, 304, 309, 312
Bermeo, Nancy, 45, 336
"big man," 19, 153, 158, 241, 244, 279,
  294: *see also* neo-patrimonialism

Guinea, 324
Gunther, Richard, 27

Hadenius, Axel, 27, 39
Hayward, Fred, 51
health, 101, 103, 110, 139, 140,
238
Hellman, Joel, 323
Higley, John, 27
HIV-AIDS, 101, 102, 150, 238, 239,
243
housing, 112
Hungary, 69, 70
Huntington, Samuel, 27, 174
hybrid regimes: *see* regimes, hybrid
Hyden, Goran, 185

identity, 284
group, 186, 187, 225: *see also* ethnic,
religious, occupational, and class
identities
national, 54, 189, 190, 201, 254
International Monetary Fund (IMF), 4,
5, 7, 13, 20, 81, 113, 116, 117, 122,
123
income (see also inequality, income),
135, 137
independence, political, 15, 20, 50, 87,
331
individualism, 38, 104, 154, 185, 197,
202, 226, 284, 291
Indonesia, 66, 70
inequality
income, 26, 124
socioeconomic, 32, 98, 123, 124, 155,
228, 248, 287–288, 345
informal sector: *see also* economy,
informal
of the polity, 143
information, 10, 40, 41, 44, 204, 209,
213, 221, 230, 232, 272, 307, 309,
347: *see also* knowledge
Inglehart, Ronald, 38, 193, 197
institutional influences, 35, 39, 267,
275, 282, 287–288, 299, 300,
302
institutional models, 266

institutions, 250, 281, 331
defined, 250
institutionalization, 19, 27, 30,
279
"the new institutionalism," 331
interest, in public affairs, 40, 41, 155,
211, 262
interest groups: *see* voluntary
organizations
Internet, 58, 208
Islam, 110, 154, 157, 164, 174, 189,
252, 254, 255, 267

Jackman, Robert, 335
jobs: *see* employment
Johnson, R. W., 53
Jonathan, Chief Leabua, 332

Kabila, Joseph, 52
Kabila, Laurent, 52
Kasfir, Nelson, 137
Kaunda, Kenneth, 78, 117, 191
Kedourie, Elie, 174
Keita, Modibo, 4, 335
Kenya, 18, 51, 52, 123, 259
King, Gary, 399
Kitschelt, Herbert, 42
knowledge, 41
of leaders, 213, 215, 219, 298, 301,
309
Konaré, Alpha Omar, 5
Korea, South, 36, 41, 274
Kraus, Jon, 251
Kuenzi, Michelle, 256
Kufuor, John, 327, 350

Lagos, Marta, 194
Lambright, Gina, 256
Latin America, 13, 34, 60, 73, 82, 94,
144, 194, 336, 347
Latinobarometro, 60
learning, popular, 10, 34–35, 45, 46,
224–225, 272, 275, 289, 294, 302,
309, 314, 335, 337, 347
in adulthood, 289
by doing, 261, 262, 267, 310
childhood socialization, 289